Principles of
CAD / CAM / CAE
Systems

Principles of
CAD / CAM / CAE
Systems

KUNWOO LEE
Seoul National University

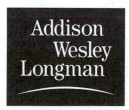

Addison
Wesley
Longman

**Addison-Wesley is an imprint
of Addison Wesley Longman, Inc.**

Reading, Massachusetts ■ Harlow, England
Menlo Park, California ■ Berkeley, California
Don Mills, Ontario ■ Sydney ■ Bonn ■ Amsterdam
Tokyo ■ Mexico City

Senior Acquisitions Editor: Denise Olson
Project Manager: Phoebe Ling
Senior Production Editor: Amy Rose
Production Coordinator: Brooke D. Albright
Compositor: Jackie Davies
Cover Designer: Joyce Weston
Text Designer: Debbie Schneck
Technical Illustrator: Paula Gentile
Copyeditor: Jerry Moore
Indexer: Nancy Fulton

Access the latest information about Addison-Wesley books from our World Wide Web site: http://www.awl.com/cseng/cad

Many of the designations used by manufacturers and sellers to distinguish their products are claimed as trademarks. Where those designations appear in this book, and Addison-Wesley was aware of a trademark claim, the designations have been printed in initial caps or all caps.

The programs and applications presented in this book have been included for their instructional value. They have been tested with care, but are not guaranteed for any particular purpose. The publisher does not offer any warranties or representations, nor does it accept any liabilities with respect to the programs or applications.

Library of Congress Cataloging-in-Publication Data

Lee, Kunwoo.
    Principles of CAD/CAM/CAE systems / Kunwoo Lee.
       p.   cm.
    Includes bibliographical references and index.
    ISBN 0-201-38036-6
    1. CAD/CAM systems.   2. Computer-aided engineering. I. Title.
TS155.6.L445   1999
670' .285—dc21   98-18040
                                                                CIP

This book was typeset in QuarkXPress 3.32 on a Macintosh Quadra 840AV. The fonts used were Times and ITC Kabel. It was printed on Rolland, a recycled paper.

3 4 5 6 7 8 9 10-MA-02

To my family and students
Without their support, this book would not have been completed

Preface

With the dramatic changes in computing power and wider availability of software tools for design and production, engineers are now using CAD/CAM/CAE systems for everyday tasks, not just for demonstrations. International competition, decreased availability of skilled labor, and increased emphasis on quality are also forcing manufacturers to use CAD/CAM/CAE systems to automate their design and production processes. As a result, educators in engineering schools are experiencing a new pressure to change the way they teach design-related courses in order to equip their students to interact with CAD/CAM/CAE systems and have a knowledge of their fundamental principles.

The objective of this book is to present the fundamental principles and concepts underlying CAD/CAM/CAE systems rather than explain the use of specific systems. Some people may argue that it is enough to teach a student how to use existing systems or even a specific popular system because the student as an engineer will be the user—not the developer—of such systems. However, in order to use existing software effectively and create usable macros or programs for automated design, the user must understand both the computing environment and the underlying system principles. With this knowledge of the fundamentals, the student can quickly learn a specific system within a specific environment and use it to its maximum capability. Furthermore, manuals and documentation that are typically provided with CAD/CAM/CAE systems tend to concentrate on the user interface and its syntax, assuming that the user has a sound theoretical background. A user who does not have this background will have trouble understanding the terminology of system documentation and will also have trouble dealing with system errors.

This book is written primarily about CAD/CAM/CAE systems in mechanical engineering. But the topics on computer graphics may also appeal to those in many other engineering fields. The book is intended as a course for seniors and first-year graduate students. Students are required to have a background only in programming, calculus, and matrix and vector algebra, with no prior knowledge of CAD/CAM/CAE systems. Thus complicated mathematical terminology and explanations have been kept to a minimum. Instead, related topics are explained in an intuitive way as much as possible. Accordingly, if chapters are selected as explained later, this book can also be used in a course for juniors or as a reference book for engineers who want a quick overview of CAD/CAM/CAE systems.

In writing the book, my goal was to explain fundamental concepts with an appropriate number of figures and examples without getting bogged down in too many details. I have seen several textbooks fail to get their main points across by trying to explain too many details. This overreliance on detail also makes a book so thick that it scares students away from using it effectively. For details, I recommend that students turn to the References section at the end of the book. The same goal applied to my choice of references. I have tried to recommend only those sources directly related to each topic so that I could keep the number of references to a minimum. Some textbooks recommend so many references that students are overwhelmed by them.

Chapter 1 introduces the role of CAD/CAM/CAE systems in the context of the product cycle. It also provides the definition of CAD/CAM/CAE systems and illustrates their use with case studies in which these systems are used to carry out design and production process. Case studies clarify how the principles explained in the remaining chapters contribute to a new design and production activity using CAD/CAM/CAE systems. Chapter 2 reviews the available hardware and software components that make up current CAD/CAM/CAE systems. The instructor should update this chapter as new hardware and software are introduced. This chapter could be given as a reading assignment rather than covered in depth.

Chapter 3 introduces all the concepts required for graphics programming with any graphics library and is not limited to a specific graphics library. However, the graphics library OpenGL was used in writing the sample graphics programs because it tends to be the de facto standard library running on both workstations and personal computers. This chapter serves as good introductory material for anyone interested in computer graphics in general. Chapter 4 reviews the basic functions provided by most computer-aided drafting systems. Similar to Chapter 3, it describes the general concepts and functions provided by most computer-aided drafting systems for product documentation. However, the example commands used in this chapter are those of AutoCAD because it is currently the most popular drafting system. The way a specific system is used can be handled in a laboratory class complementing the course.

Chapter 5 explains the fundamentals underlying geometric modeling systems. It also introduces a nonmanifold modeling system, an emerging area in geometric modeling. Some topics that are too advanced for student users are presented in the appendices for professionals' reference. For those interested only in using geometric modeling systems, these topics can be ignored. Chapters 6 and 7 cover the representation and manipulation of curves and surfaces. These topics provide the mathematical basis for geometric modeling systems and even for computer-aided drafting systems. I have tried to keep the types of curves and surfaces to a minimum, yet sufficient for most applications. To prevent students from being lost, I have moved the complicated mathematical derivations from the main text to the appendices. I have also tried to explain the mathematical concepts in an intuitive way appropriate for engineers, not for mathematicians.

Chapter 8 introduces CAE systems. It explains how the finite-element analysis program is generated and how information necessary for the analysis program is provided from the geometric model created by CAD systems. Thus it reviews the various approaches to automatic finite-element generation. Chapter 9 reviews various techniques for optimization. Emerging optimization techniques such as simulated annealing algorithm and genetic algorithm are described in detail. An example of integrating finite-element analysis and optimization is a fairly new concept called *structural optimization*. The structural optimization method can be used for initial conceptual design of a component to ensure that it has the desired loading capability.

Chapter 10 introduces various process planning methods and software as key elements in CAD/CAM integration. It also introduces the concept of group technology, which enables the encoding of parts to be produced and is the prerequisite for automated process planning. Chapter 11 describes how NC machines are programmed once the shape of a part has been defined by a CAD system and the process to be applied has been determined. Chapter 12 introduces the emerging manufacturing technology called *rapid prototyping* as another aspect of CAM. Unlike production by NC machines, this technology generates a part directly from its CAD model without requiring complicated process planning. In fact, this technology completely integrates automatic CAD/CAM for the first time. Chapter 13 introduces another emerging technology called *virtual engineering*; in this approach, geometric modeling systems, computer graphics, CAE and CAM systems are all applied during the product development process.

Chapter 14 reviews several standard data file formats that allow communication between different systems. These standards are indispensable for the integration of CAD/CAM/CAE systems.

Each chapter of the book ends with a set of problems and/or programming assignments written to deepen students' understanding of the material. Some assignments require use of the students' own systems. In these cases, documentation for those systems should be used as supplements to the text.

As mentioned earlier, this book may be used for a lower level undergraduate course. In that case, the topics in the appendices may be omitted because they are presented from the system developer's point of view. Instead, I recommend emphasizing the projects related to CAD/CAM/CAE system applications. These projects include generation of a solid, generation of the corresponding drawing, evaluation of the design by a finite-element analysis, and production of the corresponding prototype by either an NC milling machine or other machines for rapid prototyping, such as a stereo lithography apparatus. If the book is to be used in an advanced geometric modeling course for graduate students, Chapters 1, 2, 4, and 14 may be given as reading assignments with the topics presented in the appendices treated heavily.

I am indebted to the reviewers for their useful comments and suggestions which have undoubtedly enhanced the quality of this book. I want to express my appreciation to Professor David C. Gossard at the Massachusetts Institute of Technology, who gave me valuable advice during the planning stage of this book. I also want to thank Professor Kyung Ho Cho, Professor Young Il Kim, Professor Jongwon Kim, Dr. Woncheol Choi, Dr. Ha-Yong Shin, Mr. Suk Ju Kim, and Mr. Jin Pyung Chung for providing me with the related materials on optimization, virtual engineering, process planning, and standard data files. Finally, I want to thank my students, especially Junghoon Hur and Inhaeng Cho, who helped prepare the manuscript and illustrations.

Contents

Principles of
CAD / CAM / CAE
Systems

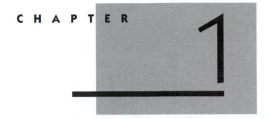

CHAPTER 1

Introduction to CAD/CAM/CAE Systems

1.1 OVERVIEW

Today's industries cannot survive worldwide competition unless they introduce new products with better quality (quality, Q), at lower cost (cost, C), and with shorter lead time (delivery, D). Accordingly, they have tried to use the computer's huge memory capacity, fast processing speed, and user-friendly interactive graphics capabilities to automate and tie together otherwise cumbersome and separate engineering or production tasks, thus reducing the time and cost of product development and production. Computer-aided design (CAD), computer-aided manufacturing (CAM), and computer-aided engineering (CAE) are the technologies used for this purpose during the product cycle. Thus, to understand the role of CAD, CAM, and CAE, we need to examine the various activities and functions that must be accomplished in the design and manufacture of a product. These activities and functions are referred to as the *product cycle*. The product cycle described by Zeid [1991] is presented here with minor modifications, as shown in Figure 1.1.

As indicated by the boxes bounded by solid lines in Figure 1.1, the product cycle is composed of two main processes: the design process and the manufacturing process. The design process starts from customers' demands that are identified by marketing personnel and ends with a complete description of the product, usually in the form of a drawing. The manufacturing process starts from the design specifications and ends with shipping of the actual products.

The activities involved in the design process can be classified largely as two types: synthesis and analysis. As illustrated in Figure 1.1, the initial design activities (such as identification of the design need, formulation of design specifications,

Figure 1.1

Product cycle

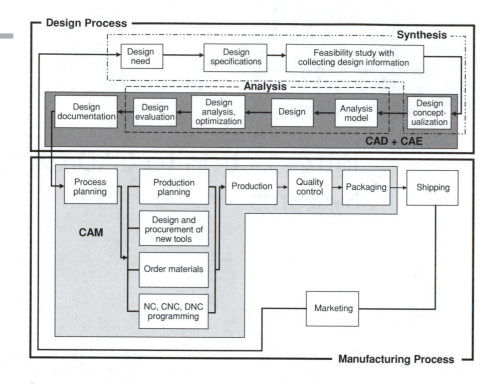

feasibility study with collecting relevant design information, and design conceptualization) are part of the synthesis subprocess. That is, the result of the synthesis subprocess is a conceptual design of the prospective product in the form of a sketch or a layout drawing that shows the relationships among the various product components. The major financial commitments needed to realize the product idea are made and the functionality of the product is determined during this phase of the cycle. Most of the information generated and handled in the synthesis subprocess is qualitative and consequently is hard to capture in a computer system.

Once the conceptual design has been developed, the analysis subprocess begins with analysis and optimization of the design. An analysis model is derived first because the analysis subprocess is applied to the model rather than the design itself. Despite the rapid growth in the power and availability of computers in engineering, the abstraction of analysis models will still be with us for the foreseeable future. The analysis model is obtained by removing from the design unnecessary details, reducing dimensions, and recognizing and employing symmetry. Dimensional reduction, for example, implies that a thin sheet of material is represented by an equivalent surface with a thickness attribute or that a long slender region is represented by a line having cross-sectional properties. Bodies with symmetries in their geometry and loading are usually analyzed by considering a portion of the model. In fact, you have already practiced this abstraction process naturally when you analyzed a structure in an elementary mechanics class. Recall that you always start with sketching the structure in a simple shape before performing the actual analysis. Typical of the analysis are stress analysis to verify the strength of the design, interference checking to detect collision between components while they are moving in an assembly, and kinematic analysis to check whether the machine to be used will provide the required motions. The quality of the results obtained from these activities is directly related to and limited by the quality of the analysis model chosen.

Once a design has been completed, after optimization or some tradeoff decisions, the design evaluation phase begins. Prototypes may be built for this purpose. The new technology called *rapid prototyping* is becoming popular for constructing prototypes. This technology enables the construction of a prototype by depositing layers from the bottom to the top. Thus it enables the construction of the prototype directly from its design because it requires basically the cross-sectional data of the product. If the design evaluation on the prototype indicates that the design is unsatisfactory, the process described is repeated with a new design.

When the outcome of the design evaluation is satisfactory, the design documentation is prepared. This includes the preparation of drawings, reports, and bills of materials. Conventionally, blueprints are made from the drawings and passed on to manufacturing.

As illustrated in Figure 1.1, the manufacturing process begins with process planning, using the drawings from the design process, and it ends with the actual products. Process planning is a function that establishes which processes—and the proper parameters for the processes—are to be used. It also selects the machines that will perform the processes, such as a process to convert a piece part from a rough billet to a final form specified in the drawing. The outcome of process planning is a production plan, a materials order, and machine programming. Other special requirements, such as design of jigs and fixtures, are also handled at this stage. The relationship of process planning to the manufacturing process is analogous to that of synthesis to the design process: It involves considerable human experience and qualitative decisions. This description implies that it would be difficult to computerize process planning. Once process planning has been completed, the actual product is produced and inspected against quality requirements. Parts that pass the quality control inspection are assembled, functionally tested, packaged, labeled, and shipped to customers.

We have described a typical product cycle. Now we will review it to show how the computer, or CAD, CAM, and CAE technologies, are employed in the cycle. As indicated earlier, the computer is not widely used in the synthesis phase of the design process because the computer does not handle qualitative information well. However, in the synthesis subprocess, for example, a designer might well collect the relevant design information for the feasibility study by using a commercial database and collect catalog information in the same way.

Nor is it easy to imagine how a computer might be used in the design conceptualization phase because the computer is not yet a powerful tool for the intellectual creative process. The computer may contribute in this phase by physically generating various conceptual designs efficiently. The parametric modeling or macro programming capability of computer-aided drafting or geometric modeling may be useful for this task. These packages are typical examples of CAD software. You may imagine a geometric modeling system to be a three-dimensional equivalent of a drafting system; that is, it is a software package by which a three-dimensional shape instead of a two-dimensional picture is manipulated. We explain computer-aided drafting in Chapter 4 and geometric modeling in Chapter 5.

The analysis subprocess of the design process is the area where the computer reveals its value. In fact, there are many available software packages for stress analysis, interference checking, and kinematic analysis, to name a few. These software packages are classified as CAE. One problem with using them is the provision of the analysis model. It would not be a problem at all if the analysis model were derived automatically from the conceptual design. However, as explained previously, the analysis model is not the same as the conceptual design but is derived by eliminating unnecessary details from the design or by reducing its dimensions. The proper level of abstraction differs, depending on the type of analysis and the desired accuracy of the solution. Thus it is difficult to automate this abstraction process; accordingly the analysis model is often created separately. It is a common practice to create the abstract shape of the design redundantly by using a computer-aided drafting system or a geometric modeling system or sometimes by using the built-in capability of the analysis packages. Analysis packages usually require the structure of interest to be represented by an aggregation of interconnected meshes that divide the problem into manageable chunks for the computer. If the analysis package being used has the capability of generating these meshes automatically, it would be necessary to create the abstract boundary shape only. Otherwise, the meshes also have to be generated either interactively by the user or automatically by appropriate software. This activity of generating meshes is called *finite-element modeling*. Finite-element modeling also includes the activity of specifying boundary conditions and external loads.

The analysis subprocess can be imbedded in the optimization iteration to yield the optimal design. Various algorithms for finding the optimal solution have been developed, and many optimization procedures are commercially available. Optimization procedures could be thought of as a component of CAD software, but it is more natural to treat optimization procedures separately.

The design evaluation phase also can be also facilitated by use of the computer. If we need a design prototype for the design evaluation, we can construct a prototype of the given design by using software packages that automatically generate the program that drives the rapid prototyping machine. These packages are classified as CAM software, which we define later. Of course, the shape of the prototype to be made should exist in advance in a type of data. The data corresponding to the shape are created by geometric modeling. We present an overview of the existing rapid prototyping technologies in Chapter 12. Even though the prototype can be constructed conveniently with rapid prototyping, it would be even better if we could use a virtual prototype, often called *digital mock-up*, which provides the same valuable information.

As the analysis tools used to evaluate the digital mock-up become powerful enough to give an analysis result as accurate as that from the equivalent experiment on a real prototype, digital mock-ups will tend to replace real prototypes. This tendency will increase as virtual reality technology[1] enables us to get the same feeling from the digital mock-up as we get from the real prototype. The activity of building digital mock-ups is called *virtual prototyping*. The virtual prototype can also be generated by a kind of geometric modeling that is specialized for that purpose. We describe virtual prototyping in detail in Chapter 13.

The final phase of the design process is design documentation. In this phase, computer-aided drafting is a powerful tool. The file-handling capability of computer drafting systems also allows the systematic storage and retrieval of documents.

Computer technologies are also used in the manufacturing process. The manufacturing process includes the activities of production planning, design and procurement of new tools, ordering materials, NC programming, quality control, and packaging, as illustrated in Figure 1.1, so all the computer technologies for these activities can be classified as CAM. For example, computer-aided process planning (CAPP) software to aid the process planning activity is one type of CAM software. As mentioned previously, process planning is difficult to automate, and thus 100 percent automatic CAPP software is not available currently. However, there are many good software packages that generate the numerically controlled (NC) programs that drive NC machines. This type of machine creates a given shape when the shape exists in the computer in the form of data. This is similar to driving the rapid prototyping machine. The NC programming capability is explained in Chapter 11. In addition, also belonging to CAM are the software packages to program robot motion to assemble components or deliver them to the various manufacturing activities, or to program a coordinate measuring machine (CMM) to inspect the product.

By now you should have an idea of how computer technologies are employed in the product cycle and which tasks are facilitated by CAD, CAM, and CAE. We define these technologies in the following section.

1.2 DEFINITIONS OF CAD, CAM, AND CAE

As described in the previous section, *computer-aided design* (CAD) is the technology concerned with the use of computer systems to assist in the creation, modification, analysis, and optimization of a design [Groover and Zimmers 1984]. Thus any computer program that embodies computer graphics and an application program facilitating engineering functions in the design process is classified as CAD software. In other words, CAD tools can vary from geometric tools for manipulating shapes at one extreme, to customized application programs, such as those for analysis and optimization, at the other extreme [Zeid 1991]. Between these two extremes, typi-

---

[1] Virtual reality is the technology concerned with making the image look like a real physical object. It enables an operator to feel and manipulate the image in the same way as he or she does the physical object.

cal tools currently available include tolerance analysis, mass property calculations, and finite-element modeling and visualization of the analysis results, to name a few. The most basic role of CAD is to define the geometry of design—a mechanical part, architectural structure, electronic circuit, building layout, and so on—because the geometry of the design is essential to all the subsequent activities in the product cycle. Computer-aided drafting and geometric modeling are typically used for this purpose. This is why these systems are considered CAD software. Furthermore, the geometry created by these systems can be used as a basis for performing other functions in CAE and CAM. This is one of the greatest benefits of CAD because it can save considerable time and reduce errors caused by otherwise having to redefine the geometry of the design from scratch every time it is needed. Therefore we can say that computer-aided drafting systems and geometric modeling systems are the most important components of CAD.

Computer-aided manufacturing (CAM) is the technology concerned with the use of computer systems to plan, manage, and control manufacturing operations through either direct or indirect computer interface with the plant's production resources. One of the most mature areas of CAM is numerical control, or NC. This is the technique of using programmed instructions to control a machine tool that grinds, cuts, mills, punches, bends, or turns raw stock into a finished part. The computer can now generate a considerable amount of NC instructions based on geometric data from the CAD database plus additional information supplied by the operator. Research efforts are concentrating on minimizing operator interactions.

Another significant CAM function is the programming of robots, which may operate in a workcell arrangement, selecting and positioning tools and workpieces for NC machines. These robots may perform individual tasks such as welding or assembly or carry equipment or parts around the shop floor.

Process planning is also a target of computer automation; the process plan may determine the detailed sequence of production steps required to fabricate an assembly from start to finish as it moves from workstation to workstation on the shop floor. Even though completely automatic process planning is almost impossible, as mentioned previously, a process plan for a part can be generated if the process plans for similar parts already exist. For this purpose, group technology has been developed to organize similar parts into a family. Parts are classified as similar if they have common manufacturing features such as slots, pockets, chamfers, holes, and so on. Therefore, to automatically detect similarity among parts, the CAD database must contain information about such features. This task is accomplished by using feature-based modeling or feature recognition. Feature-based modeling and feature recognition are explained in Chapter 5. Group technology is explained in Chapter 10.

In addition, the computer can be used to determine when to order raw materials and purchase parts and how many should be ordered to achieve the production schedule. This activity is called material requirements planning (MRP). The computer can be also used to monitor the status of the machines on the shop floor and to send them the proper orders.

Computer-aided engineering (CAE) is a technology concerned with the use of computer systems to analyze CAD geometry, allowing the designer to simulate and study how the product will behave so that the design can be refined and optimized. CAE tools are available for a wide range of analyses. Kinematics programs, for example, can be used to determine motion paths and linkage velocities in mechanisms. Large-displacement dynamic analysis programs can be used to determine loads and displacements in complex assemblies such as automobiles. Logic-timing and verification software simulates the operation of complex electronic circuits.

Probably the most widely used method of computer analysis in engineering is the *finite-element method* (FEM). This approach is used to determine stress, deformation, heat transfer, magnetic field distribution, fluid flow, and other continuous field problems that would be impractical to solve with any other approach. In finite-element analysis, the structure is represented by an analysis model made up of interconnected elements that divide the problem into manageable chunks for the computer.

As mentioned previously, a proper level of abstract model is required by the finite-element method instead of the design geometry itself. The abstract model is different from the design geometry in that it is obtained by eliminating the unnecessary details from the design geometry or by reducing the dimensions of the design geometry. For example, a three-dimensional object having thin thickness may become a two-dimensional shell model when it is converted to an analysis model [Armstrong 1994]. Thus it is necessary to generate an abstract model either interactively or automatically in order to use a finite-element method. Once the abstract model has been developed, the finite elements are generated to yield the analysis model. The software tools that enable the construction of the abstract model and generation of the finite elements are called *pre-processors*. After performing an analysis on each element, the computer assembles the results and displays it visually. Areas of high stress may be shown in red, for example. The software tools for this visualization are called *post-processors*. The finite-element method is explained in Chapter 8.

Many software tools are also available for design optimization. Although design optimization tools may be regarded as CAE tools, they are commonly classified separately. Several research activities are under way to determine design shape automatically by integrating design optimization and analysis [Bendsoe 1992]. In these approaches, the initial design shape is assumed to be a simple shape, such as a rectangular shape for a two-dimensional item composed of small elements of different densities. Then the optimization procedure is carried out to calculate the optimal values of these densities to meet a certain goal while satisfying the stress constraint. The goal often will be achieving minimum weight. Based on the optimal values of the densities, the optimal shape of the design is derived by eliminating the elements of low densities. Optimization techniques are introduced in Chapter 9.

The beauty of design analysis and optimization is that it allows the engineer to see how the product will behave and enables the engineer to catch any errors before going to the time and expense of building and testing physical prototypes. Because the cost of engineering goes up exponentially in the later stages of product development and production, the early optimization and refinement afforded by CAE analysis pays off in greatly reduced overall product development time and costs.

Thus CAD, CAM, and CAE are concerned with automating specific functions of the product cycle and making them more efficient. Because they were developed separately, they have not fully realized the potential of integrating the design and manufacturing activities of the product cycle. To solve this problem, a new technology called *computer-integrated manufacturing* (CIM) has been introduced. CIM is aimed at tying the separate "islands of automation" together into a smoothly running, efficient system. CIM is concerned with using the computer database as a way to run an entire enterprise more efficiently, having an impact on accounting, scheduling, shipping, and other management functions in addition to the engineering design and production functions of concern to CAD/CAM/CAE. CIM is often said to be more of a business philosophy than a computer system. We do not deal with CIM in this textbook.

1.3 INTEGRATING THE DESIGN AND MANUFACTURING PROCESSES THROUGH A COMMON DATABASE—A SCENARIO

We present the following scenario to show how CAD/CAM/CAE are overlaid on the product cycle to realize the goals of better quality (Q), lower cost (C), and quick delivery (D). The scenario may be a bit simplistic compared to state-of-the-art computer technologies, but it illustrates the direction in which technology development is moving. Let's consider the product development and production phases of the audio system cabinet shown in Figure 1.2. Its product cycle will be similar to that

Figure 1.2

Audio system cabinet to be designed

of, say, a mechanical assembly or building, and thus the scenario will also be applicable to such products.

Assume that the design specification calls for the cabinet to have four spaces—one for a compact disc player, one for a cassette player, one for a receiver, and one for a storage compartment of compact discs. The designer probably will sketch many design concepts before coming up with the one shown in Figure 1.2. During this phase the designer may use a computer-aided drafting system if the task is performed in two dimensions or a geometric modeling system if the task is performed in three dimensions. The design concept may also be sent to marketing via e-mail to get their reaction. Communication between the designer and marketing in real time can take place through remotely located workstations. Such communication can be easy and interactive if the right hardware and networking are used. When the design concept is complete, the information is stored in the computer database: the configuration of the furniture (the audio components are stacked vertically in this case), the number of shelves, which shelf is to be used for which component, and so on. In other words, features that we can see by looking at Figure 1.2 are cataloged and stored in the database and can be retrieved from it and modified at any time.

The next step is to determine the dimensions of the cabinet. Its overall size should be determined so that each space within it can accommodate various models of the audio components on the market. Thus it is necessary to obtain information on the sizes of the audio components available. This information may be obtained from catalogs or retrieved from manufacturers' or distributors' databases. Accessing such databases would be similar to accessing books and their contents by connecting to a library database. The designer may also copy the information into his or her database if the information is to be used often. Accumulating the design information is similar to accumulating more forms and files as with the use of word processors. From the size information retrieved, the shape in Figure 1.2 is modified as necessary to fit the required dimensions.

Now the designer has to determine the material to be used for the cabinet. The designer could specify natural oak, natural pine, particle board, steel sheet, or some other material. In this case the designer bases selection of the material on intuition or experience. However, in the case of products that operate under severe conditions, such as mechanical assemblies, the designer must be guided by the material's properties. The database is useful in this phase also because properties of many materials can be stored in it for later retrieval and use. Furthermore, an expert system can be applied to infer the material from the material properties supplied by the database. Once the material has been selected, this information is also stored in the database.

The next step is to determine the thickness of each shelf and door and the side walls. For the simple case of this cabinet design, the thickness may be based primarily on aesthetics. Even in this simple case, though, the thickness of the shelves must be sufficient to avoid deflection caused by the weight of the audio components. However, in mechanical assemblies requiring high accuracy or a structure supporting heavy loads, dimensions such as thickness must be determined to avoid excessive deformation. The finite-element method is generally used to calculate the deformation of a structure. As explained previously, the finite-element method requires an analysis model of the design. In this case, the analysis model is composed of the shell meshes on the sheet approximation of the cabinet. The sheet approximation can be derived automatically by the *medial axis transformation* (MAT) algorithm [Sudhalkar, Gursoz, and Prinz 1993]. The shell elements on the sheet approximation can also be automatically generated.[2] The load condition, in this case the weights of the audio components, are obtained from the database just as their sizes were obtained. By evaluating the deflection of the shelves while varying the thickness of the shelves, the designer can determine the proper thickness of the shelves and store that information in the database. This process may be automated by integrating the finite-element method and the optimization procedures. The thickness of the door and the side walls may be determined similarly or simply from aesthetic considerations.

The designer then considers the method to be used in assembling the shelves and the side walls. Ideally, this method can also be determined by considering the strength of the whole structure or by an expert system that has some knowledge about assembly methods.

When the design conceptualization, analysis, and optimization phases have been completed, the designer moves on to design documentation to specify the details of the cabinet. That is, the part drawings of the shelves, doors, and side walls are generated by using computer-aided drafting. In this phase, the designer can add more details for aesthetic purposes (e.g., some decorative details on the doors or side walls). These part drawings are also stored in the database for use in the manufacturing process.

To make the cabinet, each part shape is arranged on the raw material, in this case sheets of wood, and cut out with a saw. Waste can be reduced by arranging the parts efficiently on the wood sheets. The designer can try various parts layouts on the computer screen until obtaining a layout with minimum waste. The computer program can facilitate this process by calculating the amount of waste for each layout. Also a nesting program that automatically provides the most economic layout can be used. In either method, the final layout is stored in the computer and will be used to determine the path of a saw that is driven by a numerical controller. Furthermore, software tools may be used to design the jigs and fixtures for this cutting process and to program the materials handling systems. These systems may be conveyor belts or robots that transfer the raw material and the cut parts to and from the saw.

Once prepared, the parts have to be assembled. Ideally, the assembly process can also be carried out by robots that are programmed automatically from the descriptions of the final product and its parts that are stored in the database. The jigs and fixtures for the assembly process can also be designed simultaneously. In addition, a robot can be programmed to paint the cabinet after it has been assembled. Currently, the assembling jigs and fixtures are designed or selected by the process planner, and robot programming is done interactively as the programmer moves around the robot's end-effector for the desired tasks.

This scenario is summarized in Figure 1.3. It shows how the CAD, CAM, and CAE activities are integrated through the database, which is the objective of CIM.

---

[2] Fully automatic MAT and mesh generation on an arbitrary three-dimensional object are not currently available.

Figure 1.3

Integration of CAD, CAM, and CAE through the database

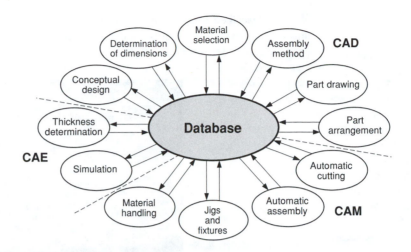

1.4 USING CAD/CAM/CAE SYSTEMS FOR PRODUCT DEVELOPMENT—A PRACTICAL EXAMPLE

In the previous section, we presented an ideal scenario in which all design and manufacturing activities were integrated through a common database. In this section, we introduce a practical example in which current CAD/CAM/CAE systems are applied to development of a product. In this case we apply CAD, CAM, and CAE systems in collaboration to the common geometric model of a part.

Assume that our task is to design and manufacture the front piece of a cellular phone shown in Figure 1.4. To simplify the problem, let's assume that we have already carried out the styling and conceptual design process with a CAD system and that the part shown is the result.

Figure 1.4

Solid model of example part

As described earlier, the next step in the product cycle would be the design analysis, for which the analysis model shown in Figure 1.5 is generated by a CAE preprocessor. The one used here is the commercial pre-processor, Pro/Mesh.[3]

Figure 1.5

Finite-element analysis model of example part: (a) finite-element meshes; (b) load condition, case 1; (c) load condition, case 2

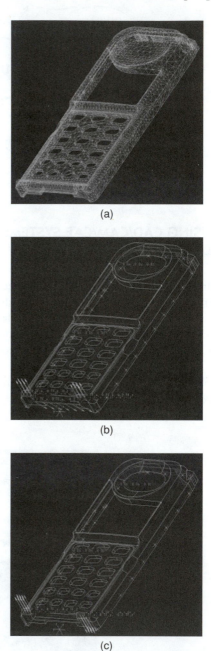

(a)

(b)

(c)

[3] Pro/Mesh is a registered trademark of Parametric Technology Corporation.

Figure 1.6

Stress distribution
on example part:
(a) result for case 1
and (b) result for
case 2

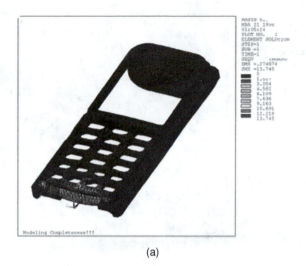

(a)

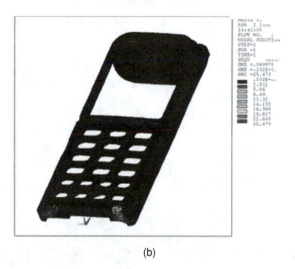

(b)

Figure 1.5(a) shows the tetrahedron elements that have been automatically generated, and Figures 1.5(b) and (c) show two different sets of the external loads applied at the hinge area.

Running a finite-element analysis on the finite-element model, we can verify
whether the designed cover is strong enough. Figure 1.6 shows the result, displaying
the stress distribution on the part by color mapping when the external loads are applied at the hinge area. Note that higher stresses exist at the hinge area, a result that
coincides with our intuition. We can also run a simulation program to check whether
the molten resin will propagate into the cavity of the injection mold. If the simulation result tells us that there are some problems with flow in the mold, we will need
to thicken the part at the proper locations. Figure 1.7 illustrates the simulation result.

Figure 1.7

Fill-time distribution
for example part

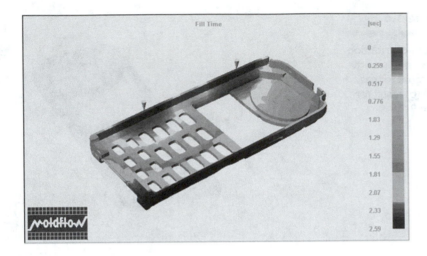

At this stage, we can also make a physical prototype, using a rapid prototyping system for a design evaluation. A physical mock-up is commonly used for aesthetic or functional evaluation of a design. Figure 1.8 shows the prototype of the example part made by a rapid prototyping system. Once the part design has been approved, a part drawing, as shown in Figure 1.9, can be generated if needed. Note that only the important dimensions are displayed to simplify the drawing.

Now we move to the manufacturing process: injection mold design, production of the mold, and injection of parts. From the part model data generated by CAD, the core, cavity, and side cores are designed interactively by using a general-purpose geometric modeling system or automatically by using a specialized injection mold design system. Figure 1.10 shows the resulting core, cavity, and side cores for the example part.

Figure 1.8

Physical prototype
of example part

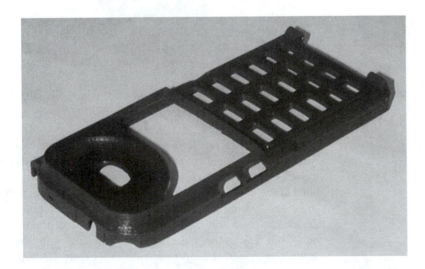

Figure 1.9

Part drawing of example part

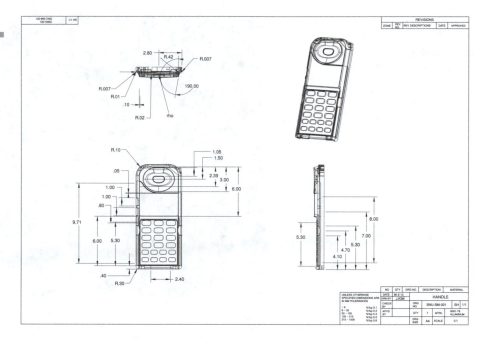

Figure 1.10

Core, cavity, and side cores for example part

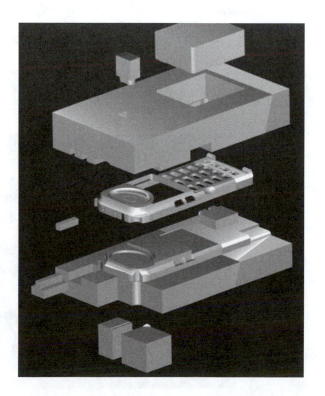

Figure 1.11

Completely de-
signed mold base

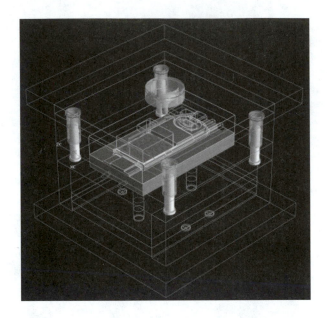

From the core, cavity, and side core data, a proper mold base can be selected from the database containing standard mold bases. Then gates, runners, cooling channels, and other mold components are designed and imbedded in the mold base, as shown in Figure 1.11. At this stage, we can run the simulation program again to predict the mold flow behavior more exactly. We can also run a heat transfer analysis to verify the cooling channel design.

Upon completion of the mold design, CAM software is used to calculate the NC tool paths required to machine the cavity plate and the core plate, as shown in Figure 1.12. When the necessary machining has been completed, the mold base is

Figure 1.12

NC tool paths re-
quired to machine
mold

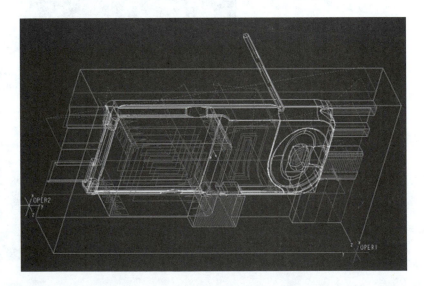

assembled and used for injection molding. Here we can also use the simulations to determine proper processing conditions, such as mold temperature, injection pressure, and resin temperature.

QUESTIONS AND PROBLEMS

1. Describe the difference between the design and analysis models.

2. Why is the analysis model different from the design model?

3. What types of analysis work are involved in the design process?

4. What are the roles of CAD tools in the design process?

5. Among the roles identified in Question 4, which is the most important role and why?

6. Based on your answer to Question 5, list the most important types of CAD tools.

7. What are the roles of CAM tools in the manufacturing process?

8. Of those roles named in Question 7, which is most mature? Explain why.

9. Which advantage can be expected from group technology if similar parts are grouped into a family?

10. What is the main advantage of using CAE tools in the design process?

2

Components of CAD/CAM/CAE Systems

Specific types of hardware and software are required for the computer-oriented approach to the design and manufacturing process illustrated in Chapter 1 Interactive shape manipulation was key to that process, so it should come as no surprise that hardware and software enabling interactive shape manipulation would be the major components comprising CAD/CAM/CAE systems. Thus, as shown in Figure 2.1, graphics devices and their peripherals for input and output operations, in addition to normal computing machines, comprise the hardware for CAD/CAM/CAE systems. The key software components are packages that manipulate or analyze shapes according to the user's interactions with them, either in two or three dimensions, and

Figure 2.1

Components of CAD/CAM/CAE systems

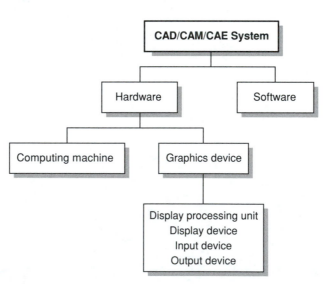

update the database. These hardware and software components are explained in detail in the following sections.

2.1   HARDWARE COMPONENTS

As illustrated in Figure 2.1, a graphics device is composed of a display processing unit, a display device (called a monitor), and one or more input devices. The display device, or monitor, functions as a screen on which a graphical image appears, but locating a specified image on the screen is a function of the display processing unit. In other words, the display processing unit accepts the signals corresponding to the graphics commands, produces electron beams, and transmits them to the proper locations on the monitor to generate the desired image.

A graphics device is usually accompanied by one or a combination of various input devices. These include a mouse, a space ball, and a data tablet with a puck or a stylus, in addition to a keyboard. These input devices facilitate the interactive shape manipulations by allowing the user to provide graphics inputs directly to the computer. Each graphics device is also usually connected to output devices such as plotters and a color laser printer. These output devices may be shared with other graphics devices. With these output devices, any image on the display device can be transferred onto paper or other media. Figure 2.2 shows three input devices; Figure 2.3 shows two output devices.

Figure 2.2

Examples of input devices: (a) mouse, (b) data tablet with a puck and a stylus, and (c) space ball

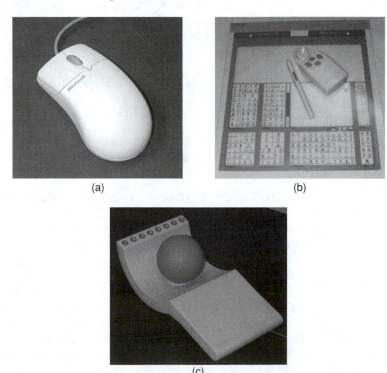

(a)   (b)

(c)

Figure 2.3

Examples of output devices: (a) plotter and (b) color laser printer

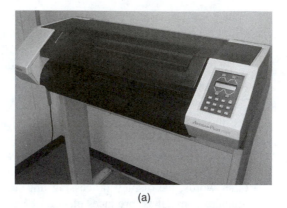

(a)

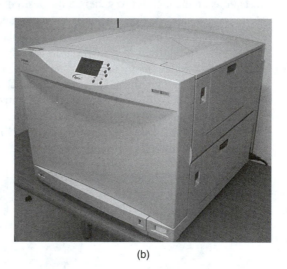

(b)

In the following sections, various graphics devices are illustrated and their operating principles are described.

2.1.1 Vector-Refresh (Stroke-Refresh) Graphics Devices

Vector-refresh graphics devices, which were introduced in the mid 1960s, are composed of a display processing unit, a display buffer memory, and a cathode ray tube (CRT), as illustrated in Figure 2.4. The basic principles of their operation can be briefly explained as follows.

The display processing unit reads the display list, which can be considered as the list of the codes corresponding to the graphics commands sent from the application program. The display list is stored in that portion of memory called a *display buffer*. The processing unit also loads the display list into the display buffer. Then, as shown in Figure 2.5, the display processing unit generates the proper voltages

Figure 2.4

Components of a
vector-refresh
graphics device

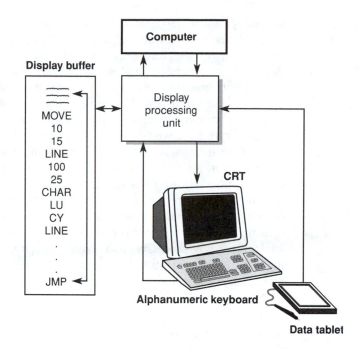

Figure 2.5

Cross-sectional
view of a cathode
ray tube (CRT)

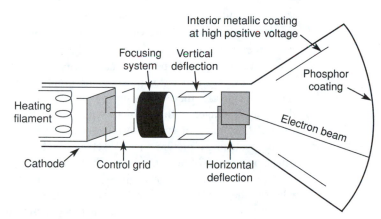

across the vertical and horizontal deflection plates so that the electron emitted from the cathode hits the correct location on the inside surface of the CRT. This location corresponds to one spot of the image to be created. The inside surface of the tube is coated with phosphor, and thus a light will glow for a short time at the location hit by an electron. In this way, as the electron beam traverses the screen, an image generated by the display list in the display buffer will appear.

However, the light emission by the phosphor lasts for only a very short time before disappearing. Therefore the image must be redrawn repeatedly and very rapidly so that the user will not see a flickering image. An image stays on the human eye about 1/30 second, so the user will not notice the disappearance of the image if it is redrawn within 1/30 second. This redrawing process, called *refresh*, is achieved by repeated reading of the display buffer from top to bottom and directing the electron beam according to each display list. The display buffer is required solely for the refresh. Depending on the complexity of the image, the refresh operation may take longer than 1/30 second. Therefore the images drawn at the beginning of the refresh operation disappear while some remaining images are still being redrawn so that the whole scene will appear to flicker. This and the high cost of vector-refresh graphics devices are the major disadvantages of such devices.

However, the voltages supplied to the vertical and horizontal deflection plates can be controlled to a resolution as fine as desired. Thus the display device may have high resolution (e.g., 4096 by 4096), and straight lines can be displayed without a jagged appearance. In addition, a dynamic display for animation is possible. A dynamic display is obtained simply by modifying the contents of the display buffer while the display processing unit is reading each line of the buffer and working on the refresh. The contents of the display buffer are modified by receipt of the graphics commands from the application program, an animation program in this case.

2.1.2 Raster Graphics Devices

Raster graphics devices were introduced in the mid 1970s as a result of the widespread availability of television technology. Since their emergence, they have become the main type of graphics device due to their high performance-to-price ratio. The basic principle of operation can be briefly explained as follows.

The display processor receives the graphics commands from the application program, converts them into a dot-by-dot representation, or raster image, and stores those raster images in that portion of memory called a *frame buffer*, as illustrated in Figure 2.6. You can easily visualize a dot-by-dot representation of an image by closely watching a picture on a TV set. The picture is simply an approximation of an image as a group of dots, or pixels. The sizes of the dots correspond to the resolution desired. The raster image is stored in the memory of the raster graphics device, whereas the display lists corresponding to the graphics commands are stored in the vector-refresh device. Therefore the memory requirement and the method of refresh of the two types of devices will differ.

While the display processor generates and stores the raster image in the frame buffer, it also reads the contents of the buffer and casts the electron beams onto the display device, reproducing the image from the frame buffer. The inside of the display device can be coated with phosphor dots as numerous as the dots in the frame buffer. Therefore the electron beam is cast onto the phosphor dots corresponding to the dots of the raster image. As in a vector-refresh device, light emission of the phosphors lasts only a brief time, and thus refresh is required. The only difference is the pattern in which the electron beam is scanned for the refresh. As illustrated in Figure 2.7, the electron beam is repeatedly scanned to the right, with scan lines

Figure 2.6

Components of a raster graphics device

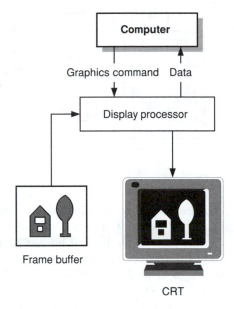

Figure 2.7

Scanning pattern for raster refresh

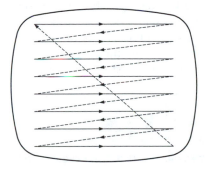

looping downward. In the course of scanning when the electron beam is positioned to point to the phosphor dots corresponding to the dots of the image, it will be simply turned on, causing the phosphor to be activated. In this way, the time required for the refresh will be constant regardless of the complexity of the image to be drawn. In fact, the refresh time is the time required to scan the electron beam from the top scan line to the bottom scan line—usually 1/30 second for normal TV sets or 1/60 second for high-end raster graphics devices. However, the frame buffer in raster graphics devices requires much more memory than the display buffer for vector-refresh devices.

The raster image stored in the frame buffer may carry color information if more than one bit is allocated for each dot (or pixel) of the raster image. Consider the use of three bits for each pixel. As shown in Figure 2.8, the frame buffer in

Figure 2.8

Example of 3-bit planes

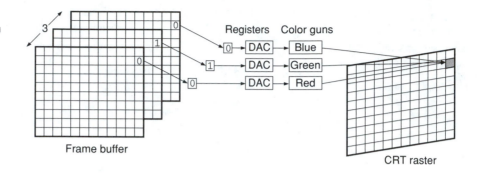

this case can be represented by three planes, each of which provides one bit for all the pixels, and thus the frame buffer is said to have 3-bit planes. With three bits for each pixel, the first bit can be used to represent the on/off state for the color red, the second bit for green, and the third bit for blue. Thus the eight colors shown in Table 2.1 can be defined and displayed simultaneously on the display device. The DACs shown in Figure 2.8 are the digital-to-analog converters that generate the analog signal controlling each color gun in accordance with the on/off signal of each color bit. Because of the declining price of memory chips, raster graphics devices with 24-bit planes (eight for each red, green, and blue), tend to be prevalent. In those devices, 256 (2^8) different levels can be defined for each color and thus a total of 16,777,216 (2^{24}) colors can be defined and displayed simultaneously on the display device. Figure 2.9 illustrates how any spe-

TABLE 2.1

Possible colors in the case of 3-bit planes

	Red	Green	Blue
Black	0	0	0
Red	1	0	0
Green	0	1	0
Blue	0	0	1
Yellow	1	1	0
Cyan	0	1	1
Magenta	1	0	1
White	1	1	1

Figure 2.9

Color definition, using 24-bit planes

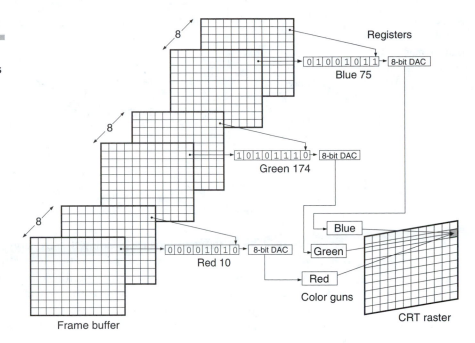

Figure 2.10

Distribution of phosphors for different colors

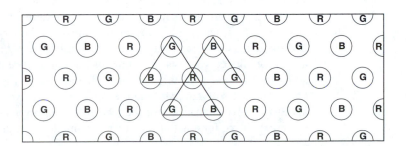

cific color can be stored in the frame buffer. The DACs in Figure 2.9 have the same function as those in Figure 2.8, except that each DAC has the resolution of eight bits instead of one bit.

Once a color has been defined for a dot of the frame buffer, the corresponding location on the monitor will be colored as in normal TV sets. The process can be briefly explained as follows. The inside of the monitor tube is coated with three different kinds of phosphor: The first one emits red light when activated by the associated gun, the second one emits green, and the third one emits blue. Those phosphors are distributed to form triangles, as illustrated in Figure 2.10. Each of these triangles corresponds to one dot in the frame buffer. Each phosphor in a triangle receives an amount of energy from the associated gun in proportion to the analog signal from a DAC (shown in Figure 2.8 or 2.9) and emits the light of the

Figure 2.11

Shadow mask

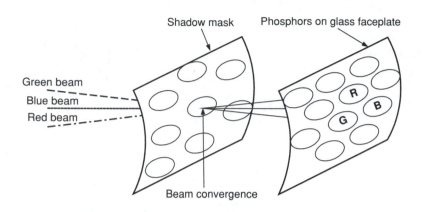

corresponding color in an intensity corresponding to the energy received. The light of the different colors from each phosphor is positioned in a triangle but will be combined in the viewer's vision and appear to be the color originally intended in the frame buffer. It's possible for an electron beam to affect a phosphor that is not associated with its gun. For example, the gun associated with the red phosphor might shoot at a green phosphor. To prevent that from happening, a shadow mask is positioned as shown in Figure 2.11. The shadow mask ensures that each electron beam will hit only the associated phosphor.

2.2 HARDWARE CONFIGURATION

The graphics devices explained in the previous section are not usually used as a single unit; instead, they are connected to form a cluster to support multiple users. There are basically three possible configurations.

The first configuration is composed of a mainframe computer and multiple graphics devices, as illustrated in Figure 2.12. The graphics devices are connected to the mainframe similar to the way alphanumeric terminals are connected to the mainframe in a normal data processing environment. Some output devices, such as plotters, are also connected to the mainframe, as printers are. Because this configuration can be considered as a natural extension of the existing computing environment, it was readily accepted by most of the large companies that already had mainframes. In fact, this approach is still used by automobile manufacturers and shipbuilders whose large databases are handled centrally. However, there are some disadvantages to this approach. It requires a big initial investment for the hardware and software, and maintenance is expensive. Maintaining a mainframe always involves expansion of the system's memory and hard disk, which is a lot more expensive for a mainframe than for smaller machines. Furthermore, updating

Figure 2.12

Hardware configuration, using a mainframe

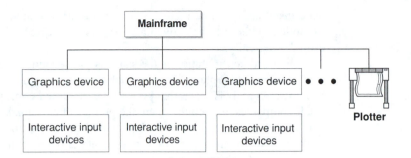

the operating system is not a simple job. Quite often CAD/CAM/CAE software has to be replaced either because much more powerful software has been introduced or because the initial selection of the software was not right. The CAD/CAM/CAE software running on a mainframe is much more expensive than the same software on smaller machines, so replacement of the software on a mainframe will involve a much bigger cost. Another serious disadvantage with the mainframe approach is system response time. With a mainframe, all the application programs in each graphics device are competing with each other for the machine's computing capability. Thus the system response for any one graphics device varies, depending on the task being ordered by another graphics device. Sometimes the system response may be too slow for the interactive graphics operation, especially when a heavy computation such as finite-element analysis is being performed by others at the same time.

The second configuration is composed of engineering workstations connected in a networked environment, as shown in Figure 2.13. Output devices such as plotters are also connected to the network. The engineering workstation can be considered a graphics device with its own computing power. This approach is widely used because of rapid progress in workstation technologies and the trend toward distributed computing. In fact, the performance of same-priced engineering workstations has been doubling every year. This approach has several advantages. The user can choose the computing power of any workstation on the network, using the most appropriate workstation for the task, with system response not affected by other people's tasks. Another advantage is the avoidance of a large initial investment. The number of workstations together with the soft-

Figure 2.13

Hardware configuration, using engineering workstations

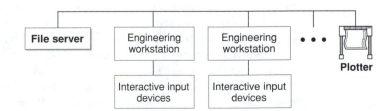

ware installation can be increased as the activities related to CAD/CAM/CAE are expanded. This is a real advantage because the price of hardware continues to drop dramatically.

The third configuration is the same as the second, except that the engineering workstations are replaced by personal computers that are run by the Microsoft Windows 95 and NT operating systems. A PC-based configuration is popular with small companies, especially where the products being made are composed of small numbers of parts of reasonable complexity. This configuration is also popular with companies whose main purpose is to generate drawings with their CAD/CAM/CAE systems. As the distinction between personal computers and engineering workstations becomes blurred, so does the distinction between the second and the third configurations.

2.3 SOFTWARE COMPONENTS

As defined in Chapter 1, any software used in the product cycle to reduce the time and cost of product development and to enhance product quality can be classified as CAD/CAM/CAE software. Specifically, the key CAD software allows the designer to create and manipulate a shape interactively on the monitor and store it in the database. However, in general, any software that can facilitate the design process can, in a sense, be classified as CAD software. For example, a customized application program for automating the design of a specific part or mechanism is also considered to be CAD software. Figure 2.14 shows a mechanical drawing, an architectural drawing, and an electrical circuit diagram generated by computer-aided drafting, a typical CAD software. Figure 2.15 shows a solid model created by a geometric modeling system, another typical CAD software.

Similarly, any software used to facilitate the manufacturing process of the product cycle is classified as CAM software. That is, any software related to planning, managing, and controlling the operations of a manufacturing plant through either direct or indirect computer interface with the plant's production resources can be considered as CAM software. For example, software that generates a process plan to manufacture a part is typical CAM software. Another example is the software that generates a part program, simulates the tool motion, and drives an NC machine tool to machine the external surfaces of a part. Figure 2.16 illustrates the simulation of the tool path of an NC milling machine generated by CAM software after the part geometry has been already created by the use of CAD software.

CAE software is used to analyze design geometry, allowing the designer to simulate and study how the product will behave. Thus the design can be refined and optimized. A typical example of CAE software is a finite-element program used to calculate factors such as the stress, deformation, and heat transfer on a part of an assembly. Figure 2.17 illustrates the contour plots of stress on a part under load. Other types of CAE systems and their functions were introduced in Chapter 1.

Figure 2.14

Example outputs of computer-aided drafting system: (a) example of a mechanical drawing; (b) example of an architectural drawing (drawing courtesy of AutoCAD® sample, drawn in AutoCAD® Release 13, Autodesk); and (c) example of an electric circuit diagram

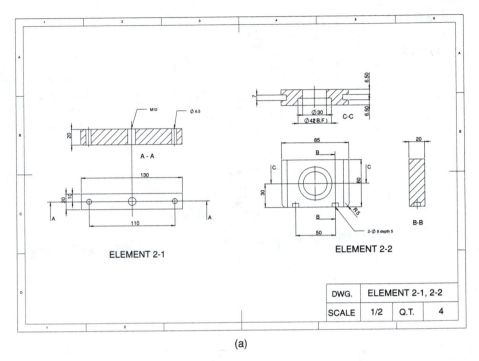

(a)

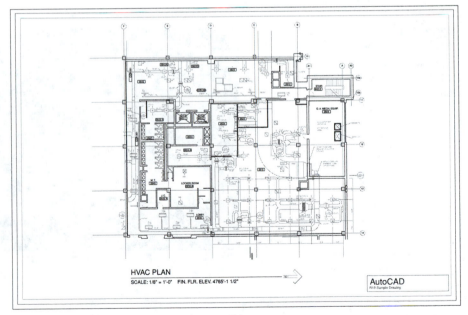

(b)

Figure 2.14

(Continued)

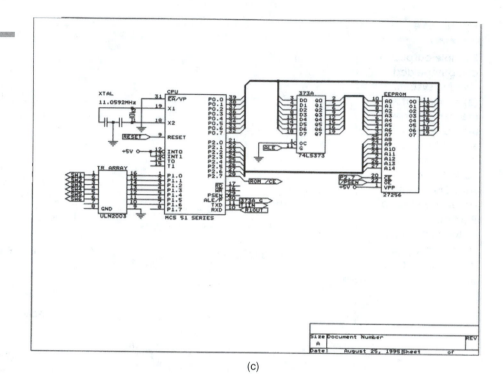

(c)

Figure 2.15

Example output of solid modeling system

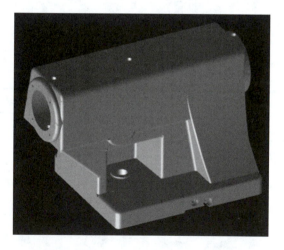

Figure 2.16

Example output of
NC tool path simu-
lation (Courtesy of
Gibbs and
Associates, Virtual
Gibbs)

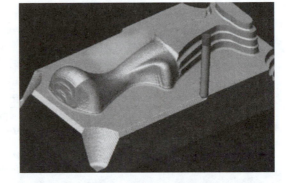

Figure 2.17

Example output of
CAE system
(Courtesy of
Unigraphics/FEA,
Unigraphics
Solutions, Inc.)

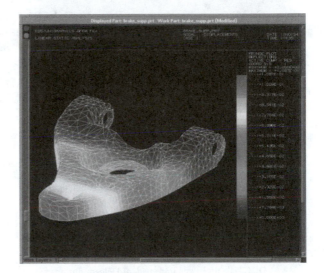

The shape created by a CAD system can be used for applications such as NC tool-path generation and three-dimensional stress analysis only if the shape was created in three dimensions. This explains the practice of designers starting their design in three dimensions by using geometric modeling.

Some commercial software widely used for CAD/CAM/CAE are presented in Table 2.2. Selection of the software packages included in the table was based on the author's familiarity with them, not because they represent each application area. Therefore some commercial software with powerful capabilities may have been omitted. The integrated systems in the right-hand column provide CAD, CAM, and CAE capabilities through their option modules. As described in Chapter 5, many PC-based systems continue to emerge. We briefly introduce PC-based CAD systems in Section 2.4.

In addition to the CAD/CAM/CAE systems listed in Table 2.2, several modeling tool kit software products are becoming popular because they provide a flexible modeling environment that can be tailored to each application. Any specific appli-

TABLE 2.2

Some typical CAD/CAM/CAE software

Application Area	Software	Integrated System
CAD—2D drafting	CADAM, AutoCAD, MicroCADAM, VersaCAD	Pro/ENGINEER
CAD—Solid modeling	Solid Edge, SolidWorks, SolidDesigner, Mechanical Desktop	Unigraphics CATIA I-DEAS
CAM	BravoNCG, VERICUT, DUCT, Camand, Mastercam, PowerMILL	I/EMS EUCLID-IS
CAE	MSC/NASTRAN, ANSYS, PATRAN, DADS, ADAMS, C-MOLD, MOLDFLOW, DesignWorks	

Notes:
ANSYS is a registered trademark of Swanson Analysis Systems, Inc.
AutoCAD is a registered trademark of AutoDesk, Inc.
BravoNCG is a registered trademark of Applicon, Inc.
CADAM is a registered trademark of CADAM, Inc.
CATIA is a registered trademark of DASSAULT SYSTEMS.
C-MOLD is a registered trademark of Adavanced CAE Technology.
Camand is a registered trademark of Structural Dynamics Research Corporation (SDRC).
DADS is a registered trademark of CADS, Inc.
DesignWorks is a registered trademark of Computer Aided Design Software, Inc.
DUCTis a registered trademark of Delcam, Int.
EUCLID-IS is a registered trademark of Matra Datavision.
I/EMS is a registered trademark of Intergraph, Inc.
I-DEAS is a registered trademark of Structural Dynamics Research Corporation (SDRC).
Mastercam is a registered trademark of CNC Software Inc.
Mechanical Desktop is a registered trademark of Autodesk, Inc.
MicroCADAM is a registered trademark of CADAM, Inc.
MOLDFLOW is a registered trademark of Moldflow Pty Ltd.
MSC/NASTRAN is a registered trademark of MacNeal-Schwendler Corporation.
PATRAN is a registered trademark of MacNeal-Schwendler Corporation.
PowerMILL is a registered trademark of Delcam International Inc.
Pro/ENGINEER is a registered trademark of Parametric Technology Corporation.
SolidDesigner is a registered trademark of Hewlett-Packard Company.
Solid Edge is a registered trademark of Intergraph Corporation.
SolidWorks is a registered trademark of SolidWorks Corporation.
VERICUT is a registered trademark of CGTech.
VersaCAD is a registered trademark of T&W Systems, Inc.
Unigraphics is a registered trademark of Unigraphics Solutions, Inc.

cation program that involves the creation and manipulation of a three-dimensional shape can be constructed by collecting just the necessary modeling tools from the kit. The result is a compact application program tailored precisely to the required function. The typical modeling tool kits available these days are ACIS, SHAPES, Parasolid, CAS.CADE, and DESIGNBASE.

2.4   WINDOWS-BASED CAD SYSTEMS

As the CAD/CAM/CAE software market has matured, things have changed radically. First, engineers and manufacturers have become accustomed to the idea that they need more than two-dimensional drafting tools. Earlier they longed for versatile three-dimensional CAD systems that could drive design and lead from design directly through manufacturing on affordable platforms. Until recently, industrial applications have dominated traditional high-end CAD tools. Fortunately, PC hardware has become incredibly fast and powerful, and many software developers have begun producing good software products that take advantage of the superior graphics environments offered by Microsoft Windows 95 and Windows NT. The earliest software releases in this category occurred in 1995; most of the products were first released in 1996.

These products have the following common features. First, they were developed by exploiting the functions provided by Windows 95 and Windows NT to the maximum and thus have user interfaces similar to other Microsoft programs. In fact, they look similar to other Microsoft office automation programs, and so users feel comfortable with them and learn to use them very quickly. In addition, they have the object linking and embedding (OLE) capabilities of other Microsoft office automation programs. That is, any image of a three-dimensional part or an assembly created by these systems can be shared by other Microsoft programs. Imagine using this feature to generate a service manual. You may simply and conveniently cut the exploded view of an assembly from the CAD system and paste it into the proper location of a text file created and edited on a word processor. Currently, this OLE capability is expanding to share even three-dimensional data,[1] and this expanded capability makes data transfer between different CAD systems much easier.

Second, these systems involve use of the approach called *component technology*, in which the best key software elements are selected from among available software. Then the system developer can simply assemble proven technologies while focusing on the capabilities that directly facilitate the design process. For example, the system developer may use ACIS from Spatial Technology, Parasolids from Unigraphics Solutions, or Designbase from Ricoh as a modeling kernel (key software for handling shape manipulation in three dimensions) and Constraint Solver from D-cubed for the parametric design. In this way, developmental time can

[1] This capability is called *OLE for Design & Manufacturing*.

be saved and only the capabilities directly facilitating the design task need be provided. Some systems also use programs developed by others for database management and for handling curve and surface equations.

Third, these systems employ object-oriented technology, three aspects of which should be considered. In terms of programming, object-oriented technology means modularizing the program according to its various functions so that each module can be reused later independently. A typical programming language supporting modular programming is C++. With C++, each function can be programmed so that it acts as an independent unit. Object-oriented technology also applies to the system's interface with the user. When a system has an object-oriented user interface, every icon comprising the interface is programmed to recognize the current situation and the response to make when it is selected. In this way, the system guides the user to give the necessary input. This guidance helps the user feel a lot easier when working with the system. Object-oriented technology is also used for the efficient storage of data. In conventional CAD systems, the data associated with a part are usually stored in several files: a file for storing its geometric model, another file for its finite element meshes, and another file for its NC tool path, and so on. However, in the object-oriented approach, all the data associated with a part are stored in one file. Common data that are stored in several files redundantly in a conventional system are stored only once in an object-oriented system, saving substantial memory.

Fourth, the systems provide the capability of either parametric modeling[2] or variational modeling. Both approaches allow a user to define a shape by using constraints instead of manipulating the shapes of elements directly. The only difference is whether the constraints are solved sequentially or simultaneously. Defining a rectangle as two sets of parallel lines separated by exact distances is an example of manipulating shape elements directly. However, defining the same rectangle by specifying constraints such as perpendicularity between adjacent lines and the distances between the parallel lines is an example of defining a shape by using constraints. Many systems that support parametric or variational modeling capability presume the self-evident constraints such as perpendicularity and parallelism from the user's initial sketch to minimize the user's input. In this case, the user is required to input only the dimensions and is allowed to change the shape by changing the dimension values. Thus we call this capability *dimension-driven modeling*. This means that the geometry of a part is determined by the part's dimensions and that its geometry can be easily modified by changing the dimension values. In these systems, the user can also specify the relationships between dimensions so that the geometry can be modified while maintaining the relationships. This is one of the mechanisms that can be used to store the designer's intent as part of the final design. However, providing all the constraints required to define the geometry completely may be difficult, especially for a complicated part. In this case, the systems supporting parametric or variational modeling still need more intelligence in order to render the design conveniently.

---

[2] We show this capability in Section 5.3.1.

Finally, the systems have Internet support for collaborative engineering. This support allows remotely located users to communicate regarding the same part while marking up the part model on their screens. A designer may also check a part by fitting its model to those of other parts designed by other people. To enable this capability, writing a part file in VRML format is a minimum requirement. Appendix L compares the features of the Windows-based CAD systems.

QUESTIONS AND PROBLEMS

1. List the components of a graphics device and explain the role of each component.

2. Explain why refresh is required in a vector-refresh or raster graphics device.

3. Explain how animation can be realized in a vector-refresh graphics device.

4. Explain why flickering does not occur in a raster graphics device regardless of image complexity.

5. Consider a raster graphics device composed of 12-bit planes (i.e., 4-bit planes for red, 4-bit planes for green, and 4-bit planes for blue). How many colors can be displayed simultaneously on this device?

6. List the advantages of a hardware configuration composed of networked engineering workstations.

7. List the two-dimensional drafting software available to you.

8. List the geometric modeling systems available to you.

9. List the CAM software available to you. Briefly describe the function of each software product.

10. List the CAE software available to you. Briefly describe the function of each software product.

3

Basic Concepts of Graphics Programming

As mentioned earlier, interactive shape manipulation plays a major role in CAD/CAM/CAE systems. Programming that creates a graphics display on a display monitor is thus an essential part of CAD/CAM/CAE software. Hence we need to review some of the terminology and concepts that are basic to graphics programming.

3.1 GRAPHICS LIBRARIES

The term *computer programming* used to mean writing a composition by using some computer commands in compliance with a predetermined grammar. The composition generated the desired numbers and characters on the terminal or in a data file when it was executed with inputs of numbers or characters. Today, however, it is not unusual for the composition, in addition to working with numbers and characters, to accept graphics information as input and produce graphics display as output. The activity that includes graphics as input and output is called *graphics programming*, and the field related to it is called *computer graphics*.

In addition to the basic software—operating system, editor, and compiler software—required for conventional programming, some basic graphics software is required for graphics programming. Graphics software may be divided into two groups: device drivers and graphics libraries.

A device driver may be considered to be a set of machine-dependent codes that directly controls the display processing unit of a graphics device so that the electron beam is cast at the desired location (see Chapter 2). Each device driver is device-dependent, as if it were hard-wired to a specific display processing unit. Thus a display processing unit of one graphics device works with a specific device driver. It is analogous to the way that one type of assembler language can be understood only by a specific type of computer and a program written in that assembler language can be executed only on that type of computer. The same thing happens when a graphics program is written directly with a device driver, as illustrated in Figure 3.1. That is, the graphics program needs to be rewritten with the proper device driver commands when a different graphics device has to be used. Furthermore, each device driver command has only a primitive capability, and so a graphics program written with such commands would be very long if any meaningful task were to be performed. A program with poor readability will result.

Programmers now want to write programs in languages of a higher level. Graphics programming cannot be an exception, especially considering the inconveniences caused by using device driver commands of a lower level. Thus it has been a common practice to equip a graphics device with a library called a *graphics library*. Similar to the math library in conventional programming, the graphics library is a set of subroutines, each of which has a specific purpose. For example, a subroutine might draw a line or a subroutine might draw a circle. The graphics library is built on top of the device driver, as illustrated in Figure 3.2. Each subroutine is created by using a supporting set of device driver commands. For example, a subroutine for drawing a circle might be composed of a series of a device driver command drawing a short straight-line segment.

The subroutines of a graphics library can be used in exactly the same way as that of a math library; that is, the necessary subroutine is called from the main program just as the sine and cosine functions in the math library are called when the values of those functions are needed. One problem with the subroutines in the graphics library is that their names and the way they are called (e.g., the input and output arguments) vary for each different graphics library. This may not be a problem if one graphics library can drive all the existing graphics devices; this arrangement is theoretically possible if all the existing device drivers support the graphics library. However, for practical reasons software vendors cannot or do not want to develop a graphics library that can be interfaced with all the device drivers, and

Figure 3.1

A type of graphics programming using a device driver directly

Figure 3.2

A type of graphics programming using a graphics library

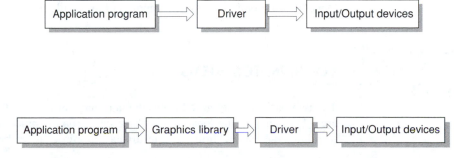

thus all graphics libraries are bundled with a limited number of different device drivers. Therefore each graphics library drives a limited number of graphics devices, and as a result, a graphics program may have to be rewritten with another graphics library if many types of graphics devices are to be used.

One of the ways to get around this problem would be for the developers of graphics libraries to use the same set of subroutines with the same name, arguments, and capability. (In practice, each subroutine is implemented by the set of device driver commands chosen independently by each developer.) In this way, graphics programs would not need to be modified at the source level, even when the graphics device changes. One example of this approach is the CORE graphics system proposed in 1977 by the Special Interest Group on Computer Graphics (SIGGRAPH) of the Association for Computing Machinery (ACM). However, the CORE graphics system does not provide enough commands to use all the capabilities of raster graphics systems because those systems were not widely available when CORE was being developed. The Graphics Kernel System (GKS) was developed by the International Standards Organization (ISO) at about the same time. The GKS is considered to be the standard for two-dimensional graphics, and it was extended to GKS-3D for three-dimensional graphics later.

Both CORE and GKS have some deficiencies with regard to supporting dynamic display and versatile user interactions. Thus ISO suggested another standard, the Programmer's Hierarchical Interactive Graphics System (PHIGS), which became a de facto standard graphics library for most workstations. Then PHIGS was extended to become PHIGS Extension to X (PEX) by including the X window system for operations related to windows (e.g., creating, manipulating, and closing windows). Thus graphics programs written in PEX can be used independently of the type of workstations in a networked environment, a benefit inherited from the X window system. (The X window system is described briefly at the end of this chapter.) Developed independently of the standards organizations, a commercial graphics library, OpenGL, is gaining popularity because of its versatility in driving both the engineering workstations and the personal computers (running under Microsoft's Windows NT) in a networked environment. OpenGL is an extension of GL, a proprietary graphics library for Silicon Graphics[1] machines. Because of the popularity of Silicon Graphics machines in computer graphics applications, OpenGL is becoming a de facto standard graphics library.

3.2 COORDINATE SYSTEMS

The two basic tasks required to display an image of an object on a graphics device are: (1) specifying the location of all the points on the object in space, and (2) determining which locations on the display monitor are to be occupied by those

---

[1] Silicon Graphics is the name of the company that manufactures graphics workstations such as Indigo and O_2.

points. Thus a coordinate system is necessary to provide a reference for specifying the location of a point both in space and on the monitor. Understanding the relationships among various coordinate systems is essential, especially in calculating where a three-dimensional point is projected onto a display monitor. This projection occurs in the same way an image is projected onto a person's retina.

One coordinate system is a *device coordinate system*, which is used as the reference in defining a location on a display monitor. In general, a device coordinate system comprises a u axis in the horizontal direction and a v axis in the vertical direction, as illustrated in Figure 3.3. Note that the origin of the coordinate system can be chosen arbitrarily. In addition, a third axis, perpendicular to both the u and v axes, is not defined because the u and v axes alone are sufficient to define any location on a display monitor. In fact, any such location is defined by two u and v integer values that give the number of pixels residing between the origin of the device coordinate system and the location of interest in the u and v directions, respectively. However, the same location on the monitor may have different u and v values, depending on the location of the origin, the direction of the u or v axis, and the range of the u and v values for the entire monitor; these may be arbitrarily set for each different graphics device, as shown in Figure 3.3. Therefore the device coordinates used in a graphics program may have to be changed if the same image has to be drawn on a different graphics device.

The *virtual device coordinate system* avoids the device coordinate system problem described. The virtual device coordinate system has the same origin, the same u and v axes, and the same range of u and v values for all workstations. The word *virtual* is used because the coordinate system exists only in a graphics programmer's imagination. Usually, it has the origin at the lower left corner of the display monitor, the u axis extending to the right, the v axis extending upward, and the range of u and v values being from 0 to 1. Thus a point specified by the values in reference to the virtual device coordinate system would always occupy the same location regardless of the type of graphics device. As a result, a graphics programmer can specify a shape consistently without having to consider a specific device coordinate system. In this case, knowing which graphics device is driven, the graphics program sends the virtual coordinate values to the device driver routine, which converts virtual coordinates to device coordinates in compliance with the device coordinate system of the specific graphics device.

Figure 3.3

Device coordinate systems

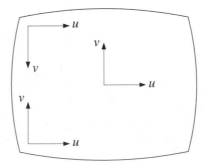

Both the device coordinate system and the virtual device coordinate system provide coordinate systems that specify the location on a two-dimensional display monitor. Let's now consider the coordinate systems that define the location of a point in three-dimensional space. There are basically three such coordinate systems: world coordinate system, model coordinate system, and viewing coordinate system.

The *world coordinate system* is a reference coordinate system used to describe what the world of interest looks like, as its name implies (i.e., what types of objects exist in the world and how they are located). For example, this system can be used to describe the locations and orientations of desks, chairs, and the blackboard if the world in which we have an interest is a classroom.

Now we have to describe the shape of each object in that world. The shape of an object is defined by the coordinates of all the points or some characteristic points on the object with respect to a coordinate system attached to the object. This coordinate system is called the *model coordinate system*. The coordinates of the points on an object defined with respect to its model coordinate system do not change their values even when the object is translated or rotated in space, but are determined solely by the shape of the object. That is, the model coordinate system moves with its object. This is why a shape of each object is defined with reference to its own model coordinate system. The location and the orientation of each object are then specified by the relative location and the orientation of its model coordinate system with respect to the world coordinate system. The relative locations and orientations of two coordinate systems are defined by the transformation matrix, which we explain in Section 3.7. With the world coordinate system and the model coordinate systems for all the objects in the world of interest, the scene of that world (i.e., the layout and the shape of all the objects in the world) is completely defined. In other words, the coordinates of all the points of the objects can be obtained in world coordinates after applying the associated transformation matrices.

The next task is to project those three-dimensional objects, or points on the objects, onto the monitor as they are projected onto the retina of the human eye. Two types of projection—perspective and parallel—are typically used in computer graphics, as illustrated in Figure 3.4.

Figure 3.4

Two types of projection: (a) perspective projection and (b) parallel projection

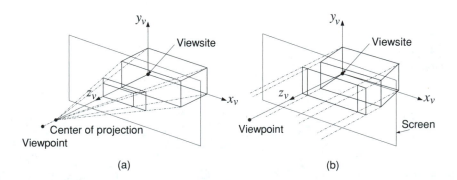

(a)   (b)

For both types of projection, the viewpoint and the viewsite need to be specified. The *viewpoint* is considered to be the viewer's eye. The *viewsite* is a point on the object; it defines the viewing direction so that the vector pointing from the viewpoint to the viewsite becomes the viewing direction.

In *perspective projection*, all the points on the object of interest are connected to the center of projection, usually located along the line from the viewsite to the viewpoint,[2] and the intersection points between these lines and the screen comprise the projected image. The screen is located between the viewpoint and the viewsite. In *parallel projection*, the parallel lines are cast from all the points on the object in the viewing direction defined by the viewsite and the viewpoint as before, and the intersection points between these lines and the screen comprise the image. Similar to perspective projection, the screen is oriented perpendicular to the projection direction for orthogonal projection.[3]

The projection points described in either of the two projection methods can be easily calculated if the coordinates of the points on the object being projected are given with respect to the $x_v y_v z_v$ coordinate system, as indicated in Figure 3.4.[4] For example, the projection points in the parallel projection can be generated by simply collecting the X_v and Y_v values of the corresponding points on the object. Thus the $x_v y_v z_v$ coordinate system is called a *viewing coordinate system* because it facilitates the viewing projection. The viewing coordinate system is constructed so that it possesses the following characteristics. As shown in Figure 3.4, the origin of the viewing coordinate system is located at the viewsite, the z_v axis points to the viewpoint from the origin, and the y_v axis is parallel with the vertical direction on the screen. The remaining axis, x_v, is determined by the cross product of the y_v and z_v axes. Most people naturally perceive the vertical direction in space to be the vertical direction on the screen, so the y_v axis is determined to be the projection of the vertical vector in space onto the screen. In most graphics libraries, the user is supposed to give this vertical vector in space, called the *up vector*, in world coordinates. The viewpoint and the viewsite are also specified in world coordinates, as illustrated in Figure 3.5.

Once the viewing coordinate system has been defined and all the coordinates of the points on the object of interest derived with respect to the viewing coordinate system, the next task is to calculate the locations of their projections on the screen. We already know that those projection points can be easily derived for the parallel projection. Therefore we need only describe the procedure to calculate the projection points for the perspective projection. Let's consider the top and side views from Figure 3.4(a), as shown in Figure 3.6. The point of interest is marked ⊙, and its coordinates with respect to the viewing coordinate system are denoted X_v, Y_v, and Z_v.

---

[2] In the oblique projection, the center of projection is not located along the line from the viewsite to the viewpoint.

[3] The screen may have an arbitrary orientation for oblique projection.

[4] It is also possible to locate the origin of the viewing coordinate system at the viewpoint with the z_v axis pointing from the viewpoint to the viewsite. Meanwhile, the x_v and y_v axes are determined in the same way, and the resulting coordinate system becomes the left-handed coordinate system. This leads to the logical interpretation of larger Z values being farther from the viewer. In our convention, objects with larger Z value are nearer the viewer.

Figure 3.5

Viewpoint and viewsite

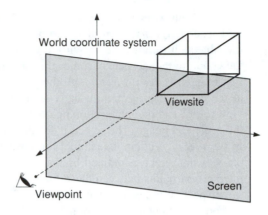

Figure 3.6

Calculation of projection point

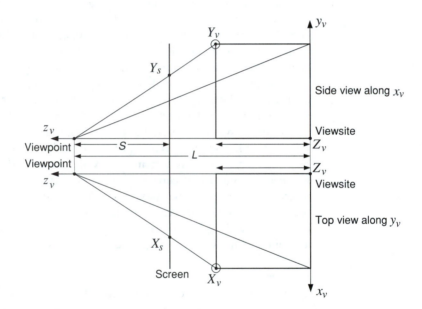

Applying the similarity rule between the triangles gives

$$X_s = \frac{S}{L - Z_v} X_v \qquad (3.1)$$

and

$$Y_s = \frac{S}{L - Z_v} Y_v \qquad (3.2)$$

In Equations (3.1) and (3.2), X_s and Y_s are the distances of the projection of the point marked ⊙. The distances are measured in the horizontal and vertical directions of the screen from the point where the z_v axis intersects the screen. Thus L is the distance between the viewsite and the center of projection, and S is the distance between the center of projection and the screen. Equations (3.1) and (3.2) indicate that a point with a bigger Z_v value would have bigger X_s and Y_s values, which makes a distant line appear smaller than a nearer line of the same length. The distances X_s and Y_s will be converted eventually to virtual device coordinates by considering the desired location of the center and the size of the image to appear on the display monitor.

The coordinate systems described are illustrated together in Figure 3.7 to clarify their relationships with each other.

The coordinate systems are related by the transformation matrices, as previously mentioned. Thus the location and orientation of each model coordinate system is specified by the corresponding transformation matrix with respect to the world coordinate system. The viewing coordinate system can also be defined by the transformation matrix with respect to the world coordinate system from the given viewpoint, viewsite, and up vector specified in the world coordinates. The procedure for calculating the projection points, using the transformation matrices, can be summarized as follows. First, the coordinate values of a point being projected are converted from model coordinates to world coordinates by applying the transformation matrix defining the relative translation and rotation between the world coordinate system and the point's model coordinate system. This operation is called *model transformation* and is shown in Figure 3.8. Second, the coordinate values of the same point are converted from world coordinates to viewing coordinates by applying the transformation matrix between the world coordinate system and the viewing coordinate system. This operation is called *viewing transformation* and is also shown in Figure 3.8. Third, the viewing coordinates of the point are converted into X_s and Y_s values by Equations (3.1) and (3.2), and again into virtual device coordinates. This operation is called *projection transformation* and is also shown in Figure 3.8. Finally, the virtual device coordinates are converted into device coordinates by the device driver routine, as shown in Figure 3.8.

Figure 3.7

Relationships among coordinate systems

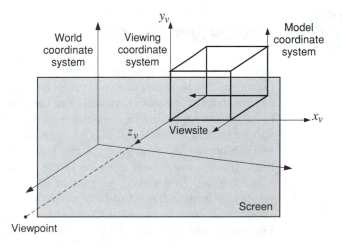

Figure 3.8

Transformations
between coordi-
nate systems

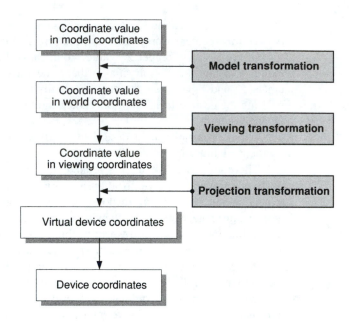

These transformations are usually performed inside the graphics library, and the graphics programmer need specify only the necessary information for each transformation. For example, the translations and rotations of the objects corresponding to their layout are provided for the model transformation; the viewpoint, the viewsite, and the up vector are provided for viewing transformation; and the type of projection together with the location of the center of projection and the screen are specified for the projection transformation. However, graphics libraries of a primitive level may require the programmer to write code for all those transformations. We explain the transformations in detail in Section 3.7.

3.3   WINDOW AND VIEWPORT

The word *window* used in the networked computing environment means the separate areas on a workstation monitor through which the user interacts with the various computational sources connected to the network. However the word *window* has a different meaning in computer graphics. It defines the region in space that will be projected onto the display monitor so that any object outside the window will not appear on the monitor. In this sense, it is analogous to the window of a house through which only a portion of the outside world is visible to a person inside the house. This analogy seems to be why the name window was selected. The window is usually defined to be a rectangle on a projection screen by the corresponding X_v and Y_v values in the viewing coordinate system, as illustrated in Figures 3.9 and 3.10. The visible region, called *viewing volume*, depends on the

Figure 3.9

Figure 3.9

Window and viewing volume for parallel projection

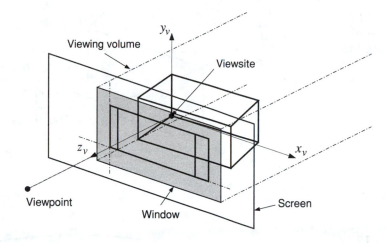

Figure 3.10

Window and viewing volume for perspective projection

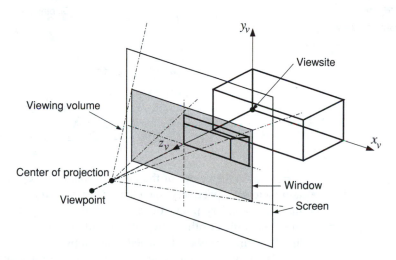

type of projection (i.e., parallelepiped for the parallel projection and pyramid for the perspective projection).

The viewing volume can yield a complicated image when projected because it may include unnecessary objects far from or near the viewer. Thus it is sometimes desirable to cut the viewing volume by both the near and far planes, as illustrated in Figure 3.11. The near and far planes for parallel projection are defined similarly.

The viewport is the area (or areas) on the display monitor where we want the projected image to appear, as shown in Figure 3.12. It is an area to which the viewing volume defined by the window is mapped. Mapping will involve a translation and a scaling to take into account the deviation of the viewport center from the center of the display monitor and the size difference between the window and the viewport. In other words, the X_s and Y_s values of the projection points obtained from Equations (3.1) and (3.2) have to be increased or decreased by certain values, respectively, so that the center of the window appears at the center of the viewport

Figure 3.11

Near plane and far plane

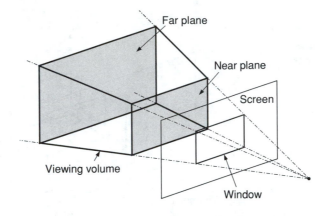

Figure 3.12

Examples of viewports

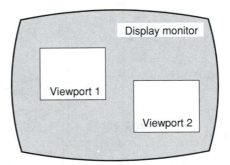

instead of at the center of the display monitor. They also have to be scaled by certain factors, respectively, such that the four boundary points of the window become the four boundary points of the viewport. The aspect ratio of the window must be the same as that of the viewport to avoid distortion of the image. Otherwise, for example, a circle may be displayed as an ellipse.

The following sample code is an example of defining a window and a viewport by using the graphics library, OpenGL. In OpenGL, the viewport is also defined as a three-dimensional volume. However, it results in the same graphics output as the two-dimensional viewport derived by ignoring the third dimension.

static GLint viewport[ ] = { 0, 0, 400, 400 };
Viewport is specified by the window[5] coordinates. The first and second arguments specify the lower left corner of the viewport, and the third and fourth arguments are the size of the viewport rectangle.

static GLclamped depth_range[ ] = { 0.0, 1.0 };
The first and second arguments represent adjustments to the minimum and maximum values that can be stored in the depth buffer.

---

[5] This window means the separate area on a workstation monitor through which the user interacts with a computer. It is opened and handled by the window manager of each operating system (e.g., an X-window client and Microsoft Windows).

static GLdouble viewing_volume[ ] = { −100.0, 100.0, −100.0, 100.0, −10.0, 100.0 };
The horizontal and the vertical ranges of the window are specified in viewing coordinates (first through fourth arguments). The fifth and sixth arguments represent the distances from the screen to the near and far planes, respectively.

glOrtho(viewing_volume[0], viewing_volume[1], viewing_volume[2], viewing_volume[3], viewing_volume[4], viewing_volume[5]);
Defines a projection type as the parallel projection and creates a matrix for an orthographic parallel viewing volume and multiplies the current matrix by it.

glViewport(viewport[0], viewport[1], viewport[2], viewport[3]);
Defines a pixel rectangle in the window opened by the window manager, and the final image is mapped into the window. If **glViewport** is not used, by default the viewport is set to the entire pixel rectangle of the window that is opened.

glDepthRange(depth_range[0], depth_range[1]);
Defines an encoding for z coordinates that is performed during the viewport transformation. The Z values can be scaled to lie within a desired range with this command.

3.4 OUTPUT PRIMITIVES

Output primitives are the graphics elements that can be displayed by a graphics library. They may be different for each specific graphics library, and thus only the output primitives supported in common by most graphics libraries are described in this section.

3.4.1 Line

A straight-line segment is displayed when the coordinates of its two end points are specified. Three-dimensional coordinates of the end points can also be used in most graphics libraries, where the three-dimensional coordinates are converted to the two-dimensional projection points automatically. The attributes of a line—such as its type, thickness, and color—can be specified. The types of lines supported by most graphics libraries are illustrated in Figure 3.13. It is essential to support these

Figure 3.13

Types of lines supported

types of lines in computer-aided drafting systems because they are frequently used in mechanical, architectural, or electrical drawings.

In GKS, PHIGS, and OpenGL, the polyline capability by which a set of connected line segments can be drawn as a whole is a default function, and thus the end points of the polyline are provided in sequence in the following matrix form. When only one line segment needs to be displayed, the matrix would hold the coordinates of the two end points only.

$$[P] = \begin{bmatrix} X_1 & Y_1 & Z_1 \\ X_2 & Y_2 & Z_2 \\ \bullet & \bullet & \bullet \\ \bullet & \bullet & \bullet \\ X_n & Y_n & Z_n \end{bmatrix}$$

The uses of the polyline function in PHIGS and OpenGL are illustrated as follows.

PHIGS
Pint   **num_of_point = 10;**
                      The number of points in the polyline to be drawn.

Ppoint3   **point3[ ] = {**
                      { 0.0, 0.0, 0.0 },
                      { 10.0, 20.0, 15.0 }, ...,
                      { 1.0, 3.0, 6.5 }};
                      The coordinates of the points on the polyline.

Ppolyline3 (num_of_points, point3);
                      Draws the polyline from the points provided.

OpenGL
GLdouble   **point[ ][3] = {**
                      { 0.0, 0.0, 0.0 },
                      {10.0, 20.0, 15.0 }, ...,
                      { 1.0, 3.0, 6.5 } };
                      The coordinates of the points on the polyline.

glBegin(GL_LINE_LOOP);
        glVertex3dv(&point[0][0]);
        glVertex3dv(&point[1][0]);
        :
        glVertex3dv(&point[9][0]);
glEnd();
                      Draws the polyline from the points provided. (The number of points is 10.)

3.4.2 Polygon

The polygon function is the same as the polyline function except that the first row and the last row of the point array [P] should be the same. Thus the same graphics output would be obtained by the polyline function. However, the polygon drawn by the polygon function carries the inside and outside information, and its interior can be filled with a pattern such as those illustrated in Figure 3.14.

In addition to the fill type shown, the interior color of a polygon (fill color) and the type, width, and color of the perimeter can also be specified as the attributes of the polygon. Even though a circle and a rectangle can be drawn by the polygon function, functions that require much less input (e.g., a center point and a radius for a circle and two end points of a diagonal for a rectangle) are provided additionally in most graphics libraries. However, these functions are realized internally by the polygon function.

3.4.3 Marker

Markers usually are used to differentiate data points in a graph. Figure 3.15 shows the markers provided in most graphics libraries.

The types of markers are specified as an attribute. Similar to the line element, polymarker is a default in GKS and PHIGS. OpenGL does not support markers explicitly but provides a mechanism by which any marker can be defined in a bitmap and invoked when needed. In this way, a graphics program written in OpenGL has much better portability across the different hardware platforms. The following sample code shows how to draw the marker * (asterisk), using PHIGS and OpenGL.

Figure 3.14

Examples of fill type

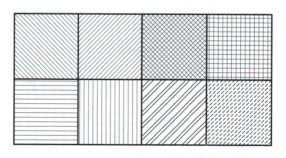

Figure 3.15

Examples of markers

PHIGS

pint num_of_point = 10;
Number of markers to be drawn.

Ppoint3 point3[] = {
{ 0.0, 0.0, 0.0 },
{10.0, 20.0, 15.0 }, ...,
{ 1.0, 3.0, 6.5 } };
Coordinates of the locations of the markers.

pset_marker_type (PMK_STAR);
Specify the type of marker to be asterisk.

ppolymarker3 (num_of_point, point3);
Draws markers from the inputs provided.

OpenGL

GLubyte asterisk[13] = { 0x00, 0x00, 0x30, 0x18, 0x0c, 0x0c, 0x0c,
0x0c, 0x0c, 0x0c, 0x0c, 0x18, 0x30 };[6]
Defines bitmap data for asterisk. First, the bottom row is drawn, then
the next row above it, and so on.

GLsizei width = 8;
Indicates the width of the bitmap in pixels.

GLsizei height = 13;
Indicates the height of the bitmap in pixels.

GLfloat origin_x = 0.0, origin_y = 0.0;
Defines the origin of the bitmap (positive values move the origin up
and to the right; negative values move it down and to the left).

GLfloat incre_x = 10.0, incre_y = 0.0;
Indicates the x and y increments that are added to the raster position
after the bitmap is rasterized.

GLfloat white[3] = { 1.0, 1.0, 1.0 };
Indicates the marker color.

GLfloat position[2] = { 20.5, 20.5 };
Coordinates of the locations of the markers.

glPixelStorei(GL_UNPACK_ALIGNMENT, 1);
Sets the pixel-storage modes, which affect the operation of **glBitmap**.

glColor3fv(white);
Sets the marker color as white

glRasterPos2fv(position);
Sets the current raster position.

glBitmap(width, height, origin_x, origin_y, incre_x, incre_y, asterisk);
Draws the bitmap specified by the last argument, which is a pointer to
the bitmap image. The raster position and size are also specified by
the first through the fourth arguments.

---

[6] The method to define bitmap data is explained in Neider, Davis, and Woo [1993].

3.4.4 Text

Two kinds of text are supported in most graphics libraries: annotation text (screen text or two-dimensional text) and three-dimensional text. Annotation text is always located on the plane of the display monitor and thus its shape is not distorted regardless of its orientation. Three-dimensional text can be placed on any plane in three-dimensional space, and thus its location and orientation are specified in world coordinates. Regardless of the kind of text, the font, the ratio of height to width, and the slant angle of the characters comprising the text must be specified in order to display a string of text. In addition, the location of the text and the direction of the text line are also specified. Two kinds of character fonts can be used in a text: the hardware font and the software font. The software font is displayed by executing the corresponding graphics programs that have been stored in advance. The software font takes longer than the hardware font to execute, but its shape is much more elaborate than that of the hardware font, which is stored as a set of straight-line segments for each character.

The following sample code shows how to draw the text string ABC, using PHIGS and OpenGL. As with markers, the characters have to be defined in bitmaps before they can be used in OpenGL.

PHIGS

Pvector3   **direction[2] = {**
                    { 0.0, 0.0, 0.0 },
                    {10.0, 10.0, 10.0 } };
The direction of the text line is specified by two position vectors.

Ppoint3   **position = { 5.5, 5.0, 5.0 };**
The location of the text is specified.

ptext3 (&position, direction, "ABC");
Draws the text from the inputs provided.

OpenGL

GLubyte   **a[13] = { 0x00, 0x00, 0x3f, 0x60, 0xcf, 0xdb, 0xd3,**
                    0xdd, 0xc3, 0x7e, 0x00, 0x00, 0x00 };

GLubyte   **b[13] = { 0x00, 0x00, 0xc3, 0xc3, 0xc3, 0xc3, 0xff,**
                    0xc3, 0xc3, 0xc3, 0x66, 0x3c, 0x18 };

GLubyte   **c[13] = { 0x00, 0x00, 0xfe, 0xc7, 0xc3, 0xc3, 0xc7,**
                    0xfe, 0xc7, 0xc3, 0xc3, 0xc7, 0xfe};
Defines bitmap data for A, B, and C. First, the bottom row is drawn, then the next row above it, and so on.

GLsizei   **width = 8;**
Indicates the width of the bitmap in pixels.

GLsizei   **height = 13;**
Indicates the height of the bitmap in pixels.

GLfloat   **origin_x = 0.0, origin_y = 0.0;**
Defines the origin of the bitmap (positive values move the origin up and to the right; negative values move it down and to the left).

GLfloat   incre_x = 10.0, incre_y = 0.0;
Indicates the *x* and *y* increments that are added to the raster position after the bitmap is rasterized.

GLfloat   white[3] = { 1.0, 1.0, 1.0 };
Indicates the font color.

GLfloat   position[2] = { 20.5, 20.5 };
Coordinates of the locations of the markers.

glPixelStorei(GL_UNPACK_ALIGNMENT, 1);
Set the pixel-storage modes, which affect the operation of **glBitmap**.

glColor3fv(white);
Sets the marker color as white.

glRasterPos2fv(position);
Sets the current raster position.

glBitmap(width, height, origin_x, origin_y, incre_x, incre_y, a);
glBitmap(width, height, origin_x, origin_y, incre_x, incre_y, b);
glBitmap(width, height, origin_x, origin_y, incre_x, incre_y, c);
Draws the bitmap specified by the last argument, which is a pointer to the bitmap image. The raster position and size are also specified by the first through the fourth arguments.

3.5   GRAPHICS INPUT

As mentioned earlier, a graphics program may need to accept graphics elements such as points, lines, or polygons as input in addition to numbers and text strings. For example, a user who wanted to calculate the area of a polygon on display or scale it up would need somehow to specify the polygon of interest among all the graphics elements on the display. Two types of physical devices are used for specifying graphics input: a locator and a button. The *locator* transfers its location, or the corresponding location of the cursor, to the graphics program. The *button* transfers the action of the user, on and off, at the current location of the cursor. The mouse, which is the most popular graphics input device these days, is a device with both of these functions. The tracking ball underneath its body acts as a locator, and the push button on its top acts as a button.

The type of input provided by a graphics input device can be characterized by three modes: sampling, requesting, and picking. The *sampling* mode continuously reads the status, mostly the location, of the input device. For example, we can use a mouse in the sampling mode to draw text on the screen by moving the mouse. As the mouse moves, it draws the cursor continuously. In the *requesting* mode the status of the input device is read only when we send a request, usually by pushing the mouse button. To clarify the difference between the sampling mode and the requesting mode, let's consider a situation where a polygon is drawn by specifying its vertices graphically by a mouse. In this case, we move the mouse until the cursor is located properly and push the button to specify that location as a vertex. The cursor moves around on the monitor display as we move the mouse, while the mouse is used in the sampling mode. Thus the location of each vertex is provided to the graphics program when we use the mouse in the requesting mode. These two modes have a common feature: They deliver the location of the mouse or the corresponding location of the cursor to the graphics program. However, in the *picking* mode, the graphics input device identifies the graphics element that the cursor is pointing to when the mouse button is pushed. We can identify the graphics elements by the names assigned by the graphics programmer when the elements were programmed. The picking mode is a very convenient way to edit an existing drawing on the screen (e.g., for deleting some polygons or changing some boundary lines of a polygon).

3.6 DISPLAY LIST

A display list is a group of graphics library commands that have been stored for later execution. Most commands of a graphics library can be either stored in display list or issued in immediate mode; this mode causes the commands to be executed immediately. Thus a set of graphics library commands can be named, organized, and handled with a display list conveniently and efficiently. For example, consider the translation of the image of a house on a display monitor. If the image of the house were composed of several hundred lines, we would have to write the translation command several hundred times—once for each line—if the lines of the image exist as separate entities. However, we may need to write the same command only once if the graphics entities for the image have been defined as a display list. The graphics elements are defined in a display list by (1) opening a display list before the program statements for drawing, and then (2) closing the display list after the statements, as illustrated in the following example.

OpenGL
glNewList(AREA_FILL, GL_COMPILE_AND_EXECUTE);
        A display list named **AREA_FILL** is opened.

        glBegin(GL_POLYGON);
            glVertex2fv(point1);
            glVertex2fv(point2);
               :
               :
    glEnd();
        A polygon entity is defined.

glEndList();
        The display list is closed.

    The display list of OpenGL is designed to optimize performance, particularly over a network, but never at the expense of performance on an individual machine.

To optimize performance, a display list is a cache of commands rather than a dynamic database. In other words, once a display list has been created, it cannot be modified. If a display list were modifiable, performance could be reduced by the overhead required to search through the display list and perform memory management. As portions of a modifiable display list were changed, memory allocation and deallocation might lead to memory fragmentation. Using display lists is typically at least as fast as not using it. In the case of OpenGL, display lists can substantially increase performance—particularly when OpenGL routines are issued over networks—because display lists reside with the server and network traffic is minimized.

Once a display list has been defined, the following operations can be applied.

- *Multiple execution:* The same display list can be executed many times.
- *Hierarchical execution:* A hierarchical display list is one that executes another display list by calling the command for executing a child display list in the parent display list. A hierarchical display list is useful for an object made of components, especially if some of those components are used more than once.
- *Deletion:* The display list can be eliminated.

3.7 TRANSFORMATION MATRIX

As we explained in Section 3.2, the conversion of coordinates from one coordinate system to another is essential in calculating the locations of projections of points on an object in space. First, we need to calculate the coordinates of the points on the object for the world coordinate system from its model coordinate system. The current position of the object is usually specified by how much the object has been translated and rotated from its initial position, at which its model coordinate system coincided with the world coordinate system. Thus the world coordinates of the points on the object at the current location are obtained by translating and rotating the corresponding points at the initial position, where their model coordinates are the same as the world coordinates. Most graphics libraries execute these transformations internally, and the graphics programmer may need provide only the amount of translation and rotation of each object. However, you still need to understand the transformation clearly in order to draw objects at their correct locations without trial and error, especially when objects are moving in a complicated way. We describe the transformation matrix to be applied to the coordinates of the points for these translations and rotations in the following section.

Once we have obtained the world coordinates of all the points of an object at its current position, we have to derive the coordinates of the same points with respect to the viewing coordinate system. This conversion of the coordinates among different coordinate systems is called *mapping*. The mapping between the world coordinate system and the viewing coordinate system is usually taken care of internally by the graphics library when the programmer provides information such as the location of viewpoint, viewsite, and the direction of the up vector, all in world coordinates. The transformation matrix for this mapping is described in Section 3.7.3.

3.7.1 Translation

When an object is translated by a, b, and c in the x, y, and z directions, respectively, from its initial position at which its model coordinate system coincides with the world coordinate system (see Figure 3.16), the world coordinates of a point on the object at the new position, (X_w, Y_w, Z_w) are obtained as follows:

$$
\begin{aligned}
X_w &= X_m + a \\
Y_w &= Y_m + b \\
Z_w &= Z_m + c
\end{aligned}
\tag{3.3}
$$

In Equation (3.3), X_m, Y_m, and Z_m also are the model coordinates of the same point. Equation (3.3) can be expressed in the following form, using matrix operations:[7]

$$
\begin{bmatrix} X_w \\ Y_w \\ Z_w \\ 1 \end{bmatrix}
=
\begin{bmatrix} 1 & 0 & 0 & a \\ 0 & 1 & 0 & b \\ 0 & 0 & 1 & c \\ 0 & 0 & 0 & 1 \end{bmatrix}
\begin{bmatrix} X_m \\ Y_m \\ Z_m \\ 1 \end{bmatrix}
\tag{3.4}
$$

$$\Downarrow$$

$$Trans(a,b,c)$$

Figure 3.16

Translation of an object

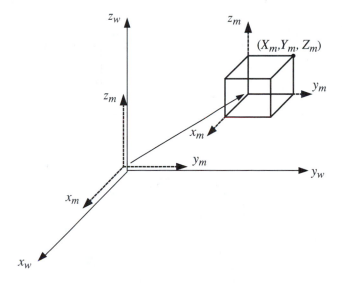

[7] It is also possible to represent the coordinates as a row vector, in which case the transformation matrix is placed after the row vector. This transformation matrix is the transpose of the one in Equation (3.4). In Equation (3.4) we are following the OpenGL convention.

Equation (3.4) can be easily verified to be the same as Equation (3.3) by simple expansion. The addition operation in Equation (3.3) could be expressed as the multiplication operation in Equation (3.4) by using homogeneous coordinates that represent a three-dimensional vector by four scalars instead of three.[8] The matrix used to transform the homogeneous coordinates is called the *homogeneous transformation matrix*. Therefore the transformation matrix on the right-hand side of Equation (3.4), denoted *Trans(a,b,c)*, is a homogeneous transformation matrix for a translation. If a point in two dimensions needs to be transformed, or translated as in this case, the homogeneous transformation matrix will be reduced to a 3×3 matrix by eliminating the third row and the third column from the 4×4 homogeneous transformation matrix. It will be applied to the coordinates of the point represented by a 3×1 column vector obtained by eliminating the z coordinates from 4×1 three-dimensional homogeneous coordinates.

3.7.2 Rotation

Suppose that an object is rotated by θ about the x axis of the world coordinate system together with its model coordinate system (which again coincides the world coordinate system at its initial position, as illustrated in Figure 3.17). The world coordinates of a point on the object at the new position, (X_w, Y_w, Z_w), can be obtained from its original coordinates, (X_m, Y_m, Z_m), as follows. Here, (X_m, Y_m, Z_m) are the coordinates of the point with respect to the model coordinate system, and thus they are equal to its world coordinates before rotation.

Figure 3.17

Rotation about the
x axis

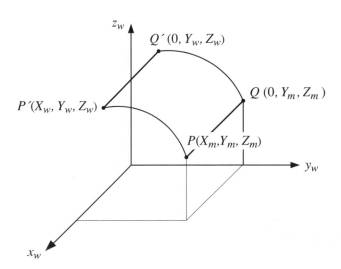

---

[8] Any vector $(x, y, z)^T$ in three-dimensional space can be expressed by the corresponding homogeneous coordinates $(x w, y w, z w, w)^T$. The superscript T indicates the transpose operation. As w can have any arbitrary value, many homogeneous coordinates exist for one vector. The value of 1 is used in Equation (3.4).

Figure 3.18

Projection onto the yz plane

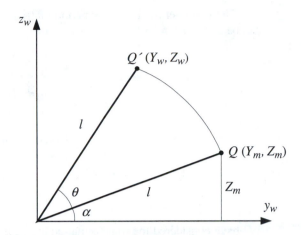

The relation between (X_w, Y_w, Z_w) and (X_m, Y_m, Z_m) becomes clear when Figure 3.17 is projected onto the yz plane, as shown in Figure 3.18.

From Figure 3.18, the following equations can easily be obtained:

$$X_w = X_m \tag{3.5}$$

$$\begin{aligned}
Y_w &= l\cos(\theta + \alpha) \\
&= l(\cos\theta\cos\alpha - \sin\theta\sin\alpha) \\
&= l\cos\alpha\cos\theta - l\sin\alpha\sin\theta \\
&= Y_m\cos\theta - Z_m\sin\theta
\end{aligned} \tag{3.6}$$

$$\begin{aligned}
Z_w &= l\sin(\theta + \alpha) \\
&= l(\sin\theta\cos\alpha + \cos\theta\sin\alpha) \\
&= l\cos\alpha\sin\theta + l\sin\alpha\cos\theta \\
&= Y_m\sin\theta + Z_m\cos\theta
\end{aligned} \tag{3.7}$$

Equations (3.5), (3.6), and (3.7) can be expressed in matrix form as

$$\begin{bmatrix} X_w \\ Y_w \\ Z_w \\ 1 \end{bmatrix} = \begin{bmatrix} 1 & 0 & 0 & 0 \\ 0 & \cos\theta & -\sin\theta & 0 \\ 0 & \sin\theta & \cos\theta & 0 \\ 0 & 0 & 0 & 1 \end{bmatrix} \begin{bmatrix} X_m \\ Y_m \\ Z_m \\ 1 \end{bmatrix} \tag{3.8}$$

The matrix on the right-hand side of Equation (3.8) is a homogeneous transformation matrix for the rotation about the x axis and thus is denoted $Rot(x,\theta)$. This homogeneous transformation matrix will also be reduced to 3×3 for a two-dimensional object, as for the translation.

The homogeneous transformation matrix for the rotation about the y or z axis can be derived similarly and expressed as

$$Rot(y, \theta) = \begin{bmatrix} \cos\theta & 0 & \sin\theta & 0 \\ 0 & 1 & 0 & 0 \\ -\sin\theta & 0 & \cos\theta & 0 \\ 0 & 0 & 0 & 1 \end{bmatrix} \tag{3.9}$$

$$Rot(z, \theta) = \begin{bmatrix} \cos\theta & -\sin\theta & 0 & 0 \\ \sin\theta & \cos\theta & 0 & 0 \\ 0 & 0 & 1 & 0 \\ 0 & 0 & 0 & 1 \end{bmatrix} \tag{3.10}$$

We have considered the transformation matrices associated with the rotations about one of the world coordinate axes. We can then infer that the rotation about an any arbitrarily oblique axis is achieved by a combination of the rotations about the x, y, and z axes. Thus the transformation matrix for an arbitrary axis is obtained by combining the matrices in Equations (3.8)–(3.10).

As mentioned earlier, the transformation matrices described in this section are usually derived by the associated routines in the graphics libraries. The following example codes illustrate how those routines are used in PHIGS and OpenGL.

PHIGS
ptranslate3 (Pvector* offset3, Pint* error_ind, Pmatrix3 result3);
> **offset3:** vector representing the translational amount and direction
> **error_ind:** error index
> **result3:** resulting transformation matrix[9]

protate_x(Pfloat angle, Pint* error_ind, Pmatrix3 result3);
protate_y(Pfloat angle, Pint* error_ind, Pmatrix3 result3);
protate_z(Pfloat angle, Pint* error_ind, Pmatrix3 result3);
> **angle:** rotational amount
> **error_ind:** error index
> **result3:** resulting transformation matrix

OpenGL
glTranslated(GLdouble offset_x, GLdouble offset_y, GLdouble offset_z);
> Multiplies the current matrix by a matrix that moves an object by the given offset_x, offset_y, offset_z values.

glRotated(GLdouble angle, GLdouble x, GLdouble y, GLdouble z);
> Multiplies the current matrix by a matrix that rotates an object counterclockwise about the ray from the origin through the point (x, y, z).

Let's consider some examples to clarify the explanations for the transformation matrix.

---

[9] In PHIGS, the transformation matrix follows the row vector representing the coordinates.

EXAMPLE 3.1

An object in space is translated by 5 units in the y direction of the world coordinate system and then rotated by 90 degrees about the x axis of the world coordinate system. If a point on the object has the coordinates $(0, 0, 1)$ with respect to its model coordinate system, what will be the world coordinates of the same point after the translation and the rotation?

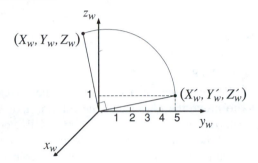

ANSWER

The coordinates (X'_w, Y'_w, Z'_w) after translation can be obtained by

$$[X'_w \; Y'_w \; Z'_w \; 1]^T = Trans(0,5,0) \cdot [0 \; 0 \; 1 \; 1]^T$$
$$= [0 \; 5 \; 1 \; 1]^T \qquad \text{(a)}$$

Then a rotation is applied:

$$[X_w \; Y_w \; Z_w \; 1]^T = Rot(x,90°) \cdot [0 \; 5 \; 1 \; 1]^T \qquad \text{(b)}$$

Thus the coordinates of the new point would be $(0, -1, 5)$. Note that Equations (a) and (b) can be merged as follows:

$$[X_w \; Y_w \; Z_w \; 1]^T = Rot(x,90°) \cdot Trans(0,5,0) \cdot [0 \; 0 \; 1 \; 1]^T \qquad \text{(c)}$$

Equation (c) is a much more convenient expression, especially when the coordinates of numerous points need to be calculated. In that case the transformation matrices $Rot(x,90°)$ and $Trans(0,5,0)$ are multiplied in advance to give an equivalent transformation matrix, and then the resulting matrix is applied to all the points involved. This process of calculating the equivalent transformation matrix by multiplying the associated transformation matrices in the proper sequence is called *concatenation*. This process is one of the benefits of using homogeneous coordinates, which enables the translation to be expressed by a matrix multiplication instead of an addition.

EXAMPLE 3.2

An object in space is rotated by 90 degrees about an axis that is parallel to the x axis of the world coordinate system and passes through a point having world coordinates $(0, 3, 2)$. If a point on the object has model coordinates $(0, 0, 1)$, what will be the world coordinates of the same point after the rotation?

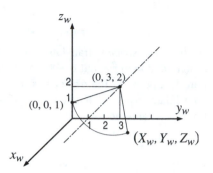

ANSWER

We have discussed rotations only about axes passing through the origin, so we have to move the object and the rotation axis together. The rotation axis must pass through the origin while the same relative position is maintained between the object and the rotation axis. Thus the object is translated by (0, –3, –2) together with the rotation axis so that the rotation axis coincides with the x axis of the world coordinate system. Then the object is rotated about the x axis by 90 degrees. Now the object is translated again, by (0, 3, 2), to return to the original position.

These operations can be expressed as

$$[X_w \ Y_w \ Z_w \ 1]^T = Trans(0,3,2) \cdot Rot(x,90°) \cdot Trans(0,-3,-2) \cdot [0 \ 0 \ 1 \ 1]^T \quad (d)$$

Note the sequence of transformation matrices in Equation (d). The result can easily be verified by applying the transformations step by step, as in Example 3.1.

Expanding Equation (d) gives

$$[X_w \ Y_w \ Z_w \ 1]^T = \begin{bmatrix} 1 & 0 & 0 & 0 \\ 0 & 1 & 0 & 3 \\ 0 & 0 & 1 & 2 \\ 0 & 0 & 0 & 1 \end{bmatrix} \begin{bmatrix} 1 & 0 & 0 & 0 \\ 0 & \cos 90° & -\sin 90° & 0 \\ 0 & \sin 90° & \cos 90° & 0 \\ 0 & 0 & 0 & 1 \end{bmatrix} \begin{bmatrix} 1 & 0 & 0 & 0 \\ 0 & 1 & 0 & -3 \\ 0 & 0 & 1 & -2 \\ 0 & 0 & 0 & 1 \end{bmatrix} \begin{bmatrix} 0 \\ 0 \\ 1 \\ 1 \end{bmatrix}$$

$$= \begin{bmatrix} 0 & 4 & -1 & 1 \end{bmatrix}^T$$

This result reflects the operations illustrated in the accompanying figure.

3.7.3 Mapping

Mapping involves calculating the coordinates of a point with respect to a coordinate system from known coordinates of the same point with respect to another coordinate system.

Let's consider the two coordinate systems illustrated in Figure 3.19. To do so, we assume that the coordinates (X_2, Y_2, Z_2) of the point P with respect to the $x_2 y_2 z_2$ coordinate system need to be calculated from (X_1, Y_1, Z_1), which are the coordinates of the same point with respect to the $x_1 y_1 z_1$ coordinate system. Furthermore,

Figure 3.19

Mapping between
two coordinate
systems

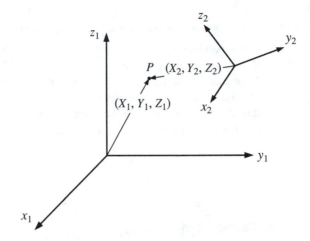

(X_2, Y_2, Z_2) are assumed to be calculated by applying the transformation matrix T_{1-2} to (X_1, Y_1, Z_1) as follows:

$$[X_2 \ Y_2 \ Z_2 \ 1]^T = T_{1-2} \cdot [X_1 \ Y_1 \ Z_1 \ 1]^T \tag{3.11}$$

Replacing T_{1-2} with its elements allows Equation (3.11) to be expressed as

$$\begin{bmatrix} X_2 \\ Y_2 \\ Z_2 \\ 1 \end{bmatrix} = \begin{bmatrix} n_x & o_x & a_x & p_x \\ n_y & o_y & a_y & p_y \\ n_z & o_z & a_z & p_z \\ 0 & 0 & 0 & 1 \end{bmatrix} \begin{bmatrix} X_1 \\ Y_1 \\ Z_1 \\ 1 \end{bmatrix} \tag{3.12}$$

To derive the elements in Equation (3.12) we first substitute $X_1 = 0$, $Y_1 = 0$, and $Z_1 = 0$ and get

$$X_2 = p_x, \quad Y_2 = p_y, \quad Z_2 = p_z \tag{3.13}$$

Thus we can say that p_x, p_y, and p_z are obtained as the coordinates of the origin of the $x_1y_1z_1$ coordinate system with respect to the $x_2y_2z_2$ coordinate system.

We now substitute the values of $X_1 = 1$, $Y_1 = 0$, and $Z_1 = 0$ into Equation (3.13) and get

$$X_2 = n_x + p_x, \quad Y_2 = n_y + p_y, \quad Z_2 = n_z + p_z \tag{3.14}$$

By subtracting Equation (3.13) from Equation (3.14), we can conclude that n_x, n_y, and n_z are, respectively, the x_2, y_2, and z_2 components of a unit vector along the x_1 axis of $x_1y_1z_1$ coordinate system. Thus n_x, n_y, and n_z are easily derived from the relative orientation between the two coordinate systems involved.

Similarly, o_x, o_y, and o_z are the x_2, y_2, and z_2 components of the y_1 axis and a_x, a_y, and a_z are those of z_1 axis.

The following example clarifies these concepts.

EXAMPLE 3.3

Corresponding to the viewpoint (−10, 0, 1), the viewsite (0, 0, 1), and the up vector (0, 0, 1), the viewing coordinate system is drawn as shown in the accompanying figure. Note that all the coordinate and component values are given in world coordinates. From the relative position between the viewing coordinate system and the world coordinate system, (i) calculate the mapping transformation T_{w-v} and (ii) calculate the coordinates of a point in viewing coordinates if it has world coordinates (5, 0, 1).

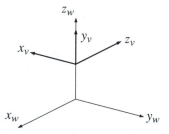

ANSWER

The first three numbers in the first column of T_{w-v} (i.e., n_x, n_y, and n_z), are (0 0 −1) because they are the x_v, y_v, and z_v components of the x_w axis. Similarly, o_x, o_y, and o_z, which are the x_v, y_v, and z_v components of the y_w axis, are (−1 0 0), and a_x, a_y, and a_z are (0 1 0). Because p_x, p_y, and p_z are, respectively, the x_v, y_v, and z_v coordinates of the origin of the $x_w y_w z_w$ coordinate system, and their values are 0, −1, and 0, respectively. Therefore we can derive T_{w-v} as follows:

$$T_{w-v} = \begin{bmatrix} 0 & -1 & 0 & 0 \\ 0 & 0 & 1 & -1 \\ -1 & 0 & 0 & 0 \\ 0 & 0 & 0 & 1 \end{bmatrix}$$

We obtain the viewing coordinates of (5, 0, 1) by applying T_{w-v} as follows:

$$\begin{bmatrix} X_v \\ Y_v \\ Z_v \\ 1 \end{bmatrix} = \begin{bmatrix} 0 & -1 & 0 & 0 \\ 0 & 0 & 1 & -1 \\ -1 & 0 & 0 & 0 \\ 0 & 0 & 0 & 1 \end{bmatrix} \begin{bmatrix} 5 \\ 0 \\ 1 \\ 1 \end{bmatrix} = \begin{bmatrix} 0 \\ 0 \\ -5 \\ 1 \end{bmatrix}$$

Thus we can conclude that the viewing coordinates of (5, 0, 1) are (0, 0, −5), as can be guessed from the figure.

EXAMPLE 3.4

The viewpoint and the viewsite are set at (5, 5, 5) and (0, 0, 0), respectively, to draw an isometric view, and the up vector is chosen to be (0, 0, 1). Derive the mapping transformation matrix T_{w-v}, and the viewing coordinates of a point represented by (0, 0, 5) in world coordinates.

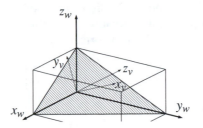

ANSWER

The viewing coordinate system can be drawn as shown in the accompanying figure. The hatched triangle on which the xv and yv axes are placed indicates a plane parallel to the screen.

To derive the elements of T_{w-v}, we have to derive the x_v, y_v, and z_v components of each x_w axis, y_w axis, and z_w axis. For this purpose, we let each unit vector along the x_v, y_v, and z_v axes be $\mathbf{i_v}$, $\mathbf{j_v}$, and $\mathbf{k_v}$, respectively. Similarly the unit vectors along the x_w, y_w, and z_w axes are denoted $\mathbf{i}$, $\mathbf{j}$, and $\mathbf{k}$, respectively.

The unit vector $\mathbf{k_v}$ acts in the direction from the viewsite to the viewpoint, so

$$\mathbf{k_v} = \frac{1}{\sqrt{3}}\mathbf{i} + \frac{1}{\sqrt{3}}\mathbf{j} + \frac{1}{\sqrt{3}}\mathbf{k}$$

As mentioned earlier in Section 3.2, the unit vector $\mathbf{j_v}$ should be in the direction of the projection of the up vector onto the screen. In other words, it will have the same direction as the vector obtained by subtracting, from the up vector, its component in the normal direction of the screen. Thus $\mathbf{j_v}$ can be expressed as follows if the up vector is denoted $\mathbf{u_p}$:

$$\mathbf{j_v} = \frac{\mathbf{u_p} - (\mathbf{u_p} \bullet \mathbf{k_v})\mathbf{k_v}}{\left|\mathbf{u_p} - (\mathbf{u_p} \bullet \mathbf{k_v})\mathbf{k_v}\right|} = \frac{-\frac{1}{3}\mathbf{i} - \frac{1}{3}\mathbf{j} + \frac{2}{3}\mathbf{k}}{\left|-\frac{1}{3}\mathbf{i} - \frac{1}{3}\mathbf{j} + \frac{2}{3}\mathbf{k}\right|} = -\frac{1}{\sqrt{6}}\mathbf{i} - \frac{1}{\sqrt{6}}\mathbf{j} + \frac{2}{\sqrt{6}}\mathbf{k}$$

The remaining unit vector $\mathbf{i_v}$ is obtained by the cross product:

$$\mathbf{i_v} = \mathbf{j_v} \times \mathbf{k_v} = \frac{1}{-\sqrt{2}}\mathbf{i} + \frac{1}{\sqrt{2}}\mathbf{j}$$

Now n_x, the x_v component of x_w axis, is derived as

$$\frac{1}{-\sqrt{2}} \text{ by } \mathbf{i} \bullet \mathbf{i_v}.$$

Similarly, n_y is

$$\frac{1}{-\sqrt{6}} \text{ by } \mathbf{i} \bullet \mathbf{j_v}.$$

and n_z is

$$\frac{1}{\sqrt{3}} \text{ by } \mathbf{i} \bullet \mathbf{k_v}.$$

The second and third columns of T_{w-v} are derived in the same way. We can ignore p_x, p_y, and p_z because the viewing coordinate system and the world coordinate system have the same origin in this example. Therefore, T_{w-v} is

$$T_{w-v} = \begin{bmatrix} -\dfrac{1}{\sqrt{2}} & \dfrac{1}{\sqrt{2}} & 0 & 0 \\ -\dfrac{1}{\sqrt{6}} & -\dfrac{1}{\sqrt{6}} & \dfrac{2}{\sqrt{6}} & 0 \\ \dfrac{1}{\sqrt{3}} & \dfrac{1}{\sqrt{3}} & \dfrac{1}{\sqrt{3}} & 0 \\ 0 & 0 & 0 & 1 \end{bmatrix}$$

and the viewing coordinates of (0, 0, 5) are

$$[X_v \ Y_v \ Z_v \ 1]^T = T_{w-v} \cdot [0 \ 0 \ 5 \ 1]^T = \left[0 \ \ \frac{5\sqrt{6}}{3} \ \ \frac{5\sqrt{3}}{3} \ \ 1 \right]^T$$

The screen coordinates for the isometric view from the viewing coordinates are

$$\left(0 \ \ \frac{5\sqrt{6}}{3} \right)$$

simply by ignoring the z coordinates. The isometric projection is one of parallel projection, so any point on the z_w axis is projected onto the y axis of the screen coordinates. In fact, specifying the up vector to be (0, 0, 1) means that the z_w axis appears as a vertical line on the screen after projection.

3.7.4 Other Transformation Matrices

In addition to the transformation matrices described in the previous sections, the transformation matrices for scaling and for mirror reflection are also often used.

To scale an object up or down s_x times in x, s_y times in y, and s_z times in the z direction, the following transformation matrix is applied:

$$\begin{bmatrix} X' \\ Y' \\ Z' \\ 1 \end{bmatrix} = \begin{bmatrix} s_x & 0 & 0 & 0 \\ 0 & s_y & 0 & 0 \\ 0 & 0 & s_z & 0 \\ 0 & 0 & 0 & 1 \end{bmatrix} \begin{bmatrix} X \\ Y \\ Z \\ 1 \end{bmatrix} \tag{3.15}$$

For translation and rotation of two-dimensional objects, the scaling transformation matrix is also reduced to a 3×3 matrix. The same scaling effect can be obtained by changing the size of the viewport or the window without changing the values of the coordinates.

The transformation matrix in Equation (3.15) is used when the object is scaled with respect to the origin. However, it may often be desirable to scale an object with respect to a point P on the object represented by (X_p, Y_p, Z_p). In this case, a translational transformation, $Trans(-X_p,-Y_p,-Z_p)$, is applied first so that the reference point for the scaling is moved to the origin, then the scaling matrix in Equation (3.15) is applied, and finally $Trans(X_p,Y_p,Z_p)$ is applied to move the object back to its original position.

With the xy plane as a mirror, the mirror reflection can be accomplished with the following transformation matrix because only the sign of the z coordinate has to be reversed:

$$\begin{bmatrix} X' \\ Y' \\ Z' \\ 1 \end{bmatrix} = \begin{bmatrix} 1 & 0 & 0 & 0 \\ 0 & 1 & 0 & 0 \\ 0 & 0 & -1 & 0 \\ 0 & 0 & 0 & 1 \end{bmatrix} \begin{bmatrix} X \\ Y \\ Z \\ 1 \end{bmatrix} \qquad (3.16)$$

The transformation matrix for other mirror reflections, with the yz plane or the xz plane as a mirror, can be derived in the same way.

3.8   HIDDEN-LINE AND HIDDEN-SURFACE REMOVAL

When an object in space is projected onto a screen, displaying only the visible lines and surfaces enhances the clarity. *Hidden-line removal* prevents display of line segments that are obscured from view; *hidden-surface removal* prevents display of any part of a surface that is obscured. Figures 3.20 and 3.21 illustrate the images of an

Figure 3.20

Image before hidden lines are removed

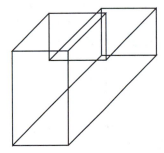

Figure 3.21

Image after hidden lines are removed

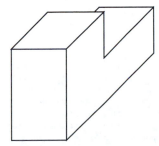

object before and after the hidden lines are removed. Obviously, understanding the image is much easier with hidden lines removed.

Many software algorithms for removing hidden lines or surfaces have been published. They attempt to improve computational efficiency or expand the range of shapes of the objects to be handled. However, the hidden-line or hidden-surface removal tends to be realized best by taking advantage of a graphics hardware device called the z-buffer,[10] and thus there is little current research on the topic. In this section, we explain several typical algorithms for eliminating hidden lines and surfaces by using software and a method for using the z-buffer for the same purpose.

3.8.1   Back-Face Removal Algorithm

The back-face algorithm uses the basic idea that a face of an object is visible if its normal vector in the direction of the outside of the object is pointing toward the viewer, and invisible otherwise. For example, the top face of the block shown in Figure 3.22 is said to be visible if its outward normal vector **N** has a positive component in the direction of **M**, which is a vector from a point on the face to the viewer. This can be expressed mathematically as follows:

If $\mathbf{M} \cdot \mathbf{N} > 0$, then the face is visible.
If $\mathbf{M} \cdot \mathbf{N} = 0$, then the face is displayed as a line.
If $\mathbf{M} \cdot \mathbf{N} < 0$, then the face is invisible.

These conditions can easily be applied to an object bounded by planar faces because the normal vector **N** is constant anywhere on each face. However, the conditions cannot be applied to a concave[11] object because a face pointing toward the viewer may be obscured by another face of the same object, as illustrated in Figure 3.23. The same situation occurs with more than one convex object when a face of

Figure 3.22

Two vectors related to the visibility of a face

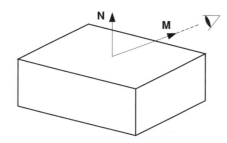

---

[10] The z-buffer is a type of memory similar to the frame buffer in that it provides a memory space for each pixel. However, instead of storing the color bits of each pixel, it stores the z coordinate of the object point that the pixel represents when projected. The z coordinate is measured with respect to the viewing coordinate system and thus is a measure of distance from the viewer.
[11] An object is called concave if at least a pair of faces meet at an edge with an inside angle bigger than 180 degrees. When all the faces meet each other with the inside angle less than 180 degrees, the object is called convex.

Figure 3.23

Example of a concave object

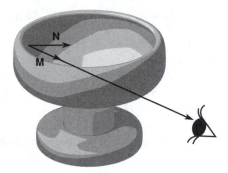

one object can be obscured by another object even though the face points toward the viewer. Therefore the back-face algorithm can be applied only to one convex object. Furthermore, the algorithm cannot handle an object such as the one shown in Figure 3.24 because the outward normal vector of each face cannot be determined unambiguously.[12]

If an object has nonplanar faces, the value of N for each nonplanar face will change, depending on which point on the face is chosen, and the sign of $M \cdot N$ will also change. This means that the face has a visible portion and an invisible portion at the same time. Thus the face should be divided along a curve on the face following the points of $M \cdot N = 0$. The curve along which $M \cdot N = 0$ is called the *silhouette line*. Once the face has been divided along the silhouette line, the sign of $M \cdot N$ for the divided segment is investigated for any one representative point selected from each segment. This process may appear to be easy, but calculating the silhouette lines is not a simple task and thus the biggest advantage of the back-face algorithm—simplicity of implementation—is lost.

After all the faces have been identified as visible or invisible, the edges of the visible faces are displayed to generate a line drawing image with hidden lines removed. If an image with hidden surfaces removed is desired, the visible surfaces are simply filled with selected colors.

Figure 3.24

An object whose outward normal vector is not determined unambiguously

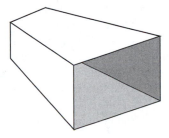

[12] In fact, representing an object like this is not a simple problem, as is explained in a discussion of the nonmanifold modeler in Chapter 5.

3.8.2 Depth-Sorting, or Painter's, Algorithm

The basic principle of the depth-sorting (or painter's) algorithm can be stated as follows. The surfaces of the objects are sorted by distance from the viewer and filled with their respective colors from the farthest face to the nearest face. By painting the surfaces in this order, the farther surfaces are automatically hidden by the nearer surfaces if they have to occupy the same region in the screen. Hence the depth-sorting algorithm is a hidden-surface removal algorithm.

The distance of a surface from the viewer is measured by the z coordinates of the points on the surface, with respect to the viewing coordinate system. That is, the point with larger Z_v coordinate can be said to be nearer the viewer.[13] (The z coordinate with respect to the viewing coordinate system will be denoted Z_v from now on.) Thus it is only necessary to compare the Z_v coordinates of the surfaces to be drawn and display the surfaces in sequence starting from the surface with the smallest Z_v coordinate.

Comparing the Z_v coordinates between two surfaces would be simple if the maximum Z_v value of one surface is smaller than the minimum Z_v value of the other surface. However, in most cases, the range of Z_v values of all the points on one surface overlaps the Z_v range of the other surface. These ambiguous situations can be avoided by splitting each of the surfaces into two or several pieces until the Z_v ranges do not overlap. There is another, simple way to overcome the problem, which is easier to implement. In this method, every surface of the objects is converted to a set of small triangles beforehand so that the Z_v range of each triangle does not overlap any other, and then each triangle is colored with the associated color in the proper sequence. As the sizes of the triangles get smaller, there is less probability that the Z_v ranges will overlap. This approximation of an object as bounded by many triangles is called *triangulation* or facet conversion.

3.8.3 Hidden-Line Removal Algorithm

As explained in the previous sections, the depth-sorting algorithm is used basically for removing hidden surfaces. The back-face algorithm can be used to generate a line drawing with hidden lines removed but has many limitations in removing hidden lines generally. In fact, only about 50 percent of the hidden lines can be eliminated if the back-face algorithm is simply applied to multiple objects, including concave objects. Thus an algorithm is needed that will eliminate all the hidden lines regardless of the number of objects involved, the convexity of the objects, and the existence of curved faces.

One such algorithm works basically in the following manner: Every edge[14] of the objects is tested to determine whether it is obscured by the faces[15] of the objects involved; the portion obscured by each overlapping face is sequentially eliminated

---

[13] In OpenGL, the point with larger Z_v coordinate is farther from the viewer because OpenGL uses a left-hand viewing coordinate system.

[14] An *edge* of an object is the intersection curve between its neighboring boundary surfaces.

[15] Surfaces bounding an object are called *faces*. Each face has a finite area because it is bounded by edges.

from the edge until no surface remains to be tested; and the remaining portions of all the edges are collected and displayed.

The following steps describe implementation of the algorithm.

Step 1. The faces pointing toward the viewer are collected by applying the back-face algorithm and stored in an array FACE-TABLE. The faces pointing away from the viewer do not have to be considered because they do not contribute to obscuring the edges. When the necessary faces have been collected, the maximum and the minimum Z_v values of each face are also stored. The curved faces are divided along their silhouette lines as in the back-face algorithm, and the proper portions are stored in FACE-TABLE, as for the planar faces.

Step 2. The edges of the faces in FACE-TABLE are collected and stored as a list. The edges of the faces not in FACE-TABLE are not considered because they are invisible. Then the edges in the list are tested in sequence to determine whether they are obscured by each face in FACE-TABLE.

Step 3. The possibility of an edge being obscured by a face can be detected by comparing the range of Z_v values of the edge and the range of Z_v values stored for the face. Three situations are possible, as shown in Figure 3.25. Figure 3.25(a) shows the situation where the Z_v values of the edge are smaller than the minimum Z_v value of the face (i.e., the face is placed in front of the edge). Figure 3.25(b) shows the situation where the Z_v values of the edge are bigger than the maximum Z_v value of the face (i.e., the edge is placed in front of the face). Figure 3.25(c) shows the situation where the ranges of Z_v values of the edge overlap those of the face (i.e., a portion of the edge is placed in front of the face, and the other portion is placed behind the face). If an edge is detected in front of the face being tested, the next face is retrieved from FACE-TABLE, and the test is repeated for this face. If an edge is detected behind or piercing a face, the following extra step is performed.

Step 4. The edge and the face being tested are projected and tested to determine whether the projected entities overlap. If there is no overlapping, it can be concluded that the edge is not obscured by the face being tested. Thus the next face in FACE-TABLE is retrieved and step 3 is repeated. If the projected entities overlap, the edge is split at the points where the edge pierces the face being tested, as illustrated in Figure 3.26. The segment obscured by the face being tested is ignored,

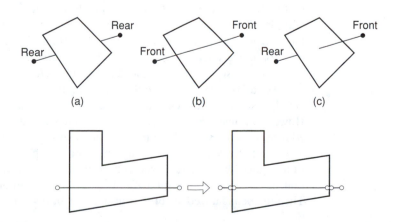

Figure 3.25

Three possible situations involving positions of faces and edges

Figure 3.26

Separation of edges

and the visible segments are added to the list. Then step 3 is repeated with these new edges. The original edge—before the split operation—should be eliminated from the list.

Step 5. The edges that pass through the test with all the faces in the FACE-TABLE are collected to form the visible edges.

3.8.4 *z*-Buffer Method

The z-buffer method is based on the same principle as the depth-sorting algorithm in that any region of the screen is occupied by an entity closest to the viewer. Here, the entities imply points, curves, or surfaces. This method involves the use of hardware memory called the z-buffer that stores, for each pixel, the Z_v value of the entity whose projection is represented by the pixel. As explained earlier, the Z_v value (i.e., z coordinate in the viewing coordinate system) is a measure of the entity's distance from the viewer. Therefore the z-buffer requires the amount of memory space needed to store as many real variables as the number of pixels.

The faces whose normal vectors are pointing away from the viewer are invisible, so only the faces whose normal vectors are pointing toward the viewer are collected and projected onto the screen. However, unlike the depth-sorting algorithm, the surfaces are projected in a random order. The reason will become clear as you go through the following procedure.

First, any arbitrary surface is projected, and the memory locations of the z-buffer corresponding to the pixels associated with the projected image are set with the Z_v values of the corresponding points on the surface represented by the pixels. At this time, the pixels are colored with the color of the first surface. Then the next surface is projected, and the associated pixels are colored with the color of this surface if those pixels have not been colored by the previous surface. If some pixels have already been colored, the stored Z_v values of those pixels are compared to the Z_v values of the points on the current surface represented by the same pixels. If the stored Z_v value of a pixel is bigger than the current value (i.e., the point on the previous surface is closer than that on the current surface to the viewer), then the color of the pixel is reserved. Otherwise, it is colored with the color of the current surface. All the Z_v values of the pixels are initialized to be the distances to the "far plane" (refer to Figure 3.11) from the viewer so that the pixels for the first surface are automatically set to the color of the first plane. Repeating the same procedure for all the surfaces involved will color every pixel on the screen with the color of the nearest surface, as illustrated in Figure 3.27.

As can be surmised from the preceding description, the z-buffer method is basically used for removing the hidden surfaces, like the depth-sorting method. However, a line drawing without hidden lines can also be generated by using the z-buffer method with a little modification as follows. First, all the surfaces are projected onto the screen by coloring the associated pixels with the background color. In this stage, the z-buffer is set with the proper Z_v values as before. Thus this operation has the effect of setting Z_v values correctly without displaying the surfaces. Then the boundary edges of the surfaces are projected onto the screen. While these

Figure 3.27

The principle of the *z*-buffer method

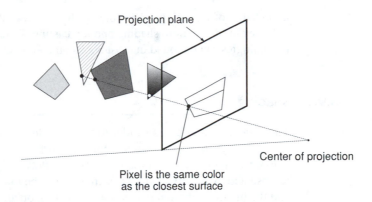

Projection plane

Center of projection

Pixel is the same color
as the closest surface

edges are being projected, the Z_v values of pixels representing the edges are compared to the Z_v values already set by the surfaces, and only the pixels with the original Z_v values smaller than the new Z_v values will be updated. In this way, the portions of the boundary edges that are obscured by surfaces will not be displayed. This procedure yields the correct line drawing—without the hidden lines. However, some boundary lines may become too thin because some of the pixels of each boundary line can be occupied by the surfaces sharing the boundary line. You can easily solve this problem by moving the entire object closer to you by a small amount when projecting the boundary lines.

3.9 RENDERING

Images drawn without hidden lines or hidden surfaces may convey shapes clearly enough in most cases. However, being able to display more realistic images for some applications is desirable at times. For example, realistic images play an especially important role in "virtual reality," a relatively new technology that simulates a real situation on a computer. For example, you might visualize the inside and outside of a building on a computer. Then you might experience the various aspects of the building as if you were walking around the inside and outside of the building. This tool could be very useful, for example, before a decision is made to invest money in building construction.

To simulate a real scene, it is necessary to recreate the effects of light on surfaces of objects. This process is called *rendering*. In fact, most of what we see is the reflection of light off surfaces, and we determine the shapes, textures, and colors of objects from this reflected light. Some rendering facilities are provided in advanced graphics libraries. With them, we need only provide a faceted model of the objects, the lighting situation, and the property of the surfaces (e.g., shiny or dull). However, you should understand the principles of rendering technologies in order to properly use them in graphics libraries. In fact, assigning the proper values to the related parameters in those facilities will not be easy if you do not have a basic knowledge of rendering. Therefore we briefly describe two major rendering technologies in this section: shading and ray casting. Detailed descriptions of rendering technologies can be found in most books on computer graphics.

3.9.1 Shading

The *shading* procedure is similar to that of hidden-surface removal, except that the pixels representing a surface are not colored with one color. Instead, each pixel is colored with the color and the intensity of reflected light at the point of the surface represented by the pixel after projection. Thus the main task is to calculate the color and the intensity of the reflected light at a point on an object. Let's consider the calculation of the intensity first.

An object's surface may be illuminated by light coming directly from light sources, or *direct illumination*, and by light reflected from other surfaces, or *ambient illumination*. Thus the reflected light at a point on an object is formed by the addition of the reflections of these two types of illumination, as illustrated in Figure 3.28.

The reflected light from many surfaces in a scene can be assumed to come from infinitely many directions, and thus the reflection of ambient illumination can be assumed to spread uniformly in all the directions. Therefore the intensity of the reflection, R_a, can be expressed as

$$R_a = K_d I_a \tag{3.17}$$

where I_a is the intensity of the ambient light and K_d is the coefficient of reflectivity (or reflectivity) of the surface. White surfaces have a reflectivity of nearly 1, whereas black surfaces have a reflectivity of nearly 0. A viewer will perceive the

Figure 3.28

Reflected light from two types of illumination

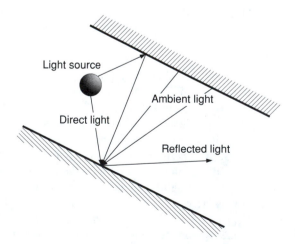

same intensity of ambient illumination regardless of the person's location in a scene because the reflection emanates from all the surfaces present and spreads uniformly in every direction.

With regard to direct illumination, we will consider only point light sources because a line light source or a surface light source can be approximated by multiple point sources. The reflection from a point light source can be assumed to be the combination of two extreme types of reflections: diffuse reflection and specular reflection.

Diffuse reflection occurs when light penetrates a surface and the surface, having absorbed the light, reemits it in all directions, as illustrated in Figure 3.29. Thus the intensity of diffuse reflection is independent of the viewer's location, as in ambient illumination. Surface details such as texture and color are revealed by diffuse reflection. For surfaces of coarse quality, diffuse reflection is dominant over specular reflection.

Specular reflection is direct reflection of light by a surface. This type of reflection is dominant for shiny surfaces such as mirrors. As shown in Figure 3.30, shiny surfaces reflect almost all incident light and therefore have bright specular highlights. The intensity of the specular reflection will be perceived differently by the viewer, depending on the person's location in a scene.

We will describe how to calculate the individual intensities of diffuse reflection and specular reflection. Then reflection at a point from illumination by a point source can be approximated by adding the intensities of these two types of reflection. The intensity of diffuse reflection is directly proportional to the cosine of the angle of incidence. The angle of incidence at a point is the angle between the normal vector of the surface at the point and a vector from the point to the light source, as shown in Figure 3.31.

Figure 3.29

Diffuse reflection

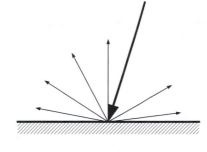

Figure 3.30

Specular reflection

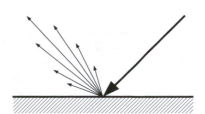

Figure 3.31

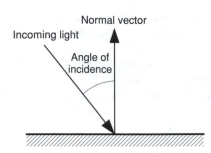

This relationship, called Lambert's cosine law, can be verified by assuming the incoming light to be a finite number of parallel lines evenly spaced, as shown in Figure 3.32. Note that the number of light rays hitting a surface decreases as the surface is tilted. This implies that the intensity of the reflected light will also decrease as the surface is tilted.

Lambert's cosine law can be expressed mathematically as follows. The intensity of the incoming light at the point of interest, I_p, is assumed to be inversely proportional to the square of the distance from the light source, D_1, so it can be expressed as follows for a light source of intensity E_p:

$$I_p = \frac{E_p}{D_1^2} \tag{3.18}$$

We usually assume that all the light sources are far enough from the surfaces involved that D_1 in Equation (3.18) can be regarded to be the same for all the points. Therefore Lambert's cosine law can be expressed, ignoring D_1, as

$$R_d = K_d E_p (\mathbf{N} \cdot \mathbf{L}) \tag{3.19}$$

where R_d is the intensity of diffuse reflection, K_d is the reflectivity as in Equation (3.17), $\mathbf{N}$ is the unit normal vector at the point of interest, $\mathbf{L}$ is the unit vector from the point to the light source, and $\mathbf{N} \cdot \mathbf{L}$ is the cosine of the angle of incidence. The vector $\mathbf{L}$ is constant for all the points because the light source is assumed to be located far away.

We can expect one problem in using Equation (3.19): Two parallel planes cannot be differentiated when they partially overlap on the screen. It would be desirable for the surface closer to the viewer to appear brighter by having the larger

Figure 3.32

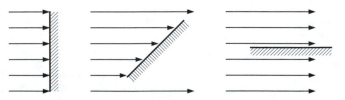

value of R_d. This effect can be imposed by modifying Equation (3.19) to obtain

$$R_d = \frac{K_d E_p}{D + D_0}(\mathbf{N} \cdot \mathbf{L}) \tag{3.20}$$

where D is the distance between the point of interest and the viewpoint or the viewer. The constant D_0 is simply introduced to avoid division by zero.

Now, let's consider the calculation of the intensity of specular reflection. There have been many efforts to model accurately the specular reflection. Here, we introduce one typical model, the *Phong model*. As illustrated in Figure 3.30, most of the reflected light exists in a small conic volume around the axis, which has the same angle as the angle of incidence from the surface normal vector at the opposite side of the incoming light. This axis is represented by the unit vector $\mathbf{R}$ in Figure 3.33. Therefore the intensity of the reflection perceived by a viewer will decrease as the line of sight vector, denoted the unit vector $\mathbf{V}$ in Figure 3.33, deviates from vector $\mathbf{R}$. Phong modeled this phenomenon as

$$R_d = \frac{E_p}{D + D_0} K_s (\mathbf{V} \cdot \mathbf{R})^n \tag{3.21}$$

where E_p, D, and D_0 have the same meaning as in Equation (3.20) and K_s is a constant similar to K_d in Equation (3.20). K_s is called *specular reflectance*. Equation (3.21) can be interpreted as the intensity of the light perceived by a viewer along a vector at an angle ϕ from $\mathbf{R}$ is proportional to $(\cos \phi)^n$. Thus the intensity of the reflection decreases rapidly as the line of sight deviates from $\mathbf{R}$ when n is much bigger than 1. This implies that the reflected light is densely packed around the axis in the $\mathbf{R}$ direction. Hence shiny surfaces such as metallic surfaces have the larger values for n. For example, a metallic surface is well represented by using an n value of 150 or larger. A dull surface such as paper or cloth has an n value close to 1.

We now obtain the intensity of the reflection at a point by summing Equations (3.17), (3.20), and (3.21):

$$I = K_d I_a + \frac{E_p}{D + D_0}\left[K_d(\mathbf{N} \cdot \mathbf{L}) + K_s(\mathbf{V} \cdot \mathbf{R})^n\right] \tag{3.22}$$

To consider the color of the reflected light, we need only express Equation (3.22) separately for each primary color: red, green, and blue. That is, the intensity of the

Figure 3.33

Vectors used in the Phong model

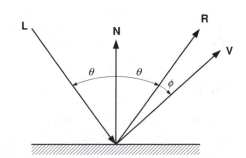

reflected light is expressed in terms of red (I_r), green (I_g), and blue (I_b). The light sources are also expressed in terms of the three colors as I_{ar}, I_{ag}, and I_{ab} for ambient light and E_{pr}, E_{pg}, and E_{pb} for direct light. Surface reflectivity is also decomposed into three components, K_{dr}, K_{dg}, and K_{db}, one for each primary color. For example, the surface of pure red color will have the value of 1 for K_{dr} but 0 for K_{dg} and 0 for K_{db}. Then Equation (3.22) can be decomposed into three components as follows:

$$I_r = K_{dr}I_{ar} + \frac{E_{pr}}{D + D_0}\left[K_{dr}(\mathbf{N}\cdot\mathbf{L}) + K_s(\mathbf{V}\cdot\mathbf{R})^n\right]$$

$$I_g = K_{dg}I_{ag} + \frac{E_{pg}}{D + D_0}\left[K_{dg}(\mathbf{N}\cdot\mathbf{L}) + K_s(\mathbf{V}\cdot\mathbf{R})^n\right] \qquad (3.23)$$

$$I_b = K_{db}I_{ab} + \frac{E_{pb}}{D + D_0}\left[K_{db}(\mathbf{N}\cdot\mathbf{L}) + K_s(\mathbf{V}\cdot\mathbf{R})^n\right]$$

Note that the specular reflectance, K_s, is not decomposed in Equation (3.23). This is because the specular reflection has almost no effect on color. The three intensities calculated by Equation (3.23) are used to set the output of the red, green, and blue electron guns in the RGB color monitor.

We have explained how to calculate the color and intensity of reflected light at a point on an object. However, when a shaded image of an object is needed, we must evaluate Equation (3.23) for all the points on each surface of the object. Obviously, this task requires a tremendous amount of computation. One way to reduce it would be to approximate each surface by a set of triangular facets. In this way, the unit normal vector at the points within each facet needs to be calculated only once. Furthermore, the vectors $\mathbf{L}$, $\mathbf{R}$, and $\mathbf{V}$ can be regarded as constants within each facet if we assume that the light sources and the viewer are located far away from the object. This assumption is commonly used for simplicity. Therefore Equation (3.23) needs to be evaluated only once for each facet. This simplification, however, does not give a smooth transition between neighboring triangular facets but leaves bent lines along the boundary between them.

One remedy for this problem would be to use smoothly varying unit normal vectors instead of a constant normal vector within each facet. In the Phong shading method, the unit normal vectors within a facet are obtained by interpolating the normal vectors at the vertices of the facet. Here, the normal vector of a vertex is obtained by averaging the normal vectors of the planar facets sharing the vertex. Another remedy would be to calculate the intensity of the reflected light at a pixel within the projected triangle of a facet by interpolating the intensities at the vertices of the facet. This method is called *Gouraud shading*.

3.9.2 Ray Tracing

The shading method described in the preceding section can be applied to simple situations in which one object is illuminated by point light sources located far away. However, it cannot be applied when multiple objects are involved, especially when

Figure 3.34

The principle of ray tracing

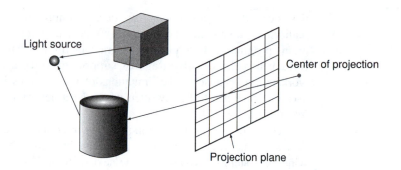

some of them are transparent and others refract light. *Ray tracing* is one of the methods applied to complicated situations.

The basic idea of ray tracing is as follows. Light rays are emitted in every direction from the light sources, and every ray is traced until it is projected onto a point on the screen. In the course of tracing, the intensity and the direction of a ray are updated whenever it hits any object in the scene. Its direction will change, depending on the amount of reflection, scattering, or refraction that occurs. Then each point on the screen, a pixel, will be set to be the intensity and the color of the ray at the last moment. Because infinitely many such paths can be considered to fill the entire screen in this way, this approach is not feasible. But, as we are interested in setting the color of a finite number of pixels on the screen, we may not have to consider infinitely many rays. That is, we need only consider a finite number of rays by tracing the rays in the reverse direction. As illustrated in Figure 3.34, a ray from the center of projection through each pixel is generated and traced back through all its reflections and refractions until the ray passes out of the viewing volume, strikes a diffuse surface, or hits the light source. A traced ray hitting the light source implies that no obstacle or only transparent objects exist between the light source and the screen, and thus the pixel should be colored with the color of the light source. A ray passing out of the viewing volume implies that no object exists to be projected onto the pixel, and thus the pixel should be colored with the background color. If the back-traced ray hits a surface that reflects light diffusely, it is not possible to trace farther. In this case, the color of the pixel is set to that of the reflection on the surface. Thus the light intensities on diffuse surfaces are evaluated in advance by the shading method described in the preceding section before ray tracing begins.

3.10 GRAPHICAL USER INTERFACE

As mentioned earlier, interaction with the user through graphics input and graphics output is an essential capability of existing CAD/CAM/CAE software. In other words, this software should have the facility for opening windows (areas for interaction and application), for displaying menus or equivalent icons, and for defining the tasks to be executed for each menu or icon. The software enabling these facilities is called a *graphical user interface*, or simply GUI. These facilities can also be realized by a so-called homemade graphical user interface, a set of graphics programs programmed with a specific graphics library. This kind of graphical user interface has the disadvantage of supporting only a limited type of graphics workstation because of the limitations of the graphics library. Thus the graphical user interface has to be rewritten whenever a new type of graphics workstation is introduced.

To avoid this problem, graphical user interfaces tend to be based on the X window system, which is supported nowadays by most graphics workstations. (The X window system is explained in the next section.) Two typical graphical user interfaces are based on the X window system: Open Look and OSF/Motif. Open Look has been supported by Sun Microsystems, and OSF/Motif has been supported by the remaining computer companies, including IBM, Hewlett-Packard, DEC, and Tektronix.

A programmer using OpenLook or OSF/Motif to develop an application program can simply use the window manager in the graphical user interface to perform such functions as opening windows, drawing menus, and defining tasks associated with the menus.[16] The graphics display generated by the window manager of Motif is illustrated in Figure 3.35.

Figure 3.35

Graphics display generated by the Motif window manager

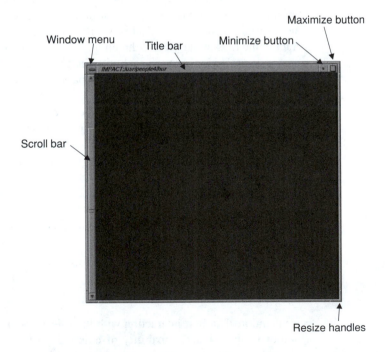

16 On personal computers running under Windows 98 or Windows NT, Microsoft Foundation Classes (MFC) provides the same capabilities.

The advantages of using Open Look or Motif in developing application programs stem from the advantages of using the X window system because both systems are built on the X window system. Therefore we cover the X window system in the next section.

3.11 X WINDOW SYSTEM

Development of the X window system, or simply X, began in 1993 at the Massachusetts Institute of Technology as the ATHENA project. It was developed on top of the window operating system called W, which was developed at Stanford University in the early 1980s. In 1986, the first commercial version, X10, was announced; later X11R5 was announced.

The X window system enables an application program to open and close windows on various workstations connected to a network. That in turn allows input and output for the application to occur in windows of the various workstations on the network. The meaning of *window* here is different from that in Section 3.3. Here, it means a separate area on a workstation through which the user interacts with the various computational resources connected to the network. For example, we can open two windows on the INDIGO2 workstation shown in Figure 3.36 and use one window as an input and output port for an application program running on the SUN machine. At the same time we can use the other window as an input and an output port for another application program running on INDIGO2 itself.

For this kind of task, the X window system should be able to accept a request from an application program, called a *client*, send the request to the proper workstation, and perform some graphics input or output task on the window. This window may be located anywhere on the network. Thus the workstation where the window is opened must have an X server program to enable the graphics operation. Furthermore, the request on the client side has to be written with the specific library functions stored in the library Xlib. The Xlib library must also be installed on the workstation where the application program is running. Transmission of the request through the network will be taken care of by the original function of the X window system. In fact, the X window system includes all the components mentioned, including X server and Xlib.

Figure 3.36

Role of X in a networked environment

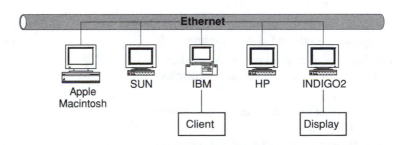

In summary, an application program written in X will have the following advantages. First, an application program running on a workstation can have the interaction of graphics input and output through a window on a different workstation on the network. Second, multiple windows can be opened on a workstation, and multiple computational resources can be used through each window at the same time. Finally, the application program written in X is generally independent of the operating system or the type of workstation. These advantages can be applied to the graphical user interface because the graphical user interface is considered to be an application program. Open Look and Motif have the same advantages.

QUESTIONS AND PROBLEMS

1. What are the disadvantages of a graphics program written directly with the device driver commands?

2. Explain why a graphics program based on a graphics library runs on a limited type of graphics devices.

3. What is the main reason for using the virtual device coordinate system instead of the device coordinate system in specifying a location in a graphics device?

4. In describing the shape of an object, what is the reason for using the object's model coordinate system?

5. Explain how the location and orientation of each object in a scene is specified.

6. Briefly describe the procedure by which the coordinates of a point on an object, measured with respect to its model coordinate system, are converted to screen device coordinates.

7. Explain the meaning of *window* used in computer graphics.

8. Explain the meaning of *viewport*.

9. Explain the difference between using a mouse in the picking mode and in the sampling mode.

10. What kinds of operations can be done when graphics elements are defined to be a display list?

11. The locations of the viewpoint and the viewsite are specified to be (1, 1, 2) and (0, 1, 2), respectively, with respect to the world coordinate

system. Similarly, the up vector is (0, 0, 1) with respect to the world coordinate system.

a. Show the relationships of the screen, the viewing coordinate system, the viewpoint, and the viewsite in a sketch.

b. Derive the transformation matrix T_{w-v} that transforms the coordinates in world coordinates to those in viewing coordinates.

c. Using the transformation matrix T_{w-v} in (b), calculate the viewing coordinates of a point represented by (5, 1, 2) in world coordinates.

12. Explain which transformation matrices have to be applied in which order to rotate the point (2, 2) on the *xy* plane by 30 degrees counterclockwise with the point (3, 4) as the center of rotation. Calculate the coordinates of the rotated point by applying the transformation matrices obtained to the point (2, 2).

13. The coordinate systems related to a projection are illustrated in the following figure. Answer the following questions.

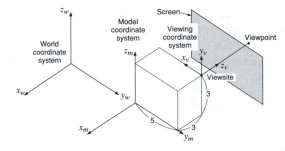

a. A point on an object to be displayed has the coordinates (−3, 0, 3) in reference to the model coordinate system. The coordinates of this point in reference to the world coordinate system, (X_w, Y_w, Z_w) can be obtained as follows once the model transformation matrix T_m has been derived.

$$\begin{bmatrix} X_w \\ Y_w \\ Z_w \\ 1 \end{bmatrix} = T_m \begin{bmatrix} -3 \\ 0 \\ 3 \\ 1 \end{bmatrix}$$

Derive the model transformation matrix T_m and calculate (X_w, Y_w, Z_w) using the preceding equation. The model coordinate system in this problem is attained when the world coordinate system is simply translated by 0, 2, and −1 in the x, y, and z directions, respectively.

b. The viewing coordinate system in the figure was established from the given viewsite, viewpoint, and up vector. That is, the viewsite is (−3, 7, 2), the viewpoint is (−10, 7, 2), and the the up vector is (0, 0, 1), all of which are measured with respect to the world coordinate system. Derive the viewing transformation matrix T_v that calculates the viewing coordinates (X_v, Y_v, Z_v) from the world coordinates (X_w, Y_w, Z_w) of a point:

$$\begin{bmatrix} X_v \\ Y_v \\ Z_v \\ 1 \end{bmatrix} = T_v \cdot \begin{bmatrix} X_w \\ Y_w \\ Z_w \\ 1 \end{bmatrix}$$

c. Calculate the coordinates in the viewing coordinate system of the point (−3, 0, 3) in the model coordinate system by applying T_m and T_v, as derived in (a) and (b).

14. Derive the transformation matrix T_{w-v} that transforms the coordinates in world coordinates to those in viewing coordinates when the locations of the viewpoint and the viewsite are specified to be (4, 5, 6) and (0, 0, 0), respectively, in the world coordinate system. Assume that the z axis of the world coordinate system is to be the the up vector.

15. Consider a triangular face of a convex object whose three vertices are A(0, 0, 0), B(1, 1, 0), and C(0, 1, 2). Determine whether this face is visible from a viewpoint V(0, 1, 5) by using the back-face removal algorithm. Assume that a point D(2, 2, 2) is also a vertex of this object.

16. Two points, A and B, constituting a portion of a two-dimensional shape are moved to points C and D, respectively, resulting in transformation of the original shape. List the required transformation matrices, in proper order, that have to be applied to all the points of the shape. The coordinates of the points are, A(2, 2), B(5, 5), C(5, 2), and D(7, 2 + 2√3).

17. A plane perpendicular to the xz plane is located as shown in the following figure.

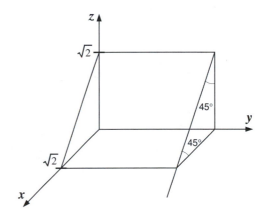

If a mirror reflection P* of a point P with respect to this plane is obtained by the following equation, express $Tp–p*$ as a combination of the elementary transformation matrices

$$[X^* \ Y^* \ Z^* \ 1] = T_{p-p^*} \cdot [X \ Y \ Z \ 1]$$

The transformation matrices such as $Trans(a,b,c)$, $Rot(x,\alpha)$ $Rot(y,\beta)$ $Rot(z,\gamma)$, Mirror-xy, Mirror-yz, and Mirror-xz belong to the elementary transformation matrices.

18. Explain the difference between Phong shading and Gouraud shading.

19. Using a graphics library available to you, write a graphics program that performs the following tasks.

    a. Display a coordinate system and a cube at its center, assuming the proper viewsite, viewpoint, and up vector for the projection. Assume the proper size of the cube, too.

    b. The cube is translated by +5 in the positive y direction when the left mouse button is pushed, and +5 in the positive z direction when the right mouse button is pushed. The cube is moved to the original position (at the center of the coordinate system) when the middle mouse button is pushed.

20. Make a two-dimensional editor running under the following popup menu.

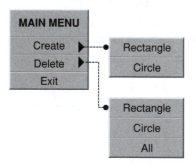

21. Write a graphics program that will draw the trajectory of the point D, the midpoint of link BC, as the input link AB rotates the slider-crank mechanism depicted in the following figure. From the drawn trajectory, determine approximately the input link angle θ at which the tangent of the trajectory becomes horizontal.

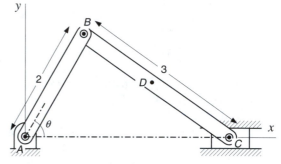

22. Describe the advantages of writing the graphical user interface portion of an application program in X.

4

Computer-Aided Drafting Systems

As explained in the previous chapters, a computer-aided drafting system is a software product that enables the creation and modification of mechanical drawings, architectural drawings, engineering drawings, electrical circuit diagrams, and various other types of drawings, according to the designer's interactive input. This software also updates a database by storing the resulting drawings and modifications to them. Thus using a computer-aided drafting system is analogous to using a word processor. The only difference is that the output is a drawing instead of a document. As a new document can be made very easily by modifying an existing document created on a word processor, so too a new drawing can be made from an existing drawing by a computer-aided drafting system. The advantage of using a word processor or a computer-aided drafting system may hardly be appreciated when a completely new document or drawing is made. However, they are very powerful tools when used to modify existing documents or drawings.

The common functions provided by most computer-aided drafting systems are described briefly in the following sections. The specific commands for each function may differ for each specific system, and thus you should refer to its user's manual for guidance about their use.

4.1 DRAWING SETUP

The first thing to do in using a computer-aided drafting system is to set factors such as units, drawing limits, grid, and layers. In order to generate a drawing accurately and quickly, these factors must be set properly. You can produce a drawing without grids and layers but will waste a lot of time doing so, and modifying the drawing will be very difficult.

4.1.1 Units

A format and the precision for the units of distance and angle measurement should be chosen. The formats of distance units, for example, are scientific, decimal, fractional, engineering, and architectural. The formats of angle units are decimal degrees, degrees/minutes/seconds, grads, radians, and surveyor's units. Figure 4.1 shows the unit control dialog box of AutoCAD[1] Release14, which is one of the most popular computer-aided drafting systems available.

4.1.2 The Size of Drawing (Limits)

When you create a drawing on paper, you are supposed to draw only within the bounds of the sheet of paper. Similarly, when you construct a drawing on a graphics device, you should limit the drawing to certain boundaries because the drawing on a display monitor eventually will be plotted on paper of a finite size. Thus you should preset the size of a drawing. The prompt sequence for setting the size of a drawing in AutoCAD Release14 is as follows.

Commands: limits
Reset Model Space Limits
ON/OFF/<Lower left corner><0.00,0.00>: 10,10
Upper right corner<12.00,9.00>: 300,200

Figure 4.1

Unit control dialog
box of AutoCAD
Release14

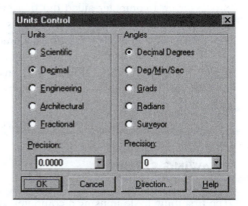

---

[1] AutoCAD is the name of a computer-aided drafting system developed by Autodesk, Inc.

The factors usually considered when determining the limits of the drawing area [Tickoo 1996] are the

- actual size of the drawing;
- space needed for dimensions, notes, bill of materials, and other necessary details;
- space between different views so that the drawing does not look cluttered; and
- space for the border and a title block if any.

Before setting such limits, you should draw a sketch of the drawing to calculate roughly the necessary area. For example, for an object that has a front view of 6×5 units, a side view of 4×5 units, and a top view of 6×4 units, the limits should be set so that the drawing area can accommodate the drawing and everything associated with it. As shown in Figure 4.2, let's assume that you want the space between the front and side view to be 4 units and between the front and top view to be 3 units. Also, let's say that you want the space between the border and drawing to be 4 units on the left, 4 units on the right, 2 units at the bottom, and 2 units at the top. The spaces used should be determined so that the complete drawing looks balanced.

After you have determined the sizes of the different views and the space required between views, the space between the border and the drawing, and the space between the border and the edges of the paper, you can calculate the limits as follows:

Limit in the x direction $= 1 + 4 + 6 + 4 + 4 + 4 + 1 = 24$
Limit in the y direction $= 1 + 2 + 5 + 3 + 4 + 2 + 1 = 18$

Therefore the limits for the drawing are 24×18 units. Note that we assumed the space between the border and the edges of the paper to be a uniform 1 unit.

Figure 4.2

Setting limits in a drawing

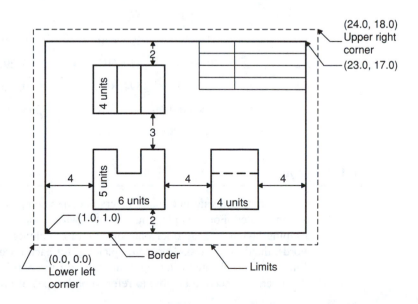

The drawing shown in Figure 4.2 was made at a 1:1 scale. However, when you want to plot a drawing to get a hard copy, you should scale the drawing up or down based on the sheet size. In fact, the sheet size determines the limits, text size, dimensioning scale factor, linetype scale factor, and other drawing-related parameters. Standard sheet sizes and the corresponding drawing limits for different scale factors (in inches and millimeters, respectively) are illustrated in the following tables.

English System

Paper Size	Sheet Size	Limits (1:1)	Limits (1:4)—Reduction	Limits (4:1)—Magnification
A	12 × 9	12, 9	48, 36	3, 2.25
B	18 × 12	18, 12	72, 48	4.5, 3
C	24 × 18	24, 18	96, 72	6, 4.5
D	36 × 24	36, 24	144, 96	9, 6
E	48 × 36	48, 36	192, 144	12, 9

Metric System

Paper Size	Sheet Size	Limits (1:1)	Limits (1:5)—Reduction	Limits (5:1)—Magnification
A4	210 × 297	210, 297	1050, 1485	42, 59.4
A3	297 × 420	297, 420	1485, 2100	59.4, 84
A2	420 × 594	420, 594	2100, 2970	84, 118.8
A1	594 × 841	594, 841	2970, 4205	118.8, 168.2
A0	841 × 1189	841, 1189	4205, 5945	168.2, 237.8

4.1.3 Layer

Organizing a drawing into many layers is convenient, especially when the drawing is complicated. For example, you can work with much simpler drawings if you draw a piping layout and the floor plan of an entire building in separate layers. In other words, the drawing tasks, including picking, for each layer is much easier than handling one complicated drawing containing all the entities that need to be shown. However, you need to be able to refer to both types of drawing at the same time to get a feel for the relative locations of the entities from the different layers (e.g., the relative position of, say, the pipes and the walls of the building). Layering allows you to overlap layers without increasing the complexity of a drawing, at least in terms of the graphics operations being performed. The layer on which you are currently working is active while the other layers are inactive. Just as in a background role, the graphics elements belonging to the inactive layers are insensitive to graphics operations such as picking and deleting. Therefore the complexity of the drawing appears to be the same as if you were working with the active layer alone.

The layer function can be used efficiently in drawing the layout of each layer of a multiple-layered printed circuit board. In this application, the layout of each layer can be drawn separately while some related layers are overlapped for relative position information. The layer function can also be used conveniently to generate component drawings for an assembly. If each component has been drawn on a separate layer for an assembly layout, any component drawing can easily be generated by bringing up the proper layer and modified by adding some details. Figure 4.3 shows the layer control dialog box in AutoCAD Release14.

4.1.4   Grid and Snap

It is a common practice in manual drafting to draw construction lines beforehand, using a T-square, so that the boundary and other lines of a drawing can be drawn easily and uniformly over them. The grid lines provided by a computer-aided drafting system have the same purpose as the construction lines in manual drafting. That is, the horizontal and vertical grid lines are drawn at a regular interval conforming to the desired resolution, and the lines composing the drawing are drawn on top of them. Note that only the grid points are drawn in some computer-aided drafting systems.

To draw a straight line on top of a grid line, you must specify the locations of the two end points. To do so, you can provide its coordinates through the keyboard or push the mouse button when the cursor is at a desired position. Recall that the cursor tracks the movement of the mouse when the mouse is in the locator mode. The location of the point specified by the latter method may not be exact because of

Figure 4.3

Layer control dialog box of AutoCAD Release14

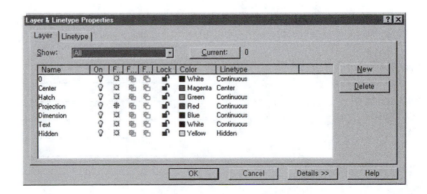

the unstable motion of the human hand or the imprecise mechanism of the mouse. To avoid this problem, you can set the cursor to snap to the nearest intersection point of the grid lines. The coordinate values returned when you push the mouse button are those of the intersection point. Therefore the accuracy limits of the point coordinates are determined by the resolution of the grid drawn on the screen, which you can adjust. This feature is called *snapping*. The grid command is activated in AutoCAD Release14 as follows.

Command : grid
Grid spacing(X) or ON/OFF/Snap/Aspect<0>: 0.75 /*the gap between the grid lines are set to be 0.75 screen unit*/

4.2   BASIC DRAWING FUNCTIONS

4.2.1   Straight Line

There are many ways of drawing a straight line in a computer-aided drafting system. The most popular method is by specifying the line's two end points. Again, the location of a point can be specified in various ways. We introduced two methods in the previous section: providing the coordinates of the point and pushing the mouse button in the locator mode. In addition, you can specify the location of a point by picking an existing point.

You can also draw a line without specifying the two end points explicitly. One way is to ask a system to draw a tangent line to an existing curve from a specified point. In this case you have to specify only one point explicitly, and the system determines the other end point. The type and thickness of a line can be specified as its attributes. Figure 4.4 shows the types of lines generally supported by most computer-aided drafting systems. Drawing a straight line in AutoCAD Release14 involves the following.

Command: line
From point: 1, 1
To point: 5, 2
To point: return

Figure 4.4

Various types of straight lines

4.2.2 Circle and Circular Arc

The basic method of defining a circle is to provide a center point and a radius or three points on the circle. Most computer-aided drafting systems also allow the generation of a circle by other methods. For example, they can generate a circle tangent to two straight lines or tangent to a circle and a straight line. In either case, you have to pick the related entities. The circular arc is a special case of a circle and can be defined by specifying the starting and ending points in addition to the parameters for a complete circle. You can draw a circle in AutoCAD Release14 as follows.

Command: circle
3P/2P/TTR/<Center point>: 5, 5
Diameter/<Radius><current>: 3

A circular arc can be drawn by the following command. In this case the arc is drawn to pass through the three input points.

Command: arc
Center/<Start point>: 7, 4
Center/End/<Second point>: 6, 5
End point: 6, 3

4.2.3 Spline

The spline function is used to draw an arbitrary curve in the same way it is drawn manually with adjustable curves. That is, the points on the desired spline are provided, and a curve interpolating those points is created. The resulting curve is usually represented by a third-order equation. Sometimes, a curve can be generated from some control points instead of the points lying on the curve, but the control points to define a curve do not have to lie on the curve. We explain control points in Chapter 5.

4.2.4 Deleting

The delete function acts as the eraser does in manual drafting. When you pick graphics entities such as points, lines, and curves, the picked entities disappear from the screen. We explained the picking input in Chapter 3.

4.2.5 Filleting and Chamfering

Filleting or rounding is adding a circular arc between two intersecting lines (Figure 4.5a) so that the added circular arc is tangent to both the lines, as illustrated in Figure 4.5(b). More specifically, filleting is used for concave corners, whereas rounding is used for convex corners. Chamfering is the same as filleting, except

Figure 4.5

Filleting and chamfering

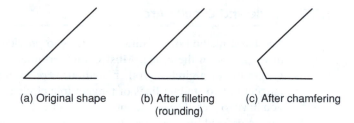

(a) Original shape   (b) After filleting (rounding)   (c) After chamfering

that it adds a straight-line segment instead of a circular arc, as shown in Figure 4.5(c). Filleting and chamfering are executed in the following sequence.

1. The fillet radius or chamfer size is provided.
2. Two intersecting lines are picked. A fillet or chamfer will be added at the corner of the picked lines.
3. Unnecessary portions of the original lines are deleted after a fillet or a chamfer is added. This deletion is done automatically in some systems but has to be done manually in other systems.

You can add a fillet in AutoCAD Release14 as follows.

Command: fillet
(TRIM mode) Current fillet radius = 10.00
Polyline/Radius/Trim/<Select first object>: r
Enter fillet radius<current>: 3
(TRIM mode) Current fillet radius = 3.00
Command: fillet
Polyline/Radius/Trim/<Select first object>: /*The first line is picked*/
Select second line: /*The second line is picked*/

4.2.6   Hatching

Hatching fills a closed polygon with a specific pattern. It is often used to indicate the cross sections in mechanical drawings and different materials in architectural drawings. Figure 4.6 shows some typical patterns provided in most computer-aided drafting systems.

The first task in hatching is to specify the closed polygon to be hatched. That can be done by using either of the following two methods. In some systems, you may

Figure 4.6

Types of hatching patterns

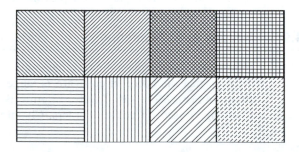

have to pick all the boundary lines composing the polygon. Or, you may need pick only one boundary element because some systems then find all the other boundary elements automatically. If there are some regions in the polygon for which hatching is not desirable, such as holes, the boundaries for those regions have to be specified too. Hatching is one of the features of computer-aided drafting systems that increase the drafter's productivity. Figure 4.7 shows a drawing containing hatched portions.

Figure 4.7

Drawing with dimensions, hatching, and a note

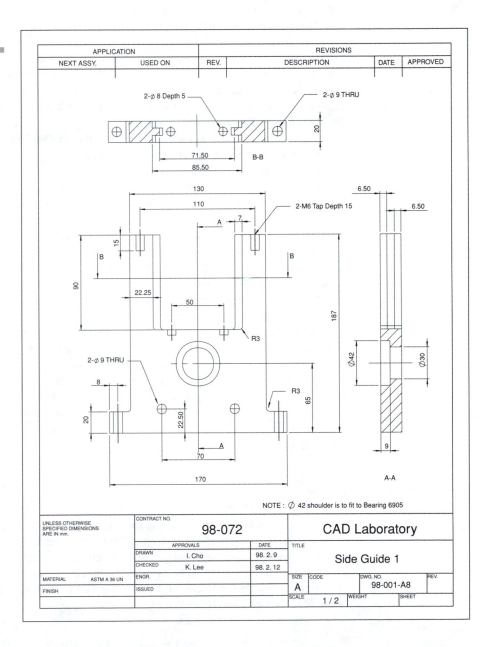

4.3   ANNOTATION FUNCTIONS

4.3.1   Dimensioning

The dimensioning capability is considered to be the most attractive feature of computer-aided drafting systems—one that cannot be rivaled in manual drafting practice. With a computer-aided drafting system the dimensioning task is performed as follows. To assign a horizontal or a vertical dimension, you have only to specify the two graphics elements, usually points, and the desired location of the dimension line. In this case, the dimension value (i.e., the distance between the elements) is automatically measured from the drawing. The arrowheads, dimension lines, dimension values, and the extension lines are then drawn by the system. It automatically measures the vertical distance if the graphics elements are located on a vertical line, or it measures the horizontal distance if they are on a horizontal line. If they are on neither a horizontal nor vertical line, the system will ask whether you intend horizontal, vertical, or real distance.

A radial or diametric dimension can be assigned by picking a circle or a circular arc to be dimensioned and by specifying the desired location of the dimension value in the drawing. Similarly, an angular dimension is assigned by picking two lines and the location of the dimension value. The internal or external angle is implied by the order of picking the two lines. As every system uses a different ordering convention, you should refer to the manual for the specific system. Figure 4.7 shows a dimensioned drawing.

You might wonder why dimensioning has to be done interactively even when an exact drawing already contains all the size and location information. Complete automatic dimensioning may be possible in theory, but it would have the following problems. There are many ways of dimensioning the same drawing. In fact, a designer considers the manufacturing, inspection, and assembling aspects of the part represented by the drawing and chooses the best dimensioning scheme for it. The designer's choice is based primarily on experience, which is very difficult to replicate on a computer. Furthermore, finding just one complete and nonredundant dimensioning scheme for a drawing is not simple. In fact, some researchers are working on a solution to this problem.

4.3.2   Notes

In order to insert notes or a text string on a drawing, the location and the orientation of the string have to be specified together with the size and the font of the characters in the string. There is usually a default setting for character size, its font, and the string orientation that will be assumed when no specific input for them is given. An example of a note is shown on Figure 4.7. You can insert notes with MTEXT in AutoCAD Release14 as follows.

Command: text
Justify/Style/<start point>: 2, 1
Height<0.20>: 0.25
Rotation angle<0>:
Text: MTEXT

4.4 UTILITY FUNCTIONS

4.4.1 Copy

The copy function works in the same way as cut and paste do in the word processor (i.e., a set of graphics elements already drawn can be selected, stored in the buffer, and copied at any place in the same or different drawings). The graphics elements to be copied are selected by enclosing them within a rectangle of a proper size. The rectangle can be drawn on a graphics screen to an arbitrary size in the same way that a rectangle is drawn to define a viewport. If some graphics elements are cut by the boundary of the rectangle, you can choose an option to include those elements in the set to be copied or exclude them from it. The cursor is dragged to the location where the selected elements are to be copied. The copy function can be conveniently used when a drawing has a repetitive pattern, as in an architectural drawing of an apartment complex. The copy function also facilitates the task of component drawing because some related portions from the entire assembly drawing can be copied and detailed further.

As a special form of a copy function, a mirror reflection function is used to draw a shape with symmetry axes. That is, a complete shape is generated from an axis of symmetry and a set of graphics elements is folded about the symmetry axis. This function is useful for drawing shapes with one or many axes of symmetry. Furthermore, many computer-aided drafting systems provide a function that lays out a given set of graphics elements in various patterns. For example, some systems can lay out a bolt head along a circumference at a regular angular increment after you draw only one bolt head. You can use the copy function in AutoCAD Release14 as follows.

Command: copy
Select objects: /*A set of graphic elements are selected*/
<Base point or displacement>/Multiple: /*First point is specified*/
Second point of displacement: /*Second point is specified to fix the orientation*/

4.4.2 Window

Sometimes you may want to enlarge a portion of a drawing when you are working on a complicated drawing. Often, you may not be able to pick a graphics entity if it is not far enough from other entities on the display monitor. You can solve this problem by enlarging the portion that contains the entity to be picked. Using a smaller window with mapping to the same viewport will give the effect of enlargement without changing the numerical data of the graphics elements. You can specify the window by its two diagonal points similar to the way you define the region to be copied in the copy function. You can define a window in AutoCAD Release14 as follows.

Command: zoom
All/Center/Dynamic/Extents/Left/Previous/Vmax/Window/Scale(X/Xp)>: w
First corner: /*One diagonal point is specified by moving the cursor*/
Second corner: /*The other diagonal point is specified using the cursor*/

4.4.3   Symbol

Shapes that are used frequently in drawings can be stored as symbols and drawn any time by simply invoking them. For example, creating mechanical drawings is greatly facilitated if the shapes of standard components such as bolts and nuts and the symbols for surface texture and tolerance are registered as symbols and can be invoked whenever needed. This symbol function is the same as the copy function in principle and thus it is implemented in the same way. You can draw a symbol in AutoCAD Release14 as follows.

Command: block
Block name(or ?): name of the symbol registered

Figure 4.8 shows typical symbols used frequently in drawings.

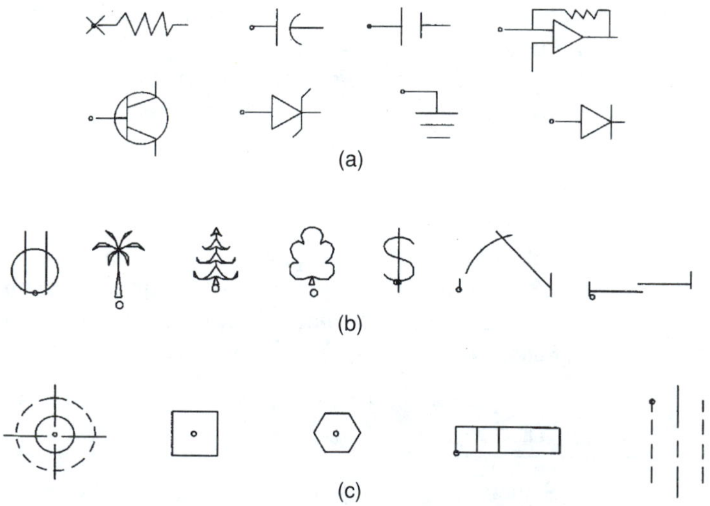

Figure 4.8

Typical symbols used in drawings: (a) electrical symbols, (b) architectural symbols, and (c) mechanical symbols

4.4.4   Macro or Parametric Programming

Macro programming is used to merge a set of graphics commands into one graphics command. When a sequence of graphics commands is composed into a program, called a *macro program*, some conditional statements and arithmetic operations in normal computer language can also be inserted between graphics commands. Furthermore, the parameters to be input to the graphics commands in the macro program can be defined as variables so that a different set of values can be assigned to yield various graphics outputs. In this case the macro program is called a *parametric program* because the resulting shape to be drawn changes according to the specific numerical values passed to the corresponding parameters. For example, an automatic drawing program for screws is an application of parametric programming. The program receives the loading condition from the user, calculates the dimensions of the screw from the loading condition, and then draws the screw to the calculated dimensions. As expected, the parametric program has the arithmetic operations needed to calculate the dimensions and the sequence of graphics commands needed to draw the screw with the calculated dimensions. This macro function is very important because it allows a commercial computer-aided drafting system to be customized for different applications. In fact, the variety of the parametric programs developed by a company can be a measure of how efficiently the company uses its computer-aided drafting system.

4.4.5   Measurement

The measurement function allows calculation from the finished drawing or a drawing in process. In other words, the system reveals the area of any shape of interest, an angle between two lines, or the minimum distance between two graphics elements, and so on. This function can be very useful when drafting and designing are performed simultaneously with a computer-aided drafting system. For example, the designer can check whether the resulting design satisfies the required heat transfer area or the minimum space for maintenance purposes. You can use the measurement function in AutoCAD Release14 as follows.

Command: dist
First point: /*One end point is picked*/
Second Point: /*The other end point is picked*/
Distance = <Calculated distance>
Angle in XY plane = <Angle>
Angle from XY plane = <Angle>
Delta X = <Change in X>, Delta Y = <Change in Y>, Delta Z = <Change in Z>

4.4.6   Miscellaneous Functions

In addition to the functions described in the previous sections, there are some miscellaneous functions that relate to manipulations to update drawing files in the database, retrieve files from the database, and make up bills of materials.

4.5 COMPATIBILITY OF DRAWING FILES

We have previously shown that the real advantage of using a computer-aided drafting system is the ability to store a drawing file in a database so that it can be shared by people in various departments. This advantage may be easily realized if all these people use the same drafting system and if they have no trouble reading drawing files made somewhere else. However, this advantage can easily be lost if different departments in the same company use different computer-aided drafting systems that cannot read the drawings, which is not unusual. The problem becomes even worse if the systems of various vendors cannot read the drawings. In such cases drawings created on paper and reproduced mechanically will be the only feasible medium of communication, as in the past.

One way to avoid this type of problem would be to require all computer-aided drafting systems to store drawing files in a standard format. The most popular standard format currently is the Initial Graphics Exchange Specification (IGES), which is ANSI Standard Y14.26M. In fact, almost all the commercial computer-aided drafting systems support IGES. Therefore the drawing files generated by one system should be transferable to other systems. However, some symbols defined in one system still cannot be transferred correctly to other systems through IGES. In addition to IGES, DXF file format, the drawing file format of AutoCAD files, is becoming a de facto standard format because of the popularity of AutoCAD.

QUESTIONS AND PROBLEMS

1. Copy the following drawings, using any computer-aided drafting system available. The dimensions are in millimeters. You do not have to insert the dimensions.

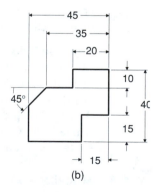

(b)

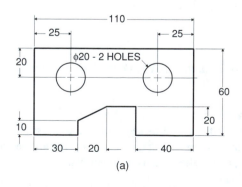

(a)

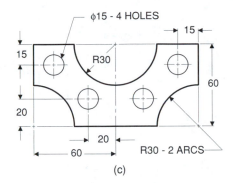

φ15 - 4 HOLES

R30

R30 - 2 ARCS

(c)

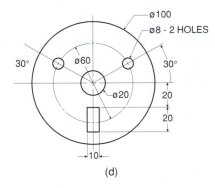

ø100

ø8 - 2 HOLES

ø60

ø20

(d)

2. Draw the top, front, and right side views of the following objects. Use third angle layout of views. The dimensions are in inches, with millimeters in parentheses. You do not have to insert the dimensions.

(*Source:* J. Luckow, *The Technical Drawing Workbook*, Addison-Wesley Publishing Company, 1994)

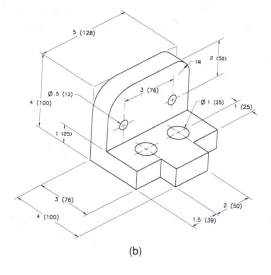

(b)

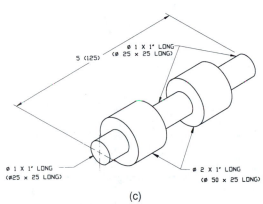

(c)

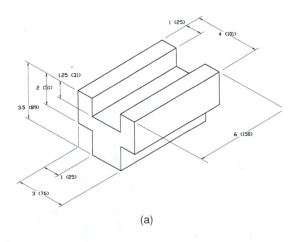

(a)

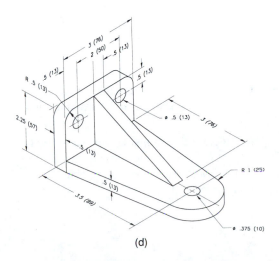

(d)

3. Copy the following drawings, including the dimensions. Dimensions are in millimeters.

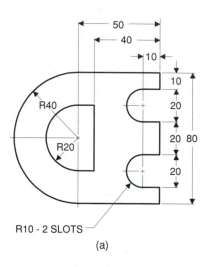

(a)

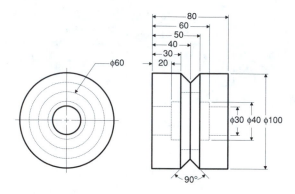

b. Show the front view as a half-section and show the corresponding cutting plane in the top view. Include any notes that are necessary.

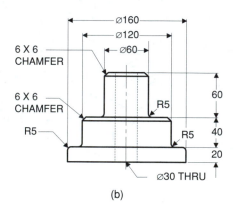

(b)

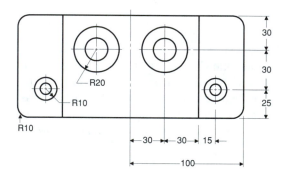

4. Create the following drawings, including the dimensions. The dimensions are in millimeters.

a. Replace the right side view shown with a sectional view. The vertical centerline of the front view is the cutting plane line for the sectional view.

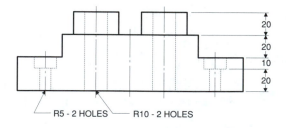

c. Create the auxiliary view of the slanted surface.

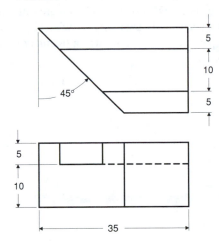

5. Copy the following drawing, including the dimensions and tolerances. The dimensions are in millimeters.

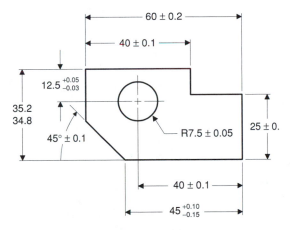

6. Prepare an assembly drawing and parts list based on the following information. First, create the detail drawings of parts 1 and 2. Join part 2 to part 1, using two 5.00—13 UNC × 25 LONG HEX-HEAD BOLTS. Include 5.00—13 UNC NUTS on each bolt. Locate a 6.25 × 12.5 × 1.25 WASHER under the head of each bolt, between part 1 and part 2, and

between part 1 and NUT. Each bolt will have three washers and a nut.

(*Source:* S. Lockhart, *A Tutorial Guide to AutoCAD, Release 12*, Addison-Wesley Publishing Company, 1994)

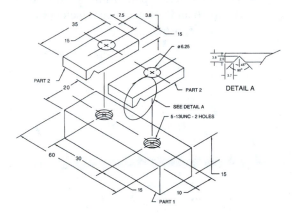

7. Design a clock pendulum that will satisfy the constraints given.

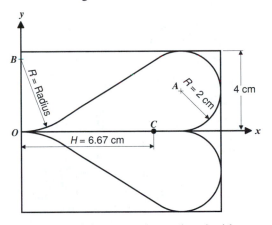

- The pendulum must be enclosed with a rectangle 10 cm × 8 cm.

- The pendulum should be symmetric about the x axis.

- The top-half boundary of the pendulum is composed of a circular arc centered at *B*, a straight line, and a circular arc of radius 2 cm. The straight line between the two circular arcs must be tangent to the arcs.

- The pendulum rod is connected to the pendulum at C, its centroid. This location must be 6.67 cm from O, as shown in the figure.
- The area of the pendulum should be between 36 and 44 square centimeters to meet a weight constraint.

Determine the location of B and the radius of the arc centered at B by trying various drawings until the constraints given are satisfied. You can easily try many drawings by making a parametric program, using the macro capability.

5

Geometric Modeling Systems

The design process can be thought of as the detailing of a shape as the designer's idea evolves. Thus CAD software as a design aid is just a tool to facilitate this detailing process. As mentioned in Section 2.3, typical CAD software can be classified as two groups. One is the computer-aided drafting system that enables the designer to realize the design idea by manipulating the shape in two dimensions, as described in Chapter 4. The other is the geometric modeling system by which the designer manipulates shapes in three dimensions.

The following example illustrates how a geometric modeling system can be used in the design process. Envision a child making something from "play dough." The child progresses toward a final shape by deforming and sometimes by adding and cutting pieces off the dough. This process can be considered to be a design process because it involves detailing a shape as the design idea evolves. In fact, the child is immersed in the design process without any knowledge of technical drawings—even without pen and paper. If the child wants to deliver the result to others, say, for prototyping or mass production, the child can just give them the real model from which all the necessary information can be obtained. This natural use of the design process raises questions such as Are technical drawings indispensable to the design process? Do computer-aided drafting systems support our activities naturally in the design process? We can justify the use of drawings by saying that the detailing process involving the use of a material such as play dough cannot realize a complicated shape while at the same time satisfying exact size or dimension requirements. Furthermore, it is very difficult in most cases to extract the necessary information from real models in order to make an exact reproduction.

Geometric modeling systems came into being to overcome the problems encountered with the use of physical models in the design process. These systems provide an environment similar to the one in which the physical model is created and naturally manipulated. In other words, using a geometric modeling system, the designer deforms, adds, and cuts pieces off the visual model in the process of detailing a shape just as the child does with the physical model of play dough. The visual model may look the same as the physical model, but it is intangible. However, the three-dimensional visual model is accompanied by its mathematical description and thus eliminates the need for measurement for prototyping or mass production, which is the major disadvantage of using a physical model. Geometric modeling systems are classified as wireframe modeling systems, surface modeling systems, solid modeling systems, and nonmanifold modeling systems, in order of their evolutionary history. We explain each category in the following sections.

5.1   WIREFRAME MODELING SYSTEMS

Wireframe modeling systems represent a shape by its characteristic lines and end points. The systems use these lines and points to display three-dimensional shapes and allow manipulation of the shapes by modifying the lines and points. In other words, the visual model is simply a wireframe drawing of the shape, and the corresponding mathematical description is the list of curve equations, coordinates of the points, and connectivity information for the shape's curves and points. Connectivity information identifies which points are the end points of which curves and which curves are adjacent to each other and at which points. Wireframe modeling systems were popular when geometric modeling was first introduced. Their popularity was due to the fact that wireframe modeling systems require only simple user input to create a shape and that it is relatively easy for users to develop systems themselves. However, a visual model composed only of lines is sometimes ambiguous, as illustrated in Figure 5.1. Furthermore, the corresponding mathematical description does not include information about the inside and outside boundary surfaces of the object being modeled. Without this information, it is impossible to calculate the object's mass properties, derive the tool paths to machine its surfaces, or generate its finite meshes for finite-element analysis even though it appears to be a three-dimensional

Figure 5.1

Ambiguous wire-
frame models

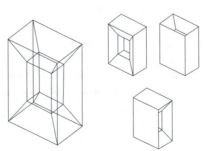

shape. Therefore, because these capabilities are an essential part of the design process, wireframe modeling systems have tended to be replaced by surface modeling systems and solid modeling systems.

5.2 SURFACE MODELING SYSTEMS

In surface modeling systems, the mathematical description corresponding to a visual model includes surface information in addition to the information about the characteristic lines and their end points contained in the wireframe description. Thus a list of surface equations, a list of curve equations, and the coordinates of end points are updated as the visual model is manipulated on the graphics screen. The visual model in a surface modeling system may appear to be the same as that in the wireframe model when the surfaces are neither colored nor shaded.

The mathematical description may include the information about surface connectivity (i.e., information on how surfaces are joined and which surfaces are adjacent to each other at which curves, and so on). This adjacency information is very helpful in some application programs. For example, a program to generate the tool paths of an NC milling machine may use this information to check gouging (unexpected machining) of a surface adjacent to the surface being machined. However, the mathematical description of the surface model created by a surface modeling system has typically included only a list of surface equations (or the characteristic attributes defining the surface equations) of infinite surfaces without connectivity information. The location, direction of the center axis, and radius of a cylindrical surface are examples of the characteristic attributes defining a cylindrical surface equation. Without surface connectivity information, the application program (e.g., an NC tool path program) has to derive the boundaries of the surfaces and their connectivity information. Because of that inconvenience, the surface modeling systems now being developed include surface connectivity information.

Typically, three methods are used to create a surface in surface modeling systems: (1) by interpolating the input points, (2) by interpolating the curve nets specified, and (3) by translating or revolving a specified curve. The input method for each of these surface creation methods may differ, depending on the particular surface modeling system. However, the basic input mode for a system can easily be guessed from the representations of the curves and surfaces presented in Chapter 6 and 7.

Surface modeling systems are used to create models with complex surfaces mainly for two purposes—the visual model is used to evaluate the model aesthetically, and the mathematical description is used to generate the NC tool paths to machine its surfaces. Figure 5.2 illustrates evaluation of the appearance of an automobile body modeled by a surface modeling system. Figure 5.3 shows the calculation and verification of NC tool paths generated for an object created by a surface modeling system.

Figure 5.2

Modeling of an automobile body

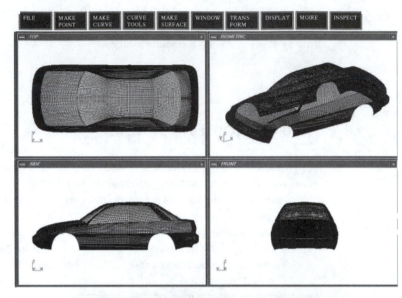

Figure 5.3

Calculation and verification of NC tool paths (Courtesy of OPEN MIND Software Technologies GmbH., HyperMILL®)

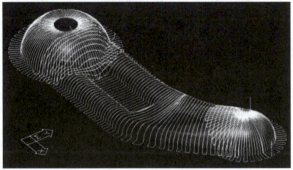

5.3 SOLID MODELING SYSTEMS

Solid modeling systems are used to model a shape having a closed volume, called a *solid*. Unlike wireframe modeling systems or surface modeling systems, a simple set of surfaces or a simple set of characteristic lines is not allowed if it cannot form a closed volume. In addition to the information provided in a surface modeling system, the mathematical description of a shape created by a solid modeling system contains information that determines whether any location is inside, outside, or on the closed volume. Therefore any information related to the volume of the solid can be derived, and thus application programs can be written to do operations at the level of volume instead of at the level of surface.

For example, an application program can be written to generate automatically the finite elements of a solid type from a solid model. Furthermore, an NC tool path generation program can be written to generate automatically all the tool paths to machine the volume to be removed from the workpiece. It can do so without generating the tool paths surface by surface that would require user input for each surface. These capabilities are realized when the model is created as a complete solid. But creating a model as a complete solid requires a large amount of input data in proportion to the amount of data stored in the mathematical description. This is one reason why nonmanifold modeling systems have been developed. Nonmanifold modeling systems allow a mixture of surfaces and solids. Nonmanifold modeling systems are explained in Section 5.4.

If a solid modeling system requires direct input of all the information for the mathematical description, users will feel that it is too complicated and not use it. The process of detailing a shape then will be unlike the intuitive process of physical modeling, and the result would be contrary to the original intent of geometric modeling systems. Hence the developers of solid modeling systems try to provide simple and natural modeling functions so that users can manipulate the shape of a solid as they do for a physical model without having to consider the details of the mathematical description. Modeling functions such as primitive creation, Boolean operations, lifting, sweeping, swinging, and rounding typically require only a simple input from the user. They then take care of all the bookkeeping tasks needed to update the mathematical description.

5.3.1 Modeling Functions

The modeling functions supported by most solid modeling systems can generally be classified as five groups. The first group includes the modeling functions that are used to create a simple shape by retrieving a solid, which is one of the primitive solids stored in the program in advance, and by adjusting its size. Hence they are called *primitive creation functions*. The functions of adding to or subtracting from a solid also belong to this group. These functions are called *Boolean operations*. The modeling functions in the first group enable a designer to model a shape that will be close to the final shape quickly, as the child does when using play dough to make an approximate physical model.

The second group is composed of the modeling functions that create a solid by moving a surface. Thus the sweeping and skinning functions belong to this group. The *sweeping* function creates a solid by translating or revolving a predefined planar closed domain. The modeling function using the revolution of a planar domain is also called *swinging*. When defining the planar closed domain, the user may impose geometric constraints and/or enter dimension data instead of specifying the shape directly. Here the geometric constraints are the relations between shape elements (e.g., perpendicularity between two lines, tangency between neighboring circular arc and line, and so on). In this case the system will generate the exact shape satisfying the dimension data. Thus changing the geometric constraints and/or dimension data will yield a different planar closed region and resulting solid. This approach is called *parametric modeling* because various solids are generated by changing the parameters. The parameters may be some constants involved in the geometric constraints and/or dimension values. The *skinning* function generates a solid by creating the skin surface to enclose a volume when the cross sections of the desired solid are given. The functions in the second group enable a designer to start the modeling from a shape very close to the final shape because the cross sections alone will describe the final solid accurately.

The third group includes the modeling functions used mainly for modifying an existing shape. The rounding (or blending) and lifting functions are typical of this group. The fourth group comprises the functions by which the lower level entities of a solid, such as vertices, edges, and faces, are directly manipulated. The use of these functions, called *boundary modeling*, is similar to that of the functions provided in surface modeling systems. The last group includes the functions by which a designer can model a solid by using familiar shapes. For example, the designer can use commands such as "make a hole of a certain size at a certain place" and "make a chamfer of a certain size at a certain place." The use of these functions is called *feature-based modeling*. It is receiving a great deal of attention these days because a model created this way carries manufacturing feature information, without which the process plan for the part cannot be generated automatically. Note that a model created with other modeling functions carries only the simple geometric information on faces, edges, vertices, and so on.

Primitive creation functions   These functions retrieve a solid of a simple shape from among the primitive solids stored in the program in advance and create a solid of the same shape but of the size specified by the user. Figure 5.4 illustrates the

Figure 5.4

Primitives generally supported

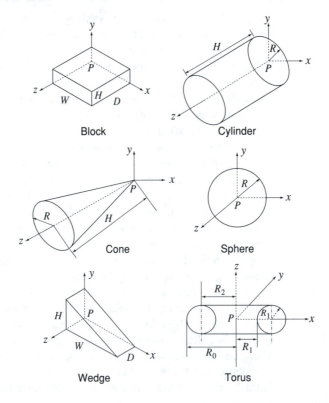

primitives supported by most solid modeling systems. The dimensions identified by alphabetic characters are the size parameters to be specified by the user. The primitives are stored by procedure as they are created, and parameter values are passed to the corresponding procedure as arguments. Creating a primitive is described in Appendix C.

Boolean operations   Modeling the desired solid by simply retrieving a primitive would be great. However, because of the numerous possible applications, it is not possible to store every possible shape in advance. But a combination of primitives can increase dramatically the repertoires of the shapes to be modeled. The Boolean operations of set theory have been applied as a method of combining primitives in solid modeling. In other words, each primitive solid is assumed to be a set of points, a Boolean operation is performed on point sets, and the result is a solid composed of the points resulting from the operation.

The Boolean operations supported by most solid modeling systems are union, intersection, and difference, as illustrated in Figures 5.5, 5.6, and 5.7, respectively. The relative locations and orientations of the two primitives have to be defined before the Boolean operations can be performed. Furthermore, the Boolean operations can be applied to two solids other than the primitives even though only the operations for the primitives are shown in the figures.

Another modeling function is implemented in the same way as the Boolean operations: cutting a solid by a plane so that the result is a solid containing two portions. You can obtain the same result by applying the difference operation on the

Figure 5.5

Example of a union operation

Figure 5.6

Example of an intersection operation

Figure 5.7

Example of a difference operation

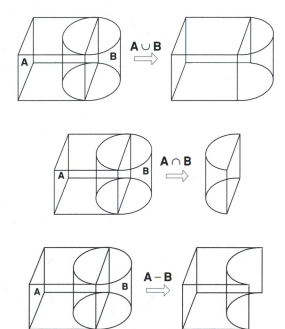

solid to be cut and a cube including the cutting plane as one of its faces and thus could implement the cutting operation as a special case of a Boolean operation.

When using the Boolean operations, be careful to avoid situations that do not result in a valid solid. Figure 5.8 illustrates what can happen when a solid is not obtained by the operation. Some solid modeling systems give a warning when this kind of situation is expected; others may simply crash. Nonmanifold modeling systems can handle these special situations, too, because they support a mixed form of wireframes, surfaces, and solids.

Sweeping *Sweeping* is a modeling function in which a planar closed domain is translated or revolved to form a solid. When the planar domain is translated, the modeling activity is called *translational sweeping*; when the planar region is revolved, it is called *swinging*, or *rotational sweeping*. If the planar shape to be translated or revolved is not closed, the result after the sweeping is a surface instead of a solid. In fact, this is the sweeping function provided in surface modeling systems.

Figures 5.9 and 5.10 illustrate the two types of sweeping operations, respectively. Even though Figure 5.10 depicts a revolution of 360 degrees, revolutions of less than 360 degrees are also allowed in most solid modeling systems.

Skinning *Skinning* is a modeling function used to form a closed volume or a solid by creating a skin surface over prespecified cross-sectional planar surfaces, as illustrated in Figure 5.11. This is analogous to constructing a structure by covering its frames, which are the boundaries of the cross sections, with a skin surface of cloth or vinyl. If two end faces corresponding to the two end cross sections are not added to the skin surface, the resulting model would be a surface instead of a solid. This is the skinning modeling function provided in surface modeling systems.

Rounding (or blending) *Rounding* or *blending* is a function used to modify an existing model so that a sharp edge or vertex is replaced with a smooth curved sur-

Figure 5.8

Example of a
Boolean operation
to be avoided

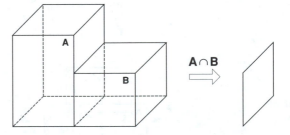

Figure 5.9

Example of translational sweeping

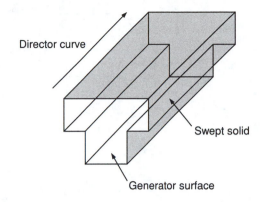

Figure 5.10

Example of rotational sweeping

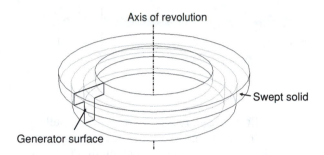

face whose normal vectors are continuous with those of the surfaces meeting at the original sharp edge or vertex. Figure 5.12(a) shows replacement of a sharp straight edge with a cylindrical surface. The normal vectors of the cylindrical surface are continuous with those of each adjacent planar surface at the common boundary. Figure 5.13 shows replacement of a sharp vertex with a spherical surface. Again, the normal vectors are continuous at the common boundaries. *Filleting* is a special case of rounding in which a rounding effect is obtained by the addition, instead of the elimination, of extra material, as illustrated in Figure 5.12(b).

Figure 5.11

Example of creating a solid by skinning

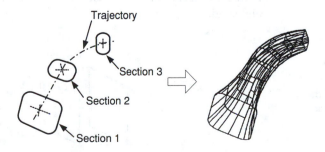

Figure 5.12

Examples of edge
rounding

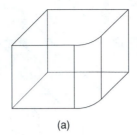 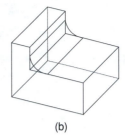

(a)　　　　　　　　　　(b)

Figure 5.13

Example of vertex
rounding

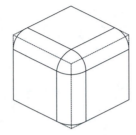

Lifting　*Lifting* is a function used to pull a portion or entire face of a solid in a certain direction, lengthening the solid accordingly. Figure 5.14(a) illustrates the lifting operation. If only a portion of a face is to be lifted, as shown in Figure 5.14(b), the face should be split beforehand. You may simply add a splitting edge for this purpose. However, other tasks have to be carried out internally to cause the effect of face splitting. A typical task involves updating the face connectivity information. These tasks are handled internally by the Euler operators, which we explain in Section 5.3.3.

When using the lifting function, you must specify properly the lifting direction or distance to avoid interference between the extended portion and the original solid, as illustrated in Figure 5.15. This may not be a problem if the lifting function is implemented so that it gives the same effect in the case of self-interference as would be obtained by the union of the extended portion and the original solid. However, the lifting function was developed originally for making local, minor modifications, and thus the special situation shown in Figure 5.15 will result an invalid solid.

Figure 5.14

Examples of the
lifting operation

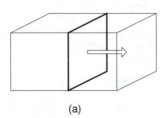 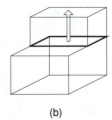

(a)　　　　　　　　　　(b)

Figure 5.15

Self-interference caused by lifting

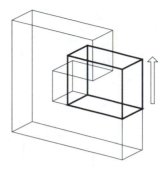

Boundary modeling   *Boundary modeling functions* are used to add, delete, or modify the lower entities of a solid, such as vertices, edges, and faces, in order to manipulate it directly. Thus the procedure that uses the boundary modeling functions would be the same as that in the surface modeling systems. In other words, points are created, then edges are created by connecting the points, and finally surfaces are defined by the bounding edges. However, in solid modeling systems, unlike surface modeling systems, you have to define all the surfaces until a closed volume is formed. Figure 5.16 illustrates modeling a wedge with the boundary modeling functions. The procedure involves the creation of points, edges, and surfaces.

As shown in Figure 5.16, the procedure for creating a solid by using only the boundary modeling functions is tedious. In fact, these functions are used mainly to create only two-dimensional shapes that in turn are used for sweeping or skinning. However, boundary modeling functions can be applied effectively to modify a shape of an existing solid. A vertex can be moved to a new location accompanying modifications of its related edges and faces, as illustrated in Figure 5.17. A straight edge can be replaced by a curved edge, resulting in modification of the related faces and vertices, as illustrated in Figure 5.18. A planar surface can be replaced with a new

Figure 5.16

Example of solid modeling, using boundary modeling functions

Figure 5.17

Modification by vertex moving

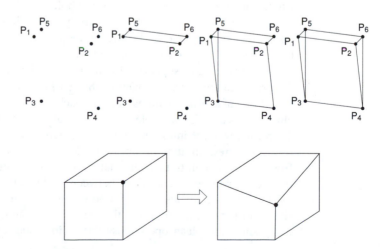

Figure 5.18

Modification by
edge replacement

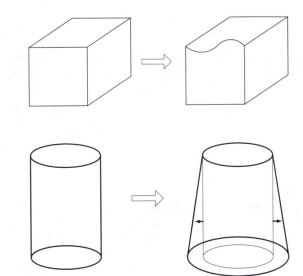

Figure 5.19

Modification by
surface replace-
ment

curved surface accompanying modification of the related edges and vertices, as illustrated in Figure 5.19. Sometimes, the planar surface can also be replaced with a curved surface imported from a surface modeling system. These modeling functions are called *tweaking functions*. They are useful in modeling a solid bounded by curved surfaces because it can be modeled easily from a planar polyhedron.

Feature-based modeling   *Feature-based modeling* enables the designer to model solids by using familiar shape units. A solid being created carries information about those shape units in addition to information about the elementary shape entities (vertices, edges, faces, etc.). For example, the designer can use commands such as "make a hole of a certain size at a certain place" and "make a chamfer of a certain size at a certain place," and the resulting solid will carry the information on the existence, the size, and the location of the hole and the chamfer. The shape units are called *features* and the modeling activity using those features is called *feature-based modeling*. The set of features to be provided in a solid modeling system can be determined by its most frequent applications.

Popular features supported by most feature-based modeling systems are manufacturing features such as chamfer, hole, fillet, slot, pocket, and so on. They are called manufacturing features because each one can be matched to a specific machining process. For example, a hole is created by drilling and a pocket by milling. Therefore, with the information on the existence, size, and location of the manufacturing features, an attempt can be made to generate process plans automatically from a solid model. In fact, automatic process planning, if it is developed to a practical level, will provide a bridge between CAD and CAM; these systems currently exist as separate islands. Thus, for now, it is better to model a solid such as the one shown in Figure 5.20 by using the feature commands Slot and Hole instead of by using simple Boolean operations. The solid model created by feature commands

Figure 5.20

Examples of modeling using Slot and Hole features

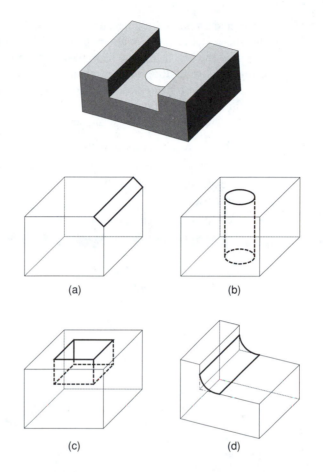

Figure 5.21

Examples of modeling using other features: (a) chamfering, (b) hole, (c) pocket, and (d) fillet

(a)

(b)

(c)

(d)

will make process planning easier, if not fully automatic. Figure 5.21 illustrates the use of various features in modeling.

One problem with feature-based modeling is that it cannot provide all the features necessary for many applications. As mentioned earlier, each application may require a different set of features. To get around this problem, many feature-based modeling systems provide a language in which a feature can be defined whenever it is needed. When a feature is defined, the parameters specifying the size of the feature also have to be defined. Just as primitives of various sizes could be created by assigning different values to the parameters, features can be created in many different sizes by changing parameters. Creating models of different sizes by assigning different values to the parameters is one type of parametric modeling.

Parametric modeling   In *parametric modeling* the designer models a shape by using geometric constraints and dimension data on its elements. The geometric constraints describe the relation between the elements—for example, two faces are parallel, two edges lie in a plane, a curved edge is tangent to a neighboring straight edge, and so on. The dimension data include not only the dimensions assigned on the shape but also the relations between the dimensions. These relations are provided by the designer in the form of mathematical equations. Thus parametric modeling constructs the required shape by solving the equations that express the geometric constraints, those derived from the dimensions, and those obtained from the dimensional relations.

In parametric modeling, a shape is usually constructed in the following manner.

1. Input a two-dimensional shape as a rough sketch.
2. Input geometric constraints and dimensional data interactively.
3. Reconstruct the two-dimensional shape for the given geometric constraint and dimensional data.
4. Repeat steps 2 and 3, modifying the geometric constraints and/or dimensional data until the desired model is obtained. This step is illustrated in Figure 5.22.
5. Create a three-dimensional shape by sweeping or swinging the two-dimensional shape. The values used in this step for thickness or rotation angle can also become the dimensional data, and thus the generated three-dimensional shape can be easily modified if necessary.

Note that the steps in parametric modeling modify a shape through the use of geometric constraints, dimensional data, and/or dimensional relations rather than by directly modifying the shape elements. Hence the designer can generate many design alternatives without considering the details of the shape's elements and concentrate on the functional aspects of the design.

The two types of parametric modeling are based on the way they solve the equations that express the geometric constraints—those derived from the dimensions, and those obtained from the dimensional relations. One type solves the equations sequentially, whereas the other type solves them simultaneously. With the former, the shape varies, depending on the sequence in which the constraints are assigned. With the latter, the same shape is obtained regardless of the sequence of the constraints but it may be in trouble when conflicting constraints are assigned.

5.3.2 Data Structure

In the preceding section, we described the types of modeling functions provided in solid modeling systems. Thus we know that a mathematical description of a solid is

Figure 5.22

Modifying a shape by changing constraints

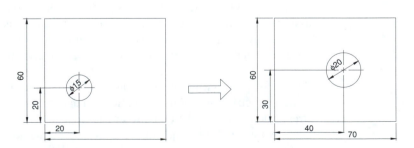

stored in the computer when a solid is created with these modeling functions. How then is such information stored in various formats to represent mathematical descriptions describing a solid without ambiguities? In this section, we discuss data structures that store mathematical descriptions in that way.

The *data structures* needed to describe a solid can be classified into three types generally according to the entities stored. The first structure stores in a tree the history of applying Boolean operations on the primitives. This history is called a *constructive solid geometry* (CSG) *representation*, and the tree is called a *CSG tree*. The second structure stores the boundary information for a solid (i.e., vertices, edges, and faces, together with the information on how they are connected). This way of describing a solid is called *boundary representation* (B-Rep), and its data structure is called a *B-Rep data structure*. Many types of B-Rep data structures are devised based on which entity has the main role in providing connectivity information, as we explain later. The third structure stores a solid as an aggregate of simple solids such as cubes. A solid model described in this way is called a *decomposition model*. Although many possible decomposition models can be used, according to the selection of the simple solid, none of the decomposition models can describe a solid exactly.

CSG tree structure   Recall that a CSG tree structure stores the history of applying Boolean operations on the primitives. Consider the solid shown in Figure 5.23(a). Its Boolean operation history can be envisioned to be a binary tree, as shown in Figure 5.23(b). That tree also can be represented by the interrelated data elements shown in Figure 5.23(c). The data elements are implemented, as shown in Figure 5.24, by using the C language.

Figure 5.23

Example of a CSG tree

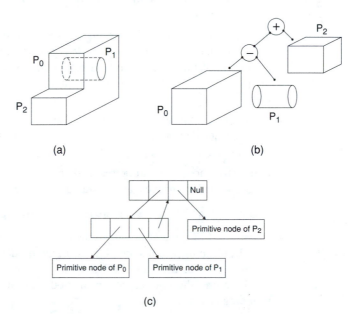

(a)

(b)

(c)

Figure 5.24

Implementation of
a CSG tree struc-
ture in C language

```
struct operator {
    int     op_type,          /* union, intersection or difference operator */
            L_type;           /* left node type: 0=operator, 1=primitive */
            R_type            /* right node type: 0=operator, 1=primitive */
    void    *L_ptr;           /* left node */
            *R_ptr;           /* right node */
            *p_ptr;           /* parent node */
}


struct primitive {
    int     prim_type;              /* type of primitive */
    double  pos_x, pos_y, pos_z;    /* position of instance */
    double  ori_x, ori_y, ori_z;    /* orientation of instance */
    void    *attribute;             /* the value of dimensions of the primitive */
}
```

A CSG tree data structure has the following advantages.

- The data structure is simple and stores compact data. Accordingly, the management of data is easy.

- The solid stored in a CSG tree is always a valid solid. A valid solid implies a solid for which the inside and outside regions can be clearly identified. An example of an invalid solid would be a solid with a strut edge. In that case, the notion of inside and outside is not clear around the vertex where the strut edge is attached.

- CSG representation of a solid can always be converted to the corresponding B-Rep. Thus CSG tree representation can be interfaced with the application programs written for B-Rep.

- Parametric modeling can be realized easily by changing the parameter values of the associated primitives, as illustrated in Figure 5.25.

However, a CSG tree structure has the following disadvantages.

- Because a CSG tree structure stores the history of applying Boolean operations, only Boolean operations are allowed in the modeling process. With Boolean operations alone, the range of shapes to be modeled is severely restricted. Furthermore, the convenient local modification functions such as lifting and rounding cannot be used.

Figure 5.25

Modification of a
solid by changing
parameters

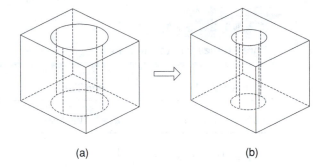

(a)   (b)

- It requires a great deal of computation to derive the information on the boundary surfaces, their boundary edges, and the connectivity between these boundary entities from CSG tree representation. Unfortunately, many applications require this boundary information. One example is the display of solids. Whether a shaded image or a line drawing of a solid is to be displayed, as explained in Chapter 3, information about the faces and/or edges is required. Thus CSG tree representation is felt to be inappropriate for the interactive display and manipulation of solids. Another example is the calculation of NC tool paths to machine the surfaces of a solid by a milling machine. In this application, information about the surface to be machined and its boundary edges is necessary. Furthermore, the adjacent surfaces need to be derived for gouging detection. Deriving all this boundary information from a CSG tree representation of a solid is not a simple task.

Because of these drawbacks, solid modeling based on CSG tree representation tends to accompany the corresponding boundary representation. This combination is called a *hybrid representation*, in which maintaining consistency between the two representations is very important.

B-Rep data structure The basic elements composing the boundary of a solid are the vertices, the edges, and the faces.[1] Thus a *B-Rep data structure* stores these entities with the information about how they are interconnected. One of the simplest data structures, if not the simplest, is shown in the three parts of Table 5.1. The data structure represents the solid shown in Figure 5.26. The face table stores the list of bounding edges for each face. The sequence of edges for each face is given by traversing it counterclockwise when the solid is viewed from the outside. By listing the edges in a consistent way, each face can be stored together with information about what represents the inside and the outside of the solid. In other words, you can determine whether any point is located on the inside or outside of the solid from the information given about the faces. The vertices, edges, and faces shown in

[1] A face is a portion of a boundary surface, the boundary of which comprises the curve segments across which the normal vector of the face changes radically. The curve segments bounding a face are called *edges*. The points at which the neighboring edges meet are the *vertices*.

Three tables for storing B-Rep

Face Table		Edge Table		Vertex Table	
Face	*Edges*	*Edge*	*Vertices*	*Vertex*	*Coordinates*
F_1	E_1, E_5, E_6	E_1	V_1, V_2	V_1	x_1, y_1, z_1
F_2	E_2, E_6, E_7	E_2	V_2, V_3	V_2	x_2, y_2, z_2
F_3	E_3, E_7, E_8	E_3	V_3, V_4	V_3	x_3, y_3, z_3
F_4	E_4, E_8, E_5	E_4	V_4, V_1	V_4	x_4, y_4, z_4
F_5	E_1, E_2, E_3, E_4	E_5	V_1, V_5	V_5	x_5, y_5, z_5
		E_6	V_2, V_5	V_6	x_6, y_6, z_6
		E_7	V_3, V_5		
		E_8	V_4, V_5		

Figure 5.26 are numbered arbitrarily by a geometric modeling system when the boundary representation shown in Table 5.1 is stored.

Each row of the edge table stores the vertices at the ends of each edge, and the vertex table stores the *x*, *y*, and *z* coordinates of the vertices. These coordinates are usually defined with respect to the body coordinate system attached to the solid. If you ignore the face table, you can use the same data structure to store shapes created by wireframe modeling systems. The data structure for a wireframe model can also be used as a basic frame of the data structure for computer-aided drafting systems if two-dimensional coordinates are allowed for the points.

Figure 5.26

Example of a solid for which data are to be stored

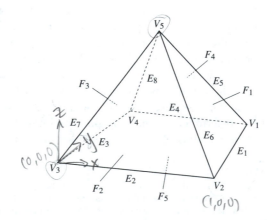

The data structure looks very simple and compact. However, it is not used in elaborate solid modeling systems because of the following drawbacks.

- The data structure is basically designed for storing planar polyhedra. If a solid having curved faces and curved edges is to be stored, each row of the face table and the edge table should be modified to include the surface equation and the curve equation, respectively.[2] The surface equations for planar faces do not have to be stored because the surface equation can be derived from the vertices on a face.

- A face with external and internal boundaries, as shown in Figure 5.27(a), cannot be stored in the face table because it requires multiple lists of edges instead of a single list. Such faces are encountered, for example, when a solid with a through hole is being modeled. A simple treatment of this situation would be to add an edge connecting the external and the internal boundaries, as shown in Figure 5.27(b). In this way, two lists of edges can be merged into one list. This connecting edge is called a *bridge edge* and will appear twice in the merged list.

- As shown in Table 5.1, the number of edges for faces may be different. Furthermore, the number of columns (one for each edge) required for each face cannot be predetermined because they can change as modeling proceeds. Therefore the number of columns should be set as a variable when the face table is declared. However, managing a table of variable size may cause some inconvenience.

- Deriving the connectivity information solely from the information stored in the three tables can be cumbersome. Consider the case of searching two faces sharing an edge when the boundary representation of a solid is given by the three tables. For this task, the entire face table will be searched to identify the rows storing the given edge. Now consider the case of searching all the edges sharing a vertex. For this task, the entire edge table will be searched to identify the rows with the given vertex. You can easily see that these searching tasks will become very inefficient when the tables are large.

Two typical data structures can be used to store the boundary representation of a solid without encountering these problems. They are the half-edge data structure and the winged-edge data structure.

Figure 5.27

One method of treating a face with multiple boundaries

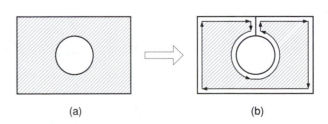

(a)   (b)

[2] The information on the surface equation, the curve equation, and the point coordinates are generally referred to as *geometry information*, whereas the interrelationships among faces, edges, and vertices are referred to as *topology information*. The data in any B-Rep data structure can be classified as either geometry data or topology data.

Figure 5.28

Doubly linked list
for face F_1

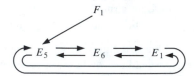

Half-edge data structure   As a remedy for the variable size of the face table, a list of edges for each face can be stored in a doubly linked list, as shown in Figure 5.28.[3] The face simply stores the pointer to the starting edge of the list instead of the entire list, and each edge has pointers to the previous and next edge in the list. In this way, the face table has a fixed number of columns. However, we can still reconstruct the edge list by following the pointers (e.g., the edge list E_5, E_6, and E_1 for face F_1). Face F_1 may point to edge E_6 or E_1 as its starting edge, in which case the pointers for each edge should be changed to give the same edge list.

However, we encounter another problem immediately when we consider face F_2 that shares edge E_6 with face F_1 in Figure 5.26. The doubly linked list for face F_2 can be obtained as shown in Figure 5.29. That is, E_6 has E_7 as the next edge pointer and E_2 as the previous edge pointer. This will change the previous and the next edge pointers of E_6 in the edge list of face F_1 and accordingly destroy the edge list of F_1.

We can solve this problem by splitting each edge into halves and using these halves separately for the two faces sharing the original edge. Specifically, each edge is split into two half edges of opposite directions, as shown in Figure 5.30,

Figure 5.29

Doubly linked list
for face F_2

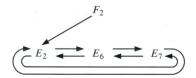

Figure 5.30

Half edges of the
example solid

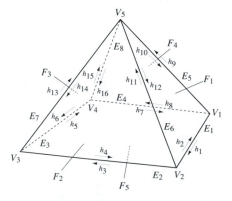

<hr />

[3] The same problem may be also solved by using a single linked list. A doubly linked list is chosen here to give the same half-edge data structure suggested by Mäntylä [1988].

and each face stores the doubly linked list of half edges instead of the edges. The half edges of each face are collected into a list so that each half edge has the direction consistent with the overall counterclockwise sequence for the boundary of the face when the face is viewed as before from outside the solid. Therefore the doubly linked list of half edges for faces F_1 and F_2 are obtained as shown in Figure 5.31. Destruction of the previous linked list for E_1 does not now occur.

Loops can be used to take care of faces having inner holes without adding redundant bridge edges. A *loop* is a list of edges forming a closed circuit, and thus any face is bounded by one peripheral loop corresponding to the external boundary and several hole loops corresponding internal boundaries.[4] With the introduction of loops, each face can refer to the lists of half edges through loops instead of pointing to them directly. In other words, each face stores the list of the loops in a doubly linked list, and each loop stores the corresponding list of half edges. In this way, a face with any number of internal holes can be treated without adding redundant bridge edges.

Figure 5.32 illustrates how a face with internal holes is stored, using loops. Typically, the face points to the peripheral loop as the starting entity and the hole loops are pointed to by other loops in the doubly linked list of the loops. Every hole loop has a list of half edges in the direction opposite to that of the peripheral loop. In other words, the half edges of a hole loop are collected into a list so that each

Figure 5.31

Doubly linked list using half edges

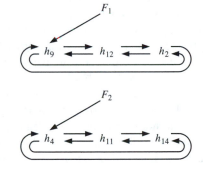

Figure 5.32

Treatment of a face with holes, using loops

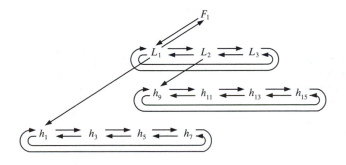

---

[4] The peripheral loop and the hole loop are also called the *parent loop* and the *child loop*, respectively.

half edge has a direction consistent with the overall clockwise sequence for the internal boundary when the loop is viewed from outside the solid. In Figure 5.32, the half edges in the direction consistent with the overall clockwise sequence are collected into a doubly linked list for loops L_2 and L_3, respectively, whereas the half edges in the counterclockwise sequence are collected for loop L_1.

The half edges for the hole loops are stored in the opposite direction from those of the peripheral loop to provide the in and out information for the face. In fact, the directions of the peripheral loop and the hole loops have been determined so that the inside domain of a face always resides at the left-hand side when any loop is traversed in its direction.

The introduction of half edges and loops into the data structure has many advantages over the data structure that uses only the vertex, edge, and face tables. Connectivity information for vertices, edges, and faces also can be stored in the data structure by using half edges and loops, and adjacency information for these entities can be derived from the stored connectivity information. We have already shown that this kind of derivation from the original simple table structure is not an easy task. However, the task becomes simple once the connectivity between the vertices, edges, and faces has been provided through the half edges and the loops; these have the role of agents providing connections for the vertices, edges, and faces. In other words, the vertices, edges, and faces point to the corresponding half edges or loops, and the adjacency information for the half edges and loops is provided. To establish a connection between each edge and its half edges, each edge points to its two half edges and each half edge points to its parent edge. Similarly, each vertex points to any one of the half edges connected to the vertex while each half edge points to its starting vertex,[5] and each face points to its peripheral loop while each loop points to its parent face, as shown in Figure 5.32. The adjacency information for the half edges and the loops is specified as shown (i.e., each loop is represented by a doubly linked list of half edges).

Now we will derive the adjacency information for the vertices and the edges from the stored information to demonstrate that all the necessary connectivity information is stored in the structure. For example, we will search all the edges connected to a vertex, denoted V_1 in Figure 5.33. This search starts from the half edge

Figure 5.33

Finding adjacency information for edges and vertices

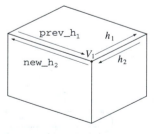

---

[5] Two vertices connected to a half edge can be classified as a starting and ending vertex according to the direction of the half edge.

pointed to by the vertex, which could be any arbitrary half edge connected to the vertex. Let's denote it h_1 as in Figure 5.33 and then use the following procedure.

Step 1. If vertex V_1 is the starting vertex of h_1, as shown, then the previous half edge of h_1 (denoted **prev_h$_1$**) is selected and its parent edge becomes one of the edges connected to V_1. Then the conjugate half edge of **prev_h$_1$** (called **new_h$_1$**) takes the role of h_1, and Step 1 is repeated with **new_h$_1$**. If V_1 is the ending vertex of h_1, the next half edge of h_1 is selected and its parent edge is derived as the connecting edge. Then the conjugate of this next half edge takes the role of h_1, and Step 1 is repeated with **new_h$_1$**.

Step 2. The process is repeated until the conjugate half edge of the original h_1 is reached.

Implementation of the half-edge data structure is illustrated in Appendix A. In fact, the data structure in Figure A.1 is the one used in the GWB solid modeling system developed by Mäntylä [1988]. Some additional pointers are explained in that reference. Sometimes, it is better to store the redundant pointers in the data structure instead of deriving them, especially when the information needs to be retrieved often. In fact, the questions of how many redundant pointers to allow and to what extent they are to be used must be resolved when the data structure is designed. Figure A.2 illustrates how the procedure used to search for all the edges connected to a vertex is implemented on the data structure.

Winged-edge data structure   As described earlier, the half-edge data structure basically stores a list of faces, each of which is represented by a linked list of edges. Thus the face plays the major role in describing a solid. In contrast, the edges play the major role in a winged-edge data structure. Each edge stores the faces sharing the edge, the neighboring edges sharing any of the vertices of the edge, and the vertices at its ends. The list of edges for each face is not explicitly stored in this data structure because it can be derived from any of the face's edges and its neighboring edges. Therefore the problem encountered with varying numbers of edges for faces is solved without introducing the linked list and, consequently, half edges. Because half edges are not introduced, the connectivity of vertices, edges, and faces is specified directly in the winged-edge data structure. This connectivity was described indirectly through half edges in the half-edge data structure. We have mentioned some of this connectivity information already; that is, for each edge, the faces sharing the edge, the neighboring edges, and the vertices are stored.

The winged-edge data structure was first introduced by Baumgart [1972]. It was extended by Braid to handle a solid with through holes by introducing the use of loops [Braid, Hillyard, and Stroud 1978]. Now we will define the winged-edge structure, with reference to Figure 5.34. Edge E_1 has four neighboring edges, E_2, E_3, E_4, and E_5, each of which shares one of E_1's two vertices. If you envision E_1 as the fuselage of an airplane, the four edges E_2, E_3, E_4, and E_5 suggest wings. Thus these four edges are called the *winged edges* of E_1. Each of these edges must be stored under a different name to specify its relative position with respect to E_1. They are named as follows. First, assign a direction to edge E_1, as illustrated in

Figure 5.34

Definition of the
winged-edge struc-
ture

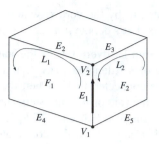

Figure 5.34. Here the edge is directed from vertex V_1 to vertex V_2. Then orient yourself as if you were lying along E_1 with your head pointed toward vertex V_2. (Of course, your body is outside the solid.) Now stretch your arms and legs as if you were flying. Your left arm will touch edge E_2, your right arm will touch E_3, your left leg will touch E_4, and your right leg will touch E_5. Therefore E_2 is called the left-arm edge, E_3 the right-arm edge, E_4 the left-leg edge, and E_5 the right-leg edge of E_1. If E_1 was set in the opposite direction, E_5 would be the left-arm edge, E_4 the right-arm edge, E_3 the left-leg edge, and E_2 the right-leg edge. The direction of each edge is set arbitrarily when a solid is created and stored in the winged-edge data structure as its number is assigned.

In addition to specifying the connectivity of edges in terms of winged edges, we need to specify the connectivity of faces and edges. This is why each edge points to two sharing faces. For example, edge E_1 in Figure 5.34 points to F_1 and F_2 as the left face and the right face, respectively, with the name of each face determined by the direction of E_1. The two faces are stored under different names for the same reason that the winged edges have different names. Braid introduced loops to allow a solid with through holes to be stored in the winged-edge data structure as in the half-edge data structure. That is, the connection between the face and its edges is specified indirectly through loops. Thus each edge points to its left and right loop instead of its left and right face, but a face has to point to its loops in this case. For example, E_1 in Figure 5.34 points to L_1 as its left loop and L_2 as its right loop. The role of each loop will be switched if the direction of E_1 is reversed. In response to being pointed to by the edges, each loop points to each edge belonging to itself. This provides the starting edge from which neighboring edges are traversed to give the list of edges of the loop. This is similar to the process of deriving the list of half edges, starting from any arbitrary half edge pointed to by a loop in the half-edge data structure.

Now let's consider the connection between edges and vertices. Recall that each edge has vertices at its ends. These vertices are stored under the names *previous vertex* (or tail vertex) and *next vertex* (or head vertex), because each edge has a direction. In Figure 5.34, V_1 is the previous vertex of E_1 and V_2 is the next vertex. In addition to the pointers from each edge to its vertices, it is common for each vertex to point to one of the edges connected to it. This provides the starting edge from which all the edges connected to a vertex are searched. These neighboring edges of a vertex need to be searched often in implementing the modeling functions, especially the Euler operators residing in them. (Euler operators are explained in Section 5.3.3.)

Figure 5.35

Connections of vertices, edges, and faces

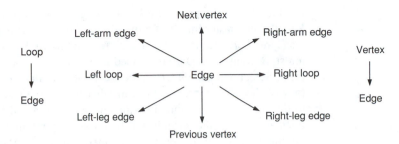

The connections of vertices, edges, and loops explained so far are illustrated in Figure 5.35. The origin is the entity from which an arrow emanates, and the arrow points to the entity that is connected to the origin.

In addition to the connections described, each face and its loops are connected, as in the half-edge data structure. Namely, each face points to its peripheral loop, and the peripheral loop points to a hole loop if the face has a hole. Then the hole loop points to another hole loop if the face has multiple holes; otherwise, it points back to the peripheral loop, as shown in Figure 5.36. Each loop also points to its parent face. Note that a single linked list is used here instead of the doubly linked list used in Figure 5.31. The decision whether to use a single linked list or a doubly linked list is based on the relative importance of the efficiency of data retrieval and compactness of the structure.

Figure B.1 in Appendix B presents one example of winged-edge data structure implementation in C language. The data structure is used in the solid modeling system SNUMOD, developed at the Seoul National University in Korea. The figure contains a new entity called a *shell*. A shell is a three-dimensional extension of a loop, implying a list of faces forming a closed volume. Generally, a solid has only one shell unless it has some voids. The *void* of a solid is the three-dimensional extension of the hole loop of a face. Therefore the shell concept provides for a solid with voids, just as the hole loop concept provides for a face with holes.

Decomposition model structure   A solid model can be described approximately as an aggregate of simple solids such as cubes. A solid model described in this way is called a *decomposition model*. Many decomposition models are possible for a solid. The one selected depends on the choices of the simple solid to be used for the approximation and the method of aggregation. Typical decomposition models and the data structures for storing them include the voxel representation , the octree representation, and the cell representation.

1.   Voxel representation

The *voxel representation* of a solid is simply a three-dimensional extension of a raster representation of a two-dimensional shape. To explain voxel representation we

Figure 5.36

Connection of a face and its loops

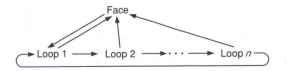

need to review the procedure for deriving a raster representation or a raster image. Recall that a raster image of a two-dimensional object is generated as follows. First, a square is created to have a size corresponding to the two-dimensional space of interest. Second, the square is divided into many small squares by imposing grid lines on it. Selection of the intervals between the grid lines is based on the desired accuracy of the raster representation. In other words, the raster image will be very close to the shape of the original two-dimensional object if the intervals between the grid lines are small; otherwise, it will be a rough approximation. Third, the square containing many small squares is represented in a computer by a two-dimensional array, which has the same number of elements as there are small squares. Finally, the large square is superimposed on the two-dimensional object and the array elements corresponding to the small squares overlapping the object are assigned the value of 1, and the remaining elements are assigned the value of 0. Thus the resulting array filled with 1s and 0s becomes the raster representation of the two-dimensional object.

A voxel representation of a solid is generated by the same procedure as the raster representation. However, instead of starting with a large square and small squares, a large cube is divided into small cubes, called *voxels*,[6] by grid planes equally spaced along the x, y, and z axes. The starting cube is represented by a three-dimensional array that has the same number of elements as there are small cubes, and each element of the array has the value of either 1 or 0, depending on the position of the element in the solid being represented. Even though the overall process is almost the same as the process of rasterization, the overlap detection between the solid and a small cube requires more complicated computation than does the same task in rasterization.[7] Figure 5.37 is a voxel representation of a doughnut-shaped solid by voxels having the value of 1.

Using a voxel representation to describe a solid has the following advantages.

- A solid of arbitrary shape can always be described accurately by a voxel representation, or described at least approximately. For instance, models of human bones and organs are often voxel representations of digital tomography data.

Figure 5.37

Visualization of a voxel representation (By A.H.J. Christensen, *SIGGRAPH '80 Conference Proceedings, Computer Graphics,* Vol. 14 No. 3, July 1980. Courtesy of Association for Computing Machinery, Inc.)

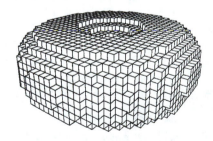

[6] A voxel is a three-dimensional extension of the pixel in two dimensions. In fact, the last three characters "xel" are borrowed from "pixel," and the first two characters come from "volume."
[7] The three-dimensional equivalent to rasterization is called *exhaustive enumeration*.

Modeling these shapes by using conventional modeling functions is very difficult. Even after application of the complicated procedures described in Section 5.3.1, the resulting models are still inaccurate.

- Calculating the mass properties of a solid, such as mass and moments of inertia, from the voxel representation of the solid is easy. Deriving any mass property of a solid by summing the mass properties of each voxel also is easy. Finally, obtaining the result of Boolean operations on two solids if both are represented by voxels is easy. In fact, calculating the Boolean operation on the integer values of 1 or 0 for the corresponding voxels of the two solids is all that's necessary.

- Even though a voxel representation is generated to describe a solid in space, it also represents the space excluding the solid. Hence this feature is useful in calculating the capacity of a shell structure. It also is useful in calculating the paths of robots to avoid obstacles because the available space can be obtained from the voxel representations of the obstacles.

However, using a voxel representation to describe a solid has the following drawbacks.

- The memory space required to store a voxel representation increases dramatically as the size of the voxels decreases. The size of the voxels determines how closely the representation approximates the original solid, so the use of very small voxels may be necessary.

- A voxel representation is inherently an approximation of the original solid. Therefore not many solid modeling systems use only voxels as the mathematical representation of a solid. Instead, voxels are often used as an auxiliary representation to increase computational efficiency.

2. Octree representation

An *octree representation* is similar to a voxel representation in that it represents a solid as an aggregate of hexahedra (a cube is a regular hexahedron), but it reduces the memory requirement considerably by dividing the space differently. In voxel representation, the original cube is divided by grid planes equally spaced along x, y, and z axes, regardless of the solid being represented. In the octree representation, however, the original hexahedron is divided into eight hexahedra each time by introducing mid planes along width, depth, and height, respectively, as shown in Figure 5.38(a). Thus each hexahedron is one-eighth of its parent octant in size and is called an *octant*. Furthermore, all the octants can be represented as the nodes of a tree in which every node has eight branches, as shown in Figure 5.38(c). This tree is called an *octree*.[8] If each octant is always divided into eight octants, regardless of the solid being represented, the generated octants will be the same as voxels of uniform size in the voxel representation. In the octree representation, however, some octants are divided into eight while others are left untouched based on their relative locations with respect to the solid being represented.

---

[8] A two-dimensional object can be represented similarly (i.e., the object is enclosed by a square or a rectangle and it is divided into four squares or rectangles during each subdivision). In this case, the tree is called a *quadtree*.

Figure 5.38

Example of octree
generation

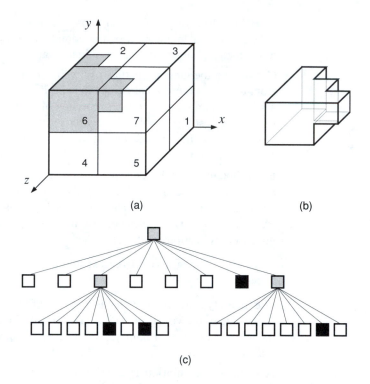

(a)

(b)

(c)

The procedure for generating an octree representation is as follows. First, a hexahedron is created to enclose completely the solid to be represented. This hexahedron is called a *root octant*. Second, the root octant is divided into eight octants and the spatial relation of each octant with respect to the solid is investigated. If an octant is completely inside the solid, it is marked "black." If it is completely outside the solid, it is marked "white." If it is partially inside and partially outside, it is marked "gray" and divided into eight octants. The octants marked black or white are not subdivided further. Finally, the second step is repeated until the current octants being generated by the subdivision are as small as prespecified. Then the collection of the octants marked black will represent the original solid.[9]

Figure 5.38(c) illustrates the octree generated for the solid shown in Figure 5.38(b). The number of octants to be stored is much less than the number of voxels because the octants marked black or white do not participate further in the subdivision. The octree illustrated in Figure 5.38(c) is stored in a computer in data structure. Figure 5.39 shows one such data structure, written in C language. Figure 5.40 illustrates the procedure for generating an octree from the data structure illustrated in Figure 5.39. The procedure is simply a restatement in computer language of the previously described steps. Even though the procedure looks simple, the routine **classify(p,t)** requires a complicated geometry computation because it has to deter-

---

[9] The octant marked "gray" at the terminal nodes can also be included in the representation. This will give the upper limit on the volume of the solid, whereas the representation with "black" octants only will give the lower limit.

Figure 5.39

Data structure for
storing octrees

```
struct       octreeroot
{
        float                          xmin, ymin, zmin;          /*space of interest*/
        float                          xmax, ymax, zmax;
        struct      octree    *root                      /*root of the tree*/
};


struct      octree
{
        char                       code;/*BLACK, WHITE, GREY*/
        struct      octree    *oct[8];     /*pointers to octants, present if GREY*/
};
```

Figure 5.40

Procedure for oc-
tree generation

```
make_tree( p, t, depth)
primitive  *p;        /* p = the primitive to be modeled */
octree     *t;        /* t = node of the octree, initially
                         the initial tree with one grey node */
int        depth;     /* initially max. depth of the recursion */
{
          int       i;
          switch( classify( p, t ) )
          {
                  case WHITE:
                      t–> code = WHITE;
                      break;
                  case BLACK:
                      t-> code = BLACK;
                      break;
                  case GREY:
                      if (depth == 0 )
                      {
                          t–> code = BLACK;
                      }
                      else
                      {
                          subdivide( t );
                          for( i = 0; i < 8; i++ )
                              make_tree( p, t–> oct[i], depth–1 );
                      }
                      break;
          }
}

/* classify octree node against primitives */
classify( ... );

/* divide octree node into eight octants */
subdivide( ... );
```

Figure 5.41

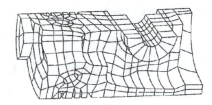

mine whether an octant is inside, outside, or overlapping the solid. In addition, the gray octants are converted to black octants when the subdivision process stops. Therefore the octree representation derived by this procedure would have more volume than the exact solid.

3. Cell representation

Cell representation is also a method of representing a solid as an aggregate of simple cells, as in voxel representation. However, as implied by the name *cell*, it does not impose a strict restriction on the allowable shape of the cells to be used. As a result, any solid can be represented by only a small number of simple cells. Figure 5.41 shows an example of cell representation. As can be inferred from the figure, generating the finite elements for the finite-element analysis is a typical example of cell decomposition.

5.3.3 Euler Operators

We now turn to the tasks required to modify the data in the data structure used in solid modeling systems. These tasks are important because the modeling functions are basically implemented by bookkeeping operations that update the data.

As most solid modeling systems are built on the B-Rep data structure, we will review the operations manipulating data in that B-Rep structure. You know that the topology entities stored in B-Rep data structures are the shell, face, loop, edge, and vertex. Therefore you can simply think of the operators that manipulate these entities separately (e.g., an operator to make an edge, an operator to delete a vertex, etc.). If these operators are used in implementing the modeling functions, however, the following problems will occur.

First, there is an inherent contradiction in trying to handle independently each topology entity that is not independent of the others. In fact, the following relation, called the *Euler–Poincare formula* [Mortenson 1985; Braid, Hillyard, and Stroud 1978], applies to the topology entities:

$$v - e + f - h = 2(s - p) \tag{5.1}$$

where v represents the number of vertices, e the number of edges, f the number of faces or peripheral loops, h the number of hole loops, s the number of shells, and p the number of passages (through holes of a solid). Equation (5.1) can be verified by applying it to a solid such as the one shown in Figure 5.42. Here $v = 16$, $f = 10$, $h = 2$, $s = 1$, and $p = 1$ (found by counting the entities). Substituting these values into

Figure 5.42

Example of a solid

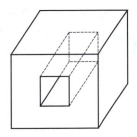

Equation (5.1) yields

$$16 - 24 + 10 - 2 = 2(1 - 1)$$

which satisfies Equation 5.1. From Equation (5.1), we can conclude that all six topology entities cannot be manipulated independently, whereas any five of them can be manipulated independently.

Second, it is not efficient to manipulate each topology entity separately because, in most cases, the addition or deletion of one means a change in the others. For example, as Figure 5.43 shows, the addition of a diagonal edge increases the number of faces by splitting an original face. It would therefore be efficient to have an operator that would take care of these secondary effects at the same time.

Thus it would be desirable to have operators that would manipulate topology entities in a small group rather than individually. As there are five independent topology entities in Equation (5.1), the number of operators required to increase or decrease the six topology entities in the equation would be five. Thus we need to define no more than five such operators. In addition, it would be helpful to define each operator to handle simultaneously the topology entities that frequently change as a group when a solid is modified. Forecasting which subset of topology entities will be changed most frequently as a group in the process of manipulating a particular solid may not be easy. However, the operators should include the topology entities that can at least satisfy the Euler–Poincare formula. For example, an operator making an edge and a vertex would be an appropriate choice because it would increase the number of edges and vertices by 1 and thus Equation (5.1) would hold after the operator is applied. In this way, an originally valid solid can be guaranteed to still be valid after the topology change. The operators satisfying these requirements are called *Euler operators*. There are many possible sets of Euler operators, and every solid modeling system has its own set. The modification shown in Figure 5.43 is an example of the Euler operator called Make an Edge and a Loop (MEL). This operator increases the number of loops by connecting two vertices in the loop with an edge. We can easily imagine this oper-

Figure 5.43

Change in a face caused by the addition of an edge

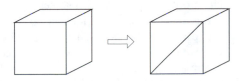

Figure 5.44

Euler operators

MEVVLS (KEVVLS)	make (kill) edge, two vertices, loop, shell	
MEL (KEL)	make (kill) edge, loop	
MEV (KEV)	make (kill) edge, vertex	
MVE (KVE)	make (kill) vertex, edge	
MEKH (KEMH)	make (kill) edge, kill (make) hole	
MZEV (KZEV)	make (kill) zero length edge, vertex	
MPKH (KPMH)	make(kill) peripheral loop, kill (make) hole loop	Peripheral loop

ator being activated when we split a face to extrude part of it. Figure 5.44 shows the Euler operators repeatedly referred to in this text.

In Appendix C, we introduce the Euler operators used in the SNUMOD solid modeling system and describe how they are used in implementing typical modeling functions. These operators are basically same as the Euler operators suggested by Chiyokura [1988]. Detailed descriptions of the Euler operators and their implementation are presented in Mäntylä [1988], Chiyokura [1988], and Park [1990].

5.3.4 Boolean Operations

Boolean operations are the most difficult modeling functions to implement, yet they provide the most powerful modeling capability available. As mentioned earlier, Boolean operations perform union, intersection, or difference on any two solids and store the resulting solid in the data structure of the specific solid modeling system being used. If this system represents and stores solids in a CSG tree or in a decomposition model, the solid resulting from a Boolean operation can easily be represented in the same structure. In other words, the CSG tree of the solid resulting from any Boolean operation is obtained by simply combining the CSG trees of the two solids with the specific Boolean operation. Similarly, the decomposition model of the resulting solid can easily be derived by evaluating the Boolean operation on the corresponding spatial elements of the decomposition models of the two solids. For example, the voxel representation of a solid resulting from a Boolean operation can easily be obtained by applying the Boolean operation on the values of each pair of voxels occupying the same space in the two solids—one voxel from the representation of each solid. Therefore we have only to calculate the Boolean operation on the numbers of either 1 or 0 for each pair, a process called a *bitwise Boolean operation*.

However, if a solid modeling system stores its solids in a B-Rep structure, the situation is different. In this case, the B-Rep of the resulting solid has to be derived from the B-Reps of the solids on which the Boolean operation is applied. This process is called *boundary evaluation*.

The algorithm for boundary evaluation was first introduced by Requicha and Voelcker [1985] as the *boundary evaluation and merging process* and later refined by Miller [1988]. Their approach consists basically of three steps. Although, for purposes of illustration, we use the two-dimensional example shown in Figure 5.45, the same approach applies to three-dimensional solids. First, we denote the two faces (solids in the three-dimensional case) on which the Boolean operation is to be applied as face A and face B and the face resulting from the Boolean operation as face C (see Figure 5.45a). In step 1, all the edges of A and B and the edges obtained by the intersection of the two faces are collected to form an edge pool. This edge pool includes all the edges of C as a subset. In step 2, each edge in the edge pool is classified according to its relative location with respect to faces A and B individually. As a result, each edge in the edge pool has two classifications: (1) inside, on, or outside face A, and (2) inside, on, or outside face B (see Figure 5.45b). In step 3, the edges are collected; they are grouped by relative location and the specific Boolean operation being applied. Note that we do not have to collect edges that are "in A" and "in B" for "A union B" in Figure 5.45(b). Similarly, the edges "out A" and "out B" have to be discarded for "A intersection B." Once the edges have been collected, they are formed into a face by filling in the necessary connectivity information for vertices, edges, loops, and so on. For a solid, this approach requires heavy geometric computation to classify the edges as inside, on, or outside the solid and a complicated topological operation to construct a B-Rep of the resulting solid from the collected edges.

To avoid the difficulties just described, Mäntylä [1986] suggested an algorithm called a *vertex neighborhood classifier*. Unlike the edge-by-edge approach by Requicha and Miller, Mäntylä's algorithm takes a face-by-face approach. Hoffmann, Hopcroft, and Karasick [1989] and Chiyokura [1988] also suggested boundary evaluation algorithms based on a face-by-face approach. In Appendix D,

Figure 5.45

Classification of edges

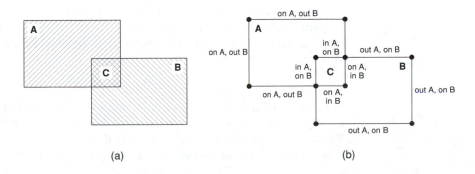

(a)   (b)

we introduce the algorithm implemented in SNUMOD, which is also based on a face-by-face approach.

5.3.5 Calculation of Volumetric Properties

We previously mentioned that one of the advantages of a solid model is the ability to calculate directly the volumetric properties of an object from its mathematical description. In fact, the early solid modeling systems were mainly used to visualize an object's shape, and thus the calculation of volumetric properties was one of the few engineering capabilities that they provided. Volumetric properties of an object include its volume, centroids, moments of inertia, and products of inertia, which are defined as follows.

Volume:
$$V = \iiint_V dV$$

Centroid:
$$x_c = \frac{1}{V} \iiint_V x \, dV$$

$$y_c = \frac{1}{V} \iiint_V y \, dV$$

$$z_c = \frac{1}{V} \iiint_V z \, dV$$

Moments of inertia:
$$I_{xx} = \iiint_V (y^2 + z^2) \, dV$$

$$I_{yy} = \iiint_V (x^2 + z^2) \, dV$$

$$I_{zz} = \iiint_V (y^2 + x^2) \, dV$$

Products of inertia:
$$I_{xy} = \iiint_V xy \, dV$$

$$I_{yz} = \iiint_V yz \, dV$$

$$I_{zx} = \iiint_V zx \, dV$$

The symbols $\iiint_V$ represent an integral over the volume of the object of interest. These definitions become those of the corresponding mass properties if the density of the object is included. The density does not need to be included if it is uniform over the object; in that case, each mass property simply becomes the volumetric property multiplied by the constant density.

The value of any volumetric property can be obtained by evaluating the volume integral in the form

$$\psi = \iiint_V F(x, y, z) \, dV \tag{5.2}$$

For a voxel or an octree representation, the volume integral in Equation (5.2) will simply be the summation of the volume integrals over the voxels or octants. Therefore it is necessary to calculate only the volume integral of $F(x, y, z)$ over a single voxel or octant. Because a voxel or an octant is defined by eight corner points, the volume integral over a voxel or an octant can be expanded to be a function of the coordinates of the eight corner points, and the value of the integral over any voxel or octant can be obtained by substituting the coordinate values into the function. Then the resulting volumetric property can be obtained by summing these values for all the voxels or octants by applying the parallel axis theorem [Crandall, Karnopp, Kurtz, and Pridmor-Brown 1968]. Doing so compensates for the difference between the origin of the local coordinate system for each voxel or octant and that of the global coordinate system. When an object is represented by a CSG tree, a similar procedure of adding or subtracting the volume integrals for the primitives can be used, depending on the Boolean operations applied.

If an object is represented by a B-Rep, however, the evaluation of the volume integral in Equation (5.2) is not so simple. Timmer proposed a method of evaluating the volume integral for an object of an arbitrary shape represented by a B-Rep [Timmer, Stern 1980]. Timmer's approach, step by step, is as follows.

Step 1. The volume integral in Equation (5.2) is converted to the surface integral over the bounding surface of the volume by Gauss's theorem. Gauss's theorem is expressed as [Kreyszig 1988]:

$$\iiint_V (\nabla \bullet \Phi) \, dV = \iint_S (\Phi \bullet \mathbf{n}) \, ds \qquad (5.3)$$

where ∇ is the gradient operator implying

$$\left(\frac{\partial}{\partial x} \mathbf{i} + \frac{\partial}{\partial y} \mathbf{j} + \frac{\partial}{\partial z} \mathbf{k} \right)$$

$\iint_S$ is a surface integral over the bounding surface of volume V, and $\mathbf{n}$ is the outward unit normal vector at the point on the infinitesimal area ds of surface S. Generally, $\mathbf{n}$ is a function of x, y, and z because it varies for each infinitesimal area as the surface integral is evaluated. Detailed explanations of Gauss's theorem are presented in calculus textbooks such as Kreyszig [1988] and Hildebrand [1976].

Applying Gauss's theorem, we can convert the volume integral in Equation (5.2) to a surface integral by substituting $\Phi(x, y, z)$, satisfying $\nabla \bullet \Phi = F(x, y, z)$, into the right-hand side of Equation (5.3). Then we can expand Equation (5.2) to

$$\psi = \iint_S G(x, y, z) \, ds \qquad (5.4)$$

where $G(x, y, z)$ is a function of x, y, and z obtained by $\Phi \bullet \mathbf{n}$.

There are many possible choices for $\Phi(x, y, z)$; accordingly, many $G(x, y, z)$ can be obtained. Even though any $\Phi(x, y, z)$ satisfying $\nabla \bullet \Phi = F(x, y, z)$ can be chosen, a function of a simple form is recommended.

Step 2. The bounding surface S in Equation (5.4) can be considered to be a set of faces S_i of the object. Thus the surface integral in Equation (5.4) can be obtained by summing the surface integral over each face:

$$\iint_S G(x, y, z) \, ds = \sum_{i=1}^{n_f} \psi_i \qquad (5.5)$$

where ψ_i is $\iint_{Si} G(x, y, z) \, ds$ and n_f is the number of faces.

Step 3. Each surface integral ψ_i in Equation (5.5) can be converted to a double integral over the domain of the parameters defining the surface equation of face S_i. To be more specific, the double integral can be expressed as follows when the equation for the surface involving face Si is represented by $\mathbf{P}(u, v) = x(u, v)\mathbf{i} + y(u, v)\mathbf{j} + z(u, v)\mathbf{k}$:[10]

$$\psi_i = \iint_{Ri} G[x(u,v), y(u,v), z(u,v)] \, |\, \mathbf{J}\, | \, du\, dv \tag{5.6}$$

where R_i is the finite domain in the uv plane corresponding to S_i, which is the portion of the surface $\mathbf{P}(u, v)$, and $|\mathbf{J}|$ is the Jacobian. The Jacobian compensates for the difference between the infinitesimal area ds and the infinitesimal area in the parametric domain $du\, dv$ and is defined as

$$|\mathbf{J}| = \left| \frac{\partial \mathbf{P}(u,v)}{\partial u} \times \frac{\partial \mathbf{P}(u,v)}{\partial v} \right| \tag{5.7}$$

The integrand in Equation (5.6) can be expanded to be a function of u and v, $H(u, v)$, by substituting the right-hand side of Equation (5.7) for $|\mathbf{J}|$. Hence Equation (5.6) becomes[11]

$$\psi_i = \iint_{Ri} H(u, v) \, du\, dv \tag{5.8}$$

If the domain R_i is a square represented by $0 \le u \le 1$ and $0 \le v \le 1$, the double integral in Equation (5.8) can be evaluated numerically by using Gaussian quadrature as follows [Dewey 1988]:

$$\psi_i = \iint_{Ri} H(u, v) \, du\, dv \cong \sum_{i=1}^{m} \sum_{j=1}^{n} w_i w_j H(u_i, v_j) \tag{5.9}$$

As Equation (5.9) shows, Gaussian quadrature can be used to evaluate an integral by selecting the proper number of sample values of the integrand, putting a proper weight on each sample value, and summing the weighted sample values. Thus the accuracy of the result depends on the number, n and m, of the samples and their parameter values. Figure 5.46 shows the recommended values of the u and v parameters for the samples and the corresponding weights for given values of n and m, respectively. If different values of n and m are used, two different groups would be used in Figure 5.46, based on the specific values of n and m. Furthermore, Gaussian quadrature can be applied only when the integral interval ranges from 0 to 1.

Step 4. Face S_i is not generally mapped to a square in its parametric domain. That is, it may have more than four irregular boundary edges and some holes inside it. Thus the general domain for the double integral in Equation (5.8) would look like the one shown in Figure 5.47. Double integrals over irregular domains cannot

---

[10] Various forms of $\mathbf{P}(u, v)$ for various types of surfaces are introduced in Chapter 7.
[11] Because all the area properties are expressed by double integrals, the approach used to evaluate Equation (5.8) may be used to calculate the area properties.

FIGURE 5.46

Sample parameter values and corresponding weights for Gaussian quadrature

i, j	w_i	u_i, v_j
	$n, m = 2$	
1	0.500 000 000	0.211 324 865
2	0.500 000 000	0.788 675 135
	$n, m = 3$	
1	0.277 777 778	0.112 701 665
2	0.444 444 444	0.500 000 000
3	0.277 777 778	0.887 298 335
	$n, m = 4$	
1	0.173 927 423	0.069 431 844
2	0.326 072 577	0.330 009 478
3	0.326 072 577	0.669 990 522
4	0.173 927 423	0.930 568 156
	$n, m = 5$	
1	0.118 463 443	0.046 910 077
2	0.239 314 335	0.230 765 345
3	0.284 444 444	0.500 000 000
4	0.239 314 335	0.769 234 655
5	0.118 463 443	0.953 089 923
	$n, m = 6$	
1	0.085 662 246	0.033 765 243
2	0.180 380 787	0.169 395 307
3	0.233 956 967	0.380 690 407
4	0.233 956 967	0.619 309 593
5	0.180 380 787	0.830 604 693
6	0.085 662 246	0.966 234 757

Figure 5.47

Irregular domain for double integral

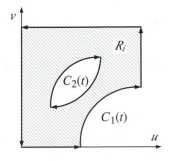

be evaluated by Gaussian quadrature. However, they can be converted to line integrals along the boundary of the irregular domain by applying Green's theorem:

$$\iint_{Ri}\left[\frac{\partial\alpha(u,v)}{\partial u}-\frac{\partial\beta(u,v)}{\partial v}\right]du\,dv = \oint\left[\beta(u,v)\,du+\alpha(u,v)\,dv\right] \tag{5.10}$$

where $\oint$ represents the line integral along the closed boundary of the domain R_i. For a multiply connected domain such as R_i in Figure 5.47, this integral implies the summation of the line integrals, one along the outer boundary and the other along the inner boundary. The direction of the inner boundary, denoted $C_1(t)$, is opposite to that of the outer boundary, denoted $C_2(t)$, so that the line integral along $C_1(t)$ will be subtracted automatically during the summation. The line integral along $C_1(t)$, has to be subtracted because it is the double integral over the domain surrounded by $C_1(t)$.

To use Equation (5.10), we need to derive $\alpha(u,v)$ and $\beta(u,v)$ to satisfy the equation

$$H(u,v) = \frac{\partial\alpha(u,v)}{\partial u}-\frac{\partial\beta(u,v)}{\partial v} \tag{5.11}$$

Many possible combinations of $\alpha(u,v)$ and $\beta(u,v)$ satisfy Equation (5.11). One simple set of $\alpha(u,v)$ and $\beta(u,v)$ may be obtained from the following equation by setting $\beta(u,v)$ to zero:

$$H(u,v) = \frac{\partial\alpha(u,v)}{\partial u} \tag{5.12}$$

However, it is not easy to derive $H(u,v)$ and $\alpha(u,v)$ in closed form when the surface equation of S_i is provided in a form that cannot be easily expanded, such as a B-spline equation.[12] Timmer got around this problem by approximating $H(u,v)$ as a polynomial in u and v from the numerical values evaluated for $H(u,v)$. Thus $H(u,v)$ is expressed as

$$H(u,v) = \sum_{i=0}^{M}\sum_{j=0}^{M} a_{ij}u^i v^j \tag{5.13}$$

Substituting Equation (5.13) into (5.12) yields

$$\alpha(u,v) = \sum_{i=0}^{M}\sum_{j=0}^{M}\frac{1}{i+1}a_{ij}u^{i+1}v^j \tag{5.14}$$

Therefore Equation (5.8) can be expanded as follows:

$$\psi_i = \oint\alpha(u,v)\,dv \tag{5.15}$$

---

[12] The B-spline equation is introduced in Chapters 6 and 7.

Step 5. The line integral along the closed boundary in Equation (5.15) can be evaluated by summing the line integral along each curve segment of the closed boundary. Thus Equation (5.15) can be expressed as

$$\psi_i = \sum_{l=1}^{L} \int_l \alpha(u,v)\,dv \tag{5.16}$$

where $\int_l$ is a line integral along a curve segment of the boundary in the direction of the entire boundary, as described in Step 4, and $\sum_{l=1}^{L}$ is the summation for all the curve segments on the boundary.

Any curve segment along the boundary in the uv domain can be represented by the following parametric equation:[13]

$$u = u(t), \qquad v = v(t) \qquad 0 \le t \le 1 \tag{5.17}$$

Substituting Equation (5.17) into Equation (5.16) yields

$$\psi_i = \sum_{l=1}^{L} \int_0^l \alpha[u(t), v(t)]\frac{dv}{dt}\,dt \tag{5.18}$$

where each integral inside the summation can be evaluated exactly by using the curve equation of each curve segment or evaluated numerically by using Gaussian quadrature.

5.4   NONMANIFOLD MODELING SYSTEMS

In the preceding section, we mentioned that a solid modeling system allows a user to create only a shape having a closed volume or the manifold model in mathematical terminology. In other words, it disallows such nonmanifold conditions as two surfaces touching at a single point, two surfaces touching along an open or closed curve, two distinct enclosed volumes sharing a face, edge, or vertex as a common boundary, a wire edge emanating from a point on a surface, and faces forming a cellular structure. Figure 5.48 illustrates some examples of nonmanifold models.

We can clarify the difference between the manifold model and the nonmanifold model in mathematical terminology as follows. In a manifold model, every point on a surface is two-dimensional; that is, every point has a neighborhood that is homeomorphic to a two-dimensional disk [Weiler 1988]. In other words, even though the surface exists in three-dimensional space, it is topologically "flat" when the surface is examined closely enough in a small area around any given point. Historically, all the B-Rep–based solid modeling systems have used manifold representations for their models [Baumgart 1972, 1975; Braid, Hillyard, and Stroud 1978; Eastman and

---

[13] Parametric equations of various curves are introduced in Chapter 6.

Figure 5.48

Examples of non-manifold models

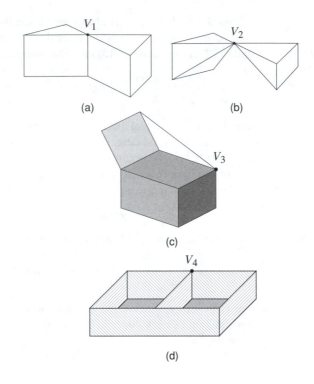

Weiler 1979]. In a nonmanifold model, however, a given point on a surface need not necessarily be "flat" in that the neighborhood of the point need not be a two-dimensional disk. In this case, the point is essentially the intersection of two or more topologically two-dimensional surfaces (V_1, V_2, and V_4 in Figures 5.48a, b, and d are examples), or a two-dimensional surface and a one-dimensional curve (V_3 in Figure 5.48c is an example).

You may wonder about the need to create nonmanifold models, such as those shown in Figure 5.48. In fact, disallowance of nonmanifold models has been considered to be one of the good features of solid modeling systems because they yield only manufacturable models. However, it is a different story when you want to use a geometric modeling system for the entire design process. A designer who wants to design a plastic container, for example, might start from a model such as the one shown in Figure 5.48(d) without considering its thickness. Similarly, the geometric model in Figure 5.48(c) would be a natural initial design for a structure composed of a solid block holding a plate with a cord.

Thus an abstract model of mixed dimensions is useful in supporting the designer's reasoning process. A model of mixed dimensions might include some dangling edges, laminar plates, and solids. In addition, an abstract model is also useful in providing a basis for analysis. Various analytic tools can be applied to verify the design at each stage in the design process. For example, when we need to perform a finite-element analysis on a component, we generate the shell elements from an abstract shape, such as the one shown in Figure 5.48(d) rather than generating solid elements from the corresponding solid model having the required thickness. In conclusion, we can say that a nonmanifold model is indispensable in capturing the evolution of a design from incomplete lower level prescriptions to a true solid.

Unfortunately, conventional geometric modeling systems, whether wireframe modelers, surface modelers, or solid modelers, do not support the representation of the nonmanifold models shown in Figure 5.48. Most abstract models, as an intermediate result in the design process, have representations composed of mixture of one-, two-, and three-dimensional elements, as shown in Figure 5.48(c) or of only the elements that are less than three-dimensional, as shown in Figure 5.48(d). Therefore we need a modeling system that supports a representation scheme in which the transitions between one-, two-, and three-dimensional geometric entities can be performed within the same representation. Such a modeling system is called a *nonmanifold modeling system* and encompasses both the manifold and nonmanifold object domains. This system allows the unified representation of wireframe, surface, solid, and cellular models simultaneously in the same modeling environment while increasing the representable range of models beyond what is individually achievable in these other modeling systems. In addition, analysis such as finite-element analysis can be carried out in the same representation as the original modeling representation, allowing the possibility of automated feedback rather than manual feedback, as currently, in the design and analysis cycle.

As in (manifold) solid modeling systems, a data structure has to be established and the operators manipulating the entities in the data structure have to be implemented in the development of a nonmanifold modeling system. Then the upper level modeling commands are developed by ordering the operators in the proper sequence, as modeling commands were developed from the Euler operators in a solid modeling system. In fact, the upper level modeling commands in nonmanifold modeling systems appear to be similar to those of solid modeling systems even though they make use of a different set of basic operators. In Appendix E, we briefly explain the issues associated with the data structure storing the boundary of a nonmanifold model and the operators manipulating the entities in the data structure.

5.5 ASSEMBLY MODELING CAPABILITIES

Geometric modeling systems, whether they are wireframe, surface, or solid modeling systems, have been used mainly to design or model an individual part rather than for the assembly of parts. Until recently, engineers designed parts individually and then assembled them later in the development cycle to determine whether they fit properly and the product functioned as intended. Such an approach was fine for small design teams working on simple products. However, this approach is unworkable when the design is performed by several teams spread around the world and the assembly to be designed is complex.

A designer may change a component configuration and fail to let others know or forget to make corresponding changes in other affected components. Considerable time is spent manually tracking part designs, part-to-part interfaces, engineering changes, product specifications, test results, and other essential information to be sure that individual part designs fit with one another. In the early 1990s, the growing need for collaborative engineering in industries was a primary driving force for the development of assembly design capabilities. These capabilities accurately keep track of parts and their relationships to one another so that designers can create part geometry in the context of other parts.

Probably the greatest use of assembly design capabilities is in the automotive and aerospace industries. There the design of highly complex products must be coordinated not only for engineers throughout the world but also with second- and third-tier suppliers [MacKrell 1997].

5.5.1   Basic Functions of Assembly Modeling

Assembly modelers provide a logical structure for grouping and organizing parts into assemblies and subassemblies. The structure enables a designer to identify individual parts, keep track of associated part data, and maintain relationships among parts and subassemblies. Relationship data maintained by an assembly modeling system include a wide range of information about a part and its association with others in the assembly. Mating conditions between parts in the assembly are among the most important pieces of relationship data. Mating conditions identify how the part is connected to others (e.g., two planar faces of a pair of parts are in contact or two cylindrical faces are coaxial). *Instancing information* identifies other places in the assembly where the same part is used; instancing is a useful concept, especially for standard parts, such as fasteners, because the part data can be stored only once even when the part is used many places in the assembly. Data on fit, position, and orientation specify exactly how parts are joined in the assembly and often include allowable tolerances. The position and orientation data of parts are derived from the mating conditions in many systems.

Assembly modeling systems also provide the capability to create parametric constraint relationships between parts and to measure size and dimension information from one part and apply it to another, thus freeing the user from having to reenter geometric data where parts interface. Interpart constraint relationships are helpful when many dimensions in an assembly depend on some key dimensions. Once such relationships have been input, the designer need change only the key dimensions; the system takes care of other related dimensions automatically. This powerful capability also provides a mechanism for propagating a complete change (e.g., if the diameter of a shaft changes, the size of a hole that fits into it is updated as well). Thus designers' time is saved because the entire assembly doesn't have to be painstakingly modified whenever part designs are modified. Figure 5.49 illustrates how the change of a dimension in a part propagates into the assembly created by the assembly module of Pro/Engineer.

In summary, assembly modeling systems enable a designer to create and manage overall assembly constraints among parts, defining the position and movement

Figure 5.49

An illustration of change propagation: (a) assembly before modification, (b) relations between part dimensions specified by the designer, and (c) assembly after modification

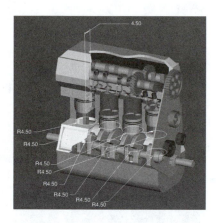

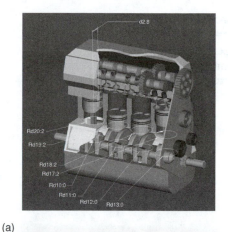

(a)

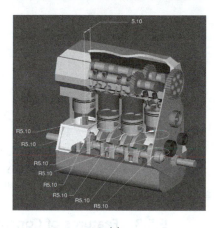

(b)

(c)

of parts in relation to each other. Assembly constraints capture design intentions, including the common dimensions of parts, positions of parts with respect to each other, alignment of parts, joint conditions, operational parameters, and general mating conditions. The distance by which a part can move with respect to mating parts, the number of degrees a part can rotate, and the linear distance a pin can move in and out of a hole are examples of operational parameters.

5.5.2 Browsing an Assembly

All assembly design systems have some type of browser, allowing users to interact with the system in locating parts, identifying their relationships, and accessing CAD models, drawings, and associated parts data. The browser displays parts and subassemblies in a treelike structure, with nodes connecting the various levels of detail. Figure 5.50 shows a tree structure of an assembly created by the assembly module of

Figure 5.50

An example of an
assembly tree
structure

Pro/Engineer. As shown, many browsers help users find parts by simultaneously displaying the assembly tree and the CAD model on the screen. Clicking on a part in the browser immediately highlights that part on the CAD model and vice versa.

5.5.3 Features of Concurrent Design

Assembly modeling capabilities are virtually indispensable for groups that are developing a product composed of multiple parts. These capabilities provide the functions needed to manage effectively multiple users' access of the same assembly at the same time. In some CAD systems, check-in/check-out procedures control who works on what parts and prevent two designers from modifying the same part design at the same time. Assembly modeling systems that support concurrent engineering also have the ability to bring the parts together into a unified assembly and perform kinematic studies, finite-element analysis, and other types of engineering analysis.

When many people are allowed to work on one assembly, communicating part-design changes without disrupting the work of others is a challenge. Most users don't want their CAD screens flickering with updates every time their colleagues make design changes. One way to solve this problem is to transmit routine updates only at certain times or when users request the most current configuration. However, crucial design changes to a mating part will have an impact on other parts and should be sent to the affected designers immediately.

5.5.4 Use of Assembly Models

Assembly models created by assembly modeling systems can be used in various ways for efficient product design. Most assembly modelers let users make measurements between parts in an assembly. Generating exploded views from an assembly model is another useful application. Exploded views are helpful in clearly showing the physical relation of all the parts in complex assemblies, as illustrated in Figure 5.51. These views are especially helpful in describing assembly instructions.

Also, color-shaded renderings can show the assembly of thousands of parts in realistic detail. Digital mock-ups enable users to view not only complex assemblies but also to perform packaging studies, interference checks, kinematic analysis, and other operations. A digital mock-up even allows a walk-through of the assembly in a virtual reality environment to see how the assembly works and verify that the parts interact properly.[14]

Assembly modelers also facilitate the generation of a bill-of-materials (BOM), a document that lists the various materials needed for a product, the parts required for an assembly, and the like. A BOM can easily be produced by traversing the assembly structure and summarizing the part data.

5.5.5 Simplification of Assemblies

Most geometric modeling systems with standard assembly modeling capabilities have no trouble handling an assembly of hundreds of parts. However, handling large assemblies with thousands of parts is more difficult. System performance also depends on the number of features of the individual parts and subassemblies. The blending surface is a typical example of a feature that affects performance. The

Figure 5.51

An exploded view

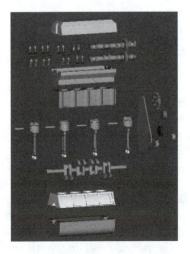

---

[14] We explain *virtual reality environment* in detail in Chapter 13.

number of parts in an assembly and complex parts features overpower many systems, greatly reducing modeler performance and making information hard to find. Thus many systems provide various ways for simplifying complex assemblies to make them manageable.

One method is to use instancing, as mentioned earlier. Instancing can simplify assemblies significantly by having to model commonly used parts, such as fasteners, only once and then being able to specify multiple locations where they are used. Instances refer back to a single master-part definition containing the geometric model and all relevant information about the part. This approach obviously eliminates the need to model the part whenever it is used at many locations. Also, the instances can be easily changed by modifying only the master-part definition.

Another technique, called *agglomeration*, groups an entire assembly or subassembly into a single model. In this way, the internal features at the contacts between parts would disappear and only outer details would remain. The single model can then be manipulated more efficiently if the exterior shape is all that the user cares about. Interactive display is an application that can be improved by agglomeration.

Model complexities can also be reduced by ignoring detailed features temporarily when they are not needed. They remain as part of the geometric model, however. In producing a display, geometric intricacies that are too tiny to be seen from a distance can be ignored. Also, many details such as small holes and minor fillets can be eliminated when the model is being used for finite-element analysis or kinematic studies. Geometry in the assembly model can also be turned off by zone for simplification. One way is to divide the model into geometric cubes or blocks, allowing the user to work in one specific area without dealing with details in the others. The model can also be divided functionally; mechanical, electrical, and hydraulic subsystems can be treated separately so that data the user doesn't need at the moment are not carried along.

5.6 WEB-BASED MODELING

CAD/CAM/CAE system vendors are all moving toward integrating their systems with the Internet. Thus Internet capabilities from inside geometric modeling systems are either already in place or about to become available. By using the Internet as an extension to a geometric modeling system through the use of browsers and browser plug-ins, an entire project team and its clients can view and manipulate models and drawings in various Web formats early in the design process [Knoth 1997].

One way of making geometric data available via the Web is to save it in a format that a Web browser can read and put it on a Web page. That way, someone with a browser can type in the universal resource locator (URL) for the page and view an image of the geometric model. This is called *publishing* the geometric model.

Geometric modeling system vendors support publishing by giving their systems the ability to export geometric data in one or more of the browser-compatible formats. That could be a format such as Virtual Reality Modeling Language

(VRML), which is accepted by standard Web browsers. Or it could be a format such as Computer Graphics Metafile (CGM) or Autodesk's Drawing Web Format (DWF), which requires the addition of a special plug-in to the browser before the model can be viewed [Potter 1997].

VRML is a standard file format for three-dimensional graphics data, whereas CGM and DWF are two-dimensional formats. Although VRML has limitations, such as loss of accuracy and large file sizes, most geometric modeling system vendors have opted to go with the VRML output capability because of VRML's support for three-dimensional work. Some even go a step further, providing the ability to put the VRML model into a Web page and add information such as text and hyperlinks to the page. Just as in Hypertext Markup Language (HTML) hypertext links—now used to link to other World Wide Web (WWW or the Web) data—VRML files contain URLs that can point to any other type of file on the Web, including other VRML files. When VRML files are read by a viewer, a navigable three-dimensional model appears. Hot spots (links to other URLs) are identified by a graphical change in the cursor, much like the user encounters on HTML pages [Beazley 1996]. Clicking the mouse on a hot spot loads the file associated with the hot spot. By clicking on the different parts of a model, for instance, a user can open a window that displays information written by another member of the design team. When clicking on a different corner of the image, the user can read technical characteristics about the model and can see concerns posted by someone else on the team. Another hypertext link from a different part of the design may connect to a part catalog, a standards manual, or even an embedded e-mail address of the project design manager [Knoth 1996].

QUESTIONS AND PROBLEMS

1. What are the two main applications of a surface modeling system in a product cycle?

2. As perceived by most users, what is the primary disadvantage of a solid modeling system compared to a surface modeling system?

3. List the solid modeling methods that are used to generate a solid object by defining the planar closed domains.

4. Show some examples in which an invalid solid is generated after a Boolean operation is applied.

5. What do you have to be concerned about when you modify an object by lifting a portion of its face?

6. Assuming that the modeling functions described in Section 5.3.1 are provided, which modeling functions would you apply in which order to model the objects shown? Recall that many combinations of the modeling functions will result in the same object.

(Tallen wheel was designed by Zetec Ltd. www.zetec.co.nz using SolidWorks solid modeling software for NZ Wheels International Ltd.)

7. What is the main advantage of modeling an object by using manufacturing features in a feature-based modeling system?

8. Explain the advantage of the parametric modeling approach whereby the part shape is specified by geometric constraints or dimensional relations.

9. Describe the advantages and disadvantages of storing an object in a CSG tree.

10. In a boundary representation, one way to store a face is to store the list of its bounding edges. If the face has a hole in it, how is the boundary of the internal hole handled in this list?

11. List the advantages and disadvantages of using voxel representation for an object.

12. Explain why the octree representation requires less memory space than the voxel representation for the same resolution.

13. Evaluate the area in the accompanying figure.

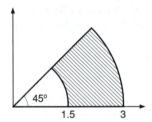

The area can be expressed as

$$A = \int_0^{\pi/4} \int_{1.5}^{3} r^3 \, dr \, d\theta$$

   a. Evaluate the integral by using the Gaussian quadrature using three samples for each variable.

   b. Evaluate the integral exactly and compare the value with the results obtained in (a).

14. Describe the advantages of nonmanifold modeling systems over conventional solid modeling systems.

15. Model the following objects and calculate the locations of their centroids by using a solid modeling system.

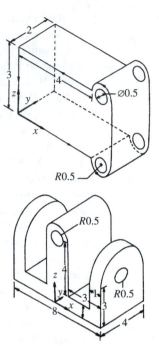

16. Two pipes are to be welded, as illustrated in the accompanying figure. The diameters of the pipes are the same: 7.6 cm. To avoid the large pressure drop of the inside flow, the elliptic area at the intersection of the pipes must be 65 ± 6 cm². What angle θ and welding length (perimeter of the ellipse) will satisfy the design requirement? Solve this problem interactively by using a surface modeling system or a solid modeling system.

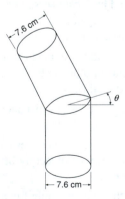

6

Representation and Manipulation of Curves

As mentioned in Section 5.3.2, we have to store the curve equation itself or its equivalent characteristic attributes[1] for each curved edge. This information is required in computer-aided drafting systems as well as in solid modeling systems. We also showed that it is necessary to calculate the intersection points of the curves to determine the limits of "xegments"[2] for evaluating the Boolean operations explained in Appendix D. The limits of a xegment are derived by calculating the intersection points between the boundary curve of the intersecting surfaces and the intersection curve between the surfaces, each of which belongs to a separate solid. Once the limits of each xegment have been obtained, a further step is required to cut the intersection curve at the intersection points. Similar processing is required to create and deform the curves in computer-aided drafting systems and surface modeling systems. Therefore in this chapter we briefly review various methods of representing curve equations and manipulation techniques such as intersection and composition of curves. More detailed discussions of the topics in this chapter are presented in books on computational geometry [Faux and Pratt 1979; Farin 1990; Piulin 1987; Hoschek and Lasser 1993; Boehm and Prantzsch 1984].

---

[1] The center point, radius, and normal vector of the plane on which a circle lies are examples of the characteristic attributes equivalent to the equation of a circle.

[2] A *xegment* is defined as a portion of an intersection curve between two faces, each of which belongs to a different solid. The xegment lies inside both faces.

6.1   TYPES OF CURVE EQUATIONS

Curve equations can be classified primarily as two groups. One is the parametric equation, which relates the x, y, and z coordinates of the points on a curve with a parameter. The other is the nonparametric equation, which directly relates the x, y, and z coordinates with a function. We can clarify this distinction with an example. Consider a circle of radius R centered at the origin of the reference coordinate system. If the circle is located in the xy plane, the parametric equation of the circle can be expressed as

$$x = R\cos\theta, \quad y = R\sin\theta, \quad z = 0 \quad (0 \le \theta \le 2\pi) \tag{6.1}$$

However the same circle may be expressed without using the parameter θ as

$$x^2 + y^2 - R^2 = 0, \quad z = 0 \tag{6.2}$$

or

$$y = \pm\sqrt{R^2 - x^2}, \quad z = 0 \tag{6.3}$$

Equation (6.2) is in *implicit nonparametric form*, whereas Equation (6.3) is in *explicit nonparametric form*.

Each form shown in Equations (6.1), (6.2), and (6.3) has its own advantages and disadvantages, depending on the application for which the equation is used. Here we focus on the equation's application in the display of curves because interactive graphics is one of the most important features of CAD/CAM/CAE systems. When a curve is displayed on a graphics screen, it is actually drawn as a set of short straight-line segments. Thus we often need to calculate the points at a certain interval along a curve, which is called *curve evaluation*. We easily expect that the points on the circle represented by Equation (6.1) can be generated in sequence along the curve by substituting small increments of the parametric values into the equation every time. If we want to use Equation (6.2), however, we are not sure which variable to choose as the independent variable and thus to increment at each evaluation. Even if we choose the independent variable, two values (positive and negative) will be obtained for the dependent variable. This means that one of the two points has to be selected every time as the neighbor of the last point drawn. Equation (6.3) also has the same inherent problem, even though it differentiates the independent variable from the dependent variable.

Because of the disadvantages of the other forms of the curve equation, the parametric equation is the most popular form for representing curves and surfaces in CAD systems.[3] Therefore, in this chapter we discuss only parametric equations of curves.

---

[3] Intersection points between two curves are sometimes calculated efficiently when one curve is represented by a parametric equation and the other one is represented by a nonparametric equation. Thus a conversion process from a parametric form to a nonparametric form or vice versa is also used in some systems. The conversion process is discussed in Hoffmann, Hopcroft, and Karasick [1989].

6.2 CONIC SECTIONS

The curves, or portions of the curves, obtained by cutting a cone with a plane are referred to as *conic sections*. Based on the location and orientation of the cutting plane with respect to the cone, the section curve may be a circle, an ellipse, a parabola, or a hyperbola. Most of the profile curves of mechanical components can be represented by conic sections because most mechanical components have axial symmetry.

6.2.1 Circle or Circular Arc

A circle or its portion on the xy plane with radius R and center at (X_c, Y_c) can be represented by the equations

$$x = R\cos\theta + X_c$$
$$y = R\sin\theta + Y_c \tag{6.4}$$

As mentioned previously, curves can be evaluated by substituting in them the values of θ with an increment of $\Delta\theta$, starting from 0. The value of θ is incremented to 2π for a complete circle or to a certain value for a circular arc. The value $\Delta\theta$ has to be chosen properly because a value that is too small causes computational inefficiency, whereas a value that is too large draws a circle like a polygon. The equation of a circle or circular arc lying on planes other than the xy plane can be derived by applying the proper transformation matrices to Equation (6.4). (Transformation matrices were explained in Section 3.7.)

EXAMPLE 6.1

A circle of unit radius is centered at $(0, 1, 1)$ and located on the yz plane, as illustrated in the accompanying figure.[4] Derive the parametric equation of the circle by applying the proper transformation matrices to Equation (6.4).

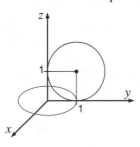

[4] The equation of this circle can be stored by attributes such as the normal vector $(1, 0, 0)$, the center $(0, 1, 1)$, and the radius 1. As described earlier, these are the characteristic attributes equivalent to the equation.

ANSWER

We drew the original unit circle on the xy plane in dotted lines, and we drew the circle of interest in solid lines. Thus we obtained the solid circle by rotating the dotted circle by –90 degrees about the y axis and then translating it by 1 in the y and 1 in the z directions. If the x, y, and z coordinates of the points on the solid circle are denoted x^*, y^*, and z^* and those of the dotted circle are denoted x, y, and z, the following equation will hold:

$$\begin{bmatrix} x^* & y^* & 0 & 1 \end{bmatrix}^T = Trans(0,1,1)Rot(y,-90°)\begin{bmatrix} x & y & 0 & 1 \end{bmatrix}^T$$

$$= \begin{bmatrix} \cos(-90°) & 0 & \sin(-90°) & 0 \\ 0 & 1 & 0 & 0 \\ -\sin(-90°) & 0 & \cos(-90°) & 0 \\ 0 & 0 & 0 & 1 \end{bmatrix}\begin{bmatrix} x \\ y \\ 0 \\ 1 \end{bmatrix}\begin{bmatrix} 1 & 0 & 0 & 0 \\ 0 & 1 & 0 & 1 \\ 0 & 0 & 1 & 1 \\ 0 & 0 & 0 & 1 \end{bmatrix}$$

$$= (0 \ y+1 \ x+1 \ 1)$$

Therefore

$$x^* = 0$$
$$y^* = y + 1 = R\sin\theta + 1$$
$$z^* = x + 1 = R\cos\theta + 1 \qquad (0 \le \theta \le 2\pi)$$

6.2.2 Ellipse or Elliptic Arc

As we did for a circle, we introduce the parametric equation of an ellipse centered at the origin and located in the xy plane of the reference coordinate system. We further assume that the major axis is in the x direction with length a and the minor axis is in the y direction with length b. Then the parametric equation is

$$x = a\cos\theta$$
$$y = b\sin\theta \qquad\qquad (6.5)$$
$$z = 0$$

The range of the parameter θ would be from 0 to 2π for an ellipse and from 0 to the value corresponding to the end point for an elliptic arc. A general ellipse on an arbitrary plane with arbitrary directions of the major and the minor axes can be obtained by applying the proper transformation matrices, as was done for a circle.

EXAMPLE 6.2

Derive the parametric equation of an ellipse in the xy plane, which has a center at (X_c, Y_c) and the major and the minor axes as illustrated in the accompanying figure.

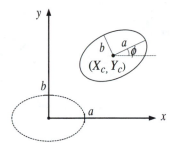

ANSWER

The ellipse of interest can be obtained by rotating the reference ellipse at the origin by ϕ about the z axis and translating it by X_c in the x direction and by Y_c in the y direction. If the x, y, and z coordinates of the points on the ellipse of interest are denoted x^*, y^*, and z^* and those of the reference ellipse are denoted x, y, and z, the following equation will hold:

$$\begin{bmatrix} x^* & y^* & 0 & 1 \end{bmatrix}^T = Trans(X_c, Y_c, 0)Rot(z, \phi)(x \ y \ 0 \ 1)^T$$

$$= \begin{bmatrix} \cos\phi & -\sin\phi & 0 & 0 \\ \sin\phi & \cos\phi & 0 & 0 \\ 0 & 0 & 1 & 0 \\ 0 & 0 & 0 & 1 \end{bmatrix} \begin{bmatrix} x \\ y \\ 0 \\ 1 \end{bmatrix} \begin{bmatrix} 1 & 0 & 0 & X_c \\ 0 & 1 & 0 & Y_c \\ 0 & 0 & 1 & 0 \\ 0 & 0 & 0 & 1 \end{bmatrix}$$

$$= (x\cos\phi - y\sin\phi + X_c \ \ x\sin\phi + y\cos\phi + Y_c \ \ 0 \ 1)$$

Therefore

$$x^* = x\cos\phi - y\sin\phi + X_c = a\cos\theta\cos\phi - b\sin\theta\sin\phi + X_c$$
$$y^* = x\sin\phi + y\cos\phi + Y_c = a\cos\theta\sin\phi + b\sin\theta\cos\phi + Y_c$$
$$z^* = 0 \quad (0 \le \theta \le 2\pi)$$

6.2.3 Hyperbola

We know that the hyperbola shown in Figure 6.1 can be represented by the following implicit equation:

$$\frac{x^2}{a^2} - \frac{y^2}{b^2} = 1 \tag{6.6}$$

Figure 6.1

A Hyperbola

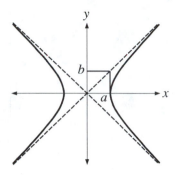

Equation (6.6) can be converted to parametric equations as follows:[5]

$$x = a\cosh u$$
$$y = b\sinh u$$

(6.7)

This conversion has been made by using the formula $(\cosh u)^2 - (\sinh u)^2 = 1$. The range of the parameter u in Equation (6.7) is determined from the end points of the portion of the hyperbola to be represented. As was done for the circle and the ellipse, the equation of the general hyperbola at any location and of any orientation can be derived by applying the proper transformation matrices to Equation (6.7).

6.2.4 Parabola

A reference parabola that is symmetric about the x axis and passes through the origin can be represented by the following explicit equation:

$$x = cy^2$$

(6.8)

Equation (6.8) can be converted to the following parametric equations:

$$x = cu^2$$
$$y = u$$

(6.9)

Note that Equation (6.9) is not a unique parametric equation equivalent to Equation (6.8), and thus any convenient parametric equation can be chosen. The range of the parameter u in Equation (6.9) is determined from the end points of the portion of the parabola to be represented. As was done for the hyperbola, the equation of the general parabola in any location and orientation can be derived by applying the proper transformation matrices to Equation (6.9).

---

[5] Note that $\cosh u = \dfrac{e^u + e^{-u}}{2}$ and $\sinh u = \dfrac{e^u - e^{-u}}{2}$. Other parametric equations can also be derived from Equation (6.6).

6.3 HERMITE CURVES

Most of the equations for curves used in CAD software are of degree 3 because of the following advantages: Two curves each represented by equations of degree 3 can be combined so that continuity to their second derivatives is guaranteed at the connection point. This implies that the curvature is continuous across the connection point and that the two curves appear to be one. The same continuity can be guaranteed with degrees higher than 3. However, use of a higher degree causes small oscillations in curve shape and requires heavy computation.

The simplest parametric equation of degree 3 we can think of is

$$\mathbf{P}(u) = [x(u)y(u)z(u)]$$
$$= \mathbf{a}_0 + \mathbf{a}_1 u + \mathbf{a}_2 u^2 = \mathbf{a}_3 u^3 \quad (0 \le u \le 1) \tag{6.10}$$

In Equation (6.10), $\mathbf{a}_0$, $\mathbf{a}_1$, $\mathbf{a}_2$, and $\mathbf{a}_3$ are the vector coefficients of the parametric equation and thus are row vectors with x, y, and z components.[6] These coefficients are simply algebraic coefficients,[7] and thus the change of the curve's shape cannot be intuitively anticipated from changes in their values.

To avoid this problem with the algebraic coefficients, we replace them with vectors having geometric meanings. One possible choice would be the position vectors of the two end points of the curve, $\mathbf{P}_0$ and $\mathbf{P}_1$, and the tangent vectors at the end points, $\mathbf{P}_0'$ and $\mathbf{P}_1'$. Imposing the boundary conditions of $\mathbf{P}_0$, $\mathbf{P}_1$, $\mathbf{P}_0'$, and $\mathbf{P}_1'$ on Equation (6.10) yields

$$\begin{aligned}
\mathbf{P}_0 &= \mathbf{P}(0) = \mathbf{a}_0 \\
\mathbf{P}_1 &= \mathbf{P}(1) = \mathbf{a}_0 + \mathbf{a}_1 + \mathbf{a}_2 + \mathbf{a}_3 \\
\mathbf{P}_0' &= \mathbf{P}'(0) = \mathbf{a}_1 \\
\mathbf{P}_1' &= \mathbf{P}'(1) = \mathbf{a}_1 + 2\mathbf{a}_2 + 3\mathbf{a}_3
\end{aligned} \tag{6.11}$$

Equations (6.11) can be solved for $\mathbf{a}_0$, $\mathbf{a}_1$, $\mathbf{a}_2$, and $\mathbf{a}_3$ to obtain

$$\begin{aligned}
\mathbf{a}_0 &= \mathbf{P}_0 \\
\mathbf{a}_1 &= \mathbf{P}_0' \\
\mathbf{a}_2 &= -3\mathbf{P}_0 + 3\mathbf{P}_1 - 2\mathbf{P}_0' - \mathbf{P}_1' \\
\mathbf{a}_3 &= 2\mathbf{P}_0 - 2\mathbf{P}_1 + \mathbf{P}_0' + \mathbf{P}_1'
\end{aligned} \tag{6.12}$$

Substituting Equation (6.12) into (6.10) gives the new expression of the curve equation:

$$\mathbf{P}(u) = [1 - 3u^2 + 2u^3 \quad 3u^2 - 2u^3 \quad u - 2u^2 + u^3 \quad -u^2 + u^3] \begin{bmatrix} \mathbf{P}_0 \\ \mathbf{P}_1 \\ \mathbf{P}_0' \\ \mathbf{P}_1' \end{bmatrix} \tag{6.13}$$

---

[6] The coordinates of a point were represented by a column vector in applying the transformation matrices to follow the convention used in OpenGL. Here we use row vector for a convenient representation of the geometric coefficient matrix shown in Figure 6.2.

[7] Accordingly, Equation (6.10) is called the *algebraic equation*.

Note that the curve equation no longer includes the algebraic coefficients; instead it contains $\mathbf{P}_0$, $\mathbf{P}_1$, $\mathbf{P}_0'$, and $\mathbf{P}_1'$. These new coefficients are called *geometric coefficients*, and Equation (6.13) is called the *Hermite curve*.[8] Its advantage is that the change in curve shape can be anticipated intuitively from changes in the geometric coefficients. For example, a change in $\mathbf{P}_0$ and/or $\mathbf{P}_1$ will modify the curve so that its end points pass through the new $\mathbf{P}_0$ and $\mathbf{P}_1$ end points. Similarly, a change in $\mathbf{P}_0'$ and $\mathbf{P}_1'$ will modify the curve so that the tangents at the ends are equal to the new $\mathbf{P}_0'$ and/or $\mathbf{P}_1'$. Figure 6.2 illustrates the change of a curve's shape as $\mathbf{P}_0'$ and $\mathbf{P}_1'$ are changed. Here [**B**] is the geometric coefficient matrix that includes $\mathbf{P}_0$, $\mathbf{P}_1$, $\mathbf{P}_0'$, and $\mathbf{P}_1'$. Specifically, the first row is $\mathbf{P}_0$, the second row is $\mathbf{P}_1$, the third row is $\mathbf{P}_0'$, and the fourth row is $\mathbf{P}_1'$. Thus Figure 6.2 shows only the effect of the tangent vectors on the curve's shape. Note how the curve changes as the magnitudes of the tangent vectors are changed but with their directions held constant. We can conclude that the magnitude of the tangent vector determines how far the effect of the tangent vector propagates toward the center of the curve.

Equation (6.13) can also be interpreted as follows. The vectors $\mathbf{P}_0$, $\mathbf{P}_1$, $\mathbf{P}_0'$, and $\mathbf{P}_1'$ affect the shape of the curve, with their relative importance determined by the functions

$$\begin{aligned}
f_1(u) &= 1 - 3u^2 + 2u^3 \\
f_2(u) &= 3u^2 - 2u^3 \\
f_3(u) &= u - 2u^2 - u^3 \\
f_4(u) &= -u^2 + u^3
\end{aligned} \tag{6.14}$$

These functions can be said to blend the effects of the prescribed boundary conditions $\mathbf{P}_0$, $\mathbf{P}_1$, $\mathbf{P}_0'$, and $\mathbf{P}_1'$. Thus they are called *blending functions*.

Figure 6.2

Effect of $\mathbf{P}_0'$ and $\mathbf{P}_1'$ on curve shape

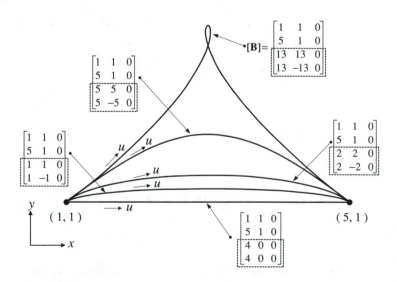

[8] As the Hermite curve is defined by $\mathbf{P}_0$, $\mathbf{P}_1$, $\mathbf{P}_0'$, and $\mathbf{P}_1'$, the curve is created from these four vector inputs and stored by these four vectors.

6.4   BEZIER CURVE

Even though the algebraic equation of a curve is converted to the form of the Hermite equation to allow curve modification to be like the intuitive approach of designers, the Hermite form does not fulfill this requirement completely. As we have shown in Figure 6.2, it is not easy to predict curve shape according to changes in magnitude of the tangent vectors, $\mathbf{P}_0'$ and $\mathbf{P}_1'$.

Bezier, an employee of the French auto company Renault, suggested a new form of curve equation and used it in Renault's surface modeling system, UNISURF, in the early 1960s [Bezier 1986]. This curve, called the *Bezier curve*, is defined by the vertices of a polygon that enclose the resulting curve. In other words, the effects of the vertices are weighted by the corresponding blending functions and blended as in the Hermite curve. Bezier selected the blending function so that the resulting curve has the following properties.

- The curve passes through the first and last vertex of the polygon.
- The tangent vector at the starting point of the curve has the same direction as the first segment of the polygon (see Figure 6.3). Similarly, the last segment of the polygon gives the slope of the tangent vector at the ending point.
- The nth derivative of the curve at the starting or ending point is determined by the first or last $(n + 1)$ vertices of the polygon. In fact, the second property is a special case of this property. This property is used very effectively when two Bezier curves need to be combined so that they satisfy the continuity of the higher order derivatives at the connection point.
- The same curve is generated when the order of the vertices of the polygon is reversed.

With these properties in mind, Bezier selected the Bernstein polynomial function as the blending function:

$$B_{i,n}(u) = \binom{n}{i} u^i (1-u)^{n-i} \qquad (6.15)$$

where

$$\binom{n}{i} = \frac{n!}{i!(n-i)!}$$

When the blending function defined by Equation (6.15) is applied to the vertices of the polygon, the equation of the Bezier curve is obtained:

$$\mathbf{P}(u) = \sum_{i=0}^{n} \binom{n}{i} u^i (1-u)^{n-i} \mathbf{P}_i \qquad (6.16)$$

where $\mathbf{P}_i$ is the position vector of the ith vertex. These vertices are called *control vertices* and the polygon obtained by connecting these vertices is called a *control polygon* because together they control the shape of the Bezier curve. Equation (6.16) indicates that the highest degree term is u^n for the curve defined by $(n + 1)$ control points. This means that the degree of the Bezier curve is determined by the number of control points. Figure 6.3 shows examples of Bezier curves of different degree for different numbers of control points.

Now we can show that the Bezier curve defined by Equation (6.16) satisfies the four properties described at the beginning of this section. First, let's examine whether the curve passes through the first and the last control points. This can be verified simply by substituting the values 0 and 1 for the parameter u. Hence we expand Equation (6.16) as follows:

$$\mathbf{P}(u) = \binom{n}{0}(1-u)^n \mathbf{P}_0 + \binom{n}{1}u(1-u)^{n-1}\mathbf{P}_1 + \binom{n}{2}u^2(1-u)^{n-2}\mathbf{P}_2$$

$$+ \cdots + \binom{n}{n-1}u^{n-1}(1-u)\mathbf{P}_{n+1} + \binom{n}{n}u^n\mathbf{P}_n$$

We obtain $\mathbf{P}(0)$ and $\mathbf{P}(1)$,

$$\mathbf{P}(0) = \binom{n}{0}\mathbf{P}_0 = \mathbf{P}_0$$

$$\mathbf{P}(1) = \binom{n}{n}\mathbf{P}_n = \mathbf{P}_n$$

and conclude that the curve passes through the first and the last control points.

The second and third properties can be verified from the differentiation of the Bezier curve equation, which we consider in the next section. The fourth property is verified by considering two curves defined as

$$\mathbf{P}(u) = \sum_{i=0}^{n} \binom{n}{i}u^i(1-u)^{n-i}\mathbf{P}_i \qquad (0 \le u \le 1) \tag{6.17}$$

and

$$\mathbf{P}^*(v) = \sum_{j=0}^{n} \binom{n}{j}v^j(1-v)^{n-j}\mathbf{Q}_j \qquad (\mathbf{Q}_j = \mathbf{P}_{n-j}, 0 \le v \le 1) \tag{6.18}$$

From Equations (6.17) and (6.18), $\mathbf{P}(u)$ can be interpreted to be a Bezier curve running from $\mathbf{P}_0$ to $\mathbf{P}_n$ while $\mathbf{P}^*(v)$ runs from $\mathbf{P}_n(=\mathbf{Q}_0)$ to $\mathbf{P}_0(=\mathbf{Q}_n)$. If we introduce a new parameter u^* and replace v with $(1 - u^*)$, the direction $\mathbf{P}^*$ will be reversed (i.e., it will run from $\mathbf{P}_0$ to $\mathbf{P}_n$ as u^* varies from 0 to 1). Thus we can say that the two curves $\mathbf{P}$ and $\mathbf{P}^*$ are identical if $\mathbf{P}^*(1 - u^*)$ is expanded to the same form as $\mathbf{P}(u)$, ex-

Figure 6.3

Bezier curves of different degrees

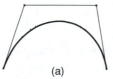

(a)

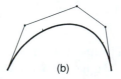

(b)

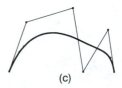

(c)

cept that a variable u^* is used instead of u. Therefore, it is necessary only to show that $\mathbf{P}^*(1-u)$ is the same as $\mathbf{P}(u)$. We obtain $\mathbf{P}^*(1-u)$ by substituting $(1-u)$ for v in Equation (6.18):

$$\mathbf{P}^*(1-u) = \sum_{j=0}^{n} \binom{n}{j} (1-u)^j u^{n-j} \mathbf{P}_{n-j} \tag{6.19}$$

We reformulate Equation (6.19) by replacing $(n-j)$ with i:

$$\mathbf{P}^*(1-u) = \sum_{i=n}^{0} \binom{n}{n-i} (1-u)^{n-i} u^i \mathbf{P}_i$$

$$= \sum_{i=0}^{n} \binom{n}{n-i} (1-u)^{n-i} u^i \mathbf{P}_i \tag{6.20}$$

As

$$\binom{n}{n-i}$$

equals

$$\binom{n}{i},$$

we conclude that Equation (6.20) is the same as Equation (6.17).

In addition to the properties of a Bezier curve described previously, another important property of a Bezier curve is the *convex hull property*. A convex hull of a Bezier curve is a convex polygon formed by connecting the control points of the curve, as illustrated by the hatched areas in Figure 6.4. Note that each of these Bezier curves resides completely inside its convex hull.

The convex hull property of a Bezier curve is based on each blending function for the curve having a value between 0 and 1, with their sum being 1 for any arbitrary value of u. We can easily verify this statement for a Bezier curve defined by two control points. A Bezier curve defined by $\mathbf{P}_0$ and $\mathbf{P}_1$ would be a straight line, and its convex hull would be the same straight line. Any point on this Bezier curve would be obtained by $\mathbf{P}_0 B_{0,1} + \mathbf{P}_1 B_{1,1}$. Because the blending functions $B_{0,1}$ and $B_{1,1}$ are positive and their sum equals 1 for any u, the point obtained by $\mathbf{P}_0 B_{0,1} + \mathbf{P}_1 B_{1,1}$ would be a point internally dividing the straight line from $\mathbf{P}_0$ to $\mathbf{P}_1$ in the ratio $B_{1,1} : B_{0,1}$ for any u. The straight line from $\mathbf{P}_0$ to $\mathbf{P}_1$ is a degenerate convex hull in this case, so we can say that all the points on the curve lie in the convex hull. Similarly, the statement for a Bezier curve defined by three or more control points can be verified as in Farin

Figure 6.4

Examples of convex hulls

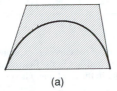

(a)

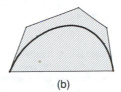

(b)

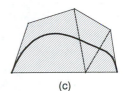

(c)

[1990]. The convex hull property is useful in calculating the intersection points of Bezier curves. A convex hull of a Bezier curve encloses the curve completely, so two Bezier curves cannot intersect each other if their convex hulls do not overlap. Thus we can skip the complicated intersection calculation for Bezier curves if their convex hulls do not overlap. The overlap test for convex hulls requires much less computation than the intersection calculation.

6.4.1   Differentiation of a Bezier Curve Equation

In addition to calculating the coordinates on a curve, calculating the curve's first- or higher order derivatives is also often required. For example, we need to calculate the first- and second-order derivatives to obtain the curvature of a curve. We also need the first-order derivative to calculate the intersection points of the curves, using the Newton–Raphson iteration [Conte and de Boor 1980].[9]

In this section, we derive the expression for the derivatives of a Bezier curve. This expression shows the relation between the derivatives of a Bezier curve and its original control points. For our derivation, we rewrite Equation (6.16) as

$$\mathbf{P}(u) = \sum_{i=0}^{n} \binom{n}{i} u^i (1-u)^{n-i} \mathbf{P}_i$$

We then differentiate this equation with respect to u:[10]

$$\frac{d\mathbf{P}(u)}{du} = \sum_{i=0}^{n} i \binom{n}{i} u^{i-1} (1-u)^{n-i} \mathbf{P}_i - \sum_{i=0}^{n} (n-i) \binom{n}{i} u^i (1-u)^{n-i-1} \mathbf{P}_i$$

$$= \sum_{i=1}^{n} i \binom{n}{i} u^{i-1} (1-u)^{n-i} \mathbf{P}_i - \sum_{i=0}^{n-1} (n-i) \binom{n}{i} u^i (1-u)^{n-i-1} \mathbf{P}_i \qquad (6.21)$$

$$= \sum_{j=0}^{n-1} (j+1) \binom{n}{j+1} u^j (1-u)^{n-j-1} \mathbf{P}_{j+1} - \sum_{i=0}^{n-1} (n-i) \binom{n}{i} u^i (1-u)^{n-i-1} \mathbf{P}_i$$

The terms

$$(j+1) \binom{n}{j+1}$$

and

$$(n-i) \binom{n}{i}$$

in Equation (6.21) can be expanded as follows:

$$(j+1) \binom{n}{j+1} = \frac{(j+1) n!}{(j+1)!(n-j-1)!} = \frac{n(n-1)!}{j!(n-j-1)!} = n \binom{n-1}{j} \qquad (6.22)$$

---

[9] The method used to calculate the intersection points of the curves is explained in Section 6.8.
[10] In the second line, the term corresponding to $i = 0$ vanishes in the first summation, and the term corresponding to $i = n$ vanishes in the second summation. In the third line, j is substituted for $i - 1$.

and

$$(n-i)\binom{n}{i} = \frac{(n-i)n!}{i!(n-i)!} = \frac{n(n-i)!}{i!(n-i-1)!} = n\binom{n-1}{i}$$

(6.23)

Substituting Equations (6.22) and (6.23) in Equation (6.21) gives

$$\frac{d\mathbf{P}(u)}{du} = \sum_{j=0}^{n-1} n\binom{n-1}{j}u^j(1-u)^{n-j-1}\mathbf{P}_{j+1} - \sum_{i=0}^{n-1} n\binom{n-1}{i}u^i(1-u)^{n-i-1}\mathbf{P}_i$$

$$= n\sum_{i=0}^{n-1}\binom{n-1}{i}u^i(1-u)^{n-i-1}\left(\mathbf{P}_{i+1} - \mathbf{P}_i\right)$$

(6.24)

By replacing $\mathbf{P}_{i+1} - \mathbf{P}$ with $\mathbf{a}_i$, we can express Equation (6.24) as

$$\frac{d\mathbf{P}(u)}{du} = n\sum_{i=0}^{n-1}\binom{n-1}{i}u^i(1-u)^{n-1-i}\mathbf{a}_i$$

(6.25)

The right-hand side of Equation (6.25), if the n in front of the summation symbol is ignored, is the same as the equation of a Bezier curve defined by the control points $\mathbf{a}_0, \mathbf{a}_1, \ldots, \mathbf{a}_{n-1}$. Thus the equation will hold:

$$\left[\sum_{i=0}^{n-1}\binom{n-1}{i}u^i(1-u)^{n-1-i}\mathbf{a}_i\right]_{u=0} = \mathbf{a}_0$$

(6.26)

and

$$\left[\sum_{i=0}^{n-1}\binom{n-1}{i}u^i(1-u)^{n-1-i}\mathbf{a}_i\right]_{u=1} = \mathbf{a}_{n-1}$$

(6.27)

Equations (6.26) and (6.27) are the mathematical expressions of the statement that a Bezier curve passes through the first and last control points.

From Equations (6.25), (6.26), and (6.27), we get the derivatives at the starting and the ending points as

$$\left.\frac{d\mathbf{P}}{du}\right|_{u=0} = n\mathbf{a}_0 = n(\mathbf{P}_1 - \mathbf{P}_0)$$

(6.28)

and

$$\left.\frac{d\mathbf{P}}{du}\right|_{u=1} = n\mathbf{a}_{n-1} = n(\mathbf{P}_n - \mathbf{P}_{n-1})$$

(6.29)

Thus we can say that the tangent vectors at the starting and ending points of a Bezier curve are in the same directions as the first and last segments of the control polygon, respectively. In addition, Equation (6.25) can be used recursively for higher order derivatives because its right-hand side has the form of the Bezier curve equation. Hence the second-order derivative is

$$\frac{d^2\mathbf{P}(u)}{du^2} = n(n-1)\sum_{i=0}^{n-2}\binom{n-2}{i}u^i(1-u)^{n-2-i}\mathbf{b}_i \qquad (6.30)$$

where $\mathbf{b}_i$ is $\mathbf{a}_{i+1} - \mathbf{a}_i$. Equation (6.30) tells us that the second-order derivative at the starting point is determined by $\mathbf{P}_0$, $\mathbf{P}_1$, and $\mathbf{P}_2$ and that $\mathbf{P}_{n-2}$, $\mathbf{P}_{n-1}$, and $\mathbf{P}_n$ determine the second-order derivative at the ending point. If we keep differentiating Equation (6.30), we can derive the higher order derivatives in the same way and show that the rth derivatives at the starting and ending points are determined by the first and last $(r+1)$ control points.

6.4.2   Evaluation of a Bezier Curve

Even when a curve is represented by an equation, say, a Bezier curve equation, the equation would be useless if the coordinates of the points on the curve could not be calculated efficiently. We know that simply to display the curve it is necessary to calculate the coordinates of the points on a curve at the parameter values of a small interval and to do so efficiently. Reviewing the equation of the Bezier curve given in Equation (6.15), we can expect that the combination function

$$\binom{n}{i}$$

in the blending function $B_{i,n}(u)$ has to be evaluated often, which requires a fair amount of computation. Thus we may need an algorithm that enables a direct evaluation of a point on a Bezier curve without calculating

$$\binom{n}{i}.$$

This algorithm is called the *de Casteljau algorithm* and is explained in Appendix F.

6.5   B-SPLINE CURVE

Recall that the degree of a Bezier curve is determined by the number of control points and also that any one control point affects the shape of the entire curve. These Bezier curve properties have two drawbacks. First, when a curve of a complicated shape is represented by a Bezier curve, inevitably many control points are used; this in turn results in a higher degree Bezier curve. The higher degree curve may cause oscillation as well as increase the computational burden. Why not then represent the same curve with many Bezier curves of lower degree to avoid these problems? The reason is that connecting the curves while maintaining continuity in the derivatives of the desired order at the connection points is not easy.

Second, modifying the shape of a curve locally is difficult. It would seem natural to adjust the control points near the portion of the curve to be modified, and it is actually possible to modify the desired portion in this way. However, moving a control point affects the shape of the entire curve, including the portion to be modified, and thus the portions that were not supposed to be modified may also change shape. This characteristic is called the *global modification property*. Global modification is undesirable when a curve of a specific shape is to be created because a curve is always created or designed by continuously modifying the rough shape of the initial curve. Thus the opposite characteristic of a curve, called the *local modification property*, is desirable in CAD systems.

The drawbacks to a Bezier curve described are due to the properties of its blending functions. Therefore we need to select a new set of blending functions with the following properties. First, contrary to $B_{i,n}(u)$ of a Bezier curve, the new blending function should not involve n in its definition. As a result, the degree of the blending function and thus the degree of the curve are independent of the number of control points because n is related to the number of control points. Second, all the blending functions should have nonzero values over only a limited portion of the parameter interval of the entire curve, and this limited portion is different for each blending function. Then the shape of a curve segment corresponding to a finite interval of the parameter value is affected only by those control points that are the counterparts of the blending functions with nonzero values over the same interval.

To satisfy these requirements, Cox [1972] and de Boor [1972] suggested the blending functions $N_{i,k}(u)$ defined by the recursive formulas in Equations (6.32) and (6.33). The curve based on these new blending functions is called the *B-spline curve* and is expressed as

$$\mathbf{P}(u) = \sum_{i=0}^{n} \mathbf{P}_i N_{i,k}(u) \qquad (t_{k-1} \le u \le t_{n+1}) \tag{6.31}$$

where

$$N_{i,k}(u) = \frac{(u - t_i)N_{i,k-1}(u)}{t_{i+k-1} - t_i} + \frac{(t_{i+k} - u)N_{i+1,k-1}(u)}{t_{i+k} - t_{i+1}} \tag{6.32}$$

$$N_{i,1}(u) = \begin{cases} 1 & t_i \le u \le t_{i+1} \\ 0 & \text{otherwise} \end{cases} \tag{6.33}$$

and t_i are the *knot values*, or the parameter values limiting the finite intervals over which the blending functions have nonzero values.[11] In Equation (6.32), 0/0 is presumed to be zero. As can be inferred from Equation (6.32), $(n + k + 1)$ knot values from t_0 to t_{n+k} need to be specified to define the $(n + 1)$ blending functions from

---

[11] We have to be cautious when u has the limit value of the interval because only one of $N_{i,1}(u)$ is allowed to have the nonzero value for any value of u. This is the presumption for the definition in Equation (6.32). When u equals t_1, for example, only one of $N_{0,1}(t_1)$ and $N_{1,1}(t_1)$ is allowed to have the value of 1 even though both of them can be interpreted to be 1 from Equation (6.33). Either choice will give the same value for $\mathbf{P}(t_1)$.

$N_{0,k}$ to $N_{n,k}$. According to the method used to specify these knot values, different B-spline blending functions and curves are derived. We explain later how to specify the knot values. Note from Equation (6.32) that all the knot values can be shifted (increased or decreased) by the same amount without affecting the curve's shape. In this case, the range of the parameter u also increases or decreases by the same amount, as indicated by Equation (6.31).

Let's now examine whether the blending function defined in Equations (6.32) and (6.33) satisfies the properties described at the beginning of this section. From Equation (6.32), we find that $N_{i,k}(u)$ is one degree higher in u than $N_{i,k-1}(u)$ and $N_{i+1,k-1}(u)$. Thus $N_{i,2}(u)$ is a function of degree 1 because $N_{i,1}(u)$ is a constant, and $N_{i,3}(u)$ has degree 2 for the same reason. Continuing the same reasoning shows that $N_{i,k}(u)$ has degree $(k-1)$. Thus we can select the degree of a B-spline curve regardless of the number of its control points by specifying k to be greater than the desired degree by 1. This value of k is called the *order of the B-spline curve*.

To show that a portion of a B-spline curve is affected only by a finite number of the control points, we focus on the curve segment corresponding to the parameter values in the closed interval $[t_i, t_{i+1}]$, that is, the ith knot span. Thus the control points that affect the shape of this segment would be those whose counterpart blending functions of order k are nonzero over the interval $[t_i, t_{i+1}]$. Among the blending functions of order 1, only $N_{i,1}(u)$ is nonzero over that interval. If we substitute this $N_{i,1}(u)$ in one of the two terms on the right-hand side of Equation (6.32), we can expect to get the nonzero blending function $N_{i,2}(u)$ or $N_{i-1,2}(u)$. That is, we obtain $N_{i,2}(u)$ by substituting $N_{i,1}(u)$ in the first term and $N_{i-1,2}(u)$ by substituting it in the second term. Then we propagate the effects of $N_{i,2}(u)$ and $N_{i-1,2}(u)$, respectively, into the blending functions of order 3, and so on until we reach the blending functions of order k. This pattern of propagation is illustrated in Figure 6.5.

From Figure 6.5, we conclude that only the blending functions $N_{i-k+1,k}$, $N_{i-k+2,k}$, ..., $N_{i,k}$ have nonzero values over the interval $[t_i, t_{i+1}]$. Therefore the control points affecting the shape of this curve segment would be $\mathbf{P}_{i-k+1}$, $\mathbf{P}_{i-k+2}$, ..., $\mathbf{P}_i$. That is, only k control points affect the shape of this segment. For example, only four control points will affect the shape of this segment if a B-spline curve of order 4 is used, and all other control points will have no effect on it.

Figure 6.5

Propagation pattern of the effect of $N_{i,1}(u)$

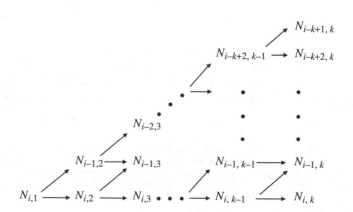

We now need to determine $(n + k + 1)$ knot values from t_0 to t_{n+k}. There are basically two types of knots: periodic knots and nonperiodic knots. *Periodic knots* are determined from

$$t_i = i - k \quad (0 \le i \le n + k) \tag{6.34}$$

and *nonperiodic knots* are determined from

$$t_i = \begin{cases} 0 & 0 \le i < k \\ i - k + 1 & k \le i \le n \\ n - k + 2 & n < i \le n + k \end{cases} \tag{6.35}$$

The main difference between the two types of knots is that the first and last nonperiodic knots are duplicated k times. These multiple knots make a nonperiodic B-spline curve pass through the first and the last control points as with a Bezier curve. In a periodic B-spline curve, however, the first and the last control points make the same contribution to the curve shape as the other control points, and thus the curve does not pass through them. In fact, the blending function for periodic knots repeats itself identically over successive intervals of the parametric variable, which is the reason for the name *periodic knot*. The nonperiodic B-spline curve is more popular in CAD systems because most designers are familiar with curves that pass through the first and last control points.

Equations (6.34) and (6.35) reveal that the gap between neighboring knots is always uniform, with a value of 1. These knots are called *uniform knots*, and a B-spline curve based on uniform knots is called a *uniform B-spline curve*. A uniform B-spline curve can be either periodic or nonperiodic. As we modify the shape of a curve, we often add[12] or delete knot values and so produce nonuniform gaps between the knots. In this case, the resulting B-spline curve is a nonuniform B-spline curve. Because uniform knots can be considered to be a special case of nonuniform knots, nonuniform B-splines are considered the general form of B-spline curves. Thus most CAD systems provide the capability of creating and modifying nonperiodic and nonuniform B-spline curves.

The following examples will help clarify the concepts introduced so far.

EXAMPLE 6.3

Expand the equation of a nonperiodic uniform B-spline curve of order 3 in polynomial form. Assume that the control points of the curve are $\mathbf{P}_0$, $\mathbf{P}_1$, and $\mathbf{P}_2$.

ANSWER

From Equation (6.35), the knot values t_i are

$$t_0 = 0, \quad t_1 = 0, \quad t_2 = 0, \quad t_3 = 1, \quad t_4 = 1, \quad t_5 = 1$$

---

[12] When we create a surface from a set of B-spline curves, we have to make the knot values of all the curves the same by adding knot values of other curves. A detailed description is presented in Tiller [1983].

and the parameter u ranges from 0 to 1. Let's use Equation (6.33) to obtain the blending functions of order 1, $N_{i,1}(u)$:

$$N_{0,1}(u) = \begin{cases} 1 & t_0 \leq u \leq t_1 \quad (u = 0) \\ 0 & \text{otherwise} \end{cases}$$

$$N_{1,1}(u) = \begin{cases} 1 & t_1 \leq u \leq t_2 \quad (u = 0) \\ 0 & \text{otherwise} \end{cases}$$

$$N_{2,1}(u) = \begin{cases} 1 & t_2 \leq u \leq t_3 \quad (u \leq 1) \\ 0 & \text{otherwise} \end{cases}$$

$$N_{3,1}(u) = \begin{cases} 1 & t_3 \leq u \leq t_4 \quad (u = 1) \\ 0 & \text{otherwise} \end{cases}$$

$$N_{4,1}(u) = \begin{cases} 1 & t_4 \leq u \leq t_5 \quad (u = 1) \\ 0 & \text{otherwise} \end{cases}$$

From among $N_{0,1}(u)$, $N_{1,1}(u)$, and $N_{2,1}(u)$, we choose $N_{2,1}(u)$ to be the blending function having nonzero value at $u = 0$. Similarly, we choose $N_{2,1}(u)$ from among $N_{2,1}(u)$, $N_{3,1}(u)$, and $N_{4,1}(u)$ to be the blending function having nonzero value at $u = 1$. Thus $N_{2,1}(u)$ becomes the only nonzero blending function of order 1 in the parameter range [0,1] and has a constant value of 1 over the entire range.

Thus we obtain the nontrivial blending functions of order 2 from Equation (6.32) as follows:[13]

$$N_{1,2}(u) = \frac{(u - t_1)N_{1,1}}{t_2 - t_1} + \frac{(t_3 - u)N_{2,1}}{t_3 - t_2} = \frac{(1 - u)N_{2,1}}{1}$$

$$= (1 - u)$$

$$N_{2,2}(u) = \frac{(u - t_2)N_{2,1}}{t_3 - t_2} + \frac{(t_4 - u)N_{3,1}}{t_4 - t_3} = \frac{uN_{2,1}}{1}$$

$$= u$$

Similarly, we get the blending functions of order 3, $N_{i,3}(u)$:

$$N_{0,3}(u) = \frac{(u - t_0)N_{0,2}}{t_3 - t_1} + \frac{(t_3 - u)N_{1,2}}{t_4 - t_2} = \frac{(1 - u)N_{1,2}}{1} = (1 - u)^2$$

$$N_{1,3}(u) = \frac{(u - t_1)N_{1,2}}{t_3 - t_1} + \frac{(t_4 - u)N_{2,2}}{t_4 - t_2} = u(1 - u) + (1 - u)u = 2u(1 - u)$$

$$N_{2,3}(u) = \frac{(u - t_2)N_{2,2}}{t_4 - t_2} + \frac{(t_5 - u)N_{3,2}}{t_5 - t_3}$$

$$= u^2$$

---

[13] In the equation for $N_{1,2}(u)$, the first term containing $N_{1,1}$ is zero because it is 0/0.

Then the expanded equation of the B-spline curve is

$$P(u) = (1-u)^2 P_0 + 2u\,(1-u)P_1 + u^2 P_2 \tag{6.36}$$

The equation of the Bezier curve defined by the control points P_0, P_1, and P_2 can be expanded as

$$P(u) = \binom{2}{0}_0 u^0 (1-u)^2 P_0 + \binom{2}{1}_1 u^1 (1-u)^1 P_1 + \binom{2}{2}_2 u^2 (1-u)^0 P_2$$

$$= (1-u)^2 P_0 + 2u(1-u)P_1 + u^2 P_2 \tag{6.37}$$

Comparing Equations (6.36) and (6.37) shows that the nonperiodic, uniform B-spline curve of order 3 defined by the control points P_0, P_1, and P_2 is the same as the Bezier curve defined by the same control points. Thus, in general, we can say that a nonperiodic, uniform B-spline curve is the same as the Bezier curve defined by the same control points if order k equals the number of the control points $(n+1)$. In other words, a Bezier curve is simply a special case of a B-spline curve.

EXAMPLE 6.4

Expand the equation of a nonperiodic, uniform B-spline curve of order 3 defined by the control points P_0, P_1, ..., P_5 in polynomial form and show its local modification capability.

ANSWER
From Equation (6.35), the knot values t_1 are

$$t_0 = 0, \quad t_1 = 0, \quad t_2 = 0, \quad t_3 = 1, \quad t_4 = 2, \quad t_5 = 3, \quad t_6 = 4, \quad t_7 = 4, \quad t_8 = 4$$

and the parameter u will range from 0 to 4. Let's use Equation (6.33) to obtain the blending functions of order 1, $N_{i,1}(u)$:

$$N_{2,1}(u) = \begin{cases} 1 & 0 \leq u \leq 1 \\ 0 & \text{otherwise} \end{cases}$$

$$N_{3,1}(u) = \begin{cases} 1 & 1 \leq u \leq 2 \\ 0 & \text{otherwise} \end{cases}$$

$$N_{4,1}(u) = \begin{cases} 1 & 2 \leq u \leq 3 \\ 0 & \text{otherwise} \end{cases}$$

$$N_{5,1}(u) = \begin{cases} 1 & 3 \leq u \leq 4 \\ 0 & \text{otherwise} \end{cases}$$

We ignore $N_{0,1}(u)$ and $N_{1,1}(u)$ by choosing $N_{2,1}(u)$ to be the only nonzero blending function at $u = 0$. Similarly, we ignore $N_{6,1}(u)$ and $N_{7,1}(u)$. Now we obtain the nontrivial blending functions of order 2 from Equation (6.32) as follows:

$$N_{1,2}(u) = \frac{(u - t_1)N_{1,1}}{t_2 - t_1} + \frac{(t_3 - u)N_{2,1}}{t_3 - t_2} = (1 - u)N_{2,1}$$

$$N_{2,2}(u) = \frac{(u - t_2)N_{2,1}}{t_3 - t_2} + \frac{(t_4 - u)N_{3,1}}{t_4 - t_3} = uN_{2,1} + (2 - u)N_{3,1}$$

$$N_{3,2}(u) = \frac{(u - t_3)N_{3,1}}{t_4 - t_3} + \frac{(t_5 - u)N_{4,1}}{t_5 - t_4} = (u - 1)N_{3,1} + (3 - u)N_{4,1}$$

$$N_{4,2}(u) = \frac{(u - t_4)N_{4,1}}{t_5 - t_4} + \frac{(t_6 - u)N_{5,1}}{t_6 - t_5} = (u - 2)N_{4,1} + (4 - u)N_{5,1}$$

$$N_{5,2}(u) = \frac{(u - t_5)N_{5,1}}{t_6 - t_5} + \frac{(t_7 - u)N_{6,1}}{t_7 - t_6} = (u - 3)N_{5,1}$$

Similarly, we get the blending functions of order 3, $N_{i,3}(u)$:

$$N_{0,3}(u) = \frac{(u - t_0)N_{0,2}}{t_2 - t_0} + \frac{(t_3 - u)N_{1,2}}{t_3 - t_1} = (1 - u)N_{1,2} = (1 - u)^2 N_{2,1}$$

$$N_{1,3}(u) = \frac{(u - t_1)N_{1,2}}{t_3 - t_1} + \frac{(t_4 - u)N_{2,2}}{t_4 - t_2} = uN_{1,2} + \frac{2 - u}{2} N_{2,2}$$

$$= \left[u(1 - u) + \frac{(2 - u)u}{2} \right] N_{2,1} + \frac{(2 - u)^2}{2} N_{3,1}$$

$$N_{2,3}(u) = \frac{(u - t_2)N_{2,2}}{t_4 - t_2} + \frac{(t_5 - u)N_{3,2}}{t_5 - t_3} = \frac{u}{2} N_{2,2} + \frac{3 - u}{2} N_{3,2}$$

$$= \frac{u^2}{2} N_{2,1} + \left[\frac{u(2 - u)}{2} + \frac{(3 - u)(u - 1)}{2} \right] N_{3,1} + \frac{(3 - u)^2}{2} N_{4,1}$$

$$N_{3,3}(u) = \frac{(u - t_3)N_{3,2}}{t_5 - t_3} + \frac{(t_6 - u)N_{4,2}}{t_6 - t_4} = \frac{u - 1}{2} N_{3,2} + \frac{4 - u}{2} N_{4,2}$$

$$= \frac{(u - 1)^2}{2} N_{3,1} + \left[\frac{(u - 1)(3 - u)}{2} + \frac{(4 - u)(u - 2)}{2} \right] N_{4,1} + \frac{(4 - u)^2}{2} N_{5,1}$$

$$N_{4,3}(u) = \frac{(u - t_4)N_{4,2}}{t_6 - t_4} + \frac{(t_7 - u)N_{5,2}}{t_7 - t_5} = \frac{u - 2}{2} N_{4,2} + (4 - u)N_{5,2}$$

$$= \frac{(u - 2)^2}{2} N_{4,1} + \left[\frac{(u - 2)(4 - u)}{2} + (4 - u)(u - 3) \right] N_{5,1}$$

$$N_{5,3}(u) = \frac{(u - t_5)N_{5,2}}{t_7 - t_5} + \frac{(t_8 - u)N_{6,2}}{t_8 - t_6} = (u - 3)N_{5,2} = (u - 3)^2 N_{5,1}$$

Then the expanded equation of the B-spline curve is

$$\mathbf{P}(u) = (1-u)^2 N_{2,1}\mathbf{P}_0 + \left\{ \left[u(1-u) + \frac{(2-u)u}{2} \right] N_{2,1} + \frac{(2-u)^2}{2} N_{3,1} \right\} \mathbf{P}_1$$

$$+ \left\{ \frac{u^2}{2} N_{2,1} + \left[\frac{u(2-u)}{2} + \frac{(3-u)(u-1)}{2} \right] N_{3,1} + \frac{(3-u)^2}{2} N_{4,1} \right\} \mathbf{P}_2$$

$$+ \left\{ \frac{(u-1)^2}{2} N_{3,1} + \left[\frac{(u-1)(3-u)}{2} + \frac{(4-u)(u-2)}{2} \right] N_{4,1} + \frac{(4-u)^2}{2} N_{5,1} \right\} \mathbf{P}_3 \quad (6.38)$$

$$+ \left\{ \frac{(u-2)^2}{2} N_{4,1} + \left[\frac{(u-2)(4-u)}{2} + (4-u)(u-3) \right] N_{5,1} \right\} \mathbf{P}_4$$

$$+ (u-3)^2 N_{5,1}\mathbf{P}_5$$

The form of Equation (6.38) may lead you to expect that modification of any one control point will change the shape of the entire curve. However, rewriting Equation (6.38) separately for each subinterval of parameter u would show that each curve segment is affected only by the subset of the control points.

Consider the subinterval $0 \leq u \leq 1$ and let $\mathbf{P}_1(u)$ denote the curve equation of the corresponding portion (i.e., the first curve segment). For the parameter value in $0 \leq u \leq 1$, all $N_{i,1}$ except $N_{2,1}$ can be ignored and $N_{2,1}$ has a value of 1. Hence we can simplify Equation (6.38) as follows:

$$\mathbf{P}_1(u) = (1-u)^2 \mathbf{P}_0 + \left[u(1-u) + \frac{(2-u)u}{2} \right] \mathbf{P}_1 + \frac{u^2}{2} \mathbf{P}_2 \quad (0 \leq u \leq 1) \quad (6.39)$$

Similarly, we can obtain the curve equation $\mathbf{P}_2(u)$ corresponding to $1 \leq u \leq 2$ by leaving only the terms involving $N_{3,1}(u)$:

$$\mathbf{P}_2(u) = \frac{(2-u)^2}{2} \mathbf{P}_1 + \left[\frac{u(2-u)}{2} + \frac{(3-u)(u-1)}{2} \right] \mathbf{P}_2 + \frac{(u-1)^2}{2} \mathbf{P}_3 \quad (1 \leq u \leq 2) \quad (6.40)$$

We also obtain the curve equations $\mathbf{P}_3(u)$ and $\mathbf{P}_4(u)$, corresponding to $2 \leq u \leq 3$ and $3 \leq u \leq 4$, respectively, in the same way:

$$\mathbf{P}_3(u) = \frac{(3-u)^2}{2} \mathbf{P}_2 + \frac{1}{2}(-2u^2 + 10u - 11)\mathbf{P}_3 + \frac{(u-2)^2}{2} \mathbf{P}_4 \quad (2 \leq u \leq 3) \quad (6.41)$$

$$\mathbf{P}_4(u) = \frac{(4-u)^2}{2} \mathbf{P}_3 + \frac{1}{2}(-3u^2 + 20u - 32)\mathbf{P}_4 + (u-3)^2 \mathbf{P}_5 \quad (3 \leq u \leq 4) \quad (6.42)$$

We can draw each segment of the B-spline curve by assigning the proper values to control points $\mathbf{P}_0$, $\mathbf{P}_1$, . . ., $\mathbf{P}_5$ in Equations (6.39)–(6.42); Figure 6.6 illustrates one example of this approach. Note the following important properties of B-spline curves from Figure 6.6.

Figure 6.6

A B-spline curve
composed of curve
segments

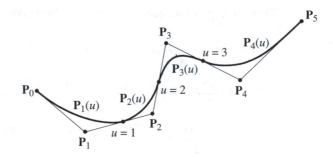

- Any B-spline curve is a composite curve of several different curves (e.g., $\mathbf{P}_1(u)$, $\mathbf{P}_2(u)$, $\mathbf{P}_3(u)$, and $\mathbf{P}_4(u)$ in this example). These separate curves are joined at the points at which the parameter values are the knot values. For the curve in this example, the relations $\mathbf{P}_1'(1) = \mathbf{P}_2'(1)$, $\mathbf{P}_2'(2) = \mathbf{P}_3'(2)$, and $\mathbf{P}_3'(3) = \mathbf{P}_4'(3)$ hold at the connection points. This can be verified by evaluating the derivatives of Equations (6.39)–(6.42). These relationships mean that first-order continuity holds between the curve segments. In the same way we can also verify that second-order continuity is not satisfied at the connection points. This result can be easily anticipated from the fact that Equations (6.39)–(6.42) have degree 2. In general, the derivatives of up to order $(k-2)$ are continuous across the curve segments comprising an original B-spline curve because each segment has degree $(k-1)$. For example, a B-spline curve of order 4 will have first- and second-order continuity across the curve segments.

- Each curve segment is affected by k control points, as shown by Equations (6.39)–(6.42). Thus the first k (order) control points starting from the first control point specify the shape of the first segment, the next k control points starting from the second control point do the same for the second segment, and so on until the last k control points specify the $(n-k+2)$th curve segment, as illustrated in Figure 6.7.

- Figure 6.7, reveals that the maximum number of curve segments affected by one control point equals order k. We can verify this statement by counting the groups containing a control point P_{k-1}, for example. Therefore we conclude that any control point affects the shape of at most k curve segments in its neighborhood. This implies the local modification capability of B-spline curves.

Figure 6.7

Grouping of con-
trol points for each
curve segment

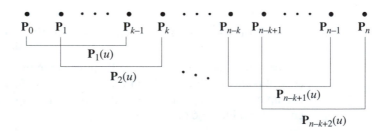

6.5.1 Evaluation of a B-Spline Curve

As we demonstrated in the preceding examples, it is not easy to expand the blending functions of a B-spline curve in polynomial form. This task is especially tedious if the order k is very high. Thus we usually do not resort to use of the polynomial form of a B-spline equation in evaluating the coordinates of points on the curve. Instead, we keep substituting specific u values into the recursive formula in Equation (6.32) to get the numerical coordinates of the points corresponding to those u values. Meanwhile, Cox [1972] and de Boor [1972] suggested that Equation (6.32) be rearranged so that the recursive substitution be replaced by an iteration similar to the one in the de Casteljau algorithm. Thus their method also gives the control points of the B-spline curves subdivided at the point being evaluated, as shown in Appendix G.

6.5.2 Composition of B-Spline Curves

Besides subdividing a B-spline curve into two B-spline curves, we can also find a composite B-spline curve equivalent to two B-spline curves of the same order connected at one end of each B-spline curve. This is called a *composition of B-spline curves*, and the task involved is to find the control points and the knot values of the composite curve. For those interested in this procedure, Appendix H describes it.

6.5.3 Differentiation of a B-Spline Curve

We have shown that the derivative of a Bezier curve is expressed in the form of a Bezier curve equation of 1 degree less than the original curve. Similarly, the derivative of a B-spline curve is expressed in the form of a B-spline curve equation of 1 degree less than the original curve. The derivative of a B-spline curve, when u is in the interval $t_l \le u \le t_{l+1}$ (the proof is given in Appendix I) is

$$\frac{d\mathbf{P}(u)}{du} = \sum_{i=l-k+2}^{l} \mathbf{P}_i^1 N_{i,k-1}(u) \tag{6.43}$$

where P_i^1 is defined as

$$\mathbf{P}_i^1 = (k-1)\frac{\mathbf{P}_i - \mathbf{P}_{i-1}}{t_{i+k-1} - t_i} \tag{6.44}$$

As the right-hand side of Equation (6.43) has the form of a B-spline curve equation, we can expect that higher order derivatives can also be derived by applying Equation (6.43) recursively. Hence the rth derivative of a B-spline curve is

$$\frac{d\mathbf{P}^r(u)}{du^r} = \sum_{i=l-k+r+1}^{l} \mathbf{P}_i^r N_{i,k-r}(u) \tag{6.45}$$

where

$$\mathbf{P}_i^r = (k - r) \frac{\mathbf{P}_i^{r-1} - \mathbf{P}_{i-1}^{r-1}}{t_{i+k-r} - t_i} \tag{6.46}$$

Equation (6.45) holds when u is in the interval $t_l \leq u \leq t_{l+1}$, and P_i^r in Equation (6.46) implies P_i, as before. Furthermore, the numerical values of the derivatives can be evaluated by the Cox–de Boor algorithm because Equations (6.43) and (6.45) have the form of a B-spline curve equation.

EXAMPLE 6.5

Calculate the first-order derivative of a B-spline curve at its end points, using Equations (6.43) and (6.44). The B-spline curve has order k and control points $\mathbf{P}_0$, $\mathbf{P}_1, \ldots, \mathbf{P}_n$.

ANSWER

The parameter value corresponding to the starting point of the B-spline is $t_0 = t_1 = \cdots = t_{k-1}$, and the curve segment of interest is the first one corresponding to the parameter interval $t_{k-1} \leq u \leq t_k$. Hence we obtain the derivative at the starting point by substituting $(k - 1)$ for l and t_{k-1} for u in Equation (6.43):

$$\frac{d\mathbf{P}(t_{k-1})}{du} = \sum_{i=1}^{k-1} \mathbf{P}_i^1 N_{i,k-1}(t_{k-1})$$

The term on the right-hand side of this equation has the form of a B-spline curve, and $u = t_{k-1}$ corresponds to the starting point of the curve. Therefore $\sum_{i=1}^{k-1} P_i^1 N_{i,k-1}(t_{k-1})$ should equal the first control point, $\mathbf{P}_1^1$. Hence the first-order derivative of the original B-spline curve at the starting point is

$$\frac{d\mathbf{P}(t_{k-1})}{du} = \mathbf{P}_1^1 N_{1,k-1}(t_{k-1}) = \mathbf{P}_1^1 = (k - 1) \frac{\mathbf{P}_1 - \mathbf{P}_0}{t_k - t_1}$$

We can obtain the derivative at the other end in the same way. The parameter value corresponding to the ending point equals t_{n+1}, and the curve segment of interest has the parameter interval $t_n \leq u \leq t_{n+1}$. Thus, substituting n for l in Equation (6.43) gives

$$\frac{d\mathbf{P}(t_{n+1})}{du} = \sum_{i=n-k+2}^{n} \mathbf{P}_i^1 N_{i,k-1}(t_{n+1})$$

The term on the right-hand side of this equation is again a B-spline curve, and $u = t_{n+1}$ corresponds to the ending point of the curve. Therefore $\sum_{i=n-k+2}^{n} P_i^1 N_{i,k-1}(t_{n+1})$ equals the last control point, $\mathbf{P}_n^1$. The first-order derivative of the original B-spline curve then is

$$\frac{d\mathbf{P}(t_{n+1})}{du} = \mathbf{P}_n^1 = (k - 1) \frac{\mathbf{P}_n - \mathbf{P}_{n-1}}{t_{n+k-1} - t_n}$$

In the preceding example, we identified yet another important property of a B-spline curve: The tangent vector at the starting or ending point is in the same direction as the direction of the first or last edge of the control polygon. We already know that Bezier curves have this property, too.

6.6 NONUNIFORM RATIONAL B-SPLINE (NURBS) CURVE

A *nonuniform rational B-spline curve*, or simply a NURBS curve, is similar to a nonuniform B-spline curve in that it uses the same blending functions derived from the nonuniform knots as those of nonuniform B-spline curves. However, the control points are given in the form $(x_i \cdot h_i, y_i \cdot h_i, z_i \cdot h_i, h_i)$, using the homogeneous coordinates h_i instead of (x_i, y_i, z_i), and these four coordinates are blended by the blending functions. Thus the coordinates of a point on a NURBS curve in the homogeneous space, $(x \cdot h, y \cdot h, z \cdot h, h)$, are obtained from

$$x \cdot h = \sum_{i=0}^{n} (h_i \cdot x_i) N_{i,k}(u) \tag{6.47}$$

$$y \cdot h = \sum_{i=0}^{n} (h_i \cdot y_i) N_{i,k}(u) \tag{6.48}$$

$$z \cdot h = \sum_{i=0}^{n} (h_i \cdot z_i) N_{i,k}(u) \tag{6.49}$$

$$h = \sum_{i=0}^{n} h_i N_{i,k}(u) \tag{6.50}$$

The x, y, and z coordinates of a point can be obtained by dividing $x \cdot h$, $y \cdot h$, and $z \cdot h$ by h, so the equation of NURBS curve $\mathbf{P}(u)$ is derived by dividing Equations (6.47), (6.48), and (6.49) by Equation (6.50):

$$\mathbf{P}(u) = \frac{\sum_{i=0}^{n} h_i \mathbf{P}_i N_{i,k}(u)}{\sum_{i=0}^{n} h_i N_{i,k}(u)} \tag{6.51}$$

where $\mathbf{P}_i$ is a position vector composed of (x_i, y_i, z_i), which are the x, y, and z coordinates of the ith control point in three-dimensional space, as for the nonrational B-spline curves. The parameter interval of the curve is $t_{k-1} \le u \le t_{n+1}$, as in the B-spline curve in the preceding section.

Equation (6.51) reveals the following properties of a NURBS curve.

• Similar to a nonrational B-spline curve, a NURBS curve represented by Equation (6.51) passes through the first and the last control points if nonperiodic knots are used. This statement can be proved as follows. The numerator in Equation (6.51) can be considered to be a B-spline curve whose control points are $h_i \mathbf{P}_i$. Thus the coordinates corresponding to the lower and upper limits of the parameter value would be $h_0\mathbf{P}_0$ and $h_n\mathbf{P}_n$, respectively, because the B-spline curve with nonperiodic knots should pass through the first and last control points. Similarly, the denominator of Equation (6.51) can again be considered to be a B-spline whose control points are h_i. Thus its values corresponding to the lower and the upper limits of parameter values would be h_0 and h_n, respectively. Therefore the values of $\mathbf{P}(u)$ at the lower and the upper limits of the parameter value will be $\mathbf{P}_0$ and $\mathbf{P}_n$, which are the first and last control points.

- The tangent vector at the starting point is in the same direction as $\mathbf{P}_1 - \mathbf{P}_0$, and at the ending point it is in the same directions as $\mathbf{P}_n - \mathbf{P}_{n-1}$. Verification of this statement is given in Section 6.6.2.

- The denominator in Equation (6.51) becomes 1 when all h_is equal 1 because $\sum_{i=0}^{n} N_{i,k}(u)$ is 1.[14] Equation (6.51) then becomes the equation of a B-spline curve. Therefore we can say that the NURBS curve equation is a general form that can represent both B-spline and NURBS curves. A Bezier curve is considered to be a special case of a B-spline curve, so the NURBS equation can also represent Bezier and rational Bezier curves.[15]

A NURBS curve equation has some advantages over a B-spline equation.

- The shape of a B-spline curve is modified by changing the x, y, and z coordinates of the control points; that is, three degrees of freedom are allowed for each control point. However, the homogeneous coordinates h_i in addition to the x, y, and z coordinates of each control point can be changed in a NURBS curve. Thus a more versatile modification of a curve becomes possible if the curve is represented by a NURBS equation. Increasing the value of the homogeneous coordinate of a control point has the effect of drawing a curve toward the control point.

- The conic curves—circles, ellipses, parabolas, and hyperbolas—can be exactly represented by NURBS equations. By contrast, these curves can be represented by B-spline equations only in an approximate manner. Thus the curves such as conic curves, Bezier curves, rational Bezier curves, and B-spline curves can be converted to their corresponding NURBS representations as required. This conversion may reduce the amount of computer coding enormously. For example, we may need develop only one intersection program for NURBS curves and use it for the intersections of any two curves if they belong to the types mentioned because those curves can be converted to the corresponding NURBS representations.

To demonstrate how to derive the NURBS representation of conic curves, we give an example of representing a circular arc in a NURBS equation by simply extracting the result given in Piegl and Tiller [1987]. In other words, we present the order, the coordinates of the control points (including the homogeneous coordi-

---

[14] The proof of $\sum_{i=0}^{n} N_{i,k}(u) = 1$ is presented in Bartels, Beatty, and Barsky [1987].
[15] The rational Bezier curve equation is obtained by substituting $B_{i,n}(u)$ for $N_{i,k}(u)$ in Equation (6.51). That is, the blending functions for Bezier curves are used with the control points specified by using homogeneous coordinates.

Figure 6.8

Control points of a NURBS curve equivalent to a circular arc

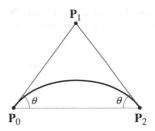

nates), and the knot values of the NURBS curve equivalent to a circular arc. The NURBS representation of other conic curves is also discussed in Piegl and Tiller [1987]. A circular arc is a quadric curve of degree 2, so we can expect the NURBS curve of the circular arc to have order 3. Piegl showed that just three control points are sufficient if the center angle of a circular arc is less than 180 degrees. Thus we will use three control points, as illustrated in Figure 6.8. From the properties of a NURBS curve described previously, we know that the control points $\mathbf{P}_0$ and $\mathbf{P}_2$ should be located at the end points of the circular arc and that $\mathbf{P}_1$ is obtained by the intersection of the tangent lines through the end points.

Now we have to determine the homogeneous coordinates h_0, h_1, and h_2. If all these homogeneous coordinates were 1s, the resulting curve would be a regular B-spline curve and would not represent a circular arc exactly. However, Piegl found that the homogeneous values $h_0 = h_2 = 1$ and $h_1 = \cos\theta$ result in a circular arc exactly. Here, θ is the angle between either tangent line and the line segment $\mathbf{P}_0\mathbf{P}_2$, as shown in Figure 6.8. Thus $\mathbf{P}_1$ will not be defined and, accordingly, θ will not be defined when the center angle for a circular arc is greater than or equal to 180 degrees. In this case, we split the circular arc into pieces so that each piece has a center angle less than 180 degrees. Then a NURBS representation is derived for each piece, and the individual NURBS representations are composed into one composite NURBS curve. We can derive a composite NURBS curve from NURBS curves the same way that we derived a composite curve from B-spline curves in Appendix G. That is, the control points of the composite curve become the simple union of each control point set of each NURBS curve. The knot values of the composite curve are obtained by merging the several sets of knot values after shifting each set so that there are no abrupt jumps in the knot values at the connections. Then some of the knot values are eliminated so that they are repeated only $(k-1)$ times at every connection.

EXAMPLE 6.6

Derive a NURBS representation of a half circle of radius 1 in the xy plane. In other words, determine its order, the coordinates of the control points (including the homogeneous coordinates), and the knot values.

ANSWER

Consider the accompanying drawing of a half circle. The order k is 3 because a circle is a quadric curve. We will split the half circle into two circular arcs, 1 and 2, because the half circle has a center angle of 180 degrees. Of course, there are many ways to split the given arc.

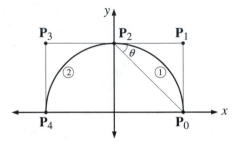

Let's consider arc 1 first. The x, y, and z coordinates of its control points are

$$\mathbf{P}_0 = (1, 0), \quad \mathbf{P}_1 = (1, 1), \quad \mathbf{P}_2 = (0, 1)$$

and their homogeneous coordinates are $h_0 = 1$, $h_1 = \cos 45° = 1/\sqrt{2}$, and $h_2 = 1$. The knot values are derived to be 0, 0, 0, 1, 1, 1 for $n = 2$ and $k = 3$.

Following the same procedure for arc 2 we obtain

$$\mathbf{P}_2 = (0, 1), \quad \mathbf{P}_3 = (-1, 1), \quad \mathbf{P}_4 = (-1, 0)$$

and

$$h_2 = 1, \qquad h_3 = \frac{1}{\sqrt{2}}, \qquad h_4 = 1$$

The knot values are 0, 0, 0, 1, 1, 1 but are shifted to 1, 1, 1, 2, 2, 2 for the composition to be followed.

The two NURBS representations are formed into a composite curve, which has $\mathbf{P}_i$ and h_i of

$$\mathbf{P}_0 = (1, 0), \quad \mathbf{P}_1 = (1, 1), \quad \mathbf{P}_2 = (0, 1), \quad \mathbf{P}_3 = (-1, 1), \quad \mathbf{P}_4 = (-1, 0)$$

and

$$h_0 = 1, \qquad h_1 = \frac{1}{\sqrt{2}}, \qquad h_2 = 1, \qquad h_3 = \frac{1}{\sqrt{2}}, \qquad h_4 = 1$$

The knot values are 0, 0, 0, 1, 1, 2, 2, 2.

EXAMPLE 6.7

Expand the NURBS equation of arc 1 in Example 6.6 and show that it represents the circular arc exactly.

ANSWER

The NURBS equation of arc 1 is

$$\mathbf{P}(u) = \frac{h_0 \mathbf{P}_0 N_{0,3}(u) + h_1 \mathbf{P}_1 N_{1,3}(u) + h_2 \mathbf{P}_2 N_{2,3}(u)}{h_0 N_{0,3}(u) + h_1 N_{1,3}(u) + h_2 N_{2,3}(u)} \tag{a}$$

We obtain the blending functions $N_{0,3}(u)$, $N_{1,3}(u)$, and $N_{2,3}(u)$ recursively as follows:

$$N_{2,1} = \begin{cases} 1 & 0 \le u \le 1 \\ 0 & \text{otherwise} \end{cases}$$

$$N_{1,2}(u) = \frac{(t_3 - u)N_{2,1}(u)}{t_3 - t_2} = (1 - u)$$

$$N_{2,2}(u) = \frac{(u - t_2)N_{2,1}(u)}{t_3 - t_2} = u$$

$$N_{0,3}(u) = \frac{(t_3 - u)N_{1,2}(u)}{t_3 - t_1} = (1 - u)^2$$

$$N_{1,3}(u) = \frac{(u - t_1)N_{1,2}(u)}{t_3 - t_1} + \frac{(t_4 - u)N_{2,2}(u)}{t_4 - t_2} = 2u(1 - u)$$

$$N_{2,3}(u) = \frac{(u - t_2)N_{2,2}(u)}{t_4 - t_2} = u^2$$

Hence we can expand the NURBS equation, Equation (a), as follows:

$$P(u) = \frac{1 \cdot \begin{pmatrix} 1 \\ 0 \\ 0 \end{pmatrix}(1-u)^2 + \frac{\sqrt{2}}{2}\begin{pmatrix} 1 \\ 1 \\ 0 \end{pmatrix}2u(1-u) + 1 \cdot \begin{pmatrix} 0 \\ 1 \\ 0 \end{pmatrix}u^2}{1 \cdot (1-u)^2 + \frac{\sqrt{2}}{2} \cdot 2u(1-u) + 1 \cdot u^2} \tag{b}$$

Let's denote the x and y terms in Equation (b) $x(u)$ and $y(u)$, respectively. Then $x(u)$ and $y(u)$ can be expressed as

$$x(u) = \frac{(1 - \sqrt{2})u^2 + \sqrt{2}(1 - \sqrt{2})u + 1}{(2 - \sqrt{2})u^2 + (\sqrt{2} - 2)u + 1}$$

$$y(u) = \frac{(1 - \sqrt{2})u^2 + \sqrt{2}u}{(2 - \sqrt{2})u^2 + (\sqrt{2} - 2)u + 1}$$

We can show that $x(u)$ and $y(u)$ satisfy the equation

$$\{x(u)\}^2 + \{y(u)\}^2 = \frac{\left\{(1 - \sqrt{2})u^2 + \sqrt{2}(1 - \sqrt{2})u + 1\right\}^2 + \left\{(1 - \sqrt{2})u^2 + \sqrt{2}u\right\}^2}{\left\{(2 - \sqrt{2})u^2 + (\sqrt{2} - 2)u + 1\right\}^2}$$

$$= 1$$

Therefore we can conclude that the NURBS curve expressed by Equation (b) represents the circular arc 1 exactly.

6.6.1 Evaluation of a NURBS Curve

The x, y, and z coordinates of a point on a NURBS curve corresponding to the parameter value $u = u_0$ are obtained by evaluating the formula

$$\mathbf{P}(u_0) = \frac{\sum\limits_{i=0}^{n} h_i \mathbf{P}_i N_{i,k}(u_0)}{\sum\limits_{i=0}^{n} h_i N_{i,k}(u_0)} \tag{6.52}$$

Both numerator and denominator in Equation (6.52) have the form of B-spline equation, and thus they can be evaluated by an algorithm to evaluate a B-spline curve such as the Cox–de Boor algorithm given in Appendix G. Specifically, the $h_i \mathbf{P}_i$ have the role of the control points $\mathbf{P}_i$ in the Cox–de Boor algorithm when the numerator is evaluated, and the h_i are used when the denominator is evaluated.

6.6.2 Differentiation of a NURBS Curve

The first-order derivative of a NURBS curve can be obtained by differentiating Equation (6.51) with respect to u as follows:

$$\frac{d\mathbf{P}(u)}{du} = \frac{\dfrac{d}{du}\left[\sum\limits_{i=0}^{n} h_i \mathbf{P}_i N_{i,k}(u)\right] \cdot \sum\limits_{i=0}^{n} h_i N_{i,k}(u) - \sum\limits_{i=0}^{n} h_i \mathbf{P}_i N_{i,k}(u) \cdot \dfrac{d}{du}\left[\sum\limits_{i=0}^{n} h_i N_{i,k}(u)\right]}{\left[\sum\limits_{i=0}^{n} h_i N_{i,k}(u)\right]^2} \tag{6.53}$$

The terms $\sum_{i=0}^{n} h_i N_{i,k}(u)$ and $\sum_{i=0}^{n} h_i \mathbf{P}_i N_{i,k}(u)$ in Equation (6.53) can be evaluated by using an algorithm to evaluate a B-spline curve—for example, the Cox–de Boor algorithm presented in Appendix G. The derivatives in the numerator of Equation (6.53) can be evaluated by the method described in Section 6.5.3. Specifically, the $h_i \mathbf{P}_i$ act as the control points $\mathbf{P}_i$ in Equation (6.44) when

$$\frac{d}{du}\left[\sum\limits_{i=0}^{n} h_i \mathbf{P}_i N_{i,k}(u)\right]$$

is evaluated as do the h_i when

$$\frac{d}{du}\left[\sum\limits_{i=0}^{n} h_i N_{i,k}(u)\right]$$

is evaluated.

EXAMPLE 6.8

By expanding Equation (6.51) show that a NURBS curve based on nonperiodic knots passes through the first and last control points. By using Equation (6.53) show that the NURBS curve has tangent vectors at the end points in the directions $\mathbf{P}_1 - \mathbf{P}_0$ and $\mathbf{P}_n - \mathbf{P}_{n-1}$, respectively.

ANSWER

The parameter value corresponding to the starting point of the NURBS curve would be $t_0 = t_1 = \cdots = t_{k-1}$. The first curve segment corresponds to the parameter interval $t_{k-1} \le u \le t_k$ and $N_{k-1,1}$ is the only nonzero blending function of order 1 for that interval. Thus $N_{k-1,1}$ is the only blending function of order 1 to be considered in deriving the equation of the first curve segment. Thus it will be the only nonzero blending function of order 1 when $u = t_{k-1}$ is substituted to evaluate the starting point. Hence all the blending functions $N_{i,k}(t_{k-1})$ are zeroes except $N_{0,k}(t_{k-1})$, which has a value of 1. You should pursue the recursive formula to verify this last statement. Therefore the starting point can be obtained from Equation (6.52) as

$$\mathbf{P}(t_{k-1}) = \frac{\displaystyle\sum_{i=0}^{n} h_i \mathbf{P}_i N_{i,k}(t_{k-1})}{\displaystyle\sum_{i=0}^{n} h_i N_{i,k}(t_{k-1})} = \frac{h_0 \mathbf{P}_0 N_{0,k}(t_{k-1})}{h_0 N_{0,k}(t_{k-1})} = \frac{1 \cdot \mathbf{P}_0 \cdot 1}{1 \cdot 1} = \mathbf{P}_0$$

Similarly, the parameter value corresponding to the ending point of the NURBS curve would be $t_{n+1} = t_{n+2} = \cdots = t_{n+k}$. As $N_{n,1}$ is the only nonzero blending function of order 1 for $t_n \le u \le t_{n+1}$, it is the only blending function of order 1 to be considered in deriving the equation of the last curve segment. Accordingly, it will be the only nonzero blending function of order 1 for $u = t_{n+1}$. Hence all the blending functions $N_{i,k}(t_{n+1})$ are zeroes except $N_{n,k}(t_{n+1})$, which has a value of 1. Therefore the ending point can be obtained from Equation (6.52) as

$$\mathbf{P}(t_{n+1}) = \frac{\displaystyle\sum_{i=0}^{n} h_i \mathbf{P}_i N_{i,k}(t_{n+1})}{\displaystyle\sum_{i=0}^{n} h_i N_{i,k}(t_{n+1})} = \frac{h_n \mathbf{P}_n N_{n,k}(t_{n+1})}{h_n N_{n,k}(t_{n+1})} = \frac{1 \cdot \mathbf{P}_n \cdot 1}{1 \cdot 1} = \mathbf{P}_n$$

The first-order derivative at the starting point is arrived at by using Equation (6.53). The left-hand side derivative in the numerator of Equation (6.53) is evaluated by substituting $h_1 \mathbf{P}_1$ for $\mathbf{P}_1$ and $h_0 \mathbf{P}_0$ for $\mathbf{P}_0$ in the result of Example 6.5. Similarly, the right-hand side derivative is evaluated by substituting h_1 for $\mathbf{P}_1$ and h_0 for $\mathbf{P}_0$. Furthermore, $\sum_{i=0}^{n} h_i N_{i,k}(t_{k-1})$ in Equation (6.53) is h_0. Hence the first-order derivative at the starting point is

$$\left. \frac{d\mathbf{P}(u)}{du} \right|_{u=t_{k-1}} = \frac{(k-1) \cdot \dfrac{h_1 \mathbf{P}_1 - h_0 \mathbf{P}_0}{t_k - t_1} \cdot h_0 - h_0 \mathbf{P}_0 (k-1) \cdot \dfrac{h_1 - h_0}{t_k - t_1}}{h_0^2}$$

$$= \frac{\dfrac{(k-1) h_0 h_1}{t_k - t_1} (\mathbf{P}_1 - \mathbf{P}_0)}{h_0^2} = \frac{(k-1) h_1}{(t_k - t_1) h_0} (\mathbf{P}_1 - \mathbf{P}_0)$$

Similarly, the first-order derivative at the ending point is

$$\frac{d\mathbf{P}(u)}{du}\bigg|_{u=t_{n+1}} = \frac{(k-1)\cdot\dfrac{h_n\mathbf{P}_n - h_{n-1}\mathbf{P}_{n-1}}{t_{n+k-1}-t_n}\cdot h_n - h_n\mathbf{P}_n(k-1)\cdot\dfrac{h_n - h_{n-1}}{t_{n+k-1}-t_n}}{h_n^2}$$

$$= \frac{\dfrac{(k-1)h_{n-1}h_n}{t_{n+k-1}-t_n}(\mathbf{P}_n - \mathbf{P}_{n-1})}{h_n^2} = \frac{(k-1)h_{n-1}}{(t_{n+k-1}-t_n)h_n}(\mathbf{P}_n - \mathbf{P}_{n-1})$$

6.7 INTERPOLATION CURVES

When we are using a geometric modeling system and want to visualize a curve, it is natural to approximate the shape of the curve by providing several points on the curve. In fact, drafters have been drawing curves in this intuitive way for many years. They place several points that are in agreement with their mental image of the shape and connect them smoothly, using a drafting tool called a *spline*. Similarly, in a CAD system, designers provide the points on a curve to be visualized, and the system, instead of using a spline, produces an interpolation curve through those points and displays the curve. The equation of the interpolation curve is also stored for later manipulation of the curve. You could create a curve by directly specifying the control points of a Bezier or a B-spline curve. However, most designers prefer to create a curve initially by specifying the points on the curve and then making small modifications by adjusting the characteristic points of the interpolation curve. The control points of a Bezier or a B-spline curve can be used as the characteristic points if the interpolation curve is in Bezier or B-spline form. Furthermore, the ability to derive the interpolation curves from data points is a very useful capability when a geometric model is to be created from an existing physical model. For example, suppose that we need to derive the mathematical description of the curves and surfaces from a clay model of an automobile. The mathematical description of the surfaces can be used for die-face design and thereafter for the automatic generation of the NC tool paths for milling the die face. In such applications, we would like to be able to specify the points on the curves (or the surfaces) and let the system derive the equations of the interpolation curves (or surfaces). Thus we need to understand how to derive two typical types of interpolation curve equations: for a Hermite curve and a B-spline curve.

6.7.1 Interpolation Using a Hermite Curve

The basic idea in this approach is to express each segment between two neighboring data points by a Hermite curve. Because a Hermite curve has a degree of 3, this approach is analogous to the use of a spline drafting tool, illustrated in Figure 6.9, to draw a curve passing through the data points.

Figure 6.9

A spline, a tool used in mechanical drafting

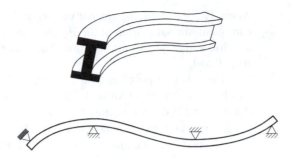

Figure 6.10

Static model of a spline

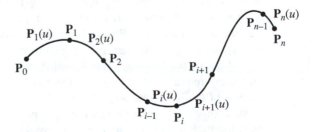

When a spline is being used to draw a curve passing through data points, its static situation can be represented as a beam simply supported at the locations of the data points, as illustrated in Figure 6.10. The shape of each segment between neighboring supports is governed by the following beam equation:

$$\frac{d^2y}{dx^2} = \frac{\mathbf{Q}_0 x + \mathbf{M}_0}{EI} \tag{6.54}$$

Equation (6.54) is a differential equation to be satisfied by the neutral axis $y = y(x)$ of the beam segment when a reaction force $\mathbf{Q}_0$ and the moment $\mathbf{M}_0$ are exerted at its left support. Here, E is the Young's modulus of the beam material, and I is the area moment of inertia of the beam cross section.[16] Equation (6.54) can be integrated twice to yield $y(x)$ of degree 3 in x. Thus we can use a Hermite curve to represent each segment between the data points.

Now we will derive the Hermite equation for each segment when the data points $\mathbf{P}_0, \mathbf{P}_1, \ldots, \mathbf{P}_n$ are specified. From these $(n + 1)$ data points, we have to derive n Hermite curves, denoted $\mathbf{P}_1(u), \mathbf{P}_2(u), \ldots, \mathbf{P}_n(u)$, as illustrated in Figure 6.11.

The ith Hermite curve, $\mathbf{P}_i(u)$, can be expressed by using Equations (6.10) and (6.12) as follows:

$$\mathbf{P}_i(u) = \mathbf{P}_{i-1} + \mathbf{P}_{i-1}'u + [3(\mathbf{P}_i - \mathbf{P}_{i-1}) - 2\mathbf{P}_{i-1}' - \mathbf{P}_i']u^2$$
$$+ [2(\mathbf{P}_{i-1} - \mathbf{P}_i) + \mathbf{P}_{i-1}' + \mathbf{P}_i']u^3 \tag{6.55}$$

Figure 6.11

$(n + 1)$ data points and n Hermite curves

---

[16] The derivation of Equation (6.54) can be found in any strength of materials textbook.

where $\mathbf{P}'_{i-1}$ and $\mathbf{P}'_i$ are the tangent vectors at data points $\mathbf{P}_{i-1}$ and $\mathbf{P}_i$, respectively. We can obtain the same form of the Hermite curve equation for all $\mathbf{P}_i(u)$ by substituting specific values of i in the equation. The parameter value for every segment ranges from 0 to 1.

There is one problem with the form of Equation (6.55)—the coefficients $\mathbf{P}'_{i-1}$ and $\mathbf{P}'_i$ are not usually provided. Thus we must modify Equation (6.55) somehow so that $\mathbf{P}'_{i-1}$ and $\mathbf{P}'_i$ do not appear. To be able to evaluate the values of $\mathbf{P}'_{i-1}$ and $\mathbf{P}'_i$ from the given data points, we have to impose the following constraint equation to guarantee second-order continuity across the curve segments:

$$\frac{d^2\mathbf{P}_i(u)}{du^2}\bigg]_{u=1} = \frac{d^2\mathbf{P}_{i+1}(u)}{du^2}\bigg]_{u=0} \qquad (i = 1, 2, \ldots, n-1) \qquad (6.56)$$

Substituting Equation (6.55) in Equation (6.56) gives

$$2(-3\mathbf{P}_{i-1} + 3\mathbf{P}_i - 2\mathbf{P}'_{i-1} - \mathbf{P}'_i) + 6(2\mathbf{P}_{i-1} - 2\mathbf{P}_i + \mathbf{P}'_{i-1} + \mathbf{P}'_{i+1}) =$$
$$2(-3\mathbf{P}_i + 3\mathbf{P}_{i+1} - 2\mathbf{P}'_i - \mathbf{P}'_{i+1}) \qquad (6.57)$$

Note that the first line in Equation (6.57) is obtained by differentiating Equation (6.55) twice and substituting $u = 1$ in the resulting equation. The second line is obtained by a similar procedure after we derive $\mathbf{P}_{i+1}(u)$ by substituting $i + 1$ for i in Equation (6.55). Rearranging Equation (6.57) gives

$$\mathbf{P}'_{i-1} + 4\mathbf{P}'_i + \mathbf{P}'_{i+1} = 3\mathbf{P}_{i+1} - 3\mathbf{P}_{i-1} \qquad (i = 1, 2, \ldots, n-1) \qquad (6.58)$$

Then we can derive the following matrix equation by substituting the values of i from 1 to $(n - 1)$ in Equation (6.58):

$$
\begin{bmatrix}
4 & 1 & 0 & \cdot & \cdot & \cdot & 0 & 0 \\
1 & 4 & 1 & 0 & \cdot & \cdot & 0 & 0 \\
0 & 1 & 4 & 1 & 0 & \cdot & \cdot & \\
 & & & & & & & \\
0 & 0 & \cdot & \cdot & & 1 & 4 & 1 \\
0 & 0 & \cdot & \cdot & & 0 & 1 & 4
\end{bmatrix}
\begin{bmatrix}
\mathbf{P}'_1 \\
\mathbf{P}'_2 \\
\cdot \\
\cdot \\
\cdot \\
\mathbf{P}'_{n-1}
\end{bmatrix}
=
\begin{bmatrix}
3\mathbf{P}_2 - 3\mathbf{P}_0 - \mathbf{P}'_0 \\
3\mathbf{P}_3 - 3\mathbf{P}_1 \\
3\mathbf{P}_4 - 3\mathbf{P}_2 \\
\cdot \\
\cdot \\
3\mathbf{P}_n - 3\mathbf{P}_{n-2} - \mathbf{P}'_n
\end{bmatrix}
\qquad (6.59)
$$

If we know the values of $\mathbf{P}'_0$ and $\mathbf{P}'_n$ on the right-hand side of Equation (6.59), the values of $(n - 1)$ unknown variables $\mathbf{P}'_1, \mathbf{P}'_2, \ldots, \mathbf{P}'_{n-1}$ can be obtained from $(n - 1)$ equations. Once all the $\mathbf{P}'_i$ have been determined, they are substituted in Equation (6.55), defining all the Hermite curve equations.

We now need to determine $\mathbf{P}'_0$ and $\mathbf{P}'_n$, which are the tangent vectors at the ends of the entire curve. Basically, two methods can be used to determine them, but the shapes of the interpolation curve will differ, depending on the method used. In the first method, the curve designer simply provides the values of these two tangent vectors. In this case, we say that an interpolation curve is derived under a *clamped-end condition*. The second method is based on the assumption that no bending moments are applied at either of the two ends. This assumption is equivalent to assuming that $\mathbf{P}_0''$ and $\mathbf{P}_n''$ are zeros at the ends because the second-order derivative is proportional to the bending moment in a simply supported beam. Thus the following extra constraint equations can be derived:

$$\frac{d^2\mathbf{P}_1(u)}{du^2}\bigg]_{u=0} = -3\mathbf{P}_0 + 3\mathbf{P}_1 - 2\mathbf{P}_0' - \mathbf{P}_1' = 0 \tag{6.60}$$

$$\frac{d^2\mathbf{P}_n(u)}{du^2}\bigg]_{u=1} = 2[3(\mathbf{P}_n - \mathbf{P}_{n-1}) - 2\mathbf{P}_{n-1}' - \mathbf{P}_n']$$

$$+ 6[2(\mathbf{P}_{n-1} - \mathbf{P}_n) + \mathbf{P}_{n-1}' + \mathbf{P}_n'] = 0 \tag{6.61}$$

Rearranging Equations (6.60) and (6.61) yields

$$2\mathbf{P}_0' + \mathbf{P}_1' = 3\mathbf{P}_1 - 3\mathbf{P}_0 \tag{6.62}$$

$$2\mathbf{P}_n' + \mathbf{P}_{n-1}' = 3\mathbf{P}_n - 3\mathbf{P}_{n-1} \tag{6.63}$$

We rewrite Equation (6.59), moving $\mathbf{P}_0'$ and $\mathbf{P}_n'$ from the right-hand side into the variable vector on the left-hand side and adding Equations (6.62) and (6.63) at the beginning and end of the equations in Equation (6.59). Then the following equation is derived.

$$\begin{bmatrix} 2 & 1 & 0 & \cdot & \cdot & \cdot & 0 & 0 \\ 1 & 4 & 1 & 0 & \cdot & \cdot & 0 & 0 \\ 0 & 1 & 4 & 1 & 0 & \cdot & \cdot & \\ & & & & & & & \\ 0 & 0 & \cdot & \cdot & & 0 & 1 & 4 & 1 \\ 0 & 0 & \cdot & \cdot & & & 0 & 1 & 2 \end{bmatrix} \begin{bmatrix} \mathbf{P}_0' \\ \mathbf{P}_1' \\ \cdot \\ \cdot \\ \cdot \\ \mathbf{P}_n' \end{bmatrix} = \begin{bmatrix} 3\mathbf{P}_1 - 3\mathbf{P}_0 \\ 3\mathbf{P}_2 - 3\mathbf{P}_0 \\ 3\mathbf{P}_3 - 3\mathbf{P}_1 \\ \cdot \\ \cdot \\ \cdot \end{bmatrix} \tag{6.64}$$

We can solve Equation (6.64) for $(n + 1)$ unknowns, $\mathbf{P}_0', \mathbf{P}_1', \ldots, \mathbf{P}_n'$, from $(n + 1)$ equations.

Figure 6.12 illustrates two different interpolation curves obtained from the same data points: one under the clamped-end condition and the other under the free-end condition. Note that the interpolation curve under the free-end condition tends to be flat near the ends.

Figure 6.12

Two interpolation curves for different end conditions

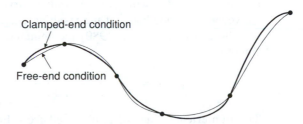

Clamped-end condition

Free-end condition

6.7.2 Interpolation Using a B-Spline Curve

In this approach, a B-spline curve is derived to pass through data points $\mathbf{Q}_0, \mathbf{Q}_1, \ldots,$ $\mathbf{Q}_n$. Specifically, the order, the number of control points (including their coordinates), and the knot values of the interpolating B-spline curve are determined. We could make any B-spline curve defined by $(n + 1)$ or more control points pass through $(n + 1)$ data points because the curve would have $(n + 1)$ or more degrees of freedom. A B-spline curve with more than $(n + 1)$ control points would provide a designer with more freedom to manipulate curve shapes such as tangent slopes at the ends while satisfying the data points. In this section, for simplicity, we explain a method of deriving a B-spline curve with $(n + 1)$ control points.

First, the order of the B-spline curve has to be selected. It is a common practice to use order 4 because degree 3 is the lowest degree satisfying second-order continuity. Then we have to determine the knot values. Because we are using $(n + 1)$ control points, we have to determine $(n + k + 1)$ knot values. Even though there are many possible choices of these knot values, we assign the following values by combining the results given in Hartley [1980] and Lee [1989]:

$$t_i = 0 \qquad\qquad (i = 0, 1, \ldots, k-1)$$

$$t_i = t_{i-1} + \frac{\displaystyle\sum_{j=i-k}^{i-2} d_j}{\displaystyle\sum_{m=k}^{n+1}\sum_{j=m-k}^{m-2} d_j} \qquad\qquad (i = k, k+1, \ldots, n) \qquad\qquad (6.65)$$

$$t_i = 1 \qquad\qquad (i = n+1, n+2, \ldots, n+k)$$

where

$$d_j = \sqrt{\left|\mathbf{Q}_{j+1} - \mathbf{Q}_j\right|} \qquad\qquad (6.66)$$

and $\mathbf{Q}_j$ are the data points already specified.

Let $\mathbf{P}_0, \mathbf{P}_1, \ldots, \mathbf{P}_n$ be the $(n + 1)$ control points to be derived. They have to satisfy the relation

$$\mathbf{Q}_j = \sum_{i=0}^{n} \mathbf{P}_i N_{i,k}(u_j) \qquad (j = 0, 1, \ldots, n) \qquad\qquad (6.67)$$

where u_j are the parameter values to be assigned to data points $\mathbf{Q}_j$. Any set of u_j between t_{k-1} and t_{n+1} will give a B-spline curve passing through the data points. However, the smoothness of the resulting curve will vary severely, depending on the choice of u_j. Hartley [1980] recommended the following values of u_j for a smooth curve:

$$u_j = \frac{t_{j+1} + t_{j+2} + \cdots + t_{j+k-1}}{k - 1} \qquad (j = 0, 1, \ldots, n) \qquad\qquad (6.68)$$

The numerical values of u_j obtained from Equation (6.68) are substituted in

Equation (6.67), and the following simultaneous equations for $\mathbf{P}_i$ are derived:

$$\begin{bmatrix} \cdot & N_{i,k}(u_0) & \cdot & \cdot \\ \cdot & N_{i,k}(u_1) & \cdot & \cdot \\ \cdot & \cdot & \cdot & \cdot \\ \cdot & N_{i,k}(u_n) & \cdot & \cdot \end{bmatrix} \begin{bmatrix} \mathbf{P}_0 \\ \mathbf{P}_1 \\ \cdot \\ \mathbf{P}_n \end{bmatrix} = \begin{bmatrix} \mathbf{Q}_0 \\ \mathbf{Q}_1 \\ \cdot \\ \mathbf{Q}_n \end{bmatrix} \tag{6.69}$$

We can solve for $\mathbf{P}_i$ from Equation (6.69) to obtain the control points of the B-spline curve that interpolates the data points $\mathbf{Q}_i$.

6.8   INTERSECTION OF CURVES

We have already shown that the intersection points of curves need to be calculated to implement the Boolean operations. The intersection points are also required in trimming a curve where it is cut by other curves. Here, we briefly explain the basic idea underlying the algorithms that find the intersection of curves represented by parametric equations. The method described in this section holds for the intersection of any arbitrary curves of the following types: Hermite curve, Bezier curve, B-spline curve, or NURBS curve. The intersection calculation for curves of nonparametric equations or of mixed equations, one in parametric and the other in nonparametric form, can be found in Hoffmann [1989].

Let's assume that two curves to be intersected have the parametric equations of $\mathbf{P}(u)$ and $\mathbf{Q}(v)$, respectively. Then the parameter values corresponding to the intersection points are determined by

$$\mathbf{P}(u) - \mathbf{Q}(v) = 0 \tag{6.70}$$

Note that Equation (6.70) is composed of three scalar equations with two unknowns. Thus we will select only two of the three components (say, x and y):

$$P_x(u) - Q_x(v) = 0 \tag{6.71}$$
$$P_y(u) - Q_y(v) = 0 \tag{6.72}$$

We solve Equations (6.71) and (6.72) for u and v and use the remaining scalar equation—the z component of Equation (6.70)—to verify the derived u and v values. Nonlinear simultaneous equations such as Equations (6.71) and (6.72) usually are solved by using numerical methods such as the Newton–Raphson method [Conte 1980]. In the Newton–Raphson method, the derivatives of $\mathbf{P}_x$, $\mathbf{Q}_x$, $\mathbf{P}_y$, and $\mathbf{Q}_y$ need to be evaluated, which is one application of the derivations given in Sections 6.4.1, 6.5.3, and 6.6.2.

We can expect the following problems when we solve Equations (6.71) and (6.72) by any numerical method.

- The iteration may diverge if the initial values for u and v are too far from the real solution.

- Not all the solutions may be given when more than one intersection point exists. The solution nearest the initial guess of the solution usually is given.

- Inherently, a situation in which a portion of one curve exactly overlaps another curve cannot be handled. In this case, an arbitrary number of intersection points may be returned.

- When the distance between two curves is very small at some locations, those locations may be detected as the intersection points, depending on the value of an inside tolerance.

The first and second problems can be avoided by separately providing initial values close to the real solutions for all the intersection points. In the cases of the Bezier and B-spline curves, initial guesses close to the real solutions for all the intersection points can be made by calculating the intersections of the straight-line segment approximations of the original curves. We have already shown in the Appendix that the straight-line segment approximation of a Bezier or a B-spline curve is generated by subdivision. The third problem usually occurs in the case of intersections of simple curves (e.g., straight lines or circular arcs). For example, we may try to solve numerically the intersection of two circular arcs lying on the same circle after converting the equation of each arc to a NURBS equation. Recall that the curve equations are sometimes converted into a NURBS equation so that only one program handles all the curve intersections. A numerical method cannot detect the overlapping situation and will give an arbitrary number of intersection points based on the initial values provided. Therefore it is necessary to check the possibility of overlapping before handing over a problem to a numerical method. This check may be done by comparing the characteristic features of the curves to be intersected. For example, we may compare the center points and the radii of the circular arcs before they are converted into NURBS representations. The fourth problem can be avoided in most cases, but not completely, by careful tuning of the tolerance values used in a numerical method.

We now introduce a simpler method of calculating intersection points when one of the two curves is a straight line. Let's assume that $\mathbf{P}(u)$ is an equation of a straight line and $\mathbf{Q}(v)$ is an equation of a curve. If the straight line passes through the points located by the position vectors $\mathbf{P}_0$ and $\mathbf{P}_1$, the equation $\mathbf{P}(u)$ can be expressed as

$$\mathbf{P}(u) = \mathbf{P}_1 + u(\mathbf{P}_1 - \mathbf{P}_0) \tag{6.73}$$

Thus the parameter values u and v corresponding to the intersection points will satisfy the relation

$$\mathbf{P}_0 + u(\mathbf{P}_1 - \mathbf{P}_0) = \mathbf{Q}(v) \tag{6.74}$$

Applying the internal product to both the left-hand and right-hand sides of Equation (6.74) with $(\mathbf{P}_0 \times \mathbf{P}_1)$ gives[17]

$$(\mathbf{P}_0 \times \mathbf{P}_1) \cdot \mathbf{Q}(v) = 0 \tag{6.75}$$

Equation (6.75) is a nonlinear equation in v and can be solved numerically for v. Thus we have to be careful to avoid the aforementioned problems of numerical methods in using this approach, too.

---

[17] This equation is obtained because the internal product of $\mathbf{P}_0$ or $\mathbf{P}_0$ with $(\mathbf{P}_0 \times \mathbf{P}_1)$ is zero.

QUESTIONS AND PROBLEMS

1. To draw the ellipse shown in the accompanying figure, you need to derive the expressions for the x and y coordinates of the boundary points in parametric equations.

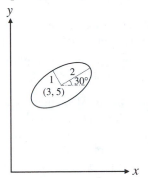

a. Derive the expression for the ellipse that is located at the origin and oriented with its major axis in the x direction.

b. Apply the proper transformations to the expression derived in (a) to get the parametric equation of the ellipse shown.

2. Consider a Hermite curve in the xy plane defined by the following geometric coefficients:

$$\begin{bmatrix} 2 & 3 \\ 4 & 0 \\ 3 & 2 \\ 3 & -4 \end{bmatrix} \begin{matrix} \mathbf{P}(0) \\ \mathbf{P}(1) \\ \mathbf{P'}(0) \\ \mathbf{P'}(0) \end{matrix}$$

a. Find a Bezier curve of degree 3 that represents the given Hermite curve as exactly as possible. In other words, determine the four control points of the Bezier curve.

b. Expand both of the curve equations in polynomial form and compare them.

3. The Bezier curve defined by the control points A_0, A_1, and A_2 is to be transformed to the Bezier curve defined by B_0, B_1, and B_2, as shown in the accompanying figure. The transformation should move point A_0 to B_0 and A_2 to B_2. This means that scaling is also required.

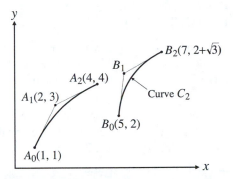

a. Explain which transformation matrices are applied and in which order.

b. Calculate the coordinates of control point B_1.

c. Derive the parametric equation of the resulting curve, C_2.

4. Determine a Bezier curve of degree 3 that approximates a quarter circle centered at $(0, 0)$. The end points of the quarter circle are $(1, 0)$ and $(0, 1)$. Calculate the coordinates of the middle point of this Bezier curve and compare them with those of the midpoint of the quarter circle.

5. Consider the two Bezier curves shown in the accompanying figure. Curve 2 is to be attached to curve 1 by moving point D to point C. In addition, slope continuity is to be maintained at the junction. What will be the control points of the composition curve?

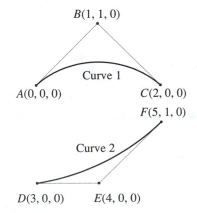

6. A nonperiodic B-spline curve of order 4 is defined by four control points:

$$\mathbf{P}_0 = (0, 0, 0), \quad \mathbf{P}_1 = (6, 8, 0),$$
$$\mathbf{P}_2 = (12, 8, 0), \quad \mathbf{P}_3 = (18, 0, 0)$$

If you rotate this curve around the x axis by 180 degrees, what will be the rotated curve? If it is a B-spline curve, what are its order and control points?

7. Answer the following questions for a nonperiodic B-spline curve of order 3 defined by the control points $\mathbf{P}_0$, $\mathbf{P}_1$, $\mathbf{P}_2$, $\mathbf{P}_3$.

a. What are the knot values?

b. How many different curves is the B-spline curve composed of?

c. Expand the B-spline curve equation to get the separate equations of the curves in (b).

8. Represent a unit circle centered at (0, 0) by the NURBS curve defined by 7 control points, as shown in the accompanying figure. In other words, derive the order k, knot values, and coordinates $(x \cdot w, y \cdot w, z \cdot w, w)$ of the control points.

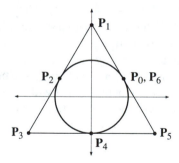

9. Interpolate the three points $\mathbf{P}_0(0, 0)$, $\mathbf{P}_1(1, 2)$, $\mathbf{P}_2(3, 2)$ by using two Hermite curves $\mathbf{P}_1(u)$ and $\mathbf{P}_2(u)$. Assume the free-end condition at $\mathbf{P}_0$ and $\mathbf{P}_2$.

10. Using any CAD system available to you, demonstrate

- global modification of cubic spline and Bezier curves,
- local modification of B-spline curves,
- the convex hull properties of Bezier curves, and
- the effect on Bezier and B-spline curves of repeating control point selection.

11. Write a program having the following menus and the corresponding functions.

CP input menu—This menu allows the user to input the control points of a nonperiodic B-spline curve of order 3 in the xy plane. The maximum number of the control points is 10. Draw a marker that follows the movement of the mouse until the desired position is selected by pushing the mouse button. This means the mouse is used in a sampling mode.

Input end menu—This menu is used when all the control points are input. When this menu is selected, the program should display the B-spline curve with the corresponding control polygon.

CP modify menu—This menu allows the user to change the location of the control points one at a time. The user should be able to pick any one control point and drag it to the new location. As the control point is moved, the system should display the new control polygon and the new B-spline curve dynamically.

Delete menu—This menu allows the user to delete a B-spline curve by picking any edge of the corresponding control polygon.

Exit menu—This menu terminates the program.

7

Representation and Manipulation of Surfaces

In geometric modeling systems, the curve equation (or its equivalent characteristic attributes) has to be stored for each edge and, for each face, so does the surface equation (or its equivalent characteristic attributes). Therefore we need to know what types of surface equations are available and what attributes can be used to store these equations. We have also shown that it is necessary to calculate the intersection curves of faces to evaluate the Boolean operations. Similarly, in surface modeling systems, the intersection curves of surfaces need to be calculated in order to manipulate the surfaces. For example, an intersection curve might need to be determined when a surface is cut by another surface and trimmed along the cut in the course of modeling a surface. This task requires evaluation of the points on the surfaces and the derivatives of the curve equations at those points, too. Therefore, in this chapter we briefly review various types of surface equations and the techniques of manipulating them, including evaluation, differentiation, and intersection. More detailed discussions of these topics are presented in books on computational geometry [Bartels, Beatty, and Barsky 1987; Faux and Pratt 1979; Farin 1990; Qiulin 1987; Hoschek and Lasser 1993; Méhauté et al. 1997].

7.1   TYPES OF SURFACE EQUATIONS

Surface equations, like curve equations, can be classified mainly as two types. One is the *parametric equation*, which relates the x, y, and z coordinates of the points on a surface with a parameter. The other is the *nonparametric equation*, which directly relates the x, y, and z coordinates with a function. The following example will clarify these definitions. Consider a sphere of radius R centered at the origin of the reference coordinate system. Then the parametric equation of the sphere can be expressed as

$$\mathbf{P}(u, v) = R \cos u \cos v \, \mathbf{i} + R \sin u \cos v \, \mathbf{j} + R \sin v \, \mathbf{k} \quad (0 \le u \le 2\pi, -\pi/2 \le v \le \pi/2) \quad (7.1)$$

where the parameter u is equivalent to the longitude and v is equivalent to the latitude. The same sphere may be expressed without using the parameters u and v as in

$$x^2 + y^2 + z^2 - R^2 = 0 \quad (7.2)$$

or

$$z = \pm\sqrt{R^2 - x^2 - y^2} \quad (7.3)$$

We call Equation (7.2) an *implicit nonparametric form* and Equation (7.3) an *explicit nonparametric form* of the curve equations.

Even though each form shown in Equations (7.1)–(7.3) has its own advantages and disadvantages, depending on the application, we focus only on the parametric equations in this chapter. As mentioned in Chapter 6, the parametric equation of a surface enables us to evaluate efficiently the points on the surface at fine intervals and thus facilitates the interactive display and manipulation of the surface. This is one of the main reasons for using parametric equations to represent surfaces in most CAD systems.[1]

7.2 BILINEAR SURFACE

A *bilinear surface* is derived by interpolating four data points, using linear equations in the parameters u and v so that the resulting surface has the four points at its corners, denoted $\mathbf{P}_{0,0}$, $\mathbf{P}_{1,0}$, $\mathbf{P}_{0,1}$, and $\mathbf{P}_{1,1}$, as illustrated in Figure 7.1 Deriving the equation of a bilinear surface would be equivalent to finding the expression of the coordinates of an arbitrary point corresponding to the parameter values u and v. We assume that this point is obtained by dividing the line segment between $\mathbf{P}_{0,v}$ and $\mathbf{P}_{1,v}$ in the ratio $u : (1 - u)$, as illustrated in Figure 7.1. We also assume that $\mathbf{P}_{0,v}$ and $\mathbf{P}_{1,v}$ are to be the internal division points of the line segments $\mathbf{P}_{0,0}\mathbf{P}_{0,1}$ and $\mathbf{P}_{1,0}\mathbf{P}_{1,1}$, respectively, in the ratio $v : (1 - v)$. The point $\mathbf{P}(u, v)$ defined in this way will traverse the entire surface consistently with the increment of the parameter values u and v from 0 to 1. Based on these assumptions, $\mathbf{P}_{0,v}$ and $\mathbf{P}_{1,v}$ are

$$\mathbf{P}_{0,v} = (1 - v)\mathbf{P}_{0,0} + v\mathbf{P}_{0,1} \quad (7.4)$$

$$\mathbf{P}_{1,v} = (1 - v)\mathbf{P}_{1,0} + v\mathbf{P}_{1,1} \quad (7.5)$$

---

[1] Intersection curves of two surfaces are sometimes calculated efficiently when one surface is represented by a parametric equation and the other is represented by a nonparametric equation. Thus, in some systems, nonparametric equations of a surface are also used internally even though they are not stored explicitly. In this case, conversion from a parametric form to a nonparametric form or vice versa is required. The conversion process is discussed in Hoffmann, Hopcroft, and Karasick [1989].

Figure 7.1

A bilinear surface and its data points

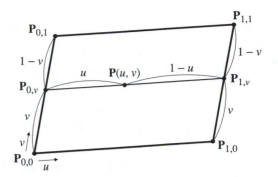

Similarly, $\mathbf{P}(u, v)$ is obtained from $\mathbf{P}_{0,v}$ and $\mathbf{P}_{1,v}$ as

$$\mathbf{P}(u, v) = (1 - u)\mathbf{P}_{0,v} + u\mathbf{P}_{1,v} \qquad (7.6)$$

Substituting Equations (7.4) and (7.5) in Equation (7.6) gives the following equation of a bilinear surface:

$$\mathbf{P}(u,v) = (1 - u)[(1 - v)\mathbf{P}_{0,0} + v\mathbf{P}_{0,1}] + u[(1 - v)\mathbf{P}_{1,0} + v\mathbf{P}_{1,1}]$$

$$= [(1-u)(1-v) \quad u(1-v) \quad (1-u)v \quad uv] \begin{bmatrix} \mathbf{P}_{0,0} \\ \mathbf{P}_{1,0} \\ \mathbf{P}_{0,1} \\ \mathbf{P}_{1,1} \end{bmatrix} \quad (0 \le u \le 1, 0 \le v \le 1) \qquad (7.7)$$

We can verify that the four data points are at the corners of the bilinear surface by substituting the proper combinations of 0 and 1 for u and v in Equation (7.7). Equation (7.7) also tells us that a bilinear surface is obtained by simply blending the effects of the corner points after they are weighted by the blending functions $(1 - u)(1 - v)$, $u(1 - v)$, $(1 - u)v$, and uv.[2] Because of these linear blending functions, a surface represented by a bilinear equation generally tends to be flat.

7.3 COON'S PATCH

The corner points are blended in a bilinear surface, but four boundary curves are blended to form a surface in a *Coon's patch*. The word *patch* is used to indicate explicitly that the surface being generated is a surface segment corresponding to the parameter region $0 \le u \le 1$, $0 \le v \le 1$. Thus any arbitrary surface is composed by many of these patches.

The equation of a Coon's patch is derived as follows. We assume that the equations of the four boundary curves are given by $\mathbf{P}_0(v)$, $\mathbf{P}_1(v)$, $\mathbf{Q}_0(u)$, and $\mathbf{Q}_1(u)$,

---

[2] Hence the attributes to be stored would be only four corner points because Equation (7.7) can be reconstructed from these attributes.

Figure 7.2

Four boundary curves defining a Coon's patch

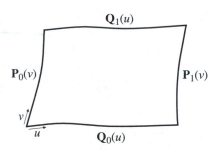

as illustrated in Figure 7.2. We also assume that the curves $\mathbf{Q}_0(u)$ and $\mathbf{Q}_1(u)$ have the interval of u from 0 to 1 and the same direction. In Figure 7.2, we assume that their direction is to the right, as indicated by the arrow for u. Similarly, $\mathbf{P}_0(v)$ and $\mathbf{P}_1(v)$ have the interval of v from 0 to 1 and the same direction, upward in this case. If boundary curves are provided without satisfying these assumptions, their equations have to be converted. The direction or the parameter interval can easily be changed by reversing or scaling the parameter [Mortenson 1985]. After all the boundary curves have been adjusted to satisfy these assumptions, the curves are interpolated as follows.

First, two curves facing each other are selected, say, $\mathbf{P}_0(v)$ and $\mathbf{P}_1(v)$. Then they are interpolated in the u direction by a linear equation:

$$\mathbf{P}_1(u, v) = (1 - u)\mathbf{P}_0(v) + u\mathbf{P}_1(v) \tag{7.8}$$

The surface defined by Equation (7.8) is bounded by $\mathbf{P}_0(v)$ at $u = 0$ and $\mathbf{P}_1(v)$ at $u = 1$. However, the other pair of boundary curves will be the straight lines between the corner points. We can verify this by substituting $v = 0$ or $v = 1$ in Equation (7.8). Thus we find that the surface defined by Equation (7.8) is not bounded by $\mathbf{Q}_0(u)$ and $\mathbf{Q}_1(u)$

Now let's try to define another surface by interpolating $\mathbf{Q}_0(u)$ and $\mathbf{Q}_1(u)$ in the v direction:

$$\mathbf{P}_2(u, v) = (1 - v)\mathbf{Q}_0(u) + v\mathbf{Q}_1(u) \tag{7.9}$$

By substituting the limit values of u and v in Equation (7.9), we can show that the surface defined by Equation (7.9) is bounded by $\mathbf{Q}_0(u)$ and $\mathbf{Q}_1(u)$ but not by $\mathbf{P}_0(v)$ and $\mathbf{P}_1(v)$. So let's try yet another surface, $\mathbf{P}_3(u, v)$, defined by adding $\mathbf{P}_1(u, v)$ and $\mathbf{P}_2(u, v)$ to determine whether it can be bounded by all the boundary curves. Then $\mathbf{P}_3(u, v)$ becomes

$$\mathbf{P}_3(u, v) = (1 - u)\mathbf{P}_0(v) + u\mathbf{P}_1(v) + (1 - v)\mathbf{Q}_0(u) + v\mathbf{Q}_1(u) \tag{7.10}$$

and substituting the limit values of u and v in Equation (7.10) yields

$$\mathbf{P}_3(0, v) = \mathbf{P}_0(v) + \underline{(1 - v)\mathbf{Q}_0(0) + v\mathbf{Q}_1(0)} \tag{7.11}$$

$$\mathbf{P}_3(1, v) = \mathbf{P}_1(v) + \underline{(1 - v)\mathbf{Q}_0(1) + v\mathbf{Q}_1(1)} \tag{7.12}$$

$$\mathbf{P}_3(u, 0) = \mathbf{Q}_0(u) + \underline{(1 - u)\mathbf{P}_0(0) + u\mathbf{P}_1(0)} \tag{7.13}$$

$$\mathbf{P}_3(u, 1) = \mathbf{Q}_1(u) + \underline{(1 - u)\mathbf{P}_0(1) + u\mathbf{P}_1(1)} \tag{7.14}$$

The terms underlined in Equations (7.11)–(7.14) should be eliminated if $\mathbf{P}_3(u, v)$ can satisfy the boundary curves. Note that each underlined term is the linear interpolation between the end points of the corresponding boundary curve. In other words, the terms to be eliminated are the expressions of the boundary curves of a bilinear surface. Therefore the correct equation of a Coon's patch is obtained by subtracting the bilinear surface equation from $\mathbf{P}_3(u, v)$:

$$\begin{aligned}\mathbf{P}(u, v) = (1 - u)\mathbf{P}_0(v) + u\mathbf{P}_1(v) + (1 - v)\mathbf{Q}_0(u) + v\mathbf{Q}_1(u) - (1 - u)(1 - v)\mathbf{P}_{0,0} \\ - u(1 - v)\mathbf{P}_{1,0} - (1 - u)v\mathbf{P}_{0,1} - uv\mathbf{P}_{1,1} \quad (0 \le u \le 1, 0 \le v \le 1)\end{aligned} \quad (7.15)$$

where $\mathbf{P}_{0,0}$ is given by $\mathbf{P}_0(0)$ or $\mathbf{Q}_0(0)$, $\mathbf{P}_{1,0}$ by $\mathbf{Q}_0(1)$ or $\mathbf{P}_1(0)$, $\mathbf{P}_{0,1}$ by $\mathbf{P}_0(1)$ or $\mathbf{Q}_1(0)$, and $\mathbf{P}_{1,1}$ by $\mathbf{P}_1(1)$ or $\mathbf{Q}_1(1)$.

The Coon's patch has been used widely because of its simplicity. However, it is not appropriate for precise modeling of a surface because the internal shape of the surface cannot be controlled from the boundary curves alone.

7.4 BICUBIC PATCH

A *bicubic patch* is a surface represented by an equation in polynomial form of degree 3 in the parameters u and v as in

$$\mathbf{P}(u,v) = \sum_{i=0}^{3} \sum_{i=0}^{3} \mathbf{a}_{ij} u^i v^j \quad (0 \le u \le 1, 0 \le v \le 1) \quad (7.16)$$

Equation (7.16) can be rewritten as a matrix equation as follows:

$$\mathbf{P}(u,v) = \begin{bmatrix} 1 & u & u^2 & u^3 \end{bmatrix} \begin{bmatrix} \mathbf{a}_{00} & \mathbf{a}_{01} & \mathbf{a}_{02} & \mathbf{a}_{03} \\ \mathbf{a}_{10} & \mathbf{a}_{11} & \mathbf{a}_{12} & \mathbf{a}_{13} \\ \mathbf{a}_{20} & \mathbf{a}_{21} & \mathbf{a}_{22} & \mathbf{a}_{23} \\ \mathbf{a}_{30} & \mathbf{a}_{31} & \mathbf{a}_{32} & \mathbf{a}_{33} \end{bmatrix} \begin{bmatrix} 1 \\ v \\ v^2 \\ v^3 \end{bmatrix} \quad (7.17)$$

In Equations (7.16) and (7.17), $\mathbf{a}_{ij}$ are algebraic vector coefficients with x, y, and z components. These algebraic coefficients do not have an intuitively obvious relationship with the shape of the surface as did the algebraic coefficients in Equation (6.10) for a curve. That makes it desirable to replace them with geometric coefficients, as we did in deriving the Hermite curve. Because there are 16 algebraic coefficients, we have to impose 16 boundary conditions.

We derive the first set of boundary conditions by requiring that the four corner points, $\mathbf{P}(0, 0)$, $\mathbf{P}(0, 1)$, $\mathbf{P}(1, 0)$, and $\mathbf{P}(1, 1)$, satisfy Equation (7.17). To derive the second set of boundary conditions we specify the tangent vectors of the boundary curves of the surface at the corner points to be $\mathbf{P}_u(0, 0)$, $\mathbf{P}_u(0, 1)$, $\mathbf{P}_u(1, 0)$, $\mathbf{P}_u(1, 1)$ and $\mathbf{P}_v(0, 0)$, $\mathbf{P}_v(0, 1)$, $\mathbf{P}_v(1, 0)$, $\mathbf{P}_v(1, 1)$ in the u and v directions, respectively. The boundary conditions introduced so far specify the shape of the boundary curves of the surface because they determine the end points and the tangent vectors for each boundary curve. Infinitely many surfaces can satisfy the given boundary curves, so we have to introduce boundary conditions that will determine the internal shape of the surface. To do so, we require that the surface have the specific values, $P_{uv}(0, 0)$, $P_{uv}(0, 1)$, $P_{uv}(1, 0)$, $P_{uv}(1, 1)$ for the second-order derivative

$$\frac{\partial^2 P(u, v)}{\partial u \, \partial v}$$

at the corner points. This second-order derivative is called a *twist vector*. We explain later how the twist vectors at the corner points determine the internal shape of a surface.

Substituting the 16 boundary conditions in Equation (7.17) gives 16 linear equations with respect to a_{ij}. The linear equations are solved simultaneously for a_{ij}, and the result is substituted back in Equation (7.17)[3] to give the following equation of the bicubic patch:

$$P(u, v) =$$

$$[F_1(u) \; F_2(u) \; F_3(u) \; F_4(u)] \begin{bmatrix} P(0,0) & P(0,1) & P_v(0,0) & P_v(0,1) \\ P(1,0) & P(1,1) & P_v(1,0) & P_v(1,1) \\ P_u(0,0) & P_u(0,1) & P_{uv}(0,0) & P_{uv}(0,1) \\ P_u(1,0) & P_u(1,1) & P_{uv}(1,0) & P_{uv}(1,1) \end{bmatrix} \begin{bmatrix} F_1(v) \\ F_2(v) \\ F_3(v) \\ F_4(v) \end{bmatrix} \quad (7.18)$$

$$(0 \le u \le 1, 0 \le v \le 1)$$

where the blending functions F_1, F_2, F_3, and F_4 are defined as

$$\begin{aligned} F_1(u) &= 1 - 3u^2 + 2u^3 \\ F_2(u) &= 3u^2 - 2u^3 \\ F_3(u) &= u - 2u^2 + u^3 \\ F_4(u) &= -u^2 + u^3 \end{aligned} \quad (7.19)$$

These blending functions are the same as those used in the Hermite curve equation. In fact, Equation (7.18) is a simple extension of the Hermite curve equation to a surface equation. We can reduce it to the curve equation by substituting a specific value v_0 for v in Equation (7.18). First, multiplication of the last two matrices in the right-hand side of Equation (7.18), which yields a column matrix, can be interpreted as follows. The first row is the curve equation of the left-hand side boundary curve between $P(0, 0)$ and $P(0, 1)$, and the second row is the curve equation of the right-hand side boundary curve between $P(1, 0)$ and $P(1, 1)$, as shown in Figure 7.3. Thus, when the value v_0 is substituted, the first two rows become the end points, A and B. Meanwhile, the last two rows of the column matrix for $v = v_0$ are the tangent vectors in the u direction at A and B, respectively, which we verify later. Therefore Equation (7.18) simply is a composition of Hermite curve equations at many v values, and the boundary curves corresponding to $v = 0$ and $v = 1$ will also be Hermite curves. By a similar derivation, we can also show that the boundary curves corresponding to $u = 0$ and $u = 1$ are Hermite curves.

---

[3] This is similar to the procedure by which the Hermite curve equation is derived.

Figure 7.3

Isoparametric curve
corresponding to
$v = v_0$

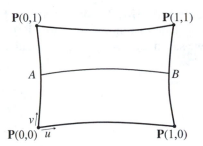

There is one problem with using Equation (7.18): Providing the values of the twist vectors is not easy because their effects on the surface shape are difficult to visualize intuitively. Thus sometimes they are assigned the value of zero for simplicity. In this case, the resulting surface is called the *F-patch* or *Ferguson's patch*. As zero twist vectors tend to generate a relatively flat patch, an F-patch cannot accurately describe a surface having large curvature values. However, it closely describes a surface that has a zero curvature in at least one direction at every point on the surface.

We now show how the twist vectors determine the internal shape of a surface. If we can show that the twist vectors determine the shape of the isoparametric curve at $v = v_0$ in Figure 7.3, we can say that the twist vectors specify any internal isoparametric curve and therefore the internal shape of the surface. Points A and B are determined from the boundary curves, which are Hermite curves defined irrespective of the twist vectors. Thus we need to show that the twist vectors determine the tangent vectors at points A and B. We do so by differentiating Equation (7.18) with respect to u:

$$
\frac{\partial \mathbf{P}(u,v)}{\partial u}
$$

$$
= \left[\frac{d\mathbf{F}_1(u)}{du} \;\; \frac{d\mathbf{F}_2(u)}{du} \;\; \frac{d\mathbf{F}_3(u)}{du} \;\; \frac{d\mathbf{F}_4(u)}{du} \right]
\begin{bmatrix}
\mathbf{P}(0,0) & \mathbf{P}(0,1) & \mathbf{P}_v(0,0) & \mathbf{P}_v(0,1) \\
\mathbf{P}(1,0) & \mathbf{P}(1,1) & \mathbf{P}_v(1,0) & \mathbf{P}_v(1,1) \\
\mathbf{P}_u(0,0) & \mathbf{P}_u(0,1) & \mathbf{P}_{uv}(0,0) & \mathbf{P}_{uv}(0,1) \\
\mathbf{P}_u(1,0) & \mathbf{P}_u(1,1) & \mathbf{P}_{uv}(1,0) & \mathbf{P}_{uv}(1,1)
\end{bmatrix}
\begin{bmatrix}
\mathbf{F}_1(v) \\
\mathbf{F}_2(v) \\
\mathbf{F}_3(v) \\
\mathbf{F}_4(v)
\end{bmatrix}
$$

$$
= \left[-6u + 6u^2 \;\; 6u - 6u^2 \;\; 1 - 4u + 3u^2 \;\; -2u + 3u^2 \right]
\begin{bmatrix}
\mathbf{G}_1(v) \\
\mathbf{G}_2(v) \\
\mathbf{G}_3(v) \\
\mathbf{G}_4(v)
\end{bmatrix}
\tag{7.20}
$$

Note that we converted the multiplication of the second and third matrices in Equation (7.20) into a column matrix denoted $\mathbf{G}_1(v)$, $\mathbf{G}_2(v)$, $\mathbf{G}_3(v)$, and $\mathbf{G}_4(v)$. $\mathbf{P}_u(A)$ can be evaluated by substituting $u = 0$, $v = v_0$ in Equation (7.20). When $u = 0$, the first row matrix in Equation (7.20) becomes [0 0 1 0], and thus $\mathbf{P}_u(A)$ becomes

$\mathbf{G}_3(v_0)$. As $\mathbf{G}_3(v_0)$ is determined by $\mathbf{P}_u(0, 0)$, $\mathbf{P}_u(0, 1)$, $\mathbf{P}_{uv}(0, 0)$, and $\mathbf{P}_{uv}(0, 1)$, we conclude that the twist vectors $\mathbf{P}_{uv}(0, 0)$ and $\mathbf{P}_{uv}(0, 1)$ determine $\mathbf{P}_u(A)$. Similarly, we substitute $u = 1$, $v = v_0$ in Equation (7.20) to evaluate $\mathbf{P}_u(B)$:

$$\mathbf{P}_u(B) = [0 \ \ 0 \ \ 0 \ \ 1] \begin{bmatrix} \mathbf{G}_1(v_0) \\ \mathbf{G}_2(v_0) \\ \mathbf{G}_3(v_0) \\ \mathbf{G}_4(v_0) \end{bmatrix}$$

$$= \mathbf{G}_4(v_0) \tag{7.21}$$

$$= [\mathbf{P}_u(1, 0) \ \ \mathbf{P}_u(1, 1) \ \ \mathbf{P}_{uv}(1, 0) \ \ \mathbf{P}_{uv}(1, 1)] \begin{bmatrix} \mathbf{F}_1(v_0) \\ \mathbf{F}_2(v_0) \\ \mathbf{F}_3(v_0) \\ \mathbf{F}_4(v_0) \end{bmatrix}$$

Thus the tangent vector at point B is determined by $\mathbf{P}_{uv}(1, 0)$ and $\mathbf{P}_{uv}(1, 1)$. Therefore we conclude that the twist vectors define any internal isoparametric curve corresponding to $v = v_0$ and thus specify the internal shape of the bicubic patch.

7.5 BEZIER SURFACE

We can extend the concept of defining a curve by a control polygon in a Bezier curve to one dimension higher so that a surface is defined by a control polyhedron. The equation of this surface, called a *Bezier surface*, is

$$\mathbf{P}(u, v) = \sum_{i=0}^{n} \sum_{j=0}^{m} \mathbf{P}_{i,j} B_{i,n}(u) B_{j,m}(v) \qquad (0 \le u \le 1, 0 \le v \le 1) \tag{7.22}$$

where $\mathbf{P}_{i,j}$ are the control points at the vertices of the control polyhedron, as illustrated in Figure 7.4, and $B_{i,n}$ and $B_{j,m}$ are the blending functions used in Bezier curves. Thus the degree of the surface equations in u and v are determined by the number of control points in the respective directions.

Equation (7.22) can be expanded by evaluating the summation for j as follows:

$$\mathbf{P}(u, v) = \sum_{i=0}^{n} [\mathbf{P}_{i,0} B_{0,m}(v) + \mathbf{P}_{i,1} B_{1,m}(v) + \cdots + \mathbf{P}_{i,m} B_{m,m}(v)] B_{i,n}(u) \tag{7.23}$$

Equation (7.23) indicates that a Bezier surface is obtained by blending the $(n + 1)$ Bezier curves, each of which is defined by the control points $\mathbf{P}_{i,0}$, $\mathbf{P}_{i,1}$, $\mathbf{P}_{i,2}$, ..., $\mathbf{P}_{i,m}$ with the blending functions $B_{i,n}(u)$. Similarly, we can show that the same Bezier surface is obtained by blending $(m + 1)$ Bezier curves, defined by $\mathbf{P}_{0,j}$, $\mathbf{P}_{1,j}$, $\mathbf{P}_{2,j}$, ..., $\mathbf{P}_{n,j}$, with $B_{j,m}(v)$. Thus we can say that a Bezier surface is derived if the control points in a Bezier curve are replaced with Bezier curves.

Figure 7.4

A Bezier surface
and its control
polyhedron

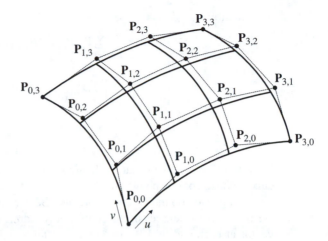

Now we turn to the properties of a Bezier curve. First, we need to show that
the four corner points of the control polyhedron lie on the surface. We do so by
substituting the limit values of u and v in Equation (7.22). Substituting $u = 0$ and
$v = 0$ yields

$$\mathbf{P}(0,0) = \sum_{i=0}^{n}\sum_{j=0}^{m}\mathbf{P}_{i,j}B_{i,n}(0)B_{j,m}(0)$$

$$= \sum_{i=0}^{n}\left[\sum_{j=0}^{m}\mathbf{P}_{i,j}B_{j,m}(0)\right]B_{i,n}(0)$$

$$= \sum_{i=0}^{n}\left[\sum_{j=0}^{m}\mathbf{P}_{i,j}\binom{m}{j}v^{j}(1-v)^{m-j}\right]_{v=0}B_{i,n}(0)$$

$$= \sum_{i=0}^{n}\binom{m}{0}\mathbf{P}_{i,0}B_{i,n}(0) \tag{7.24}$$

$$= \binom{m}{0}\sum_{i=0}^{n}\mathbf{P}_{i,0}\left[\binom{n}{i}u^{i}(1-u)^{n-i}\right]_{u=0}$$

$$= \binom{m}{0}\mathbf{P}_{0,0}\binom{n}{0}$$

$$= \mathbf{P}_{0,0}$$

Equation (7.24) tells us that control point $\mathbf{P}_{0,0}$ is a point on the surface corresponding to $u = 0$ and $v = 0$. By the same procedure, we can show that control points $\mathbf{P}_{n,0}$,
$\mathbf{P}_{0,m}$, and $\mathbf{P}_{n,m}$ lie on the surface.

In addition, we can show that the boundary curves of a Bezier surface are also
Bezier curves defined by the proper subsets of the control points. We substitute $u = 0$
in Equation (7.22) to consider the boundary curve corresponding to $u = 0$, obtaining

the equation

$$\mathbf{P}(0, v) = \sum_{i=0}^{n} \sum_{j=0}^{m} \mathbf{P}_{i,j} B_{i,n}(0) B_{j,m}(v)$$

$$= \sum_{j=0}^{m} \left[\sum_{i=0}^{n} \mathbf{P}_{i,j} \binom{n}{i} u^i (1-u)^{n-i} \right]_{u=0} B_{j,m}(v) \qquad (7.25)$$

$$= \sum_{j=0}^{m} \mathbf{P}_{0,j} B_{j,m}(v)$$

Equation (7.25) tells us that the boundary curve corresponding to $u = 0$ is a Bezier curve whose control points are $\mathbf{P}_{0,0}$, $\mathbf{P}_{0,1}$, . . ., $\mathbf{P}_{0,m}$. Similarly, we can show that the remaining three boundary curves are also Bezier curves and that their control points are the external vertices of the control polyhedron of the surface. Because a tangent vector at each end of a Bezier curve is determined by the control point adjacent to the end, $\mathbf{P}_{0,1}$ and $\mathbf{P}_{0,m-1}$ specify the tangent vectors in the v direction at $\mathbf{P}_{0,0}$ and $\mathbf{P}_{0,m}$, respectively. Thus $\mathbf{P}_{0,1}$ and $\mathbf{P}_{0,m-1}$ have the same role as $\mathbf{P}_v(0, 0)$ and $\mathbf{P}_v(0, 1)$ of a bicubic patch. If this observation is applied to a Bezier surface of degree 3 in u and v, as shown in Figure 7.4, we can make the following statement. The control point $\mathbf{P}_{1,0}$ plays the same role as $\mathbf{P}_u(0, 0)$ of a bicubic patch, $\mathbf{P}_{2,0}$ the same as $\mathbf{P}_u(1, 0)$, $\mathbf{P}_{1,3}$ the same as $\mathbf{P}_u(0, 1)$, $\mathbf{P}_{2,3}$ the same as $\mathbf{P}_u(1, 1)$, $\mathbf{P}_{0,1}$ the same as $\mathbf{P}_v(0, 0)$, $\mathbf{P}_{0,2}$ the same as $\mathbf{P}_v(0, 1)$, $\mathbf{P}_{3,1}$ the same as $\mathbf{P}_v(1, 0)$, $\mathbf{P}_{3,2}$ the same as $\mathbf{P}_v(1, 1)$. Thus these eight control points together with the four corner control points define the boundary curves of the surface. The remaining four control points $\mathbf{P}_{1,1}$, $\mathbf{P}_{2,1}$, $\mathbf{P}_{1,2}$, and $\mathbf{P}_{2,2}$ determine the internal shape of the surface, as did the twist vectors of a bicubic patch.

We mentioned that the degree of a Bezier surface is determined by the number of the control points. As higher degree surface equations have the same problem as higher degree curve equations, we usually use a Bezier surface of degree 3 in both u and v in modeling surfaces, just as we use a Bezier curve of degree 3. Thus, when the surface to be modeled is complicated, it may sometimes be necessary to create several Bezier surfaces of degree 3 and join them. In that case, we want to join the surfaces so that they look continuous across the common boundary. This can be achieved by constraining each pair of the left-hand side and right-hand side control points around the common boundary to form a straight line passing through the control point of the common boundary, as illustrated in Figure 7.5. The derivative across the common boundary is continuous at every point on the boundary if the preceding requirement is satisfied [Hoschek and Lasser 1993; Sarraga 1987; Du and Schmitt 1990].

7.5.1 Evaluation of a Bezier Surface

The x, y, and z coordinates of a point on a Bezier surface corresponding to $u = u_0$ and $v = v_0$ are calculated by

$$\mathbf{P}(u_0, v_0) = \sum_{i=0}^{n} \sum_{j=0}^{m} \mathbf{P}_{i,j} B_{i,n}(u_0) B_{j,m}(v_0) \qquad (7.26)$$

Figure 7.5

Composition of
Bezier patches

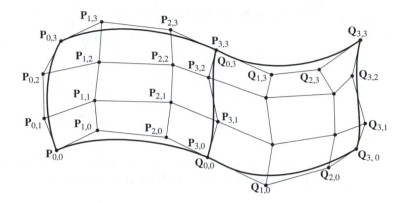

We can rewrite Equation (7.26) as follows by expanding the summation for i in it:

$$\mathbf{P}(u_0, v_0) = \sum_{i=0}^{n} \sum_{j=0}^{m} \mathbf{P}_{i,j} B_{i,n}(u_0) B_{j,m}(v_0)$$

$$= \left[\sum_{j=0}^{m} \mathbf{P}_{0,j} B_{j,m}(v_0) \right] B_{0,n}(u_0) \tag{7.27}$$

$$+ \left[\sum_{j=0}^{m} \mathbf{P}_{1,j} B_{j,m}(v_0) \right] B_{1,n}(u_0) + \cdots + \left[\sum_{j=0}^{m} \mathbf{P}_{n,j} B_{j,m}(v_0) \right] B_{n,n}(u_0)$$

In Equation (7.27), $[\sum_{j=0}^{m} \mathbf{P}_{0,j} B_{j,m}(v_0)]$ can be evaluated by applying the de Casteljau algorithm for the control points $\mathbf{P}_{0,j}$. The de Casteljau algorithm is explained in Appendix F. Similarly, the summations $[\sum_{j=0}^{m} \mathbf{P}_{1,j} B_{j,m}(v_0)], \ldots, [\sum_{j=0}^{m} \mathbf{P}_{n,j} B_{j,m}(v_0)]$ can also be evaluated. If these evaluated values are denoted $\mathbf{C}_0, \mathbf{C}_1, \ldots, \mathbf{C}_n$, Equation (7.27) can be expressed as

$$\mathbf{P}(u_0, v_0) = \mathbf{C}_0 B_{0,n}(u_0) + \mathbf{C}_1 B_{1,n}(u_0) + \cdots + \mathbf{C}_n B_{n,n}(u_0)$$

$$= \sum_{i=0}^{n} \mathbf{C}_i B_{i,n}(u_0) \tag{7.28}$$

Equation (7.28) can be evaluated again by applying the de Casteljau algorithm for the control points $\mathbf{C}_i$.

7.5.2 Differentiation of a Bezier Surface

Often the normal vector has to be evaluated at an arbitrary point of a surface. For example, we might need to calculate the angle between the incident light and the normal vector of a surface at every point to display a shaded image of the surface. We might also need the normal vectors of a surface in order to calculate the center locations of a tool when the surface is to be machined by an NC milling machine.

Therefore we have to be able to evaluate

$$\frac{\partial \mathbf{P}(u,v)}{\partial u}$$

and

$$\frac{\partial \mathbf{P}(u,v)}{\partial v}$$

at any point on a surface because the normal vector is determined by the cross product of these partial derivatives. We evaluate

$$\frac{\partial \mathbf{P}(u,v)}{\partial u}$$

for a Bezier surface at $u = u_0$ and $v = v_0$ in the following manner. (The other derivative

$$\frac{\partial \mathbf{P}(u,v)}{\partial v}$$

is evaluated in the same way.)

Differentiating Equation (7.23) with respect to u gives

$$\frac{\partial \mathbf{P}(u,v)}{\partial u} = \frac{d}{du}\left[\sum_{i=0}^{n}\mathbf{P}_{i,0}B_{i,n}(u)\right]B_{0,m}(v)$$

$$+ \frac{d}{du}\left[\sum_{i=0}^{n}\mathbf{P}_{i,1}B_{i,n}(u)\right]B_{1,m}(v) + \cdots \qquad (7.29)$$

$$+ \frac{d}{du}\left[\sum_{i=0}^{n}\mathbf{P}_{i,m}B_{i,n}(u)\right]B_{m,m}(v)$$

We rewrite the coefficient of $B_{0,m}(v)$,

$$\frac{d}{du}\left[\sum_{i=0}^{n}\mathbf{P}_{i,0}B_{i,n}(u)\right]$$

in Equation (7.29) by using the result from section 6.4.1 as follows:

$$\frac{d}{du}\left[\sum_{i=0}^{n}\mathbf{P}_{i,0}B_{i,n}(u)\right] = \sum_{i=0}^{n-1}\binom{n-1}{i}u^{i}(1-u)^{n-1-i}\mathbf{a}_{i,0} \qquad (7.30)$$

where $\mathbf{a}_{i,0}$ is $\mathbf{P}_{i+1,0} - \mathbf{P}_{i,0}$.

The right-hand side of Equation (7.30) can be evaluated for an arbitrary value of u_0 by applying the de Casteljau algorithm, as explained in Section 6.4.1. In the same way, the coefficients of $B_{1,m}(v)$, $B_{2,m}(v)$, . . ., $B_{m,m}(v)$ are evaluated for u_0. If these evaluated values are denoted $\mathbf{C}_0$, $\mathbf{C}_1$, . . ., $\mathbf{C}_m$, Equation (7.29) can be expressed as

$$\frac{\partial \mathbf{P}(u,v)}{\partial u} = \mathbf{C}_0 B_{0,m}(v) + \mathbf{C}_1 B_{1,m}(v) + \cdots + \mathbf{C}_m B_{m,m}(v)$$

$$= \sum_{j=0}^{m} \mathbf{C}_j B_{j,m}(v)$$

(7.31)

Equation (7.31) can be evaluated again by applying the de Casteljau algorithm for the control points $\mathbf{C}_j$.

7.6 B-SPLINE SURFACE

As we have extended the Bezier curve equation to that of a Bezier surface, we can also extend the B-spline curve equation to derive the equation of a *B-spline surface*:

$$\mathbf{P}(u,v) = \sum_{i=0}^{n} \sum_{j=0}^{m} \mathbf{P}_{i,j} N_{i,k}(u) N_{j,l}(v) \qquad (s_{k-1} \leq u \leq s_{n+1}, \ t_{l-1} \leq v \leq t_{m+1}) \quad (7.32)$$

where $\mathbf{P}_{i,j}$ are the control points located at the vertices of the control polyhedron, as for the Bezier surface, and $N_{i,k}(u)$ and $N_{j,l}(v)$ are the blending functions used in B-spline curves. These blending functions are defined by the knot values s_0, s_1, . . ., s_{n+k} and t_0, t_1, . . ., t_{l+m}, respectively. The parameter ranges $s_{k-1} \leq u \leq s_{n+1}$, $t_{l-1} \leq v \leq t_{m+1}$ are used because the blending functions $N_{i,k}(u)$ and $N_{j,l}(v)$ are defined only over these intervals, as was illustrated in Chapter 6. This is true also when the blending functions are based on periodic knots as well as on nonperiodic knots. Here we consider only the blending functions based on nonperiodic knots, as we did for B-spline curves. In this case, these blending functions become the same as those of Bezier surfaces if the orders k and l equal $(n + 1)$ and $(m + 1)$, respectively. Therefore we can say that a Bezier surface is only one special case of a B-spline surface and that Equation (7.32) is a general form representing both Bezier and B-spline surfaces. It is common practice to use the value 4 for orders k and l because a surface of degree 3 in u and v is used most.

When the definition of a B-spline surface is based on nonperiodic knots, it has properties similar to those of a Bezier surface (i.e., the four corner points of the control polyhedron lie on the surface, and the boundary curves are B-spline curves defined by the proper subsets of the control points). Let's now show that the boundary curve corresponding to $u = 0$ is a B-spline curve. Substituting $u = 0$ in Equation (7.32) yields[4]

$$\mathbf{P}(0,v) = \sum_{j=0}^{m} \left[\sum_{i=0}^{n} \mathbf{P}_{i,j} N_{i,k}(u) \right]_{u=0} N_{j,l}(v)$$

$$= \sum_{j=0}^{m} \mathbf{P}_{0,j} N_{j,l}(v)$$

(7.33)

---

[4] Equation (7.33) is derived by using the property $[\sum_{i=0}^{n} \mathbf{P}_i N_{i,k}(u)]_{u=0} = \mathbf{P}_0$.

According to Equation (7.33), the boundary curve corresponding to $u = 0$ is a B-spline curve whose control points are $\mathbf{P}_{0,0}, \mathbf{P}_{0,1}, \ldots, \mathbf{P}_{0,m}$. Similarly, we can show that the remaining three boundary curves are also B-spline curves and that their control points are the external vertices of the control polyhedron of the surface.

7.6.1 Evaluation of a B-Spline Surface

The x, y, and z coordinates of a point on a B-spline surface corresponding to $u = u_0$ and $v = v_0$ are calculated from

$$\mathbf{P}(u_0, v_0) = \sum_{i=0}^{n} \sum_{j=0}^{m} \mathbf{P}_{i,j} N_{i,k}(u_0) N_{j,l}(v_0) \tag{7.34}$$

We can rewrite Equation (7.34) as follows by expanding the summation for i in it:

$$\mathbf{P}(u_0, v_0) = \left[\sum_{j=0}^{m} \mathbf{P}_{0,j} N_{j,l}(v_0) \right] N_{0,k}(u_0)$$

$$+ \left[\sum_{j=0}^{m} \mathbf{P}_{1,j} N_{j,l}(v_0) \right] N_{1,k}(u_0) + \cdots + \left[\sum_{j=0}^{m} \mathbf{P}_{n,j} N_{j,l}(v_0) \right] N_{n,k}(u_0 \tag{7.35}$$

In Equation (7.35), $[\sum_{j=0}^{m} \mathbf{P}_{0,j} N_{j,l}(v_0)]$ can be evaluated by an algorithm such as the Cox–de Boor algorithm by using the control points $\mathbf{P}_{0,j}$ and the knots for v, as explained in Appendix G. Let this value be $\mathbf{C}_0$. Similarly, the summations $\left[\sum_{j=0}^{m} \mathbf{P}_{1,j} N_{j,l}(v_0) \right], \ldots, \left[\sum_{j=0}^{m} \mathbf{P}_{n,j} N_{j,l}(v_0) \right]$ are also evaluated and denoted $\mathbf{C}_1, \ldots, \mathbf{C}_n$. Then, Equation (7.35) can be expressed as

$$\mathbf{P}(u_0, v_0) = \mathbf{C}_0 N_{0,k}(u_0) + \mathbf{C}_1 N_{1,k}(u_0) + \cdots + \mathbf{C}_n N_{n,k}(u_0) \tag{7.36}$$

Equation (7.36) can be evaluated again by using an algorithm such as the Cox–de Boor algorithm, the control points $\mathbf{C}_i$, and the knots for u.

7.6.2 Differentiation of a B-Spline Surface

As we explained in Section 7.5.2, we often have to evaluate

$$\frac{\partial \mathbf{P}(u, v)}{\partial u}$$

and

$$\frac{\partial \mathbf{P}(u, v)}{\partial v}$$

at any point on a surface because the normal vector is determined by the cross product of these partial derivatives. We evaluate

$$\frac{\partial \mathbf{P}(u, v)}{\partial u}$$

for a B-spline surface at $u = u_0$ and $v = v_0$ in the following manner. (The other derivative

$$\frac{\partial \mathbf{P}(u,v)}{\partial v}$$

is evaluated in the same way.)

First, we expand Equation (7.32) by evaluating the summation for j:

$$\mathbf{P}(u,v) = \left[\sum_{i=0}^{n}\mathbf{P}_{i,0}N_{i,k}(u)\right]N_{0,l}(v) + \left[\sum_{i=0}^{n}\mathbf{P}_{i,1}N_{i,k}(u)\right]N_{1,l}(v)$$

$$+ \cdots + \left[\sum_{i=0}^{n}\mathbf{P}_{i,m}N_{i,k}(u)\right]N_{m,l}(v)$$

(7.37)

Differentiating Equation (7.37) with respect to u gives

$$\frac{\partial \mathbf{P}(u,v)}{\partial u} = \frac{d}{du}\left[\sum_{i=0}^{n}\mathbf{P}_{i,0}N_{i,k}(u)\right]N_{0,l}(v)$$

$$+ \frac{d}{du}\left[\sum_{i=0}^{n}\mathbf{P}_{i,1}N_{i,k}(u)\right]N_{1,l}(v) + \cdots + \frac{d}{du}\left[\sum_{i=0}^{n}\mathbf{P}_{i,m}N_{i,k}(u)\right]N_{m,l}(v)$$

(7.38)

The coefficient of $N_{0,l}(v)$,

$$\frac{d}{du}\left[\sum_{i=0}^{n}\mathbf{P}_{i,0}N_{i,k}(u)\right]$$

in Equation (7.38) is a differentiation of the B-spline curve defined by the control points $\mathbf{P}_{i,0}$ and can be evaluated for an arbitrary value u_0 as explained in Section 6.5.3. Let this value be $\mathbf{C}_0$. In the same way, the coefficients of $N_{1,l}(v)$, $N_{2,l}(v)$, . . ., $N_{m,l}(v)$ are evaluated for u_0. If these evaluated values are denoted $\mathbf{C}_1$, $\mathbf{C}_2$, . . ., $\mathbf{C}_m$, Equation (7.38) can be expressed as

$$\frac{\partial \mathbf{P}(u,v)}{\partial u} = \mathbf{C}_0 N_{0,1}(v) + \mathbf{C}_1 N_{1,l}(v) + \cdots + \mathbf{C}_m N_{m,l}(v)$$

$$= \sum_{j=0}^{m}\mathbf{C}_j N_{j,l}(v)$$

(7.39)

Equation (7.39) can again be evaluated for any arbitrary value v_0 by using an algorithm such as the Cox–de Boor algorithm, the control points $\mathbf{C}_j$, and the knots for v.

7.7   NURBS SURFACE

Just as we derived the NURBS curve equation from the B-spline curve equation by introducing homogeneous coordinates for the control points, we can derive the equation of a *NURBS surface* from that of a B-spline surface:

$$P(u,v) = \frac{\displaystyle\sum_{i=0}^{n}\sum_{j=0}^{m}h_{i,j}P_{i,j}N_{i,k}(u)N_{j,l}(v)}{\displaystyle\sum_{i=0}^{n}\sum_{j=0}^{m}h_{i,j}N_{i,k}(u)N_{j,l}(v)} \qquad (s_{k-1}\le u\le s_{n+1}, t_{l-1}\le v\le t_{m+1}) \qquad (7.40)$$

where $P_{i,j}$ are the x, y, and z coordinates and $h_{i,j}$ are the homogeneous coordinates of the control points. Note that the same knot values and parameter ranges as those in Equation (7.32) are used.

Equation (7.40) becomes that of a B-spline surface when all $h_{i,j}$ equal 1, as for the NURBS curve equation. You should show for your own satisfaction that the denominator in Equation (7.40) equals 1 when all $h_{i,j}$ are 1. Thus the NURBS surface equation is a general form that includes the B-spline surface equation. Furthermore, the NURBS surface equation has the advantage of exactly representing the quadric (or quadratic) cylindrical, conical, spherical, paraboloidal, and hyperboloidal surfaces. These surfaces are called *quadric* (or *quadratic*) because their surface equations have degree 2 in the parameters u and v. Therefore the NURBS surface equation often serves as a unified internal representation for all these surfaces.

We can illustrate the use of NURBS surface equations to represent surfaces frequently created in solid modeling systems with some examples. The first example is a surface created by translating a curve, as illustrated in Figure 7.6. We assume that the curve being translated is represented by NURBS curve. This assumption does not introduce any restrictions because any curve equation can be converted to a NURBS curve equation. The NURBS curve of interest has order l, knot values $t_p (p = 0,1,\ldots, m + l)$, and $(m +1)$ control points specified by P_j, the x, y, and z coordinates, and the homogeneous coordinates h_j, as in the following equation. Thus

$$P(v) = \frac{\displaystyle\sum_{j=0}^{m}h_{j}P_{j}N_{j,l}(v)}{\displaystyle\sum_{j=0}^{m}h_{j}N_{j,l}(v)} \qquad (t_{l-1}\le v\le t_{m+1}) \qquad (7.41)$$

A boundary curve of a NURBS surface is a NURBS curve defined by control points; these control points are the boundary vertices of the control polyhedron associated with the boundary curve. Also, the order and the knots of the boundary curve are the same as for the surface in the corresponding direction. We have al-

Figure 7.6

Surface generated by sweeping a curve

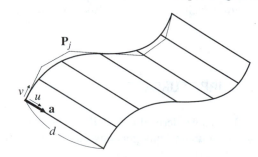

ready shown that B-spline surfaces have this property. Thus the control points, order, and knots of the surface in the parameter direction consistent with the curve being translated are obtained from the curve being translated because this curve is one of the boundary curves. To be more specific, the control points of the surface to be generated would be $\mathbf{P}_j$ at one end, as shown in Figure 7.6. Furthermore, the order and knots of the surface will be l and t_p, respectively, in the v direction if the directions for the parameters u and v are assumed as shown.

Now we need information about the surface related to the u direction; u is assumed to be in the direction of the translation, as shown in Figure 7.6, which indicates that a linear equation is sufficient for the u direction. Therefore the order is 2 and just two control points suffice in the u direction. As a result, the knot values in the u direction will be 0, 0, 1, 1 and only two sets of the control points are derived; one set is obtained from $\mathbf{P}_j$, as previously mentioned, and the other set is obtained by translating $\mathbf{P}_j$ by a distance d in the translational direction. In addition, the homogeneous coordinates for both sets will be h_j of the curve being translated. Thus the x, y, and z coordinates, $\mathbf{P}_{i,j}$, and the homogeneous coordinates, $h_{i,j}$, of the control points of the surface can be expressed as

$$
\begin{aligned}
\mathbf{P}_{0,j} &= \mathbf{P}_j \\
\mathbf{P}_{1,j} &= \mathbf{P}_j + d\mathbf{a} \\
h_{0,j} &= h_{1,j} = h_j
\end{aligned}
\tag{7.42}
$$

where d is the distance of the translation and $\mathbf{a}$ is the unit vector in the direction of the translation.

In summary, the NURBS equation of the surface to be generated can be stated as follows and can be evaluated by substituting the values obtained:

$$
\mathbf{P}(u,v) = \frac{\displaystyle\sum_{i=0}^{1}\sum_{j=0}^{m} h_{i,j}\mathbf{P}_{i,j}N_{i,2}(u)N_{j,l}(v)}{\displaystyle\sum_{i=0}^{1}\sum_{j=0}^{m} h_{i,j}N_{i,2}(u)N_{j,l}(v)} \qquad (0 \le u \le 1, t_{l-1} \le v \le t_{m+1}) \tag{7.43}
$$

Note that $N_{j,l}(v)$ in Equation (7.43) is based on the knot values t_p.

The NURBS surface equation, Equation (7.43), can be used to represent any ruled surface created by translating a curve. For example, a NURBS surface equa-

Figure 7.7

Creation of a cylindrical surface by translating a half circle

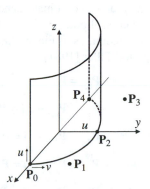

tion can be used to represent a cylindrical surface created by translating a half circle in the xy plane along the z axis, as illustrated in Figure 7.7. First, we need a NURBS representation of the half circle. From the result of Example 6.6, the coordinates of the control points, including the homogeneous coordinates, are

$$\mathbf{P}_0 = (1, 0, 0) \qquad\qquad h_0 = 1$$

$$\mathbf{P}_1 = (1, 1, 0) \qquad\qquad h_1 = \frac{1}{\sqrt{2}}$$

$$\mathbf{P}_2 = (0, 1, 0) \qquad\qquad h_2 = 1$$

$$\mathbf{P}_3 = (-1, 1, 0) \qquad\qquad h_3 = \frac{1}{\sqrt{2}}$$

$$\mathbf{P}_4 = (-1, 0, 0) \qquad\qquad h_4 = 1$$

and the order is 3 and knot values are 0, 0, 0, 1, 1, 2, 2, 2. The coordinates of the control points of the cylindrical surface then are

$$\mathbf{P}_{0,0} = \mathbf{P}_0, \qquad \mathbf{P}_{1,0} = \mathbf{P}_0 + H\mathbf{k}, \qquad h_{0,0} = h_{1,0} = 1$$

$$\mathbf{P}_{0,1} = \mathbf{P}_1, \qquad \mathbf{P}_{1,1} = \mathbf{P}_1 + H\mathbf{k}, \qquad h_{0,1} = h_{1,1} = \frac{1}{\sqrt{2}}$$

$$\mathbf{P}_{0,2} = \mathbf{P}_2, \qquad \mathbf{P}_{1,2} = \mathbf{P}_2 + H\mathbf{k}, \qquad h_{0,2} = h_{1,2} = 1$$

$$\mathbf{P}_{0,3} = \mathbf{P}_3, \qquad \mathbf{P}_{1,3} = \mathbf{P}_3 + H\mathbf{k}, \qquad h_{0,3} = h_{1,3} = \frac{1}{\sqrt{2}}$$

$$\mathbf{P}_{0,4} = \mathbf{P}_4, \qquad \mathbf{P}_{1,4} = \mathbf{P}_4 + H\mathbf{k}, \qquad h_{0,4} = h_{1,4} = 1$$

where $\mathbf{P}_{0,0}$, $\mathbf{P}_{0,1}$, $\mathbf{P}_{0,2}$, $\mathbf{P}_{0,3}$, $\mathbf{P}_{0,4}$ correspond to the control points of the bottom arc, $\mathbf{P}_{1,0}$, $\mathbf{P}_{1,1}$, $\mathbf{P}_{1,2}$, $\mathbf{P}_{1,3}$, $\mathbf{P}_{1,4}$ are those of the upper arc, and $\mathbf{k}$ is the unit vector in the z axis. Then the NURBS equation of the cylindrical surface is obtained by substituting these $\mathbf{P}_{i,j}$ and $h_{i,j}$ in Equation (7.43) together with $l = 3$ and $m = 4$. The knot values for the v direction are 0, 0, 0, 1, 1, 2, 2, 2, and those for the u direction are 0, 0, 1, 1.

Let's consider another example of a surface created by revolving a curve. The curve being revolved lies in the xz plane, the revolution axis is the z axis, and the direction of the curve corresponds to that of the parameter v of the surface being created, as shown in Figure 7.8. We assume a NURBS curve representation with order l, knot values $t_p (p = 0,1, \ldots, m + l)$, and $(m + 1)$ control points specified by $\mathbf{P}_j$, the x, y, and z coordinates, and homogeneous coordinates h_j. Then we can guess that each control point $\mathbf{P}_j$ should be split into nine control points to define the circular cross section, as in Figure 7.8. Detailed explanation of this method is presented in Piegl and Tiller [1987]. The nine control points of the surface are

$$\mathbf{P}_{0,j} = \mathbf{P}_j, \qquad\qquad h_{0,j} = h_j$$

$$\mathbf{P}_{1,j} = \mathbf{P}_{0,j} + x_j\mathbf{j} = \mathbf{P}_j + x_j\mathbf{j}, \qquad\qquad h_{1,j} = h_j \cdot \frac{1}{\sqrt{2}}$$

$$\mathbf{P}_{2,j} = \mathbf{P}_{1,j} - x_j\mathbf{i} = \mathbf{P}_j - x_j(\mathbf{i} - \mathbf{j}), \qquad\qquad h_{2,j} = h_j$$

$$\mathbf{P}_{3,j} = \mathbf{P}_{2,j} - x_j\mathbf{i} = \mathbf{P}_j - x_j(2\mathbf{i} - \mathbf{j}), \qquad\qquad h_{3,j} = h_j \cdot \frac{1}{\sqrt{2}}$$

$$\mathbf{P}_{4,j} = \mathbf{P}_{3,j} - x_j\mathbf{j} = \mathbf{P}_j - 2x_j\mathbf{i}, \qquad\qquad h_{4,j} = h_j$$

Figure 7.8

Surface creation by revolving a curve

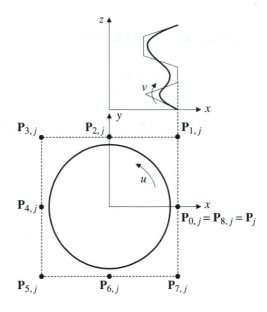

$$\mathbf{P}_{5,j} = \mathbf{P}_{4,j} - x_j\mathbf{j} = \mathbf{P}_j - x_j(2\mathbf{i} + \mathbf{j}), \qquad h_{5,j} = h_j \cdot \frac{1}{\sqrt{2}}$$

$$\mathbf{P}_{6,j} = \mathbf{P}_{5,j} + x_j\mathbf{i} = \mathbf{P}_j - x_j(\mathbf{i} + \mathbf{j}), \qquad h_{6,j} = h_j$$

$$\mathbf{P}_{7,j} = \mathbf{P}_{6,j} + x_j\mathbf{i} = \mathbf{P}_j - x_j\mathbf{j}, \qquad h_{7,j} = h_j \cdot \frac{1}{\sqrt{2}}$$

$$\mathbf{P}_{8,j} = \mathbf{P}_{0,j} = \mathbf{P}_j, \qquad h_{8,j} = h_j$$

and the surface equation can be expressed as

$$\mathbf{P}(u,v) = \frac{\displaystyle\sum_{i=0}^{8}\sum_{j=0}^{m} h_{i,j}\mathbf{P}_{i,j}N_{i,3}(u)N_{j,l}(v)}{\displaystyle\sum_{i=0}^{8}\sum_{j=0}^{m} h_{i,j}N_{i,3}(u)N_{j,l}(v)} \qquad (0 \le u \le 4, t_{l-1} \le v \le t_{m+1}) \quad (7.44)$$

Note that the order of the surface in the u direction is 3 because degree 2 is sufficient to represent circles in that direction. The knot values for $N_{j,l}$ are obtained from the NURBS representation of the curve being revolved, and those for $N_{i,3}$ are obtained by composing those of a quarter circle, or 0, 0, 0, 1, 1, 2, 2, 3, 3, 4, 4, 4.

To evaluate the x, y, and z coordinates of a point on a NURBS surface at arbitrary parameter values $u = u_0$ and $v = v_0$, we substitute these parameter values in Equation (7.40). Then we note that the numerator and denominator have the same form as a B-spline surface equation. Thus we can use the method we used to evaluate a B-spline surface with minor modifications: The $h_{i,j}\mathbf{P}_{i,j}$ are used for $\mathbf{P}_{i,j}$ in calculating the numerator, and the $h_{i,j}$ are used for $\mathbf{P}_{i,j}$ in calculating the denominator.

In addition, we evaluate the derivative of a NURBS surface by applying the methods used to evaluate a B-spline surface together with its derivative. We will leave the verification for your practice.

7.8 INTERPOLATION SURFACE

As we create a curve by interpolating data points, we often generate a surface from the data points, especially when a geometric model of an existing physical model is needed. There are many methods for interpolating data points; these methods are based on the surface equations used for the interpolation surface. In this section, we derive a B-spline surface passing through data points.

We denote the data points $Q_{p,q}$ ($p = 0, 1, \ldots, n$ and $q = 0, 1, \ldots, m$), as illustrated in Figure 7.9. Because $(n + 1) \times (m + 1)$ constraints have to be satisfied, any B-spline surface with at least $(n + 1) \times (m + 1)$ control points can be used. For simplicity, however, let's consider a B-spline surface with $(n + 1) \times (m + 1)$ control points:

$$\mathbf{P}(u, v) = \sum_{i=0}^{n} \sum_{j=0}^{m} \mathbf{P}_{i,j} N_{i,k}(u) N_{j,l}(v) \tag{7.45}$$

where $\mathbf{P}_{i,j}$ are the control points required for the resulting surface to pass through all the data points $\mathbf{Q}_{p,q}$. If we assume that the parameter values for each data point $\mathbf{Q}_{p,q}$ are u_p and v_q,[5] then we get

$$\mathbf{Q}_{p,q} = \sum_{i=0}^{n} \sum_{j=0}^{m} \mathbf{P}_{i,j} N_{i,k}(u_p) N_{j,l}(v_q) \tag{7.46}$$

We can rewrite Equation (7.46) by letting the term $\sum_{j=0}^{m} \mathbf{P}_{i,j} N_{j,l}(v_q)$ be $\mathbf{C}_i(v_q)$:

$$\mathbf{Q}_{p,q} = \sum_{i=0}^{n} \mathbf{C}_i(v_q) N_{i,k}(u_p) \tag{7.47}$$

Figure 7.9

The data points to be interpolated

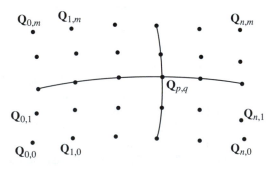

$Q_{0,m}$ $Q_{1,m}$ $Q_{n,m}$

$Q_{p,q}$

$Q_{0,1}$ $Q_{n,1}$

$Q_{0,0}$ $Q_{1,0}$ $Q_{n,0}$

[5] The value of u_p can be obtained by the method described in Section 6.7.2 from the knot values derived when the points $\mathbf{Q}_{0,q}, \mathbf{Q}_{1,q}, \ldots, \mathbf{Q}_{n,q}$ are interpolated by a B-spline curve. Similarly, v_q is obtained from the knot values derived when $\mathbf{Q}_{p,0}, \mathbf{Q}_{p,1}, \ldots, \mathbf{Q}_{p,m}$ are interpolated.

Substituting the values 0–m for q in Equation (7.47) gives

$$\mathbf{Q}_{p,0} = \sum_{i=0}^{n} \mathbf{C}_i(v_0)N_{i,k}(u_p)$$

$$\mathbf{Q}_{p,1} = \sum_{i=0}^{n} \mathbf{C}_i(v_1)N_{i,k}(u_p) \tag{7.48}$$

$$\cdots$$

$$\mathbf{Q}_{p,m} = \sum_{i=0}^{n} \mathbf{C}_i(v_m)N_{i,k}(u_p)$$

If we substitute the values 0–n for p in the first line of Equation (7.48), we get $\mathbf{C}_i(v_0)$ ($i = 0, 1, \ldots, n$) as the control points of the B-spline curve interpolating $\mathbf{Q}_{0,0}$, $\mathbf{Q}_{1,0}$, $\mathbf{Q}_{2,0}$, ..., $\mathbf{Q}_{n,0}$, which is the first horizontal curve shown in Figure 7.10. Similarly, $\mathbf{C}_i(v_1)$ ($i = 0, 1, \ldots, n$) are the control points of the B-spline curve interpolating $\mathbf{Q}_{0,1}$, $\mathbf{Q}_{1,1}$, $\mathbf{Q}_{2,1}$, ..., $\mathbf{Q}_{n,1}$, which is the second horizontal curve. In general, $\mathbf{C}_i(v_q)$ ($i = 0, 1, \ldots, n$) are the control points of the B-spline curve interpolating $\mathbf{Q}_{0,q}$, $\mathbf{Q}_{1,q}$, $\mathbf{Q}_{2,q}$, ..., $\mathbf{Q}_{n,q}$, which is the ($q + 1$)th horizontal curve. Recall that these control points of interpolating B-spline curves are obtained by the method described in Section 6.7.2.

Now let's obtain the control points $\mathbf{P}_{i,j}$ from $\mathbf{C}_i(v_q)$ ($q = 0, 1, \ldots, m$) in the preceding step. To do that, we write the definition of $\mathbf{C}_i(v_q)$ again:

$$\mathbf{C}_i(v_q) = \sum_{j=0}^{m} \mathbf{P}_{i,j}N_{j,l}(v_q) \tag{7.49}$$

If we substitute the values 0–m for q in Equation (7.49), we note that $\mathbf{P}_{i,j}$ are the control points of the B-spline curve interpolating $\mathbf{C}_i(v_0)$, $\mathbf{C}_i(v_1)$, ..., $\mathbf{C}_i(v_m)$. Specifically, $\mathbf{P}_{0,j}$ are the control points of the B-spline interpolating $\mathbf{C}_0(v_0)$, $\mathbf{C}_0(v_1)$, ..., $\mathbf{C}_0(v_m)$, which are the leftmost control points in Figure 7.10, $\mathbf{P}_{1,j}$ are those of the B-spline interpolating $\mathbf{C}_1(v_0)$, $\mathbf{C}_1(v_1)$, ..., $\mathbf{C}_1(v_m)$, which are the second control points from the left of the control polygons in the figure, and so on.

Figure 7.10

$\mathbf{C}_i(vq)$ obtained by interpolation in the *u* direction

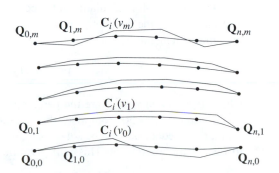

We can summarize the procedure for deriving $\mathbf{P}_{i,j}$ in the following way.

- The data points are interpolated by B-splines in one direction, as illustrated in Figure 7.10.

- The control points of the B-splines in the first step are interpolated in the direction across the B-splines in the first step. That is, the ith control points of all the B-splines derived in the first step are collected and interpolated by a B-spline. Then the control points of this B-spline will be $\mathbf{P}_{i,0}$, $\mathbf{P}_{i,1}$, $\mathbf{P}_{i,2}$, . . ., $\mathbf{P}_{i,m}$. Repeating this step for all i from 0 to n gives all the $\mathbf{P}_{i,j}$.

Once we have derived the control points of the interpolation surface, we have to determine orders k and l and the knot values in the u and v directions, respectively. A surface of degree 3 in u and v is used the most, so both k and l usually have the value 4. The knot values in the u and v directions are determined as follows. We know that the knot values are obtained when an interpolation curve is derived, as explained in Section 6.7.2. Thus we would have $(m + 1)$ different sets of knot values in the u direction for each interpolation shown in Figure 7.10. One representative set from these $(m + 1)$ sets may be derived by averaging these sets. In other words, the ith knot value is obtained by averaging the ith values of all the $(m + 1)$ sets. Knot values in the v direction are derived in the same way.

7.9 INTERSECTION OF SURFACES

In this section we calculate the intersection curves of two surfaces. More precisely, because of the inherent limitation of numerical methods, we calculate the points on the intersection curves. We have shown that the intersection curves of surfaces need to be calculated in order to implement the Boolean operations. The intersection curve is also needed when a surface is cut by other surfaces in a surface modeling system. Here we briefly explain the basic idea underlying the algorithms that calculate the intersection curves of the surfaces represented by parametric equations. We consider only the surfaces in parametric equations because the parametric equation is the form used most to represent a surface.

The methods for calculating intersection curves fall mainly into two categories. The methods in the first category basically solve the following nonlinear equation by numerical methods:

$$\mathbf{P}(u, v) - \mathbf{Q}(s, t) = 0 \qquad (7.50)$$

where $\mathbf{P}(u, v)$ and $\mathbf{Q}(s, t)$ are the parametric equations of the surfaces being intersected. Equation (7.50) comprises three scalar equations with four unknowns, u, v, s, and t. The equations can be solved simultaneously by assigning an arbitrary value to one of the unknowns. This will give the parameter values corresponding to a point on the intersection curves. Repeating the same procedure by changing the arbitrary value numerous times will give many points on the intersection curves. The disadvantage of this approach is that convergence depends on the initial values of the unknowns used to solve Equation (7.50) simultaneously [Faux and Pratt 1979]. Furthermore, this approach may not provide all the intersection curves. In other words, it may lose the points on some intersection curves entirely; the points on some intersection curves may be skipped altogether when the arbitrary values have a large interval.

The methods in the second category are based on the subdivision theory [Cohen, Lyche, and Riesenfeld 1980]. In these methods, each surface being intersected is subdivided recursively until all the surface segments are close to the planar quadrilaterals. Then the quadrilaterals from the surface are tested for intersection with those in the set generated from the other surface. Thus the pairs of intersecting quadrilaterals are obtained and the intersection curve segments from these pairs provide a good initial guess for use in Equation (7.50). However, it may not be easy to perform the intersection calculation on the pairs in the right sequence so that the resulting intersection points form the intersection curves as we expect them to. A different approach was suggested to avoid this problem [Peng 1984; Koparkar and Mudur 1986]. In Peng's approach, only one pair of quadrilaterals is searched from the subdivided quadrilaterals of each surface, and this pair is intersected to provide the two ends of the initial intersection segment. Then any one end is selected as a starting point from which the search for the next intersection point begins. In other words, the pair that will give an adjacent intersection segment sharing this end is searched. The intersection calculation on this new pair will give two end points; one is the same as one end of the previous intersection segment, and the other is a new end. This new end is used again to search for the next neighboring pair. Peng stored the subdivided quadrilaterals in a quadtree[6] structure, as suggested by Samet [1982], to provide an efficient search for the neighboring pair. The search procedure continues until the boundary of either surface is reached and starts again from the other end of the initial intersection segment. Exact intersection points are obtained by solving Equation (7.50), using the end points of the intersection segments as the initial values once these end points have been determined. Then the same procedure is repeated with other initial intersection segments to find all the intersection curves. In Appendix J, we explain how to try all the necessary intersection segments.

The methods based on the subdivision theory may require longer computation time compared to the methods in the first category, but they have less chance of missing some intersection curves. In Appendix J, we also describe the intersection calculation for NURBS surfaces based on Peng's approach.

---

[6] A *quadtree* is a two-dimensional form of an octree. Thus the root rectangle enclosing the original shape is divided into four rectangles repeatedly until the original shape is approximated to a specified resolution by the rectangles lying completely inside (or overlapping) the shape.

QUESTIONS AND PROBLEMS

1. A conical surface is generated by revolving a straight line between two points (2, 0, 0) and (1, 2, 0) about the *y* axis by 180 degrees.

   a. Derive the parametric equation of the conical surface. Assume that parameter *u* moves a point along a circle on a plane perpendicular to the *y* axis as it varies from 0 to 1 and that parameter *v* changes the height of the circle in the *y*-direction as it varies from 0 to 1.

   b. Approximate the conical surface by a bicubic patch. In other words, derive the geometric coefficient matrix in Equation (7.18).

   c. Evaluate the coordinates of the bicubic patch at $u = 0.5$, $v = 0.5$ and compare the result with those from the exact parametric equation.

2. Represent the conical surface shown in the accompanying figure, using a bilinear surface, by doing the following.

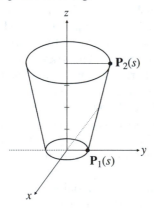

   a. Derive $\mathbf{P}_1(s)$ and $\mathbf{P}_2(s)$ so that each represents the entire circle as *s* varies from 0 to 1.

   b. Represent the conical surface by $\mathbf{r}(s,t)$, which blends $\mathbf{P}_1(s)$ and $\mathbf{P}_2(s)$ linearly. Assume that *t* also varies from 0 to 1.

   c. Substitute $t = 0.5$ in $\mathbf{r}(s,t)$ and explain what it represents.

3. Approximate the surface bounded by three circular arcs shown in the accompanying figure by using a Coon's patch. All the arcs are centered at the origin of the coordinate frame. You may divide the circular arc in the *xy* plane at (0, 1, 0) to have four boundary curves. The equations of the boundary curves should be derived carefully so that they have consistent directions.

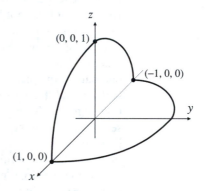

4. A cylindrical surface is generated by sweeping a quarter circle in the *xy* plane along the *z* axis by 4 units as shown in the accompanying figure. The quarter circle has a unit radius and is centered at (0, 0, 0). Do the following.

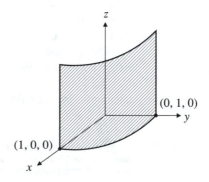

a. Derive the exact parametric equation of the cylindrical surface. Determine the parameters u and v so that the entire surface is represented as u and v vary from 0 to 1.

b. Approximate the cylindrical surface with a Coon's patch.

c. Approximate the cylindrical surface with a bicubic patch.

d. Approximate the cylindrical surface with a Ferguson's patch.

e. Compare the surfaces in (b)–(d) with the exact surface in (a) at the parametric midpoint.

5. Represent the cylindrical surface in Problem 4 by the NURBS surface equation. In other words, determine the knot values and the orders in the u and v directions, respectively, and the coordinates of the control points, including the homogeneous coordinates.

6. To represent the cylindrical surface in Problem 4 by the Bezier surface equation, do the following.

a. Approximate the half circle by a Bezier curve composed of three control points.

b. Use the result in (a) to derive the control points of the Bezier surface.

c. Compare the coordinates of the parametric midpoint with those in Problem 4.

8

Finite-Element Modeling and Analysis

In modern mechanical design, designers commonly use various computer-aided engineering (CAE) software packages to evaluate their designs at each stage in the design process. These CAE tools may be used to analyze the kinematic, or dynamic, response (with large displacements) of an assembly being designed. Software tools such as ADAMS and DADS introduced in Chapter 2 belong to this category. For these tools, each component in the assembly is assumed to have a lumped mass. Sometimes CAE tools are used to evaluate the distribution of stresses or temperatures in a mechanical component that is undergoing force or heat loading. A vibration analysis of a component is also possible when it is undergoing dynamic loading. Each of these types of problems can be solved by using finite-element analysis tools. Commercial software such as NASTRAN and ANSYS introduced in Chapter 2 are examples of finite-element analysis tools.

Early applications of the finite-element method were all in structural mechanics. In fact the name *finite element* was coined in a paper by Clough [1960] in which the technique was presented for plane stress analysis. Thus many of the commercial finite-element packages were originally designed to make a finite-element solution of structural problems more readily available to engineers. However, it soon became apparent that finite-element methods could be applied more generally to the solution of heat transfer, electrostatic potential, fluid mechanics, vibration analysis, and various other types of engineering problems. As the power of computers increased, the range and complexity of problems that could be tackled by finite-element methods also increased. Figure 8.1 illustrates the output obtained by applying finite-element analysis to the door handle of a refrigerator to calculate the temperature distribution after its injection mold is filled with the molten resin. In the application of finite-element analysis to fluid mechanics problems, tools such as C-MOLD and MOLDFLOW simulate molten plastic flow in an injection mold.

Figure 8.1

Application of the
finite-element
method to analyze
temperature distri-
bution

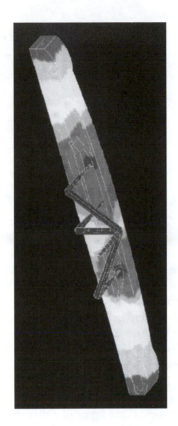

The main difference between finite-element analysis programs and kinematic, or dynamic analysis, programs is that the former consider the domain of the problem as a continuum and the latter consider it as a group of lumped elements. In this chapter we introduce the basic concepts of finite-element analysis tools. We do not consider kinematic, or dynamic, CAE tools because those programs are easy to understand and their manuals provide all the necessary information for their use.

8.1 INTRODUCTION TO FINITE-ELEMENT ANALYSIS

Practical engineering designs almost always involve complicated shapes that are often composed of several different materials. Consider, for example, the problems shown in Figure 8.2. Calculating the stress distribution of the cantilever beam shown in Figure 8.2(a) by using an analytical method is extremely difficult. If the beam is a composite beam made of many different materials, the problem is virtually impossible. Similarly, we cannot derive an analytical expression for the temperature distribution in the object shown in Figure 8.2(b).

Figure 8.2

Problems that cannot be solved analytically

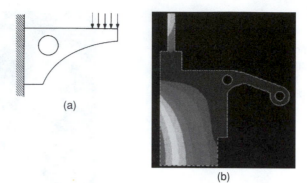

(a)

(b)

The finite-element method is perhaps the most popular numerical technique for solving such problems. The generality of the finite-element method fits the analysis requirements of today's complex engineering systems for which closed-form solutions of governing equilibrium equations usually are not available. In the finite-element method, analysis begins with an approximation of the region of interest (the domain of the problem) and its subdivision into a number of meshes. In Figure 8.3(a), each mesh is connected to associated nodes indicated by the black dots and thus becomes a finite element. Figure 8.3(a) and (b), respectively, show the approximation of the original objects in Figure 8.2(a) and (b) by the aggregation of finite elements—triangular and quadrilateral elements.

Even though we approximated the original object by the triangular elements with three nodes and the quadrilateral elements with four nodes in the preceding examples, other types of finite elements can be chosen, depending on the type of problem, its domain, and the variety of elements provided by the specific finite-element analysis package. In fact, one of the most important decisions to be made by a user of the finite-element method is the choice of the proper element(s) with the proper number of nodes from the available element library. In addition, the total

Figure 8.3

Approximation of each object by an assemblage of finite elements

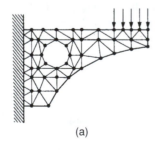

(a)

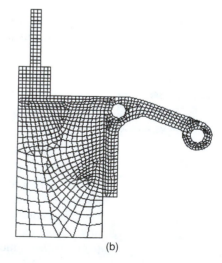

(b)

number of elements (the size of the elements, in other words) to be used in solving any particular problem is also a matter of engineering judgment. As a general rule, the larger the number of nodes and elements (in the *h* version)[1] or the higher the degree of the shape function[2] (in the *p* version), the more accurate is the finite-element solution, but also the more expensive is the solution. We introduce the various types of finite elements in Section 8.3. Another problem is the generation of meshes for an object, especially when the object has a complicated geometry. Creating three-dimensional finite-element meshes is usually a labor-intensive and error-prone process. Many studies are under way to develop an automatic mesh generation capability that can be added to solid modeling systems. With this capability, CAD and CAE can be fully integrated. We briefly review this topic in Section 8.4.

Once the original object has been approximated by finite elements with the proper nodes, each node is associated with the unknowns to be solved. For the example in Figure 8.3(a), displacements in the *x* and *y* directions would be the unknowns to be solved for. This implies that every node has two degrees of freedom and that the solution process will have to solve $2n$ degrees of freedom when there are *n* nodes in total. As we explain in Section 8.2, displacement at any location within an element can be derived from the displacements at its nodes by the presumed shape functions for the element and thus only the displacements at the nodes can be the unknowns. Shape functions simply provide the values of the unknowns, displacements in this example, within an element by interpolating the unknowns at its nodes.[3] Once the displacements have been computed, the strains are derived by the partial derivative of the displacement function and then the stresses are computed from the strains.

After approximating the domain of a problem by an assemblage of discrete finite elements, we specify the properties of the materials in each element and the boundary conditions. By specifying different properties of materials for different finite elements, we can analyze an object comprising regions of numerous materials. We usually know the boundary conditions (e.g., displacement, external force, or temperature) along the continuous boundary portion of the object. These boundary conditions must be expressed as sets of values for displacements, forces, or temperatures on specific nodes of the finite elements. After all the boundary conditions have been provided at the external nodes, the finite-element analysis code generates a formula—*system equations*—that relates the boundary conditions to the unknowns such as the displacements or the temperatures at the nodes and/or the coefficients of the shape functions (in the *p* version), and solves them for the unknowns. We explain this process of generating and solving system equations in Section 8.2.

---

[1] In the classical form of the finite-element method called the *h version*, piecewise polynomials of fixed degree are used as the shape function and the mesh size is decreased for accuracy. In the *p version*, a fixed mesh is used and the degree *p* of the shape function is allowed to increase. For details, refer to MacNeal [1994] and Iszabo and Babuska [1991].

[2] *Shape functions* are independent polynomials defining the approximation of the variable to be solved over the elements.

[3] In the *p* version, the shape function is a high-order polynomial and the coefficients of the polynomial are also the unknowns to be solved as part of the solution process.

Once the unknowns at the nodes have been obtained, the values of the unknowns at any location within any element can be derived by using the same shape function assumed for the generation of the system equations. These outputs from the finite-element analysis code are primarily in numerical form. For example, in solid mechanics problems the output is displacements and stresses. In heat transfer problems, the output is temperatures and element heat fluxes. However, it is difficult from numerical data to capture the trend of the behavior of these output variables. In fact, graphics outputs usually are more informative in showing the trend of behavior over an entire problem domain. To show a trend, curves and contours of the solved variable can be plotted and displayed by the post-processor interfaced with the finite-element analysis package. Deformed shapes can also be displayed—superposed on undeformed shapes for structural mechanics problems. This is the area in which computer graphics plays an important role for CAE.

We close this introductory section by discussing the limitations of the finite-element method. Many engineers are overly confident about the power of the finite-element method without recognizing its limitations; they accept wrong results without question. The great advantages of the finite-element method are its abilities to handle truly arbitrary geometry and to handle nonhomogeneous materials. These two features alone mean that we can treat an arbitrary shape that is made up of regions of various materials. However, the method is based on the technique of dividing the region or domain of the problem into a number of finite elements and then finding the best possible solution that is continuous "inside" the elements but that may not be continuous at the boundary between elements. For example, there may be a jump in the strain across the boundary between the elements in the cantilever shown in Figure 8.3(a), a jump that is not physically possible. The amount of such a jump is often used to evaluate the accuracy of a finite-element solution. This inaccuracy depends on the number and size of the elements and the degree of the shape function used within the element.

8.2 FORMULATION OF THE FINITE-ELEMENT METHOD

As mentioned earlier, the finite-element analysis code generates the system equations composed of nodal unknown variables with accommodating boundary conditions. It also solves the system equations for these unknowns and from them derives other quantities of interest within an element. In this section, we briefly discuss the procedure in which these system equations are formulated in the classical finite-element analysis code (*h* version). To derive the system equations for solid and structural mechanics problems we use the principle of virtual displacement. We use the same notations for the variables as those in Bathe [1982] so that those interested can easily refer to that discussion for details. A different procedure is used to derive the system equations starting from the governing differential equation. We present this procedure in Appendix K.

Figure 8.4

General three-di-
mensional object
under various force
loadings

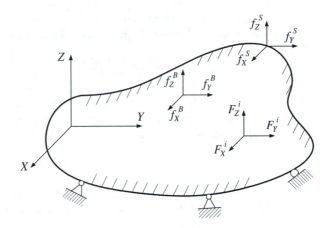

Consider an equilibrium of a three-dimensional object under loading, as shown in Figure 8.4. The external surface tractions are denoted $\mathbf{f}^S$, body forces are denoted $\mathbf{f}^B$, and concentrated external forces are denoted $\mathbf{F}^i$. In general, these forces have three components along the coordinate axes:

$$\mathbf{f}^B = \begin{bmatrix} f_X^B \\ f_Y^B \\ f_Z^B \end{bmatrix}, \qquad \mathbf{f}^S = \begin{bmatrix} f_X^S \\ f_Y^S \\ f_Z^S \end{bmatrix}, \qquad \mathbf{f}^i = \begin{bmatrix} F_X^i \\ F_Y^i \\ F_Z^i \end{bmatrix} \tag{8.1}$$

Let's denote the displacements of any point (X, Y, Z) of the object from the un-loaded configuration as $\mathbf{U}$. Then

$$\mathbf{U}^T = [U(X, Y, Z)\ V(X, Y, Z)\ W(X, Y, Z)] \tag{8.2}$$

where the superscript T implies the transpose of a matrix. The displacements $\mathbf{U}$ will cause the strains

$$\varepsilon^T = [\varepsilon_{XX}\ \varepsilon_{YY}\ \varepsilon_{ZZ}\ \gamma_{XY}\ \gamma_{YZ}\ \gamma_{ZX}] \tag{8.3}$$

and the corresponding stresses

$$\tau^T = [\tau_{XX}\ \tau_{YY}\ \tau_{ZZ}\ \tau_{XY}\ \tau_{YZ}\ \tau_{ZX}] \tag{8.4}$$

Our goal is to calculate $\mathbf{U}$, ε, and τ in Equations (8.2)–(8.4) at point (X, Y, Z) from the given external forces. You may be familiar with the following approach to solving the problem: The governing differential equations of equilibrium are established by considering the equilibrium condition on differential elements of the object and then solved, subject to appropriate boundary and compatibility conditions.

An equivalent approach is used to express the equilibrium of the object: the principle of virtual displacements. It states that the equilibrium of the object requires that, for any compatible, small virtual displacements (which satisfy the essential boundary conditions) imposed on the object, the total internal virtual work equals the total external virtual work. Thus the equilibrium can be expressed as

$$\int_V \bar{\varepsilon}^T \tau \, dv = \int_V \overline{\mathbf{U}}^{\mathbf{T}} \mathbf{f}^B \, dV + \int_S \overline{\mathbf{U}}^{S^T} \mathbf{f}^S \, dS + \sum_i \overline{\mathbf{U}}^{i^T} \mathbf{F}^i \qquad (8.5)$$

The left-hand side of Equation (8.5) represents the internal virtual work done as the actual stresses τ go through the virtual strains $\bar{\varepsilon}$ caused by the imposed virtual displacements $\overline{\mathbf{U}}$, where

$$\bar{\varepsilon}^T = \left[\bar{\varepsilon}_{XX} \ \bar{\varepsilon}_{YY} \ \bar{\varepsilon}_{ZZ} \ \bar{\gamma}_{XY} \ \bar{\gamma}_{YZ} \ \bar{\gamma}_{ZX} \right] \qquad (8.6)$$

The terms on the right-hand side of Equation (8.5) represent the external work done by the actual forces $\mathbf{f}^B$, $\mathbf{f}^S$, and $\mathbf{F}^i$ as they go through the virtual displacements $\overline{\mathbf{U}}$, where

$$\overline{\mathbf{U}}^T = \left[\overline{U}(X,Y,Z) \ \overline{V}(X,Y,Z) \ \overline{Z}(X,Y,Z) \right] \qquad (8.7)$$

The superscript S in $\overline{\mathbf{U}}^S$ denotes the virtual displacements on the surface, and the superscript i in $\overline{\mathbf{U}}^i$ denotes the displacements at the point where the concentrated forces $\mathbf{F}^i$ are applied. Equation (8.5) also contains the compatibility and constitutive requirements for continuous displacement functions that are compatible and satisfy the displacement boundary conditions. The stresses are evaluated from the strains by using the appropriate constitutive relations. Thus the principle of virtual displacements embodies all the requirements that need be met in analyzing a problem in solid and structural mechanics.

Now, let's consider the use of Equation (8.5) to generate finite-element equations. First, we approximate the object in Figure 8.4 as an assemblage of discrete finite elements. These elements are interconnected at nodal points on the element's boundaries. The displacements at any point (x, y, z) measured with respect to a local coordinate system for an element are assumed to be a function of the displacements at the nodes.[4] That is, for element m we assume that

$$\mathbf{u}^{(m)}(x, y, z) = \mathbf{H}^{(m)}(x, y, z)\widehat{\mathbf{U}} \qquad (8.8)$$

where $\mathbf{H}^{(m)}$ is the displacement interpolation matrix and $\widehat{\mathbf{U}}$ is a vector of the three global displacement components u_i, v_i, and w_i at all nodes. If there are N nodes in total, $\widehat{\mathbf{U}}$ is expressed as

$$\widehat{\mathbf{U}}^T = [u_1 \ v_1 \ w_1 \ u_2 \ v_2 \ w_2 \ \cdots u_N \ v_N \ w_N] \qquad (8.9)$$

Equation (8.9) can be rewritten as

$$\widehat{\mathbf{U}}^T = [U_1 \ U_2 \ U_3 \ \cdots U_n] \qquad (8.10)$$

---

[4] In the p version, the displacement is composed of two parts: One part is the quantity determined from the displacements at the nodes, as in Equation (8.8), whereas the other part is the "hierarchical" displacement defined by a polynomial of any arbitrary degree. For details on the p version, refer to MacNeal [1994] and Szabó and Babuška [1991].

where U_i may correspond to a displacement in any direction, and n describes the total number of degrees of freedom. We use the expression for $\hat{\mathbf{U}}$ in Equation (8.10) from now on.

Even though all nodal point displacements are listed in Equation (8.10), and thus in Equation (8.8), for a given element only the displacements at the nodes of the element affect the displacement within the element. We use all the nodes in Equation (8.8) to facilitate the process of assembling the element matrices into the whole structure matrix, as will be shown later.

From Equation (8.8), the strains in each element can be evaluated as follows:

$$\varepsilon^{(m)}(x, y, z) = \mathbf{B}^{(m)}(x, y, z)\hat{\mathbf{U}} \tag{8.11}$$

The rows of the strain–displacement matrix, $\mathbf{B}^{(m)}$, in Equation (8.11) are obtained by appropriately differentiating and combining rows of the matrix $\mathbf{H}^{(m)}$. The derivations of $\mathbf{H}^{(m)}$ and $\mathbf{B}^{(m)}$ are shown later in Example 8.1.

Now the stresses within an element can be expressed as

$$\tau^{(m)} = \mathbf{C}^{(m)}\varepsilon^{(m)} + \tau^{I(m)} \tag{8.12}$$

where $\mathbf{C}^{(m)}$ is the elasticity matrix of element m and $\tau^{I(m)}$ are the element's initial stresses. The elasticity matrix, which is a matrix simply relating strains to stresses, is described in most elementary strength of materials textbooks [Budynas 1977]. We can use different $\mathbf{C}^{(m)}$ for each element of the structure made of composite materials. In addition, $\mathbf{C}^{(m)}$ can be that of isotropic or anisotropic material.

Before we substitute the expressions of Equations (8.8), (8.11), and (8.12) in the formula for the principle of virtual displacements, we rewrite Equation (8.5) as a sum of integration over the volume and areas of each finite element:

$$\sum_m \int_{V^{(m)}} \bar{\varepsilon}^{(m)^T} \tau^{(m)} \, dV^{(m)} = \sum_m \int_{V^{(m)}} \bar{\mathbf{u}}^{(m)^T} \mathbf{f}^{B(m)} \, dV^{(m)}$$
$$+ \sum_m \int_{S^{(m)}} \bar{\mathbf{u}}^{S(m)^T} \mathbf{f}^{S(m)} \, dS^{(m)} + \sum_i \bar{\mathbf{U}}^{i^T} \mathbf{F}^i \tag{8.13}$$

where m varies from 1 to the total number of elements.

When we substitute Equations (8.8), (8.11), and (8,12) in Equation (8.13), we assume that the virtual displacements within the element $\bar{\mathbf{u}}^{(m)}$ are related to the virtual nodal displacements $\bar{\mathbf{U}}$ by the same $\mathbf{H}^{(m)}$ in Equation (8.8). These substitutions yield

$$\bar{\mathbf{U}}^T \left[\sum_m \int_{V^{(m)}} \mathbf{B}^{(m)^T} \mathbf{C}^{(m)} \mathbf{B}^{(m)} \, dV^{(m)} \right] \hat{\mathbf{U}} = \bar{\mathbf{U}}^T \left[\left\{ \sum_m \int_{V^{(m)}} \mathbf{H}^{(m)^T} \mathbf{f}^{B(m)} \, dV^{(m)} \right\} \right.$$
$$+ \left\{ \sum_m \int_{S^{(m)}} \mathbf{H}^{S(m)^T} \mathbf{f}^{S(m)} \, dS^{(m)} \right\}$$
$$\left. - \left\{ \sum_m \int_{V^{(m)}} \mathbf{B}^{(m)^T} \tau^{I(m)} \, dV^{(m)} \right\} + \mathbf{F} \right] \tag{8.14}$$

where the surface displacement interpolation matrices, $\mathbf{H}^{S(m)}$, are obtained from the volume displacement interpolation matrices, $\mathbf{H}^{(m)}$, in Equation (8.8) by substituting the element surface coordinates, and $\mathbf{F}$ is a vector of the external concentrated forces applied to the nodes. The ith component in $\mathbf{F}$ is the concentrated nodal force corresponding to the ith displacement component in $\widehat{\mathbf{U}}$. You should note that in Equation (8.14) the virtual nodal displacement vector $\widehat{\mathbf{U}}$ is moved in front of the summation because it is independent of the element considered.

For Equation (8.14) to hold for arbitrary virtual displacement, which is a condition for equilibrium, the following equation must be satisfied:

$$\left[\sum_m \int_{V^{(m)}} \mathbf{B}^{(m)^T} \mathbf{C}^{(m)} \mathbf{B}^{(m)} \, dV^{(m)} \right] \widehat{\mathbf{U}} = \sum_m \int_{V^{(m)}} \mathbf{H}^{(m)^T} \mathbf{f}^{B(m)} \, dV^{(m)} + \sum_m \int_{S^{(m)}} \mathbf{H}^{S(m)^T} \mathbf{f}^{S(m)} \, dS^{(m)}$$
$$- \sum_m \int_{V^{(m)}} \mathbf{B}^{(m)^T} \tau^{I(m)} \, dV^{(m)} + \mathbf{F} \tag{8.15}$$

If we denote the nodal point displacements $\mathbf{U}$ from now on for simplicity, we can rewrite Equation (8.15) as

$$\mathbf{K} \, \mathbf{U} = \mathbf{R} \tag{8.16}$$

where

$$\mathbf{K} = \sum_m \int_{V^{(m)}} \mathbf{B}^{(m)^T} \mathbf{C}^{(m)} \mathbf{B}^{(m)} \, dV^{(m)} \tag{8.17}$$

$$\mathbf{R} = \mathbf{R}_B + \mathbf{R}_S - \mathbf{R}_I + \mathbf{R}_C \tag{8.18}$$

$$\mathbf{R}_B = \sum_m \int_{V^{(m)}} \mathbf{H}^{(m)^T} \mathbf{f}^{B(m)} \, dV^{(m)} \tag{8.19}$$

$$\mathbf{R}_S = \sum_m \int_{S^{(m)}} \mathbf{H}^{S(m)^T} \mathbf{f}^{S(m)} \, dS^{(m)} \tag{8.20}$$

$$\mathbf{R}_I = \sum_m \int_{V^{(m)}} \mathbf{B}^{(m)^T} \tau^{I(m)} \, dV^{(m)} \tag{8.21}$$

and

$$\mathbf{R}_c = \mathbf{F} \tag{8.22}$$

Note that summation of the element volume integrals in Equation (8.17) expresses the direct addition of the element stiffness matrices $\mathbf{K}^{(m)}$ to obtain the stiffness matrix of the total element assemblage. In the same way, the body force vector of the entire structure $\mathbf{R}_B$ is calculated by summing the element body force vectors. Other force vectors $\mathbf{R}_S$, $\mathbf{R}_I$, and $\mathbf{R}_C$ are obtained similarly.

Equation (8.16) describes the static equilibrium of the problem. If the applied forces vary with time, Equation (8.16) describes equilibrium at any specific point in time. However, if the loads are applied rapidly, inertia forces need to be considered. Using d'Alembert's principle, we can simply include the element inertia forces as part of the body forces. If we assume that the accelerations at any point within an element are related to its nodal point accelerations by $\mathbf{H}^{(m)}$, as for the displacements, the contribution from the total body forces to the load vector $\mathbf{R}$ would be

$$\mathbf{R}_B = \sum_m \int_{V^{(m)}} \mathbf{H}^{(m)^T} \left[\mathbf{f}^{B(m)} - \rho^{(m)} \mathbf{H}^{(m)} \ddot{\mathbf{U}} \right] dV^{(m)} \tag{8.23}$$

where $\ddot{\mathbf{U}}$ are the nodal point accelerations and $\rho^{(m)}$ is the mass density of element m. In Equation (8.23), $\mathbf{f}^{B(m)}$ no longer includes inertia forces.

Substituting Equation (8.23) instead of Equation (8.19) in Equation (8.15) gives the equilibrium equation

$$\mathbf{M}\ddot{\mathbf{U}} + \mathbf{K}\mathbf{U} = \mathbf{R} \tag{8.24}$$

where $\mathbf{M}$, the mass matrix, is

$$\mathbf{M} = \sum_m \int_{V^{(m)}} \rho^{(m)} \mathbf{H}^{(m)^T} \mathbf{H}^{(m)} \, dV^{(m)} \tag{8.25}$$

Note that $\mathbf{U}$ and $\mathbf{R}$ in Equation (8.24) are time dependent.

We can introduce damping forces as additional contributions to the body forces to include the damping effect. In this case, Equation (8.23) becomes

$$\mathbf{R}_B = \sum_m \int_{V^{(m)}} \mathbf{H}^{(m)^T} \left[\mathbf{f}^{B(m)} - \rho^{(m)} \mathbf{H}^{(m)} \ddot{\mathbf{U}} - \kappa^{(m)} \mathbf{H}^{(m)} \dot{\mathbf{U}} \right] dV^{(m)} \tag{8.26}$$

where $\dot{\mathbf{U}}$ is a vector of the nodal point velocities, and $\kappa^{(m)}$ is the damping property parameter of element m.

Therefore the equilibrium equation is

$$\mathbf{M}\ddot{\mathbf{U}} + \mathbf{C}\dot{\mathbf{U}} + \mathbf{K}\mathbf{U} = \mathbf{R} \tag{8.27}$$

where $\mathbf{C}$ is the damping matrix of the structure expressed as

$$\mathbf{C} = \sum_m \int_{V^{(m)}} \kappa^{(m)} \mathbf{H}^{(m)^T} \mathbf{H}^{(m)} \, dV^{(m)} \tag{8.28}$$

In general, the matrix $\mathbf{C}$ is constructed from experimental results on the amount of damping by using the mass matrix and stiffness matrix because it is difficult to determine the element damping parameters. The following example clarifies the procedure for deriving the system equations described.

EXAMPLE 8.1

Derive and solve the system equations of the plate loaded as shown in Figure 8.5(a), using a two-element model, as shown in Figure 8.5(b). The Young's modulus and the Poisson's ratio of the plate are E and v, respectively, and the plate has a constant thickness 1 cm. Assume that the load P_y is applied very slowly so that inertial effect can be ignored.

Figure 8.5

Structure being analyzed

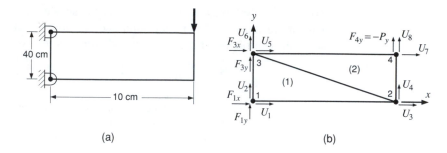

(a)　　　　　　　　　　　　　(b)

ANSWER

The first step is to construct $\mathbf{H}^{(m)}$ and $\mathbf{B}^{(m)}$ for $m = 1, 2$, which corresponds to $\mathbf{U}^T = [U_1\ U_2\ U_3\ U_4\ U_5\ U_6\ U_7\ U_8]$. Then to derive the displacement transformation matrix $\mathbf{H}^{(i)}$ of any element, consider the triangular element shown in Figure 8.6. Displacements within the triangular element with three nodes can be assumed to be linear. That is, the displacements within each element in the x and y directions are, respectively,[5]

$$u = \alpha_1 + \alpha_2 x + \alpha_3 y \tag{8.29}$$

$$v = \beta_1 + \beta_2 x + \beta_3 y \tag{8.30}$$

Thus the displacements of each node are,

$$u_1 = \alpha_1 + \alpha_2 x_1 + \alpha_3 y_1, \quad v_1 = \beta_1 + \beta_2 x_1 + \beta_3 y_1$$

$$u_2 = \alpha_1 + \alpha_2 x_2 + \alpha_3 y_2, \quad v_2 = \beta_1 + \beta_2 x_2 + \beta_3 y_2$$

$$u_3 = \alpha_1 + \alpha_2 x_3 + \alpha_3 y_3, \quad v_3 = \beta_1 + \beta_2 x_3 + \beta_3 y_3$$

When these equations are solved simultaneously, the constants α_i, β_i can be deter-

Figure 8.6

Triangular element with three nodes

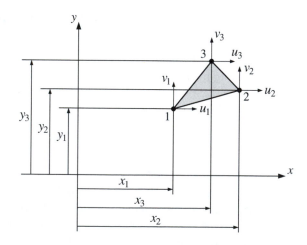

[5] The functions $\alpha_1 + \alpha_2 x + \alpha_3 y$ and $\beta_1 + \beta_2 x + \beta_3 y$ assume the role of interpolation functions.

mined in terms of u_i, v_i and x_i, y_i. Hence we get the following expressions for α_i and β_i:[6]

$$\alpha_1 = \frac{a_1 u_1 + a_2 u_2 + a_3 u_3}{2a}$$

$$\alpha_2 = \frac{b_1 u_1 + b_2 u_2 + b_3 u_3}{2a}$$

$$\alpha_3 = \frac{c_1 u_1 + c_2 u_2 + c_3 u_3}{2a}$$

$$\beta_1 = \frac{a_1 v_1 + a_2 v_2 + a_3 v_3}{2a}$$

$$\beta_2 = \frac{b_1 v_1 + b_2 v_2 + b_3 v_3}{2a}$$

$$\beta_3 = \frac{c_1 v_1 + c_2 v_2 + c_3 v_3}{2a}$$

where

$$
\begin{aligned}
a_1 &= x_2 y_3 - x_3 y_2, & b_1 &= y_2 - y_3, & c_1 &= x_3 - x_2 \\
a_2 &= x_3 y_1 - x_1 y_3, & b_2 &= y_3 - y_1, & c_2 &= x_1 - x_3 \\
a_3 &= x_1 y_2 - x_2 y_1, & b_3 &= y_1 - y_2, & c_3 &= x_2 - x_1
\end{aligned}
$$

and

$$2a = a_1 + a_2 + a_3$$

Substituting the values of x_1, x_2, x_3, y_1, y_2, and y_3 of element 1 into these equations gives

$$
u = u_1 + \left(-\frac{1}{10}u_1 + \frac{1}{10}u_2\right)x + \left(-\frac{1}{4}u_1 + \frac{1}{4}u_3\right)y
$$

$$
v = v_1 + \left(-\frac{1}{10}v_1 + \frac{1}{10}v_2\right)x + \left(-\frac{1}{4}v_1 + \frac{1}{4}v_3\right)y
$$

(8.31)

Equation (8.31) can be rewritten as

$$
\begin{bmatrix} u \\ v \end{bmatrix}^{(1)} =
\begin{bmatrix}
\left(1 - \frac{1}{10}x - \frac{1}{4}y\right) & 0 & \frac{1}{10}x & 0 & \frac{1}{4}y & 0 & 0 & 0 \\
0 & \left(1 - \frac{1}{10}x - \frac{1}{4}y\right) & 0 & \frac{1}{10}x & 0 & \frac{1}{4}y & 0 & 0
\end{bmatrix}
\begin{bmatrix} U_1 \\ U_2 \\ U_3 \\ U_4 \\ U_5 \\ U_6 \\ U_7 \\ U_8 \end{bmatrix}
$$

(8.32)

---

[6] When the expressions for α_i and β_i are substituted back in Equations (8.29) and (8.30), the displacements u and v can be expressed in the form of $u = B_1(x, y)u_1 + B_2(x, y)u_2 + B_3(x, y)u_3$, $v = B_1(x, y)v_1 + B_2(x, y)v_2 + B_3(x, y)v_3$. The functions $B_1(x, y)$, $B_2(x, y)$, and $B_3(x, y)$, respectively, are called *shape functions*.

Similarly, the displacements within element 2 can be expressed as

$$
\begin{bmatrix} u \\ v \end{bmatrix}^{(2)} = \begin{bmatrix} 0 & 0 & \left(1-\dfrac{y}{4}\right) & 0 & \left(1-\dfrac{x}{10}\right) & 0 & \left(-1+\dfrac{x}{10}+\dfrac{y}{4}\right) & 0 \\ 0 & 0 & 0 & \left(1-\dfrac{y}{4}\right) & 0 & \left(1-\dfrac{x}{10}\right) & 0 & \left(-1+\dfrac{x}{10}+\dfrac{y}{4}\right) \end{bmatrix} \begin{bmatrix} U_1 \\ U_2 \\ U_3 \\ U_4 \\ U_5 \\ U_6 \\ U_7 \\ U_8 \end{bmatrix} \tag{8.33}
$$

The next step is to determine the strains, or the matrix $\mathbf{B}^{(m)}$, using the following two-dimensional strain-displacement relations:

$$
\varepsilon_x = \frac{\partial u}{\partial x}
$$

$$
\varepsilon_y = \frac{\partial v}{\partial y}
$$

$$
\gamma_{xy} = \frac{\partial v}{\partial x} + \frac{\partial u}{\partial y}
$$

Hence $\varepsilon^{(1)}(x, y, z)$ and $\varepsilon^{(2)}(x, y, z)$ are obtained from Equations (8.32) and (8.33):

$$
\varepsilon^{(1)} = \begin{bmatrix} \varepsilon_x \\ \varepsilon_y \\ \gamma_{xy} \end{bmatrix}^{(1)} = \begin{bmatrix} -\dfrac{1}{10} & 0 & \dfrac{1}{10} & 0 & 0 & 0 & 0 & 0 \\ 0 & -\dfrac{1}{4} & 0 & 0 & 0 & \dfrac{1}{4} & 0 & 0 \\ -\dfrac{1}{4} & -\dfrac{1}{10} & 0 & \dfrac{1}{10} & \dfrac{1}{4} & 0 & 0 & 0 \end{bmatrix} \begin{bmatrix} U_1 \\ U_2 \\ U_3 \\ U_4 \\ U_5 \\ U_6 \\ U_7 \\ U_8 \end{bmatrix} \tag{8.34}
$$

$$
= \mathbf{B}^{(1)}\mathbf{U}
$$

$$
\varepsilon^{(2)} = \begin{bmatrix} \varepsilon_x \\ \varepsilon_y \\ \gamma_{xy} \end{bmatrix}^{(2)} = \begin{bmatrix} 0 & 0 & 0 & 0 & -\dfrac{1}{10} & 0 & \dfrac{1}{10} & 0 \\ 0 & 0 & 0 & -\dfrac{1}{4} & 0 & 0 & 0 & \dfrac{1}{4} \\ 0 & 0 & -\dfrac{1}{4} & 0 & 0 & -\dfrac{1}{10} & \dfrac{1}{4} & \dfrac{1}{10} \end{bmatrix} \begin{bmatrix} U_1 \\ U_2 \\ U_3 \\ U_4 \\ U_5 \\ U_6 \\ U_7 \\ U_8 \end{bmatrix} \tag{8.35}
$$

$$
= \mathbf{B}^{(2)}\mathbf{U}
$$

The stress–strain relations for a homogeneous, isotropic plane-stress element are

$$\tau^{(m)} = \begin{bmatrix} \sigma_x \\ \sigma_y \\ \tau_{xy} \end{bmatrix} = \frac{E}{1-v^2} \begin{bmatrix} 1 & v & 0 \\ v & 1 & 0 \\ 0 & 0 & \frac{1}{2}(1-v) \end{bmatrix} \begin{bmatrix} \varepsilon_x \\ \varepsilon_y \\ \gamma_{xy} \end{bmatrix} \tag{8.36}$$

We assumed that there is no initial stress on the structure.

The stiffness matrix of each element is derived by substituting the results from Equations (8.34)–(8.36) in Equation (8.17). The two elements are made of the same material, so the expression for $\mathbf{C}^{(m)}$ in Equation (8.36) can be used for both elements. (In the following derivation, the volume integral is converted to the area integral because of the unit thickness.)

$$\mathbf{K}^{(1)} = \int_{V^{(1)}} \mathbf{B}^{(1)^T} \mathbf{C}^{(1)} \mathbf{B}^{(1)} \, dV^{(1)}$$

$$= \int_{A^{(1)}} \mathbf{B}^{(1)^T} \mathbf{C}^{(1)} \mathbf{B}^{(1)} \, dA^{(1)}$$

$$= \int_0^{10} \mathbf{B}^{(1)^T} \mathbf{C}^{(1)} \mathbf{B}^{(1)} \left(4 - \frac{4}{10} x \right) dx$$

$$= \frac{E}{1-v^2} \int_0^{10} \begin{bmatrix} -\frac{1}{10} & 0 & \frac{1}{10} & 0 & 0 & 0 & 0 & 0 \\ 0 & -\frac{1}{4} & 0 & 0 & 0 & \frac{1}{4} & 0 & 0 \\ -\frac{1}{4} & -\frac{1}{10} & 0 & \frac{1}{10} & \frac{1}{4} & 0 & 0 & 0 \end{bmatrix}^T \begin{bmatrix} 1 & v & 0 \\ v & 1 & 0 \\ 0 & 0 & \frac{1-v}{2} \end{bmatrix}$$

$$\begin{bmatrix} -\frac{1}{10} & 0 & \frac{1}{10} & 0 & 0 & 0 & 0 & 0 \\ 0 & -\frac{1}{4} & 0 & 0 & 0 & \frac{1}{4} & 0 & 0 \\ -\frac{1}{4} & -\frac{1}{10} & 0 & \frac{1}{10} & \frac{1}{4} & 0 & 0 & 0 \end{bmatrix} \left(4 - \frac{4}{10} x \right) dx \tag{8.37}$$

$$= \frac{20E}{1-v^2} \begin{bmatrix} \frac{1}{100}+\frac{1-v}{32} & \frac{1+v}{80} & -\frac{1}{100} & -\frac{1-v}{80} & -\frac{1-v}{32} & -\frac{v}{40} & 0 & 0 \\ \frac{1+v}{80} & \frac{1}{16}+\frac{1-v}{200} & -\frac{v}{40} & -\frac{1-v}{200} & -\frac{1-v}{80} & -\frac{1}{16} & 0 & 0 \\ -\frac{1}{100} & -\frac{v}{40} & \frac{1}{100} & 0 & 0 & \frac{v}{40} & 0 & 0 \\ -\frac{1-v}{80} & -\frac{1-v}{200} & 0 & \frac{1-v}{200} & \frac{1-v}{80} & 0 & 0 & 0 \\ -\frac{1-v}{32} & -\frac{1-v}{80} & 0 & \frac{1-v}{80} & \frac{1-v}{32} & 0 & 0 & 0 \\ -\frac{v}{40} & -\frac{1}{16} & \frac{v}{40} & 0 & 0 & \frac{1}{16} & 0 & 0 \\ 0 & 0 & 0 & 0 & 0 & 0 & 0 & 0 \\ 0 & 0 & 0 & 0 & 0 & 0 & 0 & 0 \end{bmatrix}$$

$$\mathbf{K}^{(2)} = \int_{V^{(2)}} \mathbf{B}^{(2)^T} \mathbf{C}^{(2)} \mathbf{B}^{(2)} \, dV^{(2)}$$

$$= \int_{A^{(2)}} \mathbf{B}^{(2)^T} \mathbf{C}^{(2)} \mathbf{B}^{(2)} \, dA^{(2)}$$

$$= \int_0^{10} \mathbf{B}^{(2)^T} \mathbf{C}^{(2)} \mathbf{B}^{(2)} \frac{4}{10} x \, dx$$

$$= \frac{20E}{1-v^2}
\begin{bmatrix}
0 & 0 & 0 & 0 & 0 & 0 & 0 & 0 \\
0 & 0 & 0 & 0 & 0 & 0 & 0 & 0 \\
0 & 0 & \dfrac{1-v}{32} & 0 & 0 & \dfrac{1-v}{80} & -\dfrac{1-v}{32} & -\dfrac{1-v}{80} \\
0 & 0 & 0 & \dfrac{1}{16} & \dfrac{v}{40} & 0 & -\dfrac{v}{40} & -\dfrac{1}{16} \\
0 & 0 & 0 & \dfrac{v}{40} & \dfrac{1}{100} & 0 & -\dfrac{1}{100} & -\dfrac{v}{40} \\
0 & 0 & \dfrac{1-v}{80} & 0 & 0 & \dfrac{1-v}{200} & \dfrac{1-v}{80} & \dfrac{1-v}{200} \\
0 & 0 & -\dfrac{1-v}{32} & -\dfrac{v}{40} & -\dfrac{1}{100} & -\dfrac{1-v}{80} & \dfrac{1}{100}+\dfrac{1-v}{32} & \dfrac{1+v}{80} \\
0 & 0 & -\dfrac{1-v}{80} & -\dfrac{1}{16} & -\dfrac{v}{40} & -\dfrac{1-v}{200} & \dfrac{1+v}{80} & \dfrac{1}{16}+\dfrac{1-v}{200}
\end{bmatrix}
\tag{8.38}$$

The stiffness matrix of the structure as a whole is obtained by assembling Equations (8.37) and (8.38). Hence

$$\mathbf{K} = \frac{20E}{1-v^2}
\begin{bmatrix}
\dfrac{1}{100}+\dfrac{1-v}{32} & \dfrac{1+v}{80} & -\dfrac{1}{100} & -\dfrac{1-v}{80} & -\dfrac{1-v}{32} & -\dfrac{v}{40} & 0 & 0 \\
\dfrac{1+v}{80} & \dfrac{1}{16}+\dfrac{1-v}{200} & -\dfrac{v}{40} & -\dfrac{1-v}{200} & -\dfrac{1-v}{80} & -\dfrac{1}{16} & 0 & 0 \\
-\dfrac{1}{100} & -\dfrac{v}{40} & \dfrac{1}{100}+\dfrac{1-v}{32} & 0 & 0 & \dfrac{1+v}{80} & -\dfrac{1-v}{32} & -\dfrac{1-v}{80} \\
-\dfrac{1-v}{80} & -\dfrac{1-v}{200} & 0 & \dfrac{1}{16}+\dfrac{1-v}{200} & \dfrac{1+v}{80} & 0 & -\dfrac{v}{40} & \dfrac{1}{16} \\
-\dfrac{1-v}{32} & -\dfrac{1-v}{80} & 0 & \dfrac{1+v}{80} & \dfrac{1}{100}+\dfrac{1-v}{32} & 0 & -\dfrac{1}{100} & \dfrac{v}{40} \\
-\dfrac{v}{40} & -\dfrac{1}{16} & \dfrac{1+v}{80} & 0 & 0 & \dfrac{1}{16}+\dfrac{1-v}{200} & -\dfrac{1-v}{80} & -\dfrac{1-v}{200} \\
0 & 0 & -\dfrac{1-v}{32} & -\dfrac{v}{40} & -\dfrac{1}{100} & -\dfrac{1-v}{80} & \dfrac{1}{100}+\dfrac{1-v}{32} & \dfrac{1+v}{80} \\
0 & 0 & -\dfrac{1-v}{80} & -\dfrac{1}{16} & -\dfrac{v}{40} & -\dfrac{1-v}{200} & \dfrac{1+v}{80} & \dfrac{1}{16}+\dfrac{1-v}{200}
\end{bmatrix}$$

$$\tag{8.39}$$

The load vector, **R**, equals $\mathbf{R}_c$ because only concentrated forces act on the nodes. Hence

$$\mathbf{R} = \begin{bmatrix} F_{1x} \\ F_{1y} \\ 0 \\ 0 \\ F_{3x} \\ F_{3y} \\ 0 \\ -P_y \end{bmatrix} \qquad (8.40)$$

where P_y is the known external force and F_{1x}, F_{1y}, F_{3x}, and F_{3y} are the unknown reaction forces at the supports.

Now we have to solve for the unknown nodal point displacements from the following equation:

$$\begin{bmatrix} k_{11} & k_{12} & k_{13} & \cdot & \cdot & \cdot & k_{17} & k_{18} \\ k_{21} & k_{22} & k_{23} & & & & k_{27} & k_{28} \\ \cdot & \cdot & \cdot & & & & \cdot & \cdot \\ \cdot & \cdot & \cdot & & & & \cdot & \cdot \\ \cdot & \cdot & \cdot & & & & \cdot & \cdot \\ \cdot & \cdot & \cdot & & & & \cdot & \cdot \\ k_{71} & k_{72} & k_{73} & \cdot & \cdot & \cdot & k_{77} & k_{78} \\ k_{81} & k_{82} & k_{83} & \cdot & \cdot & \cdot & k_{87} & k_{88} \end{bmatrix} \begin{bmatrix} U_1 \\ U_2 \\ U_3 \\ U_4 \\ U_5 \\ U_6 \\ U_7 \\ U_8 \end{bmatrix} = \begin{bmatrix} F_{1x} \\ F_{1y} \\ 0 \\ 0 \\ F_{3x} \\ F_{3y} \\ 0 \\ -P_y \end{bmatrix} \qquad (8.41)$$

where the elements of the stiffness matrix in Equation (8.39) are denoted k_{ij}.

You may determine that the stiffness matrix in Equation (8.39) is singular and that therefore Equation (8.41) cannot be solved as it is. This is analogous to the idea that a unique solution of a differential equation cannot be obtained without imposing the proper boundary conditions. Similarly, the solution of Equation (8.41) can be obtained by applying the boundary conditions as follows:

$$\begin{bmatrix} k_{11} & k_{12} & k_{13} & \cdot & \cdot & \cdot & k_{17} & k_{18} \\ k_{21} & k_{22} & k_{23} & & & & k_{27} & k_{28} \\ \cdot & \cdot & \cdot & & & & \cdot & \cdot \\ \cdot & \cdot & \cdot & & & & \cdot & \cdot \\ \cdot & \cdot & \cdot & & & & \cdot & \cdot \\ \cdot & \cdot & \cdot & & & & \cdot & \cdot \\ k_{71} & k_{72} & k_{73} & \cdot & \cdot & \cdot & k_{77} & k_{78} \\ k_{81} & k_{82} & k_{83} & \cdot & \cdot & \cdot & k_{87} & k_{88} \end{bmatrix} \begin{bmatrix} 0 \\ 0 \\ U_3 \\ U_4 \\ 0 \\ 0 \\ U_7 \\ U_8 \end{bmatrix} = \begin{bmatrix} F_{1x} \\ F_{1y} \\ 0 \\ 0 \\ F_{3x} \\ F_{3y} \\ 0 \\ -P_y \end{bmatrix} \qquad (8.42)$$

Equation (8.42) can be partitioned into two parts:

$$
\begin{bmatrix}
k_{33} & k_{34} & k_{37} & k_{38} \\
k_{43} & k_{44} & k_{47} & k_{48} \\
k_{73} & k_{74} & k_{77} & k_{78} \\
k_{83} & k_{84} & k_{87} & k_{88}
\end{bmatrix}
\begin{bmatrix}
U_3 \\
U_4 \\
U_7 \\
U_8
\end{bmatrix}
=
\begin{bmatrix}
0 \\
0 \\
0 \\
-P_y
\end{bmatrix}
\tag{8.43}
$$

$$
\begin{bmatrix}
k_{13} & k_{14} & k_{17} & k_{18} \\
k_{23} & k_{24} & k_{27} & k_{28} \\
k_{53} & k_{54} & k_{57} & k_{58} \\
k_{63} & k_{64} & k_{67} & k_{68}
\end{bmatrix}
\begin{bmatrix}
U_3 \\
U_4 \\
U_7 \\
U_8
\end{bmatrix}
=
\begin{bmatrix}
F_{1x} \\
F_{1y} \\
F_{3x} \\
F_{3y}
\end{bmatrix}
\tag{8.44}
$$

We can solve Equation (8.43) for the unknown nodal point displacements U_3, U_4, U_7, and U_8 and substitute these values in Equation (8.44) to get the unknown reaction forces F_{1x}, F_{1y}, F_{3x}, and F_{3y}. In fact, most finite-element analysis code follows this solution procedure.

Once we have obtained the nodal point displacements, we calculate the strains and the stresses within each element from these displacements by using Equations (8.34)–(8.36). Therefore we conclude that displacements play a major role in the analysis of a structure. This is one of the reasons why the formulation introduced in this section is called a *displacement-based formulation*.

8.3   FINITE-ELEMENT MODELING

Even though finite-element analysis is a powerful technology for simulating structural, thermal, and other phenomena such as fluid flow and electromagnetics, the main hurdle remains preparation of the data for an analysis: building the geometry, making the finite-element mesh, adding boundary conditions and loads, providing properties of materials, and specifying analysis type (e.g., static or dynamic, linear or nonlinear, plane stress, plane strain, etc.). These activities, called *finite-element modeling*, usually are performed by a pre-processor designed for a specific finite-element analysis (FEA) code.

The pre-processor begins its task from the geometry of the object or the domain of problem. Traditional FEA systems had only rudimentary modeling functions, but most of today's systems either offer advanced modeling capabilities or have close ties to CAD systems (and sometimes both) [Mills 1997]. Systems that rely on CAD for geometric modeling either work directly on the CAD model or translate and import the geometry. The *direct on CAD* approach is becoming increasingly popular because it eliminates translation steps and loss of data and shortens the design–analyze–update loop. Moreover, using the CAD system eases modeling and provides more powerful functions for creating and changing complex geometry. Indeed, today's hybrid modeling systems (with integrated solid, surface, and wire-frame modeling[7] and parametric, feature-based methods) can build just about any geometry needed for analysis. Most FEA systems also emphasize being able to import geometry, either through standards such as IGES[8] or directly from specific CAD systems. However, using CAD geometry is not always straightforward. A model that looks perfect to the designer may actually contain flaws that are not allowed in the FEA system, especially with regard to meshing. Some systems now offer functions that can "clean up" imported geometry. Moreover, even when CAD geometry comes without flaws, not all its details may be needed for analysis and some of them may be eliminated. For example, details such as fillets may or may not be included in the geometry. Such decisions are made by the designer and based partially on the expected mesh size and on insight as to which regions of the object are critical. Some programs offer functions for "defeaturing" geometry to hide temporarily features that do not affect the accuracy of the analysis. This abstraction process is the main reason why the design team and the analysis team carry different models for the same object and why modification by one team is not directly reflected to the other team. Currently research is under way to achieve automatic abstraction of solid models [Armstrong et al. 1995].

The next step is creation of the meshes and distribution of the nodes. When each mesh is associated with the nodes, it becomes a finite element. Generation of the meshes is the most important and difficult stage in finite-element modeling. To ease the task, virtually all systems today offer some type of automatic meshing. The typical approach is to offer automatic tetrahedral meshing for solid geometry and quadrilateral or triangular elements for three-dimensional surface, shell, or two-dimensional geometry. Many systems allow users to tinker with automatic meshing parameters such as mesh densities. They also provide local refinement functions to fine-tune critical regions. Many systems also associate the mesh with the geometry so that a change in the geometry is reflected automatically onto the mesh.

The mesh complexity used will determine the size of the global stiffness matrix, the numerical complexity, and the computing resources required. The accuracy of the solution can be improved by increasing the number of meshes (elements) or by using higher order shape functions within each element. The following constraints should be satisfied in generating the finite elements. First, element dimensionality should be the same as the dimensionality of the domain of the problem. That is, one-dimensional elements are used for a one-dimensional problem, two-dimensional elements for a two-dimensional problem, and so on. Second, the element being generated should be supported by the finite-element analysis code to be used. In other words, the finite-element code should have a procedure to compute the specific element contribution to the stiffness matrix. The various elements supported by a particular finite-element analysis code are together known as the *element library*. The greater the number of elements in the library, the larger the number of problems it can handle. Figure 8.7 illustrates the typical finite elements

[7] Nonmanifold modeling systems support integrated solid, surface, and wire-frame modeling in the most general way.
[8] IGES is explained in Chapter 14.

Figure 8.7

Element types for each dimension: (a) one-dimensional elements, (b) two-dimensional elements, and (c) three-dimensional elements

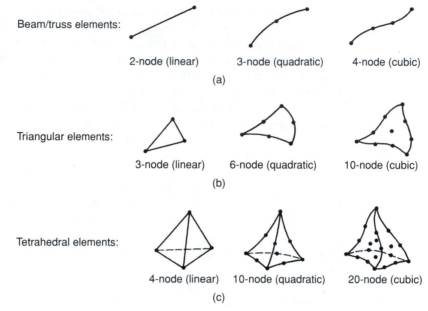

Beam/truss elements:

2-node (linear)   3-node (quadratic)   4-node (cubic)

(a)

Triangular elements:

3-node (linear)   6-node (quadratic)   10-node (cubic)

(b)

Tetrahedral elements:

4-node (linear)   10-node (quadratic)   20-node (cubic)

(c)

supported by most finite-element codes. Note that the same mesh can become different finite elements, depending on how many nodes are associated with the mesh. Finally, zones of expected abrupt change in the behavior of the unknowns to be solved (such as stress concentration around holes) should have a greater node and element density than zones of expected gradual change.

Another approach to the meshing quandary is to use the *p* version FEM. It relies on a simpler, automatically generated mesh, but then it automatically varies the degree of the shape functions. Although many *p* version FEA programs are available, two programs—PTC's Pro/MECHANICA and CADSI's PolyFEM—were designed specifically for *p* version analysis. In addition to easy meshing, the advantages of this approach are the ability to specify accuracy limits and closer approximation of CAD geometry. By using a lower accuracy level, the designer can get the analysis results quickly at the preliminary design stage.

After the element layout has been chosen, the type of analysis (e.g., static or dynamic, linear or nonlinear, plane stress, and plane strain) is specified. Also the unknowns or the degrees of freedom are associated with each node. Unknowns include displacements, rotations, temperature, heat flux, and so on. Then the boundary conditions are specified. Boundary conditions such as displacement, external force, and temperature usually are known for the continuous boundary portion of the object. These boundary conditions must be expressed as a set of values for displacements, forces, or temperatures on specific nodes of the finite elements. Sometimes, however, the finite elements have to be generated without having the boundary conditions. If point loads are to be considered, nodes have to be generated at these points. Most CAD-linked systems allow the user to define the boundary conditions on the CAD geometry, in which case the boundary conditions are converted to the equivalent boundary conditions on the nodes by the system. Most FEM modelers also provide a number of ways of defining loads and boundary conditions to handle a wide range of problems and to model real-world conditions more closely.

Properties of materials must be also assigned to each element. These properties are typically Young's modulus and Poisson's ratio for structural mechanics problems. The thickness of shell and plate elements is treated more like a property of a material than a geometric property to avoid having to solve the problem in three dimensions. Other properties of materials include heat capacity and viscosity for other types of problems. A single property need not be assumed; different regions of elements may be assigned different properties. This feature enables the user to analyze an object made of composite materials, as mentioned earlier. In problems dealing with composite materials, the treatment of the interface between these materials is a crucial modeling decision.

Once the finite-element model has been defined by choosing all the parameters of the corresponding mesh, the model is input to the code that performs the finite-element analysis. After the FEA problem has been solved, the results are viewed in a step traditionally known as *post-processing*. Most packages provide various ways to tabulate, evaluate, and display results, which typically include stress, strain, and deformed shape. The traditional type of display is a contour plot, which shows color-coded stress levels directly on the object. However, most packages now go well beyond simple contour plots. Tools such as iso-surface displays allow users to view surfaces with the same values, and cross-sectional displays let users cut across models to peer inside them. Animation is also offered for dynamic analysis, for showing various models and deformed shapes, and for time-base nonlinear analyses. Increasingly important is the ability to output displays and animations in standard formats for use elsewhere, as in documents, presentations, videos, e-mail, or posting to a Web site.

8.4 AUTOMATIC MESH GENERATION

Mesh generation implies the generation of nodal coordinates and elements. It also includes the automatic numbering of nodes and elements based on a minimal amount of user interaction. Thus fully *automatic mesh generation* methods are supposed to require only the geometric model (both geometry and topology) of the object to be meshed, the mesh attributes, such as mesh density and element type, and the boundary conditions, including loading conditions as input. Other methods requiring additional input, such as subdividing the object into subdomains or regions, are classified as semiautomatic methods. We briefly introduce mesh generation methods based on the classification scheme proposed by K. Ho-Le [1988]. In some places, we reproduce the developers' wording and illustrations without change.

8.4.1 Node Connection Approach

The node connection mesh generation approach is very popular because it is conceptually simple. The two main phases in the approach are node generation, as shown in Figure 8.8(a), and element generation, as shown in Figure 8.8(b).

Node generation   Published works on node generation include the following.

- *Cavendish's method* [Cavendish 1974]—In this method, the nodes are first added to the object boundary manually. Then interior nodes are generated automatically to satisfy mesh density requirements. The object is divided into a number of zones of different desired element sizes. In zone i, a square grid of gauge $r(i)$ is superimposed. Figure 8.9 shows a superimposed single grid, based on the assumption that uniform mesh density is desired. For each square of the grid, one interior node is randomly generated. This can be done by generating random numbers between 0 and 1 twice, one for the x direction and the other for the y direction, and calculating the position equivalent to the x and y values. If the interior node generated falls inside the object and has a distance greater than $r(i)$ from the boundary and from previously generated nodes, it is accepted. If not, another node is generated randomly and checked. If an acceptable node cannot be found in a fixed number of attempts (say, five), then the current square is skipped and the next square is considered. This method can be extended for node generation in three dimensions by superimposing the three-dimensional grid at the beginning.

- *Shimada's method* [Shimada and Gossard 1992]—This method envisions the inside of the object being meshed to be filled with bubbles, as shown in Figure 8.10, and takes the center points of the bubbles as the nodes. The size of each bubble is determined by the temperature distribution, which corresponds to the desired mesh density. Then the locations of the bubbles are determined to satisfy the equilibrium of all the reacting forces between the bubbles.

Figure 8.8

Node connection approach

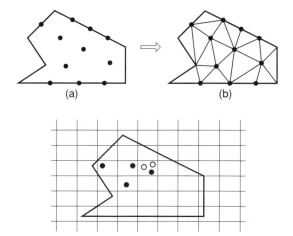

(a)   (b)

Figure 8.9

Node generation by Cavendish's method

Figure 8.10

Node generation
by Shimada's
method [Shimada &
Gossard, 1992]

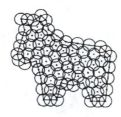

Element generation   In this phase, nodes generated in the previous phase are connected to form elements so that no elements overlap and the entire object is covered. We introduce Lee's method of element generation because it can result in quadrilateral elements. However, the Delaunay triangulation method is the most popular method of node connection. In the following explanations, we consider only the elements having nodes at their vertices. If elements with intermediate nodes are desired, these nodes can easily be generated from the corner nodes. Therefore we do not bother with the intermediate nodes in describing other mesh generation methods in this chapter.

- *Lee's method* [Lee 1983]—In this method, a square grid whose spacing is the same as the desired element size is superimposed on the object. Then the nodes generated in the previous phase are associated with the grid cells. The cells and the corresponding nodes are visited column to column from left to right and, within the same column, from bottom to top. Within a cell, the nodes are sorted in ascending *x*-coordinate values. Nodes having the same *x* coordinates are sorted in ascending *y*-coordinate values. The nodes are visited in turn and, for each node, neighboring nodes are found so as to form the nodes of a good quadrilateral. When a good quadrilateral element cannot be formed, a triangular element is formed.

- *Delaunay triangulation* [Watson 1981]—This is perhaps the most popular method of generating triangles by connecting the given nodes because it maximizes the sum of the smallest angles in all the triangles being generated. Thus thin elements are avoided as much as possible in Delaunay triangulation.

A typical Delaunay triangulation starts from a Voronoi diagram or Dirichlet tessellation [Green and Sibson 1977]. A Voronoi diagram of a set of N points, $\mathbf{P}_i (i = 1, 2, \ldots, N)$, consists of N polygons (polyhedra in three dimensions), V_i, each centered on point $\mathbf{P}_i$ so that the locus of points in the plane (space in three dimensions) nearest node i are included in V_i. Mathematically, V_i is expressed as

$$V_i = \{\mathbf{x} : |\mathbf{x} - \mathbf{P}_i| < |\mathbf{x} - \mathbf{P}_j| \quad \text{for all } j \neq i\} \tag{8.45}$$

where | | means the magnitude of the vector inside and each V_i is a convex polygon (polyhedron) bounded by the lines (planes) bisecting perpendicularly the lines between $\mathbf{P}_i$ and its neighboring nodes. This division of (two- or three-dimensional) space by a set of V_i is called Dirichlet tessellation. Each Voronoi polygon (polyhedron) has a node associated with it. After generating the Voronoi diagram, we can create triangular (tetrahedral, in three dimensions) elements by connecting the

Figure 8.11

Voronoi diagram and Delaunay triangulation

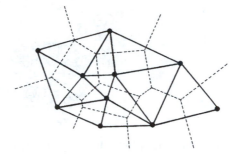

points associated with neighboring Voronoi polygons (polyhedra). Figure 8.11 illustrates the Voronoi diagram and the corresponding Delaunay triangulation for 10 node points in two-dimensional space.

Delaunay triangulation can be generated directly from the given set of points (nodes) without first constructing the Voronoi diagram by using Watson's algorithm for two-dimensional triangulation [Watson 1981]. In this algorithm, a triangle is formed from three noncollinear points when a circle passing through the points, called the *circumcircle* of the triangle, does not include any other points. The algorithm is implemented as follows. First, a triangle T_0 is formed, enclosing all the nodes; extra points may have to be introduced as the vertices of T_0. Then we introduce nodes from the given set, one by one, and find the triangles each of whose circumcircle encloses the node. These polygons, called *intersection polygons*, are eliminated. In Figure 8.12(b), the intersection polygons are marked by **X** when a new node marked ⊙ is introduced to the existing triangles, as in Figure 8.12(a), that are generated by the nodes already introduced; Figure 8.12(c) shows the result after these intersection polygons are eliminated. Then new triangles are formed by connecting the new node to the vertices of the intersection polygons, as shown in Figure 8.12(d). Finally, the triangles connected to the extra points to form T_0 are eliminated. This procedure can easily be extended for three-dimensional element generation by using circumspheres of four nodes instead of circumcircles of three nodes [Cavendish, Field, and Frey 1985]. However, the three-dimensional Delaunay triangulation may contain very thin tetrahedra, while the two-dimensional Delaunay triangulation is, in some sense, the optimal triangulation on a given point set.

Figure 8.12

Watson's algorithm for triangulation

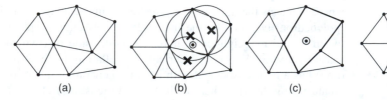

(a)   (b)   (c)   (d)

8.4.2 Topology Decomposition Approach

The two-dimensional *topology decomposition approach* was developed by Wordenweber [1984]. In this approach, an object is approximated to be a polygon and the polygon is decomposed into a set of gross elements by connecting its vertices to form triangles, as shown in Figure 8.13(a). Then these gross elements are refined to satisfy the required mesh density distribution, as shown in Figure 8.13(b). Element sizes and shapes cannot be controlled externally because the gross elements are determined solely from the original object topology, specifically the distribution of vertices. The vertices belonging to the same gross element may be found by the Delaunay triangulation method described in the preceding section.

In the course of generating a set of triangles from the vertices, Wordenweber introduced and applied the operators the way that Euler operators are used in solid modeling. As illustrated in Figure 8.14, first the Wordenweber [1984] operator OP_j is applied to eliminate the holes in the object. Then triangles are formed from the vertices and separated from the object by applying operator OP_1 recursively until only three vertices are left. Finally, operator OP_2 is applied to form the last triangle.

Once the object has been converted to a set of gross triangles, each triangle is refined to satisfy the required mesh density. The following three methods, illustrated in Figure 8.15, can be used for the refinement. Figure 8.15(a) shows a

Figure 8.13

Example of the topology decomposition approach

(a)   (b)

Figure 8.14

Operators used to form triangles

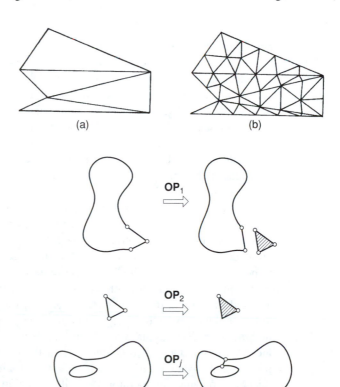

Figure 8.15

**Methods of refining
triangles**

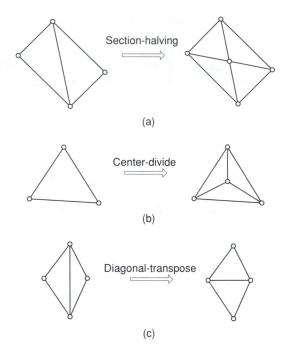

The topology decomposition approach can be extended to three-dimensional mesh generation. An object is approximated to be a polyhedron, and the polyhedron is decomposed into tetrahedral elements by connecting its vertices. Then the tetrahedral elements are refined by the subdivision. Woo and Thomasma [1984] proposed the operators similar to those proposed by Wordenweber to facilitate the formation of the tetrahedral elements. These operators, illustrated in Figure 8.16, are used in forming the tetrahedra as follows. First, the operator T_3 is applied to eliminate the holes in the object by cutting the proper portion of the object so that the hole is exposed, as shown in Figure 8.16(c). Note that three tetrahedra are produced as by-products in this stage. Then the convex corners where three edges meet, called *convex trivalent vertices* (corners), are sliced and separated from the object by applying the operator T_1, as illustrated in Figure 8.16(a). This operator is applied recursively until there is no convex trivalent vertex. If all the remaining

method to be applied when two thin triangles meet at their longest edge. That is, a node is added on the common edge, and the neighboring elements are subdivided by connecting their nodes to the new node. In Figure 8.15(b), a large triangular element is subdivided by adding a new node at its centroid. When we subdivide it by the methods previously described, thin triangles may meet as shown in Figure 8.15(c); these triangles are already small enough for the given mesh density. In this case, we can improve the quality of the mesh by switching the diagonal of the quadrilateral formed by the vertices of the two original triangles. Note that the result of the finite-element analysis may not be accurate enough if there are too many thin elements.

Figure 8.16

Operators for topology decom-position in three dimensions

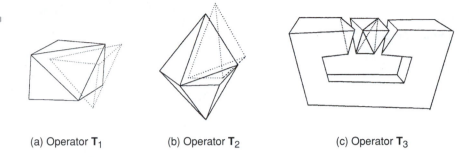

(a) Operator T_1　　　　(b) Operator T_2　　　　(c) Operator T_3

vertices are not convex trivalent, then the operator T_2 is applied to dig out a tetrahe-dron, as illustrated in Figure 8.16(b). This operator provides the new convex triva-lent vertices and thus T_1 is applied again. This process is continued until the object is reduced to a single tetrahedron.

8.4.3 Geometry Decomposition Approaches

Geometry decomposition approaches fall into two categories: one based on recur-sion and the other on iteration. We explain only the recursive method because of its potential ability for three-dimensional mesh generation.

The *recursive geometry decomposition method* generates triangular or quadri-lateral elements in two dimensions in the following way. First, the original object is divided into convex parts either manually or automatically. Automatic decomposi-tion of an object into convex parts is described in Bykat [1976]. For each convex part, nodes are inserted into the boundary of a convex part to satisfy the mesh den-sity distribution. Then each convex part is divided roughly in the middle of its "longest axis," as shown in Figure 8.17. Then more nodes are inserted into the split line according to the mesh density distribution, and the two halves are recursively divided until they become triangles or quadrilaterals. Some methods repeat the sub-division until hexagons or octagons are left and generate the triangular or quadrilat-eral elements from them according to prestored templates. In this way, we may get more regular triangular or quadrilateral elements. Figure 8.18 shows an example of mesh generation by a recursive method.

The basic method described can be extended to three-dimensional mesh gener-ation. In this case the object is divided into two subvolumes by a "best splitting

Figure 8.17

Subdivision by a split line

Candidate split line

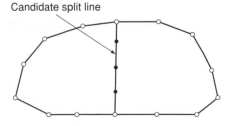

Figure 8.18

Example of mesh generation by a recursive method

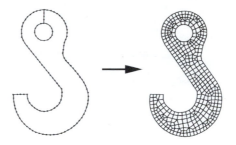

plane," until all subvolumes have been reduced to tetrahedra. In contrast to the two-dimensional case wherein quadrilaterals can be produced, hexahedrons cannot be generated directly. However, each tetrahedron may be subdivided into four hexahedrons, or brick elements, if desired.

8.4.4 Grid-Based Approach

The *grid-based approach* arises from the observation that a grid looks like a mesh and that it can be made into a mesh provided that the grid cells along the object boundary can be turned into elements. We get better meshes in general with a finer grid because internal elements that are well-shaped become dominant. The many different methods used are based on how the boundary elements are created.

The method of Thacker and colleagues is probably the first published one that used the grid-based approach [Thacker, Gonzalez, and Putland 1980]. In this method an object is first overlapped by a triangular grid and the grid points that fall outside the object are eliminated, leaving a zigzag boundary. The grid points on the zigzag boundary are then moved onto the object boundary to create the finished mesh. Kikuchi [1986] extended this method to create meshes of predominantly quadrilaterals, but with some triangles, by using a rectangular grid, as shown in Figure 8.19. One problem with both methods is that small features, with edges too short for the grid spacing, are lost. In other methods the grid points on the zigzag boundary are not moved to the object boundary. Instead, the triangular elements are created in the region between the zigzag boundary and the object boundary by use of a triangulation algorithm.

Yerry and Shephard [1983] used a quadtree representation of an object to gen-

Figure 8.19

Use of a rectangular grid for a grid-based approach

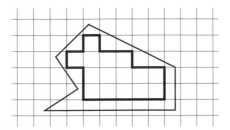

Figure 8.20

Quadtree representation

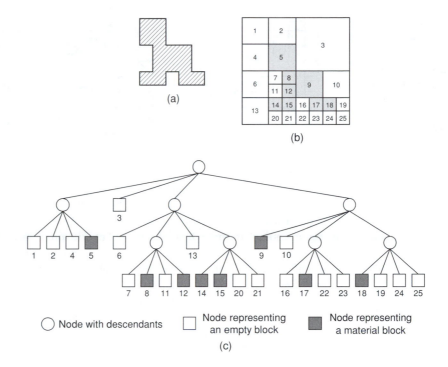

(a)

(b)

(c)

○ Node with descendants   □ Node representing an empty block   ■ Node representing a material block

erate meshes. A quadtree is a two-dimensional concept similar to the octree described in Chapter 5. It represents a two-dimensional object, such as the one shown in Figure 8.20(a), as a set of squares of different sizes by recursively subdividing the root square enclosing the object. Figure 8.20(b) shows the process of subdividing the object, and Figure 8.20(c) shows the quadtree representation of this subdivision. The meshes are generated as follows.

Step 1 A root square enclosing the object is created and subdivided into four quadrants by halving its sides. Then each quadrant is classified according to its relative location with respect to the object. If the quadrant is neither completely inside nor completely outside the object, it is subdivided again. This subdivision process is repeated until the mesh density distribution is satisfied and the quadrants either "completely inside" or "overlapping" the object are collected. When the "overlapping" quadrants are collected, they are modified to include only the inside of the object. Thus the object represented by the collection of the "completely inside" quadrants and the modified "overlapping" quadrants will look like that shown in Figure 8.21(a).

Step 2 Each modified "overlapping" quadrant is divided into the triangular elements by using the prestored template based on the shape of the quadrant. Then the "completely inside" quadrant is also subdivided to satisfy the mesh conformity with the adjacent meshes. Two adjacent elements are said to be conforming if they share an entire edge (an entire face for three-dimensional elements). Figure 8.21(b) shows the result of mesh generation.

Figure 8.21

Mesh generation, using quadtree representation

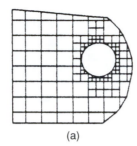 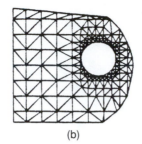 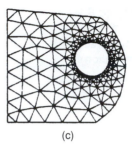

(a)　　　　　　　　　　　(b)　　　　　　　　　　　(c)

Step 3 The nodes of the elements are adjusted to improve the mesh shapes. Figure 8.21(c) shows the result of mesh smoothing. The method of mesh smoothing is described later. This method has been extended to three dimensions by using octree encoding. In three dimensions, the "overlapping" octants are modified so that they occupy only the inside space of the object and then split into tetrahedra as the modified "overlapping" quadrants are split into triangles in two dimensions. The modified "overlapping" octant should be split into tetrahedra that satisfy the mesh conformity with the neighboring octants. Considering all the special cases, this requires a very complicated algorithm. In fact, splitting the modified "overlapping" quadrant in two dimensions is not a simple problem, either.

Jung and Lee [1993] proposed a new method, starting from a triangular root (tetrahedral root in three dimensions) instead of a square root (cubic root) to avoid the difficulty just mentioned. In this method, the quadtree representation of a two-dimensional object is the approximation of the object as a set of triangles. Similarly, the octree representation of a three-dimensional object would be a set of tetrahedra. Thus we can get the meshes by collecting the "completely inside" and "overlapping" triangles (tetrahedra in three dimensions) after moving the vertices of the "overlapping" triangles (tetrahedra) onto the original object boundary. Figure 8.22(a) shows how a triangular root is split into four triangles, and Figure 8.22(b) shows how a tetrahedral root is split into eight tetrahedra.

Figure 8.22

Subdivision of triangle and tetrahedron

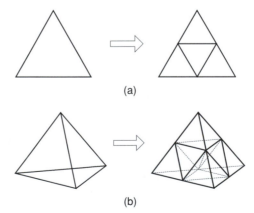

(a)

(b)

8.4.5 Mapped Element Approach

The *mapped element approach* is used in most commercial mesh generators. This approach requires subdividing the object to be meshed into regions with specific topologies. In two dimensions, these regions have three or four sides; in three dimensions, these regions are boxlike. Within each region, the mesh is generated automatically by mapping the region to a regularized domain (a regular triangle or square in two dimensions and a cube in three dimensions), slicing the regularized domain by considering the mesh density distribution, and remapping the sliced domain to the original region. The total mesh is then obtained by merging the individual meshed regions. The common sides shared by neighboring regions must have the same number of nodes to satisfy mesh conformity. This requirement can be enforced manually or algorithmically while the meshes of the neighboring regions are being generated.

Various mapping methods can be used. Two typical methods are transfinite mapping and isoparametric mapping.

Transfinite mapping   *Transfinite mapping* enables regions—three- or four-sided in two dimensions and boxlike in three dimensions—to be mapped to the regularized domain without introducing any geometric errors. In other words, the points on the region's boundary are always mapped to the boundary of the regularized domain.

A four-sided region, as shown in Figure 8.23(a), can easily be mapped to a unit square in the uv parametric domain shown in Figure 8.23(b) by the method used in the derivation of Coon's patch in Chapter 7. The mapping between the four-sided region and a regularized domain is provided by

$$\mathbf{P}(u, v) = (1 - u)\,\mathbf{P}_0(v) + u\,\mathbf{P}_1(v) + (1 - v)\,\mathbf{Q}_0(u) + v\,\mathbf{Q}_1(u)$$
$$- (1 - u)(1 - v)\mathbf{P}_{0,0} - u(1 - v)\mathbf{P}_{1,0} - (1 - u)v\mathbf{P}_{0,1} - uv\mathbf{P}_{1,1} \qquad (8.46)$$
$$(0 \leq u \leq 1, 0 \leq v \leq 1)$$

Then a rectangular grid is imposed on the parametric domain shown in Figure 8.23(b), and the u,v values of the grid points are substituted in Equation (8.46) to evaluate the nodal coordinates. The values of u and v can be biased so that nodes are more closely spaced in some areas than in others.

Figure 8.23

Mapping of a four-sided region

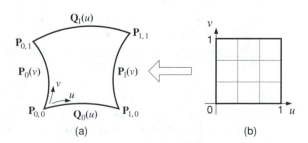

(a)   (b)

Figure 8.24

Mapping of a
three-sided region

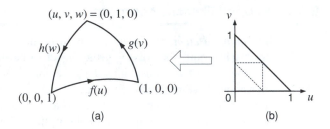

(a)   (b)

A three-sided region can be similarly divided into a mesh of triangular elements by the use of a trilinearly blended interpolant, as described by Barnhill, Birkhoff, and Gordon [1973]. The three-sided region shown in Figure 8.24(a) can be mapped to the parametric domain shown in Figure 8.24(b) by

$$P(u,v,w) = \frac{1}{2}\left[\frac{ug(v)}{1-v} + \frac{wh(1-v)}{1-v} + \frac{vh(w)}{1-w} + \frac{uf(1-w)}{1-w} \right.$$
$$\left. + \frac{wf(u)}{1-u} + \frac{vg(1-u)}{1-u} - wf(0) - ug(0) - vh(0)\right]$$

(8.47)

The parametric domain for Equation (8.47) is expressed as

$$u + v + w = 1 \quad 0 \leq u \leq 1, \quad 0 \leq v \leq 1, \quad 0 \leq w \leq 1 \tag{8.48}$$

The parametric domain in this case can be sliced by incrementing u,v values between 0 and 1 and evaluating the corresponding w values from each set of u and v.

Transfinite mapping for a boxlike region can be derived as for a four-sided region. The only difference is that six equations from the boundary faces are blended instead of four equations from the boundary edges [Zeid 1991].

Isoparametric mapping *Isoparametric mapping* is a special case of transfinite mapping. This method maps four-sided (two-dimensional) or boxlike (three-dimensional) regions to a unit square or unit cube in a parametric space, respectively, so that only the specified points on the region boundary (*not* the entire boundary) map to the corresponding points on the boundary in the parametric space, as illustrated in Figure 8.25. In other words, boundaries are matched only at a finite number of points. Thus the mapping equation is derived by replacing the exact equations of the boundary curves in Equation (8.46) with the equations interpolating the specified points. Similarly, the equation of the boundary surfaces will be replaced by the interpolating surface equations for a boxlike region. For example, if two points are specified for each boundary curve, as in Figure 8.25(a), linear interpolation equations would be substituted in Equation (8.46). Quadratic interpolation equations would be used for three points along each boundary, as shown in Figure 8.25(b), and cubic interpolation equations would be used for four points along each boundary, as shown in Figure 8.25(c).

Figure 8.25

Isoparametric mapping

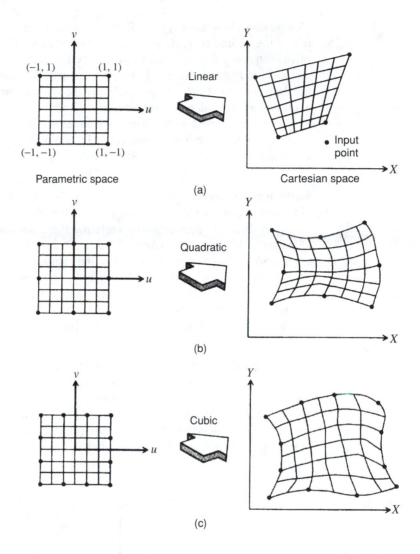

Parametric space   Cartesian space

(a)

(b)

(c)

8.4.6 Improvement of Mesh Quality

Some mesh generation methods, notably those based on the topology decomposition approach, do not generate an initial mesh that is good enough for analysis. Thus we have to rely on a three-step post-processing approach to improve the mesh.

- If the elements generated are not of the desired type, then subdivide them into elements of the desired type.
- If the elements do not have sizes compatible with the desired mesh density distribution, then refine them.
- If the elements are not well-shaped, then apply a mesh smoothing technique.

Conversion of element types If the elements generated by a mesh generator are not of the desired type, they can be converted to another type. Quadrilaterals and bricks can easily be converted to well-shaped triangles and tetrahedra, respectively, as shown in Figure 8.26. Similarly, triangles and tetrahedra may be subdivided into quadrilaterals and bricks, respectively, as shown in Figure 8.27. In this case, however, the resulting elements may not be well-shaped because the angles around the newly introduced nodes are necessarily large. It is also possible to convert a mesh of triangles into a mesh of quadrilaterals by combining every two adjacent triangles into a quadrilateral [Heighway 1983].

Refinement of meshes When a mesh is refined to satisfy the desired mesh density, some elements are subdivided into smaller elements while others remain unchanged. Thus the possibility of violating the conformity between neighboring elements, as illustrated in Figure 8.28(a), may arise. Recall that two neighboring elements are said to be *conforming* when they share an entire edge or an entire face. For triangular elements, two neighboring elements can be made to conform simply by bisecting the longest side of a larger triangle. The solution is not so simple for rectangular elements. The quadrilateral elements shown in Figure 8.28(a) are modified to conform as illustrated in Figure 8.28(b).

Mesh smoothing Quite often the elements produced by an automatic mesh generator are not well-shaped, and a mesh smoothing technique has to be applied. The most popular mesh smoothing technique is *Laplacian smoothing*, which seeks to reposition the nodes so that each internal node is at the centroid of the polygon formed by its connected neighbors. This repositioning is usually done iteratively. However, the Laplacian smoothing technique does not work well in some cases. As

Figure 8.26

Conversion of quadrilaterals and bricks into triangles and tetrahedra, respectively

Figure 8.27

Conversion of a triangle and tetrahedron into quadrilaterals and bricks, respectively

Figure 8.28

Nonconforming
meshes and their
modification

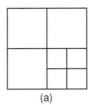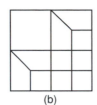

(a)   (b)

Figure 8.29

Neighborhood
nodes of an inter-
nal node i

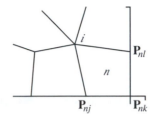

a result Herrmann [1976] proposed the following formula for the repositioning:

$$P_i = \frac{1}{N(2-w)} \sum_{n=1}^{N} (P_{nj} + P_{nl} - wP_{nk}) \tag{8.49}$$

where N is the number of elements around node i and w is the weighting factor be-tween 0 and 1. The neighboring nodes P_{nj}, P_{nl}, and P_{nk} are defined, as shown in Figure 8.29. When w equals to 0, the smoothing equals Laplacian smoothing, and it equals isoparametric smoothing when w is 1.

8.5 CASE STUDY

In this section, we demonstrate how finite-element meshes are generated and finite-element analysis is performed on the cellular phone body introduced in Chapter 1. In this case study we use Pro/MESH, a commercial finite-element modeler, and ANSYS, a commercial finite-element analysis program. In Section 8.3, we ex-plained the overall process used in this case study, which is illustrated in the flow chart in Figure 8.30. Here we explain each step in the flow chart in detail. We as-sumed that the geometric model of the part, as shown in Figure 8.31(a), had been generated already.

 Step 1: Simplifying the part's geometry. Before generating the finite-ele-ment meshes of the design model, we need to consider the part carefully to deter-mine whether we can simplify it for analysis purposes. In many cases, it is not desirable to include all the details of the part model in the finite-element analysis. The reason is that fine details produce an undesirably large number of small mesh elements that eventually increase calculation time.[9] Thus we may want to simplify

---

[9] This problem may be avoided if we use the p version finite-element analysis in which large-size ele-ments can approximate the boundary fairly well by using higher order shape functions.

Figure 8.30

Flowchart of the
case study

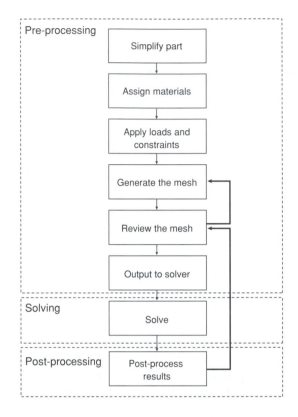

Pre-processing

Simplify part

Assign materials

Apply loads and
constraints

Generate the mesh

Review the mesh

Output to solver

Solving

Solve

Post-processing

Post-process
results

Figure 8.31

Simplification of
part geometry: (a)
part model before
simplification and
(b) part model
after simplification

(a)   (b)

the part's geometry by using a feature suppression technique to remove features that are not pertinent to the analysis, such as rounds, chamfers, and small holes. Furthermore, thin parts are often converted to shell models, resulting in shell elements rather than solid elements. In our example, however, we will use solid elements. Figure 8.31(b) shows the part model after we suppressed the narrow grooves on the top face and the rounds around the button holes.

Step 2: Assigning materials. Before we analyze our model, we must define the properties of materials that we want to assign to it, as shown in Figure 8.32.

Step 3: Adding coordinate systems. Coordinate systems are used as a reference for specifying the vector components of loads and constraints. Thus we must specify a coordinate system—cartesian, cylindrical, or spherical—before we define the loads and constraints. Figure 8.33 shows the coordinate system selected.

Step 4: Applying constraints. The model is now ready for the loads and constraints to be applied. First, we provide the displacement constraints to impose zero displacement on the back face for all six (rotational and translational) degrees of

Figure 8.32

Assigning properties of materials

```
                       MATERIAL  HANDPHONE

                 This file may be edited using available editor.
                 Just type on the necessary lines appropriate values
                 after the "=" sign. Comments are not permitted on
                 lines containing material properties names.

                 YOUNG_MODULUS                        =     2.000000e-01
                 POISSON_RATIO                        =     4.500000e-01
                 SHEAR_MODULUS                        =
                 MASS_DENSITY                         =
                 THERMAL_EXPANSION_COEFFICIENT        =
                 THERM_EXPANSION_REF_TEMPERATURE      =
                 STRUCTURAL_DAMPING_COEFFICIENT       =
                 STRESS_LIMIT_FOR_TENSION             =
                 STRESS_LIMIT_FOR_COMPRESSION         =
                 STRESS_LIMIT_FOR_SHEAR               =
                 THERMAL_CONDUCTIVITY                 =
                 EMISSIVITY                           =
                 SPECIFIC_HEAT                        =
                 HARDNESS                             =
                 CONDITION                            =
                 INITIAL_BEND_Y_FACTOR                =
                 BEND_TABLE                           =
                 PRO_UNIT_MASS                        =
                 PRO_UNIT_LENGTH                      =
```

Figure 8.33

Adding a coordinate system

Figure 8.34

Defining boundary
conditions

freedom. These displacement constraints are indicated by **X** markers on the back face in Figure 8.34.

For structural loads and constraints, the following loads and constraints can be applied in Pro/MESH: Pressure, Force, Moment, Displacement, Edge Pressure, Structural Temperature, Acceleration, Angular Velocity, and Total Force, as shown in Figure 8.35.

Five types of displacement constraints can be imposed, as shown in Figure 8.36.

- 3components: Specifying translations for points, edges, or faces.

- Immovable: Specifying a point, edges, or face to have zero displacement for all three translational degrees of freedom.

Figure 8.35

Menu for imposing
structural loads
and displacement
constraints

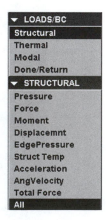

Figure 8.36

Menu for imposing displacement constraints

- 6components: Specifying translations and rotations for points, edges, or faces.
- Fixed: Specifying a point, edge, or face to have zero displacement for all six (rotational and translational) degrees of freedom.
- Along Surf: Constraining nodes on the selected plane or cylinder to move only along the selected surface. Nodes on a cylinder may be further constrained to move only in an axial or angular direction.

Step 5: Adding a region. Now we need to define a region in which the loads are applied. In our example, the loads should be applied where the flip cover joins the phone body. This region is part of a face, so we need to define a portion of a face. The region is defined by datum curves sketched directly on the part surface.

Step 6: Applying loads—Case 1. The first loading situation is where the flip cover is opened all the way and pushed down. To simulate the situation, we apply upward force on the upper half-surface of the hinge area and apply downward force on the narrow contact area where the flip cover touches the phone body when it is pushed down. Figure 8.37 illustrates the load condition. The applied total load is 0.1 N in the x direction and -0.2 N in the z direction at the contact region, and the total load at the hinge area is 0.2 N in the z direction. As shown in Figure 8.37, the system calculates the corresponding distributed load when we apply the total force on a specified region.

Figure 8.37

Load and boundary conditions for the first loading situation

Figure 8.38

Load and boundary conditions for the second loading situation

Step 7: Applying loads—Case 2. Another loading situation occurs when the flip cover is opened and twisted. It can be simulated by the load condition shown in Figure 8.38. In this case, the magnitudes of two applied forces at the hinge area are the same but their directions are opposite. The magnitude of the forces is 0.2 N.

Step 8: Reviewing the mesh. We can now generate the finite-element mesh. Two types of mesh control parameters can be used to control the size of the elements prior to meshing the part. *Global mesh controls* define the maximum and minimum element size allowed over the entire model. *Local mesh controls* define the maximum or minimum element size on a part edge, surface, or a point. In general, it is a good practice to mesh the part without any specific parameter values initially and see the resulting mesh with the default values, which gives a good starting place. From the initial result, if any additional refinements are required, we reassign the parameters and follow the same process.

Two types of elements are available:

- three-dimensional tetrahedral elements to model solid or thick-bodied components, and
- Two-dimensional triangular and quadrilateral shell elements to model thin-bodied components.

As mentioned before, we use tetrahedral elements in this case study to skip the process of converting the solid model to a shell model before mesh generation.

After we view the mesh and check its quality, we may want to improve the mesh in some areas. Perhaps we would like to specify some additional mesh control parameters and mesh the model again. In general, getting an acceptable mesh may take several iterations.[10]

---

[10] If we use the *p* version solver, we will iterate on the polynomial degree instead of the mesh size.

Figure 8.39

Initial mesh generated

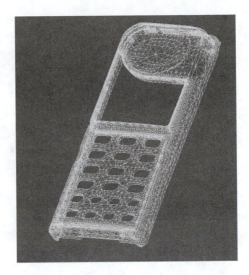

Step 9: Regenerating the mesh. The number of meshes in Figure 8.39 is about 70,000, which makes the analysis difficult and requires the use of too many system resources. Thus we need to reduce the number of meshes. We do so by adjusting the mesh control parameters, increasing the local minimum element size on portions that do not affect the analysis. Consequently, we can reduce the number of meshes to about 20,000, as shown in Figure 8.40.

Step 10: Outputting FEM data. If we want to perform a finite-element analysis on our model by using another FEA program, we must create an output file for the model's mesh data that includes

- the model's mesh elements and nodes written in a format compatible with the particular FEA program to be used,

Figure 8.40

Regenerated mesh

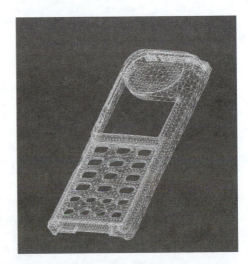

Figure 8.41

Analysis results: (a) stress distribution—Case 1 and (b) stress distribution—Case 2

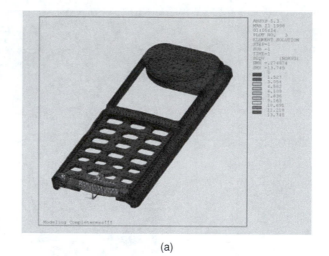

(a)

(b)

- all the constraint cases applied to the model, and
- all the material data assigned to the model.

In this case study, we create an output file for ANSYS.

Step 11: Solving, then reviewing the results. In this step, the output file is parsed in ANSYS and a finite-element analysis for the model proceeds. After the finite-element analysis is performed, we review the results (e.g., stress distribution and displacement), as illustrated in Figure 8.41. The results coincide with our intuition that higher stress exists at the hinge area.

QUESTIONS AND PROBLEMS

1. Suppose that you want to design and manufacture a hanger bracket. Before making this hanger bracket, you must build a model, obtain the displacement and stress distribution of the model, analyze the efficiency of the initially designed model, and revise the shape of the model. Finite-element modeling and analysis can be used for this purpose. Using a commercial FEM software package such as NASTRAN or ANSYS, solve (a)–(c).[11]

   a. Enter the pre-processor of the FEM tool, build the initially designed model of the hanger bracket shown, and assign the properties of materials to the model.

   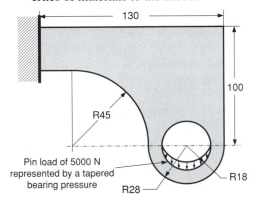

   *All dimensions are in mm

   Thickness: 10 mm

   Properties: Young's modulus $E = 2.07 \times 10^{11}$ N/m^2

   Density $\rho = 7.8 \times 10^{-6}$ kg/mm^3

   Poisson's ratio $\mu = 0.3$

   b. Enter the solver of the FEM tool, and obtain a solution for the model given the load shown in the figure. (*Hint:* Calculate the bearing pressure load, using $BP = F/td$, where $F = 5000$ N. Also, use a value of 0.001 at the side elements.)

   c. Enter the post-processor of the FEM tool and obtain displacement and stress displays.

2. A window having an uninsulated extruded metal frame is to be analyzed for steady-state thermal behavior on a winter day. Using a commercial FEM software package, build a model and generate meshes by using an element type appropriate to thermal analysis. To build the model you can generate area primitives and perform Boolean operations on them. This model is composed of composite materials, so meshes with multiple element attributes must be generated. (Assumption: The window effectively is infinitely long for purposes of this analysis. Use a lane, unit-thickness model.)

   The cross section of the window and all dimensions are shown in the accompanying figure. All dimensions are in inches.[12]

   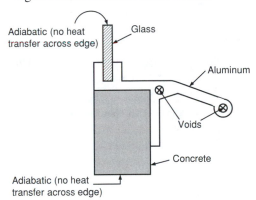

   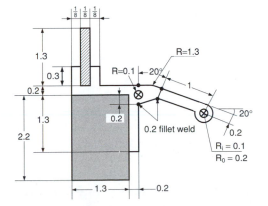

3. Obtain the solution of the window described in Problem 2 when the load is as shown in the accompanying figure, and display the temperature distribution of the window.[13]

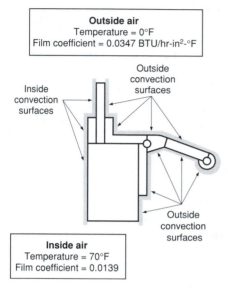

4. Build a model of the socket shown and perform a static analysis, using the finite-element method. You can generate the model by using three primitives (e.g., cylinder, prism, and block) and two Boolean operations. All dimensions are in inches.[14]

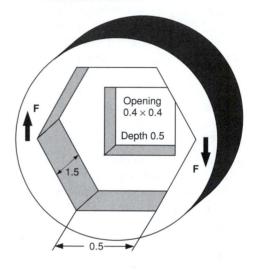

Radius of the cylinder = 0.55

Length of the cylinder = 2.0

Force = 100 lb

[11] [12] [13] [14] Figures in problems from Introduction to ANSYS for Revision 5.0A: Volume II, Solutions to Exercises, Reprinted with permission from ANSYS, Inc. (Canonsburg, PA).

Optimization

As we showed in Chapter 1, optimization is a component of the design process of a product cycle, and thus the technologies related to optimization are also regarded as a part of CAD. In fact, the entire design process can be considered to be an optimization process in which several design alternatives are generated and a specific one is selected. This statement is true if the word *optimization* is interpreted in a very general sense. However, optimization is not usually used to choose between concept alternatives (e.g., a rivet, a bolt, or a fastener); rather, optimization is used to select the best size of rivet. In this sense, optimization is a component of a design process rather than being the entire design process.

9.1 FORMULATION OF THE OPTIMIZATION PROBLEM

In design optimization, a design must be parameterized so that its alternatives can be obtained by changing the values of those parameters. For example, if we were designing a cylindrical pressure vessel, the parameters would be the mean diameter, the thickness, the height, and the material to be used. Possible alternative pressure vessels would be generated by using different sets of parameter values. However, depending on the situation, some parameters may not have any degree of freedom because of a certain constraint. For the pressure vessel, we may have to use a specific material in the inventory, and thus only the mean diameter, thickness, and height can be adjusted to obtain a better performance or optimized to gain the best performance. For the pressure vessel, the maximum allowable pressure divided by the weight may be a measure of performance, and the mean diameter, the thickness, and the height may be the design parameters to be varied. We might try to find the optimal values of these design parameters that would result in the maximum value of this performance index. We might derive the performance index as a function of the design parameters by using the knowledge gained in a strength of materials class. The parameters to be optimized are called *optimization variables*, and the performance index derived from these variables is called the *objective function*. Obviously, we select the optimization variables and objective function according to the design intent.

We can describe design optimization in mathematical terms as follows. Denoting the optimization variables **X**, which is an *n*-dimensional vector having *n* optimization variables as its components, and the objective function $F(\mathbf{X})$, we can state the optimization problem simply as minimize or maximize $F(\mathbf{X})$. However, the actual optimization process is not quite so simple. First, there are few design problems for which the performance index can be represented by a single function. Thus we have to choose among various performance measures or formulate one that is a composite of several measures, with weighting factors applied. The latter process can be viewed as the formulation of a *composite objective function*. Alternatively, we may decide to use certain measures of performance as constraints. For example, instead of maximizing the allowable pressure per unit weight and the internal volume of the pressure vessel simultaneously, we may maximize the allowable pressure per unit weight and enforce the constraint that the volume exceeds a certain value. In this case, these constraints have to be included in the mathematical formulation somehow. (Later, we show how the constraints are included in the formulation.)

We can also expect situations in which optimization variables are allowed to vary only in certain ranges. For example, the height of the pressure vessel may not exceed a certain value because of limited space. Therefore we have to satisfy certain constraints or design restrictions while selecting the trial vector, **X**. The components of the trial vector are the optimization variables, of course. A design that meets all requirements is called a *feasible design*, or an *acceptable design*. A constraint that restricts the upper and lower limits on the optimization variables is called a *regional constraint*, or *side constraint*. A constraint derived from performance or a functional requirement explicitly considered is called a *behavior constraint*, or *functional constraint* [Akin 1990].

Considering these constraints, the simple statement on optimization can be formulated as: search for

$$\mathbf{X}^* \in R^n \text{ so that } F(\mathbf{X}^*) = \min F(\mathbf{X}) \tag{9.1}$$

subject to

$$\mathbf{X}_l \le \mathbf{X}^* \le \mathbf{X}_u \tag{9.2}$$

$$G_i(\mathbf{X}^*) \ge 0 \qquad i = 1, 2, \ldots, m \tag{9.3}$$

and

$$H_j(\mathbf{X}^*) = 0 \qquad j = 1, 2, \ldots, q \tag{9.4}$$

where m is the number of inequality constraints and q is the number of equality constraints. The inequality sign in Equation (9.3) can be reversed if the G_is are negated. Here R^n denotes the design space made up by varying each of the n optimization variables. The regional constraints on the optimization variables are shown in Equation (9.2) where $\mathbf{X}_l$ and $\mathbf{X}_u$ are the lower and the upper limits on the optimization variables, respectively. Note that the functional constraints can be expressed in the form of both an equality constraint and an inequality constraint, as in Equations (9.3) and (9.4). The optimization problem for maximizing an objective function can easily be converted to the minimization problem by inverting or negating the original objective function.

The objective function $F(\mathbf{X})$ in Equation (9.1) can be interpreted to be a "surface" of dimension n embedded in a space of dimension $n + 1$. For a design problem with two optimization variables, this can easily be visualized as a surface in three-dimensional space. That is, the z coordinate of a point on the surface is the value of the objective function corresponding to its x and y coordinates that represent the values of the optimization variables, respectively. Thus the optimization process can be compared to mountain climbing in a dense fog [Taylor 1992]. The climber can determine the local altitude with an altimeter and look around to determine downhill or uphill directions but cannot identify local ridges and canyons that make certain paths difficult. The climber also has to be careful not to fall into a pit, which is equivalent to violating the constraints in Equations (9.2)–(9.4).

9.2　TREATMENT OF CONSTRAINTS

Most design optimization problems have accompanying constraints, as discussed in the preceding section, which fall into three categories. The first type of constraint gives bounds on the design variables. It can easily be satisfied by restricting the optimization variables to stay within the bounds during search. In equality constraints—the second type—each constraint effectively reduces the dimension of the design space by 1. Algebraically eliminating one design variable from each equality constraint, if possible, is the best way to handle equality constraints. However the variable-elimination method is applicable only so long as the equality constraints can be solved explicitly for a given set of independent variables. In the presence of several equality constraints, the elimination process may become unwieldy. Moreover, in certain situations it may not be possible to solve the constraints explicitly to eliminate a variable. An alternative method is the penalty function method (explained later) [Avriel 1976].

The third category consists of inequality constraints. The standard approach to the optimization problem with inequality constraints is to modify the objective function to include the effect of these constraints. The objective function is modified by adding a *penalty function* so that a large value is added when the constraints are violated. The intuitive idea behind all penalty function methods is simple: An infinitely large number is added to the objective function when the constraints are violated; otherwise, the objective function is left as it is. Thus the penalty function $P(\mathbf{X})$ can be defined as

$$P(\mathbf{X}) = \begin{cases} 0 & \text{for } \mathbf{X} \in R_f^n \\ +\infty & \text{for } \mathbf{X} \notin R_f^n \end{cases} \tag{9.5}$$

where R_f^n is the subset of R^n corresponding to the feasible design satisfying the constraints. Now we can consider the unconstrained minimization of the augmented objective function, or descent function $D(\mathbf{X})$, given by

$$D(\mathbf{X}) = F(\mathbf{X}) + P(\mathbf{X}) \tag{9.6}$$

The unconstrained optimization cannot be carried out (except perhaps in some trivial cases) because of the discontinuity in $D(\mathbf{X})$ on the boundary of R_f^n and the infinite values outside R_f^n. Replacing $+\infty$ by some "large" finite penalty would not simplify the problem because the numerical difficulties would still remain. Two types of penalty functions, exterior and interior, have been introduced to solve these problems.

9.2.1   Exterior Penalty Functions

Exterior penalty function methods usually are used to solve Equation (9.1). They involve the use of a sequence of unconstrained minimization problems, whose optimal solutions approach the solution of Equation (9.1) from outside the feasible region. In the sequence of unconstrained optimization, a penalty is imposed on every $\mathbf{X} \notin R_f^n$, increasing the penalty during the sequence and thereby forcing the unconstrained optima toward the feasible region.

The following function can be defined as an approximation of the penalty function in Equation (9.5) when the inequality and the equality constraints are those in Equations (9.3) and (9.4):

$$S(X) = \sum_i \delta_i |G_i(\mathbf{X})|^\alpha + \sum_j |H_j(\mathbf{X})|^\beta \tag{9.7}$$

where

$$\delta_j = \begin{cases} 0 & \text{if } G_j(\mathbf{X}) \geq \mathbf{0} \\ 1 & \text{if } G_j(\mathbf{X}) < \mathbf{0} \end{cases} \tag{9.8}$$

and α and β are constants, usually having values of 1 or 2, and the functions G_i and H_j are those in Equations (9.3) and (9.4). Note that

$$S(X) = 0 \quad \text{if } \mathbf{X} \in R_f^n \tag{9.9}$$

and

$$S(X) > 0 \quad \text{if } \mathbf{X} \notin R_f^n \tag{9.10}$$

For any positive number ρ, we can define the augmented objective function as

$$D(\mathbf{X}, \rho) = F(\mathbf{X}) + \frac{1}{\rho} S(\mathbf{X}) \qquad (9.11)$$

and observe that $D(\mathbf{X}, \rho) = F(\mathbf{X})$ if and only if $\mathbf{X}$ is in the feasible region; otherwise $D(\mathbf{X}, \rho) > F(\mathbf{X})$. The $S(\mathbf{X})/\rho$ term approximates the discontinuous penalty function $P(\mathbf{X})$ in Equation (9.5) as $\rho \to 0$. Thus the exterior penalty function method consists of solving a sequence of unconstrained optimizations for $k = 0, 1, 2, \ldots$, given by

$$\min D(\mathbf{X}, \rho_k) = \min\left[F(\mathbf{X}) + \frac{1}{\rho_k}\left(\sum_i \delta_i |G_i(\mathbf{X})|^\alpha + \sum_j |H_j(\mathbf{X})|^\beta \right) \right] \qquad (9.12)$$

using a strictly decreasing sequence of positive numbers ρ_k. The optimal values $\mathbf{X}_k$ for ρ_k will converge to the real optimal values $\mathbf{X}^*$ as k increases and ρ_k approaches 0. We demonstrate this convergence with the following example.

EXAMPLE 9.1

Find the minimum of

$$F(x) = x^2 \quad (x \in R)$$

subject to the constraint $x - 1 \geq 0$. The optimal solution clearly is $x^* = 1$, so we need to show that the solution obtained by the exterior penalty method converges to this solution.

ANSWER

Let's form the augmented objective function, as in Equation (9.12), with $\alpha = 2$. Then we have the unconstrained optimization problem

$$\min D(x, \rho_k) = \min\left[x^2 + \frac{1}{\rho_k} \delta(x - 1)^2 \right]$$

Here δ has the value of 1 for $x < 1$ and 0 otherwise.

For any positive ρ_k, the function D is convex downward, as shown in Figure 9.1, and its minimum is at the point

$$x_k = \frac{1}{\rho_k + 1}$$

Note that, for every positive ρ_k, this point is infeasible for the original problem because it is smaller than 1. As ρ_k approaches 0, points x_k approach $x = 1$ from outside the feasible region. The procedure described is carried out by a numerical algorithm in practice. Any numerical algorithm stops its iteration when a certain convergence criterion is satisfied, so the solution obtained by the exterior penalty method is the optimal solution that violates the constraint. This is the inherent problem caused by the exterior penalty function, which is activated only when the constraint is violated (i.e., exterior to the feasible design space).

Figure 9.1

Augmented objec-
tive function

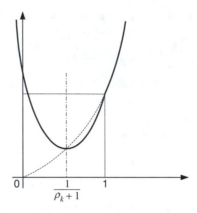

9.2.2 Interior Penalty Function

In the *interior penalty function* method, problems involving inequality constraints
are solved through a sequence of unconstrained optimization problems whose minima are at points that strictly satisfy the constraints, that is, in the interior of the feasible region. Staying in the interior can be ensured by formulating a *barrier
function* by which an infinitely large penalty is imposed for crossing the boundary
of the feasible region from the inside. Because the algorithm requires the interior of
the feasible region to be nonempty, no equality constraints can be handled by the
following method.[1]

Consider therefore the optimization problem

$$\min F(\mathbf{X}) \tag{9.13}$$

subject to

$$G_i(\mathbf{X}) \geq 0 \quad i = 1, 2, \ldots, m \tag{9.14}$$

A good choice for the barrier function that will provide the walls at the boundaries
of the feasible region would be

$$B(\mathbf{X}) = \frac{1}{G_i(\mathbf{X})} \tag{9.15}$$

Note that $B(\mathbf{X})$ has positive infinite values as $\mathbf{X}$ approaches the boundary from the
feasible region, and thus $B(\mathbf{X})$ plays the role of the barrier. To consider all m constraints in Equation (9.14), we can simply include a summation sign Σ_i in Equation
(9.15). As we have done for the exterior penalty function, we can define the augmented objective function as

$$D(\mathbf{X}, \rho) = F(\mathbf{X}) + \rho B(\mathbf{X}) \tag{9.16}$$

[1] In this case, a mixed penalty method is used in which the exterior penalty function from the equality
constraints and the interior penalty function from the inequality constraints are added in composing the
augmented objective function.

where ρ is a positive number. Similarly, the interior penalty method consists of solving a sequence of unconstrained optimizations for $k = 0, 1, 2, \ldots$, given by

$$\min D(\mathbf{X}, \rho_k) = \min\left[F(\mathbf{X}) + \rho_k \sum_i \frac{1}{G_i(\mathbf{X})} \right] \tag{9.17}$$

using a strictly decreasing sequence of positive numbers ρ_k. The optimal values $\mathbf{X}_k$ for ρ_k will converge to the real optimal values $\mathbf{X}^*$ as k is increased and ρ_k approaches 0. We demonstrate this convergence with the following example.

EXAMPLE 9.2

Find the minimum of

$$F(x) = \frac{1}{2}x \qquad (x \in R)$$

subject to the constraint $x - 1 \geq 0$. The optimal solution clearly is $x^* = 1$, so we need to show that the solution obtained by the interior penalty method converges to this solution.

ANSWER

Let's form the augmented objective function, as in Equation (9.17). Then we have the unconstrained optimization problem

$$\min D(x, \rho_k) = \min\left[\frac{1}{2}x + \rho_k \frac{1}{x-1} \right]$$

Hence the unconstrained minimum of D is[2]

$$x_k = 1 + \sqrt{2\rho_k}$$

and the minimum value of D is

$$F(x_k) = \frac{1}{2} + \sqrt{\frac{\rho_k}{2}}$$

Note that, for every positive ρ_k, the optimal point is in the feasible region for the original problem because it is greater than 1. As ρ_k approaches 0, the points x_k approach $x = 1$. The original and the augmented objective functions for a few values of ρ_k are illustrated in Figure 9.2. When the procedure described is carried out by use of a numerical algorithm, the initial value for the search has to be chosen in the feasible region.

---

[2] Differentiating D with respect to x and solving for x corresponding to the zero value of the differentiation will give x_k.

Figure 9.2

Augmented objective functions when interior penalty functions are used

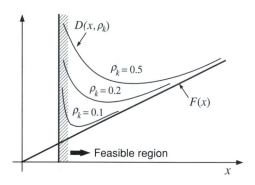

9.3 SEARCH METHODS

Various search techniques can be used to find the minimum or the maximum of an objective function. In general, these techniques, as illustrated in Figure 9.3, can be grouped into three broad classes: calculus-based, guided random search, and enumerative technique [Kumar 1993]. In Figure 9.3, we show only the search techniques that can be used efficiently for multivariable optimization. We have not included simple search techniques such as the Fibonacci method and Golden section techniques because these methods are used mainly for one-dimensional problems.

Calculus-based algorithms can be classified further as those that directly obtain the optimal solution of the problem and those that look for it indirectly by solving the usually nonlinear set of equations resulting from setting the gradient of the objective function to zero. Direct methods seek the solution by "hopping" around the search space and assessing the gradient of the new point; this process guides the direction of search. The notion is one of hill-climbing—finding the best local point by "climbing" the steepest possible slope. As shown in Figure 9.3, direct methods

Figure 9.3

Classification of search techniques

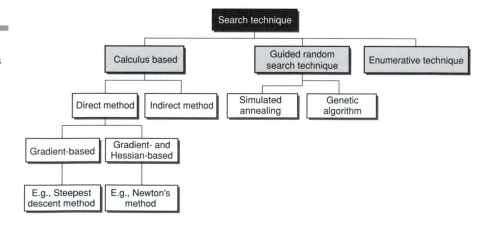

are divided into two categories. The methods in the first category involve use of the function values $F(\mathbf{X})$ and its first partial derivatives

$$\frac{\partial F}{\partial x_i}$$

Here F is the objective function and $\mathbf{X}$ is the optimization variable vector composed of x_i. Examples include the steepest descent method and the conjugate gradient method. The methods in the second category require use of the Hessian matrix composed of second-order partial derivatives

$$\frac{\partial^2 F}{\partial x_i \partial x_j}$$

in addition to the first partial derivatives and the function values. Newton's method belongs in this second category. In the following discussion we briefly describe the key ideas behind various direct methods, which can be utilized only with a restricted set of "well-behaved" problems. Details of such methods and applications for unconstrained and constrained problems are presented in textbooks such as Haftka and Gurdal [1992], Morris [1982], Avriel [1976], and Reklaitis, Ravindran, and Ragsdell [1983].

Direct gradient-based algorithms, such as steepest descent for unconstrained optimization, are insufficient for many applications because they use local information to move only in the direction of steepest descent. In fact, the direction of steepest descent is opposite that of the local gradient vector, and thus these algorithms perform poorly when the objective function is badly scaled or ill-conditioned with respect to the variables. Figure 9.4 illustrates a two-dimensional objective function in which the steepest-descent algorithm exhibits oscillatory behavior and converges slowly. Constant-value contours of the objective function in its two-dimensional design space are shown. The gradient is orthogonal to the constant-contour curve. Thus the steepest direction is nearly orthogonal to the direction toward the minimum at every iteration.

Steepest-descent methods do not take into account the second derivatives or the Hessian matrix of the objective function. Meanwhile, Newton methods and modified Newton methods involve use of the Hessian matrix in addition to the gradient. Modified Newton methods exhibit better convergence for ill-conditioned problems than do steepest-descent methods. However, the Hessian matrix is, in

Figure 9.4

Oscillatory behavior of the steepest-descent algorithm

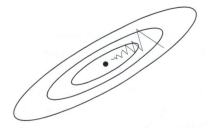

Figure 9.5

Example of multiple
local minima

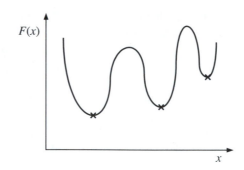

general, expensive to compute. As a result, even though modified Newton methods theoretically have a fast rate of convergence or fewer iterations, in practice they are not very efficient because of the high computational cost per iteration. To avoid this problem, quasi-Newton methods are used to obtain an approximation to the Hessian matrix (actually, the inverse of the Hessian matrix), using the gradients at each iteration. This approach therefore does not require evaluation of the Hessian matrix at each iteration. Quasi-Newton methods are among the most efficient methods for minimizing unconstrained optimization problems. In the preceding section we showed that constrained problems can be converted to unconstrained problems. Thus quasi-Newton methods can also be used for the constrained problems.

The methods described so far typically converge to a local minimum of the optimization. Except for convex optimization problems, there is no guarantee that the minimum obtained is a global minimum. Figure 9.5 illustrates an objective function that has multiple local minima for a one-dimensional problem. Enumerative techniques will solve this problem because they search every point in the design space, or the domain of the optimization variables, one point at a time. They are easy to implement but may require significant computation, and the design space of many applications is too large to search with these techniques. Guided random search techniques or probabilistic search techniques improve enumerative techniques in that the design space is searched more efficiently. However, they still search a large space of the design domain and hence tend to identify the global optimum. These techniques are well suited for parallel computing, and computation time can be reduced even though the amount of computation is still larger than calculus-based techniques. The two most popular probabilistic algorithms are the simulated annealing algorithm and the genetic algorithm. We discuss these two methods in detail because they are emerging optimization techniques for various applications.

9.4 SIMULATED ANNEALING

As early as 1953, Metropolis and colleagues proposed an algorithm for the efficient simulation of the evolution of a thermal equilibrium. It took almost 30 years for Kirkpatrick, Gelatt, and Vecchi [1983] and, independently, Cerny [1985] to realize that a profound analogy exists between minimizing the cost function of a combinatorial optimization problem and the slow cooling of a solid until it reaches its low-energy ground state and that the optimization process can be realized by applying the Metropolis criterion. By substituting cost for energy and by executing the Metropolis algorithm at a sequence of slowly decreasing temperature values, Kirkpatrick and co-workers obtained a combinatorial optimization algorithm, which they called *simulated annealing*. Since then, the research into this algorithm and its applications have evolved into a field of study of its own [Laarhoven and Aarts 1987].

9.4.1 Combinatorial Optimization

In the 1950s and 1960s, the algorithms for searching for an optimum of a function of continuous variables represented major breakthroughs in optimization research. However, we often need to choose a "best" solution from a large number of possible solutions in dealing with many important practical or theoretical problems. For example, if optimization variables are allowed to have only certain discrete values, the optimization problem would be to select the best combination of their values. Such problems are called *combinatorial optimization* problems. The main results from combinatorial optimization research were obtained in the 1970s. For many of these problems, a solution can be considered as an arrangement of a set of discrete objects according to a given set of constraints. A solution is also called a *configuration*. The set of all solutions is referred to as the *solution space*. Our goal is to develop efficient algorithms for determining a configuration that minimizes the value of the cost function or objective function. An example of a combinatorial optimization problem is the well-known traveling salesman problem (TSP), which involves determining a traveling salesman's route (a route that passes through each of several cities only once and returns finally to the starting city) with minimum cost. In this case, the cities are the discrete objects to be rearranged and the fact that each city must be visited only once is the constraint that must be satisfied [Wong, Leong, and Liu 1989]. We can also interpret this problem in terms of a conventional optimization concept. That is, the cities visited are the optimization variables, and each city is allowed to have the discrete value corresponding to its turn of being visited. We can also realize the constraints previously mentioned by imposing some constraints on each city's value.

Significant progress has been made recently in the study of combinatorial optimization. However, for many important combinatorial problems encountered in practice and classified as NP-complete [Garey and Johnson 1979], efficient algorithms for determining optimal solutions are still unknown. NP-complete problems are those that are unlikely to be solvable by an amount of computational effort that is bounded by a polynomial function of the problem size. In fact, all known algorithms for these problems require a computing effort that increases exponentially with problem size and do not produce optimal but rather near-optimal solutions [Wong, Leong, and Liu 1989].

Figure 9.6

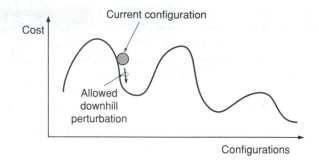

One method of solving NP-complete problems is to use an approximation algorithm, yielding an approximate solution in an acceptable amount of computation time. A general strategy for designing approximation algorithms is the method of iterative improvement, based on the simple technique of trial and error. In this method we start with an initial solution and examine its neighbors until a neighboring solution with a lower cost is discovered. The algorithm terminates when it arrives at a solution that has no neighboring solution with a lower cost. This strategy seems reasonable, but it has a serious problem: It is easily trapped in local minima, as shown in Figure 9.6. Solutions that look good in some small neighborhood of the cost surface are not necessarily the global optimum. Standard iterative improvement is a downhill-only style, and thus it does not guarantee a good solution [Wong, Leong, and Liu 1989; Rutenbar 1989].

Simulated annealing offers a strategy similar to that of iterative improvement, but with one major difference: Annealing allows perturbations to move uphill in a controlled way. Thus it is possible to jump out of local minima and potentially fall into a more promising downhill path [Rutenbar 1989].

9.4.2   Algorithm

Statistical mechanics is the study of the behavior of complex systems consisting of a large number of interacting atoms in thermal equilibrium at a finite temperature. Researchers have found that the probability that a system is in a given state S is $e^{-E(S)/k_b T}$, where $E(S)$ is the energy associated with state S, and k_b is Boltzmann's constant. Thus the most probable states of the atoms in thermal equilibrium at any temperature are those with lowest energy [Wong, Leong, and Liu 1989].

The analogy between a combinatorial optimization problem and that of determining the lowest energy ground state of a physical system with many interacting atoms was first observed by Kirkpatrick, Gelatt, and Vecchi [1983] and by Cerny [1985]. This analogy is summarized in Figure 9.7. The states of a system correspond to the configurations of the combinatorial optimization problem. The ground states of the system correspond to optimal configurations, namely, configurations that minimize the cost function. Finally, the problem of determining an optimal

Figure 9.7

Analogy between physical systems and optimization problems

Physical Systems	Optimization problems
State	Configuration
Energy	Cost function
Ground state	Optimal solution
Rapid quenching	Iterative improvement
Careful annealing	Simulated annealing

configuration in combinatorial optimization corresponds to that of determining a low-temperature ground state of the system.

In 1953, Metropolis and co-workers [Metropolis et al. 1953] introduced a computational procedure for efficient simulation of the equilibrium states of a many-body system at a given finite temperature. The Metropolis procedure is shown in Figure 9.8. In each step, a small perturbation of the configuration is chosen at random and the resulting change in the energy of the system, Δ, is computed. The new configuration is accepted with probability 1 if $\Delta \leq 0$ and with probability $e^{-\Delta/k_bT}$ if $\Delta > 0$. For $\Delta > 0$, S' is accepted when the random number generated between 0 and 1 is less than $e^{-\Delta/k_bT}$. This implies that the larger $e^{-\Delta/k_bT}$ is, the greater is the probability of S' being accepted. This is equivalent to saying that S' is accepted with the probability $e^{-\Delta/k_bT}$.

We can easily adapt the procedure to the solution of optimization problems. To do so we replace states in the physical system by configurations in the optimization problem and replace the energy function of a given state by the cost function or the objective function of the corresponding configuration. Then we can use this proce-

Figure 9.8

The Metropolis procedure

```
<Metropolis Procedure>

begin
      Choose some random initial configuration S;
      repeat
            S' := some random neighboring configuration of S;
            Δ := E(S') − E(S);
            Prob := min(1, e^−Δ/kbT);
            if random (0, 1) ≤ Prob then S := S';
            Until false;
      end;
```

dure to simulate the optimization process of the combinatorial problem with the given cost function.

Kirkpatrick and co-workers generalized this basic approach by introducing a multitemperature approach in which the "temperature" is lowered slowly in stages. At each temperature, the system is simulated by the Metropolis procedure until the system reaches equilibrium. The generic simulated annealing optimization procedure is given in Figure 9.9. Note that in the simulated annealing procedure for combinatorial optimization, Boltzmann's constant is combined with the temperature, and we will use the term *temperature* to refer to their product. Temperature can also be viewed as nothing but a control parameter for the optimization procedure.

Intuitively, the simulated annealing optimization procedure can be viewed as an enhanced version of iterative improvement. The simulated annealing procedure randomizes the iterative improvement procedure and also allows occasional "uphill moves" (moves that worsen the current solution) in an attempt to reduce the probability of being stuck at a locally optimal solution. These uphill moves are controlled probabilistically by the temperature T and become less and less likely toward the end of the process, as the value of T decreases (at high temperature, the probability of large uphill moves is large and vice versa). Thus the probability $e^{-\Delta/k_b T}$ can have a large value even for a large Δ when the temperature T has a large value.

Theoretical analysis shows that the simulated annealing algorithm converges with probability 1 to a globally optimal solution, provided certain conditions on the

Figure 9.9

Generic simulated annealing algorithm

```
<Generic Simulated Annealing Algorithm>

begin
    S := Initial olution S₀;
    T := Initial temperature T₀;
    while (stopping criterion is not satified) do
        begin
            while (not yet in equilibrium) do
                begin
                    S' := some random neighboring configuration
                        of S;
                    Δ := C(S') − C(S);
                    Prob := min(1, e^(−Δ/T));
                    if random (0, 1) ≤ Prob then S := S';
                end;
            Update T;
        end;
    Output best solution;
end;
```

number of iterations for each temperature T and a certain rule for updating the value of T are followed. However, no single general principle can be applied in choosing these conditions and rules for the implementation of various applications. Consequently, most of the current applications of the simulated annealing involve the simple and yet effective approach of Kirkpatrick, Gelatt, and Vecchi [1983] or its variations to choose these parameters.

The method of simulated annealing as an optimization technique is very appealing because it produces solutions of high quality and, in general, is easy to implement even in the absence of deep insight into the problems themselves. However, simulated annealing is a general design methodology rather than a completely specified algorithm. Thus application of this technique to a particular problem requires careful design of the basic ingredients: (1) formulating the problem with a concise description of the configurations, (2) generating systematically the neighboring solutions of each solution, (3) choosing a suitable cost function, and (4) defining an annealing schedule (i.e., specifying the initial temperature, the rule for changing the temperatures, the duration of search at each temperature, and the termination condition of the algorithm).

9.4.3 Applications

Recent research has demonstrated the effectiveness of simulated annealing in optimization fields such as

- VLSI circuits placement and wiring,
- floor-plan design,
- routing or path optimization,
- layout design,
- two-dimensional compaction (nesting),
- digital filter design,
- pattern recognition, and
- image processing.

We will use two case studies to demonstrate the solution of optimization problems by simulated annealing algorithm.

Application to the traveling salesman problem   The goal of the traveling salesman problem (TSP) lies in determining a traveling salesman's route so that it passes through each of a given set of cities once and returns finally to the starting city with minimum cost. In this case, each city must be visited only once. Thus the cost function is in general the total path length of the route.

Because many state changes are generated and evaluated in simulated annealing, it is necessary to provide efficient methods for neighborhood generation and cost evaluation. For this purpose, the neighbor typically can be generated from the current path (the list of cities in the order of being visited) in the following way.

- Choose an arbitrary portion from the current path and then reverse the visiting order

or

- Move the portion chosen to another arbitrary place in the current path.

Figure 9.10 shows four configurations in the evolution of the optimization process carried out by simulated annealing for a 100-city TSP, with the cities located on the vertices of a regular grid. The initial configuration in Figure 9.10(a) is given by a random sequence of the 100 cities, which is far from an optimal configuration. The configuration is chaotic, and the corresponding cost is large. In the course of the optimization process, the configurations obtained in Figures 9.10(b) and (c) are closer to a minimum; the configurations become less chaotic and the corresponding cost decreases. Finally, a minimum is obtained, as shown in Figure 9.10(d), with a highly regular pattern for which the cost is minimum. [Laarhoven and Aarts 1987]. Figure 9.11 shows another example of a TSP—this one for 400 cities—solved satisfactorily first by Kirkpatrick, Gelatt, and Vecchi [1983], using simulated annealing.

Application to optimal nesting The goal of *optimal nesting* lies in the minimization of the total use of raw sheet(s) in the fabrication of shapes. The typical con-

Figure 9.10

100-city traveling salesman problem solved by simulated annealing

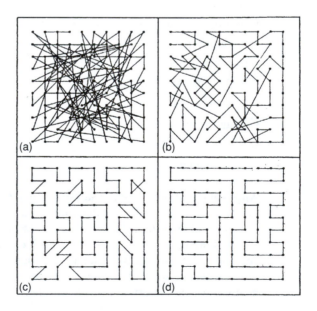

Figure 9.11

400-city traveling salesman problem solved by simulated annealing [Kirkpatrick, Gelatt Jr., & Vecchi, 1983]

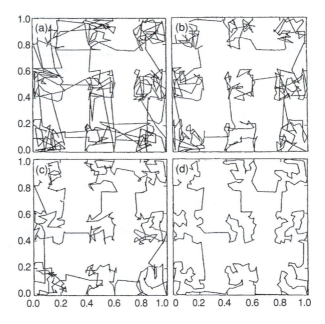

straint in the nesting problem is that there must be no overlaps of the shapes and that all the shapes must be located inside the raw sheet boundaries, avoiding any interior defects in the process. Thus the usual cost function or objective function becomes

$$F(S) = \text{scrap} + w \times \text{overlap}$$

Here, S is the current configuration of the nesting, scrap is the amount of waste of the raw sheet(s), or the difference between the raw sheet area and the total area of the nested shapes, overlap is the total area of overlaps of the shapes, and w is the weighting factor. During the optimization process overlaps are allowed occasionally, but using a large value of w will prohibit any overlap in the final nesting configuration. Note that the right-hand side of the cost function equation is the penalty function described in Section 9.2.

Neighborhood S' of the current configuration S can be generated by imposing a small perturbation on the current configuration—for example, by changing slightly the location and orientation of a shape chosen randomly among all the shapes of the current configuration. The configuration change from S to S' called *move* is executed by the Metropolis procedure, previously introduced in Figure 9.9.

Figure 9.12 shows the result of optimal blank nesting for progressive steel blanking. Figures 9.13 and 9.14, respectively, show examples of nesting 36 gar-

Figure 9.12

Optimal blank nest-
ing for progressive
blanking

Waste ratio = 17.5%

Waste ratio = 28.4%

ment patterns on a raw sheet of constant width and on an irregular raw sheet having
an interior defect. The defect area, shown in black in Figure 9.14, is a thin vertical
strip in this case. Defects often are encountered in cutting apparel parts from raw
leather sheets.

Figure 9.13

Nesting of 36 pat-
terns on the strip
of raw sheet

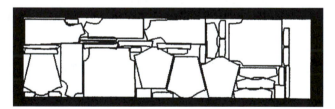

Figure 9.14

Nesting of 36 pat-
terns on an irregu-
lar raw sheet with
an interior defect

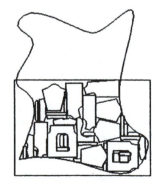

9.5 GENETIC ALGORITHMS

Genetic algorithms (GAs) are adaptive methods that may be used to solve search and optimization problems. They are rooted in the mechanism of evolution and natural genetics. Over many generations, natural populations evolve according to the principles of natural selection and "survival of the fittest." By mimicking this process, GAs are able to evolve solutions of real-world problems if they have been suitably encoded [Beasley, Bull, and Martin 1993].

The power of GAs comes from the fact that the technique is robust and can deal successfully with a wide range of problem types, including those that are difficult to solve by other methods. Although GAs may not find the global optimum solution of a problem, they usually can find "acceptably good" solutions "acceptably quickly." Of course, specialized techniques tailored for particular problems are likely to outperform GAs in both speed and accuracy of the final result. The main advantages of GAs, then, is in difficult areas where no such techniques exist. Even when existing techniques work well, improvements have been made by hybridizing them with GAs [Goldberg 1989].

The basic principles of GAs were first laid down by Holland [1975] and are described in many texts. GAs simulate those processes in natural populations that are essential to evolution: In nature, those best suited to competition for scanty resources survive, so adapting to a changing and competitive environment is essential for the survival of individuals of each species. The various features that uniquely characterize an individual determine its survival capacity, but these features in turn are determined by the individual's genetic content. Specifically, each feature is controlled by a basic unit called a *gene*. The sets of genes controlling features form *chromosomes*, which are the keys to an individual's survival. The reproduction process generates diversity in the gene pool, and evolution is initiated when the genetic material (chromosomes) from two parents recombines during reproduction. New combinations of genes are generated from previous ones, and a new gene pool is created. Specifically, the genes among chromosomes are exchanged to form new chromosomes. This mechanism of reproduction is called *crossover*. Segments of the two parent chromosomes are exchanged during crossover, improving the possibility of the "right" combination of genes for better individuals. Repeated selection and crossover cause the continuous evolution of the gene pool and the generation of individuals that have a better chance of survival.

In the early 1970s, Holland proposed GAs as computer programs that mimic the evolutionary processes in nature. GAs manipulate a population of potential solutions of an optimization (or search) problem. Specifically, they operate on encoded representations of the solutions, equivalent to the genetic material of individuals in nature and not directly on the solutions themselves. Holland's GAs encode the solutions as strings of bits from a binary alphabet. As in nature, selection provides the necessary driving mechanism for better solutions to survive. Each solution is associated with a fitness value that reflects how good it is, compared with other solutions in the population. The higher the fitness value of an individual, the higher are its chances of survival and reproduction and the greater is its existence in the subsequent generation. Recombination of genetic material in GAs is simulated through a crossover mechanism that exchanges portions between strings. Another operation, called *mutation*, causes sporadic and random alteration of the bits of strings. Mutation, too, has a direct analogy from nature and plays the role of regenerating lost genetic material [Goldberg 1983].

9.5.1 Basic Principles

In the literature, Holland's genetic algorithm is commonly called the *simple genetic algorithm*, or SGA. Essential to the SGA is a population of binary strings. Each string of 0s and 1s is the encoded version of a solution to the optimization problem. This string is equivalent to the configuration in simulated annealing. The algorithm starts with a certain number of these strings, called the *population* of the first generation. Using genetic operators—crossover and mutation—the algorithm creates the subsequent generation from the strings of the current population. The algorithm somehow forces the strings corresponding to better individuals to participate in reproduction so that the next generation has more, improved individuals. This generation cycle is repeated until a desired termination criterion is reached. Figure 9.15 summarizes the basic procedure of GAs [Goldberg 1989]. Details of the important components are given in the following sections.

Encoding mechanism   Fundamental to the GA structure is the encoding mechanism for representing the optimization problem's variables. These variables (known as genes) are joined to form a string of values (often referred to as a chromosome). For example, if our problem is to maximize a function of three variables, $F(x, y, z)$, we might represent each variable by a 10-bit binary number (suitably scaled). Our chromosome would therefore contain three genes and consist of 30 binary digits.

In genetic terms, the set of variables represented by a particular chromosome is referred to as a *genotype*. The genotype contains the information required to construct an organism, which is referred to as the *phenotype*. The same terms are used in GAs. For example, in a bridge design task, the set of variables specifying a particular design is the genotype, and the finished construction is the phenotype. The fitness of an individual depends on the performance of the phenotype. This can be inferred from the genotype (i.e., it can be computed from the chromosome using the fitness function).

Optimization variables are represented by a string, or chromosome, even though the optimization variables have continuous real values. In fact, a large number of optimization problems have real-valued continuous variables. A common method of encoding them uses their integer representation. Each variable is first linearly mapped to an integer defined in a specified range, and the integer is encoded by using a fixed number of binary bits. The binary codes of all the variables are then concatenated to obtain a binary string. For example, consider a continuous variable defined in a range from –1.28 to 1.28. We could encode this continuous variable with an accuracy of two decimal places by multiplying its real value by

Figure 9.15

Basic procedure of the genetic algorithm

<**Genetic Algorithm**>

BEGIN /*Genetic algorithm*/
    Generate initial population:
    Compute fitness of each individual

    WHILE NOT *finished* **DO**
    BEGIN /*Produce new generation*/

        FOR *population_size*/2 **DO**
        BEGIN /*Reproduction cycle*/
            Select two individuals from old generation for mating;
            /*Biased in favor of the fitter ones*/
            Recombine the two individual to give offspring;
            Compute fitness of the two offspring;
            Insert offspring in new generation;
        END

        IF population has converged **THEN**
            finished:=**TRUE**;

    END

END

100 and then discarding the decimal portion of the product. Thus the value that the variable attains is linearly mapped to integers in the range [–128, 128]. The binary code corresponding to each integer can easily be computed, as illustrated in Figure 9.16 [Chapman 1994].

Figure 9.16

The chromosome encoding process

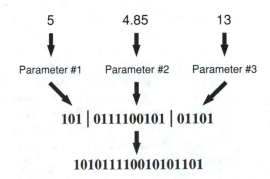

Fitness function   The objective function, the function to be optimized, provides the mechanism for evaluating each string. However, its range of values varies from problem to problem. To maintain uniformity over various problem domains, we use the fitness function that normalizes the objective function to a convenient range of 0 to 1. Thus the normalized value of the objective function is the fitness of the string, which is used by the selection mechanism to evaluate the strings of the population [Chapman 1994]. The objective function is normalized to the fitness function so that the largest fitness corresponds to the optimal situation.

Selection mechanism   A selection process models nature's survival-of-the-fittest mechanism. Fitter solutions survive while weaker ones perish. In the GAs, a fitter string receives a higher number of offspring, which are exactly same as itself, and thus it has a greater chance of survival in the subsequent generation. In the proportionate selection scheme, a string with the average fitness value of the population will be allocated one offspring and participate in the reproduction for the next generation. A string with a fitness value higher than the average is allocated more than one offspring, whereas a string with a fitness value less than the average is allocated less than one offspring. Thus the fitter strings tend to participate more actively in the reproduction while the weaker ones participate less. For example, consider a sample population of size 4:

String	Fitness (f_i)	Probability ($f_i/\bar{f} = f_i/290$)
01101	169	0.58
11000	576	1.99
01000	64	0.22
10011	351	1.21
Total	1160 ($\bar{f} = 1160/4 = 290$	4.0

In the sample population, the second string should receive one offspring, with a 0.99 probability of receiving a second offspring. Also the fourth string should receive one offspring, with a 0.21 probability of receiving a second offspring. Thus the second and fourth strings receive one offspring each. The next task is selection of the remaining two offspring. We select the first string (0.58) and the second string (0.99) as the remaining two strings because both have greater probabilities than the third and the fourth strings, which have probabilities of 0.22 and 0.21, respectively, of receiving an offspring. Note that the probabilities of the second and fourth strings have been reduced by 1 when one offspring for each was allocated previously. Through this process a new population is created, and the total fitness average is improved.

Figure 9.17

Illustration of crossover

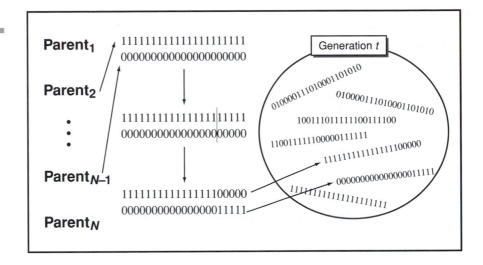

Reproduction During the reproductive phase of the GA, individuals are selected from the population and recombined, producing offspring that will comprise the next generation. Parents are selected randomly from the population. Because fitter individuals have the chance of receiving more than one offspring, they probably will be selected several times, whereas those less fit may not be selected at all.

After two parents have been selected, their chromosomes are recombined, typically using the mechanisms of crossover and mutation. Crossover takes two individuals and cuts their chromosome strings at some randomly chosen position to produce two "head" segments and two "tail" segments. The tail segments are then swapped to produce two new full-length chromosomes, as illustrated in Figure 9.17. This is known as *single-point crossover* [Chapman 1994]. Each of the two offspring inherit some genes from each parent.

Crossover is not usually applied to all pairs of individuals selected for mating. A random choice is made, where the likelihood of crossover being applied is typically between 0.6 and 1.0. This choice can be implemented by using a random number generator. That is, crossover is allowed if the random number generated between 0 and 1 at that instant is less than the likelihood number between 0.6 and 1. If crossover is not applied, offspring are produced simply by duplicating the parents. This gives each individual a chance of passing on its genes without a disruption by crossover.

Mutation is applied to each child individually after crossover. It randomly alters each gene with a small probability (typically 0.001), changing 0 to 1 or vice versa. This can also be implemented by using a random number generator as in crossover. Figure 9.18 shows the 9th gene and 17th gene of the chromosome being mutated. GAs treat mutation only as a secondary operator with the role of restoring lost genetic material. For example, suppose that all the strings in a population have converged to a 0 at a given position and that the optimal solution has a 1 at that position. Crossover cannot regenerate a 1 at that position, but mutation can.

Figure 9.18

Illustration of muta-tion

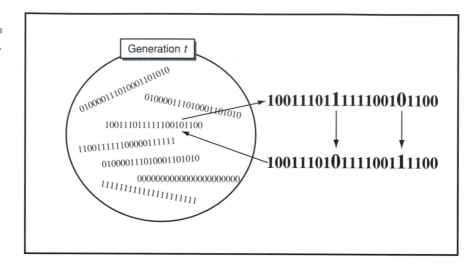

Convergence   If the GA has been correctly implemented, the population will evolve over successive generations so that the fitness of the best and the average individual in each generation increases toward the global optimum. Convergence is the progression toward increasing uniformity. A gene is said to have converged when 95% of the population share the same value [Goldberg 1989].

9.5.2 Application

The genetic algorithm can be used to find the optimal values of the molding condition in the injection molding process of a plastic part. Let's consider an upper cover of a washing machine, as illustrated in Figure 9.19. We want to find the optimal mold temperature, melt temperature, and filling time for a maximum performance

Figure 9.19

Test model

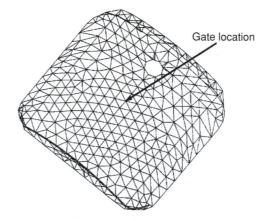

Figure 9.20

Range of molding conditions

	Minimum	Maximum	Values
Melt temperature	220	260	32
Mold temperature	50	70	32
Filling time	1	4	16

index that is related to the quality of the part to be fabricated. For simplicity, we assume that the performance index is calculated by simulation of the molding conditions. The lower and upper bounds of the optimization variables are given in Figure 9.20.

Now let's consider how to encode these variables. As shown in Figure 9.20, the melt temperature is assumed to have 32 discrete values and is thus represented by 5 digits. Similarly the mold temperature and the filling time are represented by 5 and 4 digits, respectively. Thus the chromosome in this example will be a binary string of length 14.

Figure 9.21 shows the result of the optimization and the graph of the convergence process. Note that each individual (10 individuals in this case) in each gener-

Figure 9.21

Optimal molding conditions

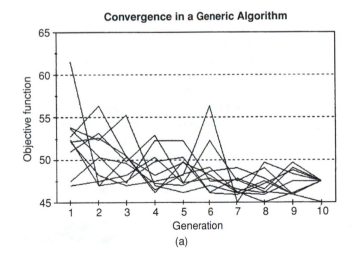

Convergence in a Generic Algorithm

(a)

	Melt temperature	Mold temperature	Filling time	Object function
Result	220.0	70.0	2.6	45.00

(b)

Figure 9.22

Population size	Crossover rate	Mutation
10	0.6	0.001

ation evolves into the fittest individual as the optimization proceeds. We used a commercial implementation of GA, called GENESIS [Grefenstette 1990]. The parameters used to run GENESIS are given in Figure 9.22.

9.6   STRUCTURAL OPTIMIZATION

In this section, we introduce the application of optimization for design purposes. *Structural optimization* is an automated synthesis of a mechanical component based on structural properties. In other words, structural optimization automatically generates a mechanical component design that exhibits optimal structural performance.

Structural optimization involves optimizing an objective function (generally stiffness, manufacturability, weight, or cost) while satisfying structural and other design constraints (locations of support points, size and weight limitations, maximum allowable stress, maximum acceptable weight, minimum heat dissipation, and the like). For this optimization, a geometric modeling tool to represent a shape, a structural analysis tool to solve the problem, and an optimization algorithm to search the optimum are needed, as illustrated in Figure 9.23.

Structural optimization techniques can be classified by the types of design variables used to describe the design geometry. The objective function and design constraints have to be expressed as functions of these design variables. Depending on the type of component attributes controlled by the design variables in a particular structural optimization, it is considered to be a sizing, shape, or topology optimization. Hence structural optimization routines iteratively modify a design's size, shape, or topology until the design reaches the optimum, subject to constraints.

Figure 9.23

Components of structural optimization [Kumar, 1993]

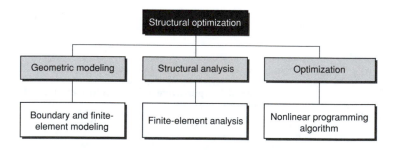

9.6.1 Sizing Optimization

Sizing optimization, the simplest method among the three structural optimization categories, performs optimization by keeping a design's shape and topology unchanged while modifying specific dimensions of the design. Optimization therefore occurs through determination of the design variable values that correspond to the component dimensions providing optimal structural behavior. The earliest attempts used simple parameterization of the design geometry and optimized easy-to-analyze structures such as trusses, frames, and plates [Kirsch 1981; Morris 1982; Haftka and Grandhi 1986].

Structural optimization of trusses and frames involves the optimal design of the cross sections of the elements. The design variables are the cross-sectional areas of the truss or frame elements. For simple trusses with only a few members, analytical expressions may be derived to express the structural properties as a function of the design variables. Larger trusses and frames can be analyzed by using the finite-element method. In the finite-element method, as described in Chapter 8, a complicated structure is subdivided into simple elements so that the results obtained for the simple elements are composed into the result for the entire structure.

Trusses and frames also can be optimized by varying their configurations. The optimal configuration of a truss can be computed by solving for the optimal nodal coordinates (the end points of the truss members). In this case, the design variables are the nodal coordinates of the truss. The topology or the connectivity of the truss is fixed and therefore there is no need to modify the analysis model when the variables are changed.

Another choice of variables for the optimal design of trusses are selection parameters for materials that indicate the material to use for each element of a truss or frame. Selecting the optimal material for each element from a given set is a combinatorial optimization problem. It is common practice to consider simultaneously a combination of these three types of sizing variables. Figure 9.24 shows an example of a 39-bar truss whose configuration, as well as the cross-sectional areas of its elements, are optimized [Morris 1982]. Figure 9.24(a) illustrates the initial configuration of the truss, and Figure 9.24(b) shows the optimal configuration and cross sections for supporting the loads acting on nodes 13, 14, and 15. The numbers pointing to the members in Figure 9.24(b) are the optimized cross-sectional areas of the corresponding members.

Similarly, the plate thickness is chosen as the design variable in the design of platelike structures. This choice of variable makes the design problem a sizing optimization problem, as the overall shape and topology of the plate remain fixed during optimization; only its thickness is allowed to vary. The thickness is assumed constant within each element but can be varied from one element to another. In this case, the mesh generated under the assumption of the smooth change in the thickness may not be adequate if the thickness varies too abruptly from element to element.

Figure 9.24

A truss example composed of 39 bars [Morris, 1982]

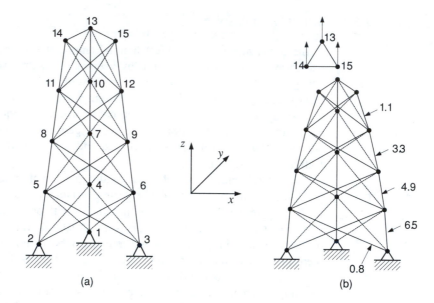

(a)   (b)

9.6.2   Shape Optimization

Shape optimization holds the topology constant while modifying the shape. Hence the design variables control the overall design shape, and the values of the design variables define the particular shape of the design. During optimization the values of the design variable that correspond to the optimal component shape are determined. Note that sizing optimization typically occurs as a by-product of the shape optimization process. In fact, sizing optimization can be considered as a special case of shape optimization.

Shape design variables can be parameters defining certain features of the shape or important dimensions. For example, the radius of a circular hole or the side of a square hole can be a design variable. Clearly changing these parameters can significantly change the geometry and in most cases require the regeneration of the finite elements for finite-element analysis. Many examples of shape variation obtained with parametric variables have been illustrated by Botkin, Yang, and Bennett [1986]. Shape optimization can also be achieved by treating some parts of the boundary of a solid as design variables. That is, the parameters for parts of the boundary are used as the design variables. For example, the nodal coordinates of the nodes on the boundary of the shape may be treated as design variables. However, one important criterion is that the finite-element model should not be deteriorated for analysis during the optimization. This may require regeneration of the finite-element mesh at each iteration. Therefore a one-to-one correspondence between the finite-element mesh and design variables is not desirable. Figure 9.25 shows an example of shape optimization. Figure 9.25(a) is the initial shape of the torque arm. Parts of the outer boundary are treated as design variables, and the

Figure 9.25

Example of shape optimization [Yang, Choi, & Haug, 1986]

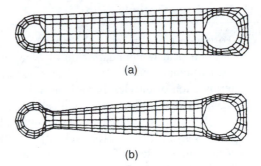

(a)

(b)

shape is optimized to obtain the final design, as shown in Figure 9.25(b). Note that the finite-element mesh was modified as the shape changed [Yang 1986].

In the shape optimization by boundary variation, the concept of a design element is often used [Imam 1982; Briabant and Fluery 1984]. Design elements are regions into which a structure is divided, and the boundaries of each such region are controlled by a set of design variables. Each design element may consist of many finite elements. Figure 9.26 illustrates a structure composed of three design elements whose boundaries are controlled by the design variables. Many methods of parameterizing boundaries have been used. Briabant and Fluery [1984] used cubic splines to represent the boundaries. That is, they used Bezier or B-spline curves and surfaces to represent the design element boundaries. The control points of these curves and surfaces then serve as the variables of the structural optimization problem. A design element parameterized with B-spline functions is illustrated in Figure 9.27.

Figure 9.26

Example of design elements [Kumar, 1993]

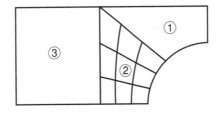

Figure 9.27

Design element with B-spline control points as design variables [Briabant & Fluery, 1984]

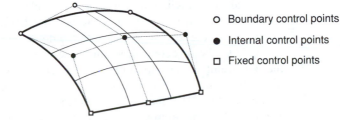

○ Boundary control points
● Internal control points
□ Fixed control points

9.6.3   Topology Optimization

To obtain globally optimal shapes topology must be also modified, allowing the creation of new boundaries. In *topology optimization*, the design variables define the particular topology of the design. Optimization therefore occurs through the determination of the design variable values that correspond to the component topology providing optimal structural behavior.

The earliest attempts to design optimal structures topologically were made for the design of trusslike (or skeletal) structures. Research in this area has been extensive and review of the literature on the optimization of skeletal structures has been compiled by Topping [1983]. The most common technique is the so-called *ground structure approach*. In this approach, the design space is covered with a grid of nodes. These nodes include locations at which loads are applied and boundary conditions are imposed. The ground structure is constructed by connecting every node to every other node. In a truss structure nodes are connected by members. A simple search technique can be used to optimize this ground structure with the objective of minimizing the weight subject to constraints on the plastic collapse load. During optimization, unnecessary members of the ground structure are removed automatically when their cross-sectional areas are reduced to zero by the optimization algorithm, yielding the optimal topology of the structure. In this approach the optimal structure is not unique, even when the optimal weight is unique. When stress or displacement constraints are to be considered, nonlinear programming techniques need to be used. Automatic removal of unnecessary members is no longer easy because the stresses in these members become large as their cross-sectional areas approach zero. Another problem is that the stiffness matrix may become singular because of the removal of some members. Many methods for overcoming these difficulties have been proposed [Topping 1983; Haftka and Gurdal 1992].

Early attempts in topology optimization involved structural analysis with a finite-element method followed by removal of elements that were understressed. This approach was unsuccessful because final shapes were found to depend on the initial mesh density used for the finite-element analysis. Strang [1986] attributed this behavior to the nonconvex nature of the problem statement. Kohn and Strang [1986], noting that the original problem was not well posed, suggested a relaxed variational problem that allows composites (or porous materials) instead of the 0–1 dichotomy between holes and materials.

Bendsoe and Kikuchi [1988] assumed that the material is porous and solved for the optimal distribution of porosity. A design domain is defined as the space within which the structure has to fit. The domain is divided into a mesh, and load is applied. The objective function is the mean compliance of the structure, and the constraint is the maximum weight. The structural behavior is analyzed by using the finite-element method. The design domain is taken as the initial shape of the structure. The material is modeled as porous by assuming a microstructure. A unit cell of the microstructure is shown in Figure 9.28(a). The material is assumed to be made up of infinite such unit cells that are assumed to be infinitesi-

Figure 9.28

(a) Dimensions and
(b) orientation of
the unit cell [Suzuki
& Kikuchi, 1991]

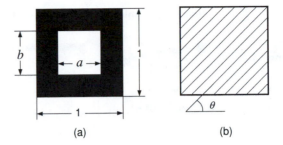

(a)   (b)

mal in the limit. Suzuki and Kikuchi [1991] assumed a rectangular void of dimensions a and b within the unit cell. The dimensions of the void within the unit cell determine the overall porosity or void fraction of the material. Each finite element is assumed to have a fixed porosity so that it is associated with its own void dimensions a_i and b_i, where i is the element number. These void dimensions, along with the orientation θ_i of the unit cells in each finite element, are taken as the design variables. Figure 9.28(b) shows the orientation of the unit cell. Modifying the void dimensions and the orientations of the unit cell will modify the property of the material.

An optimality criteria algorithm has been used [Bendsoe and Kikuchi 1988; Suzuki and Kikuchi 1991] to solve for the optimal distribution of porosity, that is, optimal value of the void dimensions and orientations for each element. The properties of the material obviously depend on the assumed microstructure and therefore on the void size in each unit cell. Thus these properties are continuous functions of the void dimensions instead of zero or nonzero constants. For a given porosity or void size, the properties of the material can be determined by using the homogenization method. Figure 9.29 illustrates the typical relation between a property coefficient and void size, where the void is square so that $1 - a^2$ represents the density of the unit cell, for a material. A finite-element analysis over the unit cell is required to evaluate the coefficient for each void-size value. In reality, to obtain the relation shown in Figure 9.29, D_{ij} is evaluated for a discrete number of values of the void dimensions a, and then the functional relationship is obtained by interpolating these values, using Legendre polynomials. The evaluation of this relation therefore requires several finite-element analyses over the unit cell. The relation obtained would be different if a different microstructure is assumed. This property,

Figure 9.29

Property of the material as a function of density [Bendsoe & Kikuchi, 1988]

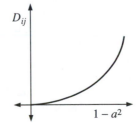

Figure 9.30

A cantilever beam optimized by using rectangular void microstructure [Bendsoe, Diaz, & Kikuchi, 1992]

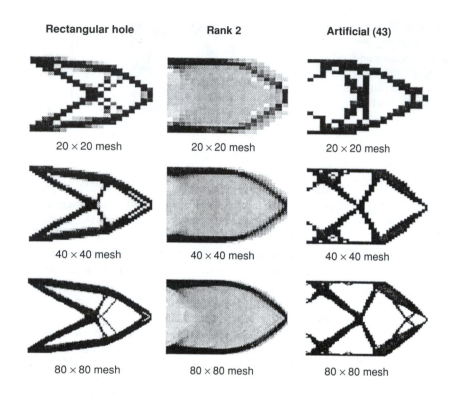

obtained by the variation of the density of the unit cell, can also be changed by the orientation of the unit cell. In the course of optimization, the properties of the material in each element should be calculated by the method described, as the design variables a_i, b_i, and θ_i are changed. The optimization algorithm approaches the optimal solution by increasing the void size for elements in which material is underutilized and by decreasing the void size where material is highly utilized, while searching the optimal orientation of each unit cell for the stiffest structure. Figure 9.30 illustrates a cantilever beam optimized for rectangular void microstructure. Note that a smoother boundary is obtained when the optimization starts with a finer mesh.

Topology optimization can be performed by using a genetic algorithm. The first efforts in this field were those of Sandgren and Jensen [1992], who applied a genetic algorithm to the topology optimization of a variety of continuum structures. They minimized the weight while satisfying displacement and stress constraints. In fact, Figure 9.31(a) was obtained with the genetic algorithm. Figure 9.31(b), (c), and (d) show the optimum shapes of the cross section of the beam for various materials. Figure 9.32 illustrates the optimum structure when loads are applied to a bicycle [Kumar 1993]. The result is striking because of its similarity to a bicycle frame.

Figure 9.31

(a) Simple, single segment beam and the optimum beam cross section for (b) plastic, (c) aluminum, and (d) steel [Chapman, 1994]

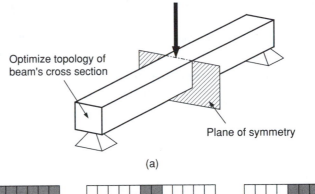

Optimize topology of beam's cross section

Plane of symmetry

(a)

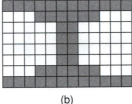

(b)

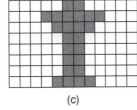

(c)

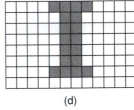

(d)

Figure 9.32

Bicycle frame [Kumar, 1993]

QUESTIONS AND PROBLEMS

1. Find the minimum of $F(x) = (x - 1)^2$ ($x \in R$), subject to the constraint $x \geq 2$.

   a. Derive the augmented objective function as in Equation (9.11) and draw $y = F(x)$ on the xy plane. Assume that $\alpha = 2$.

   b. Derive the minimum of the augmented objective function in (a) as a function of ρ and the corresponding x value.

   c. Show that the minimum in (b) approaches the real minimum and that the correspond-

ing x value approaches $x = 2$ from the infeasible region.

2. Find the minimum of $F(x) = x$ ($x \in R$) subject to the constraints $x - 2 \geq 0$, using the interior penalty method.

   a. Derive the augmented objective function as in Equation (9.16) and its minimum as a function of ρ_k.

   b. Show that the minimum in (a) approaches the real minimum and that the corresponding x value approaches $x = 2$ from the feasible region.

3. Explain the meaning of *combinatorial optimization*.

4. Select two typical search methods appropriate for combinatorial optimization from among the search techniques given in Figure 9.3.

5. Explain the meaning of *NP-complete problem*.

6. Consider a function $f(x)$, defined as shown below.

$$f(x) = \begin{cases} -\left(x - \dfrac{1}{2}\right) & x \le \dfrac{1}{3} \\ x - \dfrac{1}{6} & \dfrac{1}{3} < x \le \dfrac{2}{3} \\ -\dfrac{3}{2}(x - 1) & \dfrac{2}{3} < x \end{cases}$$

a. Write code to calculate the minimum of $f(x)$ for $0 \le x \le 1$, using the simulated annealing algorithm. The neighboring solution can be generated by a random number generator.

b. Print out the variation of x values in the optimization procedure and show that the local minimum can be overcome.

7. A fitness function is defined as $f(x) = \log x$. The optimization variable x is assumed to have one of eight values between 0 and 7 (i.e., it is represented by a string of three digits). For the initial population given in the following table, generate the population that will participate in reproduction of the next generation.

x	Chromosome
1	0 0 1
7	1 1 1
3	0 1 1
5	1 0 1

8. Suggest how to use the topology optimization method to locate the positions of ribs needed to stiffen a structure made of plastic, such as the plastic cover of a TV set.

10

CAD and CAM Integration

After a part has been designed, it is converted to a finished product by a manufacturing process. Just as the tools used in the design process are called CAD software, the tools in the manufacturing process are called CAM software. Various CAM software products can be used in the manufacturing process. For example, typical CAM software includes computer-aided process planning (CAPP) systems, in the process planning phase; NC software, for programming numerically controlled machine tools in the production phase; inspection software for use in the inspection phase; and software for programming robots, for use in the assembly phase.

Many commercial vendors of CAD and CAM systems exaggerate their benefits; the real benefits of these systems do not seem to be as great as originally touted because CAD and CAM have been poorly integrated. Therefore stronger integration of CAD and CAM is needed to increase productivity and ensure survival in increasingly competitive global markets. The need to automate process planning is the most urgent because that phase is the bridge between design and manufacturing. In fact, process planning has been the bottleneck in the integration of CAD and CAM. Thus the primary research efforts at the interface between CAD and CAM have been in the development of computer-aided process planning systems that attempt to automate communication between product engineers and manufacturing engineers. In this chapter, we describe process planning in general and discuss CAPP systems in particular. To clarify the role of process planning in the manufacturing process, we start with an overview of the discrete part production cycle.

10.1 OVERVIEW OF THE DISCRETE PART PRODUCTION CYCLE

Manufacturing systems can be classified generally as discrete part manufacturing and continuous process manufacturing. The former refers to manufacturing a product where the product undergoes a finite number of production or assembly operations. The latter refers to the production of a product that undergoes continuous changes, such as chemical reactions, that transform raw materials into final products. Here we concentrate on discrete part manufacturing and, more specifically, manufacturing by machining, which is a typical method of manufacturing discrete parts. The main phases of this manufacturing process are illustrated in Figure 10.1.

When a finished design is passed to the manufacturing department, a process planner converts the design description of parts and assemblies into production instructions. These instructions describe in detail the manufacturing processes required to transform rough billets into finished parts and the subsequent assembly operations needed to assemble parts into the final product. The procedure is therefore one of matching requirements for producing the parts to available manufacturing capabilities. Thus, in generating a process plan for a part, the process planner must interpret engineering drawings, make decisions about how cuts should be made and parts assembled, determine the order in which operations should be executed, specify which tools, machines, and fixtures are needed, and so on. This task is much easier if the process planner already has a process plan for a similar product. Thus similar parts usually are grouped in a family, using the group technology concept.

Once the process planning phase has been completed, actual production of the part begins, according to instructions generated during process planning. If numerically controlled (NC) machine tools are to be used to machine the part, the program to drive the machine tool has to be generated by an NC programmer. Many software tools needed to generate an NC program directly from the CAD database are available nowadays. Then the produced parts are inspected against specified quality standards. Parts passing inspection are assembled, packaged, labeled, and shipped to customers.

Thus the interface between the design process and the manufacturing process is process planning. Integration of design and manufacturing (or CAD and CAM) therefore cannot be automated without automating process planning. We discuss the steps in process planning and their automation in the following sections. At the end of this chapter, we introduce the product data management (PDM) system be-

Figure 10.1

Main phases of discrete part manufacturing

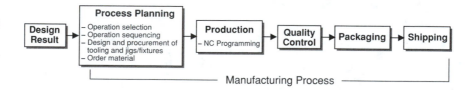

cause it is another important software component for smoothing the flow of data between CAD and CAM.

PROCESS PLANNING

Process planning is the function in a manufacturing facility that establishes which processes and parameters are to be used, as well as the machines performing these processes. The goal is to convert a rough billet to a part in final form as specified in an engineering drawing. Alternatively, process planning can be defined as the act of preparing detailed work instructions to machine or assemble a part or parts [Chang, Wysk, and Wang 1998].

The output of process planning is a *process plan* that describes the sequence of the selected manufacturing process or assembly operations. The process plan is sometimes called an operation sheet, route sheet, or operation planning summary. Figure 10.2 illustrates a process plan for producing the part shown in Figure 10.3. In addition to operation sequencing and operation selection, the selection or design of tooling and jigs/fixtures is also a major part of process planning. Selection of the tooling includes the tool itself and the machine on which the tool is used. Jigs/fixtures are devices to guide a tool or hold a workpiece for machining.

Figure 10.2

Example of a process plan

Part # SNU-SM-001				Part Name HANDLE	Date Feb. 10, 1998
Material 6061-T6 aluminum				Size $\varnothing 22 \times 206$	
Op #	Machine	Standard setup	Minutes run	Instructions	Tool and Parameters
010	Lathe	6	0.5	Chuck material exposing 45 mm length Face to clean Turn outer diameter to $\varnothing 21.8 \times 25$ long File chamfer R2	700 rpm 0.15 mm/rev Use 80 deg diamond T/F tool
020	Lathe	7	0.5	Reverse material exposing 45 mm length Face to clean Layout 30 mm dimension to shoulder Form groove $3 \times 1.5 \times R1$	Dykem Scribe Groove tool
030	Lathe	5	2	Single point M20 × 1.5 thread Finish thread with die	Threading tool 200 rpm Set feed lever to thread Set feed rate to pitch 1.5 mm M20 × 1.5 die
040	Lathe	2	1.5	Chamfer deburr thread	File #3 combined
050	Lathe	9	2	Center drill 60 deg × $\varnothing 8$ Appx.	Drill — C sink
060	Lathe	3	3	Advance stock Gripping 12 mm of raw material in chuck Advance live center to support the workpiece Knurl 125 mm	Live center Knurling tool
070	Bench	0	3	Clean, deburr, inspect	

Figure 10.3

Part to be produced

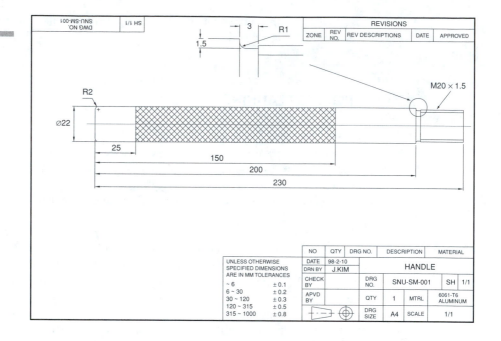

Many factors influence the process plan for a part or an assembly. These factors include the part geometry, the required accuracy and surface finish, the quantity to be produced, and the material to be used. For example, a very smooth surface finish may call for a grinding operation, whereas a less fine finish may require a turning operation, for the same part geometry. Similarly, small numbers of a part may be produced by a machining process, whereas large numbers may be produced by a forming process using a die. In addition to these part-specific factors, selection of the manufacturing process operations is also greatly influenced by available manufacturing facilities.

10.2.1 Manual Approach

Traditionally, process planning has been performed manually. In the *manual approach*, a skilled individual, often a former machinist, examines the drawing of a part and develops the necessary instructions for the process plan. The process plan being generated can be elaborate or simply an aggregation of individual operation descriptions, depending on the shop environment. For a model shop, where all the machinists are highly skilled in operating several machines and most parts produced are one of a kind, the process plan is usually nothing but a list of workstation routes and the details are left to the machinists. However, if a part is to be produced in an entirely automated transfer line, the process plan would contain the details of each operation. Regardless of the elaborateness of the process plan, its preparation depends heavily on a process planner's knowledge of manufacturing capabilities, tooling, materials, standard practices, and associated costs. Unfortunately, little of this information is documented, often existing only in the mind of the process planner. If the planner has a good memory, a process plan for a similar part might be remembered and modified for the current part. In some companies process plans are manually classified and stored in workbooks.

To develop process plans for new products, process planners often follow more or less a consistent set of steps.

- *Study the overall shape of the part.* The process planner reviews the engineering drawing to identify the basic structure of the part and potential difficulties in its production. Can the part be clamped or does it fit between the jaws? Is the part too long and thin in certain directions, causing it to bend when clamped? And so on.

- *Determine the best raw material shape to use if raw stock is not given.* With the help of the engineering drawing, the process planner can easily recognize the outer, or bounding, envelope of the part. This recognition helps the planner determine the stock shape from which the finished part can be produced with the least amount of material waste. The dimensions of a stock are typically about $1/4$ inch larger than the finished part's dimensions.

- *Identify datum surfaces and determine setups from this information.* The process planner determines the minimum number and types of setups required to machine the datum surfaces. The planner then associates each setup with the appropriate machining operations.

- *Identify part features.* The process planner identifies the individual features, or geometric shapes, that are to be cut into the stock, from which the part is to be formed. Shapes comprising the part's features or subfeatures determine the shapes of the tools needed, the movements of the machines required, and the paths the tools must follow when cutting the stock. Typical features and subfeatures for machining are illustrated in Figures 10.4 and 10.5, respectively.

- *Group the part features based on the required setups.* The process planner groups part features so that each group of features can be produced in the same setup. Some part features may be associated with the setups previously determined from the datum surfaces, but others may require new setups. Then the planner selects machining operations for the collected part features for each setup.

- *Order the sequence of the operations.* For each setup, the process planner determines the operation sequence required to produce the related datum surfaces and/or features, based on the interference and dependency between operations.

- *Select tools for each operation.* The process planner attempts to use the same tool for several operations if possible. The tradeoff between tool-change time and machining time has to be considered.

- *Select or design fixtures for each setup.* This phase of process planning depends heavily on the process planner's experience, as few standard jigs/fixtures are available. A good selection of jig/fixtures is important for good product quality.

- *Make a final check on the plan.* At this point, the process planner typically verifies the plan by checking the feasibility of the setups, verifying that clamps do not interfere with the tools, and so on.

Figure 10.4

Typical machining features

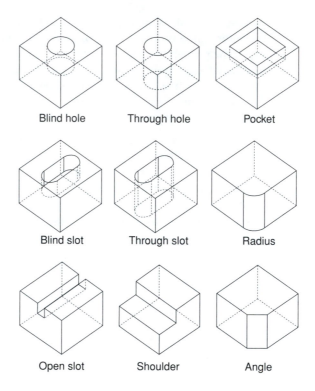

Blind hole   Through hole   Pocket

Blind slot   Through slot   Radius

Open slot   Shoulder   Angle

Figure 10.5

Typical machining subfeatures

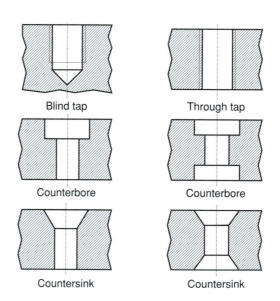

Blind tap   Through tap

Counterbore   Counterbore

Countersink   Countersink

- *Elaborate the process plan.* The process planner generates more details for producing individual features, choosing feeds and speed, estimating costs and standard times, and so on.

- *Prepare the final process plan document.* The process planner then prepares the final document and gives it to the production manager.

We can illustrate manual process planning by following these steps in Example 10.1.

EXAMPLE 10.1

Prepare a process plan for the part shown in Figure 10.6. Assume that precut bar stock and only conventional machine tools are used.

ANSWER

The part is a rotational component, so a lathe most likely will be used. The datum surfaces S1 and S2 indicated in Figure 10.7 can be machined in one setup in the lathe operation. However, at least two setups are required because of the threaded area. Specifically, part features S1, S2, S3, S4, and S5 can be machined in one

Figure 10.6

Part to be produced

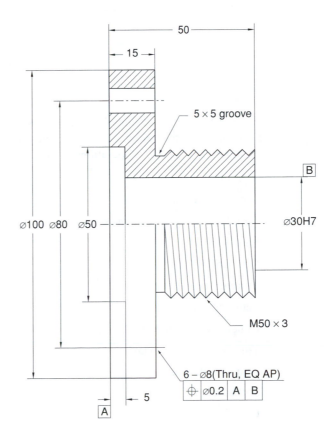

Figure 10.7

Part features to be machined

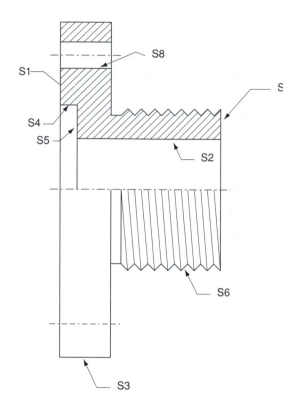

setup and S6 and S7 machined in the other setup. In addition, the holes S8 cannot be drilled on a lathe, and thus we need one more setup for a drill press. Therefore the following sequence of operations can be used to produce the part.

- Setup 1

  Chuck the workpiece.

  Turn S3 to a 100 mm diameter.

  Face S1.

  Core drill S2.

  Counter bore S4 and S5.

- Setup 2

  Chuck the workpiece on S3.

  Turn S6 to 50 mm diameter.

  Undercut the neck.

  Thread S6.

  Face S7.

- Setup 3

Locate the workpiece, using S1 and S2.

Mark six holes, S8.

Center drill and drill six holes, S8.

The elaborate process plans required, including tool and parameter selection, for this example are left for your practice.

As the preceding example demonstrates, the manual approach relies almost entirely on the individual planner's knowledge and subjective judgments, which reflect the planner's personal preferences and experiences. Consequently, process plans developed by different planners usually differ, even for the same part. Furthermore, the manual approach is very labor intensive, time consuming, and tedious. Because of these disadvantages, computerized systems have often replaced the manual approach.

10.2.2 Variant Approach

The variant approach is one of two approaches used to develop a computer-aided process planning (CAPP) system. The other approach is the generative approach, which we explain in the next section. The *variant approach* can be regarded as an advanced manual approach in which the planner's memory retrieval process is aided by the computer. In other words, the planner's workbook is stored in the computer file. A typical process plan of a similar part can then be retrieved automatically from the computer file when the specific part of interest is described according to a predefined coding system, and the retrieved process plan can be edited interactively for the specific part being planned. Thus a variant system requires a database containing a standard process plan for each family of parts. Such a plan consists of all instructions that would be included in a process plan for any part in that family. The parts are classified by family, using the group technology concept. In group technology, each part is assigned a code based on its features, and the parts are grouped into a family according to their codes. We explain group technology in Section 10.4.

A process plan is developed in the variant approach as follows. The process planning task for a new part starts with coding, which is equivalent to describing the part, using the group technology concept. Then the part is assigned to the proper family according to its code. The standard process plan for this family can then be retrieved from the computer. This plan contains general instructions for handling all the parts in the family, so some editing may be required for the specific part of interest. This editing can easily be performed with the editing capabilities provided in the variant systems. Often very little editing is required because the new plan is simply a variation of the standard process plan. Consequently, considerable time is saved in preparing the plan, and the resulting plans are much more consistent than those prepared manually. If the part being planned cannot be assigned to an existing family of parts, the planner can develop a new standard process plan interactively.

10.2.3 Generative Approach

In the *generative approach*, a process plan is generated automatically from engineering specifications of the finished part. Here the engineering specifications include textual information, such as type of material, special processing details, and special inspection instructions, as well as graphical information on part shape.

The first step in generating a process plan for a new part using a generative system is to enter the engineering specifications into the system. Ideally, these specifications would be read directly from a CAD database. For this to occur, the generative CAPP system must have the ability to recognize the machining features of a part, such as a hole, slot, or pocket at the least. This step is much easier if the part has been modeled by a feature-based modeling approach, as discussed in Chapter 5. However, the design features used in the feature-based modeling system may still have to be converted to the proper machining features. Some design features have one-to-one correspondence with machining features, but many require a complicated process. In addition, feature information alone does not provide all the information necessary for process planning. For example, most CAD models do not contain tolerance and materials information, which must be provided manually. These are some of the reasons why a truly automatic generative process planning system has not yet been developed. Instead, a manual approach to coding the engineering specifications of the part is often used. The coding scheme utilized must define all the geometric features and their associated details, such as locations, tolerances, and sizes. The coded data are accompanied by textual information. Additionally, the shape of the raw stock must be provided.

The second step is to transform the coded data and accompanying textual information into a detailed process plan. During this phase, the best sequence of operations and the detailed conditions for each operation must be determined. These conditions include tooling, fixtures, gauges, clamping, feeds, and speeds. A large database and complex built-in decision logic would certainly be required to generate a process plan for arbitrarily complex parts at this level of detail. As a result, to date the generative approach has been restricted to special classes of parts that have a relatively limited set of part features.

10.3 COMPUTER-AIDED PROCESS PLANNING SYSTEMS

Most existing computer-aided process planning systems (e.g., CAM-I CAPP, MIPLAN, MITURN, MIAPP, ACUDATA/UNIVATION, CINTURN, and COMCAPPV) are based on the variant approach. However, some systems (e.g., CPPP, AUTAP, APPAS, GENPLAN, CAR, MetCAPP, and ICEM-PART) based on the generative approach have been reported recently in the literature [Amirouche 1993]. We briefly describe several popular computer-aided process planning systems in the following sections. An in-depth comparison of various computer-aided process planning systems is available in Chang [1998].

10.3.1 CAM-I CAPP

The CAM-I CAPP system was developed by McDonnell Douglas Automation Company under contract from CAM-I and was first released in 1976. CAM-I CAPP is a database management system written in FORTRAN; it provides a structure for a database, retrieval logic, and interactive editing capability. The coding scheme for part classification and the output format are added by the user. Thus a coding scheme tailored to the user's specific environment is allowed if the code is not longer than 36 digits. For example, Lockheed–Georgia used a modified Opitz code for its CAPP system. The CAM-I CAPP coding scheme also allows the user to use any existing GT system. The range of parts that can be planned by using CAM-I CAPP depends on the capability of the coding scheme implemented.

A graphical description of the CAM-I CAPP system is shown in Figure 10.8. For each family of parts, a standard process plan (i.e., a sequence of operation codes, or *op codes*) is maintained in a standard sequence file. The detailed description of each op code is stored in the operation plan file. Standard plans and operation plans must be developed for each installation because they are a function of the machines, procedures, and expertise of a particular company. In each family matrix file, the matrix defines which parts belong to that family from the codes assigned to the parts by the coding system. One such matrix is illustrated in Figure 10.9. The columns represent the positions of the digits in the group technology code, and the rows represent the digits that can be assigned to any one position for the code. In this case, the group technology code comprises five positions, and each position can have a value of 0–9. Thus the family matrix file specifies all the possible combinations of the digits for each family. The matrix in Figure 10.9 shows that the parts represented by the codes 31632, 32646, and 35638, for example, belong to the same family.

Figure 10.8

Elements and work flow of a CAM-I CAPP system (Reprinted with permission from CAM-I (Consortium of Advanced Manufacturing-International, Inc.), Bedford, Texas, U.S.A. (www.CAM-I.org))

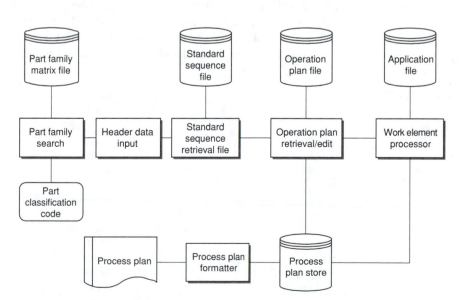

Figure 10.9

A part family matrix

	1	2	3	4	5
0					
1		×			
2		×			×
3	×			×	
4				×	
5		×			
6			×		×
7					×
8					
9					

A process plan is generated by a CAM-I CAPP system in four main steps, as illustrated in Figure 10.8.

1. After the part being planned has been classified by family, a search for the part family is performed by the system, using the stored part family matrix and the code of the part.

2. The planner inputs the header information to identify the process plan being generated. The header information includes the part number, material, planner, part name, and revision. The exact data for the header information vary with each company. Usually the type of header data needed is designated when a company installs its system.

3. The operation sequence required to manufacture a part, sometimes called a *routing*, is generated. It is created by inputting and/or modifying a standard plan consisting of mnemonic abbreviations (op codes) of available machines. Sample op codes are shown in Figure 10.10.

4. The text describing the work performed at each operation is created and/or edited. Figure 10.11 illustrates the operation plan for an op code **CNCLATH**. Once an operation plan has been completed for each operation, the operation plans of all the op codes are merged to form the complete process plan. The completed plan is stored and can be printed and edited as desired.

Figure 10.10

Sample op codes

10	**RAWMTL**
20	**SAWBAR**
30	**CNCLATH**
40	**INSP**
50	**HTRT**
60	**SAND**
70	**HOB**
80	**NCLATH**
90	**DEBUR**
100	**CNCGRIND**
110	**SLURRY**
120	**INSP**
130	**LASERMK**
140	**PKG**

Figure 10.11

Example of an operation plan

OP	OPCODE	SETUP		
30	CNCLATH		DEPTH 96-3 WORKCENTER G3JL MACH REF CNC J&L MACH CODE 0123 LOCATION 30/AA19	
		1	FIXTURE NO NCJ9 INSTRUCTIONS-REMOVE BURRS CUTTER TOOL/CODE-NCT309 TURN EDGE TURN INSIDE DIA	S/U TIME (_____) UNIT TIME (_____) HRS/PIECE (_____)
		2	FIXTURE NO NCJ9 INSTRUCTIONS-HANDLE WITH CARE CUTTER TOOL/CODE-NCT388 TURN BACKSIDE	S/U TIME (_____) UNIT TIME (_____) HRS/PIECE (_____)

For more information on these steps, see the related example in Bedworth, Henderson, and Wolfe [1991].

10.3.2 MIPLAN and MultiCAPP

MIPLAN and MultiCAPP were developed in conjunction with the Organization for Industrial Research, Inc. Both are variant systems that use the MICLASS coding system for part description. Process plan retrieval is based on part code, part number, family matrix, and code range. Part code input results in retrieval of similar parts, and each process plan displayed can be subsequently edited by the planner. These systems are similar to the CAM-I CAPP, system with MICLASS embedded as part of the system.

10.3.3 MetCAPP

MetCAPP is a typical CAPP system based on the generative approach. It was originally developed and marketed by the Software Division of the Institute of Advanced Manufacturing Science, Inc. (IAMS). Later the division became a separate company, Agil Tech. MetCAPP generates a process plans as follows. First, the feature extraction module in MetCAPP extracts the feature information from a geometric model created by a CAD system. Once the machining features have been identified, it uses the inference rules stored in the knowledge base to determine the machining methods and their orders. Thus MetCAPP can be classified as a knowledge-based generative CAPP system. It can also estimate the machining cost and time from the generated process plans.

Currently, MetCAPP has the inference rules and the necessary data for milling, turning, and hole-making processes in its knowledge base. It also provides a utility called MetScript to allow the user to define new machining features and add new process planning logic. Currently, the feature extraction module can read geometric models created by only ACIS modeler from Spatial Technology.

10.3.4 ICEM-PART

ICEM-PART was originally developed at the Laboratory of Production and Design Engineering of University of Twente in Holland and then later commercialized by ICEM. It is a generative CAPP system, mainly used for machining $2^1/_2$-dimensional prismatic parts.

ICEM-PART generates a process plan as follows. First, it reads a geometric model in either ACIS format or STEP AP203/AP214 format[1] and extracts the machining features. Then it selects the setup, cutter, and machine tool automatically and suggests the optimal order of processing. It also generates the NC tool paths for each machining feature. ICEM-PART is an example of CAD/CAPP/CAM integration.

10.4 GROUP TECHNOLOGY

As we showed in the preceding section, grouping similar parts into a family with a proper coding system is an essential step for computer-aided process planning. The concept of group technology enables this classification. One of the definitions of *group technology* (GT) can be stated as follows:

> Group technology is the realization that many problems are similar, and that by grouping similar problems, a single solution can be found to a set of problems thus saving time and effort. [Solaja and Urosevic, 1973]

This broad definition may be made more specific by stating its objective. The objective of group technology is to form a database of similar parts, design, and process and use that database to establish a common procedure for designing and manufacturing those parts. The parts are assigned to a part family based on similarities in design, such as shape, or processes, such as milling and drilling operations.

Group technology has been widely used to help simplify the flow of work through a manufacturing system. In particular, by identifying parts with similar processing characteristics, GT can support the development of efficient plant layouts by having each cell layout handle each part family. This simplifies the flow patterns of materials in a plant, which leads to reductions in transfer times of materials between machines, materials handling, and part manufacturing lead times.

---

[1] STEP format is explained in Chapter 14.

Furthermore, because similar parts are being produced on the same machines, machine setup times are also frequently reduced, and special tooling may be taken advantage of. As we stated in the preceding section, the use of GT codes to retrieve existing process plan data is also useful in process planning. Process planners, instead of starting from scratch for each new part to be planned, can review the process plan for a similar part with a similar GT code and modify it to generate the process plan for the new part.

The concept of group technology is also beneficial in the design stage. It often helps minimize unnecessary variety of parts by facilitating the search of existing similar parts and thus making designers aware of their existence. Often designers are unaware of the existence of similar designs in current production, perhaps because the part numbering system does not carry sufficient information. In such situations, parts tend to be duplicated, perhaps with minor differences that have nothing to do with the part's role in the final product. In addition, unnecessary parts would lead to a proliferation of paperwork and increased stock.

10.4.1   Classification and Coding

Classification of a part involves placing the part in a group, or family, based on the existence or absence of similar attributes. Coding of a part involves assigning symbols to the part; these symbols should reflect the attributes or features of the part.

Before constructing a coding scheme, the designer has to survey all the part features to which codes can be assigned. The selection of relevant features depends on the application of the coding scheme. For example, let's say that a designer classifies and codes parts for design retrieval (i.e., for the reduction of design effort by identifying similar parts that already exist). In this case, the features related to shape, material, and size are important, but information such as tolerances is not important. However, if the coding and classification system is to be used successfully in manufacturing, it must identify attributes such as tolerances, machinability of materials, processes, and machine tool requirements. There are three different types of code structure in GT coding system: hierarchical (monocode), chain (polycode), and hybrid.

Monocode   In hierarchical codes, or *monocodes*, each code number has a different meaning, depending on the preceding characters. Figure 10.12 illustrates the hierarchical codes for a 54xxx family, which is a frame of a facsimile machine. In this example, the fourth digit of 541xx indicates the type of plastic resin, but the same digit of 542xx indicates the existence of the ribs in the part. The hierarchical structure has the advantage of representing a large amount of information with very few codes. However, identifying the meaning of a digit is difficult because the entire hierarchy has to be traced. Also, hierarchical codes are difficult to develop and modify because all the branches in the hierarchy must be defined.

Figure 10.12

Example of a hier-
archical code

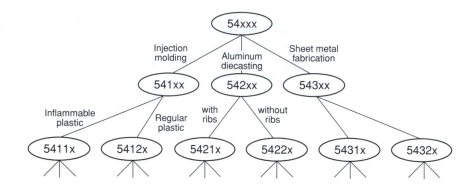

Polycode A code based on the chain structure is called a *polycode*. In polycode each digit is independent of all others, including the preceding digits, with each digit carrying self-contained information about the part. Thus polycodes are easy to construct and modify, as needed. In general, they are preferred for parts for which information is likely to change. Their primary drawback is that they can carry much less information than a monocode of the same length.

Hybrid structure In the *hybrid structure*, some digits are arranged hierarchically and others are fixed. In other words, it is a mixture of the hierarchical and chain structures. Most classification and coding systems used in industry are based on a hybrid structure in order to exploit the advantages of both structures. We describe some popular coding systems in the next section.

10.4.2 Existing Coding Systems

Various part classification and coding systems have been developed to support both design and production activities. These systems facilitate the selection of families of parts and the search for parts with similar processing requirements.

Vuoso–Praha system The *Vuoso–Praha code* is composed of four digits, three of which are arranged hierarchically to classify the part's shape, including size and proportions, and the fourth digit specifies the material. Table 10.1 explains the meaning of each digit in detail. Note that the meaning of the second and the third digits depend on the first code. Rotational parts are also coded with more detail than nonrotational parts. Let's use Table 10.1 to assign a code to the part shown in Figure 10.13. The part would be classified as 3 3 2 1 by the following reasoning.

3 ; Rotational workpiece, with through hole

3 ; $D = 75$ mm, $\dfrac{L}{D} = \dfrac{50}{75} = 0.67$

2 ; Holes not in axis

1 ; Plain steel

Table 10.1

The Vuoso–Praha coding system (Source: T. Chang, *Computer-Aided Manufacturing*, 2nd Edition, Prentice-Hall, Upper Saddle River, New Jersey, 1997)

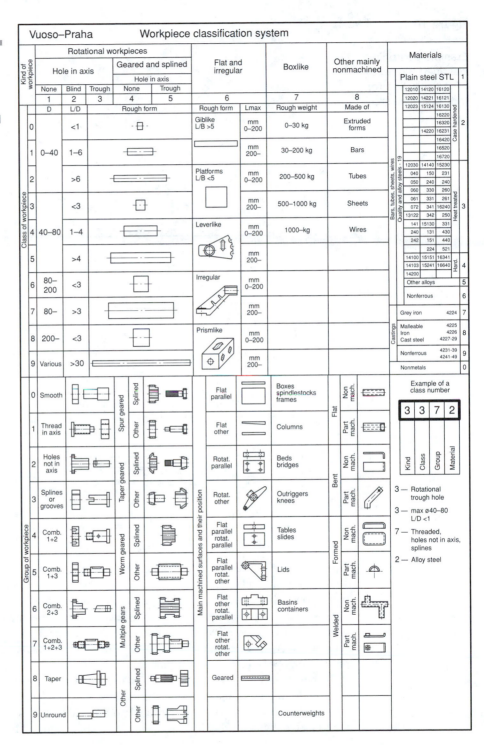

Figure 10.13

Example part being
classified (Courtesy
of Organization for
Industrial Research)

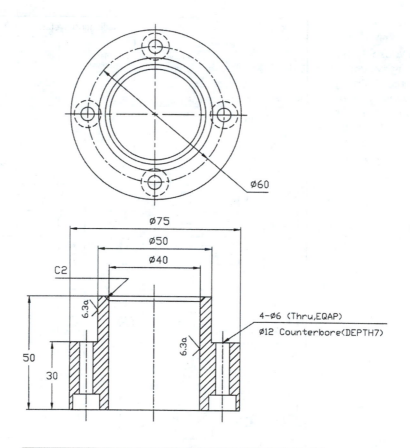

Drawing	Tolerance	Material	
Title	UNLESS OTHERWISE	Plain steel	
Bushing	SPECIFIED : DIMENSIONS		
Drawing No.	ARE IN MM TOLERANCES		
	~ 6 ± 0.1	25a	All over
SNU-SM-002	6 ~ 30 ± 0.2		except as noted
	30 ~ 120 ± 0.3		

Opitz system The Opitz coding system was developed by H. Opitz of the Aachen
Tech University in Germany. It is based on the hybrid structure, so the meanings of
the second, third, fourth, and fifth digits depend on the first digit, as shown in
Tables 10.2 and 10.3. The basic Opitz code consists of nine digits, but it can be expanded by four more. The first nine digits are called primary code, and the extra
four digits, A, B, C, and D, are secondary code. The secondary code identifies the
production operation type and sequence.

The primary code is structured so that each of the first five digits, also called
form code, represent the basic shape, component class, plane surface machining,
auxiliary holes, gear teeth, forming, and so on. Table 10.2 shows the meaning of
the first five digits for rotational parts in classes 0, 1, and 2. Meanwhile, Table 10.3

TABLE 10.2

Form code in the Opitz system for rotational parts in classes 0, 1, and 2 (Courtesy of Pergamon Press)

	Digit 1 Part Class	Digit 2 External shape, external shape elements	Digit 3 Internal shape, internal shape elements	Digit 4 Plane-surface machining	Digit 5 Auxiliary holes and gear teeth
0	$L/D \leq 0.5$ (Rotational parts)	Smooth, no shape elements	No hole, no breakthrough	No surface machining	No auxiliary hole (No gear teeth)
1	$0.5 < L/D < 3$ (Rotational parts)	No shape elements (Stepped to one end or smooth)	No shape elements (Smooth or stepped to one end)	Surface plane and/or curved in one direction, external	Axial, not on pitch circle diameter (No gear teeth)
2	$L/D \geq 3$ (Rotational parts)	Thread	Thread	External plane surface related by graduation around a circle	Axial, on pitch circle diameter (No gear teeth)
3		Functional groove	Functional groove	External groove and/or slot	Radial, not on pitch circle diameter (No gear teeth)
4		No shape elements (Stepped to both ends)	No shape elements (Stepped to both ends)	External spline (polygon)	Axial and/or radial and/or other direction (No gear teeth)
5		Thread	Thread	External plane surface and/or slot, external spline	Axial and/or radial on PCD and/or other direction (No gear teeth)
6	(Nonrotational parts)	Functional groove	Functional groove	Internal plane surface and/or slot	Spur gear teeth (With gear teeth)
7	(Nonrotational parts)	Functional cone	Functional cone	Internal spline (polygon)	Bevel gear teeth (With gear teeth)
8	(Nonrotational parts)	Operating thread	Operating thread	Internal and external polygon, groove and/or slot	Other gear teeth (With gear teeth)
9	(Nonrotational parts)	All others	All others	All others	All others (With gear teeth)

TABLE 10.3

Form code in the Opitz system for rotational parts in classes 3 and 4 (Courtesy of Pergamon Press)

	Digit 1		Digit 2		Digit 3		Digit 4		Digit 5
	Component Class		**Overall shape**		**Rotational machining**		**Plane surface machining**		**Auxiliary hole(s), gear teeth, forming**
0		0	Hexagonal bar	0	No rotational machining	0	No surface machining	0	No auxiliary hole(s), gear teeth and forming
		1	Square or other regular polygonal section	1	Machined	1	External plane surface and/or surface curved in one direction	1	Axial hole(s) not related by drilling pattern
		2	Symmetrical cross section producing no unbalance	2	With screw thread(s)	2	External plane surfaces related to one another by graduation around a circle	2	Holes axial and/or radial and/or in other directions, not related
3	$L/D \le 2$ with deviation	3	Cross sections other than 0 to 2	3	Smooth	3	External groove and/or slot	3	Axial holes
4	$L/D > 2$ with deviation	4	Segments after rotational machining	4	Stepped toward one or both ends (multiple increases)	4	External spline and/or polygon	4	Holes axial and/or radial and/or in other directions
		5	Segments before rotational machining	5	With screw threads	5	External plane surface and/or slot and/or groove, spline	5	Formed, no auxiliary holes
		6	Rotational components with curved axis	6	Machined	6	Internal plane surface and/or groove	6	Formed, with auxiliary holes
		7	Rotational components with two or more parallel axes	7	Screw thread(s)	7	Internal spline and/or polygon	7	Gear teeth, no auxiliary holes
		8	Rotational component with intersecting axes	8	External shape elements	8	External and internal spline and/or slot and/or groove	8	Gear teeth, with auxiliary hole(s)
		9	Others	9	Other shape elements	9	Other	9	Other

Digit 1 — Rotational components

Digit 2 — Around one axis, no segments (0–3); Around more than one axis (6–8)

Digit 3 — External shape (1–2); Internal shape (3–5); External and internal shape (6–7)

Digit 5 — No forming, no gear teeth (0–4); Related by a drilling pattern (3); Forming, no gear teeth (5–6)

covers the rotational parts in classes 3 and 4. The classes of parts are determined by the ratio of L/D, where L and D are the length and the diameter of the rotational part, respectively. The remaining four digits in the primary code, also called *supplemental code*, classify the size, type of material, raw material shape, and accuracy required, respectively, as illustrated in Table 10.4.

The part shown in Figure 10.13 can be recoded by using Tables 10.1, 10.2, and 10.3. The first five digits of the Opitz code of the part are 1 1 1 0 2 by the following reasoning.

$1 ; \dfrac{L}{D} = 0.67$

1 ; Stepped to one end, no shape elements

1 ; Smooth internal shape

0 ; No plane surface machining

2 ; Axial holes on pitch circle diameter

Many companies have adopted the Opitz code because it is concise and easy to use. It is probably the best-known coding system. In fact, several CAM-I CAPP systems use an Opitz-based coding system.

KK-3 system   The KK-3 coding system was developed in 1976 by the Japan Society for the Promotion of Machine Industry (JSPMI) as a general-purpose classification and coding system for parts produced by machining. It contains 21 digits, as illustrated in Table 10.5, and thus can represent more information than the Vuoso–Praha and Opitz systems. The KK-3 system allocates two digits, the first and the second, to the functional names of parts and thus can classify 100 functional names for rotational and nonrotational parts. A complete set of definitions and vocabulary for KK-3 system is presented in Chang, Wysk, and Wang [1998].

MICLASS   The Metal Institute Classification (MICLASS) System, was developed by The Netherlands Organization for Applied Scientific Research (TNO) and is currently maintained in the United States by the Organization for Industrial Research. One of the more popular commercial systems available in the United States, MICLASS uses a chain-structured code of 12 digits. These 12 digits are used to classify the design and manufacturing characteristics of a part: main shape, shape elements, position of the elements, main dimensions, ratio of the dimensions, an auxiliary dimension, tolerances, and type of material, as illustrated in Figure 10.14.

The first four digits are related to the form of a part. The first digit, main shape, indicates the form of the final product. It could be a rotational part, a boxlike part, a flat part, or some other nonrotational part. Shape elements specified by the second and third digits are part features such as holes, slots, and grooves. The positions of these elements are specified by the fourth digit. The fifth through the eighth digits provide dimensional information. The use of an auxiliary dimension varies with the main shape of the part, in general providing additional size information. The ninth and tenth digits contain tolerances, and the eleventh and twelfth digits indicate a machinability index of the material. Additional digits—as many as 18 digits—can

TABLE 10.4

Supplemental code in the Opitz system (Courtesy of Pergamon Press)

Digit 1			Digit 2		Digit 3		Digit 4	
	Diameter D or edge length A			Material		Initial form		Diameter D or edge length A
	mm	inches						
0	≤ 20	≤ 0.8	0	Cast iron	0	Round bar, black	0	No accuracy specified
1	$> 20 \leq 50$	$> 0.8 \leq 2.0$	1	Modular graphitic cast iron and malleable cast iron	1	Round bar, bright drawn	1	2
2	$> 50 \leq 100$	$> 2.0 \leq 4.0$	2	Mild steel ≤ 26.5 tonf/in^2 not hear treated	2	Bar: triangular, suare, hexagonal, others	2	3
3	$> 100 \leq 160$	$> 4.0 \leq 6.5$	3	Hard steel > 26.5 tonf/in^2 heat-treatable low-carbon and case-hardening steel, not heat treated	3	Tubing	3	4
4	$> 160 \leq 250$	$> 6.5 \leq 10.0$	4	Steels 2 and 3 heat treated	4	Angle, U–, T–, and similar sections	4	5
5	$> 250 \leq 400$	$> 10.0 \leq 16.0$	5	Alloy steel (not heat treated)	5	Sheet	5	2 and 3
6	$> 400 \leq 600$	$> 16.0 \leq 25.0$	6	Alloy steel heat treated	6	Plate and slabs	6	2 and 4
7	$> 600 \leq 1000$	$> 25.0 \leq 40.0$	7	Nonferrous metal	7	Cast or forged components	7	2 and 5
8	$> 1000 \leq 2000$	$> 40.0 \leq 80.0$	8	Light alloy	8	Welded assembly	8	3 and 4
9	> 2000	> 80.0	9	Other materials	9	premachined components	9	$2 + 3 + 4 + 5$

TABLE 10.5

Code structure of KK-3 system (Source: Courtesy of Japan Society for the Promotion of Machine Industry)

Digit	Items	(Rotational components)	
1	Parts name	General classification	
2		Detail classification	
3	Materials	General classification	
4		Detail classification	
5	Chief dimension	Length	
6		Diameter	
7	Primary shapes and ratio of major dimensions		
8	Shape details and kinds of processes	External surface	External surface and outer primary shape
9			Concentric screw threaded parts
10			Functional cut-off parts
11			Extraordinary shaped parts
12			Forming
13			Cylindrical surface
14		Internal surface	Internal primary shape
15			Internal curved surface
16			Internal flat surface and cylindrical surface
17		End surface	
18		Nonconcentric holes	Regularly located holes
19			Special holes
20		Noncutting process	
21	Accuracy		

Figure 10.14

Code structure of
MICLASS (Courtesy
of Organization for
Industrial Research)

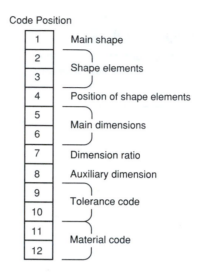

Code Position

1	Main shape
2	Shape elements
3	
4	Position of shape elements
5	Main dimensions
6	
7	Dimension ratio
8	Auxiliary dimension
9	Tolerance code
10	
11	Material code
12	

be appended to meet a company's specific needs, such as vendors, lot sizes, costs, and producibility tips.

To code manually several thousand parts using the MICLASS code of up to 30 digits would be a tedious and time-consuming job. As a result, the MICLASS is provided with several interactive computer programs to assist the user. Figure 10.15 illustrates an interactive coding session of a MICLASS interactive program for the part shown in Figure 10.13.

Figure 10.15

Coding session of a
MICLASS interactive
program (Source:
D. Bedworth,
*Computer
Integrated Design
and Manufacturing*,
McGraw-Hill, 1991)

```
VERSION-A-

3 MAIN DIMENSIONS (WHEN ROT. PART D.L AND O)?  2.9375  2  0
    DEVIATION OF ROTATION FORM?  NO
    CONCENTRIC SPIRAL GROOVES?  NO
TURNING ON OUTERCONTOUR (EXCEPT ENDFACES)?  YES
    SPECIAL GROOVES OR CONE(S) IN OUTERCONTOUR?  NO
    ALL MACH. DIAM. AND FACES VISIBLE FROM ONE END (EXC. ENDFACE + GROOVES)?   YES

INTERNAL TURNING?  YES
    INTERNAL SPECIAL GROOVES OR CONE(S)?  NO
    ALL INT. DIAM. + FACES VISIBLE FROM 1 END (EXC. GROOVES)?  YES

ALL DIAM. + FACES (EXC. ENDFACE) VISIBLE FROM ONE SIDE?  YES

ECC. HOLING AND/OR FACING AND/OR SLOTTING?  YES
    IN INNERFORM AND/OR FACES (INC. ENDFACES)?  YES
    IN OUTERFORM?  NO

ONLY KEYWAYING ETC.?  NO

MACHINED ONLY ONE SENSE?  YES
    ONLY HOLES ON A BOLTCIRCLE AT LEAST 3 HOLES?  YES

FORM-OR THREADING TOLERANCE?  NO

DIAM. ROUGHNESS LESS THAN 33 RU (MICRO-INCHES)?  YES
    SMALLEST POSITIONING TOL. FIELD?  .016
    SMALLEST LENGTH TOL. FIELD?  .0313

MATERIAL NAME?  CC15

CLASS.NR. = 1271  3231  3144
.......................

DRAWING NUMBER MAX 10 CHAR?  7
NOMENCLATURE MAX 15 CHAR?  BUSHING
CONTINUE [Y/N]?  N
PROGRAM STOP AT 4690
```

Several application programs based on MICLASS are currently available. As mentioned in the preceding section, the process planning systems such as MULTI-PLAN and MultiCAPP are based on MICLASS.

DCLASS system   The Design and Classification Information (DCLASS) System was developed by Del Allen at Brigham Young University for educational and research purposes. Although its primary use to date has been in the university environment, many companies are using it for prototype development. It is a tree-structured system that can generate codes for parts, materials, processes, machines, and tools.

For parts, the DCLASS code consists of eight digits that are partitioned into five code segments, as shown in Figure 10.16. The first segment, composed of three digits, denotes the basic shape. This segment is determined by the corresponding terminal node when the logic tree shown in Figure 10.17 is traced. Chart 1, chart 3, chart 4, chart 5, and chart 6 simply store the extension of the logic tree. The second code segment, or the fourth digit, is used to specify the complexity of the part. It is determined by the number of special features and requirements for heat treatment and special surface finishes. The third segment, or the fifth digit, indicates the overall size of the coded part. The fourth segment, or the sixth digit, de-

Figure 10.16

Structure of DCLASS code

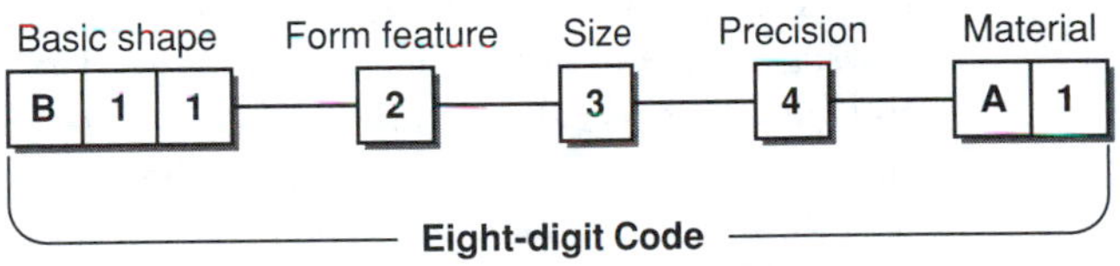

Figure 10.17

Logic tree for a DCLASS system

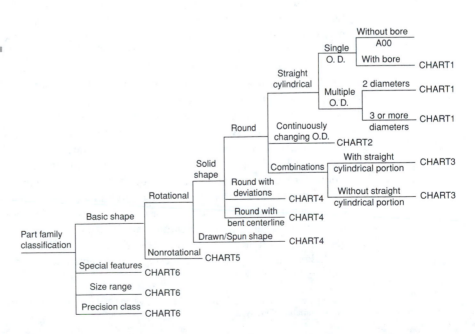

notes the required precision for the part. The final two digits are used to denote the material type and are determined by a logic tree similar to Figure 10.17. Details regarding the digits are presented in Bedworth, Henderson, and Wolfe [1991].

10.5 PRODUCT DATA MANAGEMENT (PDM) SYSTEMS

We described process planning in the preceding section as the key element for integration of CAD and CAM. However, the product development cycle, as described in Chapter 1, includes activities not only in design and manufacturing but also in analysis, quality assurance, packaging, shipping, and marketing. As the goal of using a computer is to integrate all these activities through a common database, it is necessary to have a mechanism for a smooth data flow among these activities.

In a dynamic environment, marketing concepts flow to product planning and on to the design group. The design group collaborates with manufacturing and support. Then the problems identified flow back to design and manufacturing. Purchasing and design data flow to suppliers and partners. Cost information flows to finance. All of this information is highly related, so changes in content or status must be available to all participants to avoid costly errors or duplicate effort. Engineering data become overwhelmingly large as product development proceeds, making simple browsing and searching of data extremely inefficient. Fortunately, software systems called *product data management* (PDM) systems are available to smooth data flow among all these activities. Utilizing a PDM[2] system improves data flow and communication and makes project management more efficient.

PDM systems were first developed to manage and control the volumes of electronic media that were created by CAD/CAM/CAE systems. Engineers were being buried under mountains of data and were spending too much time searching for information. PDM became especially important for managing assembly information when parts were designed on different CAD systems. Local data managers in a CAD system could effectively handle drawings and models for that particular system but often couldn't manage any data from other CAD systems or third-party products. PDM systems linked to many different application packages do a better job of managing data on an enterprisewide basis. PDM also provides ready access to associated non-CAD data, including part numbers, specifications, test results, and analysis studies.

Then PDM capabilities were expanded to support the design process by electronically routing documentation through the review cycle. This paperless workflow reduced the length of the product development cycle. Essential data could then be extracted to trace the histories of every product and its components, along with its relevant documentation, including all the data associated with different product versions and variations. Soon the areas covered by PDM systems were further extended beyond design and engineering departments into purchasing, manufacturing, and product support [Gain 1996].

---

[2] ComputerVision's Optegra, SDRC's Metaphase, and Unigraphic's IMAN are examples of commercially available PDM systems.

Recently, PDM systems have become even more popular because of the Internet, the World Wide Web, and intranets. In fact, virtually all PDM vendors are announcing Web-enabled software, and Web technology is acting as a catalyst in bringing PDM applications into corporations. The Web has become very popular because it is universal, inexpensive, and accessible. Furthermore, it is hardware-independent. Difficult end-user access has been the greatest barrier to widespread PDM acceptance. The Web solves this problem by providing a lightweight, generic, user interface at extremely low support costs [Mills 1996]. With Web capability, PDM now plays a key role in current efforts to provide multiple groups ready access to the same up-to-date information. PDM provides these users with a consistent set of data while at the same time managing the workflow process in which information is routed to the right person at the right time for appropriate action.

QUESTIONS AND PROBLEMS

1. Discuss the differences between a variant process planning system and a generative process planning system.

2. The following operations are required to manufacture a spur gear from a bar stock.

   a. Face one end

   b. Turn outer diameter

   c. Part off

   d. Face other end

   e. Machine the internal bore

   f. Perform the boring operation if necessary

   g. Machine the keyway

   h. Gear teeth cutting

   List the alternative process plans.

3. For the part shown, describe the sequence of manufacturing operations with a CNC mill/turn center. For each manufacturing operation, use the letters in the drawing to indicate which feature is to be machined.

4. Describe the sequence of manufacturing operations for the same part in Problem 3 if the mill/turn center is not available and manually operated tools must be used.

5. Discuss the similarities and differences of monocode, polycode, and mixed code and give examples.

6. Assume that a code consists of eight symbols and that the digits 0–9 are used for each symbol. Determine how many mutually exclusive characteristics can potentially be represented if the code is a monocode. What is the answer for a polycode?

7. For the part shown, develop a form code (first five digits), using the Opitz coding system.

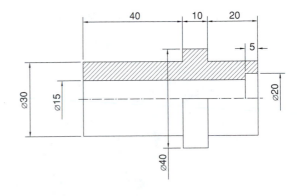

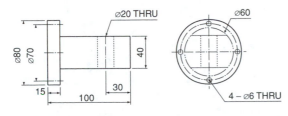

8. For the part shown, develop a form code (first five digits), using the Opitz system.

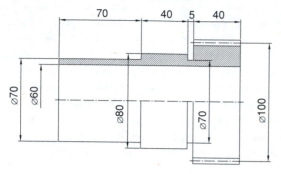

9. For the part shown, develop its code using the Vuoso–Praha system. Assume that the material is plain steel.

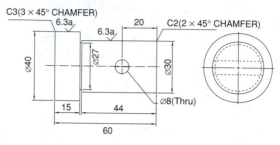

CHAPTER 11

Numerical Control

In Chapter 10 we showed that computerized process planning is essential for the integration of design and manufacturing without human intervention. If computerized process planning can be achieved, we should be able to computerize tasks such as the selection of machines to produce a part, the determination of the sequence of operations on those machines, the estimation of time for setup and production, the scheduling of production, and the identification of tooling and raw material requirements. However, computerized process planning still would not automate production itself unless the machines used can be directly driven by a computer without human intervention. This step can be realized by adding numerical control capability to conventional machine tools.

Numerical control (NC) refers to the use of coded numerical information in the automatic control of equipment positioning. To be more specific, the production steps for a part are stored in a part program, which we discuss in more detail later. This program is read by the control system of the machine tool, and the part is produced automatically without human operators. For machine tools, the object of numerical control might be to direct the motion of the cutting tool or the movement of the part against a rotating tool or to change cutting tools. Positioning and inserting electronic components in a printed circuit board line may also be directed by numerical control. In this chapter, we focus on numerical control for machine tool operation. In Chapter 12 we describe the process of accumulating material layer by layer to form the final shape and discuss briefly the various rapid prototyping processes that are also based on numerical control.

11.1 INTRODUCTION

In the late 1940s, an American named John Parsons devised a method for the manufacture of smooth shapes (e.g., templates for aircraft wing sections). The method relied on recording on punched cards the location of the centers of a large number of holes approximating the shape and feeding these cards into a machine tool to drive a cutter. The shape resulting from the many holes could be smoothed later to yield the desired profile. Until then, according to a U.S. government study in 1947, the entire U.S. metal-cutting industry could not produce the parts needed by the U.S. Army Air Corps (which later became the U.S. Air Force) alone. The Air Corps was so impressed by Parsons's idea that it contracted with the Parsons Corporation to develop the control system further. In 1951, the Parsons Corporation subcontracted the task to the Servomechanisms Laboratory of the Massachusetts Institute of Technology (MIT). In 1952, a modified 3-axis Cincinnati Hydrotel milling machine was demonstrated by MIT, and the term *numerical control* was coined. The definition of NC, as given by the Electronic Industries Association (EIA), is:

> NC is a system in which actions are controlled by direct insertion of numerical data at some point. The system must automatically interpret at least some portion of this data.

The numerical data required to produce a part is provided to a machine tool in the form of a program, called a *part program*. The program is a set of statements that can be interpreted by the machine control system and converted into signals that move the spindles and drives of the machine tool. It contains geometric information about the part and motion information to move the cutting tool with respect to the workpiece. Cutting speed, feed rate, and auxiliary functions such as coolant on/off and spindle direction are also specified in the part program to meet the required surface finishes and tolerances.

In a typical *NC machine tool*, which is a machine tool using NC technology, the part program prepared by part programmers is input for the machine controller. Part programmers usually have knowledge of manufacturing requirements such as tools and cutting fluids, as well as being capable in programming and geometric analysis. Today the burden on a part programmer tends to be much less than previously because the part program can be generated directly from the CAD database by NC software.

In this chapter, we describe three ways of generating a part program: manual part programming, computer-assisted part programming, and part programming directly from a CAD database. First, however, we need to explain some basic concepts of machine tools and their operation.

11.2   HARDWARE CONFIGURATION OF AN NC MACHINE TOOL

A typical NC machine tool contains the *machine-control unit* (MCU) and the machine tool itself, as illustrated in Figure 11.1. The MCU, considered the brain of the machine, reads the part program and controls the machine tool operation. Each of these functions is performed separately by two units of MCU: the *data processing*

Figure 11.1

Schematic of an NC machine tool

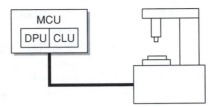

unit (DPU) and the *control loop unit* (CLU). The DPU reads the part program from tape or some other medium, decodes the part program statements, processes the decoded information, and passes information to the CLU about the position of each axis of the machine tool, its direction of motion, feed, and auxiliary function control signals. An *axis* of a machine tool is defined as a path along which relative motion between the cutting tool and workpiece occurs; machine tools may have more than one axis. The CLU receives data from the DPU and converts them to control signals. It operates the drive mechanisms of the machine, receives feedback signals about the actual position and velocity of each of the axes, and instructs the DPU to read new instructions from the part program when the operation has been completed. The DPU sequentially reads the data when each line has completed execution, as noted by the CLU.

A DPU consists of a data input device such as a paper-tape reader, data-reading circuit, and decoding circuits to determine the required axis movements. In first- and second-generation NC machine tools, the DPU had a tape drive that was able to mount and read punched tapes that contained the part programs. A typical punched tape is illustrated in Figure 11.2.

Figure 11.2

NC punched tape (Source: J. Childs, *Principles of Numerical Control*, Industrial Press, 1982)

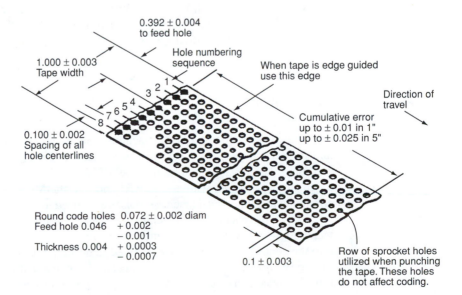

A CLU consists of an interpolator, position-control loops for all the axes of motion, velocity-control loops, deceleration and backlash take-up circuits, and auxiliary function control devices. The interpolator supplies intermediate machine-motion commands between specified data points for tool motion. The position-control loop of each motion axis controls the position of the axis. The velocity-control loops are used when feed control is required. Auxiliary function control devices handle tasks such as coolant on/off, gear changes, and spindle on/off.

11.3 TYPES OF NC SYSTEMS

There are two major types of NC controllers: *point-to-point* (PTP) and *contouring*. A PTP NC controller is used when the path of the tool relative to the workpiece is not important. This might occur when the tool is not in contact with the workpiece while traveling from one point to another. Typical examples would be drilling, punching, tapping, and component insertion in a circuit board. Motion control based on PTP is simple and thus an NC machine with such a controller is not expensive. It is able to perform simple milling operations if the machine is equipped with a feed-control mechanism to control the speed from one location to the next. This type of machine can be used to mill slots.

A contouring (continuous) control system is necessary when the motion of the tool relative to the part being machined is important. Examples of machine tools with contouring control systems are milling machines, turning machines, flame cutters, welders, and grinders. In these machine tools, two or more axes are controlled simultaneously, allowing each axis to have different velocities. For example, the tool can be driven to follow any curve in the xy plane by controlling the ratio of the two velocity components, V_x and V_y. With this capability, a circular motion can be obtained by an NC controller when the center location, the radius, and the end points of the arc are specified.

11.4 NC/CNC/DNC

Both the first generation of NC machine tools based on vacuum tube technology and the second generation based on solid-state circuits used punched tape as the medium to deliver a part program to the MCU. This implies that there was no facility to store a program within the MCU and that the MCU could process only one command at a time. Such machine tools are referred to as *NC machines*.

The third generation of machine tools uses the integrated circuit and memory technology widely used in computer hardware. That is, incorporation of a computer into the controller itself in about 1970 led to development of the modern controller. This type of machine tool is called a *computer numerical control* (CNC) machine tool. Because it has a memory unit, a part program needs to be loaded into the

MCU only once. Once the information has been stored in the computer, it can easily be recalled for further use without the controller having to reread the tape for each part of a batch, as in NC systems. In addition, the computer interface allows exchanging information between different units through integrated systems (i.e., a CNC can communicate with other units such as robots and machine tools).

Display monitors were later added to the machine to facilitate visual editing of part programs by the operator and provide diagnostic analysis. More sophisticated machines can also display the tool path for graphical verification. Figure 11.3 illustrates a typical CNC controller display. The modern CNC controller resembles a personal computer, and, in fact, it can be regarded as a special-purpose computer intended for controlling machine tools. Besides having a CPU and *read only memory* (ROM), it has *random access memory* (RAM), a hard disk, communication ports, a key pad, display monitor, and sometimes a graphics input device such as a mouse, track ball, or touch screen. PC-based NC controllers have recently become available. In these controllers, a general-purpose PC with a servo-control board is used.

An advantage of ROM is the availability of programmed cycles of machining commands, usually called *canned cycles*. They can be defined as standard subroutines and stored in the library of the machine tool. Any NC program can call and use any of these subroutines by using a special code. The word *canned* indicates that the subroutine is prewritten and stored, and the word *cycle* indicates that the subroutine is used over and over in a repetitive fashion [Zeid 1991]. The subroutines for drilling, tapping, boring, turning, and threading are typical examples of canned cycles.

Direct numerical control (DNC) refers to a manufacturing system that uses a central computer to control several machines simultaneously, as illustrated in Figure 11.4. In direct numerical control, the host computer retrieves the data on the part to be machined from either its own data storage unit or from an outside source. It then sends the instruction blocks of the part program to the NC machines to pro-

Figure 11.3

Display of a modern CNC controller. (ACRAMATIC 950 CNC controller)

Figure 11.4

Schematic of direct
numerical control

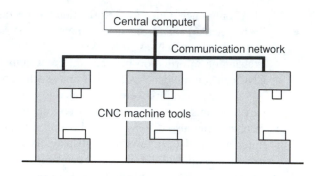

duce the desired part. This technique relies on the availability of the central computer to serve the machine tools.

Direct numerical control has been superseded by *distributed numerical control*, in which the central computer downloads complete programs to CNC machines. These machines may hold one or more programs in their local storage and thus are independent of the central computer. The acronym DNC has been used for both direct numerical control and distributed numerical control, but it has come to imply the latter as distributed numerical control systems have become popular. In some DNC systems, a satellite computer (usually a workstation or PC) local to each NC machine can be inserted to increase the speed of the entire system, to handle large computer files, and to expand the number of machine tools used. This configuration is illustrated in Figure 11.5. These satellite computers often provide facilities for reporting machine operation data to the central computer for the provision of shop management information.

Figure 11.5

Distributed numerical control (DNC)
configuration,
using satellite computers

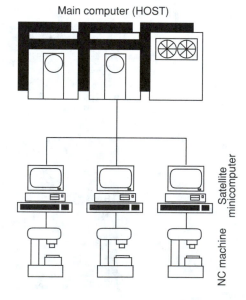

11.5 BASIC CONCEPTS FOR PART PROGRAMMING

As we have previously explained, a part program contains geometric information about the part and motion information to move the cutting tool with respect to the workpiece. This means that a part programmer must somehow describe this information in the part program. The first thing that needs to be defined in order to describe both geometry and motion is a coordinate system on which point locations can be specified. If the programmer's coordinate system is different from the default coordinate system of the machine tool, the machine tool using the part program will produce the wrong part. Therefore the NC programmer has to ensure that the orientation of the geometric coordinate system for the tool path is identical to that of the machine tool that will read and execute the corresponding NC program. If the tool path is generated from a CAD database, the coordinate system for modeling or drafting must be identical to that of the machine tool. We describe the default coordinate system of machine tools in the following section. Because the part program has its own syntax and semantics, we also explain the format of the instruction, or block,[1] as a syntax and the meaning of words in each block.

11.5.1 Coordinate Systems

The relative movement between a tool and a workpiece is achieved by the motion of the machine tool slides. The main three axes of motion are referred to as the x, y, and z axes, which form a right-hand coordinate system. The positive directions of the axes are usually defined by the manufacturer of the machine tool. However, by convention, the positive direction of the z axis moves the cutting tool away from the workpiece.

The z axis   On a machine where a workpiece is rotating, as in a lathe, the z axis is parallel to the spindle, and a motion along its positive direction moves the tool away from the workpiece, as illustrated in Figure 11.6. On a machine where a tool is rotating, as on a milling, drilling, or a boring machine, the z axis is parallel to the tool axis. As for workpiece-rotating machines, a motion in the positive z direction moves the tool away from the workpiece, as shown in Figures 11.7 and 11.8. On other machines, such as a press, a planing machine, or a shearing machine, the z axis is perpendicular to the tool set, and the positive motion increases the distance between the tool and the workpiece.

The x axis   On a workpiece-rotating machine, the x axis is in the direction of tool movement and a motion along its positive direction moves the tool away from the

---

[1] A block is a line of words in a part program. Each block is composed of several commands, as is explained in Section 11.5.2.

Figure 11.6

Coordinate system
for a lathe.
(Source:
*Manufacturing
Processes for
Engineering
Materials* by S.
Kalpakjian,
Copyright © 1991
by Addison-Wesley
Publishing
Company.
Reprinted by
permission.)

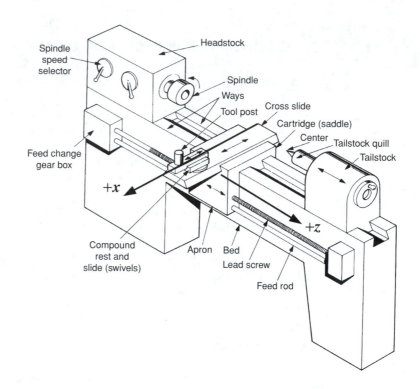

workpiece, as illustrated in Figure 11.6. On a vertical milling or drilling machine,
the positive *x* axis points to the right when the programmer is facing the machine,
as shown in Figure 11.7. On a horizontal milling machine, the *x* axis is parallel to
the table, as shown in Figure 11.8.

Figure 11.7

Coordinate system
for a vertical drill.
(Source: Y. Koren,
*Computer Control
of Manufacturing
Systems,* McGraw-
Hill, 1983)

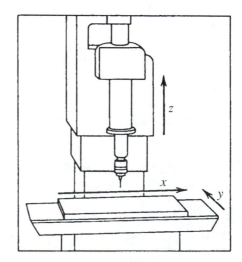

Figure 11.8

Coordinate system for a horizontal milling machine. (Source: Y. Koren, *Computer Control of Manufacturing Systems*, McGraw-Hill, 1983)

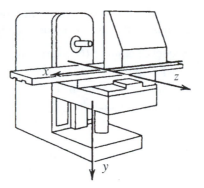

The y axis The y axis is determined from the x and z axes such that the xyz coordinate system forms a right-hand coordinate system.

In some machine tools, there may be secondary slide motions in addition to the primary slide motions in the x, y, and z directions. These axes are labeled u, v, and w. Rotary motions around axes parallel to x, y, and z may also exist, and these rotational axes are denoted a, b, and c, respectively. These notations are EIA standards.

By convention, machine tools are classified according to the number of axes of motion they can provide to control the tool position and orientation. For example, we use the terminology 2-axis, 3-axis, or 5-axis milling machines to indicate the possible axes of motion that the machine tool controller can control simultaneously. In other words, if a machine tool controller is able to control the tool along only two axes simultaneously, the machine tool is classified as a 2-axis machine. In this case, the tool is independently controlled along the third axis. This means that a cutting tool can be guided along a two-dimensional contour while an independent movement is allowed along the third axis. In a 3-axis machine, the tool can be moved along any curve by the simultaneous control of the three axes, but tool orientation does not change with tool motion. If the tool axis orientation needs to be varied with the tool motion, a machine tool with more than three axes has to be used. Up to 9-axis machine tools are commercially available.

11.5.2 Syntax of a Part Program

Information is stored in various formats when a part program is written for punched tape or equivalent media. The part program itself generally follows a fairly well-defined syntax, though there may be some variation due to differences between machines and controllers. Basically, the machine receives instructions as a sequence of blocks containing commands to set machine parameters, speed, and other operations. A block is equivalent to a line of words in a part program, and each block is composed of several commands that are equivalent to the words in each line. Each command has an identifying letter followed by an associated number. The identifying letters of the commands are as follows.

- Sequence number (N code). The sequence number is used to identify each block in a part program and provides a way to locate commands rapidly.

- Preparatory command (G code). The preparatory commands prepare the MCU for a given operation, typically involving a cutter motion. As the cutter motion is mainly determined by this G code, the program on the punched tape is often called the *G-code program*. The G codes presented in EIA Standard RS-273 are listed in Tables 11.1 and 11.2. However, many controllers do not conform to these codes (i.e., the same G code may have different meanings in different controllers).

- Dimension words (X, Y, Z, A, and B words). These words contain the location and axis orientation data of a cutter. An NC system with more than three axes uses additional words, such as an A or a B word. The locations or the coordinates are expressed by integers. The unit of these integers, called the *basic length unit* (BLU), is the position resolution of the axis of motion. Thus the number of movements along a specific axis is calculated by dividing the actual length by the BLU value. For example, to move 0.5 inch in a positive y direction in an NC system with BLU = 0.001 inch, the number of movements is 500, and it can be expressed as Y + 500 in the program. For a modern CNC, we can also write Y0.5 without using BLU. The controller pays attention to the existence of the floating point to determine whether the number is a BLU or the unit of real length.

- Feed commands (F code). The F code is used to specify the cutter feed rates to be applied. Units are inches per minute (ipm) by convention.

- Speed commands (S code). The S code is used to specify the spindle speed. Units are revolutions per minute (rpm).

- Tool selection commands (T code). The T code specifies which tool is to be used in a specific operation. The T code is required only for a machine equipped with a tool turret or automatic tool changer.

- Miscellaneous commands (M code). The M code is used to designate a particular mode of operation, typically to switch machine functions such as coolant supply and spindle on or off. The M code presented in EIA Standard RS-273 is shown in Table 11.3.

These commands are arranged to form a block in one of the following formats.

- Fixed sequential format. This format requires that each NC block be the same length and contain the same number of characters. Because the block length is invariant, it must be filled with code, even if some words or commands inserted are not required or the states of certain words do not change.

- Block address format. This format eliminates the need for specifying redundant information in subsequent NC blocks through the specification of a change code. The change code follows the block sequence number and indicates which values are to be changed relative to the preceding blocks.

TABLE 11.1

Preparatory commands—I

Code	Function	Explanation
g00	Point to point, positioning	Use with combination point-to-point/contouring systems for indicating positioning operation.
g01	Linear interpolation (normal dimensions)	A mode of contouring control used for generating a slope or straight cut, where the incremental dimensions are normal (i.e., input resolution is as specified).
g02	Circular interpolation arc CW (normal dimensions)	A mode of contouring control that produces an arc of a circle by the coordinated motion of two axes. The curvature of the path (clockwise = g02, or counterclockwise = g03) is determined when viewing the plane of motion in the negative direction of the perpendicular axis. The distances to the arc center (i, j, k) are "normal dimensions."
g03	Circular interpolation arc CCW (normal dimensions)	
g04	Dwell	A programmed (or established) time delay, during which there is no machine motion. Its duration is adjusted elsewhere, usually by the f word. In this case dimension words should be set at zero.
g05	Hold	Machine motion stopped until terminated by an operator or interlock action.
g06	Parabolic interpolation (normal dimensions)	A mode of contouring control that uses the information contained in successive blocks to produce a segment of a parabola.
g08	Acceleration	The feed rate (axes' velocity) increases smoothly (usually exponentially) to the programmed rate, which is noted later in the same block.
g09	Deceleration	The feed rate decreases (usually exponentially) to a fixed percent of the programmed feed rate in the deceleration block.
g10	Linear interpolation (long dimensions = LD)	Similar to g01, except that all dimensions are multiplied by 10. For example, a programmed dimension of 9874 will produce a travel of 98740 basic lenth-units. (Used only with incremental programming.)
g11	Linear interpolation (short dimensions = SD)	As g01, but dividing all dimensions by 10 (e.g., 987 units for the example above).

Source: Y. Koren, *Computer Control of Manufacturing Systems,* McGraw-Hill, 1983.

Preparatory commands—II

Code	Function	Explanation
g13 g14 g15 g16	Axis selection	Used to direct the control system to operate on a specific axis or axes, as in a system in which controls are not to operate simultaneously.
g17	*XY* Plane selection	Used to identify the plane for such functions as circular interpolation or cutter compensation.
g18	*ZX* Plane selection	
g19	*YZ* Plane selection	
g20	Circular interpolation arc CW (LD)	As g02 with long dimension distances.
g21	Circular interpolation arc CW (SD)	As g02 with short dimension distances.
g30	Circular interpolation arc CCW (LD)	As g03 with long dimension distances.
g31	Circular interpolation arc CCW (SD)	As g03 with short dimension distances.
g33	Thread cutting, constant lead	A mode selected for machines equipped for thread cutting
g34	Thread cutting, increasing lead	As g33, but when a constantly increasing lead is required.
g35	Thread cutting, decreasing lead	As g33, but to designate a constantly decreasing lead.
g40	Cutter compensation—cancel	Command that will discontinue any cutter compensation.
g41	Cutter compensation—left	Displacement, normal to cutter path, when the cutter is on the left side of the work surface, looking in the direction of cutter motion.
g42	Cutter compensation—right	Compensation when cutter on right side of work surface.
g43– g49	Cutter compensation if used; otherwise unassigned.	Compensation (g40–g49) is used to adjust for difference between actual and programmed cutter radii or diameters.
g60– g79	Reserved for positioning only	Reserved for point-to-point systems.
g80	Fixed cycle cancel	Command that will discontinue only fixed cycle.
g81– g89	Fixed cycles #1 through #9, respectively.	A preset series of operations that direct the machine to complete such action as drilling or boring.
g90	Absolute dimension programming	A control mode in which the data input is in the form of absolute dimensions. Used with combination absolute/incremental systems.
g91	Incremental dimension programming	A control mode in which the data input is in the form of incremental dimension.

Source: Y. Koren, *Computer Control of Manufacturing Systems,* McGraw-Hill, 1983.

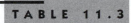

TABLE 11.3

Miscellaneous commands (M code)

Code	Function	Explanation
m00	Program stop	Stops spindle, coolant, and feed after completion of the block commands. It is necessary to push a button in order to continue the program.
m01	Optional (planned) stop	Similar to m00, but is performed only when the operator has previously pushed a button; otherwise the command is ignored.
m02	End of program	Indicates completion of the workpiece. It stops spindle, coolant, and feed after completion of all instructions in the block. May include rewinding of tape.
m03	Spindle CW	Starts spindle rotation clockwise.
m04	Spindle CCW	Starts spindle rotation counterclockwise.
m05	Spindle off	Stops spindle; coolant turned off.
m06	Tool change	Executes the change of a tool (tools) manually or automatically, not to include tool selection.
m07	Coolant no. 2 on	Turns a flood coolant on.
m08	Coolant no. 1 on	Turns a mist coolant on.
m09	Coolant off	Automatically shuts the coolant off.
m10	Clamp	Automatically clamps the machine slides, workpiece, fixture, spindle, etc. (as specified by the producer).
m11	Unclamp	Unclamping command.
m13	Spindle CW & coolant on	Combines spindle rotation and coolant on in the same command.
m14	Spindle CCW & coolant on	
m15	Motion +	Rapid traverse or feed-rate motion in either the plus or minus direction.
m16	Motion –	
m19	Oriented spindle stop	Causes the spindle to stop at a predetermined angular position.
m30	End of tape	Similar to m02 except that it must include rewinding of tape to the rewind-stop character, thus to be ready for the next workpiece.
m31	Interlock bypass	Temporarily circumvents normal interlock.
m32–m35	Constant cutting speed	The control maintains a constant cutting speed by adjusting the rotation speed of the workpiece inversely proportional to the distance of the tool from the center of rotation. Normally used with turning.
m40–m45	Gear changes if used; otherwise unassigned	

Unassigned: m12, m17, m18, m20–m29, m36–m39, m46–m99.
Source: Y. Koren, *Computer Control of Manufacturing Systems,* McGraw-Hill, 1983.

- Tab sequential format. This is a modified fixed sequential format, which allows the length of each block to vary. A TAB key is inserted before and after each word, and each block ends with an end of a block (EOB) character. Unchanged words are omitted from the block, but a TAB key must be inserted in their place. This results in consecutive TAB keys. A block can be terminated by the EOB whenever all the words needed to describe the instructions are given.

- Word address format. This is the most popular block format used currently for CNC controllers. Each word in a block is preceded by a letter that identifies the word type, and the letter is followed by a number that specifies its content. The standard sequence of words in a block is,

$$N\_, G\_, X\_, Y\_, Z\_, I\_, J\_, K\_, F\_, S\_, T\_, M\_$$

where

N is the identification number,
G are the preparatory commands given in Tables 11.1 and 11.2,
X are the coordinates along the *x* axis,
Y are the coordinates along the *y* axis,
Z are the coordinates along the *z* axis,
I, J, and K specify the arc center of circular tool motion, usually provided with algebraic signs,
F is the feed rate,
S is the spindle speed,
T is the tool number, and
M are the miscellaneous commands given in Table 11.3.

Thus the following is an example of a word address NC code:

N040 G00 X0 Y0 Z300 T01 M06

Omitted words are assumed to be zero or to be the same as the value previously defined. The F and S words were omitted from the example.

11.6 MANUAL PART PROGRAMMING

In manual part programming, the part programmer, without computer aids, records the NC blocks described in the preceding section on a document, called a *part program manuscript*, as shown in Figure 11.9. Then a Flexowriter is used to produce a typed manuscript and a punched tape simultaneously. Each line of the manuscript is equivalent to a block on the punched tape and is followed by an EOB character.

The difficulty with manual part programming is that the program has to provide the tool motions, not the configuration of the part. Therefore, in contour programming, the dimension words should describe the path of the center of the cutting tool rather than the actual part contour. The programmer may be able to

Figure 11.9

Part program manuscript

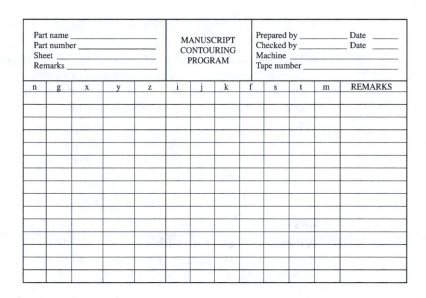

n	g	x	y	z	i	j	k	f	s	t	m	REMARKS

Part name _____
Part number _____
Sheet _____
Remarks _____

MANUSCRIPT
CONTOURING
PROGRAM

Prepared by _____ Date ____
Checked by _____ Date ____
Machine _____
Tape number _____

take advantage of the cutter radius compensation feature to avoid calculation of the cutter center locations. However, the programmer may still have to add some extra points to connect the calculated tool paths. Example 11.1 describes the tasks involved in manual (contour) part programming.

EXAMPLE 11.1

Write a part program manually to mill the edge of the plate shown in Figure 11.10. The dimensions are in millimeters, and the raw material, a rectangular plate, has a thickness of 15 mm; its bottom face has the z coordinate of 0. The characteristics of the NC controller to be used are as follows.

- Dimension words are a maximum of five digits; the resolution is BLU = 0.01 mm; both leading and trailing zeros are programmed. When a dimension word

Figure 11.10

Part to be programmed

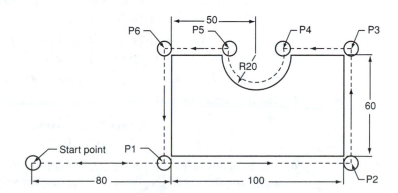

is not programmed, it means that no change is required in the corresponding coordinate.

- The feed word uses the CNC feed word (i.e., the feed rate is programmed directly in millimeters per minute, or in inches per minute times 10, using a three-digit number). In this example, we use a constant machining feed rate of 350 mm/min and a rapid traverse feed rate of 950 mm/min.

- The spindle speed word uses the three-digit magic-three code. In this example, we use a constant spindle speed of 1740 rpm and the corresponding magic-three code of 717. The derivation of magic-three code from the speed in rpm is explained in Koren [1983].

ANSWER

A cutter of 10 mm diameter is selected for this job. The cutter is initially located at the start point. We have to go through the following blocks to have the tool move along the dashed lines and arc in the direction of the arrows.

1. Set a mode such that the coordinates are provided in the form of incremental dimension instead of absolute dimension:

   N001 G91 EOB

2. Select metric unit:

   N002 G71 EOB

3. Load the tool of diameter 10 mm above the start point by 40 mm:

   N003 G00 X0.0 Y0.0 Z40.0 T01 M06 EOB

   Note that we did not use BLU in this example.

4. To move from the start point toward point P1, two blocks are programmed. At the first block, the system will accelerate to the traverse feed rate of 950 mm/min. At the second block, the tool approaches P1 at the machining feed rate of 350 mm/min. At the end of these two blocks, the center of the cutter will be located at point P1. We also have to program the z dimension to bring the cutter down to its appropriate place:

   N004 G01 X65.0 Y0.0 Z–40.0 F950 S717 M03 EOB
   N005 G01 X10.0 F350 M08 EOB

   The command M03 starts spindle rotation, and M08 starts the coolant.

5. The following blocks will move the tool from P1 to P3, through P2:

   N006 G01 X110.0 EOB
   N007 G01 Y70.0 EOB

6. The locations of P4 and P5 are calculated from Figure 11.11. Denoting their x and y coordinates (X_4, Y_4) and (X_5, Y_5), respectively, we obtain the following

relations:

$$X_4 - X_3 = -\left(55 - \sqrt{15^2 - 5^2}\right) = -40.86$$

$$Y_4 - Y_3 = 0$$

$$X_5 - X_4 = -2\sqrt{15^2 - 5^2} = -28.28$$

$$Y_5 - Y_4 = 0$$

$$I = \sqrt{15^2 - 5^2} = 14.14$$

$$J = 5$$

In the preceding equations, X_3 and Y_3, respectively, are the x and y coordinates of P3, and I and J are the quantities specifying the center of the circular interpolation, as indicated in Figure 11.11.

We can program the following blocks to move the tool from P3 to P4 along a straight line and from P4 to P5 clockwise along a circular arc:

N008 G01 X–40.86 EOB
N009 G02 X–28.28 Y0.0 I14.14 J5.0 EOB

In the second block, G02 activates the clockwise circular interpolation, X and Y words specify the end point of the circular arc (P5 in this case) with respect to the start point of the arc (P4 in this case), and I and J specify the center of the arc with respect to the start point.

7. Denoting the x and y coordinates of P5 and P6 (X_5, Y_5) and (X_6, Y_6), respectively, as before, we obtain the following relations:

$$X_6 - X_5 = -\left(55 - \sqrt{15^2 - 5^2}\right) = -40.86$$

$$Y_6 - Y_5 = 0$$

Figure 11.11

Calculation of P4 and P5

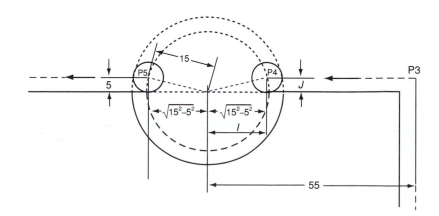

Therefore we can use the following NC blocks to move the tool from P5 to P6, from P6 to P1, and from P1 to the start point:

N010 G01 X–40.86 EOB
N011 G01 Y–70.0 EOB
N012 G01 X–75.0 Y0.0 Z40.0 F950 M30

The command M30 in the last block will turn off the spindle and coolant and rewind the tape to the beginning of the program.

As Example 11.1 demonstrates, manual part programming is tedious and involves arithmetic and trigonometric calculations that are subject to error. Some of the tedium of manual part programming can be relieved by use of the following features.

- Most CNC systems provide tool-radius compensation. This makes it possible to program directly from the part geometry instead of its offset geometry. In other words, the programmer provides the tool motion in terms of the geometry of the part, and the controller offsets the path by the tool radius and drives the tool along this offset path. This feature works with another feature, which adds offset curve segments or extends existing offset segments when the offsets of adjacent edges of the part geometry do not intersect. Figure 11.12(a) illustrates adding an extra arc; Figure 11.12(b), adding a line segment; and Figure 11.12(c), extending curve segments. These features work only for simple geometry.

- Common machining operations that involve repeated moves are stored as canned cycles so that they can be called in a part program whenever needed. In a sense, these cycles are equivalent to libraries of standard subroutines in conventional programming languages.

- In addition to the canned cycles, user-defined sequences of commands, called *macros*, can also be called repeatedly in a part program, possibly with variable parameters to provide variable numerical data to the program.

In spite of these features, for all but extremely simple parts it is obvious that the assistance of a computer would reduce a programmer's task significantly from the effort required in manual programming.

Figure 11.12

Completion of offset geometry

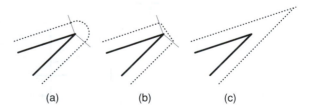

(a)   (b)   (c)

11.7   COMPUTER-ASSISTED PART PROGRAMMING

One alternative to manual part programming is to use high-level programming languages instead of the unfamiliar codes of manual part programming to define part geometry and tool motion. These languages are based on common English words and easy-to-use mathematical notations. In addition, these languages can be run on general-purpose computers. Using these languages, the part programmer has two tasks. First, the geometry of the part in terms of basic geometric elements via points, line, circles, and so on must be defined. Second, the cutting tool must be instructed to machine along these geometric elements. The offset of the part geometry is calculated automatically by the system; this capability is much more powerful and easier to use than that in manual part programming.

Programming an NC controller with one of the high-level programming languages involves use of the following procedure to obtain the punched tape or G code.

- The programmer identifies the part geometry, general cutter motions, feeds, speeds, and cutter parameters.

- The programmer codes the part geometry, cutter motions, and general machine instructions, using a programming language. This code is called a *source*. One of the most popular programming languages for this purpose is Automatically Programmed Tools (APT), which we describe in the next section.

- The source is compiled to produce the machine-independent list of cutter movements and auxiliary machine control information, known as the *cutter location data file* (CL data file). The CL data file is a binary file, but a readable version is also usually available. The CL data file contains details of cutter moves, either as a series of absolute linear GOTO moves or relative GODLTA moves[2] interspersed with post-processor statements for spindle, coolant, feedrate control, and so on. The file format of CL data is defined by the International Organization for Standardization (ISO).

- The CL data are processed by a post-processor to generate machine control data for the particular machine. Here the machine control data are the same as the NC blocks stored in the punched tape in manual part programming. Because of the variations not only in the format of machine control data file, but also even in the meaning of particular G and M codes, post-processors traditionally have been customized programs dedicated to particular machine tool–controller combinations. There are also differences in CL data formats among part programming languages.

---

[2] GOTO and GODLTA are the APT commands to move the cutting tool along a straight line. These commands are explained in Section 11.7.1.

Even though computer-assisted part programming as described is still in use, the encoding of part geometry and tool motion into a language has now been largely replaced by direct generation of cutter location data from the CAD model. We discuss this new approach in Section 11.8.

11.7.1 APT Language

Even though a great number of programming languages have been developed for NC programming, the Automatically Programmed Tool (APT) language is the most comprehensive and widely used. The first prototype of the APT system was developed at MIT in 1956. The program was developed further by the cooperative efforts of 21 companies, sponsored by the Aerospace Industries Association (AIA) with assistance from MIT. As a result of these efforts, APT II was developed in 1958, and a more effective system, APT III, was made available in 1961. The Illinois Institute of Technology Research Institute (IITRI) was selected to direct the future expansion of the program, and the capabilities of APT are being continually expanded. The present APT language can control machines with as many as five motion axes. It has also spawned many derivatives.

An APT program is composed of statements that belong to one of five types:

- identification statements, which specify part name and the specific post-processor;
- geometry statements, which define the part geometry relevant to the machining operations;
- motion statements, which define the motion of the cutting tool with respect to the part geometry;
- post-processor statements, which specify machining parameters such as feed, speed, and coolant on/off that are passed unchanged into the CL data file and dealt with by the post-processor; and
- auxiliary statements, which specify auxiliary machine-tool functions to specify the tool, tolerance, and the like.

In the following sections, we explain geometry statements and motion statements and give examples of each type. We also introduce some other important types of statements and illustrate the macro programming capability of APT.

Geometry statements   The general form of a geometry statement is as follows:

$$symbol = geometry\_word \mid descriptive\ data$$

The *symbol* is a name for the geometric element and has the same role as a variable name in other high-level languages. Up to six characters commencing with a letter can be used for the symbol. The *geometry_word* specifies the type of geometry, such as points, lines, planes, circles, cones, spheres, ruled surfaces, and tabulated cylinders. The *descriptive data* are the numeric data required to define the entity, refer to the names of the other entities used in its definition, or qualifying "minor words," such as INTOF in the following example. The minor words are used to indicate the type of geometry definition to use. We introduce the ways to define the typical *geometry_words* in the following code. We cover only point, line, circle, and plane because we use them in examples later. A complete description of the geometry statements is presented in Bedworth, Henderson, and Wolfe [1991].

There are many ways to define a point as illustrated in Figure 11.13. In the definitions of the points shown, the semicolons and the comments following them are included simply for explanation and do not appear in APT program statements.

P1 = POINT/X, Y, Z
P2 = POINT/L1, L2   ; intersection of two lines already defined
P3 = POINT/CENTER, C1   ; center of a circle
P4 = POINT/YLARGE, INTOF, L1, C1
          ; intersection of a line and a circle, one with a larger y coordinate
P5 = POINT/XLARGE, INTOF, L1, C1
          ; intersection of a line and a circle, one with a larger x coordinate
P6 = POINT/YLARGE, INTOF, C1, C2
          ; intersection of two circles, one with a larger y coordinate
P7 = POINT/XLARGE, INTOF, C1, C2
          ; intersection of two circles, one with a larger x coordinate

The lines illustrated in Figure 11.14 are defined as follows.

L1 = LINE/$X1$, $Y1$, $Z1$, $X2$, $Y2$, $Z2$; line between $(X1, Y1, Z1)$ and $(X2, Y2, Z2)$

L2 = LINE/P1, P2   ; line between predefined P1 and P2
L3 = LINE/P1, PARLEL, L0   ; line passing through P1 and parallel with predefined line L0

L4 = LINE/P1, PERPTO, L0   ; line passing through P1 and perpendicular to L0

L5 = LINE/P1, LEFT, TANTO, C1 ; line passing through P1 and tangent to the left-hand side of C1 when viewed from P1

Figure 11.13

Points defined in various ways

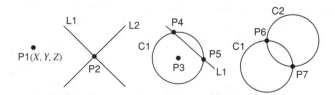

Figure 11.14

Lines defined in
various ways

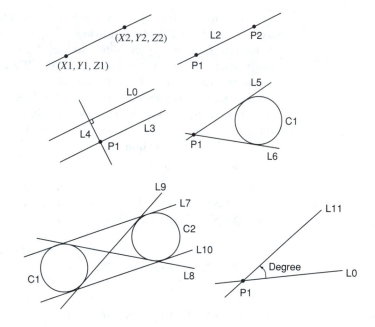

L6 = LINE/P1, RIGHT, TANTO, C1   ; line passing through P1 and tangent to
                                   the right-hand side of C1 when
                                   viewed from P1

L7 = LINE/LEFT, TANTO, C1, LEFT, TANTO, C2
                                   ; line tangent to the left-hand side of
                                   C1 and the left-hand side of C2 when
                                   viewed from C1

L8 = LINE/LEFT, TANTO, C1, RIGHT, TANTO, C2
                                   ; line tangent to the left-hand side of
                                   C1 and the right-hand side of C2
                                   when viewed from C1

L9 = LINE/RIGHT, TANTO, C1, LEFT, TANTO, C2
                                   ; line tangent to the right-hand side of
                                   C1 and the left-hand side of C2 when
                                   viewed from C1

L10 = LINE/RIGHT, TANTO, C1, RIGHT, TANTO, C2
                                   ; line tangent to the right-hand side of
                                   C1 and the right-hand side of C2
                                   when viewed from C1

L11 = LINE/P1, ATANGL, Degree, L0
                                   ; line passing through P1 at an angle of
                                   Degree with L0, counterclockwise

The circles illustrated in Figure 11.15 are defined as follows.

Figure 11.15

Circles defined in various ways

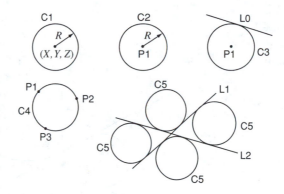

C1 = CIRCLE/X, Y, Z, R ; circle centered at (X, Y, Z) with a radius R
C2 = CIRCLE/CENTER, P1, RADIUS, R
                      ; circle centered at P1 with a radius R
C3 = CIRCLE/CENTER, P1, TANTO, L0
                      ; circle tangent to L0 with a center at P1
C4 = CIRCLE/P1, P2, P3   ; circle passing through three points
C5 = CIRCLE/{XSMALL}, L1, {XSMALL}, L2, RADIUS, R
            XLARGE   XLARGE
            YSMALL   YSMALL
            YLARGE   YLARGE

Circle C5 will be one of the four shown, depending on the modifiers used: X-SMALL, XLARGE, YSMALL, and YLARGE. The modifier indicates the relationship of the circle's center point to the tangent point of the circle and the line following the modifier. For example, the circles illustrated in Figure 11.16 can be defined as follows.

C6 = CIRCLE/XSMALL, L1, XLARGE, L2, RADIUS, 4.0 or
C6 = CIRCLE/YLARGE, L1, YLARGE, L2, RADIUS, 4.0[3]
C7 = CIRCLE/YSMALL, L1, YLARGE, L2, RADIUS, 3.0
C8 = CIRCLE/YLARGE, L1, YSMALL, L2, RADIUS, 2.0

Similar to the *geometry_words* just described, a plane can be defined in many different ways. Two of them are as follows.

PL1 = PLANE/P1, P2, P3 ; three points that are not on the same straight line define a plane
PL2 = PLANE/PARLEL, PL0, {XLARGE}, D ; a plane parallel to plane PL0
                                XSMALL   with a distance of D. A mod-
                                YLARGE   ifier is used to specify one of
                                YSMALL   the two parallel planes
                                ZLARGE
                                ZSMALL

---

[3] There are two more ways to define C6. Similarly, there are four ways of defining circles C7 and C8.

Figure 11.16

**Effect of modifiers
on circle definition**

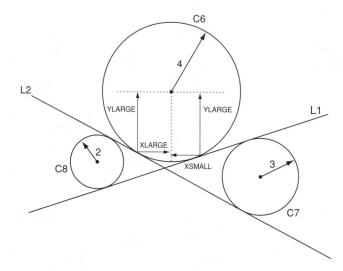

Motion statements   Once the part geometry has been defined, tool movement is specified with motion statements. Each motion statement will move the tool to a new location or along a surface, as specified by the statement. Two groups of motion statements are available: one for point-to-point operation and the other for contouring operation.

With regard to point-to-point operation, three motion statements exist for positioning the tool at a desired point:

FROM/*point_location*
GOTO/*point_location*
GODLTA/Δx, Δy, Δz

The *point_location* may be given in terms of the x, y, and z coordinates, or it may be a symbolic of the point that has been previously defined in a geometry statement. The FROM statement is the first motion statement and specifies the initial location from which a motion starts. The GOTO statement will move the tool rapidly along a straight line from the tool's present location to the point specified by this statement. The GODLTA statement will move the tool the incremental distance specified by Δx, Δy, Δz from its present location. This statement is very useful for moving a tool along one of the coordinate axes, a motion often required in a drilling operation, as demonstrated in Example 11.2.

EXAMPLE 11.2

Write an APT program to drill two 0.2-inch diameter holes in a plate, as shown in Figure 11.17. The home point P0 has a z value of 0.1 to allow for clearance of the tool when it approaches the part. Similarly, the center points of the holes will have the z value of 0.1 for the same reason. The top surface of the part corresponds to $z = 0.0$.

Figure 11.17

**Example of a
drilling operation**

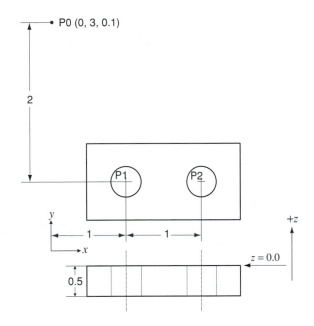

ANSWER

P0 = POINT/0.0, 3.0, 0.1
P1 = POINT/1.0, 1.0, 0.1
P2 = POINT/2.0, 1.0, 0.1
FROM/P0
GOTO/P1
GODLTA/0, 0, –0.7
GODLTA/0, 0, 0.7
GOTO/P2
GODLTA/0, 0, –0.7
GODLTA/0, 0, 0.7
GOTO/P0

In the example, note that the depth of motion was set to 0.7 to allow 0.1 inch above the top surface at the start of drilling and 0.1 inch below the bottom surface, to clear the bottom of the part. If many holes have to be drilled (instead of the two in the example), the same APT program statements would have to be repeated many times. However, the use of looping or a subroutine can greatly reduce the number of repeated statements, which we demonstrate later. A detailed description of an APT program subroutine is given in Bedworth, Henderson, and Wolfe [1991].

With regard to contouring operation, three surfaces must be defined to control the motion—part surface, drive surface, and check surface. The part surface is a surface on which the end of the tool is riding. The drive surface is a surface along which the tool slides. The check surface is a surface bounding the tool motion so that the tool motion continues until the check surface is encountered. These surfaces are illustrated in Figure 11.18.

Figure 11.18

The surfaces controlling the cutter motion

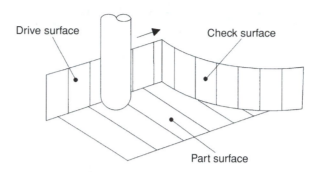

Drive surface   Check surface

Part surface

Before the tool can move along the control surfaces, the cutting tool must be brought to them. This is accomplished with a GO command:

GO/{ TO }, Drive surface, { TO }, Part surface, { TO }, Check surface

PAST	PAST	PAST
ON	ON	ON
		TANTO

We assumed that all three control surfaces were defined in the previous syntax of GO command, although that is not always the case. The modifiers TO, PAST, ON, and TANTO indicate the desired location of the cutter with respect to the associated control surface. For example, a tool moving to the check surface, denoted CS, along the drive surface, denoted DS, has three possible ending locations, as shown in Figure 11.19.

The TANTO modifier can be used only in conjunction with a check surface. Figure 11.20 shows how TANTO is used to locate a cutter with respect to the check surface. The tool positions A and B will be reached with the following commands.

Position A: GO/TO, L1, TO, PS, TANTO, C1
Position B: GO/PAST, L1, TO, PS, TANTO, C1

So far, we have considered how to locate the tool at its initial position with respect to the three control surfaces. Now let's consider moving the tool relative to the previous motion direction. The commands for this purpose are:

GOLFT/   ; move left from the previous direction and along the drive surface
GORGT/   ; move right from the previous direction and along the drive surface
GOUP/   ; move up along the drive surface (i.e., away from the part surface)

Figure 11.19

Ending locations for different modifiers

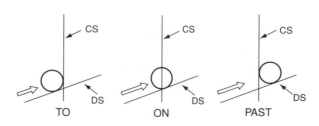

CS   CS   CS

DS   DS   DS

TO   ON   PAST

Figure 11.20

Example of the TANTO modifier

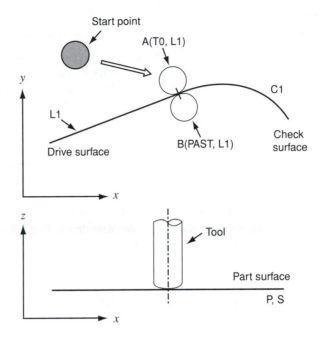

GODOWN/ ; move down along the drive surface (i.e., closer to the part surface)

GOFWD/ ; move forward from a tangent position along the tangent direction

GOBACK/ ; move backward from a tangent position along the tangent direction

The direction of the tool motion corresponding to each of these commands is illustrated in Figure 11.21.

Example 11.3 shows how to compose specific contouring motion statements.

Figure 11.21

Directions of contouring motion commands

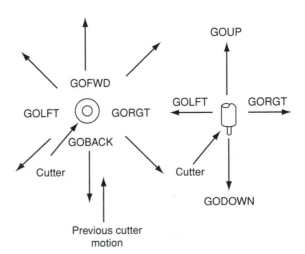

EXAMPLE 11.3

Using APT language, program the tool motion to mill the edge of the plate shown in Figure 11.22. The desired tool motion is indicated by the directed dotted lines and arc. Note that we are using the same part as in Example 11.1; doing so allows us to compare APT programming with manual part programming.

ANSWER

We assume that the lines, the circle, and the start point, SP, indicated in Figure 11.22 have been defined by the proper geometry statements. In addition, a hypothetical plane, PS, for the part surface is defined to lie just below the bottom of the plate. This part surface will control the height of the tool so that it can machine the edges of the plate to its complete depth. The following APT motion commands will give the tool motion specified in Figure 11.22. Note the different use of the GO/TO and GOTO/ statements.

```
FROM/SP
GO/TO, L1, TO, PS, ON, L4
GORGT/L1, PAST, L2
GOLFT/L2, PAST, L3
GOLFT/L3, PAST, C1
GOLFT/C1, PAST, L3
GOLFT/L3, PAST, L4
GOLFT/L4, PAST, L1
GOTO/SP
```

Comparing this example and Example 11.1 shows that circular interpolation can be specified in a much simpler way in APT programming than in manual part programming.

Example 11.4 shows how the TANTO modifier is used.

Figure 11.22

Part for contouring example

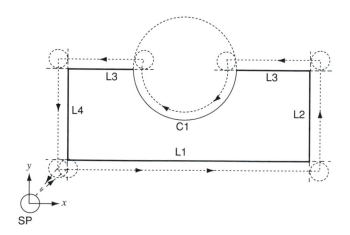

EXAMPLE 11.4

Write in APT language the motion statements required to mill the edges of the part shown in Figure 11.23. Assume that the part geometry has been already defined by the proper geometry statements. As in Example 11.3, the part surface, PS, is defined so that it is just below the bottom surface of the part.

ANSWER

```
FROM/SP
GO/TO, L1, TO, PS, TO, L6
GORGT/L1, TO, L2
GORGT/L2, TANTO, C1
GOFWD/C1, TANTO, L3
GOFWD/L3, PAST, L4
GOLFT/L4, PAST, L5
GOLFT/L5, PAST, L6
GOLFT/L6, PAST, L1
GOTO/SP
```

Additional APT statements   Geometry statements and motion statements represent about two-thirds of an average APT program. The statements composing the remainder of the program can be classified as post-processor statements, tolerance and cutter statements, and initial and termination statements.

The following are post-processor statements. They are passed into the CL data file as they are; they are processed later by the post-processor.

- **MACHIN/**

This statement is used to specify the machine tool and call the post-processor for that tool. For example,

   MACHIN/ DRILL, 2

might specify the second NC drill in the shop.

Figure 11.23

Part being programmed

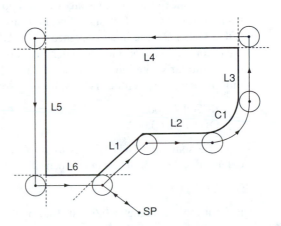

- **COOLNT/**

This statement allows the coolant fluid to be turned on and off. The modifier options are ON, OFF, FLOOD, MIST, and TAPKUL, as in

    COOLNT/MIST
    COOLNT/FLOOD
    COOLNT/OFF

- **FEDRAT/**

This statement specifies the feed rate for moving the tool—for example,

    FEDRAT/4.5

in inches per minute.

- **SPINDL/**

This statement turns on the spindle or specifies the spindle rotation speed in revolutions per minute, as in

    SPINDL/ON
    SPINDL/1250, CCLW

- **TOOLNO/**

This statement specifies the tool number to be used—for example,

    TOOLNO/3572, 6

specifies tool 3572 of 6 unit length.

- **TURRET/**

This statement can be used to call a specific tool from an automatic tool changer.

- **END**

This statement forces a machine tool to stop so that the operator can manually perform an inspection or perhaps change a tool.

Tolerance specifications are used in approximating the curved contouring motion by sequences of straight-line motions. Two tolerances, the outer tolerance (OUTTOL/) and the inner tolerance (INTOL/), are used. As shown in Figure 11.24, the outer tolerance defines the outer envelope in which the straight-line motions can exist. Similarly, the inner tolerance defines the inner envelope that the straight-line motions cannot penetrate. Their values are specified, for example, as

    INTOL/ 0.005
    OUTTOL/ 0.003

The statement CUTTER/ is used to specify the cutter diameter, which in turn determines the tool diameter compensation. For example, the statement

    CUTTER/0.6

is for a tool of diameter 0.6 unit. But, by specifying a tool diameter different from

Figure 11.24

Definitions of (a) OUTTOL and (b) INTOL

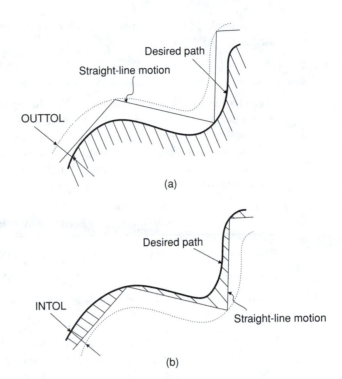

that of the actual tool, a part surface can be machined with a certain allowance. This feature is useful for rough cutting.

Other capabilities of APT   Similar to the conventional high-level programming languages, APT also provides facilities for arithmetic manipulation and looping and a subprogram feature known as the *macro facility*. This feature allows programming of repetitive operations as a subprogram and to call it repeatedly within a program. The parameters used in the subprogram can have variable names so that any values for them can be assigned when the macro is called. This is the same as the use of variable arguments in a FORTRAN subroutine. For example, we can rewrite the program in Example 11.2 as

```
P0 = POINT/0.0, 3.0, 0.1
FROM/P0
CALL/DRILL, X = 1.0, Y = 1.0, Z = 0.1, DEPTH = 0.7
CALL/DRILL, X = 2.0, Y = 1.0, Z = 0.1, DEPTH = 0.7
GOTO/P0
```

if we define the macro DRILL as

```
DRILL = MACRO/X, Y, Z, DEPTH
        GOTO/X, Y, Z
        GODLTA/0, 0, –DEPTH
        GODLTA/0, 0, DEPTH
        TARMAC
```

Example 11.5 shows how the additional statements and MACRO described are used in the APT program.

EXAMPLE 11.5

Consider the part shown in Figure 11.23. The periphery of this part is to be milled in two passes. The first pass will be a rough cut, which will leave an allowance of 0.01 inch from the final geometry specification, and the second pass will be a finish cut following the final periphery specifications. Assume that the machining conditions for these passes are as follows, with an outer tolerance of 0.002 inch for the curved section.

	Spindle speed	Feed	Coolant	Turret location of tool
Rough cut	600	3.0	ON	4
Finish cut	900	2.0	ON	6

ANSWER

Figure 11.23 is redrawn as Figure 11.25 to denote the points necessary to define the lines and the circle. It also shows that the top surface of the part corresponds to $z = 0.5$; $z = 0$ defines a plane just below the bottom surface. We will use the MACRO capability to drive the tool twice along the same path with different offsets. As shown in the following part program, the initial statement begins with the word PARTNO to identify the part or the part program. Any information may follow on the same line after PARTNO. The last statement in any APT program is FINI, which specifies the end of the program. Again, the semicolons and comments are not included in the part program.

Figure 11.25

Part, showing points necessary to define its shape

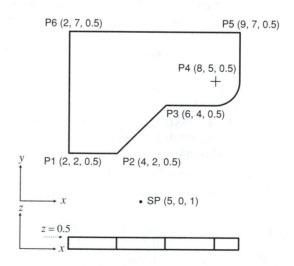

```
PARTNO        PART11
MACHIN/MILL, 3                                    ; machine selection
CLPRINT                                           ; prints out CL data file
OUTTOL/0.002
SP = POINT/5,0,1
P1 = POINT/2,2,0.5
P2 = POINT/4,2,0.5
P3 = POINT/6,4,0.5
P4 = POINT/8,5,0.5
P5 = POINT/9,7,0.5
P6 = POINT/2,7,0.5
PL1 = PLANE/P1, P2, P3
PS = PLANE/PARALEL, PL1, ZSMALL, 0.5   ; define part surface to be z = 0
C1 = CIRCLE/CENTER, P4, RADIUS, 1.0
L1 = LINE/P2, P3
L2 = LINE/P3, RIGHT, TANTO, C1
L3 = LINE/P5, LEFT, TANTO, C1
L4 = LINE/P5, P6
L5 = LINE/P6, P1
L6 = LINE/P1, P2
MILL = MACRO/CUT, SPIN, FEED, CLNT
   CUTTER/CUT
   FEDRAT/FEED
   SPINDL/SPIN
   COOLNT/CLNT
   FROM/SP
   GO/TO, L1, TO, PS, ON, L6
   GORGT/L1, TO, L2
   GORGT/L2, TANTO, C1
   GOFWD/C1, TANTO, L3
   GOFWD/L3, PAST, L4
   GOLFT/L4, PAST, L5
   GOLFT/L5, PAST, L6
   GOLFT/L6, PAST, L1
   GOTO/SP
   TERMAC
TURRET/4
CALL/MILL, CUT=0.52, SPIN=600, FEED=3.0, CLNT=ON
TURRET/6
CALL/MILL, CUT=0.5, SPIN=900, FEED=2.0, CLNT=ON
SPINDL/0
COOLNT/OFF
END
FINI
```

In the example, the cutter diameter of 0.52 inch is specified for the rough cutting, but a cutting tool of 0.5 inch is actually used. Machining with a tool having a 0.5-inch diameter will leave a layer 0.01 inch thick after rough cutting for removal during the finish cut, as illustrated in Figure 11.26.

11.7.2   Other Part Programming Languages

In addition to the APT language, many other languages operate more or less in the same manner. In this section we briefly describe several languages in widespread use.

ADAPT (ADaptation of APT) was the first attempt to adapt APT programming system for smaller computers. It was developed by IBM under contract with the U.S. Air Force. ADAPT has a flexible modular structure, making it suitable for small- to medium-sized computers by allowing removal and addition of subroutines. ADAPT is useful for positioning and simple contouring of parts in two or three dimensions, but it is not capable of programming a multiaxis contouring machine.

AUTOSPOT (AUTOmatic System for POsitioning Tools) was developed by IBM and first introduced in 1962. It is a popular program for positioning tasks, such as drilling. It was subsequently combined with ADAPT for continuous path applications.

EXAPT (EXtended subset of APT) was developed jointly in Germany in about 1964 by several universities to adapt APT for European use. It is compatible with APT and thus can use the same processor as APT. It has three versions: EXAPT I, for point-to-point machines; EXAPT II, for turning operations; and EXAPT III, for three-dimensional contouring operation.

COMPACT was developed by Manufacturing Data Systems, Inc. (MDSI), of Ann Arbor, Michigan, and its latest version, COMPACT II, and APT are the two most popular programming languages. The language used in COMPACT II statements is English-like and similar to machine shop terminology. The language statements are converted to machine control data directly, and thus post-processing is completely eliminated.

SPLIT (Sundstrand Processing Language Internally Translated) was developed by the Sundstrand Corporation, intended for its own machine tools. It can

Figure 11.26

Setting of cutter diameter for rough cutting

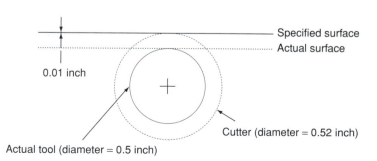

handle up to a 5-axis machine with its positioning and contouring capability. The post-processor is built into the program, so each machine tool should have its own version of SPLIT.

MAPT (Micro-APT) is a subset of APT, to be run on the microcomputers. Other than size, it has the same features as APT.

11.8 PART PROGRAMMING FROM CAD DATABASE

As we have shown in the previous examples of part programming with the APT language, a significant portion of the program consists of statements that define part geometry. If the part has already been designed in a CAD system, it would be natural for the programmer to try to use the geometry data of the part already stored in the CAD database. Even if the part has not been designed by a CAD system, defining the part geometry with a CAD system would be more convenient than using a language such as APT, especially when the part is bounded by complicated curves and surfaces. These are the ideas that underlay the development of integrated CAD/CAM systems. In an integrated CAD/CAM system, the geometry statements are derived from the CAD database by the NC program, and sometimes the tool motions are also derived automatically. These tasks had to be performed by the part programmers in the computer assisted programming described in the preceding section.

The approach to part programming involving the use of an integrated CAD/CAM system is basically as follows.

1. The aspects of part geometry that are important for machining purposes are identified and perhaps isolated on a separate layer. The geometry may be edited, or additional geometry may be added to define boundaries for the tool motion. The geometry information necessary for part programming varies, depending on the NC machine to be driven. For example, lathe operations (e.g., turning, facing, grooving, and thread-cutting) require two-dimensional profile geometry, as illustrated in Figure 11.27. This profile geometry may be obtained directly from a CAD database if the part has been designed by a computer-aided drafting system built into the integrated CAD/CAM system. The user may be required to draw the profile on a separate layer at the beginning. Otherwise, the NC program within the integrated system will ask the user to isolate interactively the profile geometry from other entities, such as drawing annotations. If the part has been designed by the solid modeling capability of the integrated system, the user may have to create the two-dimensional profile geometry by projecting the solid model or by searching the profile feature used to create the part. In either case, some interactive work may be required to define the profile geometry.

Similar to lathe operations, 2-axis or $2^1/_2$-axis milling and drilling operations require two-dimensional part geometry. For example, the profiling and pocketing operations by $2^1/_2$-axis milling, as illustrated in Figure 11.28, would be provided

Figure 11.27

Required geometry for lathe operations

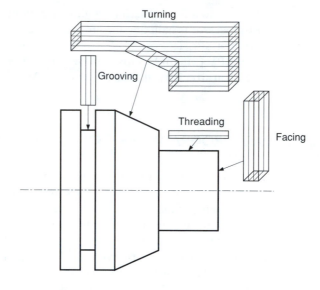

Figure 11.28

Required geometry for pocketing and profiling

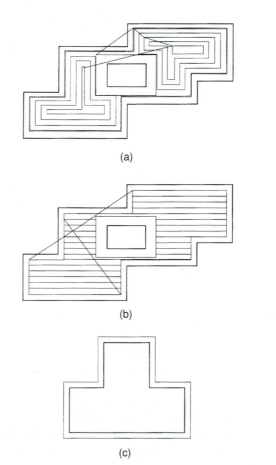

with the profile geometry from either a two-dimensional or a three-dimensional database as for lathe operations. Figure 11.28(a) and (b) show two types of pocket machining, and Figure 11.28(c) shows the profiling.

In addition to the operations mentioned, cutting operations by flame-cutting and plasma-cutting devices, and brake-press operations by NC turret presses, also require two-dimensional geometry information. Thus the two-dimensional geometry information should somehow be retrievable from the part data. Usually, the user is supposed to pick the related graphics entities making up the required geometry.

When the surfaces of a part have to be machined by using 3-axis or 5-axis contouring motion by a milling machine, geometry information of the surfaces is required. This information can be transferred to the NC program if the part has been modeled with a surface modeling or a solid modeling capability of the integrated system. In this case, the user may have to specify interactively the surfaces to be machined (describing their role as the part surfaces) and to specify their neighboring surfaces (describing their roles as the drive and check surfaces). Even when these interactive operations are involved, the advantages of the integrated CAD/CAM system will be substantial because defining complicated curved surfaces with a part programming language such as APT is difficult, often practically impossible.

2. The next step is definition of the tool geometry. The NC software usually provides the user with tool libraries that can be used to define various tools having the proper tool geometric parameters.

3. The user identifies the desired sequence of machining operations and plans the required tool path(s) with the proper cutting parameters. The *tool path* is the path that the cutting tool must follow from its home (park) position to machine the part and return to the home position. The path is usually repeated more than once as the tool is fed farther into the stock to remove additional material during each pass. The path can be planned automatically by some NC programs for simple operations such as drill and lathe operations on simple parts.

4. Once the path has been planned, x, y, and z coordinates of the necessary points on the path are calculated by the NC program, using the defined tool and the part geometry. The use of many points on each path (i.e., the use of many straight-line segments to approximate each path) will yield an accurate surface after machining. However, it may result in a long part program and slow DNC transmission speed.

5. When a tool path is generated, it can be verified on the graphics display. This usually involves the display of an animation sequence that shows the tool moving along its generated path, which is superimposed on the part geometry. If mistakes are found, the tool path can be modified accordingly and reverified. MACRO commands or other details may be added for particular machining cycles or operations.

6. A cutter location data (CL data) file is produced from the edited tool paths. Then CL data file is post-processed to machine code data (MCD file), which is transmitted to the machine tool.

In the following sections, we briefly explain how to calculate and verify the tool paths for a surface milling operation. For other operations based on two-dimensional profile geometry, such as 2-axis or $2\frac{1}{2}$-axis milling and drilling operations, cutting operations, and brake-press operations, the tool paths can easily be calculated by using simple analytic geometry and thus are not described here.

11.8.1 Tool Path Generation

Machining a surface by using milling machine with 3-axis or 5-axis contouring motion may require several paths. When significant material removal is required, two different groups of paths are normally calculated: one for roughing cuts to remove bulk material and the other for a finishing cut to produce the final shape. Sometimes an intermediate semifinishing cut is also calculated.

Tool path for rough cutting   There are two types of rough cutting process. The first type is used when the raw material has a shape already close to the final shape, as shown in Figure 11.29. In this case, the raw material has been prepared by a process such as casting. The part surfaces are first specified by offsetting the final surface by a certain interval, and the tool path for rough cutting is obtained from each offset surface in the same way as the tool paths for finish cutting are calculated. Tool path calculation for finish cutting will be explained later.

The second type of rough cutting process is applied when the raw material is provided in the form of a block and is often used to machine parts such as molds and dies. In this case, a certain thickness of raw material is removed, layer by layer, by each cut, as illustrated in Figure 11.30. The tool path for each layer is calculated

Figure 11.29

One type of rough cutting

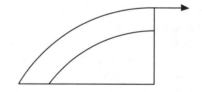

Figure 11.30

Second type of rough cutting

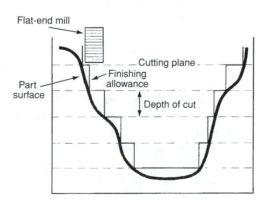

as for pocketing (see Figure 11.28). In this case, the pocket boundary curve for each layer is obtained by intersecting the surface to be machined with a horizontal plane corresponding to the layer. Once the pocket boundary has been determined, the tool path to machine the pocket is obtained by offsetting the outer boundary inward by a certain distance each time (see Figure 11.28a). The pocketing tool paths can be also obtained by calculating the parallel straight-line segments, each of which is enclosed by the pocket boundary (see Figure 11.28b). A detailed description of the procedure for calculating pocketing tool paths is presented in Held [1991].

Tool path for finish cutting Tool-path calculation for a finish cut involves approximating the curves on a part surface by a series of straight-line segments and driving the cutter along these segments. Thus the machining accuracy is determined by the accuracy of the linear approximation. It is controlled by a tolerance specifying the maximum deviation of the linear segments from the corresponding curve segments. This tolerance is equivalent to OUTTOL and INTOL in APT.

There are a number of ways to select the curves on a surface to be approximated by straight-line segments. Physically, this means that there are several ways in which the cutter can move across the surface. Figure 11.31 illustrates the various cutter paths on the surface. The cutter can follow

- curves along a surface at constant values of one of the surface parameters, either in a forward and backward motion known as *lace cutting*, or with all cuts in the same overall direction called *nonlace cutting*;
- contours on the surface; or
- paths obtained by intersecting the surface with parallel planes.

Usually, the user selects one of these three types of cutter movement during path planning. For the pattern selected, the intervals between the curves are calculated by the NC program, based on the accuracy required. As shown in Figure 11.32, this interval, called a *path interval*, determines the height of the scallop, or cusp, to be left after machining. Leaving high cusps hurts productivity because cusps have to be eliminated by the grinding process after milling, and that step may take a significant portion of the total machining time.

Figure 11.31

Various cutter paths on a surface

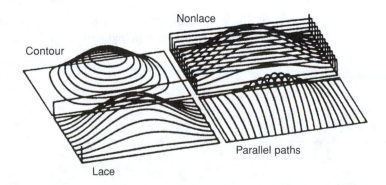

Figure 11.32

Relationship be-
tween path interval
and cusp height

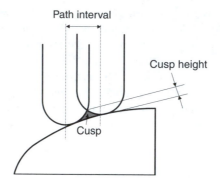

When the curves to be approximated have been obtained, the points on the curve have to be calculated. The maximum distance between any straight-line segment connecting two neighboring points and the corresponding curve segment must be less than the specified tolerance. These points are called *cutter-contact points* (CC-points) because the cutter will be in contact with the surface there. As illustrated in Figure 11.33, the deviation of the straight-line segment from the true curve will become larger as the distance between the CC-points, called the *step length*, increases. Even though smaller step length results in better accuracy, the maximum allowable step length is desirable for the compact CL data file only if it still can limit the deviation to the specified tolerance. A discussion of the procedure required to calculate the step length at any CC-point on a curve is presented in Chang [1998]. Using a technique involving subdivision of the Bezier curve, described in Appendix F, is an alternative method obtaining the CC-points on a curve. That is, as illustrated in Figure 11.34, a curve on the surface to be machined is represented by a Bezier curve, the curve is subdivided until all the convex hulls (indicated by hatching) generated by subdivision have the thickness less than the specified tolerance, and the points on the curve (D4 and D7 in the figure) are collected as CC-points.

After the CC-points have been determined, the corresponding *cutter-location points* (CL-points) are calculated. The CL-points are the data required by the NC controller. As shown in Figure 11.35, a CL-point of a ball-nosed cutter (ball-end mill) can easily be derived from the corresponding CC-point by using the formula:

$$\mathbf{r}_{cl} = \mathbf{r}_{cc} + R[\mathbf{n}(u,v) - \mathbf{a}] \qquad (11.1)$$

where $\mathbf{r}_{cl}$ and $\mathbf{r}_{cc}$ are, respectively, the position vectors of the CL-point and the CC-point, R is the radius of the ball-end mill, $\mathbf{n}(u,v)$ is the unit outward normal vector

Figure 11.33

Relationship be-
tween step length
and deviation

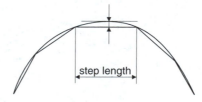

Figure 11.34

Generation of CC-points by subdivision

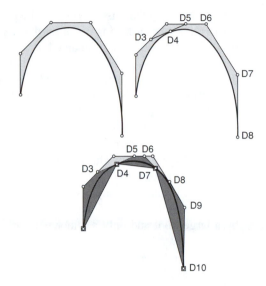

of the part surface at the CC-point corresponding to the parameter values u and v, and **a** is the unit vector along the tool axis. The tool axis vector usually will be (0, 0, 1) for 3-axis milling but an arbitrary value for 5-axis milling. In 3-axis machining, the cutter is always at a fixed angle with respect to the workpiece, normally aligned with the z axis.

For other types of cutters, a similar relationship between a CC-point and a CL-point can be derived. In 5-axis machining, the cutter axis is varied to suit the orientation of the surface being machined. In principle, the cutter could be aligned with the surface normal to minimize the cusp height, but in practice it is often inclined so that cutting occurs not on the bottom but on the side of the cutter. In this way, the cutter is more effective because it cuts the stock at the largest possible radius or maximum cutting speed. Therefore the tool-path calculation for 5-axis machining includes the complicated calculation for cutter axis orientations in addition to the cutter end locations. We do not consider the details here.

In the preceding discussion, we explained how to calculate the CL-points after derivation of the CC-points. However, it is also possible to calculate the CL-points

Figure 11.35

Relationship between the CC-point and the CL-point

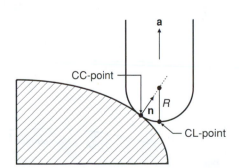

directly by using the offset surface of the part surface, especially for a ball-end mill. That is, the part surface is offset by the radius of the ball-end mill, and the curves on this offset surface are obtained as one of the patterns given in Figure 11.31. Then the points on these curves will be the locations of the center of the cutter, and the CL-points can be obtained by adding $-R\mathbf{a}$ to the position vectors of these points. The definition of R and $\mathbf{a}$ are the same as those in Equation (11.1).

When the cutter is moved along the calculated tool paths, it may cause an over-cut, called *gouging*, at some locations. Gouging can occur at the points on the concave part surface where the radius of curvature is smaller than the tool radius, as shown in Figure 11.36. This problem may be avoided by choosing a tool whose radius is smaller than the minimum radius of curvature of the part surface. However, inefficient machining may result if the selected tool is too small. In this case, the part surface has to be divided so that the major portion of the surface is machined by a larger tool and only a minor portion of the large curvature is machined by a smaller tool.

A second type of gouging can occur where the part surface meets neighboring surfaces, as illustrated in Figure 11.37. The problem occurs by taking the point (denoted A) on the boundary between the two surfaces as a CC-point. Thus the problem can be avoided by moving the limit of the CC-point to point B, as shown in Figure 11.38. The center location of the tool at its limit location can be obtained by intersecting the offset surfaces: one from the part surface by the tool radius and the other from the neighboring surface by the same amount. For different types of a tool, this calculation will be more complicated.

In 5-axis machining, gouge detection is more complicated because the entire cutter geometry at each orientation has to be considered and checked to determine

Figure 11.36

Gouging of a surface

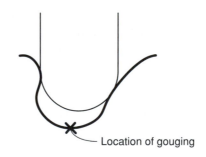

Location of gouging

Figure 11.37

Gouging at a neighboring surface

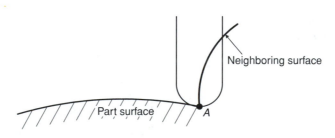

Neighboring surface

Part surface A

Figure 11.38

Tool at a new limit location

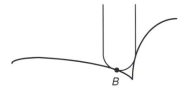

whether it collides with components such as jigs, fixtures, or spindles, as well as with the workpiece.

11.8.2 Tool-Path Simulation and Verification

The tool paths that are supposed to guide tools during actual machining usually include a lot of coordinate values that are impossible to verify manually. In the past operators used to verify and correct them by the time-consuming process of machining wooden or plastic models. Now that software is available, this time-consuming process is often replaced by the visual display of the tool paths on the graphics display. This allows machine tools to be used for cutting real parts only. This also allows the part programmer to check visually whether

- the cutter removes the necessary material from the stock,
- the cutter hits any clamps or fixtures,
- the cutter passes through the floor or side of a pocket, or through a rib, and
- the tool paths are efficient.

The simplest way of visualizing or simulating a machining process is to display the trajectory of cutter locations by line segments together with the geometric model of the desired part, as illustrated in Figure 11.39. Each line segment is displayed as the cutter location data are read line by line from the CL data file. With this kind of simulation, the programmer can get a general idea about whether the tool is moving as planned but cannot locate gouging or excess material because only the cutter locations will be seen, not the changes in the workpiece as it is machined.

The ideal way of simulating the machining process is to display the solid model of the workpiece as it is transformed by the tool movements. This can be achieved by subtracting models of the swept volumes of tool movements from the model of the workpiece. The programmer can also verify the tool paths by comparing the models of the workpiece and the desired part (i.e., by performing a Boolean difference operation between these two models). The problem with this approach is that it is computationally expensive: The cost of simulation reportedly is proportional to the fourth power of the number of tool movements. A typical CL data file for sculptured surface machining could contain 10,000 movements, making the computation virtually impossible and prohibitively expensive.

To increase efficiency in displaying the workpiece as it is machined, various approximate simulation methods have been devised. In these approximate methods,

Figure 11.39

Display of trajectory of cutter location data

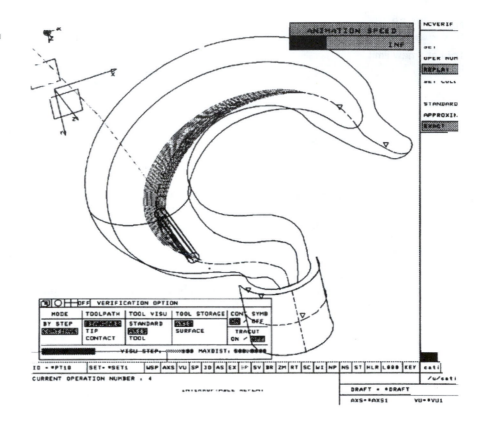

the simulation time grows linearly with the number of tool movements. One method for 3-axis machining was introduced by Anderson [1978]. He divided the base of the part into squares and represented the workpiece as the collection of rectangular columns. He called this structure a *3D histogram*. The basic idea of his approach is to update the height of the rectangular columns as they are cut by tool movements. That is, each column starts with the height of the stock, and then each tool movement updates the heights of the columns it passes over if it cuts lower than the current stored height.

Another approach is the *point-vector technique*. This technique was proposed by Chappel [1983] and enhanced by Jerard, Drysdale, Hauck, Schandt, and Magewick [1989]. In this approach, the surface to be machined is approximated by a set of points, and the direction vectors are created normal to the surface at each point, both inward and outward. During the machining simulation following each line of the CL data file, the intersection points between these vectors and the corresponding tool movement's envelope are calculated. The length of a vector is reduced if it intersects the envelope. When the last line of the CL data file is processed, the length of a final vector corresponds to the amount of excess material (if above the surface) or the depth of the gouge (if below the surface) at that point. Note that this approach can be applied to 5-axis machining as well as 3-axis ma-

Figure 11.40

Approach involving the use of direction vectors

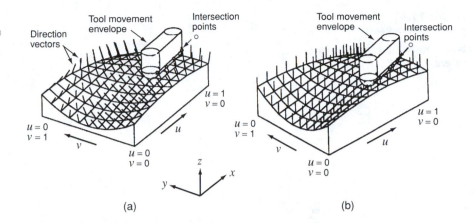

chining. For 5-axis machining, the envelope of the tool movement will be more complicated than that for 3-axis machining. Jerard and colleagues simplified the computation further for 3-axis machining simulation by using the direction vectors along the tool-axis direction, which is usually in the z direction. The direction vectors and the tool movement envelope are illustrated in Figure 11.40. In Figure 11.40(a), the direction vectors are normal to the surface, whereas those in Figure 11.40(b) are along the z axis everywhere. The method just described can also be used to display the shape of the part while it is being machined. That is, the shape of the part at any machining stage is approximated as a polyhedron by skinning the end points of the direction vectors with the polygons, and the resulting polyhedron is displayed.

11.8.3 Case Study

In this section, we demonstrate how an NC program is generated by Pro/MFG™ and Pro/NC-CHECK™, the CAM module of Pro/ENGINEER™, for part of the injection mold of the cellular phone body introduced in Chapter 1. This part will be called the *reference part* from now on. We assume that the reference part and the workpiece have already been modeled by Pro/ENGINEER, as shown in Figures 11.41 and 11.42.

We will create machining sequences required for the bottom inside of the reference part as the first operation (or setup). For the second operation (or setup), we will flip the part and generate the sequences machining the outside bottom portion of the part. For both operations, we will eventually generate the machine code data (MCD) file.

For the setups described, we need to create the proper coordinate systems, as shown in Figure 11.43. In Pro/MFG, the tool axis must be parallel with the z axis, and it approaches from the positive direction. Because the part is to be machined on both sides, two coordinate systems will be required. Figure 11.43 shows the assembly of the reference part and the workpiece with the coordinate systems defined. All the interactive operations to follow will be performed on this assembly.

Figure 11.41

Solid model of a
reference part

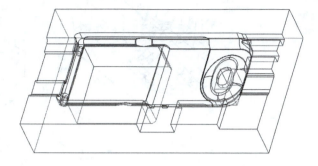

Figure 11.42

Solid model of a
workpiece

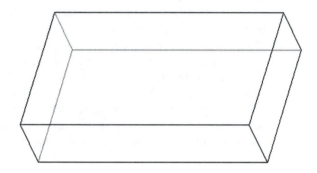

Figure 11.43

Assembly of a
workpiece and a
reference part

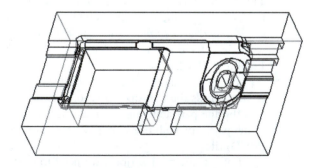

The next step is selection of the workcell among the choices Mill, Turn, and WEDM (Wire Electric Discharge Machine). After selecting the workcell (Mill in this case), we need to define the operation. The operation is a set of NC sequences machinable in one setup. Our task requires two setups, so we need to define two operations. To define the first operation, OP010, which is the setup for machining the bottom inside of the reference part, we choose OPER1 as the machining coordinate system. As shown later, OP010 comprises 21 NC sequences.

For the first sequence to machine the volume shown in Figure 11.44, we select the tool to be used from the user interface shown in Figure 11.45. Then we need to set the machining parameters for the first sequence, as shown in Figure 11.46: **STEP_DEPTH** is the depth of the cut, **STEP_OVER** is the path interval between the adjacent paths, and **PROF_STOC_ALLOW** and **ROUGH_STOCK_ALLOW** specify the machining allowance to be left for the finish cut. Detailed descriptions of other parameters are given in Parametric Technology's Pro/MFG's User's Guide [1997]. The next step is to specify the volume to be machined. To

Figure 11.44

Volume to be machined

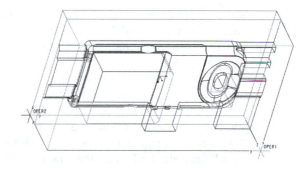

Figure 11.45

User interface for selecting a tool

TOOL_ID	6_000FEM
TOOL_TYPE	MILLING
LENGTH_UNITS	INCH
CUTTER_DIAM	6
CORNER_RADIUS	-
SIDE_ANGLE	-
LENGTH	6
NUM_OF_TEETH	4
TOOL_MATERIAL	C2
GAUGE_X_LENGTH	-
GAUGE_Z_LENGTH	-
TOOL_COMMENT	

Pro/TABLE TM Release 18.0 (c) 1988-95 by Parametric Technology Corporation. All Rights Re...

File Edit View Format Help

Figure 11.46

Specification of machining parameters

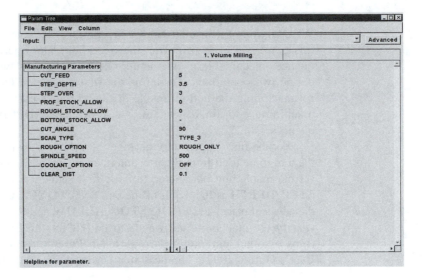

do so, we can reference the geometry of the design model, sketch the volume to be machined or excluded, intersect the volume with the workpiece or reference model, offset surfaces, and so on. In this case, we define the machining volume by sketching. As shown in Figure 11.44, the sketching method can be conveniently used to face down the workpiece. We select the top surface of the workpiece as the sketching plane and choose the extrusion operation. Then we sketch a section, using the outer boundary of the workpiece, and enter the extrusion depth. In this way, the machining volume supposed to be removed by the face milling process is finally defined. When all these steps have been taken, the system will show the tool-path simulation, as illustrated in Figure 11.47. It shows the tool path as a black solid line, with the tool starting from the lower-left corner and moving in a zigzag pattern.

The second NC sequence is defined similarly. As for the first NC sequence, the tool parameters and the machining parameters are provided. Then the machining region is specified, as shown in Figure 11.48, and the tool path is derived, as in Figure 11.49.

The remaining NC sequences are developed in the same way. Figures 11.50–11.70 show the tool-path simulations for them.

Figure 11.47

Tool-path simulation of the first NC sequence

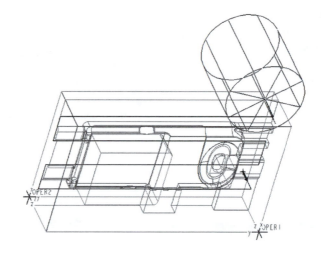

Figure 11.48

Specification of the machining region

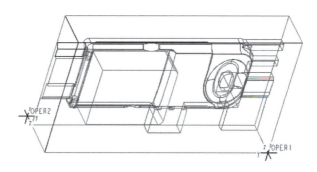

Figure 11.49

Tool-path simulation of the second NC sequence

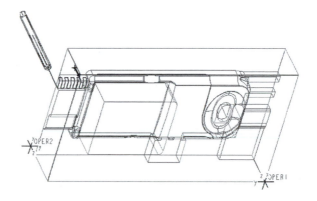

Figure 11.50

Tool-path simulation of the third NC sequence

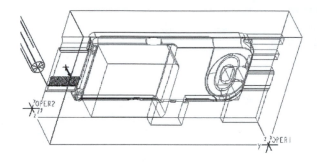

Figure 11.51

Tool-path simulation of the fourth NC sequence

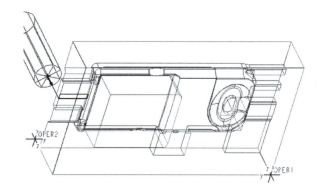

Figure 11.52

Tool-path simulation of the fifth NC sequence

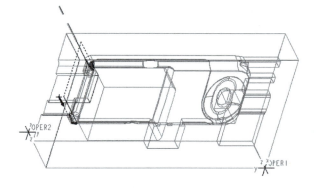

Figure 11.53

Tool-path simulation of the sixth NC sequence

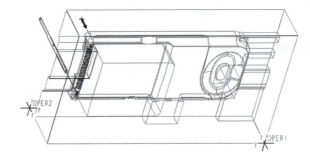

Figure 11.54

Tool-path simulation of the seventh NC sequence

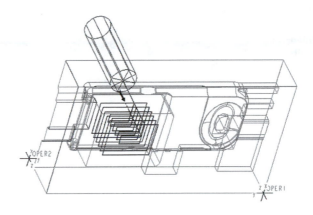

Figure 11.55

Tool-path simulation of the eighth NC sequence

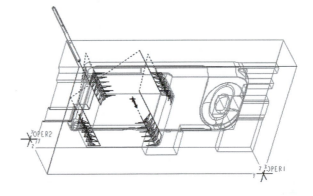

Figure 11.56

Tool-path simulation of the ninth NC sequence

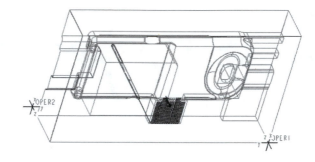

Figure 11.57

Tool-path simulation of the tenth NC sequence

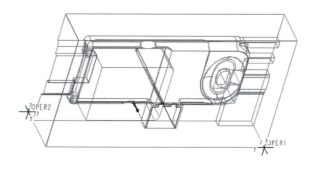

Figure 11.58

Tool-path simulation of the eleventh NC sequence

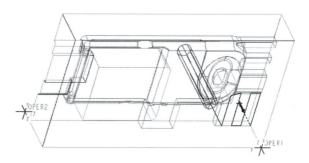

Figure 11.59

Tool-path simulation of the twelfth NC sequence

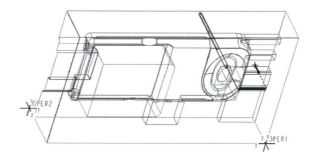

Figure 11.60

Tool-path simulation of the thirteenth NC sequence

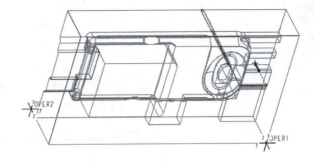

Figure 11.61

Tool-path simulation of the fourteenth NC sequence

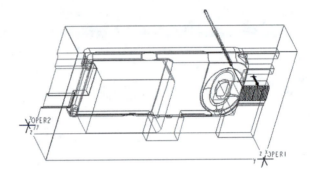

Figure 11.62

Tool-path simulation of the fifteenth NC sequence

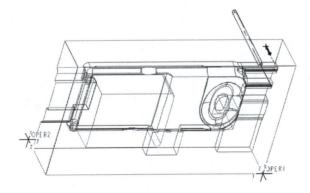

372 ■ Numerical Control

Figure 11.63

Tool-path simula-
tion of the six-
teenth NC
sequence

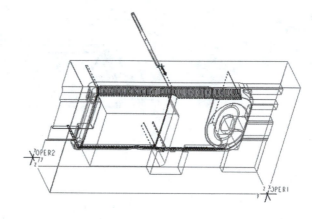

Figure 11.64

Tool-path simula-
tion of the seven-
teenth NC
sequence

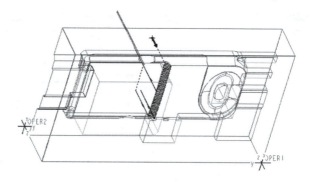

Figure 11.65

Tool-path simula-
tion of the eigh-
teenth NC
sequence

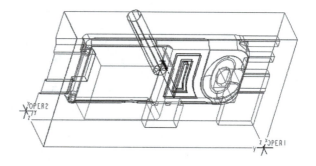

Figure 11.66

Tool-path simulation of the nineteenth NC sequence

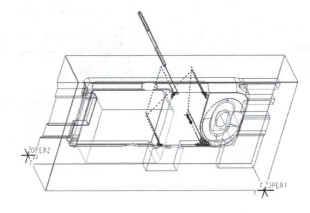

Figure 11.67

Tool-path simulation of the twentieth NC sequence

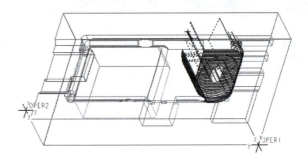

Figure 11.68

Tool-path simulation of the twenty-first NC sequence

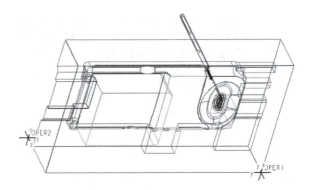

When all the sequences for the first setup have been completed, the second operation (second setup) is defined, and the NC sequences for the second operation are generated, as shown in Figures 11.69 and 11.70.

Figure 11.69

Tool-path simula-
tion of the first NC
sequence for the
second operation

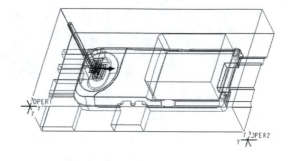

Figure 11.70

Tool-path simula-
tion of the second
NC sequence for
the second opera-
tion

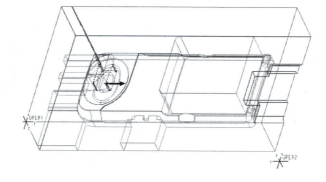

After all the NC sequences for all the operations have been generated, they are
output to the CL data file and the Machine Code Data file, as illustrated in Figures
11.71 and 11.72, respectively.

Figure 11.71

CL data file

```
$$-> MFGNO / TAC5000
PARTNO / WORKPIECE
$$-> FEATNO / 48
MACHIN / MILL, 01
UNITS / INCHES
LOADTL / 4
$$-> CUTTER / 6.000000
SPINDL / RPM, 500.000000, CLW
RAPID
GOTO / 1.5000000000, 0.0000000000, 5.0000000000
RAPID
GOTO / 1.5000000000, 0.0000000000, 4.1000000000
FEDRAT / 5.000000, IPM
GOTO / 1.5000000000, 0.0000000000, 3.0000000000
GOTO / 1.5000000000, 16.7000000000, 3.0000000000
GOTO / 3.6933333333, 16.7000000000, 3.0000000000
GOTO / 3.6933333333, 0.0000000000, 3.0000000000
GOTO / 5.8866666667, 0.0000000000, 3.0000000000
GOTO / 5.8866666667, 16.7000000000, 3.0000000000
GOTO / 8.0800000000, 16.7000000000, 3.0000000000
GOTO / 8.0800000000, 0.0000000000, 3.0000000000
GOTO / 8.0800000000, 0.0000000000, 5.0000000000
$$-> END /
$$-> FEATNO / 330
SPINDL / OFF
LOADTL / 6
$$-> CUTTER / 0.500000
SPINDL / RPM, 500.000000, CLW
RAPID
GOTO / 6.2500000000, 14.6000000000, 5.0000000000
RAPID
GOTO / 6.2500000000, 14.6000000000, 2.7000000000
FEDRAT / 5.000000, IPM
GOTO / 6.6500000000, 14.6000000000, 2.7000000000
GOTO / 6.6986072482, 14.6000000000, 2.7039639626
GOTO / 6.7405922804, 14.6000000000, 2.7140051771
GOTO / 6.7713338384, 14.6000000000, 2.7256314529
GOTO / 6.8035787860, 14.6000000000, 2.7422917221
GOTO / 6.8364736248, 14.6000000000, 2.7649944953
```

Figure 11.72

Machine Code Data file

```
N0001   G70 G90
N0002   T4 D4 M06
N0003   G0 X1.5 Y0. S500 M03
N0004   Z5.
N0005   Z4.1
N0006   G1 Z3. F5.0
N0007   Y16.7
N0008   X3.6933
N0009   Y0.
N0010   X5.8867
N0011   Y16.7
N0012   X8.08
N0013   Y0.
N0014   Z5.
N0015   M05
N0016   T6 D6 M06
N0017   G0 X6.25 Y14.6 S500 M03
N0018   Z5.
N0019   Z2.7
N0020   G1 X6.65 F5.0
N0021   G18
N0022   G2 X6.95 Z3. I-.0019 K.3019
N0023   G1 Y14.61
N0024   G3 X6.65 Z2.7 I-.3019 K.0019
N0025   G1 X6.25
N0026   Y14.62
N0027   X6.65
N0028   G2 X6.95 Z3. I-.0019 K.3019
N0029   G1 Y14.63
N0030   G3 X6.65 Z2.7 I-.3019 K.0019
N0031   G1 X6.25
N0032   Y14.64
N0033   X6.65
N0034   G2 X6.95 Z3. I-.0019 K.3019
N0035   G1 Y14.65
N0036   G3 X6.65 Z2.7 I-.3019 K.0019
N0037   G1 X6.25
N0038   Y14.66
N0039   X6.65
```

QUESTIONS AND PROBLEMS

1. In writing a part program, what is the difference between a fixed sequential format and a word address format?

2. What is a canned cycle?

3. What is the main difficulty in manual part programming compared to part programming with a computer language such as APT?

4. Explain the difference between the GOTO and GO commands in APT.

5. Write a part program manually to mill the edge of the plate shown. The dimensions are in millimeters. Assume that the raw material, a rectangular plate, has a thickness of 15 mm and that its bottom face has the z coordinate of 0. Use the NC controller, tool, feed, and spindle speed characteristics given in Example 11.1.

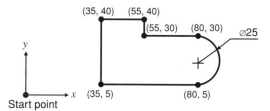

6. Sketch the geometry defined by the following APT statements.

```
P1 = POINT/0,0,0
P2 = POINT/100,50,0
L1 = LINE/P1,P2
P3 = POINT/0,50,0
P4 = POINT/100,0,0
L2 = LINE/P3,P4
C1 = CIRCLE/YLARGE, L1, XLARGE,
     L2, RADIUS, 10
```

7. From the following APT source program, sketch the geometry and the tool path. Also explain the meaning of each of the post-processor statements.

```
PARTNO PART7
MACHIN/MILL,1
INTOL/0.002
OUTTOL/0.002
CUTTER/.5
SP = POINT/–3,–3,4
P1 = POINT/0,0,0
P2 = POINT/8,0,0
P3 = POINT/4,4,0
P4 = POINT/0,4,0
L1 = LINE/P1,P2
L2 = LINE/P2,P3
L3 = LINE/P3,P4
L4 = LINE/P4,P1
PL1 = PLANE/P1,P2,P3
SPINDL/1000
FEDRAT/5
COOLNT/ON
FROM/SP
GO/TO,L1,TO,L4,TO,PL1
GORGT/L1,PAST,L2
GOLFT/L2,PAST,L3
GOLFT/L3,PAST,L4
GOLFT/L4,PAST,L1
GOTO/SP
COOLNT/OFF
FINI
```

8. For the part in Problem 5, write an APT program. Use the same machining conditions.

9. Prepare a program in APT language for the finish milling of the profile shown. Assume that the tool diameter is 1 inch, the feed rate is 8 ipm, and the spindle speed is 764 rpm.

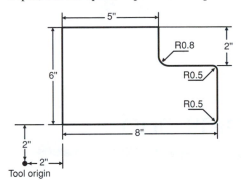

10. Use any surface modeling system available to you to model the part shown. You can assume reasonable dimensions of the part. Try to calculate the cutter paths for the finish cut, using available CAM software.

Freeform surface model of wheel (Courtesy of drawing of Autosurf®, Autodesk®, Inc.)

11. Repeat the same task as in Problem 10 for the part shown.

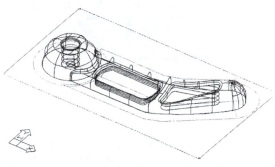

Freeform surface model of mechanical part (Courtesy of drawing of Autosurf®, Autodesk®, Inc.)

12

Rapid Prototyping and Manufacturing

In Chapter 11, we introduced machining by an NC machine tool and showed how, for a part, the geometric data in a CAD database is used in manufacturing. Even though the geometric model was used as common data, the design and manufacturing processes were not directly integrated in NC machining. That is, intermediate steps, such as process planning, jig and fixturing, and the determination of setups, had to be taken before an NC machine tool could be driven by the geometric model.

Rapid prototyping is another way in which a geometric model of a part is used in manufacturing. Various rapid prototyping processes are available, but all of them generate a prototype by laying composite material layer by layer. The main advantage of rapid prototyping processes is that they build a prototype in one step, directly from the geometric model of the part to be manufactured. Thus they do not require planning of process sequences, specific equipment for handling materials, transportation between machining stations, and so on. However, compared to NC machining, a major disadvantage of these processes is that they are currently restricted to specific materials. Because an NC machine tool can handle most of the available industrial materials, including metals, the physical objects made by rapid prototyping processes are used mainly as prototypes or patterns for other manufacturing procedures.

12.1   OVERVIEW

Based on the availability of solid modeling systems, beginning in the 1970s, attempts were made to generate physical objects directly from geometric data without traditional tools. The new technology was called *rapid prototyping* (RP), or alternatively, layered manufacturing, 3D printing, desktop manufacturing, and solid freeform manufacturing [Kochan 1993]. Since then the technology has advanced to encompass many applications of manufacturing beyond that of prototyping. Thus the terminology *rapid prototyping and manufacturing* (RP&M) now seems to be more descriptive, so we use it in this chapter.

The processes for rapid prototyping and manufacturing basically consist of three steps: form the cross sections of the object to be manufactured, lay the cross sections layer by layer, and combine the layers. Therefore RP&M processes require only cross-sectional data to generate a physical object, and they eliminate the following problems that are often encountered with other manufacturing processes.

- Feature-based design and feature recognition are unnecessary because process planning involving the use of feature information is not required. Similarly, converting design features to manufacturing features is unnecessary. A three-dimensional surface or solid model of the part, from which the cross-sectional data are generated, is sufficient.

- Defining a blank geometry is unnecessary because RP&M processes add material instead of removing material.

- Defining different setups or complex sequences of handling material is unnecessary because the part is produced in one operation.

- Considering clamping, jigs, or fixtures is unnecessary. (Some RP&M processes may require support structures to be built up together with the workpiece. We explain support structures later.)

- Designing and manufacturing molds and dies are unnecessary because RP&M processes are tool-less processes.

Thus, because RP&M processes generate a physical object without tooling, they are well suited to design and manufacturing integration without the intervention of process planning.

Forming the layers of the cross sections and combining them involve the use of one of the following methods:

- polymerization of suitable resins by laser, other light beams, or lamps,

- selective solidification of solid particles or powder by laser beams,

- binding of liquid or solid particles by gluing or welding,

- cutting and laminating the sheet materials, or

- melting and resolidification.

Typical RP&M processes based on these methods are described in the following section [Crawford 1993].

12.2   SPECIFIC RP&M PROCESSES

Table 12.1 summarizes the features of some commercially available RP&M machines for different types of processes.

TABLE 12.1

Features of RP&M machines

Process type	Stereo lithography								
Machine	SmartStart (SLA-250/30A)	SLA-250/40,50	SLA-3500	SLA-5000	LMS	JSC-1000 JSC-2000 JSC-3000	SOUP-400, -530, -600, -850	COLAMN-300	Aaroflex Soid Imager
Company	3D Systems (US)				Fockele & Schwarze (Germany)	SONY/D-MEC Ltd. (Japan)	CMET, Inc. (Japan)	Mitsui Zosen (Japan)	Aaroflexx, Inc. (US)
Work space	250 × 250 × 250 (mm)	250 × 250 × 250 (mm)	350 × 350 × 400 (mm)	508 × 508 × 584 (mm)	400 × 400 × 350 (mm)	1000 × 800 × 500 (mm)	400 × 400 × 400, 530 × 355 × 355, 600 × 400 × 400, 860 × 600 × 500 (mm)		560 × 560 × 560 (mm)
Layer thickness	0.15 mm	0.1 mm			0.1 mm	0.1 ~ 0.3 mm			0.05 mm
Accuracy	0.1 mm				0.01 mm	0.1 ~ 0.2 mm	0.05 mm		0.06 mm
Material	Any photopolymer resin								

T A B L E   1 2 . 1   Features of RP&M machines (continued)

	Laminating			Fused deposition modeling	Sintering of powder		Solid ground curing		
Machine	LOM-1015 LOM-2030H	Kira Solid Center	Hot Plot	FDM 1650, FDM 2000, FDM 8000	Sinterstation 2000, Sinterstation 2500	EOSINT P350 EOSINT M250 EOSINT S700	Solider 4600 Solider 5600	LSI-0609MA, LSI-1115MA, LSI-2224MA	SOMOS
Company	Helisys, Inc. (US)	Kira (Japan)	Sparx AB (Sweden)	Stratasys (US)	DTM (US)	EOS (Germany)	Cubital (Israel)	Light Sculpting, Inc. (US)	Teijin Seiki (Japan)
Work space	381 × 254 × 356, 813 × 559 × 508 (mm)	400 × 280 × 300 (mm)		254 × 254 × 254, 254 × 254, 457 × 457 × 609 (mm)	304.8 mmD × 381 mmH	340 × 340 × 590 (mm) 250 × 250 × 150 (mm) 720 × 380 × 380 (mm)	350 × 350 × 500, 350 × 500 (mm)	150 × 150 × 230, 280 × 280 × 380, 560 × 560 × 600 (mm)	300 × 300 × 300 (mm)
Layer thickness	0.1 mm	0.1 mm	1.0 mm	0.05 mm	0.08 mm	0.1~0.2 mm	0.1~0.15 mm	0.01 mm	0.1~0.5 mm
Accuracy	0.1 mm		0.2 mm	0.127 mm, 0.127 mm, 0.127–0.254 mm	0.38 mm	0.03 mm	0.5 mm	0.03 mm	0.05 mm (x, y) 0.15 mm (z)
Material	Coated paper	General copy paper	Coated sheet (Poly-ethylene)	ABS, wax, polyamid plastic	ABS plastic, PVC, nylon, investment casting wax, polycarbonate powdered metal ceramic, sand	polyamid, polycarbonate, polystyrene, metal alloy	Photopolymer + Water-soluble wax		

12.2.1 Stereo Lithography

In the late 1970s and early 1980s, A. Herbert of 3M Corporation in Minneapolis, H. Kodame of the Nagoya Prefecture Research Institute in Japan, and C. Hull of UVP (Ultra Violet Products, Inc.) in California worked independently on rapid prototyping concepts based on selectively curing a surface layer of photopolymer and building three-dimensional objects with successive layers. Both Herbert and Kodama stopped their work before developing a commercial product because of the lack of financial support. Obtaining continuous support from UVP, Hull developed a system that could automatically build detailed parts. Hull coined the term *stereo lithography*, founded 3D Systems, Inc., in 1986, and began producing the Stereo Lithography Apparatus (SLA).

The stereo lithography process generates a part, as illustrated in Figure 12.1(a), in the following manner.

Figure 12.1

Stereo lithography (a) process and (b) 3D Systems' SLA-3500 (Courtesy of 3D Systems, Inc.)

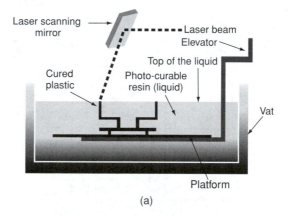

(a)

(b)

Step 1. A photosensitive polymer that solidifies when exposed to a lighting source is maintained in a liquid state.

Step 2. A platform that can be elevated is located just one layer of thickness below the top surface of the liquid polymer.

Step 3. The UV laser scans the polymer layer above the platform to solidify the polymer and give it the shape of the corresponding cross section. Note that this step starts with the bottom cross section of the part.

Step 4. The platform is lowered into the polymer bath to the layer thickness to allow liquid polymer to flow over the part to begin the next layer.

Step 5. Step 3 and step 4 are repeated until the top layer of the part is generated.

Step 6. Post-curing is performed to solidify the part completely. This step is required because some liquid regions can remain in each layer. Because the laser beam has finite size, the scanning on each layer is analogous to filling a shape with a fine color pen.

An actual Stereo Lithography Apparatus is shown in Figure 12.1(b).

Stereo lithography is the most popular RP&M process, and its interface with a solid model has become a standard for other RP&M processes. However, it requires a support structure when the part being built has undercuts, which means that the upper cross section has a larger area than the lower cross section, as illustrated in Figure 12.2. Figure 12.3 shows an impeller made by the stereo lithography process. We describe stereo lithography in detail later.

12.2.2 Solid Ground Curing

In solid ground curing (SGC) processes, each layer is cured by exposure to a lamp instead of by laser beam scanning. Thus all the locations in a layer are cured simul-

Figure 12.2

Support structures in the stereo lithography process

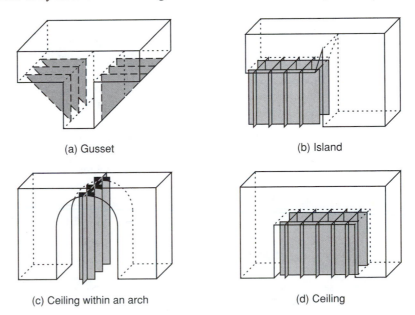

(a) Gusset

(b) Island

(c) Ceiling within an arch

(d) Ceiling

Figure 12.3

Impeller made by
the stereo lithogra-
phy process

taneously and post-curing is not required. A typical example of the solid ground curing processes is the Solider system from Cubital Israel, which works in the following manner.

Step 1. The cross section of each slice layer is calculated from the geometric model of the part and the desired layer thickness.

Step 2. The optical mask is generated conforming to each cross section.

Step 3. After leveling (Figure 12.4a), the platform is covered with a thin layer of liquid photopolymer (Figure 12.4b).

Step 4. The mask corresponding to the current layer is positioned over the surface of the liquid resin, and the resin is exposed to a high-power UV lamp (Figure 12.4c). Note that this step starts with the mask corresponding to the bottom layer.

Step 5. The residual liquid is removed from the workpiece by an aerodynamic wiper (Figure 12.4d).

Step 6. A layer of melted wax is spread over the workpiece to fill voids (Figure 12.4e). The wax is then solidified by applying a cold plate to it.

Step 7. The layer surface is trimmed to the desired thickness by a milling disk (Figure 12.4f).

Step 8. The current workpiece is covered with a thin layer of liquid polymer, and steps 4–7 are repeated for each succeeding upper layer until the topmost layer has been processed.

Step 9. The wax is melted away upon completion of the part.

The primary advantage of the solider system over the SLA process is that it does not require a support structure. The reason is that wax is used to fill the voids. In addition, the solider system eliminates the post-curing step by using a lamp instead of a laser beam. Although it can generate more accurate parts than the SLA process does, the solider system is a very complex process.

12.2.3   Selective Laser Sintering

The selective laser sintering (SLS) process developed by DTM in the United States generates a part as follows.

Figure 12.4

Solider system

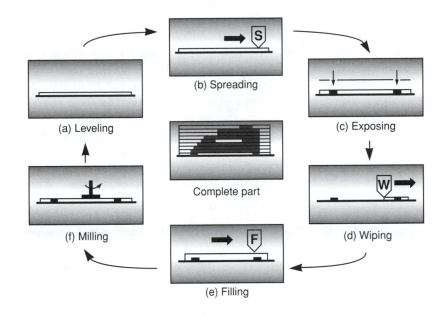

(a) Leveling

(b) Spreading

(c) Exposing

Complete part

(f) Milling

(e) Filling

(d) Wiping

Step 1. A part cylinder is located at the height necessary for a layer of powdered material to be deposited on the cylinder to the desired thickness. The powdered material being used for the prototype is applied from the feed cylinder by the leveling roller, as illustrated in Figure 12.5.

Step 2. The layer of powder is selectively raster-scanned and heated with a laser, causing particles to adhere to each other. The laser scan forms the powder into the required cross section shape. Note that this step starts with the bottom cross section.

Figure 12.5

Selective laser sintering (Courtesy of DTM Corporation)

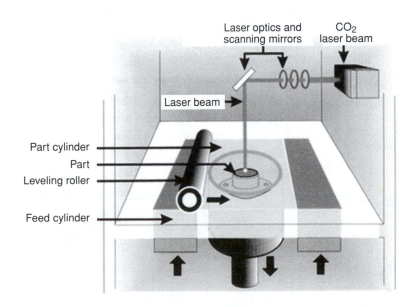

Laser optics and scanning mirrors

CO_2 laser beam

Laser beam

Part cylinder

Part

Leveling roller

Feed cylinder

Step 3. The part cylinder is lowered by the layer thickness to permit a new layer of powder to be deposited.

Step 4. The new layer is scanned, conforming it to the shape of the next upper cross section and adhering it to the previous layer.

Step 5. Steps 3 and 4 are repeated until the topmost layer of the part is generated.

Step 6. Post-curing may be required for some materials.

A support structure is not required because the voids are filled by the un-processed powder at each layer. Moreover, the selective laser sintering process is potentially usable with any meltable powder, even metal powders if the laser is powerful enough. In practice, an indirect sintering process is used for metal powders that are coated with a thermoplastic binder. When the laser is applied, the binder material melts and loosely binds the metal powders to form the desired shape, called a *green part*. In this case, the laser needs to be only powerful enough to melt the binder material. The green part is then post-processed in a furnace where the binder is burned off, and the metal powders are bonded by traditional sintering mechanics. The resulting part is called a *brown part*. Unless treated further, the part would be quite porous because of the spaces occupied previously by the binder material. To reduce the porosity, a second material, an infiltrant, is added to the furnace. This metal becomes liquid under the elevated temperature in the furnace and infiltrates the brown part via capillary action. This process is used to make an injection mold directly from its CAD model. The resulting mold is durable enough to make between 2500 and 10,000 prototype parts.

12.2.4 3D Printing

Developed at MIT, the 3D printing process was so named because of its similarity to ink-jet printing. In 3D printing, a liquid binder instead of an ink is ejected. The 3D printing process works as follows, as illustrated in Figure 12.6.

Figure 12.6

3D printing (With permission of Prof. Sachs, M.I.T.)

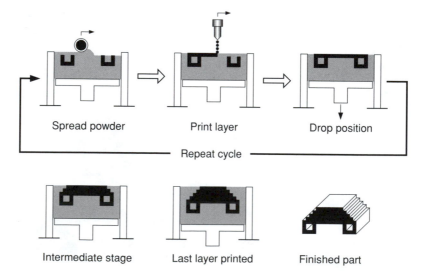

Spread powder   Print layer   Drop position

Repeat cycle

Intermediate stage   Last layer printed   Finished part

Step 1. A platform is located at the height necessary for a layer of ceramic powder to be deposited on the platform to the proper thickness.

Step 2. The layer of ceramic powder is selectively raster-scanned with a print head that delivers a liquid binder, causing particles to adhere to each other. The printer head scan forms the powder into the required cross section shape. Note that this step starts with the bottom cross section.

Step 3. The platform is lowered by the layer thickness to permit a new layer of powder to be deposited.

Step 4. The new layer is scanned, conforming it to the shape of the next upper cross section and adhering it to the previous layer.

Step 5. Steps 3 and 4 are repeated until the topmost layer of the part is generated.

Step 6. A post-process heat treatment is applied to solidify the part.

Generating a casting mold by the 3D printing process would be convenient because the mold is fabricated as a single unit, consisting of a shell and cores, and the placement of cores relative to the shell would be precise. However, casting molds generated by the current 3D printing process have inadequate surface finishes.

12.2.5 Laminated-Object Manufacturing

The laminated-object manufacturing (LOM) process, commercialized by Helisys, Inc., generates a part by laminating and laser-trimming materials that are delivered in sheet form. The sheets are laminated into a solid block by a thermal adhesive coating. The process works as follows.

Step 1. Each sheet is attached to the block, using heat and pressure to form a new layer. Sheet material is supplied from a continuous roll on one side of the machine and taken up on the opposite side, as illustrated in Figure 12.7. The heated

Figure 12.7

Laminated-object manufacturing machine (Courtesy of Helisys, Inc.)

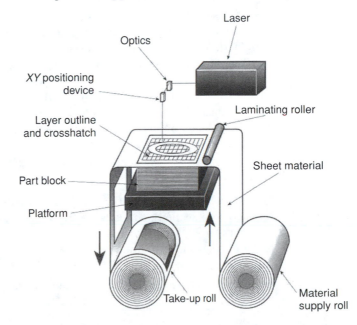

roller provides the pressure and heat needed for lamination. Note that the platform is lowered by the thickness of the sheet whenever a sheet is attached to the stack.

Step 2. After a layer (sheet) is deposited, a laser is traced on the layer along the contours corresponding to the current cross section. Usually a 25 or 50 watt CO_2 laser is used. As in the other processes, this step starts with the bottom cross section. Note that only the contours are scanned in this process. This makes the process more efficient than the RP&M processes that require a full raster scan.

Step 3. Areas of the layer outside the contours are cross-hatched by the laser (i.e., cut into small pieces called *tiles*, for removal after fabrication).

Step 4. Steps 1–3 are repeated until the top layer of the part is laminated and cut.

Step 5. After all the layers have been laminated and cut, the result is a part imbedded within a block of supporting material. This material is then broken into chunks along the cross-hatching lines.

Step 6. The resulting part may then be coated with a sealant to keep out moisture.

The presence of support material surrounding the part has both advantages and disadvantages. First, external support structures are not required. By generating the part within a form-fitted block of support material, the entire geometry is stabilized during building and is prevented from distorting under its own weight. Furthermore, we don't have to worry about the isolated "island contours" that are often generated when a CAD solid is sliced into layers. In other words, LOM avoids the need to design specialized supports to keep these islands precisely located in space until bridges to the remainder of the part are formed later in the building process. However, scrapping unnecessary material after the part is built is not a simple task, as Figure 12.8 illustrates. A careful manual cleanup process is required to ensure that only waste material is removed and that delicate sections of the part are not fractured. In addition, a hollow structure with closed surfaces cannot be fabricated as a single piece because of excess material trapped within the walls. The difficulty of removing unwanted material extends to any part with narrow passages, internal cavities with restricted access, blind holes, and so on. Also, the majority of material consumed by LOM does not contribute to the part itself. Rather, it remains with the original continuous sheet or ends up as support material, to be scrapped after building. The cost of such waste can be significant if materials more expensive than paper are used.

In addition to its advantages and disadvantages, the LOM process has the following characteristics.

- It uses a subtractive process (i.e., material is removed to create a layer having the required cross section). All other RP&M processes create layers by adding material. Thus the LOM is potentially the fastest technology for building parts with a high ratio of volume to surface area.
- The parts are formed from alternating layers of material and adhesive. Thus many of their physical properties are inhomogeneous and anisotropic.

Figure 12.8

Process of removing tiles (Courtesy of Helisys, Inc.)

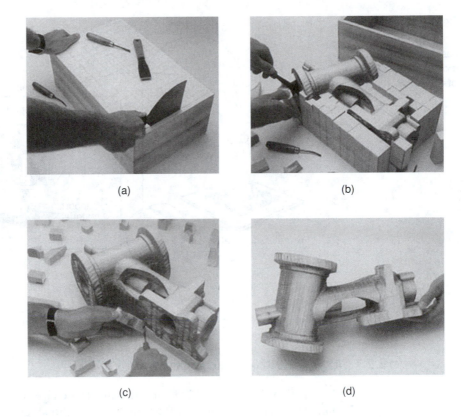

(a)

(b)

(c)

(d)

- Potential accuracy of the LOM process is high. Because any arbitrarily thin sheets can be used in the LOM process, good resolution in the part building direction is obtained. In fact, manufacturing thin, uniform sheet material is not difficult, and shrinkage during lamination is not a problem because the contours are cut after the shrinkage occurs.

- Even though the process is potentially applicable to many materials, including plastics, composites, and metals, paper sheeting is the most popular material currently.

12.2.6   Fused-Deposition Modeling

The fused-deposition modeling process commercialized by Stratasys, Inc., generates each layer by extruding thermoplastic material in a liquid state, as shown in Figure 12.9. The material is extruded at a temperature just above its solidification temperature, which is analogous to writing letters with chocolate cream on a cake. Then the part is constructed by successive extrusion of layers. This process is relatively simple but its use is limited to thermoplastic materials.

Figure 12.9

Fused-deposition modeling (Courtesy of Stratasys, Inc.)

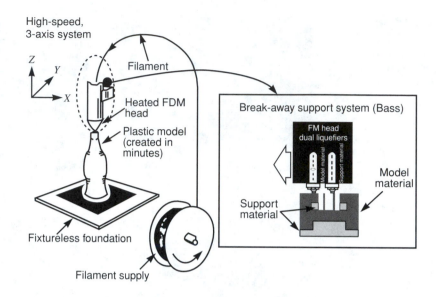

12.2.7 Low-Cost RP&M Machines

As mentioned earlier, RP&M can dramatically reduce the time and expense required to bring a new product from initial concept to production. Used early in the design process, rapid prototyping can help identify fundamental flaws that are later costly to correct if discovered when the product is ready for tooling. However, RP&M parts are not cheap, and determining how many to build in order to get maximum benefit from them is sometimes difficult. Additionally, because rapid prototypes are put to different uses at different stages in the design process, their physical requirements vary, depending on how they will be used. This is where the new class of *office* or *desktop modelers* can play a role. Less expensive to purchase and operate, modelers such as 3D Systems' Actua 2100, Stratasys' Genisys, Sanders Prototype's Model Maker II, Z Corporation's Z402, and Schroff Development's JP System 5 can be conveniently used to make relatively rough (except Model Maker II) but inexpensive prototypes for concept and design verification. By matching prototype requirements to the appropriate technology, a company can often afford to make more prototype parts for each design than if only a single technology is used for all its prototypes. Table 12.2 compares the features of low-cost RP&M machines from different companies, and Figure 12.10 illustrates the technology called *multijet modeling* (MJM) used in 3D Systems' Actua 2100. The multijet modeling technique uses a print head with 96 jets mounted in a linear array.

TABLE 12.2

Features of low-cost (desktop type) rapid-prototyping machines

Machine	Actua 2100	Genisys	Model Maker II	JP System 5
Company	3D Systems	Stratasys, Inc.	Sanders Prototype, Inc.	Schroff Development Co.
Work space	250 × 200 × 200 (mm)	203 × 203 × 203 (mm)	152 × 304 × 228 (mm)	*Standard Edition:* 305 mm width cutter *Premier Edition:* 610 mm width cutter
Technology	Print head with 96 jets delivers thermopolymer material layer by layer	A 3D printer with material fed through an extrusion head layer by layer	Liquid-to-solid inkjet plotter deposits two materials layer by layer	Cutting slices with cutter of plotter and manually position the sheets layer by layer
Software interface	Allegro Software and TCP/IP socket	AutoGen Software and TCP/IP socket	ModelWorks (operates with SLC, STL, AutoCAD DXF, HPGL, and OBJ files)	Imports STL
Layer thickness	—	—	0.013 ~ 0.13 (mm)	0.1 ~ 0.3 (mm)
Accuracy/ precision	–/300 DPI	0.356 mm/0.33 mm	0.025 mm (x, y) 0.013 (z)	No particular level of accuracy is guaranteed.
Material supply	Cartridge holding thermopolymer material (fragile plastic polymer)	Cassettes holding wafers of plastic polymer (durable plastic polymer)	Thermoplastic beads and wax beads separately poured into the reservoir become molten thermoplastic and wax	Paper
Size	1370 × 760 × 1120 (mm)	914 × 737 × 813 (mm)	685 × 381 × 685 (mm)	Approximately 610 × 1220 (mm) area
Weight	415 (kg)	84 (kg)	40.8 (kg)	

Figure 12.10

Multijet modeling (MJM) technique in Actua 2100 from 3D Systems schematic (a) Illustration of MJM mechanism (b) Illustration of part construction (Courtesy of 3D Systems, Inc.)

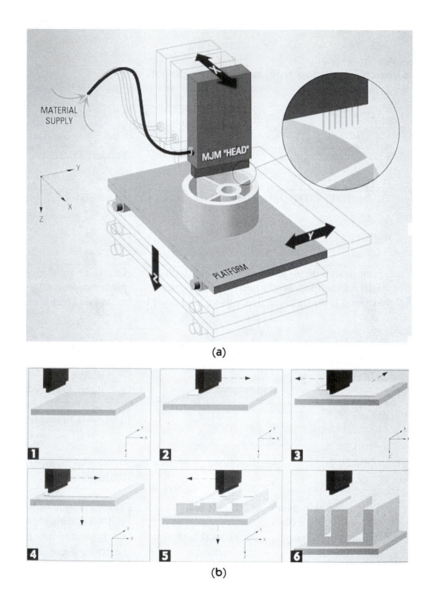

(a)

(b)

12.3   APPLICATIONS OF RP&M

The RP&M application to be used is determined by the feasible accuracy of the resulting part and the mechanical properties of the material being used, such as elongation, hardness, and tensile strength. Applications can be subdivided into three main areas:

• prototypes for design evaluation,

- prototypes for function verification, and
- models for further manufacturing processes.

When RP&M processes were first introduced, they were mainly used to visualize a designed object or to bridge the communication gap by providing actual full-size physical models that could be touched and held. This capability revolutionized the design review meeting: The constructive dialogue among members of the design team, as they passed the models to one another, suddenly allowed everyone to express concerns and suggestions with a common level of visual understanding. In some cases, this support for the designers by itself provided the main justification for investment in RP&M machines. Now the broad extension of RP&M processes into manufacturing has become the driving force for their further development.

12.3.1 Prototype for Design Evaluation

Current solid modeling systems facilitate the evaluation of a design by providing such functions as viewing, shadowing, rotating, and magnifying. However, there is no doubt that design evaluation is better when the designer can touch and hold a physical prototype of a design. No matter how experienced someone may be at reading blueprints or CAD images of a complex object, visualizing exactly what the actual part will look like is still very difficult. Features such as blind holes, complex interior passageways, and compound curved surfaces often lead to interpretation difficulties. The reduction of errors through improved part visualization can be substantial. There is no better way to be certain that a complex part contains exactly those features intended than to hold it, turn it around a few times, and look at it from all sides. In particular, aesthetic design requires a physical object for evaluation.

12.3.2 Prototype for Function Verification

Once a design has been completed, the designer has to verify that it satisfies the functions that were originally intended. Simple functional verification may include checking the practicality of assembly, kinematic performance, and aerodynamic performance.

It is often necessary to verify that a product can be assembled easily from its components or taken apart easily for maintenance. Frequently, a product can be assembled only with great difficulty or cannot even be assembled. For simple assemblies, the possibility or ease of assembly may be checked from the layout drawing. However, common practice is to perform the actual assembly in order to check it. In this case, the prototypes generated by RP&M processes are very useful because the components made of different materials are adequate enough for the assembling task. Using prototypes instead of real components results in significant savings in time and cost.

Kinematic performance verification tests whether the moving parts in an assembly function as intended. Part motion is often hindered by the unexpected interference of other components in the assembly. In fact, the failure of some components to move as intended because the motion of one component causes a collision with other components can be detected only by testing a physical prototype assembly. Because kinematic performance can be verified without components having the strength required of the final product, prototypes obtained from RP&M processes again are very useful.

A prototype made by an RP&M process can also be used to verify aerodynamic performance in a wind tunnel experiment. The geometric shape of a part plays the primary role in determining the part's aerodynamic performance, and thus a prototype made of a different material is sufficient. However, verification of other characteristics such as strength, operational temperature limits, fatigue, and corrosion resistance require that prototypes be made of the same material used in the original design. Unfortunately, because of restrictions on the materials that can be used, current RP&M processes cannot generate prototypes from many of the materials specified by designers. However, prototypes from RP&M processes can be used as the patterns for other fabrication processes, which we describe in the following section. At present, a number of techniques have been used successfully to go from an RP&M prototype to a real functional part in a relatively rapid and cost-effective manner.

For example, a significant advantage is provided by the combination of pattern-making and casting. In this case, the pattern and the cores for the casting process are made by an RP&M system and are used in the same way that the wood pattern and conventional cores are used. In connection with cutting operations, models can be used for copying. Another important application is in coating procedures. In particular, the coating of copper parts to manufacture cathodes for EDM procedures is becoming popular. The following are fabrication techniques in which RP&M prototypes can be used as a pattern [Jacobs 1992].

- Silicone room temperature vulcanizing (RTV) molding
- Vacuum casting
- Form block casting
- Spray metal molding (Tafa process)
- Resin transfer molding
- Sand casting of aluminum and ferrous metals
- Investment casting
- Abrading die EDM tools (Hauserman process)

The technique that will be most cost-effective depends on the size and geometry of the prototype, the type of the material of the functional component, the required accuracy, and the number of components to be fabricated.

12.3.3 Rapid Tooling Processes

Rapid tooling (RT) is a new term that hasn't been clearly defined. It originally was used only in connection with rapid prototyping but has since been used to describe anything that leads to making tools available quickly. This includes machining processes such as high-speed cutting (HSC) and RP&M processes.

In terms of RP&M processes, RT comprises four distinct types of methods based on the number of pattern reversals: direct tooling, single-reverse tooling, double-reverse tooling, and triple-reverse tooling. As the number of reversals increases, the durability of a product can be improved but the product cost increases and the precision decreases.

Direct tooling methods　Tools are generated directly by rapid prototyping in direct tooling. 3D Systems' ACES injection Molding (Direct AIM™), DTM's RapidTool™ process, Soliform, and direct shell production casting (DSPC) all are direct tooling methods.

In the Direct AIM process, core and cavity inserts for an injection mold are made by a stereo lithography process, using an SL photopolymer with a glass transition temperature of only 75 °C. ACES, which we discuss later, is a building technique developed by 3D Systems. Figure 12.11 shows an AIM core insert on the left and an AIM cavity insert on the right that were built by Xerox in the ACES style, using Cibatool™ resin SL5170. These inserts are assembled into the core and cavity plate of the mold base. Xerox was able to build 100 injection mold parts of the preferred material in five days. Two polystyrene switch actuators (one with the sprue still attached) are shown in the foreground [Jacobs 1996a].

DTM's RapidTool process uses a ferrous alloy with a low carbon content in particles of size 50 μm that are coated with polymer. The polymer layer of this powder is melted in a laser sintering machine. The green part created in this way is then infiltrated with a water-soluble polymer binding agent. Infiltration is obtained by dipping the green part to a depth of approximately 0.5 mm in the polymer bath. Due to capillary action, components with heights of up to 100 mm are completely infiltrated in half an hour. In this state, the components possess very little dimensional stability and must therefore be handled with great care. The infiltrated green part is dried in a vacuum oven at 50 °C in a nitrogen atmosphere.

The last step of the process involves use of the sintering furnace. First, the reinforced green part is weighed, and the result is used to determine the amount of copper alloy needed for infiltrating the part. The reinforced green part and copper alloy are placed in a graphite crucible. To begin the sintering oven process, the

Figure 12.11

Direct AIM core and cavity insert with finished part (Courtesy of 3D Systems, Inc.)

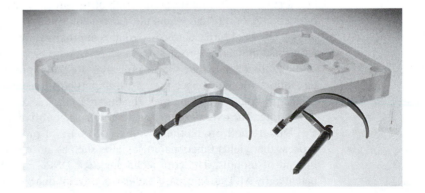

Figure 12.12

DTM's RapidTool™ process for injection molding (Courtesy of DTM Corporation.)

1 Mold Design

CAD Workstation with 3D Software for Part and Mold Design

2 The DTM™ RapidTool™ Process

Sinterstation® 2000 System

3 Infiltration and Furnace Treatment

Polymer Infiltration and Drying Oven

Green Part

Controlled-Atmosphere Furnce

Infiltration of Copper

Debinding   Fully-Dense Part

4 Injection Molding

Polish and integrate with moldbase

50,000+ Finished Parts

Injection Molding Machine

polymer binding agent is expelled in two stages. Then the part is heated to a temperature at which the iron powder begins to melt and connecting necks begin to form between the individual steel particles.

As the iron powder has not melted completely, porosity remains high. The furnace temperature is increased further, and the copper alloy that was added to the graphite crucible then melts and infiltrates the component through capillary action. After cooling to room temperature, the tool component can be removed from the furnace. The fully dense component is 60% steel and 40% copper. The overall procedure is illustrated in Figure 12.12. The time required to make the green part depends primarily on its size, not its complexity. For a base area of 180 mm × 150 mm and a height of 50 mm, laser sintering of the green part requires approximately 24 hours. Polymer infiltration and the subsequent drying process take approximately 48 hours. The final furnace process requires approximately an additional 48 hours. The entire manufacturing process thus takes five days, which is relatively independent of the tool's complexity. All the processes are accomplished without any human intervention; for the furnace processes, in particular, redundant functions or relevant safety programs are available. For this reason, weekends can be included in the scheduling. The overall setup time required is about five hours [Breitinger 1997].

Direct shell production casting (DSPC) is a proprietary patternless casting process that yields functional metal parts such as automotive cylinder heads in days instead of months. The core technology for DSPC is 3D printing—invented and patented by MIT and licensed exclusively to Soligen. The CAD file of the designed part is transferred via network or diskette to the shell design unit (SDU) of the DSPC system. The SDU operator then designs the ceramic mold for casting the metal part by adding the gating system to the part geometry and by converting the updated file into a cavity file in CAD space. This is a one-time process, after which many identical ceramic molds can be generated. The cavity file for the ceramic mold is then used to generate automatically the ceramic casting mold. The ceramic mold is created in layers, and the fabrication process involves three steps per layer. First, the ceramic shell model is "sliced" to yield a cross section of the ceramic mold. Second, a layer of fine powder is spread by a roller mechanism. Third, a multijet print head moves across the section, depositing binder in regions corresponding to the cross section of the mold. The binder penetrates the pores between the powder particles and forms them into a rigid structure. Once a given layer has been completed, the ceramic shell model is sectioned again, at a slightly higher position, and the process is repeated until all layers of the mold are concretized. The DSPC mold is then cleaned of excess powder, fired, and poured with molten metal. A DSPC mold may contain an integral ceramic core, producing a hollow metal part. Virtually any molten metal can be cast in DSPC molds. Automotive parts of aluminum, magnesium, ductile iron, and stainless steel have been manufactured. Figure 12.13 illustrates the DSPC process.

Single-reverse methods   *Single-reverse methods* are used to convert different RP patterns directly into castings with other materials. Investment casting, sand casting, spray metal molding, and silicon RTV rubber molding are single-reverse methods. Figure 12.14 illustrates the single-reverse tooling process.

Investment casting, often referred to as lost wax casting, is a precision casting process used to fabricate metal parts from almost any alloy. Although it was used largely in the production of art in the past, investment casting is now most commonly used in the production of components requiring complex, tightly toleranced, often thin-section castings of high quality. Unlike sand casting where a single pattern can be used to produce a large number of molds, a new pattern is required for every investment casting. These patterns, typically produced in injection molding machines, are made from wax specifically formulated for this use. Once a wax pattern has been produced, it is assembled with other wax components to form a metal delivery system, called the *gate and runner system*. The entire wax assembly is then subsequently dipped in a ceramic slurry, covered with a sand stucco coat, and allowed to dry. Multiple dipping and stuccoing processes are repeated until a shell of approximately 6.35–9.5 mm thick has been applied. After the ceramic has dried, the entire assembly is placed in a steam autoclave to remove most of the wax. After autoclaving, the remaining wax that had soaked into the ceramic shell is burned out in an air furnace. At this point the shell is empty. It is then usually preheated to a specific temperature and filled with molten metal. The hot mold assists with the filling of intricate shapes and thin sections. Once the casting has cooled sufficiently, the shell is chipped from the mold, and the desired casting is cut from the gates and runners. Thus the process requires that a pattern be created and destroyed for each metal casting produced.

Figure 12.13

Direct shell production casting (DSPC) process

Step 1. The part is designed on CAD software and exported in STL format

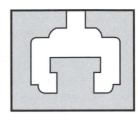

Step 2. Soligen's software designs the casting mold and "slices" it into layers.

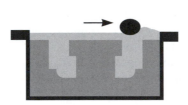

Step 3. A thin layer of powder is deposited for each layer of the casting mold or "shell."

Step 4. An ink-jet print head deposits binder that solidifies the powder into ceramic.

Step 5. The process is repeated until all layers of the shell have been formed.

Step 6. Loose powder is removed from the completed shell.

Step 7. The shell is fired and filled with molten metal.

Step 8. The shell is broken away from the part. The part is finished and shipped.

Figure 12.14

Single-reverse tooling process

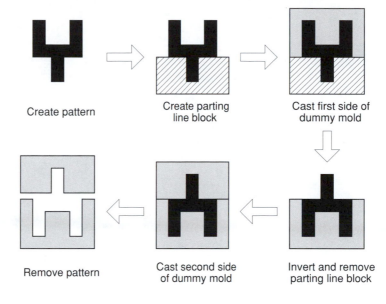

Create pattern

Create parting line block

Cast first side of dummy mold

Remove pattern

Cast second side of dummy mold

Invert and remove parting line block

Figure 12.15

Investment casting process: (a) traditional method and (b) using an RP&M part

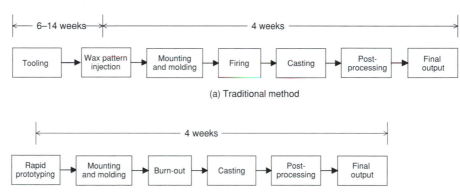

← 6–14 weeks → ← 4 weeks →

Tooling → Wax pattern injection → Mounting and molding → Firing → Casting → Post-processing → Final output

(a) Traditional method

← 4 weeks →

Rapid prototyping → Mounting and molding → Burn-out → Casting → Post-processing → Final output

(b) RP investment casting method

The traditional method of investment casting with injection molding is depicted in Figure 12.15(a). Rapid prototyping saves time by eliminating the need to manufacture the injection mold. The investment casting process involving the use of an RP&M part is presented in Figure 12.15(b). Table 12.3 compares various processes for RP&M casting.

Sand casting is used to produce metal components when high surface finish is not critical. It is a high-volume production technology that requires stable foundry patterns, cores, and core boxes. The LOM process is especially well suited for the creation of the often large, bulky patterns and cores used in sand casting. When as many as 100 components are needed, LOM parts can be finished, sealed, painted

T A B L E   1 2 . 3

Comparison of different RP&M processes for RP&M casting (Courtesy of Cercast Group, Montreal, Canada)

Vender	3D Systems	3D Systems	DTM	DTM	Helisys	Statasys	Sanders Prototype
System Process	SLA	QuickCast* SLA	SLS, WAX	SLS, Poly-Carbonate	LOM	FDM	Model-Maker (Ink-Jet)
Compatibility	low	fair to good	excellent	good	fair to good	good to excellent	excellent
Pattern accuracy in XY	excellent	excellent	fair	good	good	fair to good	superior
Pattern accuracy in Z	poor	poor	fair	good	good	fair to good	superior
Thermal expansion prior to burn-out	high	high	negligible	moderate to low	low	negligible	negligible
Melt-out burn-out time	long	moderate fast	fast	fast	long	fast	fast
Residue after melt-out burn-out	moderate to high	low	none	low	high	none	none
Surface finish	good	good	poor	fair	fair	poor	superior

* QuickCast is explained in Section 12.4.4.

Figure 12.16

Pattern for sand casting (Courtesy of Helisys, Inc.)

and used directly to create impressions in the sand. Figure 12.16 shows a prototype made by LOM to be used as a pattern for sand casting.

Spray metal molding is used to create tooling for low-volume prototype injection molding. An RP&M pattern is mounted on a wood or metal base, and parting lines are created. Generally, the model is split into two halves (unless it was originally created in a cope and drag form) by a partition made of wood or clay. It is then coated with a thin, high-temperature barrier such as stove paint and a release agent such as polyvinyl alcohol (PVA). Next, metal spray is applied to one half of the RP&M master. After spraying, the shell is framed, which establishes an outer boundary into which epoxy is poured. Within the frame's boundaries, cooling lines are strategically placed along the shell to ensure that it remains at the proper temperature to avoid cracking. The shell is backed with epoxy fill, after which the entire apparatus is turned over and the parting board is removed. At this point, only half the tool is complete. The same process must be applied to the unfinished side of the model. Once completed, the two halves are split at the parting line and the RP&M master is removed to create a two-part mold. The resultant tooling is capable of producing up to 1000 injection molded parts, making LOM ideal for this application. Almost all the thermoplastic materials can be used with this tool. Figure 12.17 illustrates the process of spray metal molding, using an RP&M model.

Silicon room-temperature vulcanizing (RTV) rubber molding is a quick and inexpensive process used to create plastic components. This process utilizes a master in the "positive" form of the final part. A sprue is attached to the master (typically with superglue), the sprue and master are cleaned with isopropyl alcohol, using a lint-free rag, and both the master and attached sprue are then carefully suspended in a clean corrugated paper box. The silicone RTV material is poured into the box, fully surrounding the RP&M master. Then the box, the uncured RTV, the master, and the attached sprue assembly are all placed in a vacuum chamber and degassed at room temperature. This step is taken to avoid trapped air bubbles that could cause mold surface defects if they happened to occur at the interface between the RP&M master and the RTV material. After the RTV has been properly degassed (for about five minutes), the box/RTV/

Figure 12.17

Process of spray metal molding, using an RP&M model

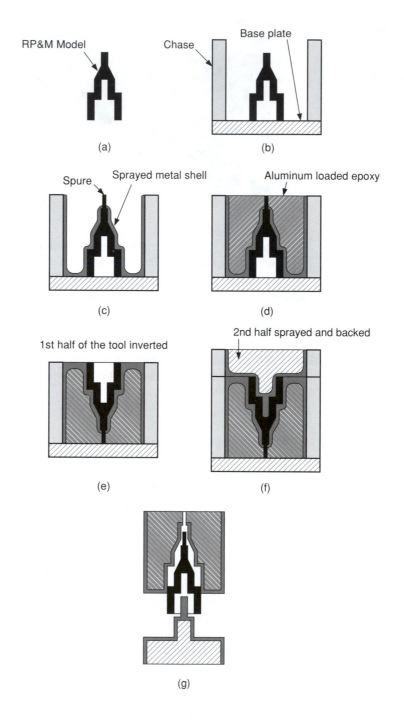

(a)

(b)

(c)

(d)

(e)

(f)

(g)

Figure 12.18

SL Pattern (lower left), RTV mold halves (top), and three polyurethane casting of a boom box housing (Courtesy of 3D Systems, Inc.)

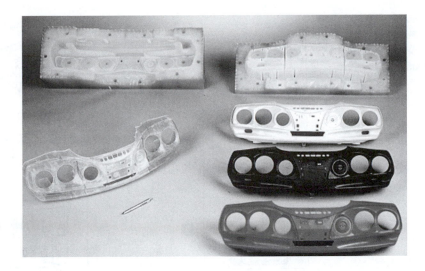

master/sprue assembly is placed in a temperature controlled oven and cured at 50 °C for about four hours.

The RTV curing process is exothermic, so the mold should be slowly cooled to room temperature (over an hour or so) to minimize distortion. The RTV is then removed form the box, and the mold is subsequently cut with a scalpel to form the parting surface. Experience has shown that it is actually better to produce a cut that is intentionally "wavy" near the outside of the mold but considerably smoother near the master. As a result, the positive and negative undulations of each half of the RTV mold can be accurately registered with respect to each other, as shown in Figure 12.18. Figure 12.19 illustrates the silicon RTV rubber molding procedure.

At this point, any of a wide range of polyurethane resins can be vacuum poured into the RTV mold. Many resins have been specifically formulated for vacuum casting and provide a range of properties such as hardness, flexural strength, flexural modulus, tensile strength, tensile modulus, elongation to break, and notched Izod impact resistance [Jacobs 1996a].

Double reverse method   If thousands of components are needed, cores and cavities can be converted to hard plastic patterns by a rubber molding process or to aluminum or steel patterns by the investment casting process. This double-reverse method emerged to overcome the disadvantages of direct tooling methods and single-reverse methods, such as the lack of durability. Figure 12.20 shows the double-reverse tooling method.

Triple reverse method   In the triple method, a mold pattern produced by single-reverse tooling (Figure 12.21a) is converted into a casting mold (Figure 12.21b). Plaster mold casting and 3D Keltool™ from 3D Systems can be categorized as triple-reverse tooling.

Plaster mold casting is used to manufacture highly complex aluminum components that require a higher surface finish than sand casting can provide. Plaster cast-

Figure 12.19

Silicon RTV rubber molding procedure

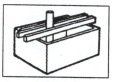 **1** RP master

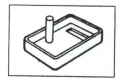 **2** Mold frame

 **3** Weighing and agitating silicone rubber

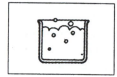 **4** Degassing silicone rubber

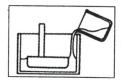 **5** Pouring silicone rubber

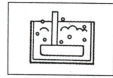 **6** Degassing mold assembly

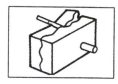 **7** Cutting parting-surface

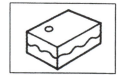 **8** Completed silicone rubber mold

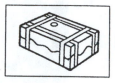 **9** Assemble silicone rubber mold

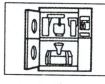 **10** Weighing polymer

 **11** Degassing polymer

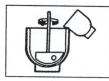 **12** Mixing and agitating polymer and hardener

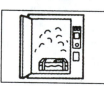 **13** Pouring polymer

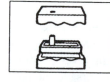 **14** Vulcanizing in oven

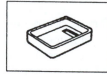 **15** Demolding

16 Finishing

Figure 12.20

Double-reverse tooling method

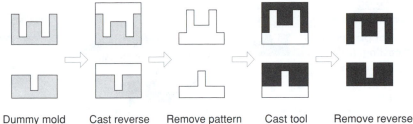

Dummy mold   Cast reverse   Remove pattern   Cast tool   Remove reverse

Figure 12.21

Triple reverse method: (a) single-reverse to create dummy molds and (b) double reverse to create tooling

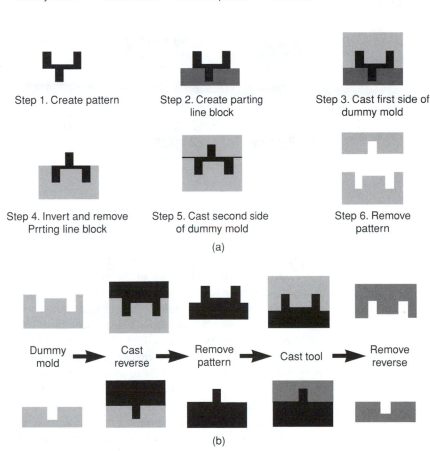

Step 1. Create pattern

Step 2. Create parting line block

Step 3. Cast first side of dummy mold

Step 4. Invert and remove Prrting line block

Step 5. Cast second side of dummy mold

Step 6. Remove pattern

(a)

Dummy mold → Cast reverse → Remove pattern → Cast tool → Remove reverse

(b)

ing is perfect for components whose surface finish must closely simulate that of die cast parts. In this process, an RP&M part is first duplicated as a flexible rubber pattern, which in turn is used to make expendable plaster molds into which molten metal can be poured. Flexible rubber is used because it can easily be removed from the relatively fragile plaster molds.

The first step in plaster mold casting is to build rubber, epoxy, or polyurethane molds by using the RP&M part as a pattern, as shown in Figure 12.22(a). This process is similar to that used to create silicone rubber molds used for epoxy cast-

Figure 12.22

Process of plaster mold casting: (a) step I; (b) step II (Source: Rapid Prototyping Report, Vol. 5, No. 1, CAD/CAM Publishing, Inc., January, 1995)

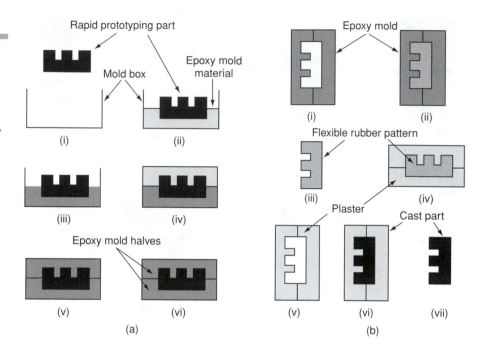

ing. First, the RP&M part is set up in a mold box. Then the liquid molding material is poured around the part, up to a designed parting line, and allowed to harden. When this half of the mold has cured, the parting surface is treated with a mold release agent, and the second half of the mold is poured and cured. For parts without a clearly definable parting line, multiple mold sections can be made. This first mold is used to make a flexible rubber pattern that is then set up in a mold box, and in a similar process, foamed plaster is poured around it. Once the plaster mold halves have set, they can be separated and the rubber pattern easily removed without breaking the plaster. After the rubber pattern has been removed, the plaster mold halves are dried in an oven for 24 to 48 hours to fully harden them.

When the plaster molds are completely dry, the halves are reassembled and filled with molten aluminum, magnesium, or zinc, as shown in Figure 12.22(b). After the metal has cooled, the plaster molds are broken off or washed away with a high-pressure stream of water. The rubber patterns usually are capable of producing 25–100 plaster molds. If additional rubber patterns are needed, they can be recast in the original epoxy tooling.

3D Keltool uses a proprietary sintered metal process to produce core and cavity tooling sets directly from an SL master. After processing, 3D Keltool molds offer tool lives (cavities and cores have a Rockwell Hardness of up to 50) similar to those of standard steel molds and actually have better heat conductivity for lower cycle times.

Once the master has been properly finished, it is ready for the 3D Keltool process. At this point, the master can be either in the form of a "positive" or a "negative," as shown in Figure 12.23. The primary advantage of positive geometry mas-

Figure 12.23

Two different routes to powder metal inserts, using the 3D Keltool process (Courtesy of 3D Systems, Inc.)

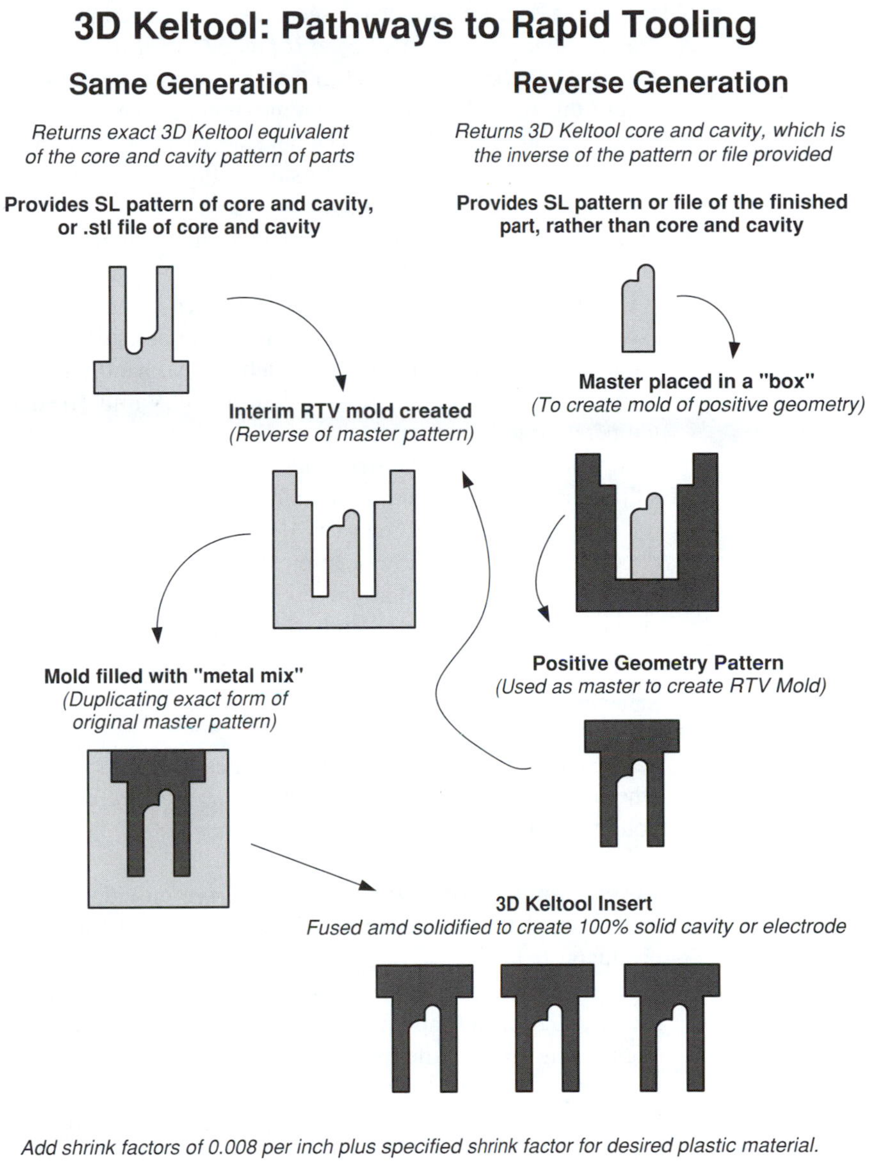

3D Keltool: Pathways to Rapid Tooling

Same Generation	Reverse Generation
Returns exact 3D Keltool equivalent of the core and cavity pattern of parts	*Returns 3D Keltool core and cavity, which is the inverse of the pattern or file provided*
Provides SL pattern of core and cavity, or .stl file of core and cavity	**Provides SL pattern or file of the finished part, rather than core and cavity**

Master placed in a "box"
(To create mold of positive geometry)

Interim RTV mold created
(Reverse of master pattern)

Mold filled with "metal mix"
(Duplicating exact form of original master pattern)

Positive Geometry Pattern
(Used as master to create RTV Mold)

3D Keltool Insert
Fused amd solidified to create 100% solid cavity or electrode

Add shrink factors of 0.008 per inch plus specified shrink factor for desired plastic material.

ters is that they are much easier to sand and polish. These positive masters used in a *reverse generation* (relative to tooling) process look very much like the final injection molded part, except for shrinkage compensation and properties of the material. The negative geometry masters used in *same generation* processes look very much like the final core and cavity inserts, again except for shrinkage compensation and properties of the material.

For the case of a properly finished SL positive master (first step on the right-hand side of Figure 12.23), the first extra step of the 3D Keltool process involves forming a "master-in-a-box" (second step on the right-hand side of Figure 12.23). Next, vacuum degassed silicone is poured to fill the box. Subsequent to curing the RTV rubber, the positive master and the silicone are removed from the box. The result of this second extra step is an interim negative geometry mold made of silicone (third step in Figure 12.23). The next step involves making an RTV "positive-in-a-box" final silicone mold (fourth step in Figure 12.23). At this point the mold is a virtual duplicate of the original positive master, except that it is now in the form of an RTV "positive-in-a-box." A patented mix of metal particles (e.g., A6 tool steel and a proprietary binder material) is thoroughly mixed and then poured into the RTV "positive-in-a-box" mold, and allowed to cure (fifth step in Figure 12.23). After curing, the result is a green part, which has sufficient strength to maintain accurately its geometric features through normal handling. The green part is then removed from the RTV "positive-in-a-box," and fired at a sufficiently high temperature to fuse the metal particles and eliminate the binder. Finally, the fused part, which is about 70% steel and 30% void, is infiltrated with copper. The end result is a mold cavity that is essentially 100% solid (sixth step in Figure 12.23).

For neat plastic, as many as 10 million injection-molded parts have been produced from a single Keltool insert. Currently, 3D Keltool inserts are restricted in size to about 150 mm in all directions, which limits the part to a maximum dimension of about 100 mm. Research to extend these dimensions is currently under way.

12.3.4   Special Application Examples

As the technology matures, RP&M applications are likely to be extended into many other areas. Some of the latest applications are reverse engineering, flow visualization, photoelastic testing, and medical models.

Reverse engineering   *Reverse engineering* provides a means by which three-dimensional data can be captured in computerized form from physical models or products. It has obvious attributes in terms of shortening the design-to-market process and effective use in conjunction with other time-compression technologies, such as RP&M and rapid replication processes. There are two phases in the reverse engineering process: the digitizing or measuring of a part and the three-dimensional modeling of the part from the digitized data. Once the surfaces have been derived from the digitized data, they are processed into a solid model, which is needed to export the STL file. As explained in Section 12.4.1, the STL file is a standard input data to any RP&M process. Once the STL file has been transferred to an RP&M machine, the replica of the scanned model can be produced. Figure 12.24 shows the general steps involved in using reverse engineering in the RP&M process.

Figure 12.24

Reverse engineering in RP&M

Flow visualization   Because of thermodynamic efficiency and endurance requirements, high-performance combustion engines require a constant flow of coolant through all the cylinders. In highly stressed areas of the cylinder head and crank case in particular, extensive testing is necessary to detect any sections insufficiently supplied with coolant. The thermodynamic consequences of uneven coolant distribution are slow burning of the fuel–air mixture and increased hydrocarbon emissions from "cold" cylinders, as well as "knocking" problems from "hot" cylinders. Coolant distribution issues are becoming increasingly important because of environmental restrictions on automotive emission.

Existing methods of coolant testing generally involve experiments on a test bench, which utilize cast components. Unfortunately, the tooling and molds necessary for these castings are often available only at a very late stage of the project. Furthermore, various adaptations required for testing, such as runners for sensors and cutouts for optical systems, may incorrectly reflect the behavior of the real configuration in an operational engine.

RP&M can be an effective alternative approach to coolant testing. RP&M enables time-saving and cost-effective generation of transparent models to investigate the flow behavior of complete cooling systems in a combustion engine. Compared to previous methods, not only are the economic advantages considerable, but the quality of the result is also improved. Additional information can be provided through visualization of the coolant flow pattern. This is accomplished by careful injection of very tiny air bubbles and then recording their motion with a high-speed video camera. Figure 12.25 shows a transparent transmission housing produced by SLA to permit observation of the flow of lubricating oil.

Photoelastic testing   The stress and strain in a physical component can be determined, under the correct conditions, through the use of *photoelastic testing*. This method is based on the temporary birefringence of a transparent material subjected to a specific load. A number of plastic materials exhibit birefringence, a characteristic that can be illustrated by irradiating the test sample with polarized white or monochromatic light. Birefringence separates a single incident beam of polarized

Figure 12.25

SLA part of a transparent transmission housing for a Porsche (Source: Rapid Prototyping Report, Vol. 6, No. 6, CAD/CAM Publishing, Inc., June, 1996)

light into two beams oscillating perpendicular to one another. If the test material is transparent and exhibits adequate birefringence, the directions of the twin-refracted beams correspond to the directions of the principal stresses. Birefringence effects disappear when the load is removed. Fortunately, an RP&M part produced by SLA with epoxy resins (e.g., SL 5170 and LMB 5353-1 from Ciba-Geigy), is highly transparent and similar to test samples made from Araldite resin, which is commonly used for photoelastic testing. Various commercial suppliers such as Ciba-Geigy, Allied Signal, and DuPont have tested literally thousands of candidate resin formulations. To date, only about 20 resins have been commercialized for stereo lithography. This low acceptance rate is evidence of the difficulty of simultaneously achieving all of the properties required for photoelastic testing: optical birefringence, optical transparency, fringe order proportional to the applied force, and an invariant photoelastic coefficient [Jacobs 1996b].

Medical models   The linking of scanning technology from the field of medicine and RP&M technology from engineering now allows anatomical image data to be viewed in a completely different manner from that previously possible. Different RP&M parts of the human anatomy can be produced from computed tomography (CT) and magnetic resonance imaging (MRI) data. Several commercial software products can convert the image data to an STL file. The RP&M parts of the human organ or bone produced with RP&M machines can be used in the following ways.

• As a tool for operative planning. Surgeons can use an RP&M model to improve their understanding of abnormal anatomy so that they can more effectively plan even the most complex surgical procedures.

• As a tool for surgical simulation of complex reconstructive procedures. Surgical procedures can now be realistically simulated with RP&M models as proxies for surgical sites. RP&M parts are made from a material having properties similar to those of bone, so surgeons can rehearse their surgical plan using the same instruments they would use in the operating theater. RP&M parts can also be sterilized for use during surgery as a real-time reference. This means more precise surgery and less operating time.

• As a communication tool for discussion between surgeon and patient and with other surgeons, surgical staff, and legal personnel.

• As a historical record of abnormal patient anatomy for later discussions and comparisons.

• As a master model for customized implant fabrication.

Figure 12.26 shows an example of a tool for rehearsal of a surgical procedure. A two-year-old boy suffering from a giant frontal encephlocele was given a CT scan, and two biomodels of his skull were produced, with a third "mirrored" across from his left side. The surgeon used two of the biomodels as guides, and rehearsed his surgical plan on the third. The result was intimate and exact advance knowledge of the required resections, resulting in reduced operating time and an enhanced surgical outcome.

Figure 12.26

Medical RP&M model for rehearsal of a surgical procedure (Courtesy of ANATOMICS™, www.qmi.asn.au/anatomics, All rights reserved))

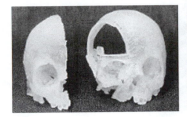

12.4 STEREO LITHOGRAPHY PROCESS

As briefly explained in Section 12.2.1, stereo lithography is a three-dimensional printing process that produces copies of geometric models in plastic. The process uses a moving laser beam directed by a computer to print or draw cross sections of the model onto the surface of a photo-curable liquid plastic. The solidification procedure is realized with a helium–cadmium or argon laser, in a layer-by-layer illumination from bottom to top. This means that the vertical elevator in the vat is controlled, step by step, from top to bottom (see Figure 12.1).

The SLA-1, the first commercial rapid prototyping machine designed at 3D Systems, was publicly introduced at the AUTOFACT show in Detroit in November 1987. The first production SLA-1 was delivered to Precision Castparts Corporation in Oregon in April 1988. The SLA-250, similar to the SLA-1 but with an upgraded resin recoating system, was announced in 1989. The SLA-5000, a larger and faster machine, became available in 1990. Its working volume is 508 mm × 508 mm × 584 mm, which is about eight times greater than that of the SLA-250 (250 mm × 250 mm × 250 mm).

In the following sections, we describe the operations performed by an SLA as it generates a prototype.

12.4.1 Geometry Input

The first step in the stereo lithography process, which is virtually identical in all the RP&M processes, is the generation of a three-dimensional geometric model of a part to be fabricated. This geometric model should be a solid model or a surface model at least. Thus a proper solid modeling system or surface modeling system is a prerequisite to using the SLA or other RP&M processes.

Usually, the geometric model of a three-dimensional object is stored in various formats, depending on the solid or the surface modeling system used. Thus SLA or other RP&M devices are designed to accept the model data in one fixed format called the *STL format*. The STL file format (files with an .stl extension) was established by 3D Systems in 1987 after development by the Albert Consulting Group.

An STL file represents an object as a mesh of connected triangles. An object represented by a mesh of triangles is called a *tessellated object* or a faceted object.

Figure 12.27

Cellular phone models: (a) original solid model and (b) tessellated model

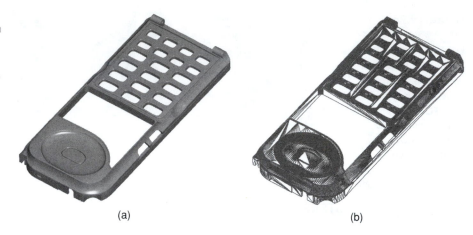

(a)   (b)

Figure 12.27(a) shows the solid model and Figure 12.27(b) shows a tessellated model of the cellular phone from Chapter 1. In the STL file, the vertices of each triangle are listed in an order that indicates which side of the triangle contains the inside volume. The normal vector points toward the exterior of the model, as shown in Figure 12.28. Figure 12.29(a) shows an STL file in ASCII format, and Figure 12.29(b) shows an STL file in binary format. Note that the ASCII and binary versions are not fully compatible. The binary version has additional attribute information that is not used currently. The ASCII format is meant for debugging and test purposes. The advantages and disadvantages of the STL file format can be summarized as follows [Kumar 1997].

Advantages

- Easy conversion. The STL file is very simple, as it contains only a list of planar triangles. A three-dimensional model can be converted to the STL format by using the standard surface triangulation algorithms. Accuracy of the output can easily be controlled, and degeneracies that can occur are minimal.

- Wide range of input. Any form of three-dimensional geometry can be converted to a triangulated model because of the wide applicability of the available surface triangulation algorithms.

Figure 12.28

Normal direction of a facet in STL file format

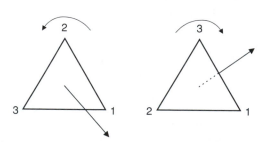

Figure 12.29

STL file formats: (a) ASCII and (b) binary

```
solid example
    facet normal 6.89114779E-02 -9.96219337E-01 -5.28978631E-02
    outer loop
        vertex 2.73239994E+01 1.08957005E+01 4.57905006E+01
        vertex 2.81019993E+01 1.09582005E+01 4.56250000E+01
        vertex 2.75955009E+01 1.09116001E+01 4.58456993E+01
    endloop
    endfacet
        :
        :
endsolid example
```

(a)

Byte	Type	Description
80	*string*	*Head information such as the CAD system used*
4	*unsigned long integer*	*Number of facets*
First Triangle Definition		
4	*float*	*normal x*
4	*float*	*normal y*
4	*float*	*normal z*
4	*float*	*vertex1 x*
4	*float*	*vertex1 y*
4	*float*	*vertex1 z*
4	*float*	*vertex2 x*
4	*float*	*vertex2 y*
4	*float*	*vertex2 z*
4	*float*	*vertex3 x*
4	*float*	*vertex3 y*
4	*float*	*vertex3 z*
2	*unsigned integer*	*Number of attributes bytes should be set to zero*
Second Triangle Definition		
		:
		:

(b)

- Simple-slicing algorithm. The algorithm for slicing an STL model is simple; it only involves processing a set of triangles.[1]
- Splitting STL models. If the workspace of the RP machine is small compared to the model size, the STL file of the model has to be split into parts to fit the workspace. This operation is easily done with STL. However, the split STL files must be individually verified for validity.

---

[1] Slicing is required to provide the cross-sectional data to an RP&M machine.

Disadvantages

- Verbosity and data redundancy. The STL file is verbose and has redundant data. The storage of the facet normal is redundant because it can be obtained from the vertex list of facets by accessing them in a specific order. Also, the coordinates of the same vertices appear several times as each vertex appears in more than one facet.

- Error due to approximation. A major problem with STL comes from its relatively poor representation of curved surfaces, which can only be approximated by the triangular facets.

- Truncation errors. Truncation errors in STL caused by floating point arithmetic are significant because of the absence of topological information about the model.

- Lack of information. The original three-dimensional model, in general, is complete and possesses useful information regarding geometry, topology, and material. By converting this information to the STL format, only the basic geometry information is stored; the other information is lost. Such information could be used in downstream processing, such as determining buildup direction and generation of support structure, or to verify the solidity of the converted model.

The disadvantages of STL files are problems intrinsic to the STL format itself. Moreover, errors can occur when a three-dimensional model is processed and converted to the STL format. Even when the original three-dimensional model has no defects, the converted STL model might have some errors, depending on the efficiency, robustness, and accuracy of the conversion algorithm. For example, the triangles may not cover the boundary faces of the original object completely. If this happens, the cross section to be generated in the next step will have an open boundary, and an incorrect prototype will result, as illustrated in Figure 12.30. A mistake in the facet approximation of the side face of the cylindrical container resulted in a gap, as indicated by the triangle in Figure 12.30(a). That caused the generation of an incorrect cross section, as shown in Figure 12.30(b). Therefore, a translator that converts a geometric model to an STL file has to be written so as not to violate any of the requirements just described.

We can set certain parameters to control the total number of the triangles in the facet approximation when we use the translator. That is, when creating an STL file of a three-dimensional model, we can control the chord height deviation between

Figure 12.30

Problem caused by a gap

(a)   (b)

Figure 12.31

Chord height of an
STL file

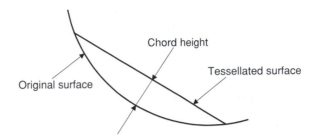

the actual model surface and the triangular facets, as shown in Figure 12.31. This value is the maximum distance that the approximated triangle can deviate from the original surface. Large STL files will result in increased slice time in cross-section generation and increased slice file size, but also in greater accuracy. They also have a negligible effect on build time.

Currently, STL files have become the de facto standard for input into all types of RP&M systems. In fact, most solid modeling systems provide the ability to output STL files. It does not require extra work by the solid modeling system because the facet representation is necessary for displaying the shaded image of the object anyway.

12.4.2 Part Orientation

The accuracy and efficiency of the stereo lithography process depend on how the object is positioned in the vat. The criteria depend on what the user wants. The user's choice of part orientation in the building chamber will have an impact on build time, part resolution, and surface finish. Obviously, minimizing the height of the geometry will reduce the number of layers required, thereby decreasing build time. Depending on the part's eventual application, the user may sacrifice a minimum build time for the benefit of increased part resolution or accuracy. Usually, part accuracy is most important, aesthetics are next in importance, and build time is somewhat less important.

Higher resolutions of curved surfaces are obtained by orienting them in the horizontal plane normal to the laser beam. Sloping surfaces that proceed along the slice axis will have a distinct stair-step appearance, as shown in Figure 12.32. The height of each step is the layer thickness used in that portion of the part. A support structure may be required, depending on the part's orientation.

Figure 12.32

Stair-stepping of a
curved surface

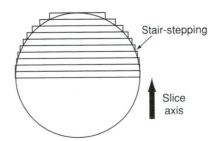

In summary, deciding which surfaces need the best finish, fitting the maximum number of parts on the platform, minimizing the number of part supports, and attaching proper supports to any cantilevered areas of the part are all considerations in optimal part orientation.

12.4.3   Support Structure

The next step is to model supports and generate their STL files. Supports in the stereo lithography process are analogous to workpiece holding devices, such as the chuck, in machining. Supports are required in stereo lithography for the following reasons. First, they ensure that the recoater blade will not strike the platform when the first (bottom) layer is swept. The recoater blade sweeps the external surface of the liquid resin to give the layer uniform thickness. Second, supports improve uniformity of layer thickness regardless of any warpage in the platform. These nonuniformities are accommodated by the layer of the supports, and thus the layer of the part has a uniform thickness. Third, they provide a simple means of removing the part from the platform upon its completion. Usually, the supports are in loose contact with the platform. To satisfy these three goals a base support should occupy at least the first 6.35 mm (0.25 inch, for the SLA-250) to 8.89 mm (0.35 inch, for the SLA-5000) above the platform [Jacobs 1992]. It also should follow the periphery of the part's bottom layer, including its corners. Supporting the entire bottom area of the part will restrain its tendency to curl as successive layers are built. However, in practice the border of the support is obtained by offsetting the periphery of the bottom layer inward by 0.254 mm (0.01 inch). This prevents part edges from being broken during support removal. A common practice is to build the base support in an "egg crate" pattern, as shown in Figure 12.33, for easy removal of the support.

Supports are also required when islands or cantilevered sections exist in the part being built. An *island* is a portion of a layer that is unconnected to any other portion of the same layer (see Figure 12.2b). In this case, the island is anchored to the platform or to the part itself by projecting the island profile downward to the platform or the previous layer of the part. Connecting to the previous layer may be preferable if the island is located many inches above the platform, because it will reduce build time. Cantilevered sections also should be supported by triangular-shaped supports called *gussets* (see Figure 12.2a). An overhang that extends beyond 1.27 mm (0.05 inch) will curl when unconstrained. Arches or convex surfaces

Figure 12.33

Generation of an egg-crate pattern for a base structure

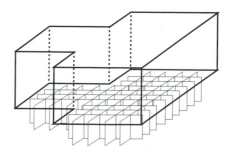

support themselves because the overhang between succeeding layers is very small, and so supports are not necessary. But if the surface is flat, down-facing areas longer than 1.27 mm (0.05 inch) must be supported (see Figure 12.2c and d).

Many solid or surface modeling systems provide an assembly mode in which the user models the supports while viewing and/or referencing the part geometry.

12.4.4 Slice and Merge

During the slice and merge stage, the part and the supports are sectioned by the computer into a series of parallel horizontal planes. The result is slice files that consist of cross sections layered one on top of another. The distance between the cross sections is the layer thickness. The layer thickness is selected by consideration of the stair-stepping effect mentioned earlier. The lower limit of the layer thickness is determined by the control resolution of the elevator while the upper limit is determined by the laser intensity and its scanning speed. In existing SLAs, the possible range of layer thickness is from 0.064 mm (0.0025 inch) to 0.762 mm (0.030 inch).

Once the slice files of the part and the supports have been generated, they are merged so that the part and the supports can be fabricated as one piece. If multiple parts are to be built concurrently on the same platform, as illustrated in Figure 12.34, the slice files of all the parts and the supports are merged so that the cross sections on the same layer are treated as the cross section of a single part.

During this stage, the necessary information for building the part, such as the intended hatch style, the desired hatch spacing, the line-width compensation value, and the shrinkage compensation factor(s) are also selected.

Hatch style and spacing *Internal hatch* is simply a method used to solidify the inside of the part, or the volume between the borders. As solidification is done by the scanning of a laser beam of a finite diameter, it is almost impossible to scan the inside completely. However, scanning the inside loosely can guarantee structural rigidity while leaving some unsolidified areas for the post-curing process. That is, the borders are drawn first and then the interior is scanned with one of the following styles. Tri-Hatch uses the scanned lines parallel to the x axis combined with lines at 60° and 120° to the x axis. This produces an internal structure of equilateral triangles. The most common spacing between these lines is 1.27 mm (0.05 inch).

Figure 12.34

Example of merging two different parts

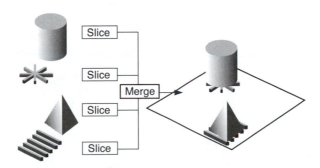

Tri-Hatch was the most widely used scanning pattern until the introduction of WEAVE, a new part-building technique developed by 3D Systems.

WEAVE normally uses hatches scanned parallel to the *x* and *y* axes. Note that the egg-crate pattern for the base support shown in Figure 12.33 can be generated by WEAVE with a large value for hatch spacing. The hatch spacing for the part portion is approximately 0.279 mm (0.011 inch, for 0.254 mm (0.010 inch) thickness) for both the *x* and *y* hatch. The spacing must be reduced when thinner layers are being built.

The advent of WEAVE improved part accuracy considerably, compared to former Tri-Hatch method. Several additional process techniques have been introduced since then. Almost all the advanced part-building processes that attempt to improve part accuracy focus on minimizing the effects of internal stress. STAR-WEAVE, QuickCast, and ACES are process techniques specifically developed to reduce distortion.

The new build style, STAR-WEAVE, a derivative of WEAVE, includes three new concepts: staggered hatch, alternate sequencing, and retracted hatch. In the term STAR-WEAVE, the ST refers to *staggered hatch*, the A to *alternate sequencing*, and the R to *retracted hatch*.

Figure 12.35 is a schematic diagram of the difference between conventional hatch and staggered hatch. In the STAR-WEAVE hatching process, because the hatch vectors in the *n*th layer are offset by exactly half the regular hatch spacing ($h_s/2$) relative to those on the $(n-1)$th layer, all evidence of microfissures vanishes. Additionally, it can reduce the stress concentrations along the relatively weaker regions between vectors.

The term *alternate sequencing* means that the drawing sequence is alternated from layer to layer. With the alternate sequencing method, the *X* and *Y* vectors will alternate in the order of the drawing sequence. Thus, for example, the *X* vectors might be drawn first on even-numbered layers, and the *Y* vectors would then be drawn first on odd-numbered layers. Furthermore, the direction of vector propagation also is alternated. Consequently, for example, on the *n*th layer, the *X* vectors might be drawn first, propagating from the front of the vat toward the back of the vat. On the $(n + 1)$th

Figure 12.35

Comparison of hatch techniques: (a) conventional hatch and (b) staggered hatch (Source: P. Jacob, Rapid Prototyping & Manufacturing; Fundamentals of Stereo Lithography, Society of Manufacturing Engineers (SME), McGraw-Hill, 1992)

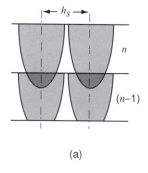

(a)

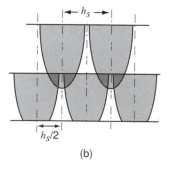

(b)

Figure 12.36

Retracted hatch (Source: P. Jacob, Rapid Prototyping & Manufacturing; Fundamentals of Stereo Lithography, Society of Manufacturing Engineers (SME), McGraw-Hill, 1992)

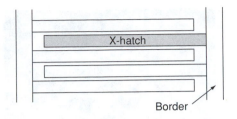

layer, the X vectors would then be drawn second (after the Y vectors), and they might then propagate from the back of the vat toward the front of the vat.

A retracted hatch scans each hatch vector, whether X or Y, so that it is attached at only one border. The other end of the hatch vector is retracted a tiny distance, typically about 0.25 mm (0.01 inch) from the adjacent border. Figure 12.36 schematically illustrates the nature of retracted hatch.

In addition to STAR-WEAVE, the QuickCast build style was designed to improve part accuracy when the SLA part functions as a master pattern in the investment casting process. After it was found that the thermal expansion of solid SL patterns cracked even the most durable shell systems, it became evident that an SL pattern had to be built with outer borders supported by an internal structure of widely spaced hatch lines. By altering the hatch pattern to allow excess resin to be removed, quasi-hollow patterns are generated that can be successfully investment-cast into a solid metal part. As the quasi-hollow structure of QuickCast patterns requires less material to be bonded between each successive layer, internal stress in the green state is reduced. Post-cure distortion is also reduced because there is less material to shrink.

To create the quasi-hollow QuickCast structure, an object must be built with large hatch spacing. Mathematically, the object must be topologically simply connected. If a drain hole is intentionally generated at any location on a topologically simply connected pattern, and a relatively small vent hole is created at a second location to relieve the partial vacuum that would otherwise be created, the uncured liquid resin can exit the pattern. Figure 12.37 shows the QuickCast hatch patterns.

The purpose of the ACES building technique is to produce accurate (A), clear (C), epoxy (E), and solid (S) parts with excellent dimensional stability, using the epoxy-based resin. This is accomplished by complete and uniform polymerization during the part-building process, virtually eliminating post-cure distortion and internal stress. To minimize the bimetallic strip effect, ACES involves the progressive curing of a layer of resin so that it is almost entirely solidified before it is bonded to the previous layer.

Line-width compensation Just as the tool center location is offset by its radius from the part boundary in the NC milling operation, the laser in an SLA must also be offset by half the line width toward the part mass to generate accurate borders. Figure 12.38(a) illustrates the absence of line-width compensation, and Figure

Figure 12.37

QuickCast hatch patterns: (a) QuickCast V1.1 uses an equilateral triangle hatch and an offset square hatch; (b) QuickCast V2.0 uses a hexagonal grid to build weaker patterns for easy burn-out in the investment casting process

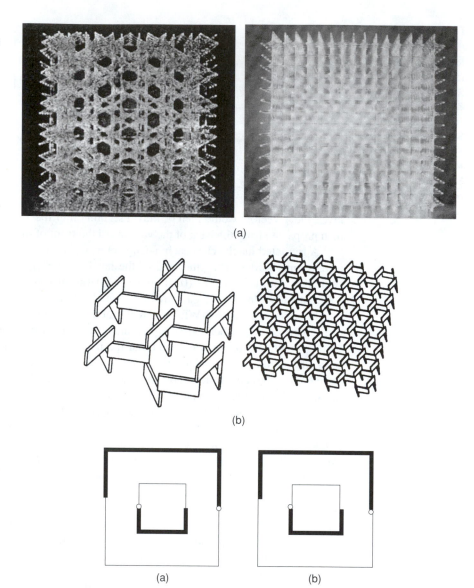

(a)

(b)

Figure 12.38

Illustration of line-width compensation

(a)   (b)

12.38(b) illustrates the presence of line-width compensation. The proper value of line-width compensation is usually determined by tests on a diagnostic part.

Shrinkage compensation factor   Polymerization leads to an increase in density of the material and thus a reduction in part volume. Thus it is necessary to enlarge the part to a certain extent to compensate for the shrinkage that occurs after solidification. The amount of enlargement is specified by the shrinkage compensation factor provided by the user. Determination of the shrinkage factor is extremely difficult, requiring careful calculation and solid experience.

12.4.5 Preparation

During the preparation step, some parameters related to part building, such as cure depths and essential recoating, are specified. The recoating parameters include the number of recoater blade sweeps per layer, the sweep period, the desired "z-wait," and the velocity and the acceleration of the elevator. We consider the cure depth in this section and the recoating parameters in the next section.

As illustrated in Figure 12.39, the cure depth is the hardening depth of the liquid polymer caused by energy absorption. The cure depth should be larger than the layer thickness. Otherwise, the successive layers will come apart. The amount of energy absorption depends on the intensity and size of the laser beam, its scanning speed, and the property of the photopolymer being used. Hence specification of the cure depth will determine the scanning speed of the laser beam for a given laser power.

12.4.6 Part Building

In this process, polymerization begins and a physical, three-dimensional part is created. This process consists of the following steps.

Step 1: Leveling. Typical SL resins undergo about 5% to 7% total volumetric shrinkage with solidification. Of this amount, roughly 50% to 70% occurs in the vat as the result of laser-induced polymerization; the remaining volumetric shrinkage occurs during the post-curing stage. This means that the free surface of the resin goes down as the polymerization proceeds, resulting in variation of its distance from the laser source. Thus the purpose of leveling is to ensure that the resin is at the proper z level for optimum laser focus.

Figure 12.39

Cure depth and layer thickness

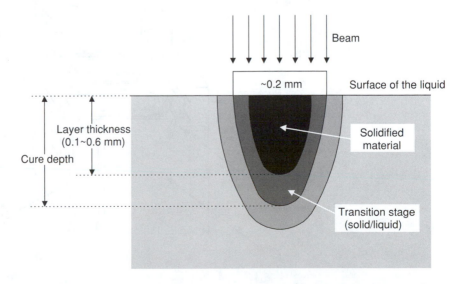

Upon completion of laser drawing on each layer, a sensor checks the resin level. If the resin level is not within the desired tolerance, a plunger is activated. The plunger motion causes fluid displacement, bringing the z coordinate of the resin surface within the specified range.

Step 2: Deep dip. The platform is lowered so that the uppermost surface of the previously cured layer lies below the resin surface. This is done to ensure that even those parts with large flat areas—comparable in size to the entire platform—can be properly recoated. This step takes about 11 seconds.

Step 3: Elevate. The platform is elevated so that the uppermost part layer lies above the resin surface and one layer thickness below the bottom edge of the re-coater blade. The recoater blade is located above the resin surface, as illustrated in Figure 12.40. This step takes about 6 seconds.

Step 4: Sweep. The recoater blade traverses the vat from front to back, or vice versa, and sweeps the excess resin from the part. The parameters specified in the preparation stage, such as the number of recoater blade sweeps per layer and the sweep period, are applied in this step. The number of sweeps ranges from 1 to 7, and the sweep period ranges from 3 to 30 seconds. The default sweep period is 5 seconds, except when trapped volumes have to be dealt with. *Trapped volumes* are spaces that hold liquid separate from the liquid in the vat. These regions may require special treatment in the recoating process and thus will slow the build rate. In this case, the sweep period may increase to 15 to 25 seconds. Note that the deep dip, elevate, and sweep processes are required only for the Doctor blade system of SLA-250/40 and the SmartStart of 3D Systems. The other SLA systems such as

Figure 12.40

Elements of the re-coating system

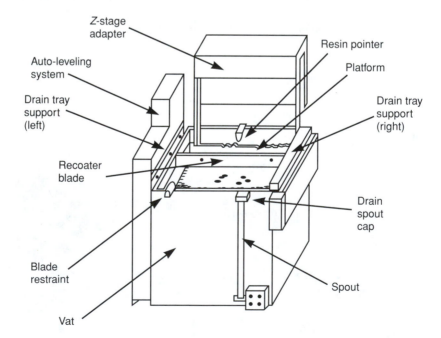

SLA-3500 and SLA-5000 utilize the 3D Systems' new Zephyr recoating process wherein the deep dip, elevate, and sweep processes are not required. The Zephyr recoating system uses a vacuum-fed blade to pick up resin from the vat and apply a thin layer of resin as the blade sweeps across the part. The Zephyr recoater greatly reduces the recoating time and speeds overall part building. It also reduces the problems caused by trapped volume. Figure 12.41 shows the process involved in the Zephyr recoating system.

Step 5: Move to build position. The platform is lowered so that the top of the layer of recoated resin is at the free surface level of the resin in the vat. Thus the top of the previous cured layer is below the free surface by one layer thickness. This step takes about 2 seconds.

Step 6: *z*-wait. Once the platform has moved to the build position, in principle the resin on top of the previous layer should blend seamlessly with the free surface of the resin in the vat. Unfortunately, due to finite surface tension effects, a small but distinct crease commonly appears at the solid–liquid interface around the perimeter of the part. The amplitude of the crease will decay with a finite relaxation time. The *z*-wait interval is intended to give the fluid surface adequate time to eliminate these nonuniformities. It ranges from 15 to 30 seconds.

Step 7: Laser drawing. When a planar photopolymer resin surface is established, laser drawing of each profile is started. The first step is to draw the part borders for the given cross section. Based on the preselected desired cure depth, the correct laser scanning speed is calculated automatically. Drawing the borders takes only a few seconds. Once the borders have been drawn, hatching of the inside is started. For most parts, the great majority of laser drawing time is spent in hatching. For profiles of all up-facing and down-facing surfaces, a scanning mode called *skin fills* is applied instead of hatching. In skin-fills mode, a series of very closely spaced parallel vectors is drawn so that the cured lines actually contact one another laterally to form a continuous skin. This arrangement prevents the unintentional draining of resin from interior portions of the part. However, resin drainage is no longer a problem with the advanced hatching styles provided by WEAVE, STAR-WEAVE, QuickCast, and ACES.

Figure 12.41

New Zephyr recoating process from 3D Systems (Courtesy of 3D Systems, Inc.)

   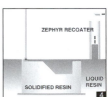

Step 1. When the laser finishes solidifying a layer, the recoater is ready to sweep across the part.

Step 2. The part is lowered only one layer thickness before recoating.

Step 3. The Zephyr recoater sweeps along the top surface of the part, applying a thin, even coat of resin.

Step 4. Upon completion of the sweep process, the laser begins solidifying the next layer, and the liquid reservoir within the recoter is refilled.

12.4.7 Part Completion and Draining

The part-building procedure is repeated for subsequent layers of the part(s). When the last layer or the uppermost layer has been completed, the platform is elevated so that both the platform and the attached part(s) lie above the free surface of the resin in the vat. If the part has trapped volumes, the uncured resin is drained back into the vat by tilting the platform on its support arms. This step is complete once the majority of excess liquid resin has been recovered.

12.4.8 Post-Processing

The post-processing stage consists of three steps: part removal and cleaning, post-curing, and part finishing.

Part removal and cleaning Together with the platform the part is tilted on edge to drain excess liquid resin back into the vat. Commonly, the perforated platform can be tipped on its edge and balanced on the platform support arms. In this way, the part can be oriented nearly perpendicular to its original position. After a few minutes of draining, both the platform and the attached part are removed from the SLA. Excess liquid resin is wiped from both the part and the platform, which extends the life of the cleaning solvent to be used in the next step.

Next, the part and the platform are placed in a cleaning apparatus. Tripropylene glycol monomethyl ether (known commercially as TPM) is a popular cleaning solvent because it produces little swelling distortion on a part if the part is immersed in the solvent briefly. To reduce cleaning time, movement of the solvent over the part is essential. For simple flat plate parts in fresh TPM, thorough cleaning takes less than 5 minutes when continuous movement is provided. If a complex part is simply immersed in TPM without movement, the cleaning may take many hours.

Once the part has been thoroughly cleaned of excess resin, it can be removed from the TPM. Because the immersion period is less than 1 hour in almost all cases, negligible swelling should occur. Next, both the platform and the part are rinsed with ordinary tap water to remove a shiny TPM film. If not removed, this TPM film could impede surface post-cure of the part in the next step. The part and the platform are dried with a stream of low-pressure (20 to 30 psi) compressed air. Even the most geometrically complex parts can be dried in about 1 minute, using compressed air.

The last thing to be done in this step is to remove the part from the platform. The best methods for part removal vary with the characteristics of the resin. Generally a variety of flat-bladed knives are used.

Post-curing The part has only been partially polymerized to this point. Recall that the laser in an SLA scans each layer along the boundary and hatching lines only. This means that inside portions of the layers may not be completely solidified. Thus the part is post-cured to complete the polymerization process and improve the final mechanical strength of the prototype.

Post-curing is accomplished with ultraviolet (UV) radiation in a specially designed apparatus. Optimizing the output wavelengths of the post-curing apparatus is important to achieve uniform polymer post-curing with minimal temperature rise and maximum part accuracy with reasonable duration [Jacobs 1992]. Post-curing causes a temperature rise inside a part because photo-polymerization is an exothermic reaction. High resin temperature may result in considerable thermal stresses and corresponding thermal strains. These strains cause post-cure distortion, and in extreme cases, fracture of the part. Thus it is desirable to find a source of radiation with significantly lower spectral irradiance to promote slower rates of polymerization, correspondingly reduced part temperatures, and hence reduced thermal stresses and strains.

How long a part must be post-cured depends on the details of the part geometry. Most parts can be completely post-cured within an hour or two, whereas very large parts may require as long as 10 hours. In general, post-cure intervals are almost always shorter than the part-building time.

Part finishing   After a part has been post-cured, part finishing is performed. If the part is to serve as only a concept model, simply removing the supports would be sufficient. With brittle polymers, the supports are removed by inserting a dull edged blade or putty knife between the part and the bottom of the supports to break off the supports. Care must be taken to avoid damaging a part that contains fragile sections. With tough resins, the supports can be cut, rather than broken off, with a sharp knife. In the case of extremely delicate part geometries, fine, sharp scissors may also work well. Machining may also be used to remove the supports made of tough resins. Once the supports have been removed, minor sanding is applied to eliminate residual traces of the supports.

If the part is to be used for other applications—for example, a pattern for soft tooling or a master for investment casting—more extensive finishing such as hand sanding, mild glass bead blasting, or some combination of the two is applied.

12.5 SOFTWARE TECHNOLOGY FOR RP&M

Just as a computer cannot function without an operating system, an RP&M machine requires operating software. Operating software has two distinct components: part preparation software and process control, or build, software. Part preparation software handles tasks such as CAD model verification, compensation and repair of STL file error, additional STL modeling, model placement and orientation, support structure generation, assignment of build and recoat attributes, production of cross-sectional slices, and the convergence of all components into an appropriate build file. The process control software uses the build file produced in the preparation phase to control the entire build process on an RP&M machine. This procedure is shown schematically in Figure 12.42. In the following section we describe the tasks performed with part preparation software.

Figure 12.42

Software required
in RP&M

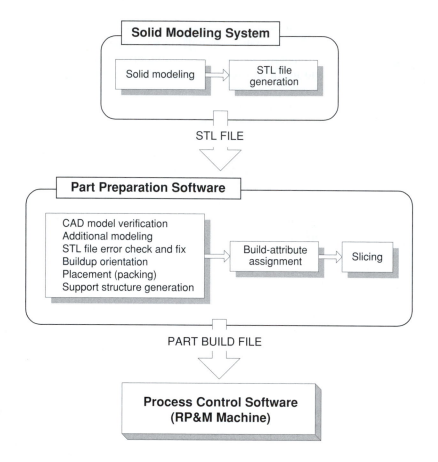

12.5.1 Part Preparation Software Tasks

STL file error-check and fix As mentioned earlier, an STL file produced by a three-dimensional solid modeler might have some errors even if the original three-dimensional model has no defects. Errors that can occur in an STL file can be summarized as follows [Kumar 1997].

Gaps: Facets of the STL data are supposed to form a set of closed shells that enclose the object. But if any of these facets is missing, then the shell is punctured—creating gaps—as shown in Figure 12.43. Thus there is no clear distinction between the inside and the outside. Also, when an STL file with gaps is sliced, it can create open contours in the slices, thereby producing stray vectors in fabrication.

Inconsistent normals: The normals of some facets could be flipped over, as shown in Figure 12.44, and therefore be inconsistent with the outward orientation of the original surface.

Figure 12.43

Gaps in an STL file

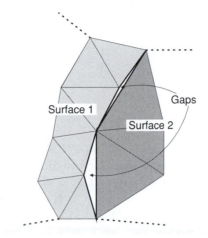

Figure 12.44

Flipped normals in a facet

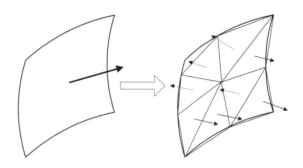

Incorrect normals: Facet normals stored in the STL file may not be the same as the normal computed from the vertices of corresponding facets.

Incorrect intersections: Facets may intersect incorrectly, at locations other than their edges; that is, there may be overlapping facets, as shown in Figure 12.45.

Internal wall and structures: Faulty geometric algorithms could erroneously generate internal walls and structures while closing gaps in STL, which can cause discontinuities in the solidification of the material. Figure 12.46 shows an internal wall error of an STL model.

Figure 12.45

Nonboundary intersection of two triangles

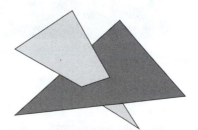

Figure 12.46

Internal wall error
of STL model

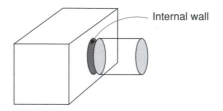

Inconsistencies: An STL file might have inconsistent tolerance values when it is created by appending two different STL files. Also, there may be gaps at the intersection of the two STL models that are appended.

Facet degeneracy: Facets may be degenerate; they might not span a finite area and consequently have no normal. There are two kinds of facet degeneracies: a topological degeneracy and a geometric degeneracy. A topological degeneracy occurs when two or more vertices of a facet coincide. It does not affect the geometry or the connectivity of the remaining facets and therefore the facet can be discarded. A geometric degeneracy occurs when all the vertices of a facet are distinct and all edges of the facet are collinear. This geometrically degenerate facet has no normal, but it does contain implicit topological information on how the neighboring facets are connected, that is, how two surfaces mate. Figure 12.47 illustrates both types of facet degeneracy.

When errors in an STL file are detected, additional operations and manipulations have to be performed on the file before slicing can be done. Repair of an incorrect STL file is computationally intensive and is a major drawback to use of the STL file. Several commercial software packages are available for use in checking and fixing an STL file. They include 3D Verify[2] from 3D Systems and MagicsRP[3] from Materialise.

Figure 12.47

Facet degeneracy
in an STL file

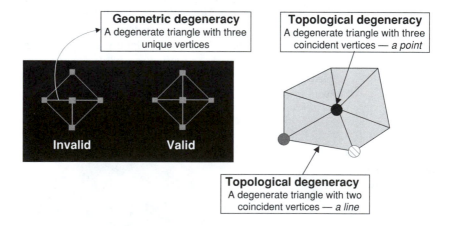

[2] 3D Verify® is a trademark of 3D Systems, Inc.
[3] MagicsRP® is a trademark of Materialise, N.V.

Figure 12.48

Optimal buildup
orientations for
four key aspects of
the RP&M process

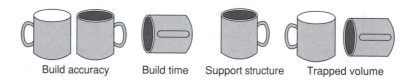

Build accuracy   Build time   Support structure   Trapped volume

Determination of buildup direction   Because each object is built layer by layer, selection of the build orientation is crucial. It affects many key aspects of the RP&M process, including quality of the surface finish, build time, amount of support structures needed, and amount of trapped volume. Currently, however, selection of the buildup orientation is based on experience or trial and error—or may not even be considered. Figure 12.48 illustrates four different optimal buildup orientations corresponding to each of the four key aspects of the process.

Trapped volume evaluation   As described earlier, a trapped volume is the amount of liquid resin in the SLA that was entrapped by the processed or solidified region. Thus trapped volumes can exist in concave regions that act as containers. The liquid resin will be trapped if it cannot be spilled out of the containers. Thus, depending on its orientation, the same concave region may or may not trap unprocessed resin. When there is a trapped volume, it is sometimes necessary to build a part with a drain hole and fill the hole after solidification. Trapped volumes are not allowed in a process such as laminated-object modeling because eliminating the region corresponding to the trapped volume is almost impossible. Figure 12.49 illustrates automatic detection of a trapped volume by software.

Part placement, or packing   Because the methodology of the RP&M process is different from that of a traditional manufacturing process, several adjustments must be made to ensure efficient use of the process. First and foremost, the time required to build multiple prototype parts with RP&M systems can be drastically reduced by building several parts simultaneously during a building cycle. In rapid prototyping, the time spent building a prototype does not depend on the number of parts but on the total number of slices required. By closely packing multiple parts into a feasible

Figure 12.49

Automatic detection of a trapped
volume [Lee, Hur,
and Kim 1997]

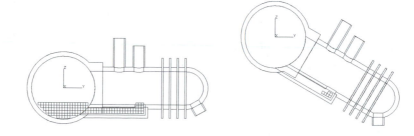

Figure 12.50

Example of optimal packing for multiple parts [Lee, Hur, Ahn, and Kim 1998]

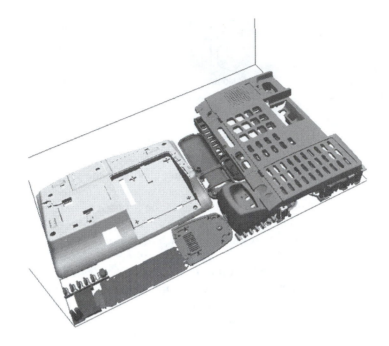

volume, several parts can be built at the same time. Thus many companies and other users are finding it advantageous to build multiple parts simultaneously. Currently, arbitrary STL files are manually chosen by the user to fit the build space by trial and error and then are set to build. However, obtaining this packing solution interactively is a tedious process that does not guarantee optimal placement of all the parts, and therefore the packing result is generally not good enough. Because a three-dimensional packing problem is nondeterministic polynomial time (NP) complete, it is impossible for an operator of an RP&M system to determine the optimal solution. For this reason, an efficient algorithm to place the multiple STL models in the working volume is required, and some commercial softwares such as MagicsRP from Materialise provide semiautomatic packing facility [Materialise 1997]. Figure 12.50 shows an example of packing multiple parts.

Support structure generation It is very important to generate efficiently the support structure reflecting the part geometry. For example, overdesign of support structures results in added design and manufacturing time, as well as finishing operations, whereas underdesigned support structures result in unusable parts. The design quality of a support structure depends completely on the capability of the RP&M software. MagicsSG[4] and Bridgeworks[5] are generally used for automatic generation of a support structure. Figure 12.51 shows examples of support structures generated by RP&M software.

[4] MagicsSG® is a trademark of Materialise, N.V.
[5] Bridgeworks® is a trademark of Solid Concepts, Inc.

Figure 12.51

Examples of support structures generated by RP&M software [Lee, Hur, and Kim 1997]

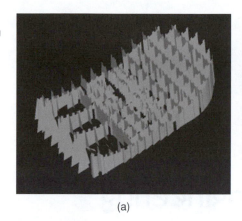 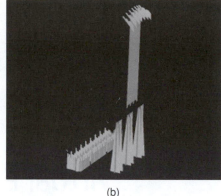

(a)   (b)

QUESTIONS AND PROBLEMS

1. What is the main difference between the stereo lithography and the solid ground curing processes?

2. List the manufacturing processes that can be used to make prototypes with the original material after a pattern is made by an RP&M process.

3. For an RP&M prototype to be used as a pattern for the investment casting process, what are the requirements for the prototype material to be used?

4. Discuss the factors to be considered when the buildup direction of a part is determined. What will be the most important factor in an LOM process?

5. Explain why the support structure is attached to the bottom face of the part in the stereo lithography process.

6. Describe the situations in which a support structure other than the base support needs to be added in the stereo lithography process.

7. What determines the lower and upper limits of the layer thickness in the stereo lithography process?

8. Use a solid modeling system available to you to get the STL file of the object shown. From the STL file try to build a prototype, using any RP&M machine available to you. Use two different part buildup directions and compare their effects on part accuracy and buildup time.

13

Virtual Engineering

The rapidly changing and diversified market demands shorter product cycles for many items. Rapid product development is critical to meeting these market demands. However, traditional product development has been based on design iterations and building costly and time-consuming physical prototypes. In order to shorten this design process, simulation-based engineering has become inevitable.

Advances in computer-aided engineering also have brought a new paradigm in design and analysis. First, geometric modeling systems have advanced greatly in the last decade so that current CAD systems are now capable of handling sophisticated geometry and assembly of part models. The assembly can be visualized, evaluated, and modified as a whole, and its motion can be simulated as done with a physical prototype. Another advance is in finite-element analysis (FEA). It could become a virtual evaluation tool for assessing product reliability and performance if its computational efficiency were improved enough to output the results in real time. It would be able to predict mechanical property and performance measures such as stress, deflection, vibration, temperature, or pressure of complex parts and systems as they are measured by means of various experiments. Furthermore, CAD producers are currently trying to integrate geometric modeling and FEA. This integration should provide a continuous flow for the design and analysis cycle. FEA would be used initially in the design process to guide design decisions, saving valuable time and costs associated with redesign.

These trends in engineering are converging to a new engineering concept: virtual engineering. In essence, virtual engineering is simulation-based engineering. Current simulation technology has improved so that it can now accomplish tasks such as numerically modeling the majority of mechanical properties of a system and detecting the collision between geometric objects in real time. Using simulation technology, industry has applied virtual engineering successfully to reduce development time and cost. The number of applications is increasing, and, when it has fully matured, virtual engineering will be the primary component in engineering activities.

In this chapter, we present the definition of virtual engineering, and discuss its components and applications. We then describe efforts to develop virtual engineering by CAD producers and present examples of industrial applications. We next introduce commercial virtual engineering software tools and hardware. Finally, we touch on research issues and obstacles.

13.1   DEFINITION OF VIRTUAL ENGINEERING

Virtual engineering is a simulation-based method used to help engineers make decisions and establish controls. The virtual environment is a computational framework in which the geometric and physical properties of real systems are accurately simulated. Virtual engineering includes simulation of various engineering activities, such as machining, assembly, production-line operation, inspection, and evaluation, as well as the design process. Thus virtual engineering can extend to an entire product development and production cycle. After a part is modeled, for example, machining of the part and part assembly are simulated. Then the assembled prototype is tested and redesigned through simulation. After the prototype is validated, the production system is modeled and operated virtually. The production cost and delivery schedule are predicted. These simulations yield an optimized final prototype and production procedures that serve as the basis for a physical system.

Virtual engineering brings an entirely new approach to engineering tasks. The use of simulation will eliminate costly physical prototypes and physical experiments. Development time will be drastically reduced, more design alternatives will be tested, and quality will be improved. Virtual engineering will also provide an excellent customer interface, allowing the customer to see three-dimensional models of the product in advance and to request design modifications. It will be possible to build a prototype of a product that is not accessible, too dangerous, or too expensive to handle in real life. Such an ability will be very valuable in the automobile and aerospace industries, where a physical mockup is costly, development time is long, products are extremely complicated, and many customer inputs are necessary.

13.2   COMPONENTS OF VIRTUAL ENGINEERING

Virtual engineering is currently approached in various ways. Because virtual engineering is an emerging technology, its terminology and definitions are not completely established. In manufacturing, the major component of virtual engineering is virtual manufacturing. *Virtual manufacturing* is defined as an integrated, synthetic manufacturing environment exercised to enhance all levels of decision and control. It can be classified as design-centered, production-centered, and control-centered [Lin, Minis, Nau, and Regli 1997]. Design-centered virtual manufacturing is a simulation environment for designing and evaluating the manufacturability of a product. Production-centered virtual manufacturing is a simulation environment for generating process plans and production plans. Control-centered virtual manufacturing is a simulation environment for shop floor production activities.

We can also classify virtual engineering in terms of production life cycle as virtual design, digital simulation, virtual prototyping, and virtual factory. Virtual design is done on virtual reality equipment. Digital simulation permits the verification and validation of the product's operation without using physical prototypes. Virtual prototyping builds a simulated prototype that possesses the same geometry and physical behavior as the real product. Virtual factory is a simulation of factory production line. Detailed descriptions are presented in the following sections.

13.2.1   Virtual Design

Virtual design is performed in a virtual environment, using virtual reality technology, as illustrated in Figure 13.1. Virtual design focuses on an alternative user interface in the design process. Employing virtual reality technologies, designers can immerse themselves in a virtual environment, build components, modify components, operate devices, and interact with virtual objects to perform design activities. Designers can see a stereoscopic view of the virtual objects and hear spatially real-

Figure 13.1

Virtual design with virtual reality equipment (Courtesy of DIVISION, Inc.)

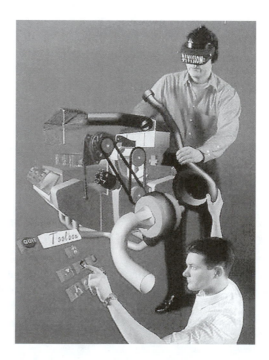

istic sound. This sight and sound occur as the designer's hand guides a virtual arm and finger. The touch of the virtual object is fed back to the designer. In this way, the designer's intent is effectively injected into the design, and the functional behavior of the design is verified.

The main objective of the virtual design is to enable a designer to use intuitive and natural actions. In geometric modeling systems, even though current CAD systems provide sophisticated modeling tools, the designer's interaction with a model is confined. The designer's view is limited to the image projected onto a monitor, and the designer's input is confined to point-wise picking with a mouse. Thus, with current CAD technology, the designer exists as a one-eyed, single-fingered creator. The more natural interaction granted by virtual reality technologies would give the designer more freedom and creativity with the model. The second purpose of virtual design is to incorporate early in the design process the viewpoint of a potential user of the product. Features such as accessibility and manipulability can be fully considered during the design process. The third purpose is to capture in the design process experts' skills in assembling or manipulating parts. These skills are complicated and difficult to formalize, but the virtual design system can reveal the user's position and interaction with objects and the sequence of assembly operations.

Virtual design will require a completely different approach to modeling three-dimensional geometry. For example, menus and buttons can be replaced by speech recognition or gesture recognition technology. Instead of pointing to a model, the designer can grip the model and stretch it to change its dimensions. New design methods and modeling schemes are bound to emerge in association with the virtual design process.

13.2.2 Digital Simulation

Process verification is one of the most important purposes of digital simulation. Machine operation must be carefully examined before actual work begins. If there is an error in the control code, a malfunction may cause serious damage to the machine. With digital simulation, the user can verify the tool path of an NC machine, the probe path of a coordinate measuring machine (CMM), and the robot arm motion before actual operation. For example, a machining process is operated graphically as if it were being done on a real machine, as illustrated in Figure 13.2. That is, a virtual NC machine executes standard NC code, and the virtual machine performs the entire machining operation in real time, including the movements of tools, fixtures, palletizers, and parts. Continuous monitoring of material removal allows the user to detect conditions that cause chatter and tool breakage, gouges, and undercuts. With simulation, the user can also detect collisions between a tool and fixture or part.

Visualization also helps engineers understand the system better. They can easily grasp the design concept and preview performance. Currently, kinematic simulation of rigid bodies is mainly used for these purposes. Simulating higher levels of models, such as fluids, human beings, and complex environments, requires the use

Figure 13.2

Digital simulation of
welding machining
(Courtesy of Deneb
Robotics, Inc.)

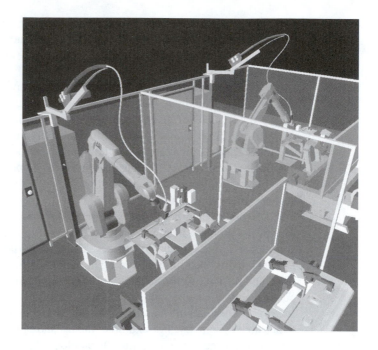

of physics-based simulation, including the effects of dynamics, vibration, acoustics, and deformation. However, sophisticated simulations involving virtual prototypes can verify performance quickly and with less expense.

13.2.3 Virtual Prototyping

Virtual prototyping refers to building a complete prototype assembly with geometric models of individual parts, as illustrated in Figure 13.3. A virtual prototype is sometimes called a *digital mockup* or *digital preassembly*. Virtual prototyping systems allow visualization of the assembly of parts and a check of the feasibility of proposed assemblies within production constraints. Through the assembly of an accurate virtual prototype, design flaws can be detected and design modifications performed so that the actual assembly can be accomplished on the first try.

The primary functionality of virtual prototyping is checking the feasibility of an assembling operation. The system checks part mating within assembly constraints and clearance requirements. Collision detection identifies interference between parts. Assembly sequence and trajectory of the parts are verified. In addition, optimal assembly trajectories can be determined. Advanced systems also perform structural and functional analysis on a virtual prototype, using integrated analysis software. Kinematic and dynamic simulation of the prototype is often performed.

Engineers will be able to base engineering decisions on virtual prototypes. Design optimization will be achieved through the iterative refinement of the virtual prototype. As virtual prototyping becomes increasingly detailed, more accurate

Figure 13.3

Virtual prototype of an engine and suspension structure

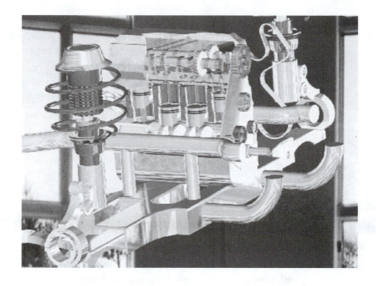

structural and functional simulation will be possible. The ultimate state of a virtual prototype is achieved when it has the comprehensive characteristics of a physical prototype. Thus virtual prototyping eventually will eliminate the need for costly and time-consuming physical prototypes.

13.2.4 Virtual Factory

A *virtual factory* is a simulation of a complete production system, as illustrated in Figure 13.4. A virtual factory system simulates workcell designs, manufacturing processes, and storage systems. Also, automated factory floor devices, such as ro-

Figure 13.4

Virtual simulation of an automotive factory (Courtesy of Deneb Robotics, Inc.)

bots, conveyors, and fixtures, can be programmed. The system models and simulates factory components such as conveyors, buffers, docks, workcells, and processes. It also models procedures such as routes, sequences, and merges. Then it analyzes the production model in terms of labor costs, inventory valuation, operating costs, processing costs, and cycle times.

With these capabilities, the virtual factory can be used for production planning, including validation of production system designs and comparison of production alternatives. When it is mature, the virtual factory will simulate the entire supply chain, allowing the entire resource management and production process to be validated and optimized.

13.3 APPLICATION OF VIRTUAL ENGINEERING

The virtual engineering process starts from geometric models, proceeds to the simulation of production systems, and finally reaches the building of a virtual prototype or virtual product. Without any physical output, the virtual engineering process may seem to involve bogus activities. However, virtual engineering is an effective design tool. It enables testing of various design alternatives so that the optimal design can be found before actual production begins. Besides its use as a design tool, virtual engineering provides various applications in actual production activities.

13.3.1 Design Tool

Virtual design provides a completely different approach to the design process. Its different user interface fosters a more interactive and immersive design environment. It helps designers understand more about the item being designed and be more creative. In addition, designs that incorporate human factors are achieved early in the design stage.

Validation and optimization can be assisted by digital simulation and virtual prototyping. A candidate design's performance can be evaluated through virtual prototyping and digital simulation. The manufacturability of the candidate design can be evaluated through production simulation in a virtual factory. From the virtual prototype, fine-tuning of the design is accomplished by interfacing with FEA or other analysis packages. Full simulation of product functionality can reveal design flaws and possible enhancements. Simulation of product performance and an evaluation of manufacturability can enable engineers to make the right decisions during the design process. Design optimization can also be performed more effectively through iterative virtual prototyping.

Another aspect of the process that virtual engineering facilitates is top-down design. Instead of the current design approach in which all the components are designed first and then fitted together, top-down modeling starts with the global functional requirements, from which the detailed design is developed. Thus a design activity starts from a conceptual design, and proceeds to detailed component designs. Unlike real prototypes, a virtual prototype can be assembled even when completely detailed components are not available. After design validation based on the virtual prototype, the detailed part design can be created from the framework of the virtual prototype. This approach fosters a more intuitive design process in the early design stage.

13.3.2 Manufacturability Assessment

Virtual engineering supports evaluation of the manufacturability of a candidate design. Manufacturability assessment provides information about processing times, cycle times, costs, and product quality. It can also predict setup times, run times, and labor costs. Of course, comprehensive models of the manufacturing process are required for this kind of assessment. Binary information is provided to demonstrate whether a design is suitable for manufacturing. Also a qualitative assessment of manufacturability can be made to determine a manufacturability rating that reflects ease of manufacturing. If the design is not manufacturable, the design attributes posing the difficulty can be identified, characterized, and modified.

13.3.3 Quality Estimation and Control

Simulated testing and operation provide an evaluation of an assembly or the performance of a product. Simulated operation can run a battery of statistical tests on a model to determine its sensitivity to design and manufacturing variations. Then a quality index can be derived with respect to a specific process capability or a design tolerance. This provides an estimation of quality before actual production.

   The process of estimating quality also identifies the main factors affecting it. The design can then be improved by modifying the factors identified as lacking in quality. Product quality can also be enhanced through improving the manufacturability of the design. As an iterative design is relatively less expensive with a virtual system, the full range of design alternatives can be explored to obtain the optimal design. Manufacturability evaluation and design optimization allow the real manufacturing process to be performed in the most effective way. These procedures lead to a better designed and made product that has minimal defects.

13.3.4 Process Validation and Optimization

Digital simulation enables verification of NC machining, robot operation, and CMM measurement before actual production begins. Tool path, robot arm trajectory, or probe trajectory specified in the process plan are visualized and validated in the simulation. From the simulation, collisions and other errors are detected and corrected. Alternatively, a collision-free path can be generated, thus avoiding costly damage that may occur during the actual processes.

Beyond overall process validation, evaluations of key process elements permit optimal process planning. Key elements include part fixturing, part feeding, component handling, and operational movements.

13.3.5 Production and Product Planning

The production activities of a manufacturing shop are simulated by discrete event simulation. It estimates throughput, utilization, operating costs, and flow of materials. Station characteristics such as cycle time, mechanism work envelopes, mechanism placement, accessibility for operation and service, and effects and interaction of tolerance variations can be analyzed. Simulation-based planning is more suitable for production lines in which all production follows similar sequences of operations. More advanced systems are required to simulate job shops that produce small batches of numerous product types with diverse production routings.

Product planning is another application of virtual engineering. Currently, rapidly changing markets demand short planning periods and fast product delivery. Simulation permits rapid cost estimation, production, and delivery schedule evaluation without any physical implementation. A company can respond efficiently to market changes with simulation-based product planning.

13.3.6 Customer Interface

Virtual engineering yields easy product customization and precise delivery time estimation to meet a customer's needs. After it has been completed, a customer can see a three-dimensional model and the simulated operation of the prototype. Then, according to the customer's desires, the prototype can be modified during a live session, transferred directly to the engineering office, and from there sent to the shop floor, speeding production. Thus a customer's desires for changes provide direct feedback to product development. Virtual engineering provides an interface that quickly and accurately captures the customer's wishes, enhancing the producer's ability to respond to customer needs in terms of both cost and timeliness.

13.3.7 Knowledge Database

As virtual engineering becomes a reality, production process information can be systematically obtained and analyzed. Production information management deals with comprehensive information about the continuous circulation of models and process instructions throughout the development cycle. In the current physical environment, expert knowledge is hard to capture, and production and development information is loosely managed; thus prior design expertise is not completely reflected in the next product generation. In virtual engineering, a large database of expert knowledge can be effectively accumulated, and all engineering information can be stored and managed. Then that knowledge base and visualization capability can guide engineering generalists working in teams on product design and modification.

13.3.8 Collaborative Engineering

Virtual engineering provides a basis for collaborative engineering. Digital product data can easily be shared among engineers and designers working on the same assignment. Shared virtual environments can allow engineers at remote locations to study a virtual prototype together and simultaneously. They can work concurrently in the context of overall production requirements. In addition, these environments give engineers and designers a better understanding of the product, improve quality, reduce time to market, and ensure that designs are right the first time, reducing the need for expensive reworking later in the process. Collaboration can be extended outside a company by sharing virtual product information with suppliers and partners, thereby creating a closer relationship in product development.

13.4 RELATED TECHNOLOGIES

13.4.1 Integration of CAD and Simulation

Before FEA analysis software or simulation software can be run, a model geometry must be created. Thus the designer works on a geometric modeling system to create a model and then exports the model to the analysis or simulation software to be used. Transferring data from one software system to another through a standard data format often results in the loss of some data. To resolve this difficulty, current CAD systems provide optional analysis and simulation modules that are tightly integrated with the modeling system.[1] With the optional modules, tasks such as kinematic simulation, FEA analysis, mesh generation, and post-processing can be performed directly from the modeling system.

The integrated solution provides a unified environment for modeling, analysis, and simulation and also avoids the data loss that often occurs in data translation. This enables an easy transition from design to design validation and provides another basis for simulation-based virtual engineering.

---

[1] SDRC's I-DEAS Masters series is one of the first systems that provide a full line of simulation, CAM, and testing modules integrated with the core design module. Parametric Technology Corporation's Pro/Engineer includes Pro/Mechanica modules that assist structure, vibration, thermal, and motion analysis. Pro/MESH and Pro/FEMPOST are pre- and post-processors of FEA analysis, respectively. Dassault System's CATIA includes CATIA Finite Element Modeler for FEM analysis and CATIA Kinematics for mechanism simulation. Unigraphics Solution's Unigraphics has UG/Scenario for pre- and post-processing and UG/FEM for analysis. UG/Mechanisms is used for kinematic analysis and design simulations.

13.4.2   LOD and Culling

Graphics for virtual engineering require a large number of assembled models and moving mechanisms to be drawn in real time. Even though current graphics hardware has advanced to an impressive level, it still is not sufficient or is too expensive to render complicated models in realistic fashion and update them in real time. Graphics hardware speed is one of the major obstacles in virtual engineering. Even with limited hardware, graphics speed can be improved by software techniques such as LOD and culling.

Level of detail (LOD) refers to the control of rendering quality. Recall that, in graphics displays, nonlinear surfaces are represented by planar facets, typically in the form of triangles. As more planar facets are used to represent a surface, a more faithful display of the surface is presented, but display time slows. Because the level of detail that a user can perceive or that hardware can display is limited, trying to draw too much detail will waste computing time. The LOD technique uses multiple representations for the same scene, which is displayed with different LODs, depending on its context. The LOD is controlled in two ways: statically and dynamically. Static control varies the LOD according to the size of the model. When an object is close, a high level of detail is displayed, but when the object is farther away, a low level of detail is displayed. Dynamic control varies the LOD according to the speed of the model. When an object is static, a high level of detail is displayed, but when an object is moving, a low level of detail is displayed.

Culling is a selective display of objects. At any instance of viewing a scene, only a portion of the entire set of models is visible to the user. A certain amount of data will be either outside the view or behind other objects in the scene. Thus sending all the object information to graphics hardware is unnecessary. There are two types of culling: view frustum and occurrence. View frustum culling removes the objects that lie outside the viewing frustum. Based on where the user is looking at the models, some of objects are inside and some are outside the field of view. The objects outside the field of view, sometimes called the *view frustum*, are not sent to the graphics pipeline for display. For example, when a user is looking at a room, the system need not send the graphics information of the ceiling fan if it is outside viewing frustum. In occurrence culling, the objects that are behind another closer object are not visible. From the user's view direction, the objects that are not visible need not be sent to the graphics pipeline. For example, when the complete assembly of a car is displayed, the car's engine compartment is not drawn because it is covered by the body of the car.

With the increasing sophistication in virtual engineering and virtual reality applications comes greater demand for high-quality graphics and high-frame rate simulation. Graphics performance is crucial to the effect of virtual engineering applications. The LOD and culling techniques help the performance of graphics by software. They increasingly are being applied to CAD and virtual engineering applications.

13.5   INDUSTRY APPLICATION CASES OF VIRTUAL ENGINEERING

- The Boeing 777 jetliner

  The Boeing 777 is the first commercial jetliner successfully designed by a paper-less approach. To design the 777, Boeing organized its workers into 238 cross-functional "design–build teams" responsible for specific products. Boeing used the CATIA CAD system from Dassault/IBM and developed its own Electronic Pre-assembly In Computer (EPIC) system. No physical prototype except the nose mockup (to check critical wiring) was built before actual assembly of the first plane. Virtual prototyping enabled Boeing to enlist customers and operators (down to line mechanics) in the plane's design. Virtual prototyping was so successful that the assembly was only 0.03 mm out of alignment when the port wing was attached.

- GM's virtual prototype of a locomotive engine

  The Electro-Motive division of General Motors developed the GM16V265H 6300 horsepower locomotive engine from what they called "virtual product development" in conjunction with Unigraphics Solutions. All the parts were represented in three-dimensional models, and subsequent analysis, design optimization, and machine tool and fixture programming were linked to those models. The model of the entire engine is shown in Figure 13.5. Modeling enabled rapid product delivery, with the first engine built in 18 months from the start of the program, a process that typically takes more than 36 months. This also allowed much faster reliability tests that enabled GM to meet more stringent reliability goals.

- Chrysler automotive interior design

  The interior of Chrysler's 1998 Dodge Durango was developed with a virtual design approach. As illustrated in Figure 13.6, a design team member sits in a

Figure 13.5

GM16V265H 6300 HP locomotive engine (Courtesy of General Motors)

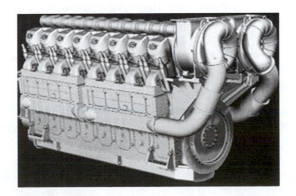

Figure 13.6

Virtual design of
automobile interior
(Courtesy of
Chrysler
Corporation)

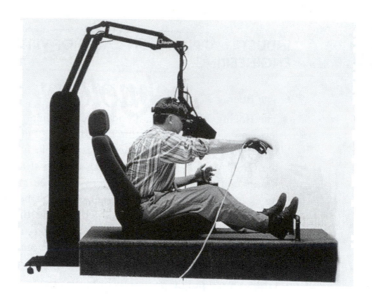

stripped car interior, consisting of just a seat, steering wheel, and pedals. Looking into virtual reality display system and wearing data gloves and tracking system, the designer sees and interacts with the virtual prototype of the car's interior components (e.g., dashboard, radio controls, glove compartment, and windows). Design changes are easily made within the virtual prototype, and visibility, accessibility, and aesthetics can also be tested. This approach enables rapid verification of various design options.

• Stockholm's Metrocar 2000

Metrocar 2000 is Stockholm's new public transportation system designed by Adtranz Sweden. Using Division's dVISE software, Adtranz demonstrated virtual prototypes of the trains that include fully furnished interiors with texture-mapped seats, floors, advertisements, and driver display panels. Looking at the virtual prototype, as shown in Figure 13.7, viewers can get a sense of the scale, spatial relationships, and aesthetics of the design. This allows the customer and engineer to review and interact with product designs in their early stages.

• Ship design for the Royal Navy, U.K.

The Naval Directorate of Future Projects of the United Kingdom has employed virtual design in its new-ship development program. Using Deneb Robotics, Inc.'s ENVISION software, the quarterdeck of a new ship was interactively designed through simulation. It included the ship's motion (with six degrees of freedom) and its effect on operating machinery, sailors, and lighting conditions in the ship's compartments. This simulation allowed engineers to evaluate the design and interactively change it as necessary.

Figure 13.7

Virtual prototype
of Metrocar 2000
(Courtesy of
DIVISION, Inc.)

13.6 SOFTWARE PRODUCTS

Companies that produce virtual engineering software products are proliferating. Most such companies provides multimodule software so that customers can get job-specific modules to match their needs. The modules are virtual assembly, digital simulations of workcell machines, and production simulations. They offer large libraries of models of currently used NC machines, robots, machine components, and production components. They are helpful for creating models for a customer's own system quickly. All the software companies are expanding their modules to incorporate broader engineering activities and improve simulation quality.

- ADAMS software by Mechanical Dynamics, Inc. (http://www.adams.com)

  ADAMS is an automobile-oriented simulation and analysis software package. Its strong point is a complete line of modeling and analysis, including kinematic, static, and dynamic, and simulation modules. Thus, unlike other simulation software packages that are mainly kinematic simulations, a dynamic simulation is accurately realized. ADAMS/Solver is the kernel of the product line that formulates and solves motion equations. The modeling modules include ADAMS/Android for animated humans, ADAMS/Driver for human response for vehicle simulation, ADAMS/Tire for tire modeling, and ADAMS/Vehicle for automobile and truck suspension modeling. An integration module provides an interface of ADAMS's modeling and analysis routines. These routines are ADAMS/FEA, ADAMS/IGES, and ADAMS/Linear. The visualization module is ADAMS/Animation. Also, ADAMS has vehicle-specific modules that include ADAMS/Car, as shown in Figure 13.8, and ADAMS/Rail.

Figure 13.8

ADAMS/Car module image (Courtesy of Mechanical Dynamics, Inc. (M.D.I.))

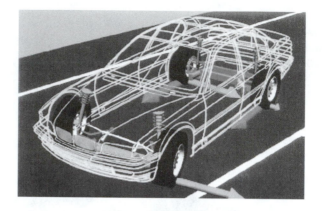

- Deneb Robotics, Inc., software (http://www.deneb.com)

  Deneb Robotics, Inc., provides virtual design, virtual prototyping, and simulation products for workcells and factories. Simulations include visualization, collision detection, and cycle time evaluation. Products include ENVISION for virtual design and prototyping, IGRIP for robot design and motion planning, and ERGO for simulation and analysis for ergonomics and human factors engineering. With IGRIP as a basic module, job-specific modules, such as UltraArc, UltraGrip, UltraPaint, and UltraSpot (shown in Figure 13.9), can be appended. QUEST is a discrete event simulation module that can be used for a factory line simulation. Also, the VirtualNC module is for the simulation of NC machines.

Figure 13.9

UltraSpot module image (Courtesy of Deneb Robotics, Inc.)

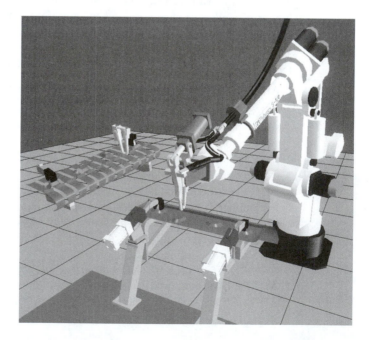

Figure 13.10

dVISE image
(Courtesy of
DIVISION, Inc.)

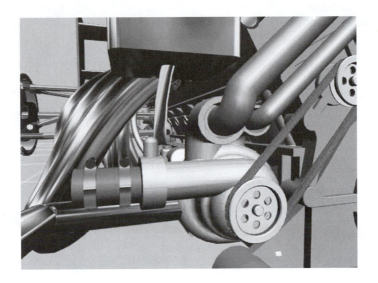

- Division, Inc., software (http://www.division.com)

  The dVISE virtual prototyping software by Division, Inc., is shown in Figure 13.10. The software provides tools for importing existing CAD data and constructing a virtual prototype. dVISE's capability includes collision detection and clearance checking during prototype creation and reviewing. The strong point of the software is its system architecture, which is distributable, has multiuser capability, and is open. The distributable system architecture allows simulation processes to run on multiple severs. The multiuser architecture supports the collaborative development by users at different locations. The open architecture allows users to extend the functionalities for customization. The product family includes dV/WebFly, dV/Player, dV/Review, dV/Mock-up, and dV/Reality.

- Engineering Animations, Inc., software (http://www.eai.com)

  VisMockUp is a virtual prototyping software product from Engineering Animations, Inc., that emphasizes on three-dimensional visualization, as shown in Figure 13.11. Users can examine an assembly and component parts with different visualization tools. The system has translators for popular CAD data format to allow importing of models into the system. Analysis functionality includes interference and collision checking. The system supports collaborative development by enabling database sharing and visual interface through standard Web browsers.

- SILMA software (http://www.silma.com)

  SILMA produces number of virtual engineering modules, including SoftAssembly, SoftMachines, CimStation, and AdeptRapid. SoftAssembly provides assembly sequence simulation, optimal trajectory recording, and visualization. Collisions are detected during assembly path simulation. SoftMachine is a simulation module for NC machining. The simulated machine executes standard G and M codes, and subsequent machining processes are simulated. From the simulation, machining errors and collisions can be checked. CimStation Robotics is a robot workcell simulation

Figure 13.11

VisMockUp image
(Courtesy of E.A.I.)

Figure 13.12

CimStation image
(Courtesy of SILMA,
A division of Adept
Technology, Inc.)

module. It uses in-house CAD data library of commercial robots to simulate a manufacturing system. CimStation Inspection, illustrated in Figure 13.12, is a CMM programming and simulation module. It has a library of kinematic models of commercial CMMs and probes.

- Prosolvia software (http://www.prosolvia.se)

Prosolvia produces the Oxygen line of modules for virtual prototyping and visualization. Oxygen Assembly is a virtual design–prototype module by which users can simulate manual assembly in a virtual environment to review and analyze assembly sequences. Oxygen Showroom allows review and evaluation of product designs in a realistic and interactive environment. Oxygen MMI simulates ergonomic analyses, whereby the user can test distances, reachability, visibility, and comfort. Oxygen Sketchmap converts two-dimensional drawings to three-dimensional models that can be used in a virtual environment. Oxygen also provides support for plug-ins: Oxygen Immersive Space supports immersive space systems; Oxygen Collaboration supports distributed environment; Oxygen Peripherals supports virtual reality equipment, such as motion tracker system, head mounted displays, and data gloves; and Oxygen CAD-Exchange offers CAD data translations.

- Tecnomatix software (http://www.tecnomatix.com)

Tecnomatix offers different lines of products for manufacturing, assembly, and tolerance analysis. ROBCAD is a set of software for design, simulation, and off-line programming of manufacturing systems. It consists of various job-specific modules, including ROBCAD/Line, ROBCAD/Spot, ROBCAD/Paint, ROBCAD/Drill, ROBCAD/Arc, ROBCAD/Fixture, ROBCAD/Man, ROBCAD/Laser, and ROBCAD/Onsite. VALISYS is a line of software tools for analysis of dimensions and tolerances, and for simulation of the CMM inspection process. It includes VALISYS/Design, VALISYS/Assembly, VALISYS/CMM Off-Line Programming, VALISYS/Inspection, VALISYS/Analyze, and VALISYS/Reverse. DYNAMO, illustrated in Figure 13.13, is a virtual prototype line of modules. The main module provides assembly simulation and service space analysis. Optional modules include DYNAMO/Engineer and DYNAMO/Link.

Figure 13.13

Dynamo image
(Courtesy of
Tecnomatix
Technologies, Inc.)

13.7 HARDWARE PRODUCTS

Virtual engineering is pure software and thus, by its nature, does not require any specific hardware. However, for human interface, virtual reality hardware is necessary. The hardware consists of both input and output devices. The output devices give a user the sense of a virtual environment. As the most effective sensory perception is visual, display systems are the main components of virtual reality systems. Display devices must provide a stereoscopic view for the user. Currently available equipment includes head-mounted displays, binocular omni oriented monitors, spatially immersive displays, and shutter glasses. Audio and touch sensory perceptions enhance the sense of virtual reality when they are used with a visual system. Headphones with spatially augmented sound systems are typical audio devices. Force-feedbacked haptic devices are touch devices. Input devices read user's reactions, including speech, position, and motion. Speech recognition systems, tracking systems, and data gloves are commonly used input devices.

- Head-mounted displays

  A head-mounted display (HMD) is a fully immersive display device. A helmet covers the eyes and permits only a straight-ahead view. A small display screen mounted in front of the user's eye gives a stereo image. A wireless tracking system is embedded in the device so that the view of the screen changes along with the position and the orientation of the user's head. More than 40 models are currently available. They include FOHMD from CAE-Electronics (shown in Figure 13.14) and Looking Glass from Polhemus Lab.

Figure 13.14

FOHMD device (Image courtesy of CAE, Inc.)

- Binocular omni oriented monitors

The binocular omni oriented monitor (BOOM) is a mechanical version of HMD. It consists of a display box that is weight balanced through the attachment to a multilink arm. The user looks into the box and the user's head motion is tracked via the mechanical link system. The main advantage of BOOM is fast and precise tracking compared to HMD. Commercially available devices are BOOM-2C from Fake Space Labs (http://www.fakespace.com) and Cyberface3 from LEEP.

- Spatially immersive displays

A spatially immersive display (SID) uses a wraparound video display that surrounds the user so that the user feels surrounded by a virtual environment. The SID provides a wide field of view and gives the freedom to walk or move around in the virtual environment. CAVE is a four-wall system developed by the University of Illinois at Chicago. CAVE is commercially available from Pyramid System. A large-scale SID includes a dome-shaped SID, such as Visionarium at Silicon Graphics, which has an 8 m diameter. Spitz ElectricHorizen built a SID that has an 8.5 m diameter, as shown in Figure 13.15.

- Shutter glasses

Shutter glasses are a low-cost display device. The user wears a glasslike device that alternatively blocks each eye. The monitor or another display device that is synchronized with the glasses has a double refresh rate, and it alternatively shows the right-eye view and the left-eye view. The user sees a stereo image on the screen of the monitor. The device can be used with currently available display monitors, so it is cost-effective. However, it is not immersive enough for the user to see the real environment, and the field of view is limited to the size of the monitor. Commercially available devices are CrystalEyes by StereoGraphics and SGS by Tektronix.

- Haptic devices

A haptic device delivers the sensation of a physical touch. A haptic device enables users to feel a real object by a force-feedback system that provides an illu-

Figure 13.15

Virtual Reality Theater (Courtesy of SPITZ, Inc., Chadds Ford, PA, U.S.A.)

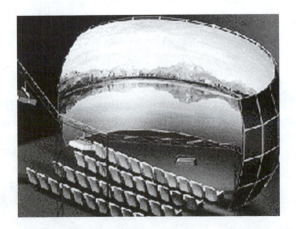

Figure 13.16

Phantom by
SensAble
Technology.
(Courtesy of
SensAble
Technology &
PennWell
Publishing
Company)

sion that the user is handling a real material. The haptic device includes a force-feedback joystick by which the user feels the reaction force on the operating hand. Commercially available joystick devices are HapticMater by Nissho Electronics and BSP Joystick by AEA Technologies. The Phantom by SensAble Technology, a pen-based haptic device that has six degrees of freedom, is shown in Figure 13.16. A more advanced type is the exoskeleton, a complicated mechanical link system that surrounds the entire hand and finger so that each finger and joint gets independent force feedback. It's a combined data glove and haptic device. The Exoskelatal Hand Master by Sarcos and the Force ArmMaster by Exos are exoskeleton devices.

• Tracking system

A tracking device uses an electromagnetic, ultrasonic, optical, or mechanical system to determine the position and orientation of the tracked object. The tracking device can be attached to an HMD to track the viewing direction and head position or to a data glove to track the hand position. The tracking device can also be attached to any body part to track its position. Flock of Birds by Ascension and ISOTRAK II by Polhemus (http://www.polhemus.com) are commercially available tracking devices. Typical devices employing ultrasonic technologies are Head-tracker by Logitech (http://www.logitech.com) and GAMS by Transition State Corporation. Devices employing a mechanical system are GyroEngine by Gyration, Inc., ADL-1 by Shooting Star Technology, and Wrightrac by Vidtronics. Finally, tracking devices utilizing optical technology include GRD-1010 by GEC Ferranti, DynaSight by Origin Instruments, and RtPM by Spatial Positioning Systems Inc.

Figure 13.17

DataGlove
(Courtesy of
Greenleaf Medical
Systems)

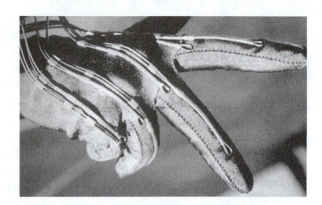

- Data gloves

  A data glove is equipped with sensors at each joint of the fingers that measure the bend of each finger. The global position of the hand is determined by a tracking system attached to the glove. Typically, the information generated from the data glove is graphically regenerated in the virtual environment and shows dynamically changing shape and position along with the user's hand motion. Commercially available gloves are Dexterous Hand Master by Exos, CyberGlove CG1801 by Virex, and DataGlove by Greenleaf Medical Systems (shown in Figure 13.17).

13.8 RESEARCH ISSUES AND CHALLENGES OF VIRTUAL ENGINEERING

Virtual engineering is an emerging field. It has the potential to become a significant activity in the engineering profession, but current systems have limited functionality and applications. For virtual engineering to become a full-fledged system, its simulation aspect must be able to reflect the complete functional behavior of physical systems. We discuss several related issues.

- New design tools

  Virtual design provides a different design environment. Viewing is stereoscopic, and interaction with a design model is multisensory. The new design environment provides room for new design methods and modeling approaches. In the near future the designer will be able to grip and stretch an object or create and modify a model by talking. The new modeling approach would allow more natural and intuitive ways of creating models.

- Process and physical modeling

  Current simulations are limited primarily to kinematics. Modeling of dynamic systems, deformable systems, and fluid systems normally require a computationally intensive finite-element analysis. This should be executed in real time to be of value as a virtual engineering tool. To enable real-time simulation, compact and accurate modeling must be possible. Furthermore, the models should carry their physical properties and the experimental data that show their physical behavior.

• Manufacturability measure

Manufacturing processes are diverse, with each process having its own unique characteristics. Thus deriving a unified metric that assesses the manufacturability of various products is difficult. Research needed includes the study of definitions of manufacturability and evaluation methodology. Besides a simple yes/no decision, the system needs to calculate a quantitative measure of manufacturability. In addition, estimated manufacturability needs to be converted into process times and costs.

• System speed

Currently, visualization and simulation quality is challenged by system speed. Because of exponentially increasing process speed and advances in distributed computing technology, simulation quality is improving. However, system speed is still relatively slow for mature virtual engineering. Visualization requires detailed three-dimensional renderings and high frame-rate animations. Design validation involves dynamic system analyses and optimizations that are computation-intensive. Also, for collaborative engineering, network speed and bandwidth and the number of channels need to be improved.

• Data interface standard

Virtual engineering involves interactions among various application software packages. Modeling of a part is normally done in a CAD system, analysis is performed in a FEA system, and simulation is performed in an interactive production simulation system. Collaborative engineering requires that these different systems work together. Interface standards for database and software are the key to virtual engineering.

• Open architecture

Open architecture provides system scalability. Virtual engineering systems need to be integrated with current engineering systems to accommodate custom-built functionality or to cope with different types of tasks. Open architecture allows the system to explore a large pool of engineering resources and to facilitate various applications.

QUESTIONS AND PROBLEMS

1. List the advantages of applying the virtual engineering concept to the product development process.

2. What are the components of virtual engineering in terms of the production cycle?

3. What extra capabilities would most likely be required for current CAD systems to help realize a virtual design?

4. For an assembly of parts created by current CAD systems to be used for digital simulation, more than the geometric models of the parts and their connections are needed. What else is required?

5. What is the most popular application of digital mockups in product development?

6. Explain why top-down design is made possible by virtual prototypes.

7. Explain why virtual engineering promotes collaborative engineering.

8. State the two typical software technologies that improve graphics speed for an assembly of many parts. Also, explain briefly the principle of each technique.

9. Explain *view frustum culling* and *occurrence culling*.

10. What is the main difference between HMD and BOOM?

11. Explain the principle by which a user wearing shutter glasses sees a stereo image.

12. When you use a data glove, how are the finger motions measured by the sensors on each joint of the glove fingers? How is the global position of the hand measured?

Standards for Communicating Between Systems

In Chapters 8 and 11, we showed that application programs—for example, those for finite-element mesh generation or NC tool-path generation—require a description of the product or the product definition data as their input. There are basically two types of product definition data. One contains the data of a drawing and thus is composed of the vector data for lines (solid lines, dotted lines, center lines, dimension lines, and extension lines) and annotation data for the dimension values, notes, and symbols in the drawing. The other type of product definition data consists of a solid model representation with some associated annotation data. Therefore product definition data are usually imported from a CAD system, either from a computer-aided drafting system or a solid modeling system. However, as we pointed out in Chapters 4 and 5, all CAD systems store design results—the product definition data—in their own system-specific data structures. These may be inconsistent with the required input format of the application program to be used. Thus a data communication problem often arises when two or more of CAD/CAM/CAE systems are tied together to form an application that shares common data. In fact, there is always the need to tie together several systems either internally within a single organization or externally as in the case of subcontract manufacturers or component suppliers.

To solve this communication problem for pairs of systems, it is necessary to translate the product definition data of one system into a form that the other system can use and vice versa. To facilitate the translation without developing translator programs for all the pairs of CAD/CAM/CAE systems, several standard formats for storing product definition data have been proposed. We briefly review the typical standard formats in this chapter.

14.1 EXCHANGE METHODS OF PRODUCT DEFINITION DATA

Different CAD/CAM/CAE systems have different structures for their product definition data, so it is necessary to convert the product definition data of one system to fit the structure of the other system in order to transfer the data. Another translator is needed to transfer the data in the opposite direction between the same systems. Therefore we need two translators for each pair of systems. As illustrated in Figure 14.1(a), the dual direction arrows for each pair of systems imply two translators. These translators between each specific pair of the systems are called *direct translators*. If we have n different systems, we have to provide $n(n - 1)$ translators because there are $n(n - 1)/2$ pairs of systems. For example, we have to develop 90 translators for the exchange of data between 10 systems. Thus this direct translation method requires too many translators to be practical when many systems have to be considered. Moreover, adding one system to the existing n systems would require writing $2n$ additional translators.

However, we can also achieve the data exchange by introducing a neutral database structure, called a *neutral file*, which is independent of existing or future CAD/CAM/CAE systems. This structure acts as an intermediary and a focal point of communication among different database structures of CAD/CAM/CAE systems, as illustrated in Figure 14.1(b). Thus each system would have its own pair of processors to transfer data to and from this neutral file format. The translator that transfers data from the database format of a given system to the neutral format is called a *pre-processor*, whereas the translator that transfers data in the opposite direction is known as a *post-processor*, as shown in Figure 14.2. Therefore a total of $2n$ processors is required for n systems to be in communication, and only two processors need to be added whenever a new system is introduced. In other words,

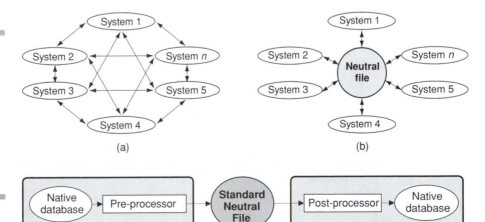

Figure 14.1

Exchanging data between different systems—two methods

(a)

(b)

Figure 14.2

Data exchange using a neutral file

this indirect approach does not suffer from the disadvantage of requiring an increasing number of programs to be written, as in the case of the direct approach. This is the main reason why the indirect approach is accepted as a typical exchange method between different systems even though it has some disadvantages relative to the direct approach. That is, direct translators run more quickly than indirect translators, and the data files they produce are smaller than the neutral file created by indirect translators. The neutral file is usually larger than the data file created by a specific system because of its general nature. When we transfer production definition data through a neutral file, some data usually are lost, especially feature-tree information and constraints in parametric modeling systems.

We introduce three typical formats of the neutral file in this chapter: the initial graphics exchange specification (IGES), drawing interchange format (DXF), and standard for the exchange of product model data (STEP). Currently, IGES is the most popular format of the neutral file, and DXF is a format used mainly for the exchange of drawing data. STEP is the standard data format used to store all the data relevant to the entire life cycle of a product, including design, analysis, manufacturing, quality assurance, testing, and maintenance, in addition to the simple product definition data. Currently, CAD systems, which used to support IGES format, are moving toward the use of STEP.

14.2 INITIAL GRAPHICS EXCHANGE SPECIFICATION

In 1979, a technical committee consisting of the Boeing Company, the General Electric Company, and the then National Bureau of Standards (now National Institute of Standards and Technology) was assigned the task of developing a data exchange method under the U.S. Air Force integrated computer-aided manufacturing (ICAM) program. As a result of this effort, IGES, version 1.0, was published in January 1980. It became an American National Standards Institute (ANSI) standard in September 1981.

IGES was the first standard exchange format developed to address the need to communicate product definition data between different CAD/CAM/CAE systems. The early versions of IGES were implicitly aimed at the CAD/CAM systems of the 1970s and early 1980s; that is, they mainly addressed the exchange of drawings. Recent revisions have extended the types of data to be exchanged. For example, version 2.0 supports the exchange of finite-element data and printed circuit-board data, version 3.0 enhances the capabilities of user-defined Macros that are essential to exchange the standard part libraries, version 4.0 supports the CSG tree of a solid, and version 5.0 handles the B-rep data of solids.

An IGES file is composed of six sections, which must appear in the following order: Flag (optional), Start, Global, Directory Entry (DE), Parameter Data (PD), and Terminate, as illustrated in Figure 14.3. The identification characters for these sections, respectively, are S, G, D, P, and T, as shown in column 73 of each record in Figure 14.4. A *record* is a line comprising 80 characters. Figure 14.4 illustrates an IGES file corresponding to the drawing shown in Figure 14.5.

Figure 14.3

Structure of IGES files

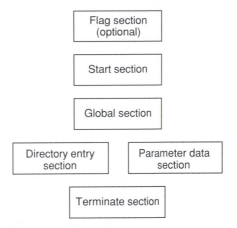

The Flag section is used only with the compressed ASCII and binary formats. IGES data in a file can be represented in two formats: ASCII and binary. The ASCII format comprises two types: a fixed 80-character record length, as shown in Figure 14.4, and a compressed form. The compressed form is simply an ASCII file compressed by eliminating spaces from the records. A detailed description of the compressed form is presented in Zeid [1991]. The binary file format is a bit-stream binary representation of the data in the fixed record length format. To identify the file as compressed ASCII, the character C is stored in column 73 of the Flag section, which is a single record (line) preceding the Start section. In the binary file format, the first byte (8 bits) of the Flag section has the ASCII letter B as the file identifier. Note that the Flag section does not appear in Figure 14.4 because it shows an IGES file in the fixed record length format.

The Start section provides a human-readable description of the file, such as the sending system that generated the original data, the pre-processor, and the product being described. In Figure 14.4, the records with the character S in column 73 belong to the Start section.

The Global section includes information describing the pre-processor and information needed by the post-processor to interpret the file. Some of the items specified in this section are

- the characters used as delimiters between individual entries and between records (commas and semicolons are used respectively in Figure 14.4),
- the name of the IGES file itself,
- the number of significant digits in the representation of integers and floating-point numbers on the sending system,
- the date and time of the file generation,
- the model space scale,
- the model units,
- the minimum resolution and maximum coordinate values, and
- the name of the author of the file and organization.

Figure 14.4

IGES file corresponding to the drawing shown in Figure 14.5

```
IGES file generated from an AutoCAD drawing by the IGES             S0000001
translator from Autodesk, Inc., translator version IGESOUT-3.04.    S0000002
,,10HB:WKEYHOLE,14HB:WKEYHOLE.IGS,27HAutoCAD-12_c2 International,12HIGESG0000001
OUT-3.04,32,38,6,99,15,10HB:WKEYHOLE,1.0,1,4HINCH,32767,3.2767D1,13H9307G0000002
06.211545,5.0D-9,5.0,13HShin Dong Koo,12H GoldStar G1,6,0;          G0000003
100    1    1    1                    0    00000000D0000001
100              1                         D0000002
110    2    1    1                         00000000D0000003
110              1                         D0000004
110    3    1    1                         00000000D0000005
110              1                         D0000006
110    4    1    1                         00000000D0000007
110              1                         D0000008
212    5    1    1                         00010100D0000009
212         256  1                         D0000010
106    6    1                              00010100D0000011
106         256  1    40                   D0000012
106    7    1                              00010100D0000013
106         256  1    40                   D0000014
214    8    1    1                         00010100D0000015
214         256  1    3                    D0000016
214    9    1    1                         00010100D0000017
214         256  1    3                    D0000018
216    10   1    1                    0    00000101D0000019
216              1                         D0000020
212    11   1    1                         00010100D0000021
212         256  2                         D0000022
106    13   1                              00010100D0000023
106         256  1    40                   D0000024
106    14   1                              00010100D0000025
106         256  1    40                   D0000026
214    15   1    1                         00010100D0000027
214         256  2    3                    D0000028
214    17   1    1                         00010100D0000029
214         256  2    3                    D0000030
216    19   1    1                    0    00000101D0000031
216              1                         D0000032
212    20   1    1                         00010100D0000033
212         256  2                         D0000034
214    22   1    1                         00010100D0000035
214         256  2    3                    D0000036
214    24   1    1                         00010100D0000037
214         256  2    3                    D0000038
206    26   1    1                    0    00000101D0000039
206              1                         D0000040
110    27   1    1                         00000000D0000041
110              1                         D0000042
110    28   1    1                         00000000D0000043
110              1                         D0000044
110    29   1    1                         00000000D0000045
110              1                         D0000046
110    30   1    1                         00000000D0000047
110              1                         D0000048
110    31   1    1                         00000000D0000049
110              1                         D0000050
110    32   1    1                         00000000D0000051
110              1                         D0000052
100,0.0,30.0,30.0,2.3D1,54.0,3.7D1,54.0;                            1P0000001
110,23.0,58.0,0.0,37.0,58.0,0.0;                                    3P0000002
110,23.0,54.0,0.0,0.0,23.0,58.0,0.0;                                5P0000003
110,37.0,54.0,0.0,0.0,37.0,58.0,0.0;                                7P0000004
212,1,2,3.2,3.0,1,,0.0,0.0,0.0,2.84D1,6.3705885482016D1,0.0,2H14;   9P0000005
106,1,3,0.0,23.0,58.0,23.0,58.0,23.0,6.4205885482016D1;            11P0000006
106,1,3,0.0,37.0,58.0,37.0,58.0,37.0,6.4205885482016D1;            13P0000007
214,1,3.0,1.0,0.0,0.0,23.0,6.2205885482016D1,30.0,6.2205885482016D1; 15P0000008
214,1,3.0,1.0,0.0,0.0,37.0,6.2205885482016D1,30.0,6.2205885482016D1; 17P0000009
216,9,15,17,11,13;                                                 19P0000010
212,1,2,4.0,3.0,1,,1.5707963267949D0,0.0,6.5399660145317D1,        21P0000011
2.95D1,0.0,2H53;                                                   21P0000012
106,1,3,0.0,37.0,58.0,37.0,58.0,6.8899660145317D1,58.0;            23P0000013
106,1,3,0.0,30.0,5.0,30.0,5.0,6.8899660145317D1,5.0;               25P0000014
214,1,3.0,1.0,0.0,0.0,6.6899660145317D1,58.0,6.6899660145317D1,    27P0000015
3.15D1;                                                            27P0000016
214,1,3.0,1.0,0.0,0.0,6.6899660145317D1,5.0,6.6899660145317D1,     29P0000017
3.15D1;                                                            29P0000018
216,21,27,29,23,25;                                                31P0000019
212,1,5,6.0,3.0,1,,4.8571836262035D-1,0.0,-3.4208387606424D0,      33P0000020
1.4053290730212D1,0.0,5H%%c50;                                     33P0000021
214,2,3.0,1.0,0.0,7.8915046446839D0,1.832890608709D1,3.0D1,        35P0000022
3.0D1,-2.7205731258678D0,1.2726781008893D1;                        35P0000023
214,1,3.0,1.0,0.0,0.0,5.2108495355316D1,4.167109391291D1,3.0D1,    37P0000024
3.0D1;                                                             37P0000025
206,33,35,37,3.0D1,3.0D1;                                          39P0000026
110,2.8D1,30.0,0.0,3.2D1,30.0,0.0;                                 41P0000027
110,3.0D1,28.0,0.0,3.0D1,32.0,0.0;                                 43P0000028
110,2.6D1,30.0,0.0,3.0,30.0,0.0;                                   45P0000029
110,34.0,30.0,0.0,57.0,30.0,0.0;                                   47P0000030
110,3.0D1,26.0,0.0,3.0D1,3.0,0.0;                                  49P0000031
110,3.0D1,34.0,0.0,3.0D1,57.0,0.0;                                 51P0000032
S0000002G0000004D0000052P0000032                                    T0000001
```

Figure 14.5

Example drawing

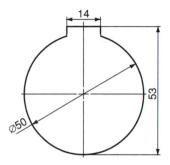

In Figure 14.4, the records with the character G in column 73 belong to the Global section.

The Directory Entry section is a list of all the entities together with certain of their attributes. In an IGES file, all product definition data are expressed as a list of predefined entities—the geometric entities such as lines, curves, planes, and surfaces and the annotation entities such as notes and dimension values. Each entity is assigned a specific entity type number. Figure 14.6 shows the geometric entities defined in each IGES version. Note that, for the first time, solids were included as geometric entities in version 4.0. The entry for each entity occupies two 80-character records that are divided into a total of twenty 8-character fields. The first and the eleventh (beginning of the second record of any given entity) fields contain the entity type number. The second field contains a pointer to the record in the Parameter Data section where the actual data defining the entity are stored. This pointer is simply the sequence number of the relevant record in the PD section. The remaining fields are used to store the attributes, such as line fonts, layer number, transformation matrix, line weight, and color.

The Parameter Data section contains the actual data defining each entity listed in the Data Entry section. For example, a straight-line entity is defined by the six coordinates of its two end points. While each entity always has two records in the DE section, the number of records needed for each entity in the PD section varies from one entity to another and depends on the amount of necessary data. Parameter data are placed in free format in columns 1 through 64. The parameter delimiter specified in the Global section is used to separate parameters, and the record delimiter—also specified in the Global section—is used to terminate the list of parameters. Usually, commas are used as parameter delimiters, and semicolons are used as record delimiters. Columns 66 through 72 in all PD records contain the pointer to point back to the corresponding entity in the DE section. Note that this pointer has the sequence number of the first of the two records of each entity in the DE section. Columns 74 through 80 contain the sequence number of its own record. The Terminate section contains a single record that specifies the number of records in each of the four preceding sections for checking purposes.

The following problems arise in practice when pre-processors and post-processors are used with IGES as a neutral file format. The first problem occurs when the

Figure 14.6

Geometric entities supported in each IGES version with their type numbers

IGES Version

Modeling type

Surfaces

IGES 2.0						IGES 3.0	
108	114	118	120	122	128	140	144
Plane	Parametric spline surface	Ruled surface	Surface of revolution	Tabulated cylinder	Rational B-spline surface	Offset surface	Trimmed parametric surface

Curves

IGES 2.0							IGES 3.0	
100	102	104	110	112	116	126	130	142
Circular arc	Composite curve	Conic arc	Line	Parametric spline curve	Point	Rational B-spline curve	Offset curve	Curve on a parametric surface

Others

IGES 2.0					IGES 3.0		IGES 4.0	
106	124	125	134	136	132	138	146	148
Copious data	Transformation matrix	Flash	Node	Finite element	Connect point	Nodal display and roration	Nodal results	Element results

Solids (IGES 4.0)

150	152	154	156	158	160	162	164	168	180	184	430
Block	Right angular wedge	Right circular cylinder	Right circular cone	Sphere	Torus	Solid of revolution	Solid of linear extrusion	Ellipsoid	Boolean tree	Solid assembly	Solid instance

internal data representation of an entity in a system is different from that of the same entity in IGES. For example, a circular arc may be defined by a center, a radius, and starting and ending angles in a particular system, but the same arc is defined by a center, a starting point, and an ending point in IGES. Thus a conversion utilizing the arc parametric equation must be performed by the designated IGES processor. Such conversion must be done twice—to and from IGES—and in each case the arc data are subject to truncation and round-off errors. The second problem is more serious and occurs when an entity is not specifically supported and thus must be converted to the closest available entity. This problem occurs often in communicating data between two systems through IGES if the processors in one system support a different version of IGES from those of the other system. The typical example is the loss of symbol information if either one of the systems uses a lower version of IGES not supporting macros.

14.3 DRAWING INTERCHANGE FORMAT

Drawing interchange format (DXF) files were originally developed to give users flexibility in managing data and translating AutoCAD[1] drawings into file formats that could be read and used by other CAD/CAM/CAE systems. Because of the popularity of AutoCAD, DXF became the de facto standard of interchanging CAD drawing files for almost all CAD/CAM/CAE systems. In fact, almost every newly introduced CAD/CAM/CAE system tends to provide translators to and from the DXF file.

A DXF file is an ASCII text file and consists of five sections: Header, Table, Block, Entity, and Terminate. The Header section describes the AutoCAD drawing environment that existed when the DXF file was created. The Table section contains information about line types, layers, text styles, and views that may have been defined in the drawing. The Block section contains a list of graphic entities that are defined as a group. Thus the Block section is equivalent to the definition of a display list in Chapter 3. The specific data of each entity of a block are stored in the corresponding Entity section immediately following the Block section. The Entity section is the main part of the DXF file, with all entities of the drawing described in it. Finally, the Terminate section indicates the end of the file. A detailed description of these sections is presented in Jones and Martin [1989].

Similar to that of the IGES files, the repertoire of the entities used in DXF files has been expanded with the introduction of the newer versions of AutoCAD. A DXF file created by a higher version of AutoCAD cannot be read by other systems based on a lower version of DXF.

---

[1] AutoCAD is a commercial two-dimensional CAD software running mainly on personal computers.

14.4 STANDARD FOR THE EXCHANGE OF PRODUCT DATA

The IGES files and DXF files were developed to exchange product definition data instead of product data. By *product data* we mean the data relevant to the entire life cycle of a product (e.g., design, manufacturing, quality assurance, testing, and support). Even though the specification of the IGES or DXF file has been broadened to encompass some of these product data, the data carried by those files are inherently insufficient to be the product data supporting the entire life cycle. As a result, a new effort called product data exchange specification (PDES) was initiated in the United States in 1983. The general emphasis of PDES was to eliminate the human presence from the exchange of product data rather than the exchange of product definition data, that is, to eliminate the need for engineering drawings and other paper documents in passing information about different product phases being performed on similar or dissimilar CAD/CAM/CAE systems. Meanwhile, the International Organization for Standardization's (ISO's) Technical Committee TC184 (Industrial Automation Systems) and its subcommittee SC4 (External Representation of Product Model Data) were formed in July 1984 to establish a single worldwide standard for the exchange of product model data, STEP (Standard for the Exchange of Product model data). Both PDES and STEP had the identical goal, so in June 1985 the IGES Steering Committee decided that PDES should represent U.S. interests in the STEP effort. As a result, the acronym PDES has been changed to stand for product data exchange using STEP, to emphasize the intention that PDES and STEP be identical.

STEP development is based on the following principles.

• It has to target product data, which encompass the data relevant to the entire life cycle of a product, including design, manufacturing, quality assurance, testing, and support. Thus it has to consider as data the tolerance information, form feature information, the finite-element model, and the kinematic analysis model, and so on, as well as the product definition data relevant primarily to the product shape.

• In STEP's data structure application-specific data should be stored in a module of the application layer separate from the generic shape information. This approach ensures that the data structure is sufficient to support a wide range of applications while disallowing redundancy in the generic data structure.

• It has to utilize a formal language to define the data structure. In IGES and DXF, the specification describes the format of a physical file that stores all the geometric and other data. In STEP, the data are described in the EXPRESS language, which then maps to the physical file. In this way, ambiguities can be avoided when product data extracted from the file are interpreted.

STEP development is being undertaken by a number of committees and working groups that are dealing with different aspects of the standards, called *parts*. These parts are grouped according to description methods, integrated-information resources, application protocols, implementation methods, and conformance methodology, as il-

Figure 14.7

STEP architecture

APPLICATION PROTOCOLS AND ASSOCIATED ABSTRACT TEST SUITES

I 201 Explicit draughting (W)*	
I 202 Associative draughting (C)	
I 203 Configuration-controlled design (C)	C 221 Process plant functional data & its schem rep (W)
C 204 Mechanical design using boundary rep (C)	W 222 Design-manuf for composite structures (W)
C 205 Mechanical design using surface rep (W)	W 223 Exc of dgn & mfg product info for cast parts (W)
X 206 Mechanical design using wireframe (X)	E 224 Mech parts def for p. plg using mach'n'g feat (W)
E 207 Sheet metal die planning and design (C)	E 225 Structural bldg elem using explicit shape rep (W)
W 208 Life-cycle product change process (W)	
C 209 Compos & metal struct, anal, & related dgn (W)	W 226 Ship's mechanical systems (W)
C 210 Electronic P-C assy: product-design data (W)	E 227 Plant spatial configuration (W)
	O 228 Building services: HVAC (O)
X 211 Electronic P-C assy: test, diag, & rem anuf (W)	W 229 Forged parts (W)
C 212 Electrotechnical design and installation (W)	W 230 Building structural frame: steelwork (W)
E 213 Num contr (NC) process plans for mach'd parts (W)	
C 214 Core data for automotive mech dgn processes (W)	W 231 Process-engineering data (W)
W 215 Ship arrangements (W)	W 232 Technical data packaging: core info & exch (W)
W 216 Ship moulded forms (W)	O Neutral optical-data-interchange format (O)
W 217 Ship piping (W)	O Product life-cycle support—NATO (O)
W 218 Ship structures (W)	O SGML and industrial data (O)
X 219 Dimension inspection (X)	
O 220 Printed-circuit assemblies: mfg planning (O)	

IMPLEMENTATION METHODS

I 21 Clear text encoding of ex ch str.	C 24 Late C (binding for #22)
E 22 Standard data access interface	X 25 Late FORTRAN
E 23 Early C++ (binding for #22)	E 26 IDL (binding for #22)

CONFORMANCE TESTING METHODOLOGY FRAMEWORK

I 31 General concepts
E 32 Requirements on testing labs and clients
X 33 Abstract test suites
C 34 Abstract test methods for Part 21 impl.
W 35 Abstract test methods for Part 22 impl. (Approved for new scope)

(a)

lustrated in Figure 14.7. The status of every part is shown beside its number. Status designators vary from O (the ISO preliminary stage) to I (International standard—the most advanced stage of standards development and acceptance). Parts designated as E, F (levels of draft international standard), and I are considered advanced enough to allow software vendors to proceed with product implementation.

The description methods group forms the underpinning of STEP. It includes part 1, Overview, which also contains definitions that are universal to STEP. Also in that group, part 11, EXPRESS Language Reference Manual, describes the data-modeling language employed in STEP. Parts in the descriptive-methods group are numbered 1 through 9.

At the next level is the integrated-information resource group, the parts that contain the actual STEP data models. These data models are the building blocks of

Figure 14.7

(continued)

DESCRIPTION METHODS
I 1 Overview and fund. principles (Amend. 1 = 0)
I 11 EXPRESS lang ref man. (Ed 2 = W)
X 12 EXPRESS I lang ref man (Type 2 tech report = W)

INTEGRATED-INFORMATION RESOURCES

INTEGRATED-APPLICATION RESOURCES

I 101 Draughting	C 104 Finite element analysis
X 102 Ship structures	I 105 Kinematics
X 103 E/E connectivity	W 106 Building core model
	A 107 Engineering anal core

INTEGRATED-GENERIC RESOURCES

I 41 Fund of prdct descr & spt (ed2 = A)	
I 42 Geom & topol rep (Amd1 = W)	I 46 Visual presentation
I 43 Repres specialization (ed2 = A)	F 47 Tolerances
I 44 Product struct config (ed2 = A)	X 48 Form features
F 45 Materials	F 49 Process structure & properties

APLLICATION-INTERPRETED CONSTRUCTS

C 501 Edge-based wireframe	C 511 Topol-bounded surface
C 502 Shell-based wireframe	C 512 Faceted B-representation
C 503 Geom-bounded 2D wireframe	C 513 Elementary B-rep
C 504 Draughting annotation	C 514 Advanced B-rep
C 505 Drawing structure & admin	C 515 Constructive solid geometry
C 506 Draughting elements	X 516 Mechanical-design context
C 507 Geom-bounded surface	C 517 Mech-design geom presentation
C 508 Non-manifold surface	C 518 Mech-design shaded presentation
C 509 Manifold surface	C 519 Geometric tolerances
C 510 Geom-bounded wireframe	C 520 Assoc draughting elements

(b)

STEP. Integrated-information resources include generic resources, application resources, and application-interpreted constructs (AICs). Integrated-generic resources are entities that are used as needed by application protocols (APs). Parts within generic resources are numbered in the 40s and are used across the entire spectrum of STEP APs. The integrated-application resources contain entities that have slightly more context than the generic entities. The parts in the integrated-application resources are numbered in the 100s. The 500 series are application-interpreted constructs. They are reusable groups of information-resource entities that make it easier to express identical semantics in more than one AP.

At the top level of the STEP hierarchy are the more complex data models that are used to describe specific product-data applications. These parts are known as application protocols and describe not only the data to be used in describing a product, but how the data are to be used in the model. The APs use the integrated-information resources in well-defined combinations and configurations to represent a particular data model of some phase of product life. Numbered in the 200s, APs currently in use are the Explicit Draughting AP 201 and the Configuration Controlled Design AP 203.

The STEP implementation-methods group, the 20s, describe mapping from STEP formal specifications to representation used to implement STEP. The conformance-testing-methodology framework group, the 30s, provides information about methods for testing of software product conformance to the STEP standards, guidance for creating abstract-test suites, and the responsibilities of testing laboratories. Figure 14.7 shows that part 31, which describes the methodology to perform conformance testing, has been approved as an international standard. The STEP standards are unique in that they emphasize testing and actually specify testing methods in the standards.

The 300 series of parts, abstract test suites, consists of test data and criteria that are used to assess conformance of a STEP software product to the associated AP. The numbers assigned to ATSs exceed the AP numbers by exactly 100. Therefore ATS 303 applies to AP 203. For further details about STEP, access the Web site http://www.nist.gov/sc4.

STEP draws more attention these days as it is expected to be accepted by Computer-aided Acquisition and Logistics Support (CALS) as a standard for product data exchange. A U.S. Department of Defense initiative, the aim of CALS is to apply computer technology to the process of specifying, ordering, operating, supporting, and maintaining the weapons systems used by the U.S. armed forces. The main thrust of the initiative is to prescribe the formats to be used for the storage and exchange of computer-based data. Even though CALS was initiated for military use, it is also becoming a standard in industry for the storage and exchange of companywide computer-based data.

QUESTIONS AND PROBLEMS

1. Discuss the advantage and disadvantage of using the standard format in exchanging product definition data between CAD/CAM/CAE systems.

2. Generate a DXF file of the drawing in Problem 1(a) of Chapter 4, using a computer-aided drafting system. Then read the file from another drafting system and display the drawing. What do you conclude?

3. Generate an IGES file of the object in Problem 8 of Chapter 12, read the file from another solid modeling system, and try the following tasks.

   a. Display the object.

   b. Calculate the centroid of the object.

   c. What do you conclude about the capability of IGES in transferring the solid data?

4. Discuss the advantage of using STEP as a standard.

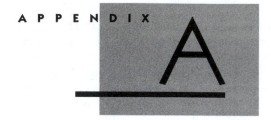

Implementation of the Half-Edge Data Structure

Figure A.1 illustrates the half-edge data structure used by Mäntylä [1988] in the solid modeling system GWB. The data structure is implemented in the C language.

The procedure shown in Figure A.2 is a C-code that searches all the edges sharing a given vertex. This procedure demonstrates that the half-edge data structure shown in Figure A.1 provides the necessary adjacency information for topologic entities.

Figure A.1

Helf-edge data
structure sug-
gested by Mäntylä

```
typedef float              vector [4] ;
typedef float              matrix [4] [4] ;
typedef short              Id ;
typedef struct solid       Solid ;
typedef struct face        Face ;
typedef struct loop        Loop ;
typedef struct halfedge    HalfEdge ;
typedef struct vertex      Vertex ;
typedef struct edge        Edge ;
typedef union nodes        Node ;

struct solid
{
        Id         Solidno ;      /* solid identifier */
        Face       *sfaces ;      /* pointer to list of face */
        Edge       *sedges ;      /* pointer to list of edges */
        Vertex     *sverts ;      /* pointer to list of vertices */
        Solid      *nexts ;       /* pointer to next solid */
        Solid      *prevs ;       /* pointer to previous solid */
} ;

struct face
{
        Id         faceno ;       /* face identifier */
        Solid      *fsolid ;      /* back pointer to solid */
        Loop       *flout ;       /* pointer to outer loop */
        Loop       *floops ;      /* pointer to list of loops */
        vector     feq ;          /* face equation */
        Face       *nextf ;       /* pointer to next face */
        Face       *prevf ;       /* pointer to previous face */
} ;

struct loop
{
        HalfEdge   *ledg ;        /* pointer to ring of halfedges */
        Face       *lface ;       /* back pointer to face */
        Loop       *nextl ;       /* pointer to next loop */
        Loop       *prevl ;       /* pointer to previous loop */
} ;

struct edge
{
        HalfEdge   *he1 ;         /* pointer to right halfedge */
        HalfEdge   *he2 ;         /* pointer to left halfedge */
        Edge       *nexte ;       /* pointer to next edge */
        Edge       *preve ;       /* pointer to previous edge */
} ;

struct halfedge
{
        Edge       *edg ;         /* pointer to parent edge */
        Vertex     *vtx ;         /* pointer to starting vertex */
        Loop       *wloop ;       /* back pointer to loop */
        HalfEdge   *nexthe ;      /* pointer to next halfedge */
        HalfEdge   *prevhe ;      /* pointer to previous halfedge */
} ;
```

Figure A.1

(continued)

```
struct vertex
{
        Id              vertexno ;      /* vertex identifier */
        HalfEdge        *vedge ;        /* pointer to a halfedge */
        vector          vcoord ;        /* vertex coordinates */
        Vertex          *nextv ;        /* pointer to next vertex */
        Vertex          *prevv ;        /* pointer to previous vertex */
} ;

union nodes
{
        Solid           s ;
        Face            f ;
        Loop            l ;
        HalfEdge        h ;
        Vertex          v ;
        Edge            e ;
} ;
```

Figure A.2

Procedure of searching for all the edges connected to a vertex

```
# define        mate ( he )   ( ( he ) ) == ( he )->edg->he1 ) ? \
                ( he )->edg->he2 : ( he )->edg->he1 )

void list_adjacent_edge ( V, list )
Vertex  *V ;
Edge    *list [ ] ;
{
    HalfEdge        *adj ;
    int             i = 0 ;

    adj = V->vedge ;

    if( adj ) do
            {
                list [ i ] = adj->edg ;
                i ++ ;
            }
            while( ( adj = mate( adj )->nexthe ) != V->vedge ) ;
    else printf( "error\n" ) ;
}
```

Implementation of the Winged-Edge Data Structure

Figure B.1 illustrates the winged-edge data structure used in SNUMOD. The data structure is implemented in the C language.

Figure B.1

Implementation of
the winged-edge
data structure in
SNUMOD

```
typedef   struct   snu_body     Body
typedef   struct   snu_shell    Shell ;
typedef   struct   snu_face     Face ;
typedef   struct   snu_loop     Loop ;
typedef   struct   snu_edge     Edge ;
typedef   struct   snu_vertxex  Vertex ;
typedef   struct   snu_surface  Surface ;
typedef   struct   snu_curve    Curve ;
typedef   struct   snu_point    Point ;


struct snu_body
{
        int       id ;          /* body identifier */
        Body      *next ;       /* pointer to next body */
        Shell     *shell ;      /* pointer to shell */
        char      *name         /* pointer to body name */
} ;


struct snu_shell
{
        int       id ;          /* shell identifier */
        Body      *body ;       /* pointer to body */
        Shell     *next ;       /* pointer to next shell */
        Face      *face ;       /* pointer to face */
} ;


struct snu_face
{
        int       id ;          /* face identifier */
        Shell     *shell ;      /* pointer to shell */
        Face      *next         /* pointer to next face */
        Loop      *loop ;       /* pointer to loop */
        Surface   *surface      /* pointer to geometry data */
} ;


struct snu_loop
{
        int       id ;          /* loop identifier */
        Face      *face ;       /* pointer to face */
        Loop      *next ;       /* pointer to next loop */
        Edge      *edge ;       /* pointer to edge */
        int       type ;        /* loop type */
} ;
```

Figure B.1

(continued)

```
struct snu_edge
{
        int         id              /* edge identifier */
        Loop        *left_loop      /* pointer to left loop */
        Loop        *right_loop     /* pointer to right loop */
        Edge        *left_arm       /* pointer to left arm ( ccw left edge ) */
        Edge        *left_leg       /* pointer to left leg ( cw left edge ) */
        Edge        *right_leg      /* pointer to right leg ( ccw right edge ) */
        Edge        *right_arm      /* pointer to right arm ( cw right edge ) */
        Vertex      *tail_vertex    /* pointer to tail vertex ( previous vertex ) */
        Vertex      *head_vertex    /* pointer to head vertex ( next vertex ) */
        Curve       *curve          /* pointer to geometry data */
} ;


struct snu_vertex
{
        int         id              /* vertex identifier */
        Edge        *edge           /* pointer to edge */
        Point       *point          /* pointer to geometry data */
} ;
```

A P P E N D I X   C

Euler Operators

C.1   EULER OPERATORS USED IN SNUMOD

C.1.1   MEVVLS and KEVVLS (make (kill) an edge, two vertices, a peripheral loop, and a shell)

MEVVLS is activated to create a shell when a solid is initially created or a void is added to an existing solid. In reality, **MEVVLS** simply allocates the memory space for a shell by declaring that a shell is created. It also creates two vertices, an edge between the vertices, and a peripheral loop traversing back and forth the vertices that will be used as the seed entity that will grow into a real shell as the modeling operation proceeds. A face is also created when a peripheral loop is created. However, the geometry information of the face is not filled when it is created by **MEVVLS** because it is a just a conceptual face used to allocate the required memory.[1] It will have the necessary geometry information when the seed edge grows into a closed circuit enclosing an area as the modeling operation proceeds.

This description of the topology change created by **MEVVLS** is illustrated by the schematic diagram shown in Figure C.1. Peripheral loop **L1** is a circuit running through **V1–V2–V1** and is not enclosing an area. However, it will have an area as the modeling proceeds, and accordingly the corresponding face will have its geometry information.

The input and output arguments of **MEVVLS** can be expressed as

$$\textbf{MEVVLS (B, \&E1, \&V1, \&V2, \&L1, \&S1, X1, Y1, Z1, X2, Y2, Z2)}$$

---

[1] Allocating a memory space for a topology entity is equivalent to assigning its number arbitrarily, as described in Section 5.3.2.

Figure C.1

Effect of MEVVLS (KEVVLS)

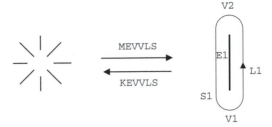

In that expression, the entities preceded by the symbol **&** are the output entities generated by **MEVVLS**, and the rest are the input entities. Therefore the expression can be interpreted to mean that new edge **E1**, new vertices **V1** and **V2** at (x1, y1, z1) and (x2, y2, z2), new peripheral loop **L1**, and a new shell **S1** are created on the solid **B**. We use the same notation to differentiate the output arguments from the input arguments in the other Euler operators.

Similarly, the inverse operator **KEVVLS** can be expressed as

KEVVLS (B, E1, V1, V2, L1, S1, &X1, &Y1, &Z1, &X2, &Y2, &Z2)

The inverse operators are very useful in implementing an *Undo* operation that cancels the modeling operation previously performed. This is why most solid modeling systems carry the inverse operators and the regular (or forward) operators at the same time.

C.1.2 MEL and KEL (make (kill) an edge and a peripheral loop)

MEL is used to add an edge **E1** connecting two vertices **V1** and **V2** in a loop **L1**, as illustrated in Figure C.2. The original loop **L1** is divided into two new loops **L1** and **L2** by the application of **MEL**. The original loop to be divided can be a peripheral loop, as shown in Figure C.2(a), or a hole loop, as shown in Figure C.2(b). Moreover, MEL should update the edge connections at vertices **V1** and **V2** and the edge–loop relations to reflect the division of the original loop **L1** into two new loops, in addition to simply adding an edge and a loop.

The input and output arguments of **MEL** and **KEL** are expressed as follows, with the input argument **B** indicating a solid as before:

MEL (B, L1, V1, V2, &E1, &L2)
KEL (B, &L1, &V1, &V2, E1, L2)

C.1.3 MEV and KEV (make (kill) an edge and a vertex)

MEV creates edge **E1** from vertex **V1** located on loop **L1** to a specified position (x, y, z) and adds the edge to **L1**, as illustrated in Figure C.3. Of course, a new vertex **V2** is also created at the specified position. An edge **E1** can be added to a peripheral loop, as shown in Figure C.3(a), or to a hole loop, as shown in Figure C.3(b).

Figure C.2

Effect of MEL (KEL)

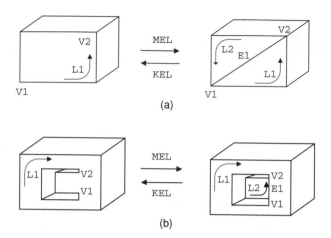

Similar to **MEL**, the edge connection at **V1** has to be updated so that new edge **E1** is included in loop **L1**, (i.e., edge **E1** will appear twice in the list of edges as the bridge edges described in Section 5.3.2 when the edge list of loop **L1** is derived from the updated connectivity information).

The input and output arguments of **MEV** and **KEV** are expressed as follows, with the input argument **B** indicating a solid as before:

MEV (B, L1, V1, &E1, &V2, X, Y, Z)
KEV (B, &L1, &V1, E1, V2, &X, &Y, &Z)

KEV is simply an inverse of **MEV**.

C.1.4 MVE and KVE (make (kill) a vertex and an edge)

MVE splits edge **E1** by adding vertex **V1** on **E1** at a position specified by (x, y, z) and accordingly replaces the original edge **E1** by two new edges **E1** and **E2**, as il-

Figure C.3

Effect of MEV (KEV)

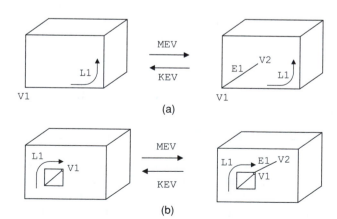

Figure C.4

Effect of MVE (KVE)

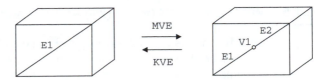

lustrated in Figure C.4. Therefore the input and output arguments of **MVE** and **KVE** can be expressed as follows, with the input argument **B** indicating a solid as before:

MVE (B, E1, &V1, &E2, X, Y, Z)
KVE (B, &E1, V1, E2, &X, &Y, &Z)

KVE can be interpreted as the inverse of **MVE**.

The effects shown in Figure C.4 are obtained by changing one vertex and the neighboring edges of **E1** and by storing similar information for **E2**. The details are given in Figure C.5, which shows implementation of the **MVE** operator in C language based on the winged-edge data structure (see Figure B.1). Going through the steps in Figure C.5 demonstrates clearly how these Euler operators are implemented. Other Euler operators can be implemented similarly.

Figure C.5

Implementation of MVE operator

```
MVE ( B, E1, V1, E2, x, y, z )
Body      *B ;
Edge      *E1 ;
Vertex    **V1 ;
Edge      **E2 ;
double    x, y, z ;
{
        ( *V1 ) = malloc ( sizeof ( Vertex ) ) ;
        ( *E2 ) = malloc ( sizeof ( Edge ) ) ;
        ( *E2 )->tail_vertex = *V1 ;
        ( *E2 )->head_vertex = E1->head_vertex ;
        ( *E2 )->right_leg = E1 ;
        ( *E2 )->left_leg = E1 ;
        ( *E2 )->right_arm = E1->right_arm ;
        ( *E2 )->left_arm = E1->left_arm ;
        ( *E2 )->right_loop = E1->right_loop ;
        ( *E2 )->left_loop = E1->left_loop ;
        ( *V1 )->edge = *E2 ;
        ( *V1 )->point.x = x ; ( *V1 )->point.y = y ; ( *V1 )->point.z = z ;
        E1->right_arm = E1->left_arm = *E2 ;
        E1->head_vertex = *V1 ;
}
```

C.1.5 MEKH and KEMH (make (kill) an edge and kill (make) a hole loop)

MEKH connects a peripheral loop and its hole loop by adding an edge to result in one peripheral loop, as illustrated in Figure C.6(a) or connects two hole loops into one hole loop, as illustrated in Figure C.6(b). More specifically, it connects vertex **V1** on loop **L1** and vertex **V2** on loop **L2** by adding edge **E1** between them and accordingly changes **L1** to include **L2**. Therefore the input and output arguments of **MEKH** and **KEMH** can be expressed as

MEKH (B, V1, V2, L1, L2, &E1)
KEMH (B, &V1, &V2, &L1, &L2, E1)

KEMH can be interpreted as the inverse of **MEKH**.

C.1.6 MZEV and KZEV (make (kill) a zero-length edge and a vertex)

MZEV splits vertex **V1** into two vertices, **V1** and **V2**, by adding edge **E1** having a zero length, as illustrated in Figure C.7. The vertex is split vertically instead of horizontally because new edge **E1** belongs to the specified loops **L1** and **L2**. Thus vertex **V1** will be split horizontally if **L3** and **L4** (in Figure 5.52) are provided as the input. Therefore the input and output arguments of **MZEV** and **KZEV** can be expressed as

MZEV (B, L1, L2, V1, &E1, &V2)
KEMH (B, &L1, &L2, &V1, E1, V2)

KZEV can be interpreted as the inverse of **MZEV**.

Figure C.6

Effect of MEKH (KEMH)

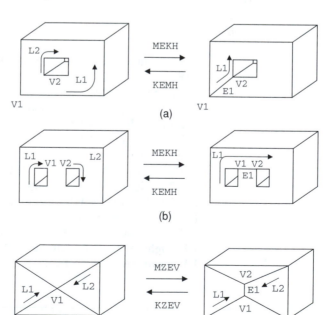

Figure C.7

Effect of MZEV (KZEV)

Figure C.8

Effect of MPKH (KPMH)

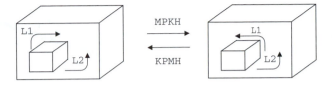

C.1.7 MPKH and KPMH (make (kill) a peripheral loop and kill (make) a hole loop)

MPKH converts a hole loop to a peripheral loop, as illustrated in Figure C.8. More specifically, it converts hole loop **L1** to a peripheral loop. It also outputs loop **L2** to keep the record that loop **L1** was originally a hole loop of **L2**. Similarly, **KPMH** converts a peripheral loop **L1** to a hole loop belonging to a peripheral loop **L2**. Therefore the input and output arguments of **MPKH** and **KPMH** can be expressed as

> **MPKH (B, L1, &L2)**
> **KPMH (B, L1, L2)**

In the application of **MPKH** and **KPMH**, when hole loop **L1** is changed to a peripheral loop, two disconnected solids may result. We can get around this problem by storing the disconnected solids under separate shells after searching through the peripheral loops comprising each shell. Similarly, it is necessary to merge two separate shells into one when loops **L1** and **L2** originally belong to the separate shells provided to **KPMH**.

C.2 APPLICATION OF EULER OPERATORS

We now present some examples to show how the Euler operators described are used to implement modeling functions. Other modeling functions can be implemented in a similar manner.

C.2.1 Translational Sweeping

We first demonstrate how the Euler operators are invoked in the translational sweeping function that creates a solid by translating a two-dimensional closed domain. We assume that the modeling function requires us to draw a two-dimensional profile in the *xy* plane. This assumption does not limit the modeling capability because a solid created in this way can be rotated to the desired orientation later. The following steps describe the entire procedure.

Figure C.9

Result after step 1

Figure C.10

Result after step 2

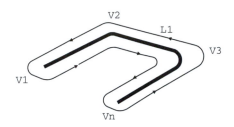

1. A seed entity is created from two points on the two-dimensional profile to be translated. More specifically, we activate **MEVVLS** to create two vertices at the points, an edge between the vertices, a peripheral loop going back and forth between the vertices, and a shell, as shown in Figure C.9. The loop is indicated by the circuit drawn with arrows. Be sure to note how loop **L1** changes as we proceed. The loop and the shell do not have physical meaning in this step, but their existence is declared for the purpose of allocating addresses in memory.

2. The points on the profile are connected to the seed edge in step 1 by applying **MEV**s, following the profile until all the points are connected, as shown in Figure C.10. If there are n points on the profile, **MEV** will be invoked $(n-2)$ times in this step.

3. A closed polygon is generated by adding an edge between the first and the last vertex by **MEL**, as shown in Figure C.11. Note that the original loop, **L1**, is divided into **L1** and **L2** by the new edge. We will find later that **L1** becomes the top face and **L2** becomes the bottom face of the solid to be generated.

4. The edges are created in the translational direction, as shown in Figure C.12. This operation involves applying **MEV** n times. Figures C.12 and C.13 show the results after we apply **MEV** once and n times, respectively. Notice how loop **L1** changes as **MEV**s are applied.

5. The side faces are created by adding proper edges, as shown in Figures C.14 and C.15. This operation involves applying **MEL** n times. Figures C.14 and C.15 show the results after we apply **MEL** once and n times, respectively. After the sweeping operation has been completed, **L1** becomes the top face.

Figure C.11

Result after step 3

Figure C.12

Result after applying **MEV** once

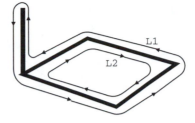

Figure C.13

Result after applying **MEV** *n* times

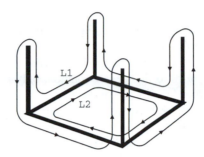

Figure C.14

Result after applying **MEL** once

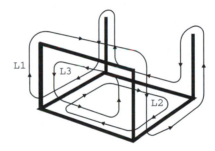

Figure C.15

Result after applying **MEL** *n* times

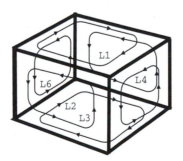

C.2.2 Rotational Sweeping or Swinging

We now consider a rotational sweeping that creates a solid by revolving a two-dimensional closed domain. We assume that the modeling function requires us to draw a two-dimensional profile in the *xz* plane with the *z* axis as the axis of rota-

Figure C.16

Figure C.16

A closed profile in
the *xz* plane

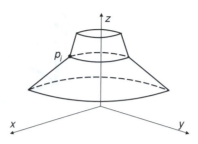

tion, as illustrated in Figure C.16. This assumption does not limit the modeling capability because a solid created in this way can be rotated to the desired orientation later. The following steps describe the entire procedure. Even though this procedure applies to 360-degree rotation, only minor modifications are needed to derive the procedure for partial revolution.

1. A seed entity is created from two points on the two-dimensional profile to be rotated, as shown in Figure C.17. This is done by using **MEVVLS** as in translational sweeping. Note that the loop is expressed as in Figure C.9.

2. The points on the profile are connected to the seed edge in step 1 by applying **MEVs**, following the profile until all the points are connected in the same way as in step 2 of translational sweeping. Thus **MEV** is invoked $(n - 2)$ times when there are n points on the profile. The result is illustrated in Figure C.18.

3. Steps 1 and 2 are repeated to generate a mirror image of the profile with respect to the *yz* plane, as shown in Figure C.19. After the mirror image has been cre-

Figure C.17

Result after step 1

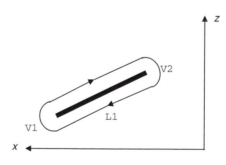

Figure C.18

Result after step 2

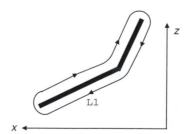

Figure C.19

Result after step 3

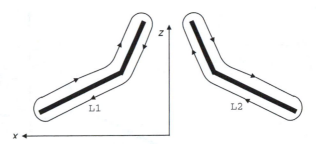

ated, **KPMH** is invoked to eliminate a shell associated with the mirror image making **L2** a hole loop of **L1**.

4. Loop **L2** is merged into **L1** by connecting them with an edge. The **MEKH** operation creates the connecting edge with the geometry of a semicircle on the xy plane, as shown in Figure C.20.

5. The corresponding vertices are connected by proper edges, as illustrated in Figures C.21 and C.22. Each edge will have the geometry of a semicircle, as before. This operation involves applying the **MEL** operator $(n - 1)$ times. Figures C.21 and C.22 show the results after applying **MEL** once and $(n - 1)$ times, respectively. Note how loop **L1** changes as **MEL**s are applied.

Figure C.20

Result after step 4

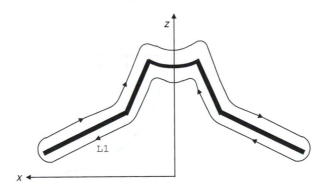

Figure C.21

Result after applying MEL once

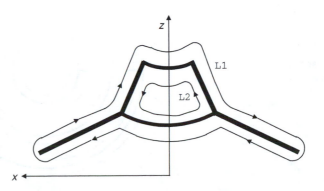

Figure C.22

Result after apply-
ing **MEL** ($n - 1$)
times

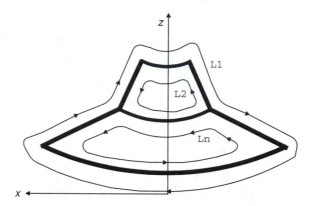

6. Step 5 is repeated to generate the faces at the rear half of the solid (i.e., **MEL** is applied n times). To understand the procedure in this step, simply follow the figures showing the topology change as **MEL**s are applied. As the rear side of the solid can be displayed better in the top view of the solid, Figures C.23, C.24, and C.25 show the top views of the solids after step 5 and after applying **MEL** once and n times, respectively. Note how loop **L1** changes as **MEL**s are applied: **L1** becomes the bottom face after the swinging operation has been completed.

Figure C.23

Result after step 5

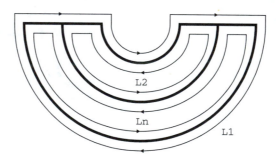

Figure C.24

Result after apply-
ing **MEL** once

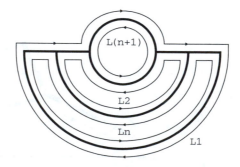

Figure C.25

Result after applying MEL *n* times

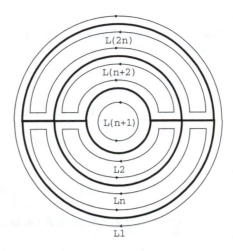

C.2.3 Primitive Creation

Recall that most solid modeling systems allow users to retrieve solids of simple shapes so that they can model complicated solids starting from these primitives. This method works because the procedures used to create these primitives are stored in advance, and they can be generated at any desired size according to the parameters specified by users. These procedures usually are composed of the Euler operators used for translational sweeping or swinging because most primitives can be generated by these modeling functions. In fact, Euler operators are indispensable for storing primitives in solid modeling systems. For example, Figure C.26 shows the procedure for creating a primitive block that has the parameters W, D, and H shown in Figure C.27.

We have applied the Euler operators in proper sequence to implement three basic modeling functions. The following example further demonstrates that any modeling function can be implemented by applying Euler operators.

EXAMPLE C.1

Show the application of a sequence of Euler operators in implementing a modeling operation that splits the hexahedron shown in Figure C.28(a) into two hexahedra, as shown in Figure C.28(f).

ANSWER

As illustrated in Figure C.28, the following Euler operators are invoked in sequence.

- The edges are split into two by **MVE**s (Figure C.28b). **MVE** is applied four times.
- **MZEV** is activated at each vertex created by **MVE** in the preceding step to get the result shown in Figure C.28(c). **MZEV** is also applied four times.

Figure C.26

Procedure for creating a block

```
Body      *Create_Block (W, D, H )
double    W, D, H;
{
        Body      *B;
        Shell     *S;
        Loop      *L1, *L2, *L3, *L4, *L5, *L6;
        Edge      *E1, *E2, *E3, *E4, *E5, *E6;
        Vertex    *V1, *V2, *V3, *V4, *V5, *V6, *V7, *V8;

        B = malloc ( sizeof ( Body ) );
        MEVVLS ( B, &E1, &V1, &V2, &L1, &S, D/2, W/2, 0, -D/2, W/2, 0 );
        MEV ( B, L1, V2, &E2, &V3, -D/2, -W/2, 0 );
        MEV ( B, L1, V3, &E3, &V4, D/2, -W/2, 0 );
        MEL ( B, L1, V4, V1, &E4, &L2 );
        MEV ( B, L1, V1, &E5, &V5, D/2, W/2, H );
        MEV ( B, L1, V2, &E6, &V6, -D/2, W/2, H );
        MEV ( B, L1, V3, &E7, &V7, -D/2, -W/2, H );
        MEV ( B, L1, V4, &E8, &V8, D/2, -W/2, H );
        MEL ( B, L1, V5, V6, &E9, &L3 );
        MEL ( B, L1, V6, V7, &E10, &L4 );
        MEL ( B, L1, V7, V8, &E11, &L5 );
        MEL ( B, L1, V8, V5, &E12, &L6 );
        return ( B );
}
```

Figure C.27

The parameters
and the coordinate
system for the
block

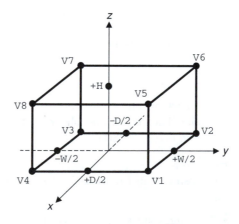

Figure C.28

Implementing a modeling function with Euler operators

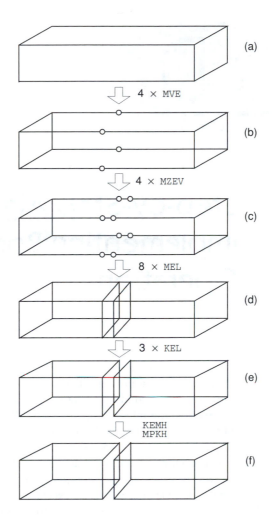

- **MEL** is applied to connect the new vertices created in the preceding steps and accordingly to create a face. **MEL** is applied eight times to create eight new edges and eight new faces (Figure C.28d). Note that four faces in the middle do not have areas.

- The edges of zero length are eliminated by **KEL** (Figure C.28e). When an edge is eliminated by **KEL**, two faces sharing the edge are merged into one at the same time. **KEL** is applied three times, leaving one connecting edge of zero length (Figure C.28e).

- The connecting edge is eliminated by **KEMH**. As **KEMH** makes one of the two loops connected by the edge being deleted into a hole loop, it is necessary to convert this loop to a peripheral loop, using **MPKH**. As mentioned earlier, **MPKH** will detect the existence of the separate shells and store the split hexahedra under two separate shells (Figure C.28f).

A P P E N D I X

D

Step-by-Step Algorithm for Implementing Boolean Operation

The Boolean operation algorithm used in SNUMOD is explained as follows for the operation illustrated in Figure D.1.

Step 1. The intersection curves of all the faces of solid *A* and all the faces of solid B are calculated; solid *A* and solid *B* are indicated in Figure D.1. Then only the portions of each intersection curve lying inside the two faces meeting at the intersection curve are obtained, as illustrated in Figure D.2. From now on, such a portion will be called an *xegment*, implying "intersection curve segment." Calculation of an intersection curve between surfaces is very difficult. However, it is a very important aspect of determining the efficiency and robustness of Boolean operation.

Figure D.1

Example Boolean operation

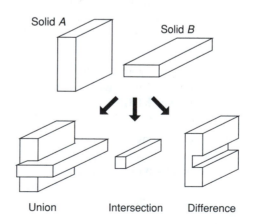

Figure D.2

Definition of xeg-ment

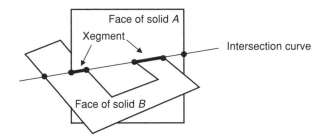

Various methods for calculating intersection curves can be used, depending on the type of surface equation used to represent each surface, as covered in Chapter 7. In addition, the end points of the xegment are obtained by the intersection points of the intersection curve and the edges of the faces involved, as covered in Chapter 6.

Step 2. The xegments obtained in step 1 are inscribed on the associated faces of solid A and solid B, as illustrated in Figure D.3. Each xegment is added as a new edge on the corresponding face of each solid by the proper Euler operators so that the division of the corresponding faces is taken care of automatically. Selection of the Euler operators is based on the relative location of the xegment with respect to the face onto which it is to be inscribed. There are five possible relative locations, as illustrated in Figure D.4. Figure D.4(a) shows the situation in which the new edge coincides with an existing edge, requiring no action. Figure D.4(b) shows the situation in which the two ends of the new edge coincide with existing vertices, but the new edge does not coincide with an existing edge; **MEL** needs to be activated

Figure D.3

Addition of new edges on solid A and solid B

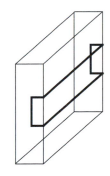
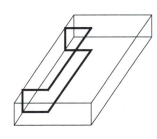

Solid A after modifiction   Solid B after modifiction

Figure D.4

Possible locations of xegment with re-spect to the corre-sponding face

(a)   (b)   (c)   (d)   (e)

in this case. Figure D.4(c) illustrates the situation in which one end of the new edge coincides with an existing vertex and the other end is located inside the face; **MEV** is applied in this case. Figure D.4(d) illustrates the case in which both ends of the new edge are located inside the face, which is handled by **MEVVLS** and **KPMH**. In this case, **KPMH** converts the loop created by **MEVVLS** to a hole loop belonging to the peripheral loop corresponding to the face. At the same time, it eliminates the redundant shell if the loop being changed to a hole loop was associated with a separate shell. Figure D.4(e) illustrates the situation in which two ends of the new edge are connected to different loops of the face; in this case, **MEKH** is applied. From these explanations, we can conclude that each xegment can be inscribed onto the corresponding face of each solid automatically if its relative location with respect to the corresponding face is identified automatically. This identification task involves testing whether the end points of the new edge are inside, outside, or on the boundary of the face. This test is called the *in/out test*.

Step 3. The faces of solid A are classified according to their relative location with respect to solid B. In other words, each face is tested to determine whether it is located inside, outside, or on the boundary surface of solid B. The faces of solid B are classified with respect to solid A in the same way.

This classification requires heavy computation, and thus we avoid it if we can infer the result from that of the neighboring faces. Fortunately, groups of faces of one solid can have the same relative location with respect to the other solid. For example, in Figure D.5, the faces in each group have the same relative location with respect to the other solid (i.e., the faces in group A_1 are outside solid B, and those in group B_1 are inside solid A). These groups also are separated by the new edges generated from xegments.

Therefore the faces in a group would be obtained by traversing the neighboring faces, starting from any seed face in the group without crossing the *xedges*, which are the new edges originated from xegments. Let's look for the faces in a group starting from the seed face hatched in Figure D.5. First, only the faces that do not share xedges with the hatched face are collected from among the neighboring faces of the hatched face. Then the same procedure is repeated by using each face in the collected faces as a secondary seed face and adding the newly collected faces to the collected face set. The process stops when all the faces in the set have been used as the secondary seed face. In this example, the faces in group A_1 will be collected. Then any face of solid A that does not belong to group A_1 will be selected as a seed

Figure D.5

Groups of faces

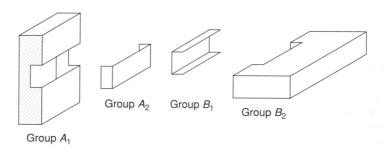

Group A_2 Group B_1 Group B_2

Group A_1

face; the same process is followed to obtain the faces in group A_2. If any face of solid A belongs to neither group A_1 nor group A_2, the faces in group A_3 (which does not exist in this example) will be collected. The same process is applied to solid B to give the face groups B_1 and B_2, as shown in Figure D.5.

Once the faces of solid A and B have been collected in groups, the relative location of each group of faces with respect to its counterpart solid should be identified. Let's consider the method for group A_1 as an example; the other groups can be handled the same way. First, one of the xedges bounding the external boundary of A_1 is arbitrarily chosen and denoted X_e as illustrated in Figure D.6. And any one of the faces of A_1 having X_e as one of its edges is denoted F_a, and the face of solid B that shares X_e with F_a is denoted F_b. Second, the respective outward normal vector N_a and N_b of F_a and F_b, and the tangent vector T at any one point on X_e are obtained, as shown in Figure D.6. The direction of the tangent vector T is counterclockwise, to be consistent with the direction of the peripheral loop L_a of F_a when viewed from outside. Finally, the classification of group A_1 with respect to solid B is derived from the value of $(N_a \times T) \cdot N_b$ as follows. Group A_1 is outside solid B if the value is positive, inside solid B if negative, and on solid B if zero. If group A_1 is determined to be on solid B, it is further classified as **ON_SAME** or **ON_OPPO-SITE**. It is **ON_SAME** if N_a and N_b are in the same direction and **ON_OPPO-SITE** if their directions are opposite.

Step 4. Groups of faces are collected according to the specific Boolean operation being applied. Table D.1 gives a rule to be followed for collecting the groups properly. We explain how to use it for the union operation, and it can be used the same way for other operations. For the union operation, Table D.1 shows that we need to collect the entities O and O(X)in the Union column. This means that we have to collect the groups of solid A that are outside solid B, the groups of solid B that are outside solid A, and groups of solid A classified as **ON_SAME** (or the groups of solid B classified as **ON_SAME**). The O(X) and X(O) symbols in Table D.1 imply that the entity in solid A corresponds to the one in solid B and that the entity has to be collected only once. If we apply this rule to the face groups in Figure D.5, we find that group A_1 and group B_2 are collected for the union operation. You can verify the rules for the intersection and difference operations in Table D.1 by applying them to the face groups shown in Figure D.5.

Figure D.6

Classification of a face group

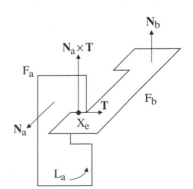

TABLE D.1

Face groups to be collected for each Boolean operation

		Union	Intersection	Difference
Solid A	OUT	O	X	O
	IN	X	O	X
	ON_SAME	O(X)	O(X)	X
	ON_OPPOSITE	X	X	O(X)
Solid B	OUT	O	X	X
	IN	X	O	O
	ON_SAME	X(O)	X(O)	X
	ON_OPPOSITE	X	X	X(O)

Step 5. Using the results obtained in step 4, the unnecessary face groups are eliminated from each solid. For the union operation example, group A_2 and group B_1 are eliminated from solid A and solid B, respectively. Figure D.7 illustrates the shape of solid A and solid B after the unnecessary face groups have been eliminated. The complicated topology operation required to form a solid can be avoided by eliminating the unnecessary face groups from the original solid instead of forming a new solid from the collected face groups. As mentioned earlier, the approaches by Requicha and Voelcker [1985] and Miller [1988] require this topology operation.

We explain the procedure for eliminating face group A_2 from solid A as an example. As illustrated in Figure D.8, the faces of group A_2 can be eliminated by deleting edges E_1 and E_2. Generally, the faces in a face group are eliminated by deleting all their edges except xedges. Xedges should not be deleted because they are also the boundary edges of other face groups that are being reserved. Edge E_1 is deleted by applying the Euler operator **KEL**, which also merges faces F_1 and F_2, as shown in Figure D.9(a). Similarly E_2 is deleted by **KEL**, as shown in Figure

Figure D.7

Solids after unnecessary face groups have been eliminated

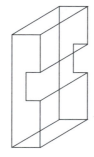
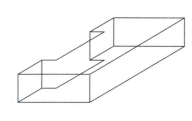

Figure D.8

Topology entities belonging to group A_2

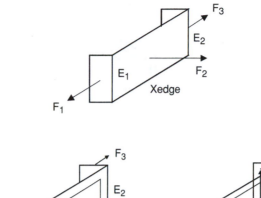

Figure D.9

Procedure for deleting E_1 and E_2

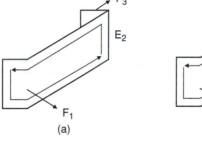

(a)   (b)

D.9(b). At this instant, the geometry information held by the merged face F_1 has no meaning, and only the information on its peripheral loop is used in the next step.

Step 6. The two solids obtained in step 5 are glued at their common boundary, as illustrated in Figure D.10. The same glue procedure needs to be applied for the different face groups when the intersection and difference operators are used.

For the example shown in Figure D.10, the glue procedure is implemented as follows. First, eight pairs of the coincident vertices and eight pairs of the coincident edges are identified, and a pair of vertices is connected by **KPMH** and **MEKH**. As explained earlier, two solids will be merged by **KPMH** to be stored under one shell. Furthermore, one of the two common boundary loops will become a hole loop of the other by applying **KPMH**. **MEKH** connects a pair of coincident vertices by appending the hole loop to the peripheral loop. The remaining seven pairs of vertices are connected by applying **MEL** seven times, as shown in Figure D.11. Second, each pair of vertices connected by an edge of zero length is deleted by **KZEV**. **KZEV** is applied eight times because eight pairs of vertices are connected by a zero length edge. Note that multiple edges and a degenerate loop still exist for

Figure D.10

Generation of solid by glue procedure

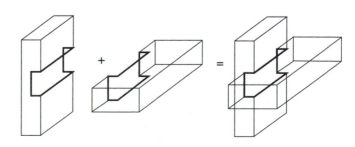

Figure D.11

Step-by-step illustration of glue procedure

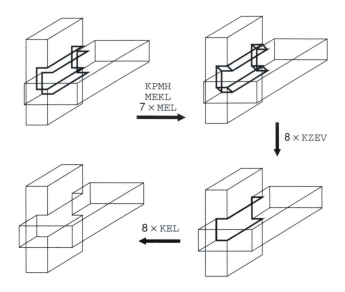

KPMH
MEKL
7 × MEL

8 × KZEV

8 × KEL

each edge, as indicated by a thick line in Figure D.11. Finally, **KEL** is applied eight times to eliminate the multiple edges and degenerate loops.

Step 7. Next, we determine whether the resulting solid has multiple separate shells. This step is necessary because multiple solids can result from the Boolean operation, as illustrated in Figure D.12.

Figure D.12

Boolean operation resulting in multiple solids

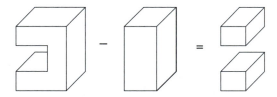

APPENDIX

E

Data Structure and Topology Operators for Nonmanifold Modeling Systems

E.1 DATA STRUCTURE

We represented a solid by three tables—face, edge, and vertex—in Section 5.3.2. We may think of storing the lists of topological entities of a nonmanifold model in a similar way. Figure E.1 illustrates such an approach, as proposed by Masuda [1990]. The object, a pyramid with a laminar face and a dangling edge in this case, is composed of a volume corresponding to the pyramid, a face corresponding to the laminar face, and an edge corresponding to the dangling edge. The volume is then defined by a shell enclosing it, and the shell is again defined by the list of faces (see the face table in Section 5.3.2). Then each face has associated loops, and each loop has a list of edges (see the edge table in Section 5.3.2). Similarly, each edge has a list of vertices (see the vertex table in Section 5.3.2). The data structure given in Figure E.1(b) appears to be very compact and clear because it is a simple extension of the data structure for manifold models. However, this data structure does not provide sufficient information for the derivation of adjacency information for the topological entities. For example, we have to identify the adjacency relation between the faces when a new face is added to the model in Figure E.1(a). If the new face generates a new shell with the existing faces, a new shell has to be derived and added with modifying shell S_1 in the data structure shown in Figure E.1(b). This requires adjacency information for the faces so that a shell composed of the faces can be derived.

Figure E.1

Representation of
a nonmanifold
model by lists of
topological entities

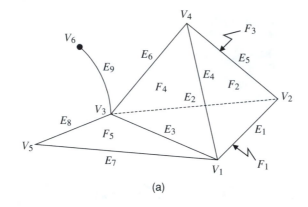

(a)

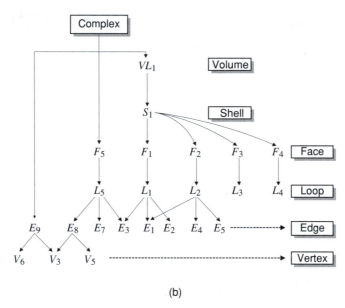

(b)

Several approaches to a description of nonmanifold topology, especially for adjacency information have been developed. The most significant work has been carried out by Weiler, who introduced the radial edge data structure to represent nonmanifold topologies [Weiler 1988a]. In the case of manifold solid models, we store two types of cyclic ordering as the adjacency information (i.e., face–edge cycle and vertex–edge cycle). The face–edge cycle is the list of edges for each face or a loop, and the vertex–edge cycle is a list of connected edges meeting at a given vertex. Review the half-edge data structure or the winged-edge data structure in Section 5.3.2 to verify that this cycle information is stored either directly or indirectly. Meanwhile, three types of cycles have to be specified to represent a general nonmanifold model: loop, radial, and disk. The loop cycle shown in Figure E.2(a) corresponds to the face–edge cycle in manifold solid models. The radial cycle shown in

Figure E.2

Three types of cycles in nonmanifold topology (a) loop cycle (b) radial cycle (c) disk cycle

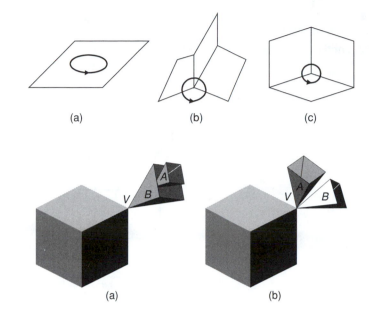

(a)   (b)   (c)

Figure E.3

Topologically different models

(a)   (b)

Figure E.2(b) is a cycle of faces connected to a certain edge. This information is not necessary for a manifold model because any edge is always shared by two faces. However, in nonmanifold models, more than two faces can share an edge, and they must be described explicitly. The disk cycle illustrated in Figure E.2(c) resembles the vertex–edge cycle in manifold solid models. However, a vertex may have several disk cycles in nonmanifold models. For example, vertex V in Figure E.3(a) and (b) has three disk cycles, each of which belong to the different shell.

Radial edge representation (RER) proposed by Weiler [1988a] is the first complete nonmanifold boundary modeling representation that explicitly represents topological adjacencies. It can represent a radial cycle as well as a loop cycle, but it does not store the disk cycle explicitly around the vertex. Even though adjacency information at a vertex can be derived from other topological information in limited cases, it is not always possible to obtain correct adjacency information at a vertex from only topological data in the radial edge data structure. Furthermore, the topologically different models illustrated in Figure E.3 are represented by the same topology in the radial edge data structure. To avoid this problem, Gursoz, Choi, and Prinz [1990] proposed vertex-based representation, which can represent both disk cycles and radial and loop cycles. Here, we explain only radial edge representation because other representations are considered to be the extensions of it. Descriptions of other representations are presented in Yamaguchi, Kobayashi, and Kimura [1991] and Gursoz, Choi, and Prinz [1990].

The basic topological entities chosen to represent a nonmanifold model in the radial edge data structure are model, region, shell, face, loop, edge, and vertex, as illustrated in Figure E.4. A model is equivalent to the complex shown in Figure E.1(b) and simply means the group of all the regions involved. A region is equiva-

Figure E.4

Topological entities
in RER

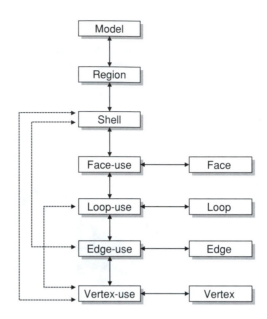

lent to the volume shown in Figure E.1(b) and thus is bounded by one or several shells. A region is bounded by several shells when it has voids inside it. In the radial edge representation, a single solid object has two regions—one for the inside of the object and the other for outside, which has an infinite extent. A shell is an oriented boundary surface of a region and has the same meaning as the shell shown in Figure E.1(b). The topological entities face, loop, edge, and vertex have the same definitions as in manifold representation.

Figure E.4 reveals that the relationships between basic topological entities are specified indirectly through four additional topological entities: face-use, loop-use, edge-use, and vertex-use. This is analogous to the introduction of half edges to specify indirectly the relationship between loops, edges, and vertices (see Section 5.3.2). A *face-use* is one of the two uses (sides) of a face, and thus a shell bounding the inside or the outside of a volume is defined by a connected set of face-uses. Face-use, the use of a face by a shell, is oriented with respect to the face geometry and has an orientation opposite to that of its mating face-use. Each face-use of a pair becomes the member of each of the two shells interfacing at the face from which the face-use is generated. In the case of a cellular structure without a closed volume, as shown in Figure E.5, these mating face-uses belong to the same shell. In this example, the list of face-uses fu_1–fu_2–fu_5–fu_6–fu_4–fu_3 forms a shell. A face-use is bounded by one or more loop-uses as a face is bounded by loops. A *loop-use* is one of the uses of a loop associated with one of the two uses of a face and is oriented with respect to the associated face-use to define its outer or inner boundary, as illustrated in Figure E.5. A loop-use is defined by a list of edge-uses. An *edge-use* is a bounding curve segment on a loop-use of a face-use and represents the use of an edge by that loop-use, or if a wire-frame edge, by its end-point vertices. The

Figure E.5

The use of additional topological entities to specify adjacency

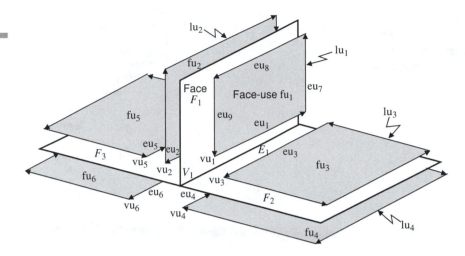

orientation of an edge-use is specified by the starting vertex-use as for the half edges. A *vertex-use* is a structure representing the adjacency use of a vertex by an edge as an end point, by a loop in the case of a single vertex loop or by a shell in the case of a single vertex shell.

Some degenerate situations are indicated by the dotted line connections in Figure E.4. First, a direct connection between a shell and a list of edge-uses allows for a shell that consists of a wire-frame. Similarly, the connection between a shell and a vertex-use allows for a shell that consists of a single vertex. An isolated point is stored as an independent shell in nonmanifold representation. In addition, the direct connection between a loop-use and a vertex-use allows storage of an isolated point located on a face as its hole loop to represent a dangling edge emanating from a point on a face. A nonmanifold model of mixed dimension can also be handled by regarding the entities of lower dimension as degenerate face-uses and storing these face-uses in a list with other face-uses belonging to the same shell.

Now we explain how the loop cycle and the radial cycle are specified in the radial edge data structure. First, the loop cycle is specified by simply storing the list of edge-uses for each loop-use. For example, the loop-use lu_1 in Figure E.5 carries the list of edge-uses eu_1–eu_7–eu_8–eu_9. To specify the radial cycle, each edge-use has two pointers—an edge-use mate pointer and an edge-use radial pointer—as illustrated in Figure E.6. Figure E.6 shows the cross-sectional view of the cellular structure depicted in Figure E.5. Figure E.6 indicates that an edge-use mate pointer is a pointer to the edge-use on the opposite side of the face and that the edge-use radial pointer points to the edge-use on the face-use radially adjacent to the face-use of the given edge-use. Owing to these pointers, the full radial ordering of faces about an edge can be obtained by tracing the pointers from any one edge-use. As mentioned previously, the radial edge representation does not store the disk cycle explicitly. However, it does store the vertex-edge cycle as in manifold representation by storing the list of vertex-uses for each vertex. Storing the vertex-uses is equivalent to storing the edge-uses because each vertex-use is associated with an

Figure E.6

Cross-sectional view with edge-use pointers

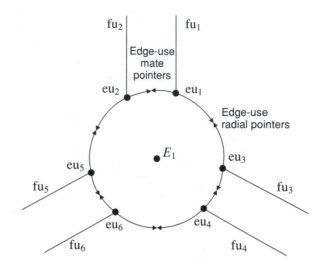

edge-use and thus is the same as storing the vertex-edge cycle. For example, vertex V_1 in Figure E.5 carries the list of vertex-uses vu_1–vu_2–vu_3–vu_4–vu_5–vu_6. Note that the vertex-uses are listed without a significant ordering. This is why the two different models shown in Figure E.3 have the same representation in the radial edge representation.

Note from Figure E.4 that the basic topology entities face, loop, edge, and vertex are redundant because all the necessary information about these entities is stored in their use entities. In fact, it is not necessary to have any direct representation of the basic face, loop, edge, and vertex elements themselves; representations of their uses are sufficient to indicate their position in the model. However, it is more convenient from a system architecture point of view if programmers using the operators to manipulate the data structure deal with the more intuitive concept of basic topological elements rather than topological uses of elements as much as possible. This is one of the few justifications for including the face, loop, edge, and vertex elements redundantly in its representation. This explanation of the radial edge data structure will become clearer if you review the detailed implementation of the radial edge data structure in Weiler [1988a].

E.2   OPERATORS USED TO MANIPULATE TOPOLOGY

Similar to the Euler operators used to manipulate the topological entities in manifold models, nonmanifold topology (NMT) operators have been proposed to manipulate topological data in nonmanifold models [Weiler 1988b]. However, these operators did not inherit the useful features of Euler operators because they were not based on an equation such as the Euler–Poincaré formula. Recall that the

Euler–Poincaré formula provides a relationship to be satisfied by the number of topological entities in a manifold model. You may be skeptical about the existence of a similar formula for a nonmanifold model, considering the flexibility of its topology. However, Masuda, Shimada, Numao, and Kawabe [1990] generalized the Euler–Poincaré formula for a nonmanifold model as follows:

$$v - e + (f - r) - (V - V_h + V_c) = C - C_h + C_c \qquad \text{(E.1)}$$

where

v = number of vertices
e = number of edges
f = number of faces
r = number of rings or holes in faces
V = number of closed volumes in all the complexes, or simply disjoint objects[1]
V_h = number of holes or passages through the volumes
V_c = number of cavities or voids in the volumes
C = number of complexes, or disjoint objects
C_h = number of holes or passages through the objects
C_c = number of cavities or voids in the objects

Equation (E.1) can be verified for the example model in Figure E.1(a). For this model, $v = 6$, $e = 9$, $f = 5$, $r = 0$, $V = 1$, $V_h = 0$, $V_c = 0$, $C = 1$, $C_h = 0$, and $C_c = 0$. Substituting these values in Equation (E.1) yields $6 - 9 + (5 - 0) - (1 - 0 + 0) = 1 - 0 + 0$, which satisfies Equation (E.1).

We can also show that the Euler–Poincaré formula given in Equation (5.1) is simply a special case of Equation (E.1). Because any disjoint object has one volume in a manifold representation, we know that $V = C$, $V_h = C_h$, and $V_c = C_c$. Substituting these relations in Equation (E.1) gives

$$v - e + (f - r) = 2(V - V_h + V_c) \qquad \text{(E.2)}$$

The number of shells, s, equals the sum of the number of volumes, V, and the number of voids, V_c, so Equation (E.2) can be rewritten as

$$v - e + (f - r) = 2(s - V_h) \qquad \text{(E.3)}$$

Hence Equation (E.3) is the same as Equation (5.1) because r and V_h have the same meanings as h and p, respectively, in Equation (5.1).

Once the relationship between the topological entities in a nonmanifold model has been determined, as in Equation (E.1), we can determine the minimum set of operators needed to manipulate them. As Equation (E.1) expresses a plane in 10-dimensional space described by (v, e, f, r, V, V_h, V_c, C, C_h, C_c), there are nine independent base vectors. Thus nine appropriate operators with their inverses are sufficient to define any object of nonmanifold topology. Figure E.7 illustrates one of these minimum sets, as suggested by Masuda et al. [1990]. Even though nine oper-

---

[1] Any disjoint object is regarded as one complex, and each complex can be composed of several volumes and dangling edges. The complex is equivalent to the model in the radial edge representation.

Figure E.7

A minimum set of operators

mvC (kvC)	make (kill) vertex, complex	
mev (kev)	make (kill) edge, vertex	
meCh (keCh)	make (kill) edge, complex_hole	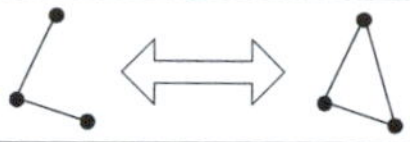
mfkCh (kfmCh)	make (kill) face, kill (make) complex_hole	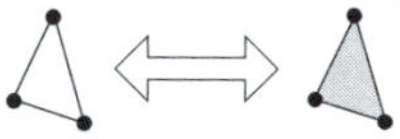
mfCc (kfCc)	make (kill) face, complex_cavity	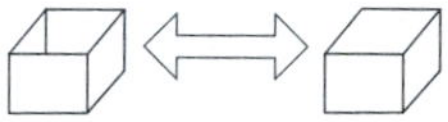
mvr (kvr)	make (kill) vertex, ring	
mVkCc (kVmCc)	make (kill) volume, kill (make) complex_cavity	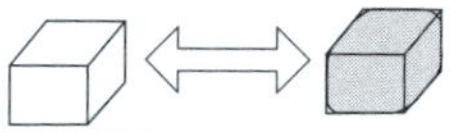
mvVc (kvVc)	make (kill) vertex, volume_cavity	
meVh (keVh)	make (kill) edge, volume_hole	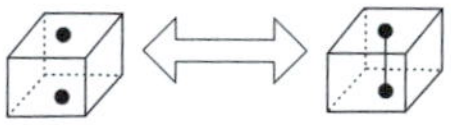

ators are sufficient to create any object, it is more efficient to add some other operators for practical use. Recall that we introduced seven Euler operators in Section 5.3.3, even though only five are sufficient to create a manifold model.

Just as all the modeling commands of higher level are implemented with Euler operators in solid modeling systems, the modeling commands in nonmanifold modeling systems are also realized by executing the proper operators in sequence. Figure E.8 illustrates how a block primitive is created by using the proposed operators listed in Figure E.7. Moreover, all other modeling commands are implemented similarly. In fact, the modeling commands provided in nonmanifold modeling systems appear to be exactly the same as those in conventional solid modeling systems and thus the user may not notice the differences involved in their use. The only differences would be the domain of the representable object and, accordingly, the data stored inside.

Figure E.8

Creation of a block primitive by the operators proposed by Masuda et al.

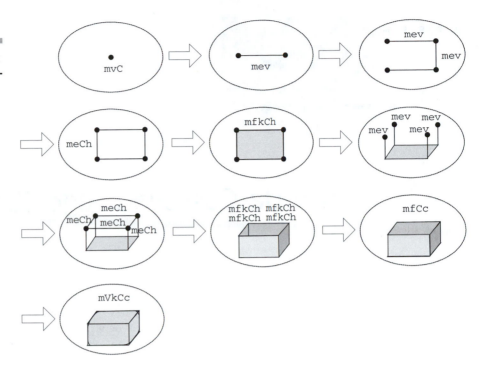

The de Casteljau Algorithm

The de Casteljau algorithm can be stated as

$\mathbf{P}(u)$, the coordinates of a point on a Bezier curve at the parameter value u, is equal to $\mathbf{P}_0^n$, which is obtained by the following recursive formula,

$$\mathbf{P}_i^r = (1 - u)\mathbf{P}_i^{r-1} + u\mathbf{P}_{i+1}^{r-1} \qquad (\text{F.1})$$

where

$$r = 1, \ldots, n$$
$$i = 0, \ldots, n - r$$
$$\mathbf{P}_i^0 = \mathbf{P}_i$$

and the initial values $\mathbf{P}_i^0$ are $\mathbf{P}_i$ which are the control points coordinates.

Equation (F.1) indicates that $\mathbf{P}_i^1$s are calculated from $\mathbf{P}_i^0$ or that the control points, $\mathbf{P}_i^2$s, are calculated from $\mathbf{P}_i^1$, and so on until $\mathbf{P}_0^n$ is obtained; this $\mathbf{P}_0^n$ is the value of $\mathbf{P}(u)$. This process is illustrated in Figure F.1 for a Bezier curve of degree 3, or $n = 3$. Note that $\mathbf{P}_0^1$ is obtained by splitting the line segment $\mathbf{P}_0\mathbf{P}_1$ by the ratio $u : (1 - u)$; $\mathbf{P}_1^1$ and $\mathbf{P}_2^1$ are obtained the same way. Then $\mathbf{P}_0^2$ is obtained by splitting the line segment $\mathbf{P}_0^1\mathbf{P}_1^1$ by the same ratio, and $\mathbf{P}_0^3$ or $\mathbf{P}_0^n$ is obtained by splitting the segment $\mathbf{P}_0^2\mathbf{P}_1^2$ by the same ratio again. This $\mathbf{P}_0^3$ gives the coordinates of the point on the curve corresponding to the parameter value, u. Remember that the parameter value determines the ratio in sectioning the associated line segments. Figure F.1 also reveals that the original Bezier curve is composed of two Bezier curves—one defined by four control points $\mathbf{P}_0$, $\mathbf{P}_0^1$, $\mathbf{P}_0^2$, and $\mathbf{P}_0^3$ and the other defined by $\mathbf{P}_0^3$, $\mathbf{P}_1^2$, $\mathbf{P}_2^1$, and $\mathbf{P}_3$. Verification of this statement is presented in Farin [1990]. Note also that the two new control polygons approximate the original Bezier curve much

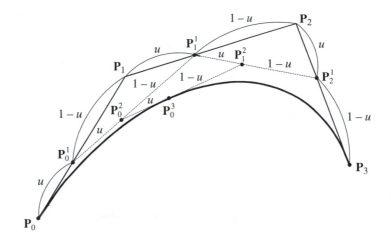

more closely than the original control polygon. Thus the de Casteljau algorithm can be applied repeatedly to approximate a Bezier curve by straight-line segments.

The process of obtaining $\mathbf{P}_0^n$ by using Equation (F.1) is illustrated schematically in Figure F.2. Any $\mathbf{P}_i^r$ is determined by its upper-left neighbor $\mathbf{P}_i^{r-1}$ and the left neighbor $\mathbf{P}_{i+1}^{r-1}$, and thus the new points created by the recursion form a lower triangle with $\mathbf{P}_0^n$ at a vertex. This schematic diagram provides additional useful information. We have shown that a Bezier curve of degree 3 can be subdivided into two Bezier curves of the same degree in the course of applying the de Casteljau algorithm. This concept can be extended to a Bezier curve of any degree. In fact, the two groups of points surrounded by the dotted loops are the control points of the two Bezier curves subdivided from an original Bezier curve defined by $\mathbf{P}_0, \mathbf{P}_1, \ldots,$ $\mathbf{P}_n$. Thus a Bezier curve of any degree can be split into many Bezier curves of the same degree by applying the de Casteljau algorithm repeatedly, and the resulting control polygons will approximate the original curve fairly closely. This straight-

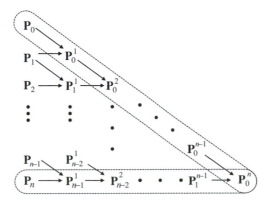

line segment approximation can be used to calculate the initial values of the intersection points between Bezier curves.

The de Casteljau algorithm can also be used to calculate the derivatives of a Bezier curve. The reason is that the derivative of any order of a Bezier curve can be expressed in the form of the Bezier curve equation, as mentioned in Section 6.4.1.

Figure F.3

Implementation of the de Casteljau algorithm in C language

```
float decas( degree, coeff, u )
/*
uses de Casteljau to compute one coordinate value of Bezier curve.
Has to be called for each coordinate( x, y, and/or z ) of control polygon.
Input :  degree : degree of curve.
         coeff : array with coefficients of curve.
         u : parameter value.
Output : coordinate value
*/
        int     degree;
        float   coeff[ ];
        float   u;
        {
                int     r, i;
                float   u1;
                float   coeffa[30];        /* an auxiliary array. Change
                                                dim. if too small */
                u1 = 1.0 - u;
                for( i=0; r<=degree; i++ )
                        coeffa[i] = coeff[i];      /* save input array */

                for( r=1; r<=degree; r++ )
                        for( i=0; i<=degree - r; i++ )
                        {
                                coeffa[i] = u1 * coeffa[i] + u * coeffa[i+1];
                        }
                return ( coeffa[0] );
        }
```

G

Evaluation of the B-Spline Curve by the Cox–de Boor Method

Here, we introduce the Cox–de Boor method of evaluating the B-spline curve. We do so by evaluating the coordinates on a B-spline curve for the parameter u in the range $t_l \le u \le t_{l+1}$. When u is in this range, only $N_{l,1}$ needs to be considered. By propagating the effect of $N_{l,1}$, as shown in Figure 6.5, we can conclude that only the blending functions $N_{l-(k-1),k}, \ldots, N_{l,k}$ can have nonzero values. Thus the expression of $\mathbf{P}(u)$ can be changed as follows:

$$\mathbf{P}(u) = \sum_{i=0}^{n} \mathbf{P}_i N_{i,k}(u) = \sum_{i=l-k+1}^{l} \mathbf{P}_i N_{i,k}(u) \tag{G.1}$$

Substituting Equation (6.32) in Equation (G.1) gives

$$\mathbf{P}(u) = \sum_{i=l-k+1}^{l} \mathbf{P}_i \left[\frac{(u-t_i)N_{i,k-1}}{t_{i+k-1}-t_i} + \frac{(t_{i+k}-u)N_{i+1,k-1}}{t_{i+k}-t_{i+1}} \right]$$

$$= \sum_{i=l-k+1}^{l} \frac{u-t_i}{t_{i+k-1}-t_i} \mathbf{P}_i N_{i,k-1} + \sum_{j=l-k+2}^{l+1} \frac{t_{j+k-1}-u}{t_{j+k-1}-t_j} \mathbf{P}_{j-1} N_{j,k-1}{}^{\dagger}$$

$$= \sum_{i=l-k+2}^{l} \frac{u-t_i}{t_{i+k-1}-t_i} \mathbf{P}_i N_{i,k-1} + \sum_{j=l-k+2}^{l} \left(1 - \frac{u-t_j}{t_{j+k-1}-t_j}\right) \mathbf{P}_{j-1} N_{j,k-1}{}^{\dagger\dagger}$$

$$= \sum_{i=l-k+2}^{l} \left[\frac{u-t_i}{t_{i+k-1}-t_i} \mathbf{P}_i + \left(1 - \frac{u-t_i}{t_{i+k-1}-t_i}\right) \mathbf{P}_{i-1} \right] N_{i,k-1}$$

$$= \sum_{i=l-k+2}^{l} \mathbf{P}_i^1 N_{i,k-1} \tag{G.2}$$

$\dagger$ j is substituted for $i + 1$.
$\dagger\dagger$ The range of each summation is reduced because $N_{l-k+1,k-1}$ and $N_{l+1,k-1}$ are zeros for $t_l \le u \le t_{l+1}$.

where $\mathbf{P}_i^1$ is defined as

$$\mathbf{P}_i^1 = \frac{u - t_i}{t_{i+k-1} - t_i}\mathbf{P}_i + \left(1 - \frac{u - t_i}{t_{i+k-1} - t_i}\right)\mathbf{P}_{i-1} \tag{G.3}$$

Thus $\mathbf{P}_i^1$ can be interpreted as an internal division point of the line segment $\mathbf{P}_i\mathbf{P}_{i-1}$, as in the de Casteljau algorithm.

Now, $N_{i,k-1}$ is expressed as the combination of $N_{i,k-2}$ and $N_{i+1,\,k-2}$ by using Equation (6.32), and this expression is substituted in Equation (G.2) for $N_{i,\,k-1}$. Then we can derive the following relation by using a process similar to that used in the derivation of Equation (G.2):

$$\mathbf{P}(u) = \sum_{i=l-k+3}^{l} \mathbf{P}_i^2 N_{i,k-2} \tag{G.4}$$

where $\mathbf{P}_i^2$ is defined as

$$\mathbf{P}_i^2 = \frac{u - t_i}{t_{i+k-2} - t_i}\mathbf{P}_i^1 + \left(1 - \frac{u - t_i}{t_{i+k-2} - t_i}\right)\mathbf{P}_{i-1}^1$$

In other words, $\mathbf{P}_i^2$ is also an internal division point of the line segment $\mathbf{P}_i^1\mathbf{P}_{i-1}^1$.

If we repeat the same procedure an arbitrary r times, we get

$$\mathbf{P}(u) = \sum_{i=l-k+r+1}^{l} \mathbf{P}_i^r N_{i,k-r}(u) \tag{G.5}$$

where

$$\mathbf{P}_i^r = \frac{u - t_i}{t_{i+k-r} - t_i}\mathbf{P}_i^{r-1} + \left(1 - \frac{u - t_i}{t_{i+k-r} - t_i}\right)\mathbf{P}_{i-1}^{r-1} \tag{G.6}$$

This $\mathbf{P}_i^r$ is called the de Boor point. Note that $\mathbf{P}_i^0$ implies $\mathbf{P}_i$ in Equation (G.6). Substituting $(k-1)$ for r in Equation (G.5) gives

$$\mathbf{P}(u) = \mathbf{P}_l^{k-1} N_{l,1}(u)$$
$$= \mathbf{P}_l^{k-1} \tag{G.7}$$

Therefore we can say that the coordinates of a point corresponding to a parameter value u in the range $t_l \leq u \leq t_{l+1}$ are those of $\mathbf{P}_l^{k-1}$, which is obtained by sectioning the line segments between the associated points recursively, starting from those between the original control points.

EXAMPLE G.1

For the B-spline curve shown in Example 6.4, calculate the coordinates of a point corresponding to $u = 2.5$ by using the Cox–de Boor algorithm.

ANSWER

As given in Example 6.4, the knot values are

$$t_0 = 0, \quad t_1 = 0, \quad t_2 = 0, \quad t_3 = 1, \quad t_4 = 2, \quad t_5 = 3, \quad t_6 = 4, \quad t_7 = 4, \quad t_8 = 4$$

Thus l becomes 4 in this case because $t_4 \le 2.5 < t_5$ and accordingly $\mathbf{P}(2.5)$ is $\mathbf{P}_4^2$ by Equation (G.7). We can use Equation (G.6) to express $\mathbf{P}_4^2$ as

$$\mathbf{P}_4^2 = \frac{u - t_4}{t_{4+k-2} - t_4}\mathbf{P}_4^1 + \left(1 - \frac{u - t_4}{t_{4+k-2} - t_4}\right)\mathbf{P}_3^1$$

$$= \frac{u - t_4}{t_5 - t_4}\mathbf{P}_4^1 + \left(1 - \frac{u - t_4}{t_5 - t_4}\right)\mathbf{P}_3^1$$

$$= 0.5\mathbf{P}_4^1 + 0.5\mathbf{P}_3^1 \tag{G.8}$$

Note that the values $k = 3$ and $u = 2.5$ were substituted in the derivation of Equation (G.8).

We also obtain $\mathbf{P}_4^1$ and $\mathbf{P}_3^1$ using Equation (G.6):

$$\mathbf{P}_4^1 = \frac{u - t_4}{t_6 - t_4}\mathbf{P}_4 + \left(1 - \frac{u - t_4}{t_6 - t_4}\right)\mathbf{P}_3$$

$$= \frac{1}{4}\mathbf{P}_4 + \frac{3}{4}\mathbf{P}_3 \tag{G.9}$$

$$\mathbf{P}_3^1 = \frac{u - t_3}{t_5 - t_3}\mathbf{P}_3 + \left(1 - \frac{u - t_3}{t_5 - t_3}\right)\mathbf{P}_2$$

$$= \frac{3}{4}\mathbf{P}_3 + \frac{1}{4}\mathbf{P}_2 \tag{G.10}$$

Note that $\mathbf{P}_i$ replaces $\mathbf{P}_i^0$, as explained before.

We can locate $\mathbf{P}(2.5)$ on the curve shown in Figure 6.6 by using Equations (G.10), (G.9), and (G.8) as illustrated in Figure G.1.

Figure G.1

Creating $\mathbf{P}_i^r$

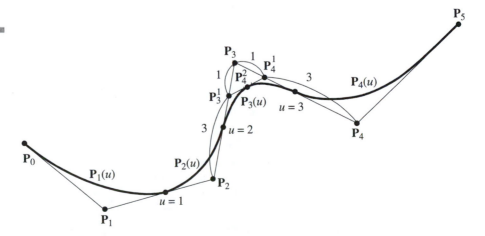

Figure G.1, shows that the original B-spline curve is subdivided by two B-spline curves of the same order as the original one, as was done for Bezier curves: one defined by $\mathbf{P}_0$, $\mathbf{P}_1$, $\mathbf{P}_2$, $\mathbf{P}_3^1$, and $\mathbf{P}_4^2$, and the other defined by $\mathbf{P}_4^2$, $\mathbf{P}_4^1$, $\mathbf{P}_4$, and $\mathbf{P}_5$. The first B-spline curve has five control points ($n = 4$) and order 3 ($k = 3$), so its knot values would be $\{0\ 0\ 0\ 1\ 2\ 2.5\ 2.5\ 2.5\}$. Similarly, the knot values of the second B-spline curve would be $\{2.5\ 2.5\ 2.5\ 3\ 4\ 4\ 4\}$.

The process of evaluating $\mathbf{P}_l^{k-1}$ using Equation (G.6) iteratively can also be illustrated schematically, as in Figure G.2. Any $\mathbf{P}_i^r$ is determined by its upper left-hand neighbor $\mathbf{P}_{r-1}^{-1}$ and the left-hand neighbor $\mathbf{P}_i^{r-1}$. Thus the new points created by the recursion form a lower triangle with $\mathbf{P}_l^{k-1}$ at a vertex. This schematic diagram provides additional useful information. We have shown that a B-spline curve of order 3 can be subdivided into two B-spline curves of the same order in the course of applying the Cox–de Boor algorithm in Example G.1. This concept can be extended to a B-spline curve of any order, as with Bezier curves. In fact, the two groups of points surrounded by the dotted loops shown in Figure 6.12 are the control points of the two B-spline curves created when the original B-spline curve defined by $\mathbf{P}_0$, $\mathbf{P}_1$, ..., $\mathbf{P}_n$ is subdivided at a point whose parameter value is $t_l \le u \le t_{l+1}$. Thus a B-spline curve of any order can be split into many B-spline curves of the same order by applying the Cox–de Boor algorithm repeatedly, and the resulting control

Figure G.2

Schematic of evaluating $\mathbf{P}_l^{k-1}$

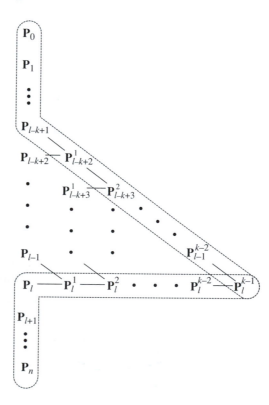

polygons will approximate the original curve fairly closely, as the de Casteljau algorithm is applied to approximate a Bezier curve. This straight-line segment approximation can be used to calculate the initial values of the intersection points between B-spline curves. The Cox–de Boor algorithm can be implemented in C language, as shown in Figure G.3.

Figure G.3

Implementation of the Cox and de Boor algorithm in C language

```
Cox_de_Boor( k, t, P, u, l, R )
int      k;        /* order of B-spline */
Knot    *t;        /* knot sequence */
Point   *P;        /* control points */
double   u;        /* parameter value */
int      l;        /* integer such that t[l] <= u < t[l+1] */
Point   *R;        /* P(u) */
{
        Point    A[MaxOrder];
        int      i, j, r;
        double   d1, d2;

        for( j=0; j<k; j++ )
                A[j] = P[l-k+1+j];

        for( r=1; r<k; r++ ) {
                for( j=k-1; j>=r; j-- ) {
                        i = l - k + 1 + j;
                        d1 = u - t[i]; d2 = t[i+k-r] - u;
                        A[j] = ( d1 * A[j] + d2 * A[j-1] ) / ( d1 + d2 );
                }
        }
        *R = A[k-1];
}
```

Composition of B-Spline Curves

To obtain the new control points and the knot values of the composite curve, we assume that the curves to be combined have the same order. Otherwise, we have to modify the lower order B-spline curve to give it the order of the other curve prior to the composition (i.e., the control points and the knot values of the equivalent curve of the higher order are obtained). Cohen, Lyche, and Schumaker [1985] cover this procedure.

Let $\mathbf{P}_1(u)$ and $\mathbf{P}_2(u)$ denote the equations of the first and the second B-spline curves of order k, respectively. Further assume that $\mathbf{P}_1(u)$ is defined by the control points $\mathbf{Q}_i$ ($i = 0, 1, \ldots, n$) with the knot values v_i ($i = 0, 1, \ldots, n + k$). Similarly, $\mathbf{P}_2(u)$ is defined by the control points $\mathbf{R}_i$ ($i = 0, 1, \ldots, m$) with the knot values w_i ($i = 0, 1, \ldots, m + k$). Note that $\mathbf{Q}_n$ is the same as $\mathbf{R}_0$, as illustrated in Figure H.1.

Then the equations $\mathbf{P}_1(u)$ and $\mathbf{P}_2(u)$ can be expressed as

$$\mathbf{P}_1(u) = \sum_{i=0}^{n} \mathbf{Q}_i N_{i,k}(u) \tag{H.1}$$

$$\mathbf{P}_2(u) = \sum_{i=0}^{m} \mathbf{R}_i N_{i,k}(u) \tag{H.2}$$

Figure H.1

Composition of
two B-spline curves

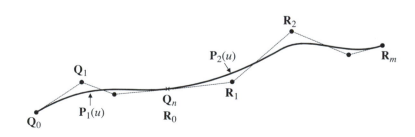

Now we determine the control points and the knot values of the composite curve (without derivation). We verify the result by showing that the composite curve represents the given curves at their corresponding portions. First, the control points of the composite curve $\mathbf{P}_i$, are the simple union of each control point set, expressed as

$$\mathbf{P}_i = \begin{cases} \mathbf{Q}_i & (i = 0, \ldots, n) \\ \mathbf{R}_{i-n} & (i = n+1, \ldots, m+n) \end{cases} \tag{H.3}$$

Note that $\mathbf{R}_0$ does not appear in Equation (H.3) because it is the same as $\mathbf{Q}_n$.

The knot values of the composite curve are derived by merging two sets of the knot values after shifting all the knots w_i so that w_0 equals v_{n+k}. We know that the shifting of all the knots by the same amount does not affect the curve equation because only the difference in knot values matters. When the two sets of the knot values are merged, some of the knot values corresponding to the connection point of the two curves are eliminated so that they are repeated only $(k-1)$ times. If this multiplicity is greater than $(k-1)$, the resulting composite curve cannot be considered as one B-spline curve and thus does not satisfy the relation of the number of control points, order, and the number of knot values. Figure H.2 illustrates generation of the knot values for the composite curve. The knot values w_i are shifted by $(v_{n+k} - w_0)$ so that the knot value w_0 equals v_{n+1}, and only $(k-1)$ knots from v_{n+1} through v_{n+k-1} are kept among the same knot values $v_{n+1}, \ldots, v_{n+k-1}$, and $w_1, \ldots, w_{k-1}$. Thus the knot values to be used for the composite curve are obtained as indicated by the dotted rectangles in Figure H.2 and can be expressed by

$$t_i = \begin{cases} v_i & (i = 0, \ldots, n+k-1) \\ w_{i-n} + v_{n+k} - w_0 & (i = n+k, \ldots, n+m+k) \end{cases} \tag{H.4}$$

Now, we verify that the composite curve defined by the control points and the knot values given in Equations (H.3) and (H.4), respectively, equals the original two B-spline curves at each corresponding portion. Let's consider the portion of the composite curve corresponding to $t_n(= v_n) \leq u \leq t_{n+1}(= v_{n+1} = v_{n+2} = \cdots = v_{n+k-1})$. We know that $N_{n,1}(u)$ is the only blending function of order 1 that does not diminish for this range of u. Propagating the effect of $N_{n,1}(u)$ as in Figure 6.5, we find that $N_{n-k+1,k}(u), N_{n-k+2,k}(u), \ldots, N_{n,k}(u)$ are the nonzero blending functions of order k. Thus the curve is determined by the control points $\mathbf{P}_{n-k+1}, \mathbf{P}_{n-k+2}, \ldots, \mathbf{P}_n$. These control points are the same as $\mathbf{Q}_{n-k+1}, \mathbf{Q}_{n-k+2}, \ldots, \mathbf{Q}_n$. Furthermore, the portion of the knot values of the composite curve participating in the evaluation of the blend-

Figure H.2

Composition of knot values

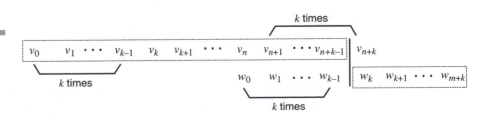

ing functions $N_{n-k+1,k}(u)$, $N_{n-k+2,k}(u)$, . . ., $N_{n,k}(u)$ would be the same as those of $P_1(u)$. Therefore we can conclude that the composite curve $P(u)$ is the same as $P_1(u)$ for u in the interval $t_n \leq u \leq t_{n+1}$. We can draw the same conclusion when u is between the knot values smaller than t_n. Similarly, we can show that $P(u)$ equals $P_2(u)$ when u is in the interval $u \geq t_{n+k}$.

EXAMPLE H.1

Two nonperiodic, uniform B-spline curves of order 4, one defined by the control points P_0, P_1, P_2, and P_3 and the other by $Q_0(= P_3)$, Q_1, Q_2, Q_3, and Q_4 are to be represented by a composite B-spline curve. Derive the knot values of the composite curve.

ANSWER

The B-spline curve defined by P_i will have the knot values 0 0 0 0 1 1 1 1 and the curve defined by Q_i will have 0 0 0 0 1 2 2 2 2. To make the first knot value of the second set equal the last knot value of the first set, the knot values of the second set are shifted by 1 and the resulting knot values will become 1 1 1 1 2 3 3 3 3. Then two sets of the knot values are merged and some of the knot value 1's are deleted so that they appear only three (= $k - 1$) times. Thus the knot values of the composite curve are 0 0 0 0 1 1 1 2 3 3 3 3.

Proof of the Formula for B-Spline Differentiation

To prove Equation (6.43), we first prove the following equation:

$$\dot{N}_{i,r}(u) = (r-1)\left\{ \frac{N_{i,r-1}(u)}{t_{i+r-1}-t_i} - \frac{N_{i+1,r-1}(u)}{t_{i+r}-t_{i+1}} \right\} \qquad (I.1)$$

To prove Equation (I.1), we rewrite Equations (6.32) and (6.33) for convenience:

$$N_{i,1}(u) = \begin{cases} 1 & t_i \le u \le t_{i+1} \\ 0 & \text{otherwise} \end{cases} \qquad (I.2)$$

and

$$N_{i,r}(u) = \frac{u-t_i}{t_{i+r-1}-t_i} N_{i,r-1}(u) + \frac{t_{i+r}-u}{t_{i+r}-t_{i+1}} N_{i+1,r-1}(u) \qquad (I.3)$$

Now, we derive Equation (I.1) by inductive reasoning. That is, we show that Equation (I.1) holds for $r = k$ if it holds for $r = k - 1$. We also show that Equation (I.1) holds for $r = 2$. Then, intuitively, Equation (I.1) holds for $r = 3$. By repeating this induction as we increase the value of r, we can prove that Equation (I.1) holds for any r.

We first show that Equation (I.1) holds for $r = 2$. Substituting $r = 2$ in Equation (I.3), we obtain

$$N_{i,2}(u) = \frac{u-t_i}{t_{i+1}-t_i} N_{i,1}(u) + \frac{t_{i+2}-u}{t_{i+2}-t_{i+1}} N_{i+1,1}(u) \qquad (I.4)$$

Differentiating Equation (I.4) gives

$$\dot{N}_{i,2}(u) = \frac{N_{i,1}(u)}{t_{i+1} - t_i} - \frac{N_{i+1,1}(u)}{t_{i+2} - t_{i+1}}$$

which is the same as Equation (I.1) for $r = 2$.

By assuming that Equation (I.1) is true for $r = k - 1$, we have

$$\dot{N}_{i,k-1}(u) = (k-2) \left\{ \frac{N_{i,k-2}(u)}{t_{i+k-2} - t_i} - \frac{N_{i+1,k-2}(u)}{t_{i+k-1} - t_{i+1}} \right\} \tag{I.5}$$

Now, we have to show that Equation (I.1) holds for $r = k$ from Equation (I.5). We substitute $r = k$ in Equation (I.3) and differentiate it with respect to u to get

$$\dot{N}_{i,k}(u) = \frac{N_{i,k-1}(u)}{t_{i+k-1} - t_i} - \frac{N_{i+1,k-1}(u)}{t_{i+k} - t_{i+1}} + \frac{u - t_i}{t_{i+k-1} - t_i} \dot{N}_{i,k-1}(u) + \frac{t_{i+k} - u}{t_{i+k} - t_{i+1}} \dot{N}_{i+1,k-1}(u) \tag{I.6}$$

We get the expressions $\dot{N}_{i,k-1}(u)$ and $\dot{N}_{i+1,k-1}(u)$ from Equation (I.5) and substitute them in Equation (I.6):

$$\dot{N}_{i,k}(u) = \left\{ \frac{N_{i,k-1}(u)}{t_{i+k-1} - t_i} - \frac{N_{i+1,k-1}(u)}{t_{i+k} - t_{i+1}} \right\}$$

$$+ \left\{ \frac{k-2}{t_{i+k-1} - t_i} \left[\frac{u - t_i}{t_{i+k-2} - t_i} N_{i,k-2}(u) - \frac{u - t_i}{t_{i+k-1} - t_{i+1}} N_{i+1,k-2}(u) \right] \right\} \tag{I.7}$$

$$+ \left\{ \frac{k-2}{t_{i+k} - t_{i+1}} \left[\frac{t_{i+k} - u}{t_{i+k-1} - t_{i+1}} N_{i+1,k-2}(u) - \frac{t_{i+k} - u}{t_{i+k} - t_{i+2}} N_{i+2,k-2}(u) \right] \right\}$$

Now, we rewrite the second term by adding and subtracting the term

$$\frac{t_{i+k-1} - u}{t_{i+k-1} - t_{i+1}} N_{i+1,k-2}(u)$$

and then applying Equation (I.3):

$$\text{Second term} = \frac{k-2}{t_{i+k-1} - t_i} \left[\frac{u - t_i}{t_{i+k-2} - t_i} N_{i,k-2}(u) + \frac{t_{i+k-1} - u}{t_{i+k-1} - t_{i+1}} N_{i+1,k-2}(u) \right.$$

$$\left. - \frac{t_{i+k-1} - u}{t_{i+k-1} - t_{i+1}} N_{i+1,k-2}(u) - \frac{u - t_i}{t_{i+k-1} - t_{i+1}} N_{i+1,k-2}(u) \right]$$

$$= \frac{k-2}{t_{i+k-1} - t_i} \left[N_{i,k-1}(u) - \frac{t_{i+k-1} - t_i}{t_{i+k-1} - t_{i+1}} N_{i+1,k-2}(u) \right]$$

$$= \frac{k-2}{t_{i+k-1} - t_i} N_{i,k-1}(u) - \frac{k-2}{t_{i+k-1} - t_{i+1}} N_{i+1,k-2}(u)$$

Then we rearrange the summation of the second and third terms in Equation (I.7):

Second term + third term

$$
= \frac{k-2}{t_{i+k-1}-t_i} N_{i,k-1}(u) + \frac{k-2}{t_{i+k}-t_{i+1}} \left[\frac{t_{i+k}-u}{t_{i+k-1}-t_{i+1}} N_{i+1,k-2}(u) \right.
$$

$$
\left. - \frac{t_{i+k}-u}{t_{i+k}-t_{i+2}} N_{i+2,k-2}(u) - \frac{t_{i+k}-t_{i+1}}{t_{i+k-1}-t_{i+1}} N_{i+1,k-2}(u) \right]
$$

$$
= (k-2) \left\{ \frac{N_{i,k-1}(u)}{t_{i+k-1}-t_i} - \frac{1}{t_{i+k}-t_{i+1}} \left[\frac{u-t_{i+1}}{t_{i+k-1}-t_{i+1}} N_{i+1,k-2}(u) + \frac{t_{i+k}-u}{t_{i+k}-t_{i+2}} N_{i+2,k-2}(u) \right] \right\}
$$

$$
= (k-2) \left[\frac{N_{i,k-1}(u)}{t_{i+k-1}-t_i} - \frac{N_{i+1,k-1}(u)}{t_{i+k}-t_{i+1}} \right]
$$

Finally, adding this result to the first term in Equation (I.7) yields

(First term) + (second term + third term)

$$
= (1) \left[\frac{N_{i,k-1}(u)}{t_{i+k-1}-t_i} - \frac{N_{i+1,k-1}(u)}{t_{i+k}-t_{i+1}} \right] + (k-2) \left[\frac{N_{i,k-1}(u)}{t_{i+k-1}-t_i} - \frac{N_{i+1,k-1}(u)}{t_{i+k}-t_{i+1}} \right]
$$

$$
= (k-1) \left[\frac{N_{i,k-1}(u)}{t_{i+k-1}-t_i} - \frac{N_{i+1,k-1}(u)}{t_{i+k}-t_{i+1}} \right]
$$

The result is the same as Equation (I.1).

Now, we prove Equation (6.43) by using Equation (I.1). We rewrite the first-order derivative of a B-spline curve at the parameter value u, which is $t_l \leq u \leq t_{l+1}$, as

$$
\frac{d\mathbf{P}(u)}{du} = \sum_{i=0}^{n} \mathbf{P}_i \dot{N}_{i,k}(u)
$$

$$
= \sum_{i=l-k+1}^{l} \mathbf{P}_i \dot{N}_{i,k}(u)
$$

From Equation (I.1), we obtain

$$
\frac{d\mathbf{P}(u)}{du} = \sum_{i=l-k+1}^{l} \mathbf{P}_i(k-1) \left\{ \frac{N_{i,k-1}(u)}{t_{i+k-1}-t_i} - \frac{N_{i+1,k-1}(u)}{t_{i+k}-t_{i+1}} \right\}
$$

$$
= \sum_{i=l-k+2}^{l} \mathbf{P}_i(k-1) \frac{N_{i,k-1}(u)}{t_{i+k-1}-t_i} - \sum_{i=l-k+1}^{l-1} \mathbf{P}_i(k-1) \frac{N_{i+1,k-1}(u)}{t_{i+k}-t_{i+1}}
$$

$$(I.8)$$

Note that we reduced the range of the summation in Equation (I.8), based on the notion that $N_{l-k+1,k-1}(u) = 0$ and $N_{l+1,k-1}(u) = 0$ for $t_l \leq u \leq t_{l+1}$.

Replacing $i + 1$ with j in the second term in Equation (I.8) yields

$$\frac{d\mathbf{P}(u)}{du} = \sum_{i=l-k+2}^{l} \mathbf{P}_i(k-1)\frac{N_{i,k-1}(u)}{t_{i+k-1}-t_i} - \sum_{j=l-k+2}^{l} \mathbf{P}_{j-1}(k-1)\frac{N_{j,k-1}(u)}{t_{j+k-1}-t_j}$$

$$= \sum_{i=l-k+2}^{l} (k-1)\frac{\mathbf{P}_i - \mathbf{P}_{i-1}}{t_{i+k-1}-t_i}N_{i,k-1}$$

$$= \sum_{i=l-k+2}^{l} \mathbf{P}_i^1 N_{i,k-1}(u)$$

Thus we have

$$\frac{d\mathbf{P}(u)}{du} = \sum_{i=l-k+2}^{l} \mathbf{P}_i^1 N_{i,k-1}(u)$$

where

$$\mathbf{P}_i^1 = (k-1)\frac{\mathbf{P}_i - \mathbf{P}_{i-1}}{t_{i+k-1}-t_i}$$

APPENDIX

J

Peng's Approach to Calculating the Intersection of NURBS Surfaces

This appendix gives a step-by-step explanation of Peng's approach.

J.1 SUBDIVISION

As we previously explained, each of the surfaces being intersected has to be continuously subdivided and stored in a quadtree structure. Because it is easier to subdivide rational/nonrational Bezier surfaces[1] than rational/nonrational B-spline surfaces, we convert each NURBS surface into multiple rational Bezier patches, as illustrated in Figure J.1. The method used to convert a NURBS surface into rational Bezier patches is explained in detail in Farin [1990].

After each NURBS surface has been converted into rational Bezier patches, the pairs of rational Bezier patches that may intersect are stored in a list called a *rival list*. For example, Figure J.2 illustrates conversion of the NURBS surfaces S1 and S2 shown in Figure J.2(a) to four rational Bezier patches, P1, P2, P3, and P4, and two rational Bezier patches, Q1 and Q2, respectively. These rational Bezier patches are stored in the quadtrees shown in Figure J.2(b). From Figure J.2(a), note that the intersections may occur between patches P3 and Q1 and between P4 and Q1. Therefore these pairs are stored in the rival list shown in Figure J.2(c). The possi-

[1] A rational Bezier surface is derived from a Bezier surface by introducing homogeneous coordinates for the control points.

519

Figure J.1

Conversion of a NURBS surface into rational Bezier patches

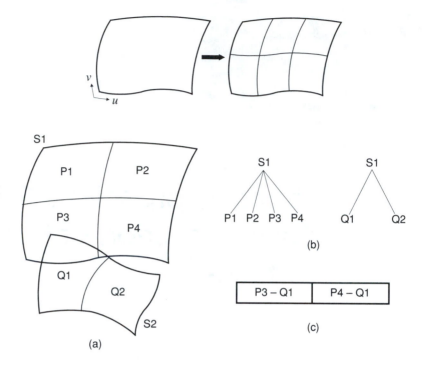

Figure J.2

Quadtree representation of rational Bezier patches and its rival list

Figure J.3

Update of quadtree and rival list after the flatness test

bility of an intersection of two patches can be detected by comparing the minimum size blocks, each of which barely encloses each patch.

Then we check to determine whether the patches stored in the rival list are flat enough to be approximated to the planar quadrilaterals. If any patch in the list is not flat enough, it is subdivided into four. In this case, the quadtree representation of the corresponding surface is updated to include these new patches. The rival list is also modified so that the pairs with the old patch before the subdivision are eliminated and the pairs with the new patches are added. Figure J.3 shows how the quadtree representation and the rival list are updated when a patch is subdivided be-

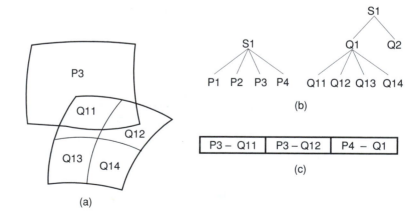

cause it cannot pass the flatness test. In this example, the patches in the pair P3–Q1 are tested for flatness, and Q1 is subdivided into four patches Q11, Q12, Q13, and Q14. Here, we assume that patch P3 passes the flatness test. Thus the quadtree shown in Figure J.2(b) is updated as shown in Figure J.3(b). Then the overlap test between the new patches and P3 is performed to update the pair P3–Q1 in the original rival list. If the new patches are located as shown in Figure J.3(a), two pairs, P3–Q11 and P3–Q12, will replace P3–Q1, as shown in Figure J.3(c).

J.2   TRACING INTERSECTION SEGMENTS

We have derived the quadtree representations of the intersecting surfaces and the rival list, so we can now trace the intersecting segments starting from a pair in the rival list. First, we can pick any pair in the rival list and calculate their intersection segment (or, more precisely, two end points). We use plane–plane intersection to calculate these end points because all the patches in the rival list have already passed the flatness test. We denote these end points A1 and A2, respectively. Recall that we always calculate the corresponding exact points whenever we obtain the end points by plane–plane intersection. The end point is used as the initial guess to solve Equation (7.50) for the corresponding exact point.

Now, we have to find the next pair of the patches that will provide the intersecting segment connected to one end of the current intersection segment. Let's assume that we trace the intersection points from A1 to A2. Thus we need to find the pair that will give the intersection segment sharing A2. The procedure for finding the next pair is illustrated in Figure J.4. We get the next pair, X1–Y2, after obtaining the most current intersection point, A2, from the current pair, X1–Y1, as follows.

- The relative location of the current intersection point, A2 in this case, is identified with respect to the patches in the current pair. Thus A2 is on the boundary of patch Y1 and inside patch X1.

- The patch completely enclosing the current intersection point, patch X1, is used for the next pair again. Then we select one of the neighbor patches of Y1 as the

Figure J.4

Searching for the next pair

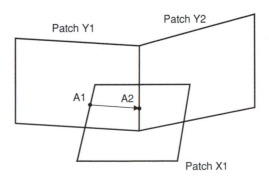

other patch of the next pair. Its selection is based on the relative location of the current intersection point with respect to Y1. Here, we choose the right-hand side neighbor of Y1 because the current intersection point, A2, is on the right-hand side boundary of Y1. Then we calculate the intersection points from this new pair, and the intersection point different from A2 will assume the role of the current intersection point in our search for the next pair.

This procedure will stop when the intersection point reaches the boundary of either of the surfaces being intersected, as illustrated in Figure J.5. When that happens, the intersection points are traced in reverse, starting from the initial intersection segment. We can assume that an intersection curve is obtained completely if it becomes a closed loop or intersects one of the surfaces at the two boundary curves. We can also find the remaining intersection curves by tracing the intersection points starting from a pair in the rival list that have not participated in the calculation of the intersection curves already obtained. Thus we can find all the intersection curves by not leaving any pair in the rival list that has not participated in the intersection calculation.

Figure J.5

Tracing in reverse

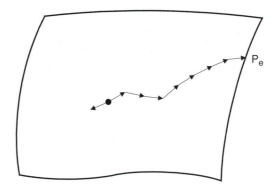

A P P E N D I X

K

Formulation of FEA System Equations from the Governing Differential Equation

In Section 8.2, we considered the formulation and solution of the system equations for finite-element analysis (FEA) directly from the integral equation describing the equilibrium condition of the problem being solved. However, most engineers are familiar with equilibrium equations expressed as differential equations. For example, we usually have differential equilibrium equations for problems involving heat transfer, vibration, and fluid flow. In this appendix, we introduce the use of weighted residuals as one method of the finite-element formulation starting from the governing differential equation.[1]

The *method of weighted residuals* is a numerical technique for obtaining approximate solutions to differential equations. It works in two steps. First, an approximate solution that satisfies the differential equation and its geometric boundary condition is chosen. The approximate solution is usually given as a linear combination of known functions with unknown coefficients. These known functions are equivalent to the shape functions, and the unknown coefficients are equivalent to nodal point displacements. When this approximate solution is substituted in the differential equation and boundary conditions, an error or residual results. Thus deriving the solution of the original differential equation would be equivalent to making this residual vanish in some average sense over the entire solution domain.

---

[1] The variational method is based on the minimization of the proper functional equivalent to the differential equilibrium equation and can also be used for the formulation from the governing differential equation. However, the weighted residual method can be used even when a functional equivalent to the differential equilibrium equation does not exist. The formulation based on the variational method is presented in Zeid [1991] and Stasa [1985].

523

This leads to the integral equations. In the second step, the integral equations are solved for the unknown coefficients and thus the approximate solution is obtained.

We review each step in a bit more detail. First, let's assume that the governing differential equation is

$$L(\phi) - f = 0 \qquad (K.1)$$

over the continuum domain D. Let's also assume that the boundary conditions are

$$\phi = \Phi \quad \text{on B}$$

where ϕ is the dependent variable to be solved for, f is a known function of the independent variable(s), L is a linear or nonlinear differential operator, and B is the boundary of the domain D.

We begin by assuming an approximate solution ϕ_a:

$$\phi \cong \phi_a = \sum_{i=1}^{n} C_i g_i \qquad (K.2)$$

where C_i are unknown coefficients to be solved for and g_i are known assumed functions of the independent variable(s). Substituting Equation (K.2) in (K.1) gives a nonzero value for $L(\phi_a) - f$ because ϕ_a is the approximate solution. Let this nonzero value be the residual R, which is expressed as

$$R = L(\phi_a) - f \qquad (K.3)$$

To minimize R over the entire solution domain, we define a weighted average, which should vanish over the domain:

$$\int_D RW_i \, dD = \int_D [L(\phi_a) - f] W_i \, dD = 0 \qquad (K.4)$$

where W_i is the weight factor. By substituting n different weight factors in Equation (K.4), we can generate n simultaneous equations from which the unknowns C_i ($i = 1, 2, \ldots, n$) can be solved for.

These weight factors may be chosen according to different criteria. The Galerkin method, for example, uses the known functions g_i in Equation (K.2) as W_i. Thus the simultaneous equations for the Galerkin method become

$$\int_D Rg_i \, dD = \int_D [L(\phi_a) - f] g_i \, dD = 0 \qquad i = 1, 2, \ldots, n \qquad (K.5)$$

In Example K.1 we show how the Galerkin method is used for the finite-element formulation in a heat transfer problem. Applications of the Galerkin method to other types of problems are described in Stasa [1985].

EXAMPLE K.1

Consider the one-dimensional heat transfer problem shown in Figure K.1(a): The temperature in the rod varies only in the axial direction. Modeling the rod as an assemblage of the linear element with two nodes, as shown in Figure K.1(b), derive

Figure K.1

Example of a one-dimensional heat transfer problem

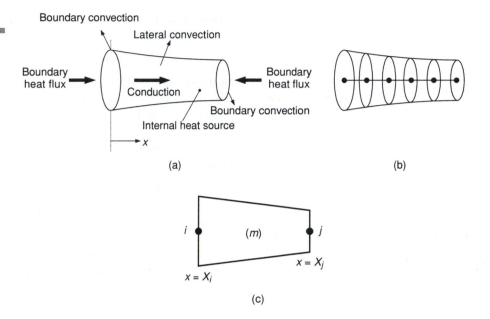

Boundary convection

Lateral convection

Boundary heat flux

Conduction

Boundary heat flux

Boundary convection

Internal heat source

x

(a)

(b)

i (m) j

$x = X_j$

$x = X_i$

(c)

the system equations for the finite-element analysis using the Galerkin method. Assume that the conductivity of the material is k, the convective heat transfer coefficient is h, the perimeter of the cross section is P, the ambient temperature is T_a, and the heat generation rate per unit volume is Q. Also assume that heat transfer by radiation can be ignored.

ANSWER

As can be found in most textbooks on heat transfer, the governing equation for the temperature T in the rod is

$$\frac{d}{dx}\left(kA\frac{dT}{dx}\right) - hP(T - T_a) + QA = 0 \tag{K.6}$$

Applying the weighted residual method, we get

$$\sum_m \int_{V^{(m)}} W_i \left[\frac{d}{dx}\left(kA\frac{dT}{dx}\right) - hP(T - T_a) + QA\right] dV^{(m)} = 0 \qquad (i = 1, 2, \ldots, n) \tag{K.7}$$

where n is the total number of nodes and Σ_m implies summation over all the elements.

For the specific case of the Galerkin method, Equation (K.7) becomes

$$\sum_m \int_{V^{(m)}} \mathbf{N}\left[\frac{d}{dx}\left(kA\frac{dT}{dx}\right) - hP(T - T_a) + QA\right] dV^{(m)} = 0 \tag{K.8}$$

where the column matrix $\mathbf{N}$ is the shape function matrix. Thus Equation (K.8) is a system of n equations, each of which corresponds to each element of $\mathbf{N}$. The shape function matrix was defined when the temperature distribution in the rod was assumed to be

$$T = \mathbf{N}^T \hat{\mathbf{T}} \qquad (K.9)$$

where $\hat{\mathbf{T}}$ is a column matrix composed of the nodal point temperatures.

Let's ignore the summation symbol in Equation (K.8) for the time being because we can apply the summation easily once we have derived the expression for a general element m. As shown in Figure K.1(c), a typical element m connects node i and j with coordinates X_i and X_j and temperatures T_i and T_j, respectively. Hence Equation (K.8) can be written as

$$\int_{X_i}^{X_j} A \left[\mathbf{N} \frac{d}{dx} \left(kA \frac{dT}{dx} \right) - hP(T - T_a) + QA \right] dx = 0 \qquad (K.10)$$

Note that the volume element dv is replaced by $A\,dx$, where A is the cross-sectional area at location X.

Integrating the first term by parts and ignoring the constant area gives

$$\mathbf{N}kA\frac{dT}{dx}\Big|_{X_i}^{X_j} - \int_{X_i}^{X_j}\frac{d\mathbf{N}}{dx} kA \frac{dT}{dx} dx - \int_{X_i}^{X_j}\mathbf{N}hPT\,dx + \int_{X_i}^{X_j}\mathbf{N}hPT_a\,dx + \int_{X_i}^{X_j}\mathbf{N}QA\,dx = 0 \quad (K.11)$$

When the summation for all the elements is applied, the first term in Equation (K.11) for each element will cancel out, with the same term coming from the next element, except for the terms from the first and last elements. Therefore this term needs to be evaluated for elements 1 and $\mathbf{M}$ only, assuming that the elements are numbered consecutively from one end of the body to the other and that $\mathbf{M}$ is the total number of the elements.

To evaluate this term for the first and the last elements, let's consider one end of the body, as shown in Figure K.2. The imposed heat flux is denoted q_s, the heat flux from conduction q_x, and heat flux from convection q_{cv}.

An energy balance on this end of the body gives

$$q_x + q_s = q_{cv}$$

or

$$q_x = q_{cv} - q_s \qquad (K.12)$$

Figure K.2

Heat exchange at a boundary of a one-dimensional heat conduction problem

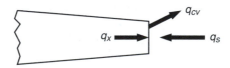

We know that the heat flux from conduction can be expressed by Fourier's law of heat conduction as

$$q_x = -k\,\frac{dT}{dx} \tag{K.13}$$

Using Equations (K.12) and (K.13), we can derive the following expression for

$$NkA\,\frac{dT}{dx}$$

in Equation (K.11)[*] at $x = X_j$:

$$NkA\frac{dT}{dx}\bigg|_{x=X_j} = N(-q_x A)\big|_{x=X_j}$$

$$= NA_j(-q_{cv} + q_s)\big|_{x=X_j} = \{-Nh_j A_j(T - T_{aj}) + NA_j q_j\}\big|_{x=X_j}^{\ *} \tag{K.14}$$

$$= (-Nh_j A_j T + Nh_j A_j T_j + NA_j q_j)\big|_{x=X_j}$$

A similar expression results for $NkA\dfrac{dT}{dx}$ at $x = X_i$:

$$-NkA\frac{dT}{dx}\bigg|_{x=X_i} = (-Nh_i A_i T + Nh_i A_i T_{ai} + NA_i q_i)\big|_{x=X_i} \tag{K.15}$$

Note that Equation (K.14) holds only for the last element, whereas Equation (K.15) holds only for the first element, as mentioned earlier.

Substituting Equations (K.9), (K.14), and (K.15) in Equation (K.11) gives

$$(-Nh_j A_j \mathbf{N}^T \widehat{\mathbf{T}} + Nh_j A_j T_{aj} + NA_j q_j)\big|_{x=X_j} + (-Nh_i A_i \mathbf{N}^T \widehat{\mathbf{T}} + Nh_i A_i T_{ai} + NA_i q_i)\big|_{x=X_i}$$

$$-\int_{X_i}^{X_j}\frac{d\mathbf{N}}{dx}\,kA\,\frac{d\mathbf{N}^T}{dx}\,\widehat{\mathbf{T}}\,dx - \int_{X_i}^{X_j}\mathbf{N}hP\mathbf{N}^T\widehat{\mathbf{T}}\,dx + \int_{X_i}^{X_j}\mathbf{N}hPT_a\,dx + \int_{X_i}^{X_j}\mathbf{N}QA\,dx = 0 \tag{K.16}$$

Taking $\widehat{\mathbf{T}}$ out of the integration in Equation (K.16) yields the following equation for element m:

$$\mathbf{K}^{(m)}\widehat{\mathbf{T}} = \mathbf{f}^{(m)} \tag{K.17}$$

where the element stiffness matrix, $\mathbf{K}^{(m)}$, is composed of three stiffness or conductance matrices:

$$\mathbf{K}^{(m)} = \mathbf{K}_x^{(m)} + \mathbf{K}_{cv}^{(m)} + \mathbf{K}_{cvB}^{(m)} \tag{K.18}$$

---

[*] The convective heat flux, q_{cv}, equals $h_j(T - T_{aj})$ where T_{aj} is the ambient temperature at $x = X_j$. Furthermore, q_s at $x = X_j$ is replaced by q_j at node j. Remember that $x = X_j$ is the location of one end.

and the element nodal force vector $\mathbf{f}^{(m)}$ is composed of four force vectors:

$$\mathbf{f}^{(m)} = \mathbf{f}_{cv}^{(m)} + \mathbf{f}_{Q}^{(m)} + \mathbf{f}_{cvB}^{(m)} + \mathbf{f}_{qB}^{(m)} \tag{K.19}$$

The matrices in Equations (K.18) and (K.19) are

$$\mathbf{K}_{x}^{(m)} = \int_{X_i}^{X_j} \frac{d\mathbf{N}}{dx} kA \frac{d\mathbf{N}^T}{dx} \ dx$$

$$\mathbf{K}_{cv}^{(m)} = \int_{X_i}^{X_j} \mathbf{N} h P \mathbf{N}^T dx$$

$$\mathbf{K}_{cvB}^{(m)} = \mathbf{N} h_i A_i \mathbf{N}^T \big|_{x=X_i} + \mathbf{N} h_j A_j \mathbf{N}^T \big|_{x=X_j}$$

$$\mathbf{f}_{cv}^{(m)} = \int_{X_i}^{X_j} \mathbf{N} h P T_a \ dx$$

$$\mathbf{f}_{Q}^{(m)} = \int_{X_i}^{X_j} \mathbf{N} Q A \ dx$$

$$\mathbf{f}_{cvB}^{(m)} = \mathbf{N} h_i A_i T_{ai} \big|_{x=X_i} + \mathbf{N} h_j A_j T_{aj} \big|_{x=X_j}$$

$$\mathbf{f}_{qB}^{(m)} = \mathbf{N} q_i A_i \big|_{x=X_i} + \mathbf{N} q_j A_j \big|_{x=X_j}$$

Once we have all the element stiffness matrices and the element nodal force vectors for all the elements, we sum them to form the system stiffness matrix and the nodal force vector in the form given in Chapter 8. The terms with the symbol B in their subscripts have nonzero values for only the first and last elements in the summation.

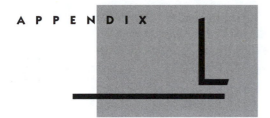

APPENDIX

L

Comparison of Windows-Based CAD Systems[1]

[1] Source: *Computer Graphics World,* Vol. 20, No. 5, May 1997, PennWell Publishing Company.

TABLE L.1

Comparison of Windows-Based CAD Systems

Product Name	CADKEY 97	Euclid Quantum 1.0	Helix Design System V4	I-DEAS Artisan Series 1.0
Price	$1195	$9995	$5695	$4995
Minimum memory requirements (MB RAM)	16	96	32	64
Disk space needed (MB)	50	2000	150	500
Disk swap space needed (MB)	20	400	120	185
Geometry modeling kernel used	ACIS 2.1	CAS. CADE	DesignBase	Proprietary
Modeling methodology used (parametric, variable, features, etc.)	Freeform hybrid modeling	Explicit, variational, parametric, features	Variational, parametric, features	Explicit, hybrid modeling, variational, parametric, features
History-based	No	Partial—using History as appropriate	Yes	Yes
Surface modeling	Yes, using 3rd party integrated software (FastSURF)	Yes	Yes	Yes
Assembly modeling	Yes, using 3rd party software	Yes	Yes	Yes
Parameters	No	Yes	Dimensional, geometric, and post parametrics for 2D	Yes
Shelling	No	Yes	Yes	Yes
Bi-directional assoc. with integrated applications	Yes	Yes with all Quantum applications	Automated layout capability with bi-directional updates	Yes, with integrated applications
Full rendering	Yes, via third party optional modules	Yes	Yes, included	Yes, included
Translator support (standard)	IGES, DXF, DWG, STL, VRML, SAT	IGES, STEP, DXF, VDA	IGES, STL, DXF, DWG, VRML, STEP	DXF, IGES, SET, VDA, STL
Optional translators	Third party .SAT translators	Custom	Custom	None
High end system directly reads and writes models	NA	Bi-directional data to and from EUCLID 3 and Strim	NA	I-DEAS Master Series reads full Artisan model, writes B-rep only

Product Name	CADKEY 97	Euclid Quantum 1.0	Helix Design System V4	I-DEAS Artisan Series 1.0
Internet Support	VRML	HTML, VRML	VRML output for commercial browsers; 3D viewer for distributing data to suppliers	Not in initial release
GUI used	Windows compliant	MOTIF and Windows	Proprietary	Proprietary
Supports OLE 2.0	OLE 2 Container—can accept OLE data, cannot serve Cadkey data to another application	Planned	Planned	No
Supports OLE for D&M	Planned	Under investigation	Under investigation	No
Integrated modules	FastSURF, FastNURBS, FastSOLIDS, DRAFT-PAK	EUCLID Machinist, EUCLID Analyst	SheetMetal, Kinematics	Surfacing, Stand alone drafting, Sheet Metal, Fastener Catalog
Product data management	Via third party products	Integrated EUCLID Design Manager or others	Helix EDMS	No
Integrated drafting module	Advanced Drafting Module (included), DRAFT-PAK (optional for $595)	Included	Bundled with modeler	Included
Integrated machining module	FastNURBS NC	EUCLID Machinist	Under development with third party	No
Company Information	Baystate Technologies Marlboro, MA	Matra Datavision Andover, MA	MicroCadam, Inc. Los Angeles, CA	SDRC Milford, OH

Product Name	Mechanical Desktop V1.2	MicroStation Modeler V5.5	Pro/Engineer 18.0 Advanced Designer Package	SolidDesigner V4.5
Price	$6250 ($2750 if upgrading from AutoCAD)	$5325 ($4975 is also purchasing Bentley SELECT maintenance)	$26,000 includes Pro/E and 13 modules	$6500
Minimum memory requirements (MB RAM)	32	32	64	96
Disk space needed (MB)	62	200	400	200
Disk swap space needed (MB)	64	48	128	96
Geometry modeling kernel used	ACIS 1.6	ACIS 2.1	Proprietary (Pro/E)	ACIS extended
Modeling methodology used (parametric, variable, features, etc.)	Explicit, Booleans, variational, parametric, features	Explicit Boolean, variational, parametric, feature	Parameters, features	Features
History-based	Yes	Yes	Yes	No
Surface modeling	Yes	Yes	Yes	Yes (optional module)
Assembly modeling	Yes	Yes	Yes	Yes
Parameters	Yes, parametric modeler using dimensional and geometric constraints	Yes, for creating features, relations and solids	Yes, parametrically-driven features, family tables, assemblies and relations as well as auto-dimension with sketcher	Optional (can apply dynamic relationships)
Shelling	No	Yes	Yes, single-feature, variable wall thickness, positive and negative direction	Yes
Bi-directional assoc. with integrated applications	Yes, with MAI integrated applications	Yes, with integrated applications	Yes, with integrated applications	No, unidirectional. Model change updates applications
Full rendering	Yes, optional modules (AutoVision 3D Studio Max)	Yes, optional module (MicroStation Masterpiece)	Yes, optional module	Yes, optional third party module
Translator support (standard)	IGES, Standard ACIS, DWG, DXF	IGES, STEP, DWG, CADKEY PRT, Versacad, ACIS SAT	IGES, SET, STL, DXF, DWG, VRML, STEP, VDA, Inventor, TIFF, CGM, JPEG, CALS	IGES, SAT, STL
Optional translators	Available with third-party partners	Many using ACIS SAT files Available via third-party partners	Catia, CADAM, PDGS, STEP, IDF 2.0	STEP

Product Name	Mechanical Desktop V1.2	MicroStation Modeler V5.5	Pro/Engineer 18.0 Advanced Designer Package	SolidDesigner V4.5
High end system directly reads and writes models	NA	NA	Yes, reads PT/Modeler files directly and writes out B-rep neutral file for use in PT/Modeler	NA
Internet Support	Yes, via Autodesk Integrated Publishing Kit and Whip! Plug-In	ModelServer Publisher for dynamic publishing of designs	HTML, VRML, CGM, and JPEG	Planned
GUI used	Windows compliant	Motif and Windows compatible	Proprietary	Motif
Supports OLE 2.0	Yes	Yes	Supports OLE 2.0, copy and paste only	Planned
Supports OLE for D&M	No	No	No	Planned
Integrated modules	Available via MAI third parties	MicroStation Masterpiece, MicroStation TeamMate 96, MicroStation 95, MicroStation PowerDraft	Over 50 integrated modules	Freeform, Dynamic Relations, Sheet Advisor, PC Blink, ME10, Solid Libraries, Dynamic Viewer
Product data management	WorkCenter (optional module)	MicroStation TeamMate 96 (optional module)	Pro/PDM and Pro/INTRALINK	Integrated with WorkManager
Integrated drafting module	Includes AutoCAD	Included	Included	ME10
Integrated machining module	Via third-party partners, for example Open Mind HYPERMILL	Via third-party partners, for example ESPRIT/MS	Pro/MFG Solutions offers several integrated products as well as fully integrated third party products such as pro/NC POST from ICAM	Via third party partners
Company Information	Autodesk, Inc. San Rafael, CA	Bentley Systems Exton, PA	Parametric Technology Corp. Waltham, MA	CoCreate Software Ft. Collins, CO

Product Name	SolidWorks 97	UniGraphics II V12	Solid Edge 3.0
Price	$3995, includes sheet metal	$17,000 average (depends on modules purchased)	$5995
Minimum memory requirements (MB RAM)	48	64	32
Disk space needed (MB)	25	150	75 to 100
Disk swap space needed (MB)	64	135	150
Geometry modeling kernel used	Parasolid	Parasolid	ACIS 2.0
Modeling methodology used (parametric, variable, features, etc.)	Parametric, features	Explicit, hybrid, Booleans, variational, parametric, features	Parameters, features
History-based	Yes	Yes	Yes
Surface modeling	Yes	Yes	No, supports B-rep solids only
Assembly modeling	Yes	Yes	Yes
Parameters	Yes, full parametric modeling, dimensional, geometric, assembly constraints using full or partial constraints	Yes, fully associative	Yes, full parametric modeler using dimensional and geometric constraints
Shelling	Yes	Yes, supports both positive and negative direction. Adds new topology (usually edges) as required.	Yes
Bi-directional assoc. with integrated applications	Yes	Yes	Yes, via OLE in-place activation in Solid Edge environment. Solid Edge supports OLE for D&M for third-party application integration
Full rendering	Yes, optional module (PhotoWorks)	Yes, optional module(UG/Photo)	Yes, optional third-party module
Translator support (standard)	IGES, SAT, STL, DXF, DWG, Parasolid Binary	IGES, DXF, STEP AP203, STEP AP214, Interleaf, VRML. Parasolid transmit files	Standard ACIS (versions 1.5–2.0), IGES, STEP, VDA/FS, DWG, DXF, DGN
Optional translators	Available via third-party partners	Several third party translators for CATIA, CADDS, Medusa, ACIS, etc.	Available via third-party partners

Product Name	SolidWorks 97	UniGraphics II V12	Solid Edge 3.0
High end system directly reads and writes models	Geometry can be read by Parasolid based modelers	Yes	Solid Edge exports design files to EMS
Internet Support	VRML, HTML	VRML	CGM
GUI used	Windows compliant	Motif, ANSI Y14	Windows compliant
Supports OLE 2.0	Yes	Planned	Yes
Supports OLE for D&M	Planned	Planned	Yes, including new Geometry and Topology extension
Integrated modules	Available via third parties	Over 30 integrated modules	Assembly, Part, Drafting, Data Management, Sheet Metal
Product data management	Fully integrated solution available from third party—SmartTeam Works as well as others. (optional modules)	UG/Manager for engineering data, IMAN for full product data management	Built-in workgroup data management in Solid Edge. Enterprise data management available via third-party partners
Integrated drafting module	Yes, included at no extra cost.	Yes, UG/Drafting can be used as a standalone package or for drafting within the context of a large assembly	Production-ready drafting tools included in Solid Edge and as standalone via Solid Edge Drafting
Integrated machining module	Via third-party partners	Fully associative and integrated machining capability. UG/Tool Path, UG/Flow Cut, UG/Lathe and others.	Via third-party partners
Company Information	SolidWorks Corp. Concord, MA	Unigraphics Solutions Maryland Heights, MO	Intergraphic Software Solutions Huntsville, AL

References

Amirouche, M. L. *A Computer-Aided Design and Manufacturing, Co*. Prentice-Hall, Englewood Cliffs, NJ, 1993.

Armstrong, C. G. "Modeling Requirements for Finite-element Analysis," *Computer-Aided Design*, Vol. 26, No. 7, pp. 573–578, 1994.

Armstrong, C. G., Robinson, D. J., Mckeage, R. M., Li, T. S., Bridgett, S. J., Donaghy, R. J., and McGleenan, C. A. "Medials for Meshing and More," 4th Annual International Meshing Roundtable, (sponsored by Sandia National Laboratories), October 16–17, 1995.

Anderson, R. O., "Detecting and Eliminating Collisions in NC Machining," *Computer-Aided Design*, Vol. 10, No. 4, pp. 231–237, 1978.

Ashley, S. "Manufacturing Firms Face the Future," *Mechanical Engineering*, pp. 70–74, June 1997.

Avriel, M. *Nonlinear Programming-Analysis and Methods*, Prentice-Hall, Englewood Cliffs, NJ, 1976.

Barfield, W. and Furness, T. A. III. *Virtual Environments and Advanced Interface Design*, Oxford University Press, New York, 1995.

Barnhill, R. E., Birkhoff, G., and Gordon, W. J. "Smooth Interpolation in Triangles," *J. Approx. Theory*, Vol. 8, pp. 114–128, 1973.

Bartels, R. H., Beatty, J. C., and Barsky, B. A. *An Introduction to Splines for Use in Computer Graphics and Geometric Modeling*, Morgan Kaufmann Publishers, Los Altos, CA, 1987.

Bathe, K.-J. *Finite Element Procedures in Engineering Analysis*, Prentice Hall, Englewood Cliffs, NJ, 1982.

Baumgart, B. "Winged-edge Polyhedron Representation," Stanford Artificial Intelligence Report No. CS-320, 1972.

Baumgart, B. "A Polyhedron Representation for Computer Vision," *Proceedings of the National Computer Conference*, 1975.

Beasley, D., Bull, D. R., and Martin, R. R. "An Overview of Genetic Algorithm: Part I, Fundamentals," *University Computing*, Vol. 19, No. 2, pp. 58–69, Inter-University Committee on Computing, 1993.

Beckert, B. A. "Venturing into Virtual Product Development," *Computer-Aided Engineering*, pp. 45–50, May 1996.

Bedworth, D. D., Henderson, M. R., and Wolfe, P. M. *Computer Integrated Design and Manufacturing*, McGraw-Hill, New York, 1991.

Beier, K. "Virtual Reality in Automotive Design and Manufacturing," SAE Technical Paper 94C030, 1994.

Bendsoe, M. P. and Kikuchi, N. "Generating Optimal Topologies in Structural Design Using a Homogenization Method," *Computer Methods in Applied Mechanics and Engineering*, Vol. 71, pp. 197–224, 1988.

Bendsoe, M. P., Diaz, A., and Kikuchi, N. "Topology and Generalized Layout Optimization of Elastic Structures," In Bendsoe and Soares (eds.), *Topology Design of Structures*, Kluwer Academic Publishers, Dordrecht, Holland, 1992.

Bezier, P. *The Mathematical Basis of the UNISURF CAD System*, Butterworths, London, 1986.

Boehm, W., Farin, G., and Kahmann, I. "A Survey of Curve and Surface Methods in CAGD," *Computer-Aided Geometric Design*, Vol. 1, pp. 1–60, 1984.

Boehm, W. and Prantzsch, H. "*Geometric Concepts for Geometric Design*," A. K. Peters, Wellesley, MA, 1994.

Botkin, M. E., Yang, R. J., and Bennett, J. A. "Shape Optimization of Three-dimensional Stamped and Solid Automotive Components," in *The Optimum Shape*, Plenum Press, New York, 1986.

Braid, I., Hillyard, R., and Stroud, I. "Stepwise Construction of Polyhedra in Geometric Modeling," CAD Group Document No. 100, Cambridge University Computer Laboratory, 1978.

Breltinger, F. "Rapid Tooling for Simultaneous Product and Process Development: Part II," *RapidNEWS*, Vol. 5, No. 6, pp. 52–57, 1997.

Briabant V. and Fluery, C. "Shape Optimal Design Using B-splines," *Computer Methods in Applied Mechanics and Engineering*, Vol. 44, No. 3, pp. 247–267, 1984.

Budynas, R. G. *Advanced Strength and Applied Stress Analysis*, McGraw-Hill, New York, 1977.

Bykat, A. "Automatic Generation of Triangular Grid: I—Subdivision of a General Polygon into Convex Subregions; II—Triangulation of Convex Polygons," *Int. J. Numer. Meth. Eng.*, Vol. 10, pp. 1329–1342, 1976.

Carrington, J. "Modeling Entire Products," *Computer-Aided Engineering*, pp. 30–34, August 1997.

Cavendish, J. "Automatic Triangulation of Arbitrary Planar Domains for the Finite Element Method," *Int. J. Numer. Meth. Eng.*, Vol. 8, pp. 679–696, 1974.

Cavendish, J. C., Field, D. A., and Frey, W. H. "An Approach to Automatic Three-dimensional Finite Element Mesh Generation," *Int. J. Numer. Meth. Eng.*, Vol. 21, pp. 329–347, 1985.

Cerny, V. "Thermodynamical Approach to the Traveling Salesman Problem: An Efficient Simulation Algorithm," *J. of Optimization Theory and Applications*, Vol. 45, No. 1, 1985.

Chang, T. C., Wysk, R. A., and Wang, H. P. *Computer Aided Manufacturing*, 2nd ed., Prentice-Hall, Englewood Cliffs, NJ, 1998.

Chapman, C. D. "Structural Topological Optimization via the Genetic Algorithm," MS thesis, Dept. of Mech. Eng., MIT, 1994.

Chappel, I. T. "The Use of Vectors to Simulate Material Removed by Numerically Controlled Milling," *Computer-Aided Design*, Vol. 15, No. 3, pp. 156–158, 1983.

Chiyokura, H. *Solid Modeling with DESIGNBASE: Theory and Implementation*, Addison-Wesley, Reading, MA, 1988.

Clough, R. W. "The Finite Element in Plane Stress Analysis," *Proceedings of 2nd A.S.C.E. Conference on Electronic Computation*, September, 1960.

Cohen, E., Lyche, T., and Riesenfeld, R. "Discrete B-splines and Subdivision Techniques in Computer-Aided Geometric Design and Computer Graphics," *Computer Graphics and Image Processing*, Vol. 14, pp. 87–101, 1980.

Cohen, E., Lyche T., and Schumaker, L. L. "Algorithms for Degree-Raising of Splines," *ACM Transactions on Graphics*, Vol. 4, No. 3, pp. 171–181, 1985.

Conte S. D. and de Boor, C. *Elementary Numerical Analysis*, McGraw Hill, New York, 1980.

Coons, S. A. "Surfaces for Computer-Aided Design of Space Forms," Technical Report MAC-TR 44, M.I.T., Cambridge, MA, 1967.

Cox, M. G. "The Numerical Evaluation of B-splines," *J. Inst. Maths. Applics.*, Vol. 15, pp. 95–108, 1972.

Crandall, S. H., Karnopp, D. C., Kurtz Jr., E. F., and Pridmore-Brown, D. C. *Dynamics of Mechanical and Electromechanical Systems*, McGraw-Hill, New York, 1968.

de Boor, C. "On Calculating with B-spline," *J. of Approx. Theory*, Vol. 6, pp. 52–60, 1972.

Deitz, D. "Re-engineering Virtual Prototypes," *Mechanical Engineering*, pp. 76–78, September 1997.

Drews, P. and Weyrich, M. "Virtual Manufacturing," *VR News*, Vol. 6, pp. 18–22, 1997.

Du, W.-H. and Schmitt, F. J. M. "On the G1 Continuity of Piecewise Bezier Surfaces: A Review with New Results," *Computer-Aided Design*, Vol. 22, No. 9, pp. 556–573, 1990.

Eastman, C. and Weiler, K. "Geometric Modeling Using the Euler Operators," Conference on Computer Graphics in CAD/CAM Systems, May 1979.

Farin, G. *Curves and Surfaces for Computer-Aided Geometric Design*, Academic Press, San Diego, CA, 1990.

Faux, I. D. and Pratt, M. I. *Computational Geometry for Design and Manufacture*, Ellis Horwood, Chichester, Sussex, UK, 1979.

Foley, J. D., van Dam, A., Feiner, S. K., and Hughes, J. F. *Computer Graphics: Principles and Practice*, Addison-Wesley, Reading, MA, 1990.

Gain, P. R. "New Generation of PDM Emerges," *Computer-Aided Engineering*, Vol. 15, No. 11, pp. 52–58, 1996.

Garey, M. R. and Johnson, D. S. "Computers and Intractability: A Guide to the Theory of NP-Completeness," Freeman, New York, 1979.

Gascoigne, B. "PDM: The Essential Technology for Concurrent Engineering," 1997 http://www.pdmic.com/articles/artefce.html

Geller, T. L., Lammers, S. E., and Mackulak, G. T. "Methodology for Simulation Application to Virtual Manufacturing Environment," *Proceedings of the 1995 Winter Simulation Conference*, pp. 909–916, 1995.

Goldberg, D. E. "Computer-Aided Gas Pipeline Operation Using Genetic Algorithm and Rule Learning," Ph.D. thesis, Civil Engineering Dept., University of Michigan, 1989a.

Goldberg, D. E. *Genetic Algorithm in Search, Optimization and Machine Learning*, Addison-Wesley, Reading, MA, 1989b.

Green, P. J. and Sibson, R. "Computing Dirichlet Tessellations in the Plane," *The Computer J.* Vol. 21, No. 2, pp. 168–173, 1977.

Grefenstette, J. J. *A User's Guide to GENESIS Version 5.0*, October 1990.

Groover, M. P. and Zimmers, E. W. *CAD/CAM Computer-Aided Design and Manufacturing*, Prentice-Hall, Englewood Cliffs, NJ, 1984.

Gursoz, E. L., Choi, Y., and Prinz, F. B. "Vertex-based Representation of Non-manifold Boundaries," in *Geometric Modeling for Product Engineering*, North-Holland, Amsterdam, 1990.

Haftka, R. T. and Grandhi, R. V. "Structural Shape Optimization—A Survey," *Computer Methods in Applied Mechanics and Engineering*, Vol. 57, pp. 91–106, 1986.

Haftka, R. T. and Gurdal, Z. *Elements of Structural Optimization*, 3rd ed., Kluwer Academic Publishers, Dordrecht, Holland, 1992.

Hartley, P. J. and Judd, C. J. "Parametrization and Shape of B-spline Curves for CAD," *Computer-Aided Design*, Vol. 12, No. 5, pp. 235–238, 1980.

Heighway, E. A. "A Mesh Generator for Automatically Subdividing Irregular Polygons into Quadrilaterals," IEEE Transaction on Magnetics, Vol. 6, pp. 2535–2538, 1983.

Held, M. *On the Computational Geometry of Pocket Machining*, Springer-Verlag, Berlin, 1991.

Helsel, S. "High-Res VR Displays," *Computer Graphics World*, pp. 49–54, May 1997.

Herrmann, L. R. "Laplacian-isoparametric Grid Generation Scheme," *J. of Eng. Mech. Div., Proceedings of Amer. Soc. Civil Eng.*, Vol. 102 (EM5), 1976.

Hildebrand, F. B. *Advanced Calculus for Applications*, Prentice-Hall, Englewood Cliffs, NJ, 1976.

Hoffmann, C. M., Hopcroft, J. E., and Karasick, M. S. "Robust Set Operations on Polyhedral Solids," *IEEE Computer Graphics and Applications*, pp. 50–59, 1989.

Ho-Le, K. "Finite Element Mesh Generation Methods: A Review and Classification," *Computer-Aided Design*, Vol. 20, No. 1, pp. 27–38, 1988.

Holland, J. H. "Adaptation in Natural and Artificial Systems," University of Michigan, Ann Arbor, 1975.

Hoschek, J. and Lasser, D. *Fundamentals of Computer Aided Geometric Design*, A. K. Peters, Wellesley, MA, 1993.

Imam, M. H. "Three-dimensional Shape Optimization," *Int. J. Num. Meth. Eng.*, Vol. 18, pp. 661–673, 1982.

ISO TC 184 / SC4 / WG5 N9, *EXPRESS Language Reference Manual*, International Organization for Standardization, 1991.

Jacobs, P. F. "Rapid Prototyping and Manufacturing," Society of Manufacturing Engineers, pp. 1–23, 153–220, 1992.

Jacobs, P. F. *Recent Advances in Rapid Tooling from Stereolithography*, 3D Systems, Valencia, CA, 1996a.

Jacobs, P. F. "Stereolithography and Other RP&M Technologies," *Soc. Manufacturing Engineers*, 1996b.

Jain, P., Fenyes, P., and Ritcher, R. "Optimal Blank Nesting Using Simulated Annealing," *Advances in Design Automation*, ASME, DE—Vol. 23, No. 2, pp. 109–116, 1991.

Jaques, M. W. S., Stickland, P., and Oliver, T. J. "Design by Virtual Manufacturing: A Review," *J. Design and Mfg.*, Vol. 5, pp. 241–250, 1995.

Jerad, R. B., Drysdale, R. L., Hauck, K., Schaudt, B., and Magewick, J. "Methods for Detecting Errors in Numerically Controlled Machining of Sculptured Surfaces," *IEEE Computer Graphics and Applications*, Vol. 9, No. 1, pp. 26–38, 1989.

Jones, F. H. and Martin, L. *The AutoCAD Database Book*, Ventana Press, 3rd ed., 1989.

Jung, Y. H. and Lee, K. "Tetrahedron-based Octree Encoding for Automatic Mesh Generation," *Computer-Aided Design*, Vol. 25, No. 3, 1993.

Kalpakjian, S. *Manufacturing Processes for Engineering Material*, 2nd ed., Addison-Wesley, Reading, MA, p. 541, 1992.

Kikuchi, N. "Adaptive Grid Design Methods for Finite Element Analysis," *Comput. Meth. Appl. Mech. Eng.*, Vol. 55, pp. 129–160, 1986.

Kirkpatrick, S., Gelatt Jr., C. D., and Vecchi, M. P. "Optimization by Simulated Annealing," *Science*, Vol. 220, No. 4598, pp. 671–680, 1983.

Kirsch, U. *Optimum Structural Design: Concepts, Methods and Applications*, McGraw-Hill, New York, 1981.

Kobayashi, K. and Nakazuka, H. "STEP Room, Part1: Parametric Definition of Geometric and Topological Representation with Three Schema," *Nikkei Mechanical*, pp. 88–99, June 1993 (In Japanese).

Kochan, D. *Solid Freeform Manufacturing*, Elsevier-North Holland, Amsterdam, 1993.

Kohn, R. V. and Strang, G. "Optimal Design and Relaxation of Variational Problems," Communic. Pure and Appl. Math., Vol. 39, (Part 1), pp. 113–137; (Part 2), pp. 139–182; (Part 3), pp. 333–350, 1986.

Koparkar, P. A. and Mudur, S. P. "Generation of Continuous Smooth Curves Resulting from Operations on Parametric Surface Patches," *Computer-Aided Design*, Vol. 18, pp. 193–206, 1986.

Koren, Y. *Computer Control of Manufacturing Systems*, McGraw-Hill, New York, 1983.

Koriyama, H., Yazaki, Y., Honbori, I., Kato, Y., and Kisakibaru, T. "Virtual Manufacturing System," *Proceedings of International Symposium on Semiconductor Manufacturing*, pp. 5–8, 1995.

Kreyszig, E. *Advanced Engineering Mathematics*, John Wiley & Sons, New York, 1988.

Krovi, V., Kumar, V., Anathasuresh, G. K., and Vezien, J. "Design and Virtual Prototyping of Rehabilitation Aides," *Proceedings of ASME Design Engineering Technical Conferences*, pp. 1–12, September 1997.

Kumar, A. V. "Shape and Topology Synthesis of Structures Using a Sequential Optimization Algorithm," Ph.D. thesis, Mechanical Engineering Dept., Massachusetts Institute of Technology, Cambridge, MA, 1993.

Kumar, V. "An Assessment of Data Formats for Layered Manufacturing," *Advanced Engineering Software*, Vol. 28, No. 3, 1997.

Laarhoven, P. J. M. and Aarts, E. H. L. *Simulated Annealing: Theory and Application*, Reidel, Dordrecht, Holland, 1988.

Lee, Y. T. "Automatic Finite Element Generation Based on Constructive Solid Geometry," Ph.D. thesis, Mechanical Engineering Dept., University of Leeds, Leeds, UK, 1983.

Lee, K., Hur, J., and Kim, G. "Computing Environment to Facilitate Stereolithographic Rapid Prototyping," *Proceedings of the 8th International Conference on Production Engineering*, Hokkaido University, Sapporo, Japan, pp. 103–112, August 1997.

Lee, K., Hur, J., Ahn, J., and Kim, G. "Geometry Manipulation Tools Applied to Rapid Prototyping Systems," Israel–Korea Bi-National Conference on New Themes in Computer Aided Geometric Modeling, Tel-Aviv, February 1998.

Lin, E., Minis, I., Nau, D., and Regli, W. C. "Contribution to Virtual Manufacturing Background Research, Phase I," (1997a).

http://www.isr.umd.edu/Labs/CIM/vm/report/report.html

Lin, E., Minis, I., Nau, D., and Regli, W. C. "Contribution to Virtual Manufacturing Background Research, Phase II," (1997b).

http://www.cs.umd.edu/~nau/vm2

MacNeal, R. H. *Finite Elements: Their Design and Performance*, Marcel Dekker, New York, 1994.

Materialise N.V., "Guide to Magics® RP V4.1," Leuven, Belgium, 1997.

Mäntylä, M. "Boolean Operations of 2-Manifolds through Vertex Neighborhood Classification," *ACM Transactions on Graphics*, Vol. 5, No. 1, pp. 1–29, 1986.

Mäntylä, M. *An Introduction to Solid Modeling*, Computer Science Press, Rockville, MD, 1988.

Martin, J. M. "Virtual Engineering on the Right Track," *Mechanical Engineering*, pp. 64–68, November 1996.

Martin, J. "Part Design Comes Together on the Net", *Mechanical Engineering*, pp. 76–78, June 1997.

Masuda, H., Shimada, K., Numao, M., and Kawabe, S. "A Mathematical Theory and Applications of Non-manifold Geometric Modeling," in *Advanced Geometric Modeling for Engineering Applications*, North-Holland, Amsterdam, 1990.

Mazzola, J. "Build and Break, Digital Style," *Computer-Aided Engineering*, pp. 62–65, May 1996.

McMahon, C., and Browne, J. *CAD/CAM from Principles to Practice*, Addison-Wesley, Reading, MA, 1993.

Mèhautè, A. L., Rabut, C., and Schumaker, L. L. *Curve and Surface with Application in CAGD*, Vanderbilt University Press, Nashville, 1997.

Metropolis, N., Rosenbluth, A., Rosenbluth, M., Teller, A., and Teller, E. "Equation of State Calculations by Fast Computing Machines," *J. Chem. Physics*, Vol. 21, pp. 1087–1092, 1953.

Mielke, B. *Integrated Computer Graphics*, West, St. Paul, 1991.

Miller, J. R. "Analysis of Quadric-Surface-Based Solid Models," *IEEE Computer Graphics and Applications*, pp. 28–42, 1988.

Mills, R. "Tackling Plane Design and Maintenance," *Computer-Aided Engineering*, pp. 44–46, November 1996.

Mills, R. "Making Models Move," *Computer-Aided Engineering*, pp. 30–38, February 1997.

Mo, J. P. T., Wang, Y., and Tang, C. K. "The Use of the Virtual Manufacturing Device in the Manufacturing Message Specification Protocol for Robot Task Control," *Computers in Industry*, Vol. 28, pp. 123–136, 1996.

Morris, A. J. *Foundations of Structural Optimization: A Unified Approach*, John Wiley & Sons, New York, 1982.

Mortenson, M. E. *Geometric Modeling*, John Wiley & Sons, New York, 1985.

Neider, J., Davis, T., and Woo, M. *Open GL Programming Guide*, Addison-Wesley, Reading, MA, 1997.

Pandelidis, I. and Zou, Q. "Optimization of Injection Molding Design Parts I and II," *Polymer Engineering and Science*, Vol. 30, pp. 873–892, 1990.

Parametric Technology Corporation, *Pro/MFG™ and Pro/NC-CHECK™ User's Guide, Release 18.0*, 1997.

Peng, Q. S. "An Algorithm for Finding the Intersection Lines between Two B-spline Surfaces," *Computer-Aided Design*, Vol. 16, pp. 191–196, 1984.

Phai, N.-V. "Automatic Mesh Generation with Tetrahedron Elements," *Int. J. Numer. Meth. Eng.*, Vol. 18, pp. 273–289, 1982.

Piegl, L. and Tiller, W. "Curve and Surface Constructions Using Rational B-Splines," *Computer-Aided Design*, Vol. 19, No. 9, pp. 485–498, 1987.

Pimentel, K. and Teixeira, K. *Virtual Reality though the New Looking Glass*, 2nd Edition, McGraw-Hill, New York, 1994.

Praun, S. V. "Digital Mock-up—Meeting the Challenges of the Future," *Prototype Technology International*, Issue 2, pp. 72–74, 1997.

Qiulin, D. *Surface Engineering Geometry for Computer-Aided Design and Manufacture*, Ellis Horwood, Chichester, West Sussex, UK, 1987.

Reed, K., Harrod, Jr., D., and Conroy, W. "The Initial Graphics Exchange Specification (IGES) Version 5.0," NISTIR 4412, September 1990.

Reklaitis, G. V., Ravindran, A., and Ragsdell, K. M. *Engineering Optimization*, John Wiley & Sons, New York, 1983.

Requicha, A. A. G. and Voelcker, H. B. "Boolean Operations in Solid Modeling; Boundary Evaluation and Merging Algorithms," *Proc. IEEE*, Vol. 73, No. 1, pp. 30–44, 1985.

Rooney, J. and Steadman, P. *Principles of Computer-Aided Design*, Prentice Hall, Englewood Cliffs, NJ, 1988.

Rutenbar, R. A. "Simulated Annealing Algorithms: An Overview," *IEEE Circuits and Devices Mag.*, pp. 16–26, January 1989.

Samet, H. "Neighbor Finding Techniques for Images Represented by Quadtrees," *Computer Graphics and Image Processing*, Vol. 18, pp. 37–57, 1982.

Sandgren, E. and Jensen, E. "Automotive Structural Design Employing a Genetic Optimization Algorithm," SAE Technical Paper #920772, *Proceedings of the 1992 SAE International Congress and Exposition*, Detroit, Michigan, 1992.

Sapidis, N. and Perucchio, R. "Advanced Techniques for Automatic Finite-Element Meshing from Solid Models," *Computer-Aided Design*, Vol. 21, No. 4, pp. 248–253, 1989.

Sarraga, R. F. "G1 Interpolation of Generally Unrestricted Cubic Bezier Curves," *Computer-Aided Geometric Design*, Vol. 4, No. 1, pp. 23–39, 1987.

Schmitz, B. "Investigating Virtual Product Development," *Computer-Aided Engineering*, p. 32, May 1996.

Schulman, M. "Fast Track to Model Display," *Computer-Aided Engineering*, pp. 52–54, November 1997.

Shimada, K. and Gossard, D. C. "Computational Methods for Physically Based FE Mesh Generation," in G. J. Olling and F. Kimura (eds.), *Human Aspects in Computer Integrated Manufacturing*, pp. 41–42, Elsevier Science, Amsterdam, 1992.

Sluiter, M. L. C. and Hansen, D. C. "A General-Purpose Automatic Mesh Generator for Shell and Solid Finite Elements," in L. E. Hulbert (ed.) *Computers in Engineering*, Vol. 3, Book No. G00217, ASME, pp. 29–34, 1982.

Solaja, V. B. and Urosevic, S. M. "The Method of Hypothetical Group Technology Production Lines," *CIRP Annals*, Vol. 22, No. 1, 1973.

Springer, S. L. and Gadh, R. "State-of-the-art Virtual Reality Hardware for Computer-Aided Design," *J. of Intelligent Mfg*, Vol. 7, pp. 457–465, 1996.

Stasa, F. L. *Applied Finite-Element Analysis for Engineers*, CBS College Publishing, New York, 1985.

Sudhalkar, A., Gursoz, L., and Prinz, F. "Continuous Skeletons of Discrete Objects," *ACM Solid Modeling A93*, pp. 85–94, Montreal, 1993.

Suzuki, K. and Kikuchi, N. "A Homogenization Method for Shape and Topology Optimization," *Comp. Meth. Appl. Mech. and Engr.*, Vol. 93, pp. 291–318, 1991.

Szabó, B. and Babuška, I, *Finite-Element Analysis*, John Wiley & Sons, New York, 1991.

Taylor, D. L. *Computer-Aided Design*, Addison-Wesley, Reading, MA, 1992.

Thacker, W. C., Gonzalez, A., and Putland, G. E. "A Method for Automating the Construction of Irregular Computational Grids for Storm Surge Forecast Models," *J. Comp. Physics*, Vol. 37, pp. 371–387, 1980.

Tickoo, S. *AutoCAD: A Problem-Solving Approach, Release13 DOS*, Delmar, Albany, NY, 1995.

Tiller, W. "Rational B-splines for Curve and Surface Representation," *IEEE Computer Graphics and Applications*, pp. 61–69, 1983.

Timmer, H. G. and Stern, J. M. "Computation of Global Geometric Properties of Solid Objects," *Computer-Aided Design*, Vol. 12, No. 6, 1980.

Topping, B. H. "Shape Optimization of Skeletal Structures: A Review," *J. Struct. Engr.*, Vol. 109, No. 8, pp. 1933–1951, 1983.

Watson, D. F. "Computing the *n*-dimensional Delaunay Tessellation with Application to Voronoi Polygons," *Comput. J.*, Vol. 24, pp. 167–172, 1981.

Weiler, K. "The Radial Edge Structure: A Topological Representation for Nonmanifold Geometric Boundary Modeling," in *Geometric Modeling for CAD Applications*, Elsevier Science, Amsterdam, 1988.

Weiler, K. "Boundary Graph Operators for Nonmanifold Geometric Modeling Topology Representations," in *Geometric Modeling for CAD Applications*, Elsevier Science, Amsterdam, 1988.

Wong, D. F., Leong, H. W., and Liu, C. L. *Simulated Annealing for VLSI Design*, Kluwer Academic Publishers, Boston, 1989.

Woo, T. C. and Thomasma, T. "An Algorithm for Generating Solid Elements in Objects with Holes," *Comp. and Struct.*, Vol. 18, No. 2, pp. 333–342, 1984.

Wordenweber, B. "Finite-Element Mesh Generation," *Computer-Aided Design*, Vol. 16, No. 5, pp. 285–291, 1984.

Yamaguchi, Y., Kobayashi, K., and Kimura, F. "Geometric Modeling with Generalized Topology and Geometry for Product Engineering," in *Product Modeling for Computer-Aided Design and Manufacturing*, Elsevier Science, Amsterdam, 1991.

Yan, X. and Gu, P. "A Review of Rapid Prototyping Technologies and Systems," *Computer-Aided Design*, Vol. 28, No. 4, pp. 307–318, 1996.

Yang, R. J., Choi, K. K., and Haug, E. J. "Numerical Considerations in Structural Component Shape Optimization," *ASME Journal of Mechanics, Transmissions and Automation in Design*, Vol. 107, No. 3, pp. 334–339, 1986.

Yerry, M. A. and Shephard, M. S. "A Modified Quadtree Approach to Finite-Element Mesh Generation," *IEEE Comput. Graph. and Appl.*, pp. 39–46, "Construction of Polyhedra in Geometric Modeling," CAD Group Document No. 100, Cambridge University Computer Laboratory, 1978.

Yokoyama, M. "Automated Computer Simulation of Two-dimensional Elastostatic Problems by the Finite Element Method," *Int. J. Numer. Meth. Eng.*, Vol. 21, pp. 2273–2287, 1985.

Zeid, I. *CAD/CAM Theory and Practice*, McGraw-Hill, New York, 1991.

Index